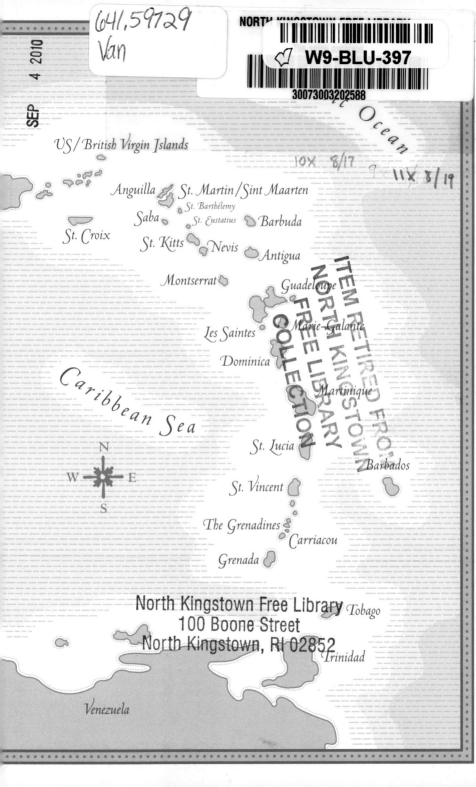

Atlantic Ocean

US / British Virgin Islands

Anguilla — St. Martin / Sint Maarten
St. Barthélemy
Saba — St. Eustatius — Barbuda

St. Croix

St. Kitts — Nevis — Antigua

Montserrat — Guadeloupe

Marie-Galante

Les Saintes

Dominica

Caribbean Sea — Martinique

N
W — E
S

St. Lucia

Barbados

St. Vincent

The Grenadines
Carriacou
Grenada

Tobago

Trinidad

Venezuela

The Spice Necklace

ANN VANDERHOOF

The SPICE *Necklace*

MY ADVENTURES IN CARIBBEAN COOKING EATING, AND ISLAND LIFE

HOUGHTON MIFFLIN HARCOURT · Boston · New York
2010

First U.S. edition

Copyright © 2009 Ann Vanderhoof

ALL RIGHTS RESERVED

For information about permission to reproduce
selections from this book, write to Permissions,
Houghton Mifflin Harcourt Publishing Company,
215 Park Avenue South, New York, New York 10003.

www.hmhbooks.com

First published in Canada by Doubleday, 2009

Library of Congress Cataloging-in-Publication Data
Vanderhoof, Ann, date.
The spice necklace / Ann Vanderhoof.
p. cm.
ISBN 978-0-618-68537-0
1. Cookery (Spices)   2. Cookery, Caribbean.   I. Title.
TX819.A1V28 2010
641.3'383—dc22   2010007136

Designed by CS Richardson

Printed in the United States of America

DOC 10 9 8 7 6 5 4 3 2 1

For Rita, who taught me the pleasure of cooking,
and Harold, who taught me the pleasure of eating
And for Steve, a second helping

· · · CONTENTS · · ·

· · · LIST OF RECIPES · · ·

STARTERS & SNACKS

DRINKS

MAINS

SOUPS, SALADS & SIDES

SWEETS & BAKING

SPICE BLENDS, CONDIMENTS & MARINADES

RECIPE NOTE: Fresh island spices pack a real flavor punch. For similar results, buy spices whole when possible, and then grate or grind them yourself right before using. (And if your spices have been in the cupboard awhile, replace them with a new supply.)

The Spice Necklace

The Spell of the Spice Necklace

A dinner invitation, once accepted, is a sacred obligation. If you die before the dinner takes place, your executor must attend. . . .

19th-century New York taste-maker Ward McAllister,

in Society as I Have Found It, *1890*

THIS TIME, I bring my rolling pin to the Caribbean.

I also bring my rat, Ramón T. Ratón (made from a small coconut), and my elderly stuffed monkey, Curious George, a companion since childhood; my best pots and knives (and a proper sharpening steel); more baking pans and serving dishes; my trusty pressure cooker; two dozen tea towels; six stemmed wineglasses; three of my favorite silicone spatulas (all the same size and color); a digital kitchen scale; and one lonely electric appliance, a wand hand-blender with attachments that whisk and chop.

Of course, my husband, Steve, comes too. He calls himself my official taster and, aided by a lightning-fast metabolism, he's an unstoppable force when it comes to food. West Indian market women adore him—setting commerce aside to chat, tucking an extra piece or two of fruit into his bag, routinely giving him big hugs hello and goodbye—and cooks can't resist spoiling him, especially since he looks like he can use a few thousand extra calories. Inevitably, he's the one who's given the largest fish, the plate with the scoop of the extra something, the invitation to "take a taste" of whatever's in the pot.

This is Phase Two.

But I'm getting ahead of myself.

. . .

In the late '90s, when Steve and I were in our mid-forties and living in Toronto, we quit our jobs—I was a magazine editor and he was a magazine art director—put our careers on hold, rented out our house, moved onto our 42-foot sailboat and sailed south to the Caribbean on a two-year midlife break. Of course, it was nowhere as straightforward as that one sentence makes it sound, and we needed a five-year plan—which stretched to seven years—to cast off the lines that held us to land.

Our new floating home was elegant, graceful, fast . . . and small, sort of like a walk-in closet with windows: only 12 feet, 3 inches across at her widest point, with most of her—from pointed bow to pinched stern—much skinnier. The U-shaped galley had a miserly 2 by 2 feet of floor space; I could reach the fridge, freezer, stove, sink and all the cupboards without moving my feet. Luckily, Steve was willing to leave the meal prep to me: two cooks squeezed in here would definitely spill the broth long before they spoiled it. No dishwasher, no microwave; actually, not a single electric appliance for two whole years.

Stowage space was at a premium, requiring a back-to-basics approach, with no duplication allowed. Every kitchen item brought aboard had to earn its keep by being used almost every day. My rolling pin didn't make the cut, and was left behind in our storage locker. When I rolled pastry, I did it with a wine bottle. I crushed garlic without a garlic press. On the upside, my arm muscles got a workout whipping cream and beating egg whites by hand.

We called our sailboat *Receta*—the Spanish word for "recipe"—reflecting our more-than-moderate interest in food. Reinforcing the point, we named *Receta*'s 10-foot, 15-horsepower dinghy *Snack*. But despite that, we apparently left Toronto with no expectations of the food we'd encounter. In fact, we arrived in the Caribbean provisioned to the gills, somehow having overlooked that people actually ate in the islands, that we would find places to buy food there. We had crammed every spare cranny with long-lasting, North America–bought edibles, the sort of canned and packaged stuff we never ate back home: losers, like gray, waterlogged asparagus and rubbery canned chicken chunks.

Never mind. The cans languished as we became devotees of island markets, seduced by glistening fish just out of the ocean; luscious-looking, new-to-us fruits that begged to be sliced open; fragrant nosegays of herbs; bundles of fresh greens with ordinary names like "spinach" but an entirely different look and taste; and, especially, tables overflowing with spices—seeds, roots, stalks, barks, buds, leaves, flowers and aromatic powders. Each time we dropped anchor, we headed to shore to investigate what delicious surprises the island held in store.

And we quickly learned that food launched conversations with strangers. "How do I know when this is ripe?" I'd ask, hefting, say, a breadfruit. "And how do you cook it for your family?" Or, pointing to a bunch of mysterious leaves that looked and smelled like thyme on steroids, "What do you call these? And what should I do with them?" Pleased by our interest, people were invariably eager to help. And we were encouraged by their warm response.

We began poking our noses into kitchens on shore too, whenever we had tasted wonderful island cooking. And when my experiments in our own galley afterward brought less than four-star reviews from the resident food taster, we went back to those who'd helped us—and asked more questions. Food became our route into island life, and strangers turned into friends.

Far too soon, however, it was time to sail back to Toronto. Our two-year break was ending, and we needed to restart our land-based life. This was like leaving a dinner party after the first course. While we were still in Grenada preparing to point *Receta* north, one of our new friends issued an invitation. "I want you to come for an oildown," Dingis Naryan said. She had taken us under wing when we anchored in a bay close to her home, teaching us island ways and showing me how to cook a few dishes "like you born Grenadian." Food, of course, had first brought us together; we met when she caught us admiring her mango tree and gave us a bag of its fruit. Oildown is Grenada's national dish, and it's synonymous with "party." "But we can't make an oildown until deh breadfruit on my tree are full," Dingis said. "How long can you stay?"

Not long enough. We had to leave with the invitation, like the breadfruit, still hanging in the air.

. . .

In the cool shadows of the outdoor market in Grenada's capital, St. George's, women sit holding long, fragrant strands of the island's spices out to passersby. "Spice necklace, spice necklace, you want a spice necklace?" they call. One slender young woman, with close-cropped hair, a high-wattage smile, and an array of elaborate necklaces draped on one arm, was bolder than the rest when I paused one day to look and breathe in their scent. Introducing herself as Adonis, she said, "I'll string some special for you. What do you want on them?"

Everything, of course. Nutmegs, the rough-ridged nuts hidden in polished mahogany shells under lacy scarlet corsets of mace. Spiky, pungent cloves. Slices of saffron-colored turmeric root and chunks of pale-gold ginger. Rough curls of cinnamon bark. Cocoa beans, fermented and roasted to a deep chocolate-brown. Bay leaves folded into tidy squares that give off a whiff of balsam forest. Small dark disks of tonka bean, which look like exotic beads and smell like the best vanilla. She'd fill the space between the spices with egg-shaped ivory river seeds, she said, and tubular golden beads cut from stalks of young bamboo, and tiny red-and-black jumbie seeds, which look like devilish glittering eyes (they're sometimes called "crab eyes"). They're said to ward off evil spirits—a "jumbie" is a spirit—and protect against spells. But they certainly didn't help us. The entire Caribbean island chain was a spice necklace to us, and we had fallen firmly under its spell.

. . .

Back in Toronto, we moved off *Receta* and back into our old house. After two years of living on a boat, I had looked forward to having space again—and a dishwasher. But soon I discovered the house felt claustrophobic, despite the square footage. We had grown happily accustomed to living on the water under vast skies, to thinking of whatever island we anchored near as an extension of our tiny living space, to taking our chances on what the market (or our fishing lines) would yield fresh for dinner. I chafed under the supposed comfort of predictable routine, and predictable ingredients.

We hung our spice necklaces in almost every room, their sight and smell reminding us of the islands. On cold evenings, I pulled out the recipes I'd developed in my galley and put a big pot of a Caribbean curry or rice pelau on the stove. Steve, meanwhile, cranked up the heat and the music—steelpan, soca or calypso.

As the aroma and sound of the islands floated through the house, we began to plan a return to the Caribbean, to pick up where we had left off. I wanted to learn to cook not only like I was born Grenadian, but like I was born Dominican, Trinidadian, and on all the islands in between. As the West Indians say, I wanted to have "sweet hand."

I'd already learned one lesson: forget the canned asparagus and chunked chicken. This time, I would use the extra space to bring along more kitchen gear. This time, our foodie bent would guide us from the start. Since spices and herbs are the heart and soul of Caribbean cooking, and the foundation of almost every dish there, we would also start with the spices. The trail would lead us to new islands, as well as back to old friends. And as we followed our taste buds farther off the beaten path, joining islanders as they gathered ingredients and set to work in their kitchens, I would jump right in and lend a hand. It's what friends do. Besides, as one cook said to me while a crowd sat at her table awaiting lunch, "You're makin' the soup today, darlin'. And the dumplin's. That's how you learn."

. . .

Little by little, we began making changes to the aging *Receta* (she had been built in 1980, by Tartan Marine) to ready her for the return trip. The galley couldn't grow, but Steve carved new storage space for me out of unused corners, and added a pair of solar panels to supplement the power brought in by our wind generator. We had a new suit of sails cut—our mainsail had worn so thin that we could see each other through it—and the rigging replaced; and, for the times when the wind didn't blow (or didn't blow in the right direction), we installed a new, more powerful, engine. "Mr. Engine, Sir," as I had respectfully called the ancient, hard-to-maintain beast I had so often worried about on our first trip, was deservedly retired.

Meanwhile, we were anything but—working hard to rebuild the kitty and coming perilously close to turning back into "wuk jumbies," as the Trinidadians disparagingly say. I had begun to wuk for myself, writing and editing; Steve had flung himself full time into his own company, publishing guidebooks for boaters; it had started as a hobby business years earlier and had grown to the point where it was now attracting interest from buyers.

It sold in the middle of a mean Toronto winter six years after we'd returned from our first trip. By that point, even six more months seemed too long to wait. So we cheated. We put our house up for rent and our belongings into storage—minus the kitchen gear I wasn't going to leave behind this time—and had *Receta* trucked to Florida. This time, we'd cast off from there.

Before we left, we hung our old spice necklaces on board to guide us.

ONE

The Nutmeg Gatherers

· · · GRENADA · · ·

It's a rampage, / The lands are savaged, / My Caribbean ruined,
Not a tree in sight, / That didn't get hit outright;
It's a rampage, / Ivan take we hostage . . .
See Barbados (stocking up) / Small Tobago (stocking up)
Poor Grenada, / Lord, what a plight;
After the storm, / All man in the same boat, / Yes, after the storm,
We've got to help each other, / (After, after)
Because livestock (blow way) / Food crop (blow way)
Nutmeg (blow way) . . .

> from *"After the Storm,"* composed by
> *Christophe Grant, sung by Denyse Plummer*

THE VILLAGE OF UNION sits about two inches south of the
northern tip of Grenada on my big multi-fold government
map—just above the spot where the capillary network of red
roads thins out and then disappears. A few old cocoa and
nutmeg estates are noted—Union Estate, Malagon Estate,
Samaritan Estate—and a few lonely squares indicate buildings.

But the map makes it clear this is the start of the island's un-developed, empty, mountainous middle.

So I shouldn't be surprised by the road we're walking (climb-ing, really), heading straight up from the village, but still it leaves me breathless, and not just from its steepness. Ahead of us, the road simply seems to end, swallowed up into lush mountains, painted thickly in a dozen shades of green. Around every bend, in every direction, is a postcard. "You see that one?" our old friend Dingis asks, puffing out the words as even she stops to rest. She points to the most imposing peak, where the white mist of a morning shower floats high up, encircling the green. "On deh other side was where all deh nutmeg trees were."

Early in the morning, Dingis, her friend Gail, and Steve and I had set out from her house in Lower Woburn, on Grenada's south coast, taking first one bus to St. George's, and then another, to travel up the leeward west coast—past Gouyave, known as the island's fishing capital, though this makes it sound much grander than it is; past Victoria, an even smaller fishing village; to Industry, where the road curves inland. Dingis keeps up an excited commentary the whole way. Her highlights are not exactly the stuff of a standard tourist spiel. "Gail mother live here," she exclaims at one point, knowing Gail is too shy to tell us herself. And a little farther along, at a spot where a cliff rises up on one side of the road and plunges into the Caribbean on the other: "Dis is where deh bus was hit by a falling boulder and everybody die." This is not particularly what one wants to hear while shoehorned into the backseat of an overcrowded, overheated-by-the-squash-of-many-bodies minivan of a bus that careens aggressively around each curve. (A longtime resident once gave new-to-Grenada drivers this advice about the island's bus drivers: "Give them a wide berth—if necessary, stop and let them pass. They are busy private entrepreneurs with an urgent appointment with death.") By the time we reach Union and Dingis announces, "Dis is where we get off," I am woozy, soggy with sweat and more than ready to continue on foot.

The bus deposits us across from a square wooden building that has seen better days. Its wide doors are pulled open, and a car sits out front, the driver hefting sacks out of the trunk. "My father used to bring our nutmegs here," Dingis says. Sure enough, this building is labeled on my map—"Nutmeg Station"—one of a scant handful of government processing stations still operating around the island, where farmers come to sell their harvest. Dingis leads us inside. Near the door, a newly arrived sack of nutmegs has been dumped onto a sorting table, and a lone woman slowly picks through them. But the rest of the downstairs is quiet; and when Dingis takes us upstairs, where the nutmegs are left to dry naturally under the roof, in the hottest part of a hot building, the tiers of screened drying racks are mostly empty.

"Before Ivan, dey were fullll," Dingis says, drawing out the word into a melancholy musical refrain. Grenadians refer to the hurricane that near-destroyed their island in September 2004 simply as "Ivan," no need to include the "H" word. They have fully anthropomorphized the storm that eventually became a Category 5, top-of-the-charts hurricane. Though he was still a Category 3 when he crossed Grenada, Ivan killed at least forty-one of the island's residents, damaged or destroyed 90 percent of its buildings and uprooted close to 90 percent of its nutmeg trees. "Ivan come lookin' for his wife Janet," Dingis had told us shortly afterward, describing the disaster. He had waited a long time: Janet, the previous hurricane to strike the island, had visited almost half a century earlier.

Back in Toronto after our first trip, we had kept in touch with Dingis, sharing from afar the milestones in her life and that of her teenage daughter, Gennel. Birthdays. Christmases. Illnesses. Funerals. And then the hurricane that "mash up" their house, and their island. "When you comin' back?" Dingis had asked at the end of every long-distance conversation.

During that first stretch in Grenada, now almost a decade ago, she had always promised to take us to "deh country," as she calls the part of the island we're now walking, where she grew up and where her father and two of her brothers still live. When we first met, her phrasing had made me laugh, since by my standards, Dingis herself lived solidly in "deh country." Her Lower Woburn house was barely visible from the road behind a dense wall of tropical greenery—banana, breadfruit, mango and papaya trees; coconut palms; pigeon pea and pepper bushes. A few sheep and goats grazed on the steep hillside behind it, and a couple of clucking chickens pecked in the yard.

But now, up here, continuing on foot along the steep road from Union, I begin to understand. We pass only scattered houses, and are passed by only the very occasional car. This part of the island—more mountainous and with more rainfall than the south—has an all-pervasive greenness, a more intense lushness, and a coolness that is different from the other end. Thanks to the morning rain, the landscape seems freshly washed—glittering, even, where the sunlight splashes the still-wet foliage. "We would climb up and over deh mountain," Dingis says, continuing her story as we walk, "to gather deh nutmegs, three hundred pounds in a day. My father had two donkeys—we would carry sacks of nutmegs partway down until we reach deh donkeys."

A nutmeg tree yields two spices. Its plump, apricot-like, yellow-orange fruit bursts open when ripe to reveal a lacy, strawberry-red corset wrapping a hard, glossy-brown shell. This delicate red lace is the spice mace; the polished shell underneath contains the nutmeg itself. When the donkeys reached their house, Dingis and her brothers would remove the mace from the nutmegs, slipping it off the shell with their fingers and sorting it into three grades, based on the size of the pieces: "deh pretty, deh not so pretty and deh broken bits"; three hundred to four hundred pounds of nutmegs are needed to yield a single pound of mace. (Even now, as we pass the occasional house along the road, we see various-sized pieces of mace drying on front porches, spread in wooden trays and on plastic tarps.) McDonald Ignatius Naryan, Dingis's father—everyone but his family calls him "Mr. Mac"—would then deliver the nutmegs to the processing station in the village.

When Dingis had first talked about bringing us to the country, her mom was alive, but a few years ago the eighty-three-year-old suffered a fatal stroke. "She pass, from deh pressure," Dingis told us in a long-distance phone call. But Mr. Mac still lives in the house where Dingis once helped with the spice harvest. Settled in a straight-backed chair, Pepsi ball cap pushed back on his head, smiling broadly at the arrival of his daughter and her friends, he looks easily a decade younger than his ninety years. Though we know Mr. Mac has had a stroke too, and has trouble getting around, it's not obvious at first meeting. With his brown trousers rolled up at the bottom, his feet bare and his face stubbly, he still looks like the farmer he once was. He is hard to understand, but we chalk this up to our difficulty with Grenadian English—the accent and vocabulary of the island's older generations, in particular, take some getting used to—rather than to infirmity.

"Why do you think he still so strong and still look so good?" his fifty-one-year-old daughter now asks us. "It's deh mountains." The bare-bones house—worn wooden floors, hot, galvanized metal roof exposed on the interior, curtains tacked across the door frames of the bedrooms, bare mattresses—has ropes strung throughout, so Mr. Mac can help himself maneuver through it. And one of Dingis's brothers, Rovel (short for Roosevelt), lives here and helps. But otherwise, the two pieces of ragged foam that cushion one of Mr. Mac's chairs are about the sum of his extra comforts.

Plastic chairs are pulled out for us, and Kimon, one of Mr. Mac's great-grandsons, is sent to climb the guava tree behind the house to get us a snack. Curling, faded family photos are thumbtacked between the exposed joists of the stained aqua wall near one of the spots where Mr. Mac regularly sits, but the real art here is what's framed by the unglazed windows: slices of tangled, jungly Rousseau-like landscape. The layered greens are punctuated with spatters of yellow, soft orange and wine red, the pods of the cocoa trees. Mr. Mac farmed cocoa in addition to nutmegs, and along the way today Dingis had picked one of the football-shaped pods. (Her eldest brother, whom we'd met briefly on our walk up the road, has taken over from their father and works the land.) Now, with the household cutlass, a wooden-handled machete with a 22-inch curving blade, she thwacks open the sunset-colored pod and offers us the beans. "Local M&M's," we've heard them called.

"Listen to me," she says, as she always does when she wants us to pay attention to some piece of information she suspects we don't know. "You don't bite deh bean—just suck it and spit it out."

I'd already learned the hard way: straight from the pod, cocoa beans are extremely bitter, lacking not only an appealing chocolate color but also any discernible chocolate taste. But they're coated with a slippery, slimy white pulp that is sweet, vaguely fruity and very delicious. Once, on a hike in Trinidad that went hours longer than anyone expected, our guide found cocoa growing wild in the rain forest and kept the diabetic of the group going by having him suck the pulp from the beans; it did the trick.

Between the sugar hit from the cocoa and the one from the ripe guavas, eaten skin and all like apples, we're ready for a hike ourselves, back into Dingis's childhood. Young Kimon leads the way, in shorts, a new-looking basketball jersey with Michael Jordan's number, and plastic thongs. Dingis has also donned a pair of flip-flops, changing out of the low-heeled "special occasion" sandals she wore (with the backs folded down under her heels) during the bus trip and walk up the road from the village. She's dressed for the day in her usual attire: modest, below-the-knee print skirt and untucked, cap-sleeved, white blouse. Meanwhile, I'm in well-worn pants and hiking shoes, sure this is what a trip to "deh country" requires.

Our first stop is a spring that Dingis had told us about many times, where the water bubbles from a rock wall and is channeled within bucket reach via a scrap of plastic eavestrough laid across a bamboo pole. "Make us a cup," Dingis instructs her grandnephew, and Kimon plucks an elephant ear–sized callaloo leaf that's growing near the water. With a few deft folds of the leaf and a wrap of the stem, he turns it into a long-handled drinking cup from which we each sip cold spring water. He spots crayfish in a nearby stream—as Dingis had predicted—and captures one with his hands so we can get a closer look. ("One day we will have a crayfish cook-up," she promises.) She then sends him a short distance into the forest to pick me a wild balisier, or heliconia, the giant red lobster claw of a flower that's related to the banana and so brilliantly colored, so exotic, and so flawless it almost seems a fake.

The beauty of this land, overflowing with stuff growing, makes my heart catch—though Dingis keeps pointing out what *isn't* here. "Before Ivan, we could have picked grapefruits and limes, but deh trees gone now." She shakes her head, still aghast at the state of the nutmegs. To our eyes, however, there are so many nutmeg trees that it's hard to imagine how many more there would have been before the hurricane. And the tourist board still trumpets that Grenada has more spices per square mile than any other place on the planet. Some of the trees are ready for harvesting, their ripe fruits (botanically, the pericarp) split open, revealing the glossy nutmeg with its lattice of mace (the aril) nestled inside: *Deh lady in deh boat wit' deh red petticoat,* says an old Grenadian rhyme. The overwhelming smell here is of rich, fertile forest after a rain, overlaid with the barest hint of spice from the open fruits.

When Dingis was a girl, she and her brothers would beat the trees with long sticks to shake the fruits to the ground, then gather the nutmegs into large sacks. Nature has already done the work today, and the ground is littered with nutmegs tossed free of their boats but still dressed in scarlet lace. Dingis insists we scoop them up to replenish our onboard supply.

· · ·

Mr. Mac has been growing nutmegs on this land for nearly half as long as nutmeg trees have existed on the island. "There are . . . some trees which I think bear nutmegs but at present no fruit," wrote Dr. Diego Álvarez Chanca, physician to Christopher Columbus's fleet during his second voyage to the

West Indies (1493–96). "I say I think because the smell and taste of the bark is like that of nutmegs." Whatever he smelled and tasted (he was on Hispaniola at the time), it was wishful thinking: nutmeg trees are only native to the Moluccas—the Spice Islands, in Indonesia—and didn't arrive in the New World until the early years of the nineteenth century. The Dutch, who ruled the Spice Islands before that, were determined to keep their monopoly on nutmeg. To ensure the trees didn't spread beyond lands they controlled, they washed the nutmegs in lime before shipping them so they couldn't be propagated elsewhere. They also destroyed trees and even part of the nutmeg crop when necessary to control production and keep prices high. When the Spice Islands briefly came under British rule beginning in 1796, however, nutmeg seedlings were sent to other British colonies for planting, including St. Vincent in 1802. Grenada came later.

Around 1840, the long arm of the British Empire was further responsible for nutmeg's spread, when successful sugar plantation managers in the British West Indies were sent to sugar plantations in the British East Indies to introduce their more efficient methods. When the Grenada-based sugarmen eventually returned home, they brought nutmegs with them. The island's first nutmeg tree is said to have been grown from seed brought from the Banda Islands by Frank Gurney and planted, in 1843, at Belvidere Estate—less than 5 miles as the crow flies from where we're walking.

Island lore doesn't give a reason for Gurney's desire for fresh nutmeg. But around the same time, Captain John Bell of the Royal Navy planted nutmeg seedlings on his Grenadian estate (which he called Penang, after his posting in Malaysia), apparently because he had become accustomed to having his rum punch with a sprinkling of the freshly grated spice on top. Steve and I can identify.

For the next two decades, nutmeg remained merely a curiosity in the Caribbean. But when a nocturnal worm took a huge bite out of the world supply of the spice in 1860, planters in Grenada jumped at the economic opportunity and started to grow nutmeg as a commercial crop. In the twentieth century, it surpassed sugar and cocoa as the island's largest export, and Grenada became the world's second-largest supplier (after Indonesia). Nutmeg remains so important to the Grenadian economy that "deh lady in deh boat wit' deh red petticoat" is depicted on the national flag. Though the island has rebounded since Ivan, nutmeg farming will be one of the last sectors to recover fully: the shallow-rooted, easily toppled nutmeg trees were among the worst casualties of the hurricane-force winds— and new nutmeg seedlings take ten to fifteen years to bear fruit.

. . .

"When you comin' back?" Rovel asks us repeatedly, as his sister Dingis used to. "You must come and spend deh night"—though the house, more than a little rustic, is unsuited to guests—"and deh next morning, I take you hiking in deh mountains." Dingis conveniently sidesteps the invitation with a more immediate plan: a stop at Kimon's house up the road to see his manicous— rough-haired, pointy-nosed, scaly-tailed, smallish, cat-sized things that are hunted (in season) for their meat.

Kimon scoops one out of a plastic barrel and sets it on the ground so we can get a good look. In the flash of an eye, one of the local mongrels lunges at it—these aren't even "Riot-Wilder" pups, like the ones listed for sale in the Classified section of one of Grenada's newspapers—and the next thing I know, the manicou is lying dead on the ground. I'm horrified—poor Kimon—and feel guilty that we're the cause of his pet being out where the dog could get it. But Kimon doesn't seem upset and neither, for that matter, does anyone else. "A manicou is an opossum," Steve whispers to me. "He's playing dead until the danger is over."

When it's time to leave, we catch a ride back to Union in a flatbed truck, Dingis and Gail sitting primly up front with the driver; Steve and I, sprawled in the back, clutching the sides and keeping low to avoid branches as we whip back down the mountain. I sleep most of the way on the two buses home, once again sandwiched into a rear seat. But this time, I'm surrounded on the first bus by the fumes of the local Rivers rum, thanks to the elderly Grenadian next to me, sleeping off his misspent afternoon.

"Listen to me," Dingis says as we hug good night back in Lower Woburn and thank her for taking us to see where she grew up, "don't forget to put deh nutmegs to dry. You know how to tell when they're ready? You shake them, and you can hear deh nut rattle in deh shell."

Sure enough, when I remember to check them a few weeks later, they click in my fingers like castanets. I put them in a jar carefully labeled *Nutmegs from Dingis's Family Land* and tuck it into *Receta*'s spice cupboard.

. . .

By this point, we are already a year and a half into our second journey, and the spice cupboard is filled to overflowing with the herbs and spices we've foraged, bought and been given along the way. Each time I open its door, some package, bottle, jar, box or bag inevitably spills out. Most are labeled with more than simply the name of a spice. Like the bag of nutmegs from Dingis's family, each has a provenance, a link to the land, a connection to a place and its people. Each wafts a scent that tells an island story.

· · · GINGER SPICE COOKIES · · ·

I use Dingis's nutmegs, plus Grenadian cloves, cinnamon and ginger (dried and fresh), to make these crisp, spicy little cookies. The white pepper adds an extra kick. Ginger's reputation as a natural seasickness remedy gives us a good excuse to bake them regularly.

2 ¼ cups	all-purpose flour	550 mL
¾ tsp	baking soda	4 mL
¼ tsp	ground cloves	1 mL
¼ tsp	freshly grated nutmeg	1 mL
1 tsp	ground cinnamon	5 mL
1 tsp	dried ginger	5 mL
1 tsp	white pepper	5 mL
½ cup	butter, at room temperature	125 mL
1 cup	granulated sugar	250 mL
1	egg, beaten	1
¼ cup	molasses	50 mL
1 tsp	white vinegar	5 mL
2 tbsp	finely chopped fresh ginger root	25 mL

1. Combine dry ingredients and spices and set aside.
2. In a large mixing bowl, cream butter and sugar well. Beat in egg.
3. Add molasses, vinegar and fresh ginger; mix well.

4. Gradually work dry ingredients into creamed mixture. Shape dough into 2 logs about 2" (5 cm) in diameter, wrap in plastic and refrigerate at least several hours or until firm.

5. When ready to bake, preheat oven to 350°F (180°C). Cut logs into scant ¼-inch (5 mm) slices. Place about ½ inch (1 cm) apart on nonstick or parchment-lined baking sheets.

6. Bake in preheated oven for 9 to 14 minutes, or until edges just start to brown. Remove from baking sheets and cool on racks.

Makes about 5 dozen cookies.

Tips:

- Use freshly ground whole white peppercorns for a stronger spicy bite.
- For crisp cookies, bake longer; for slightly chewy cookies, bake a little less.
- If you don't want to wait for your logs to get firm enough to slice, try this method instead: Shape dough into 1-inch (2.5 cm) balls. Place on baking sheet. Press with the bottom of a glass dipped in sugar to about ¼ inch (5 mm) thick. Bake 10 to 12 minutes. Makes about 4 dozen cookies.

· · · GRENADIAN BANANA BREAD · · ·
WITH CHOCOLATE, NUTMEG AND RUM

This dense, moist quick-bread is strongly rooted in the rain forests and fields of Grenada. The recipe was created by Canadian chef Frances Metcalf, who lives part of the year in Carriacou, Grenada's sister island. To suit our taste, I adjusted the spices and substituted dark, cocoa-rich Grenadian chocolate for coconut. The loaf contains no added fat, and is popular on Receta *for a snack or dessert. Try it toasted.*

Demerara sugar contains more molasses than regular brown sugar and gives the bread a hint of caramel flavor. It's available in some North American stores, or you can substitute dark brown sugar.

1 ½ cups	all-purpose flour	375 mL
1 ½ tsp	baking powder	7 mL
½ tsp	baking soda	2 mL
½ tsp	salt	2 mL
½ tsp	cinnamon	2 mL
½ tsp	freshly grated nutmeg	2 mL
¼ tsp	ground cloves	1 mL
1	egg, beaten	1
⅔ cup	lightly packed demerara or dark brown sugar	150 mL
¼ cup	dark rum	50 mL
1 ½ cups	mashed ripe banana (3 large bananas)	375 mL
1 tsp	freshly grated ginger (or ½ tsp/2 mL dried ginger)	5 mL
1 tsp	pure vanilla extract, or the beans of 1 vanilla pod	5 mL

| ⅓ cup | finely chopped high-quality dark chocolate (cocoa content of 65 percent or higher) (1 oz / 30 g) | 75 mL |
| ¼ cup | chopped pecans (optional) | 50 mL |

1. Preheat oven to 350°F (180°C). Grease and flour a 9" x 5" (2 L) loaf pan (or three 5"x 3"x 2" mini-loaf pans).
2. Combine dry ingredients and dry spices in a large bowl or on a sheet of waxed paper.
3. In a large bowl, combine egg, sugar, rum, mashed banana, fresh ginger, and vanilla or vanilla beans.
4. Pour dry ingredients into wet, and combine with quick, light strokes. Do not overmix.
5. Gently stir in chocolate and nuts (if using).
6. Scrape batter into prepared pan. Bake in preheated oven for 50 to 60 minutes (35 to 40 minutes for mini-loaves), or until a wooden skewer or cake tester inserted in the center of the loaf comes out clean.
7. Let stand in pan for 10 minutes, then turn out on rack to cool.

Makes 1 large loaf or 3 minis.

Self-Spicing Goats

· · · THE DOMINICAN REPUBLIC · · ·

The following rules are accepted between the rent company and the client: a) Lacknowieddce [sic] that rented equipment is in percet [sic] condition . . . b) The client must paid [sic] the cost of the car in case of theft and all the damages to the vehicle it is phisically [sic] or regally [sic] under his responsabible [sic] including robbery . . . d) Any injury for me any other rider or occupan [sic] to will not be the responsability [sic] of Odalis Rent Car. The renter agrees to Odalis Rent Car handless [sic] and no responsible for any legal action . . .

from the "Odalis Rent Car" contract, Luperón, DR

IN THE COMPARATIVE COOL of early morning, Luperón is full of life. As we walk into town from the *muelle*, where we've tied our dinghy, music already blares from Wendy's Bar, the lovesick *bachata* that makes my heart twinge. Loudspeakers squawk from produce-laden pickup trucks, announcing the availability of yucca, plantains or pineapples so unbelievably sweet they taste to our unaccustomed palates more like sugar-sweetened canned pineapple than fresh fruit.

I can see the industrious Rosa is already at work, sweeping the porch of her little cotton-candy-pink business, behind the sign that reads CAFETERÍA, MARISCOS, PESCADOS FRITOS, LAWNDRY—her imperfect English spelling perfectly anticipating how one's clothes will be handled. Farther along, Flaco, the skinny tailor, calls out "*Hola, hola*" from the doorway of his shop: always the double hello from everyone here, as if a single greeting might not be welcome enough. A wood fire smolders on the sidewalk of the main street in front of the *carnicería*, tended by the town's butcher. Wearing only shorts and a rubber apron, and wielding a long wooden paddle, he stirs a cauldron of hot oil that bubbles over the fire. *Chicharrones*—pork rinds— crisp in the boiling fat, the smell making Steve instantly ravenous. Luckily, we're on our way to Morena's small *comedor*, where she'll greet us with a kiss on each cheek, sit us under the lime tree in her backyard, tell us the progress of her daughter's difficult pregnancy and serve us a breakfast whose centerpiece is deep-fried cheese topped with fried red onions. Bliss.

We never intended to make Luperón our home for almost half a year, never expected to weave ourselves so firmly into the fabric of life in this small backwater of fishermen and farmers on the north coast of the Dominican Republic. We never anticipated that its slightly fetid smell (part sewage, part diesel exhaust, part rotting fish), its hot light, its heat—and the sleepy slowness that is heat's partner—would seep so deeply into our core. Luperón is only a scant hour's drive but a world away from the slick tourist areas of Puerto Plata and Playa Dorada.

"Let's have a written vote," Steve had said shortly after we arrived, and we both wrote *Stay* on our folded slips of paper— though I'd qualified my vote, adding, "And we'd better hope Dr. Gray is wrong." William Gray, Colorado State University's noted hurricane expert, had just predicted an unusually active hurricane season and, in a fit of clear thinking, we had just voted unanimously to spend it with our beloved *Receta* anchored smack-dab in the middle of the hurricane belt.

We had expected to be well south of the odds-on path of Caribbean hurricanes—safely out of "the box," as the insurance companies describe it—before the heart of hurricane season. "But the cruising gods are toying with us," I wrote in my journal when we were stopped much longer than we'd hoped at Great Exuma Island in the Bahamas. "For every five minutes of pure pleasure— the endless, mesmerizing, vertigo-inducing aqua of the Bahama Banks; swimming naked at Northwest Channel Light as the sun sets (why do I think it's scarier to swim naked? as if a teensy piece of thin Lycra is chain mail against a deviant barracuda or a shark), the sea-fresh crunch of a conch salad on Nassau's Potter's Cay— there are ten minutes that are frustrating or downright stressful."

Slowed by—cursed by—a series of boat breakdowns requiring days of troubleshooting followed by days of repair, we didn't arrive in the Dominican Republic until June 1, the official start of hurricane season. "We planned to be a thousand miles farther south by now," I lamented to Steve. "Plans are meant to be cast in Jell-O," he replied. "Written in the sand at low tide."

At least we won't be alone here: nearly one hundred other cruising boats are in the harbor, making Luperón their hurri- cane-season home. It's a better place than most to hide during *la temporada ciclónica,* as the Dominicans say, a proven hurri- cane hole. The mountainous backbone of the Dominican Republic holds storms south or rips them apart, Luperón harbor's narrow opening and overlapping reefs diffuse whipped-up seas, and the dense surrounding mangroves provide a protective cushion on all sides.

Granted, that protection comes at a price: the harbor's encircling arms create a placid pool, but they also cradle mangrove-
brown water "enriched" by runoff from a town without a
sewage system and from the anchored boats. No jumping off
Receta for a cooling swim, or dropping a fishing line from the
boat to catch dinner. Instead, we'll religiously carry bottles of
hand sanitizer. "Luperón," Steve says one day early in our stay,
"is the only place you have to wash your hands before you pee."

. . .

Only the *motoconchos*—100-cc bikes—move quickly here,
buzzing through the somnolent town with some outrageous
load on the back: perhaps three passengers, or a hundred-pound
propane cylinder, or (my favorite) a live, fully fattened, trussed
pig. A burro is usually tied up near the *panadería*, the bakery
where I buy still-warm bread and eggs recently delivered from
the chickens. Even a week later, their brilliant lemon-yellow
yolks sit up high in the pan, never collapsing unbidden into the
thick whites. Of course, I do have to wash off the odd feather
or splotch of shit before cracking them.

The produce trucks circulate lazily, looking for customers.
When I walk over to one that's piled with yucca, the starchy
tuber that's a staple on Dominican plates, the driver asks in
Spanish, "How much do you want?" "*Una libra*"—a pound—
I reply, pleased that my rusty Spanish, now pressed into daily
service, allows a ready response. But the driver explodes with
laughter; so too his assistant, and another customer. Nobody
buys just a pound of yucca, he explains—come to think of it,
my breakfast plate at Morena's probably contains a full pound
of boiled yucca alongside its deep-fried cheese—and hands

over what he considers the minimum acceptable amount: five big yucca, easily a good three pounds, for 20 pesos, roughly 60 cents U.S.

If we arrive early, someone will invariably be at a wooden table in front of one of the *pescaderías,* cleaning the morning's catch— red snappers, black snappers, small groupers and turquoise parrotfish—the scales spraying to the sidewalk in a glittery shower. Meanwhile, Luperón's mangy dogs—all seemingly fruit of the same family tree, indistinguishable except perhaps for varying stages of pregnancy—line up expectantly, tongues hanging out, in front of the *carnicería,* where the day's offerings are displayed on hooks in the open air: never much, just a few indeterminate cuts attracting more flies than customers. Occasionally, a herd of goats crosses the dusty main street, on its way to the outskirts of town to graze.

Last night we had *chivo guisado,* stewed goat, for dinner in a local restaurant. Goat and I have a troubled relationship, stemming mostly from an exceedingly muscular, still-hairy, fresh-killed leg I was once served for dinner on a sailboat in the Galápagos; but subsequently my antipathy has been kept alive by the odd goat roti with more bone and gristle than taste. This Dominican goat, however, was tender and flavorful, and a touch *picante*—the only spicy-hot dish we've encountered in *la comida criolla,* traditional Dominican cooking. The meat was first rubbed with garlic and oregano, then cooked with onions, peppers, a bit of tomato paste, white wine, a healthy splash of overproof Dominican rum, more garlic, and lots more oregano, the everyday herb of choice in this country. (Back home, a standard spice jar of oregano on the shelf of my local supermarket contains less than half an ounce; in one of Luperón's *colmados*— a category of food store smaller than a small supermarket—

oregano is available in three-and-a-half-pound sacks.) The chivo was served with mashed *auyama*, a basketball-sized squash that's green outside and yellow inside, with slivers of crisp fried red onion mixed in—perfect for soaking up every last bit of rich goat gravy.

"But the goat you get here isn't the best," Jaime Lantigua protests the next day, when I recount the meal. Jaime has become our go-to guy when Steve and I need a driver, and not just because his van doesn't resemble the typical Dominican vehicle. (For starters, it has usable seat belts, a functioning air conditioner, and only one small dent, a testament to Jaime's non-Dominican driving style, though he's lived in Luperón his whole life.) For that matter, Jaime (pronounced "High-mey") doesn't resemble a typical Dominican taxi driver either. He has the well-groomed look—fresh haircut, trim mustache—of a young exec, and he's always dressed as if he's on his way to the office on casual day. More importantly, he slows down the usual torrent of slurred syllables and dropped consonants that is rural Dominican Spanish—which turns *"Buenos días"* into *"Bueno día,"* for example—so I can understand almost every word, and he gently corrects the abuses I unintentionally inflict on his native tongue. Sure, his rate is almost double that of some other drivers, but the extra is just the price of the language, culture and culinary lessons we're given en route.

Although rail-thin, Jaime can be trusted when it comes to eating. He takes us to our favorite local cheesemaker to buy tangy, fresh *queso de hoja*, and explains that, for the best flavor, I shouldn't refrigerate it; and to Maimon, the town outside Puerto Plata where Dominicans line up at roadside *paradas* to eat whole, deep-fried fish, golden and crispy and carrying more than a hint of smoke from the wood fires over which they're cooked. These fish are meant to be consumed with one's fingers, Jaime says. How else to get every bit of the moist, sweet flesh from inside the crunchy skin?

"The best goat comes from Monte Cristi," Jaime continues, "because the goats there graze on hillsides where wild oregano grows." By the time the meat reaches the kitchen, it is already infused with the flavor of fresh herbs. Pre-marinated, if you will. He assures us we will see goats everywhere if we go to Monte Cristi, and goat on every *parada* menu. "You must try the Monte Cristi goat," Jaime insists.

Monte Cristi is at the very northwest edge of the country, close to the Haitian border, where the land is mostly inhospitable desert. It's time to rent a car ourselves, enlist friends to keep an eye on *Receta*, and hit the road.

. . .

I have avoided putting my name on rental-car contracts in foreign countries since the ugly day in Venezuela, almost twenty-five years ago, when I inadvertently entered a no-go zone and drove up to the front steps of the presidential palace. Our vehicle was immediately surrounded by soldiers (barely old enough to shave) with assault rifles, but, unfortunately, when I tried to back out of trouble, I couldn't get the car into reverse . . . which brought on an attack of uncontrollable nervous giggles. The youngsters cracked thin smiles and decided not to shoot us; Steve was not amused.

He, on the other hand, loves to drive in strange places, smoothly shifting from automatic to manual transmission, from twisting mountain roads to urban congestion, from left-hand to right-hand drive. Being behind the wheel, he says, also assures him he can stop whenever and wherever he pleases. He adjusts to foreign driving so easily that other people have been known to ask him to drive their rental cars.

The vehicles we rent, however, are somewhat less stellar than Steve's driving. In fact, we always seem to be assigned an SdJ or an SdS—Shitbox du Jour or Shitbox de la Semaine, depending on the term of the rental—named in memory of a car we were once saddled with in Martinique; its air conditioning was broken, but the heater worked a charm. Regrettably, there was no way to turn it off.

. . .

We christen our Dominican SdS the Odalismobile, after its owner. Odalis (we never determined whether that is his first or last name) operates out of a house on Luperón's main street, where a few unsteadily painted words on the wooden exterior are the only indication he has vehicles for rent. He takes only one form of payment (cash), offers no damage or theft insurance (unless you count The Club under the front seat of one of his rentals, or the holstered .45 under the front seat of another— we declined that insurance); and specializes in the vehicular equivalent of horses that are rode hard and put away wet. He is also the cheapest game in town. So we hand over a greasy mittful of pesos and head off in the Odalismobile—an overused Honda SUV with five balding tires.

Dominican driving lesson #1: If you ask a Dominican for directions and he tells you that you will cross two rivers, do not assume you will be crossing them by bridge.

"We can't," I say to Steve, surveying the scene in front of us with disbelief. The road we took out of Luperón, a confidence-inspiring solid black line on our map, has led us to a wide river—a raging torrent, actually, swollen by the previous night's rain. We can see the road climbing out of the fast-flowing water and continuing on the far shore. Concrete abutments topped with twisted, rusting rebar march partway across, with water swirling briskly around them, a broken promise of a bridge. Steve doesn't even put up a token argument, just jockeys the Odalismobile around so we can backtrack an hour and a half to Luperón and start again, this time heading toward the main highway from the opposite direction.

When you drive out of Luperón this way, town abruptly gives way to rural countryside just past the defunct cock-fighting ring at the end of the main street. In the morning, farmers squat along the roadside, waiting for the truck that comes twice a day to empty their milk cans. Their burros, with homemade tufted rag saddles like coats of many colors, graze patiently nearby. The approach of each small village—La Escalareta, El Estrecho, Vuelta Larga—is announced by a sign sponsored by Brugal, the largest rum producer in the DR, with 80 percent of the market. So, too, are the signs that say DESPACIO, ESCUELA—which is the Dominican equivalent to having a "Slow, School Zone" sign sponsored by Smirnoff or Absolut; none of the signs here, however, urge moderation or include a warning about drinking and driving. There are also a peculiarly high number of signs for car washes.

"So, do you think Dominicans have a thing about keeping their vehicles really clean?" Steve asks, visual evidence certainly to the contrary. Jaime eventually sets us straight: although you can get your car washed if you're so inclined, car washes are, in fact, places to drink and listen to music, to dance and ogle pretty girls. "They're a place to waste money," the exceedingly upright Jaime, father of two young daughters, says scornfully. They're called car washes, he explains, because taxes are lower for car washes than bars—the sort of hair-splitting, rule-circumventing fiddle at which Dominicans excel.

We curve onto Highway 1, the Carretera Duarte, which cleaves the country from end to end like a machete through a green coconut. We're only a dozen miles beyond the urban sprawl of Santiago, the DR's second-largest city, but already the thoroughfare has narrowed to a single bumpy lane in each direction. Rising abruptly from flat fields first of tobacco and then rice, the mountains of the Cordillera Septentrional form a luxuriant backdrop to the north, their peaks torn from tissue paper and layered one soft green sheet atop the other.

Soon, however, the land becomes more arid, and the silky neon-green rice fields are replaced by scrubby bush and tall cactus. Small, open-sided stands begin to pepper both sides of the road—one after the other—with fresh goat carcasses and "goat bacon" (sun-dried carcasses) hoisted under their sparsely thatched roofs; in case sales are brisk and the supply needs replenishing, most have meat on the hoof tethered to one of the stand's supporting posts. ("This is going to be a really bad day, Billy.") Interspersed with the stands are paradas, trumpeting their specialties on roadside signs: stewed goat, oven-roasted goat, goat picante, goat tripe. In case we still haven't got the message, the signs feature crude, horned silhouettes. Jaime was right: we have clearly arrived in goat country.

No, we don't want to buy a goat, we tell the young man presiding over the carcasses at one stand. But we'd sure like to eat some. Where should we go? Two ladies walking past chime in: "La Madonna, around the next curve."

. . .

"I'm not convinced," I say to Steve when the Odalismobile has settled into the narrow dirt clearing in front of La Madonna's two thatched-roof *palapas*, which sit only a car's length back from the road. They're furnished with plastic chairs, tables covered in burgundy leatherette, and a healthy population of flies. There's not a menu in sight.

Why bother with a menu when the only dish on offer is goat? We can have it either roasted (*horneado*) or stewed (*guisado*), we're told. We cross our fingers and order one of each, accompanied by rice and beans, salad and *tostones*—double-fried sliced green plantains, the starchy cooking cousin to bananas.

Like the goat in Luperón, the chunks of meat here have been roughly butchered. (That the meat is served on the bone is expected, but the additional slivers require a vigilant eye. "Be careful, no talking," my mother would have warned.) This goat meat, however, is a revelation—much more tender, and permeated with a rich, smoky, powerful oregano flavor. It's particularly obvious in the simply roasted horneado, which has no sauce to hide behind; both ways, it's a knockout, and we leave behind only a pile of well-cleaned bones (and slivers).

The meat carries the *"sabor del orégano,"* seventy-two-year-old Julián Tatiz confirms, because the goat did indeed graze on the wild herb. Slight and round-faced, with bright eyes and few teeth, Julián runs the kitchen at La Madonna: *"El maestro del chivo,"* his family calls him: the master of goat. Also the master of procreation: he's the father of twenty, he tells us right off the bat, when one of his granddaughters retrieves him from his cooking pots. His Spanish is almost impenetrable, quite different from what I've become accustomed to in Luperón, and my difficulty is compounded by his distinct lack of teeth. (In fact, I'm sure he spits one out into his hand while we're talking.)

Some weeks, he and his assistant cook a hundred goats, not just to serve in the restaurant, but also to fill orders from people in Santo Domingo and Santiago, he says. People travel for hours to eat at La Madonna, and those who have moved off the island—like the Dominican-born New Yorker eating at the table next to ours—insist on a visit when they return home. Can we return another day and watch him prepare his two goat dishes? Obviously proud of what he does, Julián gives the plan an unmistakable *sí, sí*. We arrange to circle back to Villa Elisa, where La Madonna is located, after a few days in the island's interior.

. . .

Dominican driving lesson #2: When you ask a Dominican if a certain road takes you where you want to go, he looks at your tires before answering—maybe even kicks them—and eyeballs the height of your vehicle off the ground. Do not ignore his advice. Because off the Carretera Duarte, the roads can be awe-inspiringly bad: steep uphills, steeper downhills, occasional washouts, the odd landslide, and deep, deep, rental-swallowing ruts, punctuated by tire-slashing rocks. That many are unpaved is a given.

Our first stop is Casabe Doña Mechi, a traditional cassava-bread bakery near Moncíon. Dominicans love their cassava bread, a bland, cracker-like flatbread made from the same stuff I'd bought so inexpertly in Luperón—yucca, a.k.a. cassava, or manioc. Andy Perailta, whose *mamá* owns the bakery, offers to show us around the decidedly low-tech operation, whose methods probably haven't changed much since the island's indigenous Tainos baked cassava bread for Columbus when he feasted with their chief on December 26, 1492. (Spiny lobster and root veg apparently completed the menu.) The only nods to modernity here are the gas-powered grinder that chips up the creamy-white yucca tubers after Andy and his brother have scraped off the dark skin, and the electric bandsaw that neatly carves the big round breads into quarters after baking. The screw press that squeezes the juice out of the grated yucca is operated by hand. The rough flour that's left after drying is mixed with water by hand, and patted by hand into molds resembling undersized hula hoops. The breads bake on a long, flat-topped griddle heated by a series of wood fires underneath.

Two types of cassava are found in the Caribbean, bitter and sweet, both containing hydrocyanic glucoside, or prussic acid, in their juice. Sweet cassava has only a little, but bitter cassava contains enough to poison a person if eaten raw, and the juice must be squeezed out or removed by thorough cooking. The Amerindians invented a long, woven, sleeve-like basket, called a *tipiti*, to squeeze the juice from bitter cassava flesh. Though their boss safely ate bitter cassava made into bread, Columbus's men likely encountered it in another form: the Tainos used the poisonous liquid to coat the tips of their spears and arrows. It was also the method of choice for those Tainos who later committed suicide to escape enslavement by the Spanish.

Like the method for making it, cassava bread itself has moved through the centuries pretty much unchanged from its Amerindian roots. To the uninitiated, it bears a taste and textural resemblance to cheap cardboard. Still, Steve and I are determined to try it straight from the source, and load up not just on Doña Mechi's big round flatbreads, but also on multiple packages of the same cassava "dough" formed into little curls and batons flavored with anise. They have an appealing, earthy, roasted-corn smell as they bake, and we are sure they will be delicious.

They aren't. The Odalismobile's backseat is now full of plain and anise-flavored cardboard.

We had heard about a sacred Taino site close to the bakery, called Los Charcos de Los Indios—the Pools of the Indians—and ask Andy if he can guide us there. The young man and his father circle the Odalismobile, eyeballing the freeboard and kicking the tires. Much discussion ensues, but the speed and the local dialect make it difficult for me to follow. I do pick up the words for "steep" and "through the river." I am immediately on high alert.

The Odalismobile apparently passes muster. Andy wedges himself into the backseat amid the multiple packages of his family's baking, and we set off.

Minutes later, we're perched atop a ridge. The view is spectacular—but the road down looks like a burro path, crazily steep, all rock and rut, interspersed with craters deep enough to swallow an SUV. "*No hay problema,*" says Andy. "No problem," agrees Steve. I just close my eyes and clutch the door handle all the way to the bottom, as we slalom around boulders and lurch through gullies at about a mile per hour.

The road ends at the edge of the rock-infested Río Gurabo. My heart sinks—until I realize that Andy's and his father's inspection had been about simply making it to the river: from here, we will continue, mercifully, on foot—wading upstream. After about a twenty-minute hike through water that varies from ankle to thigh deep, our first glimpse of Los Charcos makes me forget (at least temporarily) that the Odalismobile has to make it back up the precipice. Carved into the cliff above a waterfall that drops gently into a quiet pool is a hundred-foot-high face whose round mouth is formed by a cave, which the Tainos believed was an entrance to the spirit underworld. One side of the face has broken away over time, but otherwise the immense pre-Columbian totem is an exact, scaled-up version of the palm-sized clay Taino figurines we later see in the national museum in Santo Domingo. All alone, we soak in the magic of a place that Andy says outsiders—save for a few archaeologists—seldom see. No surprise, given what it took to get here.

· · ·

The price we pay for our glimpse of the Taino world is revealed the next day, when the Odalismobile's overworked tires start popping like balloons at a kids' birthday party. The first *pinchazo*—flat—comes as we're climbing through the paper-clip-tight turns on the narrow, shoulderless road to Constanza, a huge, rich bowl of high-altitude agriculture in the heart of the island's central mountain range. Among the non-tropical crops that grow abundantly in Constanza's comparatively cool mountain air are strawberries—such a profusion that thick, icy strawberry juice is a popular, and inexpensive, local drink.

Unfortunately, there's not even enough room to pull off this sky-high road 4,200 feet above sea level, let alone do a repair. We have no choice but to limp along on the rim until we reach a tiny, nameless pueblo consisting of just a couple of rough houses.

The Odalismobile's doors have barely opened when a swarm of men appears and surrounds the little Honda. "Maybe we should go a bit farther," I whisper nervously, taking in the unsmiling faces and remembering that Jaime had warned us not to stop even at police checkpoints off the beaten path because of the likelihood of a shakedown. "We can't," says Steve, already digging out the jack.

That's when the men spring into action, taking matters into

their own hands and the jack out of Steve's. Like a well-oiled Indy pit crew, one guy begins jacking up the vehicle, two more unbolt the spare from the rear door and another wedges stones around the wheels. Yet another stands poised with the lug wrench, ready to remove the flat the second it is clear of the ground. Now I realize their unsmiling faces are merely serious, not unfriendly: they are clearly accustomed to many flat tires on their road, and there's work to be done.

Meanwhile, I'm offered a chair to join the gathered crowd of spectators—women, children, babies and any males not helping. The Odalismobile is the afternoon's entertainment in this hardscrabble village. But the action is over quickly. Within minutes, our mountain pit crew has the fresh tire on, the flat secured to the door and the tools stowed, and they are dusting off their hands and waving us on our way.

"*Muchísimas gracias.*" I thank them profusely, feeling guilty for my initial mistrust, and I tell them that we want to reimburse them for their time and trouble. They vigorously wave off my offer of payment, with "*de nada, de nada*"—it's nothing, it's nothing, you're welcome, you're welcome—but I can't leave without somehow expressing our thanks.

Suddenly I remember the unloved bread, curls and batons in the backseat. I pile them in my arms and hand them to one of the pit crew. "Perhaps your children might enjoy these."

And as we rumble back onto the road, leaving behind a cloud of dust, I turn around to wave a final *adiós*—and see an entire mountain village, adults and kids alike, along the roadside, munching contentedly on cassava.

· · ·

Good thing we take the advice of our pit-crew Good Samaritans and get the flat fixed at a *gomería*—tire shop—ASAP. Pinchazos #2 and #3 follow in short order. (The frequency with which we pass gomerías is an excellent indicator of the Dominican need for tire repairs. Steve figures the entire DR economy rides on gomerías.) First, we heap insult on Taino injury by taking a shortcut from Constanza to another mountain town, Jarabacoa. "This dirt road [affords] stunning panoramas along the way," says our guidebook, then holds out an irresistible carrot to Steve. "Although not in very good shape, it is passable for cars, except in the days following heavy rains." I insist we ask about the road's current condition, and the Odalismobile gets the customary inspection before we're given a thumbs-up to proceed.

The panoramas are indeed stunning—though only slightly more spectacular than the ruts and boulders we weave through along the entire length of the mountain's spine. I'm reminded of Haitian writer Edwidge Danticat's description of the roads of her country, which shares the island of Hispaniola with the Dominican Republic. Quoting a friend, she said, "The roads are bad so you can truly appreciate the beauty of where you're going once you get there. These roads are there so one can *earn* the beauty." Steve finds himself changing a tire in Jarabacoa after dark.

And then, the next day, we pick up three hitchhikers: older ladies waiting patiently at the roadside with their luggage for a very infrequent bus. They're on their way to a relative's funeral in a *pueblo* so small it's not even on our detailed map, and the last stretch of road to the family's door is clearly designed only for four-legged beasts. "God will repay you," the eldest says when we finally arrive, pointing skyward and hugging first me and then Steve. God does, thereafter blessing us with a drivable slow leak, rather than a full-out flat tire.

. . .

Dominican driving lesson #3: If you don't react quickly when you see something potentially yummy along the roadside, you will most certainly miss an opportunity that won't arise again. People selling exactly the same thing—enormous white radishes, say, or baskets of perfectly ripe, fragrant strawberries, or succulent hunks of roasted pork with crackling skin from whole pigs turning on spits—are packed into a short stretch of road, one after the other after the other. Continue a mile or so, and you won't see a single place to buy what was in abundance, cheek by jowl, a short distance back.

"Pull over now," I yell as we're cruising past the village of Bayacanes on our way to the main highway, which will return us (eventually) to La Madonna. We'd let a few go by, but this is too incredible a sight to resist: giant, golden, bowl-shaped cakes at stall after stall, a woman standing guard behind each one. Steve slews onto the shoulder and parks the Odalismobile in what we henceforth call the Village of the Big Cakes.

Denise, the woman at our chosen stall, slices off a sample: it's reminiscent of a sweet corn pudding, with overtones of coconut, cinnamon and vanilla. She tells us she bakes one of these giant cornmeal cakes, called *arepas*, every day. So do all the other ladies. (The people in the Village of the Big Cakes must really like arepas.) Some stalls even have two giant cakes, one sweet and one savory, the local version of polenta. Each stall is "sponsored" by Mazorca, a popular brand of corn flour, and decorated in the colors of its packaging, a sunny yellow and a bright sky blue, and each woman has just one other item for sale besides her giant cakes: tall stacks of deep-fried, dinner plate–sized flatbreads. Crisp and wafer thin, except where the surface is raised into golden-brown bubbles, these *yaniqueques*, as Denise tells us they're called, are totally addictive.

Yaniqueques—pronounced like "johnnycakes," except with a "y" sound at the start and a stutter at the end—are a Dominican version of that typical Caribbean quick-bread. They got their Spanglish name because johnnycake (from "journey cake," since the bread was meant to be carried on journeys, including to work in the fields) came to the DR with immigrants from the English-speaking Caribbean. We encounter johnnycakes on many islands in many forms—from the pan-baked squares of the Bahamas, to the deep-fried, cake-like golf balls of St. Kitts, to Puerto Rico's flat fried biscuits called *yani-clecas*—but none can hold a candle to the Dominican yaniqueques. The only problem is, we never see them elsewhere during our travels in the DR . . . which in Steve's mind necessitates first a detour back to Bayacanes when we need another fix, and second a request for me to hone my skills as onboard yaniqueque-maker.

. . .

The kitchen at La Madonna is open-air on two sides, with a pile of firewood in the middle of its dirt floor and goat carcasses hanging from hooks in the ceiling. A series of *fogones*—blazing wood fires—runs along one of the open sides, with a heavy iron pot supported by cinder blocks bubbling above each one. At least a dozen members of the Tatiz family work at the restaurant, and they have crowded into the kitchen to watch the *gringa*'s cooking lesson.

"This chivo is entirely different from the other chivo,"

Valentin Tatiz, one of Julián's sons, shouts at me in Spanish for at least the fifth time, pointing between pots of roasted and stewed goat. He seems to believe that turning up the volume will hasten my comprehension of his father's instructions.

His father isn't so sure, and decides to test me: "*Qué pasa con el horneado?*" Julián asks. I stammer back the steps for making roasted goat, starting with hacking the carcass into stew-sized chunks and washing them in lime juice and water to rid the meat of any strong smell. (Julián switches to the juice of sour oranges when limes aren't in season.) As I list the ingredients for the seasoning mixture which is then pushed into slits cut in the meat, Valentin bellows each one back at me, and Julián smiles approvingly: *mucho* garlic and black pepper, which they grind fresh on the spot in two large, hand-cranked, table-mounted grinders (think the type used for grinding sausage meat), a little oil and lime juice, salt, crumbled dried oregano (a full shopping bag of it sits on the table), onion and green pepper.

There are no ovens here. The chivo horneado is roasted in a pot over one of the fires. Partway through its three-hour cooking time, the pot is covered with a flat metal sheet, and burning chunks of wood are shoveled on top, so that the heat comes from both a low fire underneath and hot coals above.

Julián's chivo guisado is simplicity itself. The goat, already flavored with oregano from its diet, is stewed in its own juices until tender, with only more oregano, garlic, salt and pepper. Then onion, lime juice, a bit of tomato sauce, and water are added to make a gravy. "Nothing more," shouts Valentin. The oregano-grazing goats of *la línea noroeste*—the northwest line, as the region of the Dominican Republic that borders Haiti is known, and why this style of goat is also called *chivo liniero*, goat of the line—don't need much in the way of added ingredients.

. . .

Despite all the miles we've put on the Odalismobile, we've yet to see a herd of the grazing chivos. "They're in the mountains," Julián tells us, waving a hand to indicate farther to the northwest. "I buy them from a variety of farms there."

We've yet to see a goat cheese, either. Back in Luperón, Jaime had suggested we try the creamy fresh cheeses made from goat's milk—at least I thought he had—and I've been sorely testing Steve's patience with my unsuccessful attempts to get my hands on some. "You just got another pity-the-crazy-gringa look," he says, after I make him pull over at yet another place advertising goat, ask about goat cheese, and then return to the Odalismobile empty-handed. "You're chasing red herrings."

And so in search of grazing goats (both of us) and goat cheese (me), we head 25 miles farther toward the town of Monte Cristi. The hills creep closer and the landscape becomes drier and dustier, until the highway ends at the Atlantic Ocean. The air shimmers in the afternoon heat, and we pass a surreal scene of bare-chested men shoveling snow: piling up mounds of it, then throwing it into wheelbarrows; we can see the glittering flakes. In fact, they are working the salt pans, the main occupation here besides fishing and tending goats.

As we close in on Monte Cristi, El Morro looms. The dry, scrub-covered, flat-topped mountain stands by itself, defining the landscape at the very northwestern tip of the Dominican Republic. Behind it runs long, exquisite, unimaginatively named Playa Detrás Del Morro ("Beach Behind El Morro"), where a derelict wooden lifeguard's stand is slowly returning to nature. No need for it: SOLO CRISTO SALVA—"Only Christ saves"—reads the message painted across one of its boards. A quick glance around both beach and mountain shows they are devoid of goats.

Goats don't graze there anymore, Claudio Peña tells us. Claudio—Caito, to his friends—explains that the mountain is public property, and thus any goats that once roamed wild there have long since been eaten. Although Caito works as a handyman at our hotel just outside Monte Cristi, he comes from a family of *criadores*, goat breeders. He will take us to his uncle's goat corrals that evening. "It's not far," he assures us.

Caito's idea of "not far" covers a lot more ground than mine does—especially when the much-abused Odalismobile is bumping at ten miles per hour along an unpopulated, unpaved, unlit, heavily washboarded track and dusk is falling. "Keep going, keep going," he says, when Steve slows for a small herd of goats moving along the shoulder. "There will be more, many more."

An understatement. His uncle Moreno's corrals hold hundreds of goats, as do the corrals of his neighbors—blurs of black and white and chestnut in the fading light. They are let out in the morning, Caito explains, to head, untended, into the hills, where they spend the day grazing, as do the goats from the many other corrals. At day's end, they regroup with their herd and make their own way back to the correct corral. Not just tasty, but smart. "They even look both ways before crossing the streets in town," Jaime had told us before we left Luperón.

Caito pulls a handful of pods off a tree to show us a smallish fruit the goats also eat. But I haven't seen any of the oregano that's responsible for their flavor. Several times, he says what sounds to my Spanish-as-a-second-language ears like "*matar orégano*"—to kill oregano—and I suspect the worst: the goats have overgrazed and destroyed all the oregano around here. I eventually catch on, with the help of my dictionary and Uncle Moreno's demonstration. Caito has been saying "*mata de orégano*"—which means oregano bush. But I'd been looking for small plants, like the garden-variety oregano back home. Uncle Moreno walks us to a shrub that's easily five feet high, and crumples a handful of its leaves. The air is suddenly awash with the familiar scent. "In the hills, the oregano bushes are even larger than this one," Caito says. "Like small trees."

"Do you make goat cheese from the milk?" I ask Caito and Uncle Moreno. I can feel Steve doing his trademark rolling of the eyes behind me.

No, they don't generally milk the goats, Caito explains, so they can have a self-sustaining herd. "The milk feeds the kids."

"But we do occasionally make a sweet from goat's milk," Moreno says. He will be happy to milk one goat the next morning, so Caito can bring us *dulce de leche de chiva*.

"This must have been what Jaime was talking about," I whisper delightedly to Steve, certain that my quest is ending.

Unfortunately, it turns out not to be so. The next morning, Caito returns from the hills dulce-de-leche-less: Moreno had to head off early to tend to a sick animal, and didn't have time for the milking and making. And we are heading back to Luperón that day.

As darkness falls, Moreno closes the corral and we washboard our way back down the track, back to our hotel, back to a late dinner. Goat, of course, tasting of the very land it came from.

· · · CHIVO GUISADO (STEWED GOAT) · · ·
IN THE STYLE OF LA MADONNA

By marinating the meat with oregano first and then adding a hefty quantity of it to the sauce, this stew echoes the intense, herby flavor of La Madonna's. If you can't get (or don't like) goat meat, you can substitute lamb. Serve it with steamed rice for soaking up the rich sauce.

2 lb	goat meat, cut into large cubes	1 kg
3	limes	3
4 tbsp	olive oil	65 mL
2	large cloves garlic, chopped	2
4 tsp	dried oregano	20 mL
1 tbsp	freshly ground black pepper	15 mL
	Salt	
1	medium red onion, chopped	1
1	small can (about 8 oz/125 mL) plain tomato sauce	1
	Hot pepper sauce (to taste)	

1. Put the meat in a large bowl and cover with water. Add the juice of 1 lime, swirl the meat in the liquid, and allow to stand for about 5 minutes.
2. In a small bowl, combine the juice of 1 lime, half the oil, half the garlic, half the oregano, half the pepper and some salt. Drain the meat and rub in the mixture. Cover and refrigerate for several hours or overnight.
3. In a pressure cooker or large pot, heat the remaining olive oil and sauté remaining garlic until soft.
4. Add the meat to pressure cooker or pot. Stir to coat the pieces in the oil and brown on all sides.

5. Add remaining oregano and pepper. Cover pressure cooker and cook under pressure for 30 minutes, or cover pot and cook for 1 hour.

6. Release pressure and/or open pot. Add onion, tomato sauce and the juice of the remaining lime. Cook under pressure for another 20 minutes, then allow pressure to decrease naturally. Or cover pot and cook for about 1 hour longer, or until meat is very tender.

7. Skim excess fat from sauce. Add hot pepper sauce. Taste and adjust seasoning. Serve with rice and additional pepper sauce.

Makes 4 servings.

· · · YANIQUEQUES · · ·
FROM THE VILLAGE OF THE BIG CAKES

Like the ones we discovered in Bayacanes, these crisp, crunchy, bubbled, golden flatbreads disappear way too quickly. Serve warm with drinks.

2 cups	all-purpose flour	500 mL
2 tsp	granulated sugar	10 mL
1 ½ tsp	baking powder	7 mL
1 ½ tsp	salt	7 mL
⅓ cup	vegetable shortening	75 mL
¾ cup	hot water (approx)	175 mL
	Oil (for deep frying)	

1. Toss flour, sugar, baking powder and salt in a bowl. Cut in shortening until mixture resembles fine crumbs.
2. Slowly pour in water and mix until a soft dough forms. (You may not need all the water.)
3. Cover bowl with plastic wrap and allow dough to rest for about 15 minutes. Meanwhile, in a heavy pot, heat about 2 inches (5 cm) oil to 375°F (190°C) for deep frying.
4. Divide dough into balls about the size of golf balls and dip in flour.
5. Roll each ball into a thin circle (approx 6 inches/15 cm). Slide circles individually into hot oil and fry, turning once, until golden brown on both sides (about 1 ½ minutes per side).
6. Drain on paper towels. Serve warm.

Makes about 10.

Tips:

- The yaniqueques can be fried a few hours ahead and reheated. Place them, unwrapped, on a baking sheet in a preheated 350°F (180°C) oven for about 5 minutes.
- Try them sprinkled with a little sea salt or, for a non-traditional sweet treat, cinnamon and sugar.

· · · STARBURST SALAD · · ·

This simple composed salad became a staple on Receta *in* Luperón, *where lettuce and other quick-to-spoil leafy greens were hard to come by. Crisp, mild, long-lasting* tayota—*called chayote in most North American supermarkets and christophene in the English-speaking Caribbean—is one of its cornerstones. A member of the squash family, it's good either cooked or raw. Even the large, flat seed, which tastes vaguely almond-like, is sliced and used in this salad.*

½	small clove garlic, finely chopped	½
½ tsp	Dijon mustard	2 mL
1 tbsp	red-wine vinegar or lime or lemon juice	15 mL
2 tbsp	extra-virgin olive oil	25 mL
	Salt and freshly ground black pepper	
1	cucumber, peeled, cut in half, seeded and sliced	1
1	ripe tomato, sliced	1
½	medium tayota (chayote or christophene), peeled and sliced lengthwise (including the seed)	½
1	ripe but firm avocado, peeled and sliced	1

1. Combine garlic, mustard, and vinegar or juice. Whisk in oil. Season to taste.
2. Toss the cucumber with some of the dressing and mound in the center of a large plate.

3. Around the cucumber, arrange alternating slices of
   remaining vegetables.
4. Drizzle with remaining dressing to taste and serve.

Makes 4 servings.

Tip:
• Sprinkle the salad with some chopped fresh cilantro
  or other herbs.

THREE

The Egg Ladies

· · · THE DOMINICAN REPUBLIC & HAITI · · ·

"*Ojalá que llueva café*," Juan Luis Guerra's hit merengue pleaded: "*So the people on their little farms do not suffer so much, / O Lord, let it rain coffee in the countryside.*" He sang of the peasants' dreams of filling the mountainsides and their dinner tables with strawberries, sweet potatoes, wheat, and rice.

· · ·

The memory of what happened at the Massacre River in 1937 is still vivid in the minds of the islanders. Even now, it is nearly impossible for Dominicans and Haitians to think of each other without some trace of the tragedy of their mutual history that took place that year.

from Why the Cocks Fight: Dominicans, Haitians,
and the Struggle for Hispaniola *by Michele Wucker, 1999*

STEVE LEARNED HIS LESSONS WELL from Caito and Moreno. Managing—as usual—to drive and sightsee at the same time, he spots oregano bushes along the Carretera Duarte as we leave Monte Cristi. Before I can react, he pulls onto the shoulder where the cacti are sparsest. We ease ourselves gingerly between them to the most accessible oregano bushes and break off a few well-leafed branches, depriving some goat of an easy lunch.

Back in Luperón, the faithful (if somewhat sweaty and muddy) Odalismobile is returned to its owner, who will give it only the quickest of rubdowns before passing it to the next lucky client. Later, a baking sheet full of fresh oregano from la línea noroeste dries in the sun in a breeze-protected corner of *Receta*'s cockpit.

"You're right," I tell Jaime the next day. "Monte Cristi goat is the best." He turns thoughtful, and then says, "But maybe you also need to try the Azua chivo?" Oh, please, no more goat. A second region—Azua on the south coast—has a rivalry going with Monte Cristi, he explains. The Azua goats are farm-raised, so they're fatter and meatier than the free-ranging Monte Cristi ones. And they're even more tender, since they don't have to work as hard for their food. But that means they don't forage for oregano (and it's not otherwise in their diet), which Jaime thinks gives Monte Cristi goats the clear edge. "We tried some Azua goat in Santo Domingo and we agree," I assure him, hoping he'll be satisfied that further taste tests are unnecessary.

After sampling chivo steadily for a week now, I'm more than ready for some *pica pollo*, the Dominican take on fried chicken, or a little seafood. Luperón's fishermen row or putt-putt past *Receta* before dawn each morning, my reliable snooze-button; I know I have another hour to sleep when I hear them passing gently by. And when they pass a second time, later, with their catch, we can wave them over and bargain for fish or lobster.

We also know by now that we have to arrive at Laisa's small, one-room restaurant (affectionately nicknamed the "Chicken Shack") on the main street by noon or shortly after: When the lunchtime batch of her irresistible pica pollo is gone, there's no more until dinner. The wiry local birds—well seasoned and deep-fried into extreme crispiness—give her pica pollo a satis-fying toothiness (and, admittedly, with the occasional hard-luck hen, a full-jaw workout) that's lacking in the springy, even-tex-tured, bland, mass-produced chicken we'd become accustomed to eating in North America.

The Dominican Republic hammers home connections between food and the land that produces it. In Canada and the United States, local-food movements are gaining strength; in the towns and villages here, they never lost it. Forget the 100-Mile Diet—people in Luperón are on the 5-mile one. Here, though, it's not a matter of choice: transportation costs scarce pesos, and locally grown, seasonal food is cheap. That it tastes better is just a side benefit. (That it's better in the global big picture never comes under consideration.)

When local trees are weighed down with ripe mangoes, I can buy them in every *colmado* in Luperón. But when the trees dry up, the fruit disappears entirely from our little town. Then we have to travel with Jaime 11 miles down the green road, past La Escalareta, where a *policía acostado* (lying policeman, or speed bump) guards the entrance to the village, toward Imbert, where fields of sugar cane press in from both sides of the road. Soon, we will begin to see tables with mangoes spilling out of king-size cans that once held powdered milk. Eighty pesos (less than US$2.50) buys fifteen big, fleshy, fra-grant mangoes—because beyond Luperón, there are still trees on the island heavy with fruit.

Shopping, consequently, isn't always easy. Steve, who his-torically avoids—no, abhors—grocery stores, willingly comes along here (he even volunteers), because every excursion to put food on board *Receta* is an adventure.

One of our regular stops is the shop next to the animal-feed store at the far end of Calle Duarte, Luperón's main street. Although it rarely has what we're looking for, we always give it a try, if only because the guy behind the counter is so unfailingly friendly. "*Vaya con Dios,*" he says each time we leave, albeit usually empty-handed. "Go with God."

"Do you have any *limones?*" I ask him one day, knowing the local trees are full of juicy little key limes. As usual, he shakes his head no. "Did you try next door?" he asks.

"Yes, I didn't see any."

"But did you ask?"

I go back. I ask. They have a crate full of limones. Behind the counter.

The young man who works in this colmado—barely a teenager—is eager to practice his English, and we soon strike a compromise: he talks to me in English when I come to shop, and I respond *en español.* Staple foodstuffs are sold in one-meal quantities here, for those who don't have refrigerators or can't afford to buy more than a small amount at once: a bit of tomato paste, for instance, spooned into a plastic bag from an institutional-size can around which flies buzz happily; a few ounces of cooking oil poured into a container brought from home; or a couple of tiny sprigs of cilantro. Granted, adolescent cockroaches stroll unmolested along the counter—which means I have to give my purchases serious scrutiny and dunk the fresh stuff in a bug-busting bath (an antibacterial-soap wash, followed by a chlorine-water rinse) before anything is allowed below decks on *Receta.*

Early in our stay, the young man's wizened grandmother was behind the counter one morning. "How are you today?" I asked her in my best Spanish. "*Bien, bien, gracia' a Dio',*" Grandmother replied, keeping me on my linguistic toes with the usual local dropping of "esses." I'd been impatiently waiting for mango season to start and, having seen her granddaughter come into the colmado with a mango in each hand, I asked her whether she had any for sale. "No," she replied. But she shouted after the young girl, who had disappeared into the back. The girl returned and handed one of her mangoes to her grandmother, who handed it to me. "No, no, I can't take it, it's hers," I protested. But the woman insisted the girl had another, stuffed the mango in my bag, put a hand on my elbow and steered me firmly out of the colmado before I could grab some pesos from my wallet. Generosity, even among those who have little, is another fact of life here.

. . .

Even poor Dominicans look rich compared with their Haitian neighbors. And they get to show it twice a week, at a street market in the Dominican town of Dajabón, about 22 miles south of Monte Cristi, on the border where the Dominican Republic meets Haiti at the aptly named Río Masacre, the Massacre River. The two countries share the island of Hispaniola uneasily—at times violently during the last two centuries—and huge cultural and racial prejudices exist between the two. Direct mail service between the neighbors didn't start until 1998; before that, letters were routed through Miami.

For twenty-two years, beginning in 1822, Haiti occupied its neighbor, until a separatist movement led by Juan Pablo Duarte (after whom the DR's main highway, Luperón's main street, and countless other roadways are named) recaptured the capital, Santo Domingo, in a bloodless coup. But their most horrific moment came in 1937, when Dominican dictator Rafael Trujillo, whose oppressive regime lasted thirty-one years (until his assassination in 1961), ordered the extermination of Haitian peasants living on the Dominican side of the border. The price of sugar had plummeted, Haitian workers were no longer needed in the cane fields, and Trujillo, also obsessed with ethnic cleansing, saw a way to appease Dominicans angry about their economic situation and looking to cast blame. At least fifteen thousand Haitians were killed. Before hacking them to death with machetes—less traceable to the government than shooting them, since only soldiers had guns—Trujillo's men used a simple test to separate Haitians from Dominicans: they held up a sprig of parsley—*perejil* in Spanish—and asked them to name the herb; the Creole-speaking Haitians could not properly roll the *r* and were dispatched without further formalities.

Desperately poor Haitians continue to leave their country— the poorest in the Western Hemisphere—and cross the border illegally to take on brutal work in the cane plantations and sugar mills of the DR, filling their neighbor's need for cheap labor and forming an exploited illegal underclass that subsists in company shantytowns called *bateyes*. Some have migrated to other equally scorned jobs in the cities. In *Why the Cocks Fight*, her study of the relationship between Haiti and the DR, Michele Wucker bluntly writes: "Dominicans will not do the work [the Haitians] do, and most Dominicans hardly blink at the subhuman treatment meted out to the immigrants."

This historical, cultural and political baggage is available for public inspection every Monday and Friday at the Dajabón market, when the border is opened briefly to legally allow impoverished Haitians to enter a six-block stretch of the Dominican Republic, its perimeter guarded by Dominican soldiers. They come to buy food and other household necessities, including the wood for their cooking fires, since the Haitian side of the island has been almost completely deforested and its soil washed away. The land can't produce enough of even the most basic foodstuffs—bananas, plantains, yucca, rice and beans—let alone support livestock. "What's the fastest animal in the world?" begins a telling joke making the rounds in the Dominican Republic at the expense of its desperately poor and hungry neighbor. "A Haitian chicken."

But the Haitians who come to the Dajabón market are sellers as well as buyers. To get money to buy the food and firewood they need, they sell what they don't need: the overflow of donated goods they have received in aid from the developed world. Friends in Luperón who have already made the trip to Dajabón described a frenzied, chaotic, overwhelmingly enormous, open-air version of Value Village or the Sally Ann. We need to see it for ourselves.

"We've rented a car"—another SUV Odalismobile—"to drive to Dajabón," I tell Jaime. His face drops and he shakes his head. "*Muy pobre, muy triste,*" he says. Very poor, very sad. He takes my notebook and draws a simple sketch to orient us when we arrive, showing the street leading to the border, the Dominican customs building, the so-called Friendship Bridge, and the unfriendly metal gates across its middle. Then he fills the simple map with dots of ink. "*Gente,*" he says. People. He has dotted a solid sea of humanity.

"And when you leave Dajabón afterward, you must stop at the roadblock." "Why, Jaime?" Steve asks. After all, he'd advised us in the past not to stop at any roadblocks—just to avoid eye contact with the police or soldiers and breeze on by. "The guards outside Dajabón want to make sure Haitians don't sneak from the market area farther into the country, and they will get angry if you don't stop. They have long boards filled with nails, and they will throw them onto the road to stop anyone who attempts to run the roadblock." Though the Dominicans don't want the jobs the Haitians take, they also don't want them in their country.

. . .

When we arrive in the growing dusk, Dajabón has an unsettling, almost war-zone feel to it. Young soldiers in olive-and-tan camouflage fatigues, rifles dangling casually by their sides, gather under the trees at the edges of the town park. The deserted streets are a jumble of broken concrete, jagged pipes and heavy equipment from a municipal improvement project, but they look to us more like the aftermath of a bombing.

Closer to the river, the town seems less menacing, more active. Trucks loaded with sacks of onions and garlic, crates of salted fish, heads of cabbage, stalks of plantains and bags of rice jockey for space to unload, as Dominicans who have arrived in Dajabón from across the country prepare for the next day's market.

On the evening before market day, the severe steel gates across the middle of the Friendship Bridge are locked tight as prison-cell bars. But the closed bridge isn't stopping Haitians who want to cross into the DR for a head start on the next day's commerce. Holding their goods high, they are wading or being carried across the thigh-deep river on the backs and shoulders of human beasts of burden, and pay a *mordita*, a little bite, or bribe, to land on the other side. We walk out onto the bridge as far as we can for a better look. None of the Dominican soldiers seems to be taking notice of the traffic through the river. However, after about five minutes, one of them chases us off the bridge. "Closed," he says, before asking for a little something to supplement his meager army pay.

The following morning, the bridge opens at daybreak, and a river of humanity starts to stream from Haiti into the DR. The flood is seemingly endless, completely mesmerizing, overwhelming—denser, even, than Jaime's sea of dots. The Haitians are distinguishable from the Dominicans by their high cheekbones, darker skin, and the Creole they speak among themselves. Also spelled *Kreyol* or *Kwéyòl*, reflecting how it's said, Creole developed in the seventeenth and eighteenth centuries as the contact language between French plantation owners and African slaves, as well as a way for Africans who spoke different tribal languages to communicate with each other. It is one of Haiti's two official languages, along with French.

The Haitian women, with long skirts and impassive faces, are dwarfed by the impossible bundles balanced on their heads: bales of new and second-hand clothing, shoes, leather handbags, children's toys and stuffed animals, pillows, linens. The men push and pull at heavy primitive handcarts with massive mounds of who-knows-what tied up in bedsheets. "*Donaciones*," confirms a Uruguayan United Nations aid worker who is stationed in Haiti but has crossed the border herself this morning to shop at the Dajabón market; the sweep of her arm encompasses arrays of sneakers and sandals, bras and panties, and Barbie and Ken dolls already spread on the sidewalks and alongside the gutters. Some of the new goods— bottles of cheap shampoo, cheesy housewares, frilly underwear and other clothes—are manufactured in the DR or imported by middlemen and resold at Dajabón.

Of the Haitians swarming across the bridge, women far out-number men—and a depressing number are pregnant. The Haitian birth rate is almost five children per woman, the infant mortality rate is more than 6 percent, and the overall life expectancy is only fifty-seven and a half, compared with, say, eighty-one in Canada. Few of the women smile; fewer still laugh; more often, their faces show just stoic resignation. Dominican customs officials randomly (and roughly) pull them aside and prod their bundles with metal rods and sticks. Looking for what? we wonder. It seems more harassment than anything, and the Haitians bear it without reaction. The streets are soon claustrophobically, oppressively crowded, with both buyers and sellers racing the clock. Promptly at noon, the gates across the bridge will close, and Haitians who attempt to linger will be herded back into their own country. All morning long, soldiers armed with switches and sticks—as well as rifles—are stationed around the perimeter of the market area to dissuade them from wandering farther into the Dominican Republic.

If I pause for even a second, I'm besieged: women push to get close to me, thrusting whatever they're selling in my face: heavy boots, fancy blouses, plaid plastic shopping bags. *"No, gracias; no, gracias,"* I repeat dozens of times. Steve, his high school French bridging Creole, buys a few things as he asks permission to take a photo; his art director's eye is drawn to the pride in these strong, sad faces—which turns to grim determination as the morning progresses. We become separated and, spooked by the swarm of sellers and the stifling heat, I back out of the crowd and head for the park beyond the soldier-guarded market, where we have agreed to meet.

On the park's far side, we gulp our water and join a lineup of Dominicans to buy fried-egg "sandwiches" from a wheeled cart. This breakfast is particularly luxurious in contrast to the hard drama playing out just a couple of blocks away. The cart's "cook" runs a lump of dough through a pasta machine until it is quite thin, and cuts it into foot-long pieces. When a customer arrives, he sprinkles one of the lengths with salt, folds it in half, and runs it back through the pasta machine to seal the edges, leaving just a corner open at the top. Then he cracks an egg and tips it into the opening. The dough package, like a giant ravioli, is gently lowered into a pot of hot oil, where it's left to burble until golden. The vendor then fishes it out by hooking it with a piece of bent wire. After it has cooled for a minute, he wraps it in a napkin and hands it over in exchange for 10 pesos (about 30 cents). Inside its slightly sweet, crispy pastry envelope, the egg is cooked somewhere between over easy and hard. If you prefer, you can have your envelope filled with fresh white farmer's cheese, which turns molten inside the dough, or both egg and cheese.

After breakfast, we wade back into the crush. Though it's still hours before the noon deadline, foot traffic back across the bridge has already begun. We're not accustomed to seeing people hurry—Dominican life generally proceeds at a leisurely pace—but the Haitians are almost running across, to give them time to drop off one load of purchases and return for more. Now we are slack-jawed at the sight of women balancing flats of eggs on their heads—towers twelve or thirteen crates high. Some carry double-wide flats—sixty eggs in each layer, a total of as many as 780 eggs. One misstep, unimaginable disaster.

Human mules, their faces etched with exhaustion, labor under sacks of cabbages or chayotes or enormous, institutional-size bags of pasta. The men with handcarts race them across, laden with great, sawdust-coated blocks of ice. I'm exhausted just by watching, but unable to tear my eyes away. One woman is completely engulfed by a sack of toilet paper easily three feet high and as wide as a mattress, which she balances on her head. Another, her back and face dripping, balances a 4 x 4 foot crate of live chickens—and we realize she is streaming not with sweat, but with fowl urine.

. . .

I buy my own chicken in Dajabón, on a back street outside the market. Mine is a piece of naive art: a small, clay, chicken-shaped bowl, painted yellow with black wings and a red comb and beak, just big enough to hold a handful of the shells and stones I've collected in my beach-walking. I'd wandered into the storefront of a bi-national Dominican–Haitian project that is working to help those who live along the border, "*las mujeres fronterizas,*" the frontier women. Sponsored in part by the University of Madrid, the woman in charge tells me, the project is attempting to build a network of border women, and encouraging them to turn to handicrafts as a way to make money, "to guarantee education, health and food for their children" and "to avoid emigration" from their homeland, no matter which side of the border they're on. While Haitians are fleeing into the DR, tens of thousands of Dominicans are leaving their country each year—but for *Nueva* York or Miami—in hopes of a better life.

Betterment is a slow process, however. The shelves in the little storefront are only sparsely filled, and my precious folk-art chicken costs a mere 50 pesos (about US$1.66). In the meantime the commerce at Dajabón allows the women to "*mantener sus familias,*" she says, to maintain their families, and "to live."

Leaving Dajabón, we pass through the military checkpoint,

complete with the boards and nails that Jaime had described, and decide to return home via Monte Cristi and then the north coast. Which means that before we get to Luperón, we will have to cross the Río Bajabonico—the one without a bridge, the one we turned back from when we first set out to explore this country months earlier. But we have forded other waterways since then; one infamous backroads excursion, perhaps Steve's favorite drive, involved piloting an Odalismobile through one river, two streams and an unnervingly deep pond, all in one afternoon. ("What rental cars are made for," he said happily.) Today, the Río Bajabonico is *tranquilo*, not the raging torrent it was at our last attempt. It laps gently up the door frame as Steve lowers the SUV in and I hide my face in my hands.

. . .

It's already mid-October. Back home, the World Series is under way. Here, la temporada ciclónica is drawing to a close, and without the threat of hurricanes we're running short of excuses to stay in Luperón much longer.

"But baseball season is just starting," Steve says, handing me the schedule of the five-team Liga de Béisbol Profesional de La República Dominicana. "We can't leave without seeing a game."

Since the days of the dictator Trujillo, when players were sometimes locked in jail to ensure they got a good night's rest before a game, Dominicans have been baseball crazy, and government has subsidized the sport—fully aware of its value as a distraction from economic and political troubles. There is never political unrest during baseball season, so the story goes. The entire country is a big farm team for the North American majors, providing more players than the rest of Latin America put together. In 2004, when Dominican Vladimir Guerrero was named the American League's MVP, three of the next four top vote-getters were also from the DR. In 2007, more than one in every nine players in the majors was Dominican born. Even small backwaters like Luperón have fields devoted to the sport—with seating where fans can down cold Presidente beer and eat pica pollo while they watch—and they are scoured each year by U.S. and Japanese scouts, looking for the next Alex Rodriguez or Sammy Sosa. When Sosa returned to his homeland after his 1998 MVP season, the line of cheering Dominicans who turned out to greet him stretched 25 miles. (Did I say baseball crazy?) For the kids, who start playing young, baseball is more than a game; it holds the promise of a ticket to the world of privilege, and fuels their dreams of following their heroes off the island.

Months earlier, just after *Receta* had arrived in Luperón, we'd heard the results of the annual cruisers-versus-locals baseball game held at the town field. The cruisers lost, 16–15. They had also lost (but very badly) the previous year, and (worse still) the year before that. "Two years ago, we played adults," a cruiser told us. "Last year, we played teenagers. This year we played the younger kids." The upside to this year's loss: "It was cheaper," our informant explained. When your opposition is twelve and under, you only have to buy soft drinks afterward.

Poor as the town is, the kids here have real gloves (although they often share them with opposing team members) and, frequently, team shirts, sponsored by a local business. But they also might have to contend with a burro on the infield or a chicken in the outfield. We watched the finals of the women's league, when the Luperón Strong Girls took on Las Tigresas of La Escalareta. There was absolutely no possibility of confusing it with a similar championship game back home. The Strong Girls had to ignore the motoconcho with two people aboard that crossed the field just behind second base while the second inning was in progress, and then ignore it a second time when it crossed back the other way during the third. They also ignored the Luperón pothound that wanted to assist in the outfield. They tossed back Presidentes between innings and, in an ecstatic final-inning rally, they won the game. Many of the Strong Girls wore tight-tight baseball-striped short-shorts with their team T's; one of the team assistants wore a headful of juice-can-sized rollers—the type I suffered each night when I was a teenager, to assure me fashionably straight hair the next day. Here they're worn publicly, on the streets, to work, at the ballpark. A friend even described a Luperón wedding where the bridesmaids all wore matching pink hair rollers; it sounded like a New York art event, but she swore it was real life.

Watching *béisbol* here reminds us where the word *fans* comes from. *Los fanáticos* treat each play—no matter how modest—as if it were the deciding moment of the deciding game of the World Series. A routine sac fly brings wild cheering and enthusiastic fingers-in-the-mouth whistling. A Strong Girls home run? The ear-piercing noise level ratchets up even higher.

. . .

Warmed up by the local games, we're headed to the Valley of Death, what los fanáticos call the home stadium of the professional league's Águilas Cibaeñas, in Santiago, because opposing teams always get killed there. The Águilas—Eagles—are taking on their archrivals, Los Tigres—Tigers—de Licey, from Santo Domingo, and we're told that even though it's only the second game of the season, the playing will be fierce.

"Luis Polonia, #22, Luis Polonia!" the rabid fan two rows in front turns around and shouts, to make sure the foreigners know this now-retired major leaguer is wearing an Águilas uniform tonight. A couple of decades ago, major leaguers returned home to the DR to play in the off-season, and they were joined by other non-Dominican pros, who saw winter ball as a way to supplement their income. But that was before multi-million-dollar contracts: before major league teams had a big enough carrot to discourage off-season play, with its potential for injury. Now the teams in the Dominican pro league comprise mostly up-and-comers and minor leaguers—players with something to prove, which still makes for first-rate ball.

We become instant fanáticos, screaming ourselves hoarse along with everyone else. By the end of the night, our ears are ringing; if this is only the second game of the season, I can't imagine the stretch.

The stadium has an intimacy that makes us feel part of the action: whether it's the bum-slapping players on their feet to congratulate their teammates as they arrive back at the dugout—even an easy-out bunt up the first-base line warrants an enthusiastic welcome if it advances a runner—or the Águilas mascot swooning at kisses from the Aguichicas, the all-girl cheerleaders dressed in ultra-tight black capris (with the name and logo of the country's sports lottery on the bum) and matching midriff-baring tops. Between innings, Steve and the other guys have their eyes glued on the gyrating Aguichicas, whose sexy, very suggestive routines to the high-decibel merengue that kicks in between innings are more nightclub than ballpark.

Me, I'm wearing my spanking-new black-and-orange Águilas cap, and between innings I'm ogling the food and drink that obliging vendors deliver right to the seats with the speed and finesse of a well-executed double play: an icy Presidente, followed down the row by, say, a complete pica pollo dinner, with rice and beans and tostones. Dominicans love these twice-fried slices of green plantain, also called *fritos verdes* ("fried greens"). When they're freshly, expertly made, you get a satisfying crunch from the caramelized exterior before you hit the soft, starchy, not-quite-sweet-and-not-quite-savory middle. If left to sit around, however, tostones turn into heavy unappealing lumps of greasy carbs. On reflection, maybe the ballpark isn't quite the best place to experience them at their peak. If you're craving plantains in the Valley of Death, probably better to ask one of the vendors to toss you a bag of crispy salted plantain chips.

Sadly, the Águila mojo is weak tonight, the pitching falls apart, and the Eagles blow a one-run lead in the seventh. When it becomes clear they are going to perish, the Tigres mascot— wearing a tiger suit, of course—drags a large stuffed toy eagle onto the field, falls on it, and proceeds to disembowel it with a vengeance, sending up a flurry of cotton and feathers. You just don't see that kind of action at Fenway Park.

. . .

Down to our last excuse, we arrange one final, early-November trip to La Madonna, to give the Tatiz family the photos Steve took on our previous visits and to eat one last lunch of Julián's oregano goat. During the drive, we're reminded of how long we've been here: the towering speakers on one of the ubiquitous roving pickup trucks are already blasting Christmas carols, and we see poinsettias with their green leaves now turned festive red. Nothing like the anorexic potted Christmas plants at home, these wild shrubs are as tall as . . . Monte Cristi oregano bushes.

I've arranged for Jaime to drive us to La Madonna, so we don't have to worry about an Odalismobile for the day. Secretly, I'm delighted he'll be along because it means I won't have to work quite so hard at the conversation; I know he will step in and translate when I'm confused by Julián's Spanish.

Which is exactly what happens when Julián leaves the kitchen to join us midway through our plates of stewed and roasted goat. Only afterward do I realize that Jaime was not translating what Julián said into English. He simply rephrased it in *his* Spanish, stripping out Julián's tricky local accent and unfamiliar colloquialisms. How far I've come. After five and a half months here, I've actually begun to think in Spanish.

On the way back, Steve insists we stop at one of the roadside stalls to buy some goat meat. "You won't get another chance at chivo liniero," he warns. Having just watched the vendor reduce a fresh leg to a pile of chunks replete with the usual bone bits, we compromise and I agree reluctantly to two pounds. Jaime conducts the business end—as he often has when we stop on our outings, since it assures us the local price—and then tells me what I owe.

A few days later, I tackle the chivo, doing exactly what Julián did, except substituting our on-board pressure cooker and stove for his pot and wood fire. Amazingly, the result tastes exactly like the goat at La Madonna: the meat, tender and deeply flavored with oregano; the sauce, spiked with my own Monte Cristi–picked, *Receta*-dried herb, rich and thick with flavor. We both rate it the best on-board meal ever. Although I know I will make the dish again, in other places, I also know it won't taste quite the same when the meat hasn't first grazed in the hills along la línea noroeste.

. . .

I take one last walk into Luperón, by myself, the day before we will—finally—lift the anchor and set sail for Puerto Rico. Somehow, in my half-year here, I have never tried the popular Dominican orange drink with the evocative name of *morir soñando:* to die dreaming. How could I leave the country without tasting a drink that bears such a hopeful, pleasing name? At the Casa de Jugos, near Flaco the tailor's shop on the main street, I can smell the moment the fruit hits the juicer, hear the ice crackling as the owner whirls the fresh orange juice in the blender with milk and a teensy bit of sugar. (I decline the typically overflowing Dominican spoonful.)

Morir soñando: I suspect when my time comes, I will die dreaming of other things besides this Creamsicle in a cup. But it's likely my years-from-now dreams will still include snapshots from our months in the Dominican Republic: the "hola, hola," that always greeted us on Calle Duarte, called above the blaring strains of heartbreak bachata; the burros plodding along the green road with silver jugs of milk suspended from their rag saddles, the corrugated mountains lit by morning sun, the landscape painfully beautiful, the roads merely painful. In my dreams, I will taste the salty tang of fresh cheese, the crunch of just-out-of-the-oil tostones, the glorious sweet mangoes, the oregano-infused chivo—which were all more than foods and became inextricably connected to people and places.

And when I die dreaming, my Spanish will be Jaime-perfect, of course, every idiom in place, every pronunciation perfectly Dominican. Gracia' a dio'.

· · · CHICKEN COCONUT PASTELILLOS · · ·

These Dominican-style empanadas were a hit at happy hour, and—bonus—the fresh ingredients were almost always available in Luperón's modest shops. In my version, a pastry wrapper replaces the traditional deep-fried dough.

Pastry:

2 cups	all-purpose flour	500 mL
¾ tsp	salt	4 mL
1 cup	shortening, or ½ cup butter and ½ cup shortening	250 mL
1	egg	1
2 tbsp	ice water	25 mL
1 tbsp	white vinegar	15 mL

Filling:

2 tbsp	olive oil	25 mL
3	cloves garlic, finely chopped	3
¼ cup	finely chopped onion	50 mL
¼ cup	finely chopped red or green bell pepper	50 mL
¼ to ½	hot pepper, finely chopped	¼ to ½
1 tbsp	finely chopped fresh ginger	15 mL
¾ lb	boneless chicken breast or thighs, finely chopped	375 g
2 tbsp	finely chopped cilantro	25 mL
1 tsp	lime zest	5 mL
1 tbsp	fresh lime juice	15 mL
½ cup	coconut milk	125 mL
	Salt and freshly ground black pepper	

1. To make pastry, combine flour and salt in a bowl. Cut in shortening (and butter, if using) until mixture resembles coarse crumbs.

2. Combine egg, water and vinegar. Add to flour, and mix until dough starts to form. Gather into a ball and then divide into two. Wrap in plastic and refrigerate until needed.

3. Heat olive oil in a large frying pan on medium heat and sauté garlic, onion, peppers and ginger until fragrant.

4. Add chicken, and brown on all sides.

5. Stir in cilantro, lime zest and juice and coconut milk, and season to taste. Simmer, uncovered, 8 to 12 minutes, stirring occasionally, until chicken is cooked through and mixture has thickened. Allow to cool.

6. Preheat oven to 400°F (200°C). Flour rolling pin and board or work surface. Roll out first ball of dough until it is about ⅛ inch (3 mm) thick. Cut 3-inch (8 cm) circles. Put about 1 tbsp (15 mL) of filling on half the dough, fold over other half to make a half-moon, and crimp with fork. Repeat with second ball of dough.

7. Bake on ungreased or parchment-lined baking sheets in preheated oven for about 15 minutes, until the pastelillos just start to color. Serve warm.

Makes about 2 ½ dozen.

Tips:
- For a golden crust, brush pastry with milk before baking.
- Slice the chicken into strips instead of chopping it, and the "filling" makes an excellent main dish served over rice.

· · · LOBSTER PASTELILLOS · · ·

For a luxurious variation—sure to leave an empty serving plate in record time—fill the pastelillos with lobster instead of chicken. Sauté 2 cloves of chopped garlic and 2 tbsp (25 mL) of chopped onion in 1 tbsp (15 mL) butter or olive oil. Add 3 tbsp (50 mL) of white wine, and continue cooking until wine is reduced by about half. Stir in 2 cups (500 mL) cooked lobster meat, cut into small pieces, and 2 tbsp (25 mL) of dry bread crumbs or matzoh meal. Reduce heat and add ½ cup (125 mL) light cream or evaporated milk. Cook about 5 minutes, until sauce has thickened and mixture holds together. Stir in 1 tbsp (15 mL) chopped cilantro and season to taste with salt, pepper and a couple shakes of hot pepper sauce. Allow filling to cool, then make pastelillos as above.

· · · ROSA'S AVOCADO SALAD · · ·

At the height of avocado season (late summer to early fall), our Dominican friend Rosa Van Sant brought this salad to a Luperón potluck dinner. We love the way its simplicity accentuates the rich, buttery taste of the perfectly ripened fruit. Rosa adds a bit of olive oil to her dressing, but we found we like it just as well without.

2	large ripe avocados, peeled and cut into chunks	2
¼ cup	sweet onion, finely chopped	50 mL
1	small clove garlic	
¾ tsp	salt	4 mL
2 tbsp	apple cider vinegar	25 mL
2 tbsp	extra-virgin olive oil (optional)	25 mL

1. Arrange avocado chunks in a shallow serving dish. Sprinkle with chopped onion.
2. Mash garlic with salt. Add vinegar and whisk in oil (if using), and pour on top of avocado. Serve immediately.

Makes 6 to 8 servings.

· · · TART AND SWEET LIME SQUARES · · ·

On one of our roadside stops with Jaime to buy mangoes, I also asked for a powdered-milk can full of limones—and discovered that it contained more than sixty key limes. I adapted our favorite lemon square recipe, created by Toronto friend and colleague Jill Snider, to take advantage of the bounty.

Crust:

1 ½ cups	all-purpose flour	375 mL
⅓ cup	granulated sugar	75 mL
¾ cup	butter	175 mL

Topping:

1 ¼ cups	granulated sugar	300 mL
3 tbsp	all-purpose flour	50 mL
3	eggs	3
1 tsp	grated lime zest	5 mL
½ cup	fresh lime juice	125 mL

1. Preheat oven to 350°F (180°C) and grease a 9" x 9" (2.5 L) cake pan.
2. Combine all ingredients for crust, mixing until crumbly. Press firmly into pan. Bake in preheated oven for 15 to 20 minutes, or until light golden.
3. In a small bowl, whisk topping ingredients together until smooth. Pour over crust. Bake in preheated oven 30 to 35 minutes longer, or until set. Cool in pan on rack, then cut into squares.

Makes about 3 dozen squares.

FOUR

The 151-Proof Spice

· · · ST. MARTIN & SABA · · ·

The only way to obtain Saba Spice is to actually visit Saba. . . . Several
brave souls have reportedly even tried to duplicate Spice by invent-
ing their own recipe with disastrous results . . . reportedly setting the
kitchen on fire . . .

Richard Holm and Marie van Rooyen, caribbeanconsulting.com

SOMETIMES YOU FIND YOURSELF in so deep, there's no
graceful way out but going forward.

"Did you taste this stuff before you bought it?" our friend
Chris asks bluntly, while his wife, Yani (trained as a French
chef), grimaces. Their sailboat, *Magus,* had been anchored
in Luperón almost as long as *Receta* had, and we'd come to
know each other well. It's not as if they're unaccustomed to
strong drink—their usual tipple is a Stoli martini, very dry.
But the "special" bottle I've contributed to tonight's tasting
party on another boat goes far beyond even their (or anyone
else's) tolerance.

When I tell them that I had indeed sampled first—as had

Steve—I get an incredulous look from Yani; this has obviously cast no small measure of doubt on the reliability of my palate. Meanwhile, Chris blurts, "Then why did you buy it?"

It can be hard to refuse the traditional specialty of an island—especially when it's a very small island and you've gone to some lengths to search that specialty out. I'm just thankful that I didn't bring a sample of another local drink I've been inadvertently collecting—currently, four almost-untouched bottles of guavaberry liqueur, from four separate island kitchens, are taking up valuable real estate in one of *Receta*'s lockers—because it surely would have led to an even louder chorus. On the upside, Steve is beginning to look back rather more fondly on my obsession with Dominican goat cheese; it, at least, didn't take up any of our precious storage space.

Receta and *Magus* are anchored just off the Witch's Tit in St. Martin's Simpson Bay Lagoon. Our boats float on the Dutch side of this island with a split personality, while the witch's warty, nippled mound—and most of the island's wonderful *boulangeries, marchés,* bistros and wine shops—are on the French side. But no matter: The Netherlands and France are fairly sanguine about coexisting on this 37-square-mile island, the world's smallest land mass shared by two separate governments. The border is simply a welcome sign on the road, no formalities required to cross from St. Martin (the French side) to Sint Maarten (the Dutch).

Although the two countries agreed to divide the island between them in 1648, they couldn't agree on exactly how for almost two hundred more years. The boundary was finally set, so the story goes, when a Dutchman and a Frenchman stood back-to-back and started walking the shoreline in opposite directions around the island; the line drawn to where they again met became the border. The Frenchman was faster—perhaps because he stuck to wine, while his rival carried a flask of gin—and therefore France got the larger portion. Neither of them, Steve points out snidely, was carrying guavaberry liqueur or Saba Spice.

. . .

The nearby island of Saba (pronounced "Say-ba") is also part of the Netherlands—but unlike St. Martin/St. Maarten, which is generously ringed by beaches, Saba is a 5-square-mile floating fortress where ocean meets rock without anything in between.

"Saba looks like a fairy-tale picture of a forbidden land," our guidebook says. Its deeply forested, steep central peak—a long-dormant volcano—is surrounded by smaller flying buttresses of raw rock. And as the fast ferry from St. Maarten approaches, it is indeed hard to believe anyone could come ashore here. The rock buttresses spire straight out of the sea, waves crashing against their bases and spewing foam into the air even on this day of modest wind. The island appears completely beachless—shoreless, even. High up on its steep sides, a few tiny, red-roofed white houses perch improbably, as if carefully planted by some friendly giant's hand. How else could they get there?

Having heard from other cruisers that the unprotected mooring buoys sprinkled along Saba's rugged leeward side give visiting boats a rocking-rolling stay in all but the most settled weather, we had taken the easy way out: left *Receta* at anchor in Simpson Bay Lagoon, booked a guesthouse and boarded the high-speed ferry. As it bounces toward the end of the hour-and-a-half trip, we can make out a series of steps hacked into the rock on the leeward side. This is "The Ladder," a thousand rough-hewn, near-vertical stairs that were for many years the way everything—from food to furniture to the Queen of the Netherlands—was transported onto the island. Things are somewhat easier for the Sabans now: a miniature harbor comes into view when the ferry churns around the island's southwest corner; from there, The Road (the Sabans use capital letters, because the island only has one) snakes upward.

"I want to open a transmission shop here," Steve says as our taxi grinds dizzily through the S-curves, higher and higher toward Windwardside, where we're staying, one of only four settlements on the island. Dutch engineers claimed a road couldn't be built on Saba. But that didn't stop the Sabans, who appear to come not just from hardy stock, but from tenacious, crazy stock. Josephus Lambee Hassell, a local carpenter, signed up for correspondence courses in engineering, and with his fellow citizens, built The Road by hand. Construction started in 1943; the first motor vehicle arrived on the island in 1947.

Saban men have long made their living from the water—becoming expert fishermen and sea captains (these days, taking visitors scuba diving is the big water-based business here)—career paths that traditionally meant Saban women had to fend for themselves for long stretches. Left to their own devices on this chunk of rock, they developed an unlikely pair of local products: Saba lace and Saba Spice. The first is an intricate, fastidious, old-fashioned form of needlework requiring good eyesight and steady hands; the second is an eye-crossing, steadiness-impairing, fennel-flavored liqueur based on—wait for it—151-proof rum.

Saba's population is a scant 1,200, everybody knows everybody else, and everybody seems related. (The phonebook shows a heavy predominance of three surnames: Peterson,

Hassell and Johnson. Still, there appears to be a bit of sensitivity to suggestions of too much swimming in the same gene pool. "Contrary to the popular theory of intermarriage," Saba-born Will Johnson huffs defensively in his book of island history, "Sabans have constantly sought brides and husbands overseas through the centuries.") All comings and goings are duly noted in family fashion, and every person passing on The Road—Saban or visitor, in a vehicle or on foot—is acknowledged with a wave, if not a full-fledged conversation. "You have to wave," says one of the local women when she stops us to chat, all the while continuing to note and wave to other passersby. "Otherwise, they ask, 'What's wrong? Why are you not waving?'"

Steve and I are fresh conversational blood. Everyone is happy—almost overeager—to talk to us, friendly to a fault. And so it happened: as soon as I made my first casual inquiry about where I might best find the local products, it was already too late to back out.

. . .

The Sabans have a decidedly glass-half-full approach to life, not just accepting but proud of their island's rigors and its out-of-the-ordinary charms. Everything is neat, tidy and outrageous at the same time. Clean, well-kept streets cant at roller-coaster angles. Storybook cottages—white, with green-edged shutters and gingerbread trim—cling to hillsides, with riotous tangled gardens and, often, their own graveyard. "There's no law against it," I'm told when I ask. "Even foreigners with houses here want to be buried in their gardens." The island's highest point is called Mount Scenery: a typical Saban name for a mountain whose 2,855-foot-high summit is frequently shrouded in clouds and reached via a quad-burning trail that includes 1,064 steps carved into the rock. Less optimistically, the highest mountain on nearby St. Kitts was once named Mount Misery.

This Saban outlook perhaps explains why Imelda Peterson puts a positive spin on our first shiver-inducing swallow of Saba Spice. "The longer it sits, the better it is," she says. She had poured us each a hefty slug of her cousin Marjorie's Spice almost as soon as we'd walked through the door of her cousin Peggy's shop. We were directed here (after a very long chat) by Sherrie Peterson, the curator of the local museum—and another of Imelda's cousins. (Already we beg to differ with Will Johnson; Saban family trees feature head-spinning complexities such as three first cousins—Imelda, Sherrie and Yvette—marrying three brothers. "No wonder people drink Spice," mutters Steve.)

Fennel is the most obvious spice in Spice (we can even see it growing outside the shop door), but I also taste cloves and cinnamon—all of them doing a highly inadequate job of disguising the rocket fuel they're steeped in. Probably just as flammable too: there are tales of accidental kitchen fires while making Spice, and cousin Marjorie, whom we meet the next day, tells us she purposefully ignites the pot after she's combined the knockout rum with a syrup she makes by boiling the spices with demerara sugar and water. "I don't know what that does, I just know Mommy did it." She lets the pot burn briefly before covering it and steeping the mixture for a full month.

In the eighteenth century, Saba had small sugar-cane plantations—I'm still trying to figure out where there was enough level ground—and boiling houses, which produced sufficient molasses to support several rum distilleries. But the boiling houses were abandoned by 1825, and the rum disappeared along with them. The overproof spirits are now imported from St. Maarten and St. Kitts, which in turn import them from other islands.

"Getting the rum is the hard part. I mean, who drinks 151-proof rum?" Imelda says, with not a hint of irony in her voice. The stuff is even on the breakfast menu at a local Windwardside café, in the form of a French toast that sounds suspiciously like having a couple of cocktails as an eye-opener: the bread is soaked in egg and Saba Spice before frying, then served with a pitcher of Spice to pour on top, like syrup. When I suggest to cousin Sherrie that this turbo-charged breakfast might render me useless for the rest of the day, she gives me an airy wave: "Oh, just have a cup of coffee with it."

Although most of the bottles sold on the island now apparently go to visitors, Spice is still a regular in the lineup of offerings at local bars. It's also a traditional Saban wedding drink. And Sherrie tells us she uses it to baste turkey. Each maker proudly identifies her brew with her name and address (and, often, her phone number) on the home-printed label, automatically assuming we'll want more.

Imelda's handiwork, too, is on the shelves of Peggy's tiny shop: everything from bookmarks to pillow covers to tablecloths edged with handmade lace. Lace-making got its start on Saba in the 1870s after Mary Gertrude Hassell's parents sent her off the island to a convent school in Caracas, Venezuela. The nuns taught her "Spanish threadwork," and she brought the craft back to Saba with her. The island's women developed the pastime into a business—using a ploy worthy of the cleverest direct marketer—once Saba was finally connected to the outside world with regular mail service in 1884. (There wasn't airmail delivery until 1946, when a pilot flying over the island simply threw down a bag of letters. Mail continued to leave the island by sea until 1963, when an airport was built; it still has the smallest commercial runway in the world, further testament to the scarcity of level ground.) The industrious women would copy the addresses from the boxes of goods arriving on their island, and send each company a letter explaining their work. The letters got posted on company bulletin boards, and the lace makers received orders. In its November 1940 issue, *National Geographic* reported that "Practically every girl over 16 in Saba helps to support herself and her family this way."

Like those responsive company employees, we're helpless to resist Saban guerrilla marketing—especially after yet more friendly chat. Imelda also insists we try cousin Marjorie's "guavaberry." The rum-based fruit liqueur is St. Maarten's national drink, "but Marjorie's is better than what you'll get on St. Maarten," Imelda says, firmly laying down a challenge and reeling us in. "I guess we have to get a bottle so we can compare," says Steve, even an easier mark than me, and Imelda carefully secures the lids on bottles of both guavaberry and Spice with masking tape to ensure they won't leak on the pieces of lace we're also buying.

. . .

"Go see Baker," Hilma advises us. "He makes guavaberry. You'll find him on the big pier."

Back on St. Maarten, we've checked back in with Hilma Harris, who owns a little pop-up trailer of a restaurant with four stools out front, sandwiched into a narrow strip of gravel between a car wash and a bank on the busy main road that borders Simpson Bay on the Dutch side of the island. The sign on the awning reads, HILMA'S WINDSOR CASTLE.

"Because as small as it is, this is my castle," Hilma explained when we first found the place. "I own it. It's mine. And I'm the queen." A flamboyant fifty, the queen has a flower tattoo on her upper arm, shoulder-dusting gold hoops in her ears, and a personality that the word *outgoing* can't begin to cover. Six days a week, she dishes out unpretentious local food such as bull's-foot soup ("but only on Saturdays"), fish-head soup ("sometimes"), stewed oxtail ("I'll make it for you tomorrow"), and souse. ("Do you know what souse is?" she asks, then proceeds to describe it without waiting for an answer: highly seasoned, pickled pig's parts, usually including feet, ears and snout.) Every day, Hilma offers fried local fish (marlin or shark, with or without a Creole-style tomato sauce, as you please), fried chicken (legs only), and six different types of patties (pronounced "patés" here, and including chicken, corned beef, fresh fish, and cheese)—at least until she runs out.

"Do you have saltfish?" Steve asked when we first stopped at her tin-can restaurant and he discovered his first two lunch choices were already gone. "But of course I have saltfish, it's my signature dish," Hilma replied, laughing out the words and spreading her arms wide, like a diva hitting the high note of her aria. And then she set to work, splitting open a johnnycake (hers are puffy, hollow, deep-fried disks) and stuffing it with a well-spiced mix of shredded salt cod, peppers and onions.

Coming to the Castle always turns out to be as much about good conversation as good food. "I like to cook and I like to eat—just look at me!—and I like to run my mouth too," Hilma says. "In the morning I can't sit and talk. That's when I'm doing my cooking. In the afternoon is when I can sit and gossip." If we wanted to find homemade guavaberry liqueur on St. Maarten, Hilma was clearly the person to ask. In the afternoon. After lunch.

. . .

"Tell Baker I sent you for his guavaberry," she says. She then allows that she and Baker—his first name is Hervé, "but everybody knows him as Baker"—are related by marriage. They're currently not on speaking terms. "Doesn't stop me from sending customers to him."

The dollar bus takes us into Philipsburg, the capital of the Dutch side, and from there we walk to the "big pier"—the cruise-ship dock at the edge of the city. When we arrive, we discover that Baker is inside the fenced compound, for security reasons accessible only to those with wristbands or other cruise-ship ID. Putting on my best smile, I try to talk my way past the guard, who proves implacable, humorless, completely immune to my charms. Eventually, we give up, resigned to a fruitless expedition and a hot walk back downtown.

Until I spot the hole in the fence. At the farthest corner of the cruise-ship compound, two of the iron bars have been pried ever-so-slightly apart, no doubt to create an inconspicuous shortcut for workers (at least for the slender ones) coming from town. Moments later, we have infiltrated the throng of cruise-ship passengers, hoping the security guard won't spot us by our deep, telltale sailing tans before we reach Baker's stand.

With his white pants, pale-blue sports shirt and multiple gold chains, Hervé Baker looks like he's just stepped off a cruise ship himself, or a Florida golf course. He's been making guavaberry liqueur for thirty years, having learned the art from his mother, he tells us while masticating a substantial cigar. "Carol, leddem try deh guavaberry colada," he says to the woman manning the nearby blender, who is easily a decade or two his junior. ("His girlfriend," Hilda sniffs, when I later call her his wife.)

"My mom used to do this for serenaders," he says. "If you don't have it on Christmas, nobody come to your house and serenade you." For generations, a shot of home-brewed guavaberry was the way of thanking the carolers who went door to door around the Dutch side of the island. "Good morning, good morning, I come for meh guavaberry," was their traditional refrain. It became a Christmas drink because the berries ripen and are picked (by hand, in the island's dry interior) around September or October. They are stewed and then mixed with rum (he uses 70-proof, says Baker—mercifully, says Steve) "and t'ings"—including nutmeg, cinnamon and vanilla. After fermenting for about ninety days, the deep-red liqueur is ready to drink, just in time for the holidays.

Despite its name, the blueberry-sized guavaberry is completely unrelated to the guava (it's actually a closer relative to cloves), and its other name is much more telling: the rumberry. Cuba, the Virgin Islands, and the Dominican Republic also have traditions of fermenting guavaberries in rum, and island musicians, such as Juan Luis Guerra, have celebrated the resulting drink in song. But St. Maarten holds the motherlode. The Sint Maarten Guavaberry Company—the largest producer on the island—claims St. Maarten likely has more guavaberry trees "than anyplace else on earth."

His guavaberry, Baker says, is vastly superior to the commercial brews. But is it superior to the Saban one? He offers us a taste, straight. All on its own, sans ice, the way it was traditionally drunk (and still is, by old-timers), both his and Marjorie's guavaberries have a strong—dare I suggest unpleasant?—

medicinal taste. (Taken straight on the heels of Saba Spice, however, as we had done in Peggy's shop, guavaberry had seemed positively delightful.) It's easy to see why St. Maarten's national drink is more popular these days blended into other drinks—like Baker's coladas, as well as Smartinis (St. Maarten martinis), punches, daiquiris, sunrises and slings—where other flavors cut the bitterness, leaving a fruity, spicy, woodsy flavor.

Walking out under the guard's nose would be tempting fate. With a bottle of Baker's guavaberry in my bag—how could we return from our quest empty-handed?—we sneak out through the fence the way we came in.

. . .

I don't see any guavaberry among the extravagant array of homemade fruit syrups, liqueurs and punches in Olive Augustine's market stall along the waterfront promenade in Marigot, the capital of French St. Martin. It's not that I want another bottle—the two I now have are proving a very tough sell to *Receta*'s happy-hour guests—but I know that Olive, who's become my favorite market woman on St. Martin, has a reputation for her alcoholic concoctions, and I'm wondering why she doesn't make it. "I do," she assures me, "for Christmas." By now, mid-February, she's long sold out. But that's no obstacle. Since we first met a month earlier, Olive has taken all my questions—no matter that their intent is only curiosity—as problems to be solved. "I still have a bottle or two at home. I'll bring you one."

The Marigot market is arrayed in a line of well-kept white gazebos with gingerbread trim—produce and spices at one end, fish and meat at the other. I'd first wandered into Olive's stall one busy market Saturday, clutching a bag that contained a just-purchased, whole, two-pound red hind, a fish I'd only previously encountered snorkeling or diving. I'd noticed her earlier: younger than the other market women, with a smile that lit up her whole face. She was wearing the standard Marigot market woman's madras apron, but over jeans and a T instead of the skirt the older ladies favor, and her hair was drawn back in lots of stylish little braids and piled on top of her head. Her tables overflowed with fat papayas, fragrant pineapples, green and yellow plantains, bundles of fresh herbs, and madras-wrapped sacks of dried spices: long lengths of cinnamon bark, vanilla beans, allspice, star anise, cardamom, bay, coriander, peppercorns of different colors, several blends of curry. "I just bought this," I explained, holding up my black plastic bag. "Can you tell me how you'd cook it? And sell me what I need?" She eyed my fish, broke into one of her dazzling smiles and set to work, collecting the necessary ingredients.

"Let me 'splain you," she said, using the phrase that quickly became her mantra when dealing with me. "You need to wash the fish thoroughly in fresh lime." She handed me a half-dozen limes, along with a bouquet of fresh thyme. "You should put fresh thyme in everything—you don't have to chop it—and use lots of garlic, it's good for you."

After I doused the fish with lime juice, she said, and rubbed it inside and out with salt, pepper, thyme, lots of garlic and some parsley, I should fill the cavity with slices of onion and tomato, lay more onion and tomato along the top, wrap it in foil, and bake. More than a good, simple way to treat any sort of small whole fish, the recipe marked the start of my relationship with Olive.

"I'd like to buy a few green plantains, please," I told her on my next visit, pointing to the sharp-edged, pointy-ended, oversized bananas that are treated like a vegetable in island kitchens and served boiled, fried or mashed. (In the DR, lumpily mashed plantains are topped with pickled or crispy-fried red onions to make a popular breakfast dish called *mangú* that—trust me on this—puts home fries to shame.) Olive, however, made no move toward the other side of her stall to retrieve the plantains. "What are you going to do with them?" she asked suspiciously. Dealing with Olive turns out not to be easy: she won't sell me something until she's convinced I know how to cook it. But she approved my plan to make Dominican-style tostones, though I didn't call them that, knowing that twice-fried green plantains must have another name on this French–Dutch island.

"What do you call them here?" I asked, describing what I planned to do.

"Fried green plantains," she replied. "But let me 'splain you. Put them in salt water for five minutes between the two fryings. And you have to eat them right away. Don't let them sit."

I tried to keep her flowing stream of 'splaining in my head. Never store plantains with citrus fruit because citrus will keep the plantains from ripening; always add a bit of fresh ginger root when cooking with curry to boost the flavor; a little piece of "saffron" helps brighten the color of a dish. In the Caribbean, "saffron" doesn't mean the dried stigmas of the crocus flower, which are the true—and very expensive—spice. Here, "saffron" is turmeric, the inexpensive, aromatic root of a commonly cultivated plant that's related to ginger and, like it, sold fresh as well as dried and ground. Use it once and the reason it's called saffron becomes obvious: like its namesake spice, it colors everything it touches a garish orange-yellow.

As Olive kept dishing out cooking advice, I desperately wanted to whip my notebook and pen from my bag so I didn't lose a single detail. But I was afraid it might derail the conversation.

"Next time you come, I'll 'splain you how to make *lokri*"—
a one-pot chicken, rice and lentils dish—"and lentil soup," she
said, as I prepared to leave. And then she added, "And next
time bring a pen and paper so you can write it down so you
don't forget."

. . .

Not much of St. Martin's food comes from St. Martin. (Not
many of St. Martin's 77,000 residents do, either; they've moved
here from seventy different countries.) The island is too small,
too dry and too crowded to grow much. Olive tells me all her
root vegetables—the yams, sweet potatoes and starchy dasheen
(called taro in other parts of the world)—come from Dominica,
her (and Hilma's, as chance would have it) birthplace. Her
tomatoes hail from Guadeloupe, and the papayas and avocados
from "Santo Domingo," meaning the Dominican Republic.
Olive imports all her spices too, mostly from Guadeloupe and
Dominica. "That's why everything is so expensive here," she
explained apologetically, after collecting three euros from me
for four modestly sized tomatoes, then tucking a gift avocado
into my bag. "When you get to Guadeloupe, Dominica and
Martinique, you'll see—everything is different."

I sure hope so. Steve has taken to calling St. Martin/St.
Maarten "the island of the bruised credit cards." Food shops and
restaurants rely on daily flights from France to fill in what the
other islands can't. Finding goat cheese here isn't a problem—
deciding which of the many types to buy is. Foie gras tasting
menus, salads of buttery little imported lettuces, traditional
French bistro dishes such as steak frites and steamed mussels,

braised rabbit accompanied by a tangle of (France-foraged) wild mushrooms, rare duck breast fanned under a lid of puff pastry, duty-free French wines, beignets filled with molten French dark chocolate in a pool of *crème anglaise:* we're certainly not on the island of the 5-mile diet anymore. Hilma even has to import the callaloo—the spinach-like leaves of the dasheen bush—for the popular West Indian callaloo soup she makes every Saturday; a friend brings her the greens from nearby Anguilla. Only the guavaberries, it seems, don't come from away.

. . .

We drop by Olive's stall again a few days later. She isn't there, but a bottle of guavaberry is, in one of the charming flasks she hand-paints with tropical designs. Her husband Kevin says she's left it for us. The price isn't marked, so Kevin checks the sticker on a similar bottle of another fruit liqueur, and we leave the money.

"Let me 'splain you," Olive says on our next visit. "That was meant to be a gift. Kevin wasn't supposed to sell it to you." She's determined to fix the matter, and when we next come to see her, she digs under one of her tables and pulls out a gift for us: yet another bottle of guavaberry she's brought from home—this one made by someone else, so we can compare it with hers.

"We are, without doubt, the only boat in the Caribbean with four bottles of a drink we don't even like taking up storage space," Steve says. I can see him twitching to clear them out so he can lay down more duty-free wine before we leave St. Martin. But I'm hoping to hold him off until next Christmas. You never know: we might have a surge of serenaders dinghying over to *Receta,* singing for their holiday tot.

· · · TOSTONES · · ·
(TWICE-FRIED GREEN PLANTAINS)

with Garlic–Cilantro Aïoli Dip

I couldn't resist buying a tostonera in the DR, a cute, hinged gizmo designed expressly for smashing plantains for tostones. A special tool isn't really necessary, though: the flat side of a cleaver or other broad knife, a pounder for tenderizing meat, or the bottom of a small heavy saucepan will do the job perfectly well. Eat the tostones while they're still warm. They don't keep well—but there likely won't be any left to worry about.

3 to 4	unripe (green) plantains	3 to 4
	Oil for shallow frying	
	Sea salt	
	Garlic–Cilantro Aïoli Dip	
	(recipe follows)	

1. Peel plantains: Cut off both ends and cut each plantain in half crosswise. On each half, make three slits down the length of the peel all the way through to the flesh. Remove the sections of skin with your fingers.
2. Slice the plantains crosswise about 1 inch (2.5 cm) thick.
3. Heat about ¼ inch (5 mm) of oil in a large heavy frying pan on medium heat and fry plantain slices until lightly browned on the flat sides.
4. As they brown, remove slices to paper towel to drain. Reserve oil in frying pan.
5. Cool a couple of minutes, then put slices in cold salted water (about 1 tbsp [15 mL] salt per cup [250 mL] of water) for about 5 minutes.

6. Drain. Place slices between sheets of waxed paper or plastic wrap, and pound to flatten. Slices should be about double the diameter, and a scant ½ inch (1 cm) thick.

7. Reheat oil in frying pan, and fry slices again on both sides, about 1 ½ minutes per side, until golden brown. Drain on paper towels. Sprinkle with salt and serve immediately with Garlic–Cilantro Aïoli for dipping.

Makes 4 to 6 snack-size servings.

Tip:
- Also try the tostones with the Chadon Beni Sauce in Chapter 12.

· · · GARLIC—CILANTRO AÏOLI DIP · · ·

Put 2 garlic cloves, cut into slivers, in 2 tbsp (25 mL) olive oil and set aside at room temperature to steep for about 30 minutes. Remove garlic, and combine the oil with 1 tbsp (15 mL) fresh lime juice, 1 tbsp (15 mL) finely chopped cilantro, and ½ cup (125 mL) mayonnaise. Add salt to taste.

Tips:
- For a curry aïoli: Heat the garlic oil in a small frying pan and stir in about 1 tbsp (15 mL) of curry powder. Continue to cook for a few minutes to remove the raw taste of the curry. Allow to cool, then mix with enough of the mayonnaise to thin to dipping consistency. Add salt to taste.
- Both dips can be made ahead.

· · · HAPPY HOUR BLUE CHEESE SPREAD · · ·

This quick spread became a favorite on Receta *when we got to St. Martin, because the store shelves are laden with wonderful French cheeses. I like to make it with creamy, mild Forme d'Ambert, but you can use whichever blue cheese you prefer. Although it's excellent served with slices of firm pear—also imported and available in St. Martin's marchés—for a real island twist, I serve it with thin fingers of christophene (chayote) along with crackers, breadsticks or slices of toasted baguette.*

4 oz	cream cheese	120 g
6 to 8 oz	Forme d'Ambert or other mild, creamy blue cheese	180 to 240 g
1 tbsp	dark rum	15 mL
¼ cup	chopped pecans	50 mL
	Crackers, breadsticks or slices of toasted baguette	
1	small christophene (chayote), peeled and sliced	1

1. Combine cream cheese, about 6 oz (180 g) of the blue cheese, and the rum in a small bowl and mash with a fork until mixture is smooth. Taste and add a bit more blue cheese if desired.
2. Cover and refrigerate until just before serving to give flavors a chance to blend.
3. Return spread to room temperature before serving. Mound in a small bowl and sprinkle with chopped pecans. Serve with crackers and christophene slices.

Makes about 1 cup (250 mL).

FIVE

Bay in the Mountains, Crabs in the Pot

· · · DOMINICA & ST. KITTS · · ·

The forest is so thick that you cannot distinguish tree from tree. You
cannot tell how tall they are nor how widely their branches spread. It
is all a tangle of bamboo and ferns and vine, of palms and mahogany
and mango, of cedar and bay and breadfruit trees. It is green, all green.

from "Typical Dominica," by Alec Waugh, 1948;

from his book Love and the Caribbean

ON AN ISLAND THAT'S TWO-THIRDS untouched rain forest,
a mountainside forested entirely with leafless branches stands
out. Somewhere else in the world, I might have thought these
barren trees had been ravaged by wildfire—but that's not likely
on Dominica, which gets more than four hundred inches of
rainfall annually and has a river for each day of the year. On
Dominica, the bare gray sticks just mean the bay-leaf harvest
is in progress.

I've become hopelessly addicted to the warm, spicy,
foresty scent of bay since *Receta* arrived at this island, the
southernmost of the Leeward Islands chain, some 170 miles

as the tern flies from St. Martin. The rain forest–surrounded cottage where we're staying on shore smells deliciously of it and, at first, I assumed the scent was simply being released as we brushed the shiny green leaves of the bay tree border-ing the path to our door. Then I discover that the "mopping water" used daily is spiced with a couple of drops of pure bay oil. Even Steve, he of the sensitive nose, who prefers all (non-food) products unscented, agrees this is a sweet-smelling idea, worthy of adoption on *Receta*. I have the sneaking sus-picion he hopes it will also provide soothing aromatherapy to silence the complainant responsible for cleaning our cabin floors.

We have left *Receta* at anchor under the watchful eyes of a local boatman in Prince Rupert Bay, the deep, protected harbor off Portsmouth, near Dominica's northwest tip, and headed across the island to explore the interior and the rugged, boat-unfriendly windward coast. Local lore suggests that Dominica—pronounced "Doh-min-eek-a"—is the only island Chris Columbus would recognize if he returned today, and we have no reason to doubt it. Startlingly, over-the-top green, it has an undisciplined wildness—more jungle than forest, a big, out-of-control garden, an untamed beauty compared with its prettily manicured, stylishly groomed French neighbors, Guadeloupe and Martinique. (The French and British traded control of Dominica until 1805, when the French were defeated once and for all, and the island remained part of Britain until independence in 1978.) Columbus and his colleagues weren't terribly creative, however, when it came to naming this unpolished gem in the island necklace. Dominica, like the Dominican Republic, was first sighted on Domingo, Spanish for Sunday, and christened for the day of the week.

This late-spring morning, a man walks along the road ahead of us, his gait easy despite a stout bundle of bay branches piled crosswise on his head and the steepness of the terrain. Dominica is the most mountainous of the Leeward and Windward Islands; the Caribs called it Waitukubuli—"tall is her body." Though bay trees are scattered throughout the island, they are only grown as a commercial crop here in the mountains of the southeast side, an area so rugged that as recently as ten years ago, no roads connected one village to another.

Moses James, a twenty-seven-year-old Rastafarian with a Bob Marley dogtag around his neck and an impressive set of dreads, is from one of those inaccessible villages, Delices, and knows this part of the island—its rivers, waterfalls, plants, wildlife and secrets—as well as anyone can. "*Bwa den*," he calls the bay tree in Creole, a corruption of the French *bois d'inde*—tree from India—though it is, in fact, a native species here. On some islands, such as Grenada, the Creole has devolved even farther from the French, and if you want bay, you ask for "borden" leaves.

The West Indian bay tree, a tall evergreen (*Pimenta racemosa*, a member of the myrtle family), is a very different species than the Mediterranean bay sold in North America (*Laurus nobilis*, a member of the laurel family). West Indian bay leaves are much larger and have a sharper, spicier, greener scent; those newly addicted to it—like me—face a dilemma: which type of West Indian bay to use. Dominica has three varieties, each with its own distinct, heady, instantly recognizable aroma: sweet cinnamon bay (also called common bay), anise bay and citronella bay. "All three can be used for cooking," Moses says, "or to make teas." A tea made with anise bay leaves is said to be good for the blood when the weather is cold, while one made from citronella bay cools the body.

As we meander along the mountain roads and hike through the rain forests, I quickly learn to recognize the silvery-barked tree with its shiny, leathery, teal-green leaves, and crinkle one for a sniff to identify the variety; soon I've found some of each type to add to *Receta*'s spice cupboard. However, most of the bay leaves on Dominica, Moses says, are destined not for a cooking pot or teapot, but rather are distilled for their oil. Local families harvest the leaves by hand, much as I have (albeit more methodically, breaking off large branches rather than my puny twigs), then carry them to one of the communal stills that dot the mountainscape—likely where the stranger with the branches on his head is going.

"My family brings our bay leaves here," says Moses, having led us to a rough-and-tumble structure just outside his village. Though no smoke rises from its chimney today, we can tell the primitive still ("maybe eighty or ninety years old") has been working very recently because the aroma of bay lingers heavily in the air. Already, fresh bundles of branches are piled high to one side; once forty-five such "parcels" have been gathered, the still will be fired up. The leaves are boiled under pressure, and the resulting vapor is condensed, a similar process to that of making rum—except what's collected at the end is a potent essential oil instead of a potent alcohol. "Families come and camp out, eating and drinking and listening to music as they wait for the oil to finish," Moses says. Since it takes about twelve hours from the time the bay leaves go into the boiler to the time the oil drips out the condenser, and a family might have four batches to process, this translates into a two-day work party that ends with ninety-six rum-sized bottles of bay oil. The owner of the still is paid with one bottle for every batch processed, and the rest (except for a bit held back for home use and local sales) goes to the Dominica Essential Oils and Spices Cooperative in the capital, Roseau. With 560 members harvesting and distilling bay, the cooperative is the world's largest source of bay oil. Perfume, soap and cosmetics manufacturers in the United States, Europe and the Caribbean buy almost all of the cooperative's production. The small amount of bay oil that remains is combined with alcohol in Petite Savanne, the village that is Delices' closest neighbor, to make the only other product the cooperative sells: bay rum.

This is such a popular local use for the oil that it gives the West Indian bay tree another name: the bay rum tree. Definitely not for drinking, bay rum is a skin tonic. It was the smell of coming of age in North America half a century ago—de rigueur among teenage boys just starting to shave. Barbers splashed it on their customers, and I remember from my childhood the spicy fragrance of my father's face when he patted on bay rum from the bottle given him by a well-traveled friend. Though it's fallen out of fashion in the United States and Canada, most Dominican households still have bay rum on hand for therapeutic purposes, using it as a rub to soothe aches and pains, on a compress to relieve headaches and reduce fevers, and generally for cooling the body in the steamy tropical climate. To foreigners on the island, it's marketed as an after-shower refresher.

Steve sniffs my neck suspiciously when I cozy up to him the first morning I splash some on. "You smell like rum punch," he says. "Have you been drinking?"

. . .

It only makes sense that these mountains also hide a different type of still. After all, if you've mastered the art of distillation and you just happen to be in a remote, hard-to-access spot far from prying official eyes, you might as well use your skill for another refreshing purpose.

Backyard brewing is a well-established tradition in the islands. Bush rum, babash, bushwacky, mountain dew and, of course, moonshine, the illicit alcohol is called—though not on St. Kitts, where it goes by the unlikely name of hammond. Austin Edinborough, a big-bellied, taxi-driving, poetry-writing, kitchen-loving ex-policeman who befriended us when *Receta* stopped there on our way to Dominica, sang its praises loudly. "Lovely to drink, the best drinking rum," he said, claiming it was much better than the legal stuff bottled on St. Kitts. "Someone is watching it all the time, because it's what they're going to be drinking themselves." He did admit, though, that drinking hammond requires a bit of caution because you never know what the proof is.

According to some Kittitians, Austin among them, this moonshine takes its name from the first person brought to trial on the island for doing his own distilling and thereby cheating the British government of a lucrative source of taxation. "Of course, he was convicted," Austin says, in response to my question about the outcome of the Crown v. Hammond. (Another story has it that Hammond was a customs officer rather than the renowned distiller.)

Thinking hammond might be our route to seeing a clandestine still in operation, we asked Austin if he could direct us to a bottle. Who better than an ex-cop to know where to find illicit moonshine? He merely laughed and promised he would bring us one himself instead.

Shortly after breakfast one morning, Austin arrived at the dock in Basseterre where *Receta* was moored, clutching a bottle that had once contained Jamaican Appleton Rum. He insisted we try its contents right away—standing on the dock, in scarcely the middle of the morning, without any cups or glasses—unscrewing the recycled cap and wafting the bottle under our noses so we'd learn to identify the distinctive hammond aroma. It was the smell of liquid fire. An incautious sip revealed it was the taste of liquid fire as well. Months later, we take the bottle—which we'd subsequently not reopened— to another tasting night on another boat. It was deemed "fish rum," suitable only for pouring into the gills of a large hooked fish to subdue it before bringing it on board. "Sacrilege," said Steve, carefully stowing it away for future retesting.

Austin had to drive to a friend's house in the country to get the hammond, he told us, and he bought the last two bottles. "There hadn't been any good molasses around," he explained, "and no one will make hammond unless there's good molasses." But the molasses supply had recently improved, and his friend now had the still going again. "It's not at his house," Austin quickly added, obviously anticipating my next question. "It's hidden in the mountains."

And so, foiled, we had left St. Kitts and its sister island Nevis without winkling our way to a working moonshine still.

. . .

Moses, however, has no such hesitation about taking us straight to the source in Dominica. From the bay oil still, he drives straight—or as straight as one can on a twisting mountain road—to the village of Petite Savanne. On my map, the route is a nameless, saw-toothed yellow line, warningly labeled "Steep Road"; on a map produced just eight years earlier, it's marked as a mere track, with a pictograph of hikers beside it. Moses parks in front of a tiny rum shop and leads us on foot down a path behind it into the edge of the rain forest. Past a small cultivated plot thick with bananas, dasheen, and no small amount of ganja, we come to a beyond-ramshackle building constructed from flattened Texaco oil drums: home of Ken Samuel's moonshine rum.

The dim interior is fiendishly hot, heavy with the smell of wood smoke and burnt sugar. At one end, most of the dirt floor is occupied by plastic drums filled with a bubbling witches' brew of brown sludge—cane juice in various stages of fermentation. At the other end, a wood fire burns under a boiler made from a recycled oil drum. This home-built jury-rigged pot still is tended by a skinny, bare-chested young man— probably not long out of his teens—who is smoking a little weed as he goes about his work.

Kirt Shaun Clinton Darroux—as he proudly introduced himself—learned how to make "*wa bio,*" the Creole term for bush rum, from his father, who also has a still in Petite Savanne. In fact, Moses guesstimates, this village, with its total population of three hundred, has some thirty stills. When Dominica was a British possession, such operations were illegal, which is why inaccessible Petite Savanne became a center for the manufacture of tax- and duty-free hooch. Following independence in 1978, however, "it was no longer an offense," Moses tells us. "The government understood it was part of the culture." The 1888 Rum Duty Act, which criminalized distilling without a license and put bush rum-makers on the wrong side of the law, is actually still on the books—but no one pays a whit of attention. As another still-owning Dominican puts it, "Some of the policemen who would be enforcing the law, their parents raised them by selling moonshine. They're not going to do anything about it."

The cane juice that's the basis of this rum comes from the area around the town of Canefield, on Dominica's west coast. For every two barrels of juice (which ultimately turns into fifty to sixty bottles of rum), Kirt adds 50 pounds of sugar, he says, and two quarts of molasses. (In pre-independence days, when British officialdom sporadically cracked down on illegal stills, sales of sugar on Dominica would plummet.) The mixture is allowed to ferment in the barrels for nine or ten days—as the process nears completion, the sludge sinks to the bottom and the evil-looking brew clarifies—before he moves it to the oil-drum boiler. Here, the mixture is slowly heated until its alcohol vaporizes. The vapor enters a gooseneck, which carries it to the condenser: a pipe running through a stone tank of cold, fresh water, fed continuously via a bamboo trough from a mountain stream behind the shack.

Once the boiler is fired up, it takes less than an hour for rum to start trickling out the pipe at the bottom of the condenser, where it's caught by a rusty tin that in its former life held a bottle of Johnny Walker Red. The first trickle of condensate is almost pure alcohol—not for drinking as is—followed by "ti rum," Creole for "little rum," the good stuff. There's no hydrometer here to measure the percentage of alcohol. "The brain knows by tasting when it's right," Kirt says, but he proves its potency by setting some alight to show us that it burns with a clear blue flame. He then urges me to dip a finger into a half-full bucket for a taste. Having watched him filter the rum from the rusty tin into the bucket via an old red bandanna, I'm a little concerned about the cleanliness of his product. "Are you kidding?" Steve says, nudging me forward. "No germ could ever survive in this stuff."

Whatever the exact proof, he's right, of course: it's numbingly potent, rough and raw, but, curiously, at the same time it has a pure, clean taste. To temper it—and purportedly give it medicinal properties—bush rum is often steeped with various herbs and spices; in this village, the resulting brew is called "Petite Savanne whiskey." Kirt pours us a glass from a bottle stuffed with lime skins, rosemary, cinnamon bark, *bois bandé* bark, lapsent leaves and ginger clover. (This is ginger "that has no root," he explains. "All the essence is in the leaves and sticks.") Local wisdom says this combo of herbs and spices is going to take care of whatever ails us: the rosemary and cinnamon relieve the symptoms of colds and flus; the ginger cures an upset stomach and gets rid of gas; the lapsent kills intestinal worms and helps with hangovers caused by drinking the stuff straight; and the bois bandé is a noted island remedy for erectile dysfunction, assures prostate health, and (quite the combination) is also good for gas. The lime skins, to the best of our knowledge, are included only to improve the taste.

A few days later, we stop in a restaurant in Castle Bruce, a little farther north on Dominica's windward coast; behind its bar is a lineup of three dozen different homemade herbal rums—including local medicinal favorites such as longleaf, another noted aphrodisiac, and *giroflou*, which is spiced with clove flowers and is excellent, the owner says, for treating colds. But Moses wants us to try the herbal blend of another Petite Savanne rum shop. Among the assortment of rums on its counter, we spot a plastic jug labeled *Jah Daniel:* moonshine flavored with a generous fistful of ganja. Let me report that it is a very acquired taste.

The results of Kirt's labor are for sale in the little shop that fronts the road where we parked. Cartons of empty recycled bottles are stacked near the door, and when we ask to buy some Petite Savanne whiskey, the man behind the counter retrieves a five-gallon plastic pail, uses a cup to ladle it into a bottle that once held a quart of Gordon's Gin, and tells us we owe him EC$10 (about $3.75).

But we leave Ken Samuel's still with something other than Petite Savanne whiskey: Kirt had filled a small plastic water bottle with the undrinkable alcohol that had first streamed out of the still. "For Godly purpose," he explained, handing the bottle to Steve, who had mentioned he was sore from hiking. Like the other villagers, we are now equipped to make our own bay rum. All we have to do is mix in a couple of drops of bay oil, he said, and rub it on our aching muscles at night.

. . .

Dominicans attribute gender to each of their 365 rivers; males flow directly from the source, females branch off other rivers. The White River, which borders Moses' father's land near Delices, is a female river, and as we follow her upstream—sometimes wading thigh deep, sometimes balancing on water-rounded stones, sometimes clambering along the shore over SUV-sized boulders—she cuts through dense rain forest. Moses is leading the way to Victoria Falls, where the soft, opaque, milky-blue water thunders down more than 200 feet into a foaming pool, creating its own wind and sending out swirling clouds of mist. "Moses, are there mountain chickens around here?" I ask.

Crapaud, as they're called in Creole, are the main ingredient in what has long been Dominica's national dish. I'm convinced they've been given the innocuous English name of "mountain chicken" purely for the benefit of visitors who might otherwise be put off by the idea of eating fried giant toads. This etymological fiddle is apparently aided by the taste and appearance of the dish, since mountain chicken legs—six inches long or more—resemble large drumsticks.

We are unlikely to run across any "*kwapo*," as Moses pronounces it in Creole, in the rain forest, the markets or any restaurant. The population is showing signs of decline, some diseased toads were found—and, as a result, the government banned their hunting and eating. "People blame it on global warming," he explains in his soft singsong voice. "I think more likely frogs introduced from Martinique spread the disease. But once the Dominican people think something is poisonous, they won't go near it." So much for the national dish.

But the White River is home to a new national dish, Moses says—which, frankly, sounds a lot more delectable than the banned one: freshwater crayfish, whose tails rival those of small lobsters. "The river crayfish are sweet, so sweet. And the last quarter of the moon is the best time for catching them."

How handy: the moon is waning. By the time we've reached Victoria Falls, Steve has hatched a plan. While I'm out of earshot swimming in the cold frothing water—surrounded by rock walls draped with oversize ferns, elephantine leaves and Tarzanesque vines—Steve pops the question: "Moses, can we go crayfish hunting with you?"

And so a few nights later, Moses leads us back up the White River—this time, in last-quarter-of-the-moon darkness, the inky night broken only by megawatt fireflies blinking in the rain forest and the tiny, ineffectual penlight I'm clutching. Lithe and loose-limbed, he moves effortlessly and soundlessly in bare feet, no need to switch on the larger torch he carries, except to check what's going on behind him—usually after an audible "Oh, shit," as I lose my balance teetering from rock to rock, scrape my ankles and splash into the water.

Moses' younger brother Israel and cousin Neville have joined us on the hunt. As we walk upstream, they're placing two-foot lengths of line they've baited with fresh coconut meat in the shallows and securing each one in place with a rock. They choose locations for these thirty-odd "traps" carefully—the water neither too deep nor too fast—so that (cue another round of me crashing and splashing) when we retrace our steps after a break for a bit of bush rum, we're likely to find crayfish gorging on the coconut, oblivious to the flat of the cutlass blade swooping down to stun them and the hands ready to make a quick grab.

The expedition is successful; the first-time hunters don't break their necks falling off a rock, and the cloth sack Moses brought along gradually fills with crayfish—each about a foot in length, with disproportionately long claws and meaty tails. One of the coconut traps has attracted a hefty freshwater crab, "the sweetest of them all," Moses says, giving us a "double treat" for the cook-up he has planned. "We're going to have a big broth," he explains as his battered pickup jolts along the narrow, unlit road back to Delices, the headlights shorting out each time we hit a bump. While I'm imagining a thin soup, he proceeds to describe a dish that's more a stew, full of plantains, dumplings and susbstantial pieces of crustacean.

The pickup jerks to a stop in front of a narrow, boarded-up roadside shack. Unsure of what's going on, Steve and I pile out along with the others. It's after nine-thirty, I'm starving, and this stop sure doesn't seem likely to result in any food, let alone a big crayfish "broth."

But within minutes, Moses has removed a padlock from the door and unshuttered the windows to reveal a simple rum shop—owned by another of his cousins. He turns on the lights, cranks up a sound system, and as reggae reaches into the darkness, patrons magically appear, as if conjured out of the warm night air. Soon dominoes are slapping on a table in one corner, where a Marley poster proclaiming BOB LIVES competes for wall space with one explaining osteoporosis.

Moses takes charge behind the bar, drinking Guinness and grooving to the tunes while he fills orders: a bottle of Kubuli, the local beer; a single cigarette; a glass of bush rum (almost half the price of the beer); a handful of ganja.

Cousin Neville, meanwhile, has stationed himself in the broom-closet kitchen, whose only appliance is a portable propane cooktop, and begins expertly chopping garlic and onions, washing the crayfish and crab with lime juice, and slicing green plantains. "Most Rasta men cook," he says, as he liberally shakes curry into the bowl with the cleaned seafood and sets it aside to season. "I been cooking since I twelve. I thirty now."

Moses, too, is a cook—his father taught him, sampling and critiquing his efforts, making him repeat a dish until he achieved the correct taste every time. He'd taken us to meet his father, fifty-seven-year-old Moses Sr., a few days earlier, on our way back from Victoria Falls. In the subdued light of the family kitchen, a coconut's throw from the White River, I barely registered the plantains and yams roasting over the cooking fire, or the face of the bearded older man with the long Rasta dreads at the table. Instead, I was captivated by his gnarled hands; they were busy stemming and seeding a mountain of marijuana, which is grown and smoked sacramentally by the Rastafarian faithful. Across the table, Moses' uncle had a similar mountain—but his hands were engaged in rolling a gargantuan spliff.

Afterward, Moses told us his father cooks for visitors who come to see his traditional "agricultural" way of life. "When you're anchored in Roseau, ask Seacat to bring you to my father." We promised him we would pay Moses Sr. a return visit.

Now, as Neville rolls dumpling dough into fat pencils between his palms, Moses disappears into the night to forage for a few more ingredients for the broth—leaving Steve to take over behind the bar. (Luckily, he isn't asked for anything more complicated than a beer.) Moses returns with handfuls of fresh sage and thyme—herbs, like everything else, grow ferociously here—and several cinnamon bay leaves he's plucked from a nearby tree, and they are chopped and added to the pot. The only thing he hasn't been able to find at this time of night, he says, is another coconut, to grate for coconut milk, and so the broth will go without. As it cooks, the grooving continues, spliffs are lit, fresh beers are opened.

It's after eleven when Neville finally declares the dish ready and ladles it into whatever bowls, pots and plastic containers he can find. Silence descends as we slurp broth, suck heads and legs, and lick shells, using fingers as much as spoons. The crayfish and crab are as sweet as Moses promised, and the plantains and dumplings have absorbed the flavor of the rich curry- and herb-scented broth. "This is real mountain cuisine," he says.

. . .

You'd think I would have learned a lesson stumbling up the White River at night. You'd think I would have realized that while rugged Dominica invites adventure, it's not always wise to accept the invitation. And why do I continue to listen to Steve?

"They're *land* crabs," he argues persuasively. "It will be a walk in the park compared to hunting crayfish in the river. Besides, we'll bring more lights." We're back on *Receta*, still anchored in Prince Rupert Bay off Portsmouth, and he's trying to convince me—though he's not allowing me much room for discussion—that we need to go crab hunting at the base of the Cabrits, the twin peaks that form the north wall of the bay. They were a separate island several millennia ago but are now joined to Dominica by a stretch of just-above-sea-level land—swamp, actually, if it's been raining for any length of time. Martin Carrierre—a boatman, guide and naturalist by trade, but also an accomplished cook—has offered to show us how to make another Dominican specialty: land crab and callaloo soup. Steve intends to go along to acquire the main ingredient.

So scarcely forty-eight hours after the crayfish caper, I find myself walking in the dark again. Mercifully, this time the route is flat and dry, because it hasn't rained in several days—though that could mean a slow night for crab hunting. Martin, who also answers to "Providence," the name of his wooden pirogue, has told us the crabs come out of their burrows to feed especially after a rainfall. On either side of the trail, the ground is covered with fallen leaves and pocked with substantial holes. (Land crab burrows are big enough that Sir Francis Drake used them to hide plundered gold and silver in Panama.) We need to listen for scrabbling in the leaves, Martin explains, and pan our lights in the direction of the sound to catch the glow of a crab's eyes. The light stuns it—deer-in-the-headlights fashion—"and then things need to happen fast."

These are seriously mean crabs, packing serious weapons: hefty, bone-crushing claws, quite different from the dainty pincers of a crayfish. When they emerge from underground with their weapons raised and ready for attack, the males (bigger-clawed than the females) look like something created for a bad horror flick. Scuttling sideways in the darkness, weapons and armor clacking, they even sound menacing, as British Admiral William Penn and his men discovered while setting an after-dark ambush for the Spanish on Hispaniola in 1655. The British were routed from their hiding place by the noise of approaching cavalry and ran back to their boats in alarm. But the terrifying pounding of hooves through the leaves turned out to be merely an army of land crabs. I mince cautiously along the path, avoiding piles of leaves and anything else that might serve as crab camouflage.

When we freeze a crab in one of our lights, Martin runs toward it and gets a foot on its back—spinning it with a gentle soccer kick first if necessary to get it facing away from him—so he's able to grab it swiftly from behind before one of the massive claws can twist around and lock onto his hand. Then he throws the sucker into the sack he's brought along.

I'm in charge of the sack. "Hold it closed down here," he says, suggesting a grip that I'm sure is too close to the bottom, where the claws are. "Just shake the bag if you feel them climbing up."

Right. As the catch mounts, the crabs become increasingly testy, and the sack becomes not just heavier but also noisier, as they plot their escape. The odd claw pokes through the fabric, until Martin double-bags them for security.

Clean-cut and close-shaven, Martin has the build of a footballer, and a long history of successful crab hunting. He started when he was fourteen or so—he's thirty-nine now—gathering sackloads for his father, who would take them to Guadeloupe to sell. "I'm not just a good crab hunter, I'm a *very good* crab hunter," he says, flashing us a big grin. He's making it all look so easy—sometimes picking up one in each hand before depositing both in the sack—that Steve decides he wants to give it a go.

But Steve misjudges as he tries to get a foot on his first crab, and had he been wearing lighter shoes, we could have been dealing with a toe amputation. The crab clamps a death grip on his leather runner, much to Martin's amusement, and refuses to let go. Martin suggests a gentle positioning kick with the other foot and then a rear pickup with Steve's right hand: the one wearing his heavy-duty Kevlar fishing glove.

Despite the lack of rain, we have an excellent night. "Just go for the big males," Martin advises once it becomes clear we (I use the word loosely, since after seeing Steve in action I've decided to stick to sack management) can pick and choose. Martin had told us we'd need five or six big ones for our crab soup; a half-hour's work yields a nice dozen.

Back on *Receta*, the crabs spend the night in their sack at the aft end of the cockpit. From time to time, faint rustlings can be heard as they plan their revenge.

Which comes the next morning. Martin arrives at the boat at 8:15 so we can start cooking lunch. During the subsequent five hours—*five hours*—of work the one dish requires, I vow never again to complain about the cost of any crab dish in an island restaurant.

Step #1: Get a crab out of the sack and break off its claws and legs. Funny, how a few simple words can so underdescribe the difficulty of a task. Did I say the crabs were mean? Because by now, they are really pissed off. You have to reach into the sack and grab one, steering clear of its claws and those of the eleven others. Steve counts. That's twenty-four deadly weapons. I can tell he's already worried about handling this part of the operation himself tomorrow, when Martin won't be here and we have to deal with the remaining crabs . . . who by then no doubt will be even angrier.

Step #2: Clean the crabs. Not so fast. This turns out to be an extremely messy, three-part process that involves removing the inedible bits (eyes, gills, internal organs, sex parts), scrubbing away external mud with a kitchen brush (scraping the worst of it off with a knife first, if necessary), and washing the cleaned pieces with water and then lime. "If you don't know where your crabs have come from, you need to put them in a barrel and feed them grass to purge them," Martin explains. You wouldn't want a crab that was noshing along a drainage ditch, for instance, to go straight into your pot. Some Dominicans purge their crabs by feeding them hot peppers. In Puerto Rico, a three-day diet of first coconut and then corn is recommended. "But these crabs have come from the forest, so purging isn't necessary."

Thank goodness, since I'm already regretting that the words "crab soup" ever crossed my lips. My hands are slick with crab goo, and the cockpit is slimed with muck, puddled with muddy crab-washing water, and splattered with stray crabby bits. We've been at it for several hours, and we haven't even started the peeling, chopping, mixing, kneading, grating and cooking phases. At least all our digits are still intact.

Martin is clearly comfortable in the kitchen, and handles a knife like a pro. "In the Caribbean, everyone gets involved in the kitchen vibration," he explains. As the morning progresses, he shows me how to season the cleaned crabs with onions, garlic, peppers (two types, one for flavor and the other for heat), parsley, celery and several branches of fresh thyme. While they marinate, he sets me to work grating an entire fresh coconut by hand to make coconut milk—meanwhile, I'm thinking fondly of the packages of instant coconut milk powder I have stowed in my lockers—peeling and chopping "provisions" (assorted inexpensive, abundant, starchy, filling vegetables such as yam, dasheen and green cooking bananas) and then making dumplings, "the heartbeat of a good broth." I try to follow his lead and knead the dumpling dough by squeezing it in one hand like an exercise ball. Between breaking apart the crabs, hand-grating the coconut, squeezing it in water to extract the milk, and now this one-handed style of kneading, this is cooking as hard physical labor, and I eventually cry defeat. I plunk the dough down on my board and knead it as I would bread.

Everything goes into the pot in stages, starting with the crabs and ending with the coconut milk and handfuls of young, slightly smoky-tasting island spinach, which grows abundantly in Dominica's rich, well-watered volcanic soil and is often used here instead of callaloo. When Martin sees that I have fresh anise bay leaves from our trip to the southeast coast, he calls for half a large leaf to be added to the simmering pot as well. "Your kitchen smells real good," a passing boatman calls to us.

The results aren't just real good; they're fabulous. We follow Martin's lead and dive in "with all ten." Only three things are required at the table: a full roll of paper towels, a bowl for shells, and a blind eye to the devastation wreaked in the cockpit and galley. In a fraction of the time it took to prepare, the broth is reduced to a pile of cracked claws and empty shells, and we are left happily licking sticky crab-and-coconut-flavored fingers. "This," Martin says, surveying us and the mess with approval, "is not for decent people."

· · · MOONSHINE PUNCH · · ·

We were served a similar rum punch in the Jungle Bay Resort restaurant on the southeast coast of Dominica, where it was made with "mountain dew" from Ken Samuel's still. ("Serve over plenty of ice," my notes read. "Or you won't be able to see straight after one drink.") The punch tastes just as good even if the rum isn't overproof moonshine brewed in a local backyard.

½ cup	white rum	125 mL
1 cup	guava nectar (see Tip, below)	250 mL
½ cup	passion fruit nectar (see Tip, below)	125 mL
Pinch	freshly grated nutmeg	Pinch
Pinch	cinnamon	Pinch
2	wedges lime	2

1. Combine rum with guava and passion fruit nectars; stir briskly.
2. Fill two tall glasses with ice and pour in punch.
3. Grate a little nutmeg on top, and dust with a tiny bit of cinnamon. Garnish with a lime wedge, and squeeze it into the glass before drinking.

Makes 2 drinks.

Tip:
- Tropical fruit nectars are available in many supermarkets. Look for them with the bottled juices or in the freezer case; they're also sold online. (Passion fruit is sometimes sold under its Spanish name, *chinola*, *maracuyá* or *granadilla;*

as is guava, *guayaba*.) They usually already have sugar added. If the punch needs additional sweetening, add a couple tablespoons (25 mL) of simple sugar syrup: Combine equal parts (by volume) of sugar and water in a saucepan. Bring to a boil and stir until the sugar goes into solution. Cool and store in the fridge.

· · · COCONUT DROPS · · ·

Steve, who's usually not a fan of coconut in baking, loved the fresh coconut "biscuits" he had for breakfast one morning in Dominica. Don't think light and flaky, however—these are dense and solid, even a bit crunchy—satisfying and not too sweet. Joanne Hilaire, who runs the kitchen at Jungle Bay, calls them Coconut Rough Cake. She was happy to share her recipe, pulling a much-folded, handwritten copy out of her handbag on the spot.

3 cups	all-purpose flour	750 mL
¾ cup	granulated sugar	175 mL
2 tsp	baking powder	10 mL
½ tsp	salt	2 mL
½ tsp	cinnamon	2 mL
1 tsp	freshly grated nutmeg	5 mL
¼ cup	butter or margarine	50 mL
1 cup	finely grated fresh coconut (see Tip, below)	250 mL
1 ¼ cups	milk	300 mL
1 tsp	coconut or almond extract	5 mL

1. Preheat oven to 400°F (200°C).
2. In a large bowl, combine dry ingredients. Cut in butter or margarine until mixture resembles fine crumbs. Mix in coconut.
3. Combine milk and extract. Stir into dry ingredients to make a stiff dough.
4. Drop in heaps on greased or parchment-lined baking sheets. Bake in preheated oven for 18 to 22 minutes or until golden and crisp.

Makes about 2 dozen.

Tip:

- It's much easier to get the meat out of a fresh-off-the-tree island coconut than an older North American store-bought one. To make the job simpler, bore two holes in the eyes of the coconut using a pointed utensil and drain the liquid. Bake drained coconut in a preheated 400°F (200°C) oven for about 15 minutes, until shell cracks. While nut is still warm, hit with a hammer to loosen shell, break it open and pry out the meat.

· · · CURE FOR THE COMMON COLD · · ·

If your neighborhood watering hole doesn't have a lineup of medicinal rums behind the bar, try this instead. Islanders swear it will make you feel better when you're plagued by sneezing and chills. Some proponents say the nutmeg helps sweat the illness out of your body.

¼ cup	dark rum	50 mL
2 tbsp	lime juice	25 mL
1 tbsp	honey or brown sugar	15 mL
⅛ tsp	ground cloves	0.5 mL
1	cinnamon stick	1
	Freshly grated nutmeg	

1. Place all ingredients except cinnamon stick and nutmeg in a large mug.
2. Fill mug with boiling water and stir with the cinnamon stick. Sprinkle nutmeg on top. Get into bed, pull the covers up to your chin, and drink slowly, inhaling the steam as you do.

Makes 1 dose.

SIX

The Food Critics Visit the Easy-Bake Boat

· · · GRENADA · · ·

I can still see those women performing feats of culinary magic, with
all the arrogance, intolerance to criticism, and competitiveness that is
peculiar to persons whose knowledge is based exclusively on an oral
tradition, on myth and on the inheritance of customs. My mother, and
all those other women who surrounded me, ignored the hot-cuisine
of France, convinced that what came out of their pots, resting on three
rocks placed in the shape of a triangle, was superior to anything
cooked in Europe.

from Love and Sweet Food, *Austin Clarke's*
2000 *culinary memoir about growing up in Barbados*

"LISTEN TO ME, you have to be careful when you buy
ochroes." Our old friend Dingis prods the tip of a raw okra pod
to make her point. "It has to be soft, or it won't melt when you
cook it. And do you remember how to stew lambi deh way I
show you?" We are crowded into the kitchen under her house in
the village of Lower Woburn—Steve and I; Dingis and her
daughter, Gennel; and Gennel's six-month-old daughter,

Belicia—because Dingis had insisted on cooking lunch for us to celebrate our return to Grenada. *Receta* had glided between the reefs off the southeast coast and into the placid anchorage behind Hog Island a couple of days earlier. With a surreal sense of déjà vu, we dropped the hook a scant boat's length from where we had anchored on our first visit to Grenada nine years earlier. It felt like coming home.

As we walked up the steep hill toward Dingis's house the following day, a bare-chested teenager climbed a tall palm to one side of the rutted road, knocked a few coconuts to the ground, then chased them down the hill to retrieve them. A stout lady wearing red shoes and a porkpie hat passed us going the other way, singing hymns to herself, accompanied by an appreciative contingent of the ever-present local dogs. The flamboyant trees were on fire, their red blossoms branded into pure-blue sky. But despite these reassuring slices of everyday Grenadian life, my heart was pounding, and not just from the exertion the hill required. I was nervous—we both were—about what we'd find at the top.

"You know the mess after a dog get into the garbage? That is Grenada," Prime Minister Keith Mitchell had said in 2004, a few days after Hurricane Ivan hit. Ivan had reserved the worst of his fury for the southern part of the island, his eyewall passing directly over Lower Woburn. Although Dingis's tiny house was left standing, it was seriously "mash up," she told us when we finally managed to reach her by phone from Toronto more than a week afterward. Ivan took her roof, door, windows, carport, electricity, water pipe, telephone, and most of the family's extremely modest belongings—as well as destroying the fishing boat they depended on to make a living.

After the breath-sucking winds passed, downed power and phone lines twisted through the debris like a new species of tropical vine, and the vibrant landscape became a moonscape— a still life of uprooted tree trunks and leafless bushes. Any chill was an illusion, however: the sun quickly returned with its usual searing heat—except now fewer trees were left to offer shade, shelter or food. The island where "God provide and no one ever go hungry," as Dingis had once described it to us, had suddenly been stripped of its mangoes, papayas, breadfruit, bananas, coconuts, golden apples, oranges and grapefruit, as well as the backyard gardens that those without a lot of cash relied on. And with the destruction of commercial crops— particularly nutmeg and cocoa—and the wreckage of the tourism business (the primary source of foreign exchange), cash was going to be in particularly short supply.

The island was woefully unprepared to deal with the aftermath. The only building material available for Dingis to use as a temporary roof was salvaged, second-hand corrugated galvanized sheet metal—complete with second-hand nail holes. When the daily afternoon rainy-season deluges came, they sluiced down those corrugated troughs and poured through the holes. "We livin' under a sieve," Dingis said with a resigned laugh during one of our calls to see how they were managing. "But we copin'." In the absence of land lines, the Grenadians embraced cellphones with a vengeance. But Dingis and others without generators had to rely on lanterns for light, and ice (whenever any was available) for cooling for the three months it took for the power to be restored in tiny Lower Woburn.

We happened to call again the evening after the electricity finally was turned back on, and caught them reveling in the unaccustomed brightness. "The country picking up," Gennel said, showing an enthusiasm that had been missing for months. "Things getting back green."

Now, as we get to the top of the hill and walk the last hundred yards up the main road to their house, the country sure looks like it has been "picking up" in the almost three years after Ivan—like it's in the middle of a building boom, in fact. Elaborate new houses have sprouted—all too clearly visible behind Ivan-trimmed vegetation—many of them owned by foreigners, who leapt at the opportunity when local landowners began selling off slices of glorious ocean-view property to make ends meet post-hurricane. The generous mango tree that had started our friendship with Dingis is gone. "Ivan take half and Emily"—the next year's follow-up punch to the still-in-recovery, saddled-with-debt island—"take deh other half," Dingis says. A substantial house now stands in its place.

After big hugs, she ushers us inside her own small house and pushes us into a loveseat, new since our last visit. Gennel takes the other chair with the baby, which leaves Dingis standing and her friend Gail sitting on the worn linoleum that covers the floor of the main room. A playpen and a television complete the furnishings: no tables, bookcases, lamps, tchotchkes, rugs or pictures. But it does have a solid roof and door now, Dingis proudly points out, and sturdy new windows. (As she shows off the changes, she thanks us profusely for the help we and others—many of them total strangers—provided, enabling the family to purchase building materials.)

The house no longer peeks through the trees as it once did, but stares at the road with undisguised boldness—and it is hard to miss the glaringly white tomb near the ("thanks be to God") still-standing breadfruit tree: Kellie, Dingis's long-time common-law husband (though she never called him that) and

Gennel's father, had died in an accident a few months before Ivan, suffering a heart attack while swimming back to his fishing boat after falling out in rough seas.

But happiness has returned to their lives recently, with the birth of Belicia. "Blaise and me want you to be the godparents," Gennel tells us, as the baby, nicknamed Bici, bounces happily in Steve's arms, showing off her first two teeth when he makes her laugh. She has a full head of dark hair, which has been tamed into an elaborate series of little braids and tufts, and her mother's beautiful, expressive eyes. Almost twenty-four and far from the shy teenager we remember, Gennel wears a new-to-us confidence that goes with her stylish Rasta braids. She recently arranged the sale—of necessity—of a piece of their property, left to her when her father died; it's part of the steep hillside behind their house, where we remember goats and sheep grazing. Omnipresent cellphone tucked into her cleavage, Gennel seems completely at ease with motherhood, not at all concerned when we non-parents awkwardly hold our first godchild. "We have the christening when Blaise reach back from England," she says. Meanwhile, Dingis arranges our return in a few days for a lambi lunch, remembering that nine years earlier the dish had been one of our island favorites.

. . .

When we arrive, she has just finished tenderizing and seasoning the lambi, the name used in much of the West Indies for queen conch. Floridians aside, North Americans know it more for its large, pearly, salmon-pink-and-ivory shell (it was used in Victorian England for carving ornate cameos) than for its tasty meat. A conch is essentially a vastly overgrown snail that claws its way along the ocean bottom with a large, muscular foot. When it's cleaned—eyes, organs, skin and foot removed—it's a hunk of dense white muscle that will have all the mouth appeal of a rubber ball unless it's tenderized. One high-end, restaurant-owning Grenadian chef swears the secret to tender lambi is to freeze it first, which "relaxes" the muscle, slice it almost paper-thin, and then flash-fry it. Rubbed with a spice mix heavy on sweet paprika, cumin and ginger, then dredged in seasoned flour and quickly finished in butter after mere seconds in the fryer, Brian Benjamin's sizzling lambi are outstanding. But when we take Dingis to his St. George's restaurant, BB's Crabback, for a birthday dinner, she is unimpressed. Actually, she is horrified—personally offended by his untraditional approach to island ingredients. "We need to go into his kitchen and show him how to cook," she says with disdain.

The time-honored, Dingis-approved method for tenderizing lambi is to "pong" it with a wooden club until it has flattened to twice its diameter. ("He beat him like a lambi" is an island expression to describe the damage done in a fight.) She then cuts it into bite-size pieces and "seasons it up" with fresh sive, the pungent West Indian chives, closer in size and flavor to North American green onions; fresh thyme; onion and garlic; a couple of "pounded" cloves; a sprinkling of curry powder; and a couple splurts of ketchup, which plays the same role as a dollop of tomato paste might in my kitchen. "Now let deh lambi rest," she says.

Cooked Dingis-style, lambi is sweet and tender, and extremely rich, in a fragrant sauce that gets its deep color from brown sugar caramelized in hot oil until it's almost black. Like much Caribbean cooking, however, this isn't fast food; after turning the lambi pieces in the burnt sugar, Dingis leaves them to stew for a couple of hours while she moves on to the accompanying dishes. Cooking here is never to a strict mealtime—it takes as long as it takes, and you eat whenever it's ready.

Today, she's serving the lambi with the standard mound of white rice, and with callaloo. Although it's frequently prepared as a soup, callaloo can also be served as a vegetable dish, reminiscent of creamed spinach but with a much stronger, more textured, more complex personality. Dingis cooks the callaloo leaves with chopped okra and the usual island seasonings—chief among them, sive and thyme. Since these two usually go hand in hand in cooking, that's how they're sold in the market—a few branches of thyme tied to a bunch of green onions—giving the cook exactly what she needs; she's not forced to buy an entire bundle of herbs (expensive and wasteful) to get the small quantity needed for a dish.

When the callaloo is soft, "you swizzle it," Dingis says, spinning a long wooden dowel tipped with metal coils back and forth between her palms. In less than half a minute, the simple cheap kitchen tool has turned the callaloo into a thick puree, with a few distinct bits of leaf remaining to give it interest. If the okra has been properly chosen, it will melt into the callaloo, giving it body without sliminess. The only trick to preparing the dish appears to be the salt. "It take salt quick," Dingis warns, "same as pumpkin." She tells me to add only a very little at the end, or the callaloo will be overseasoned. The warning is worth heeding, since Dingis, like many West Indian cooks, generally salts with a liberal hand.

Closer to dinnertime than lunchtime, we sit down to eat in the kitchen, which is underneath the main room of the house and connected to it by an outdoor staircase and a rough path. Sunlight floods through a Dutch door, brightening the dim space—as do the pesky flies that are everywhere on the island already, even though it's only early July and "fly season" isn't until August. One Grenadian we meet suggests we leave fresh plum leaves scattered about *Receta* as a natural repellent; Dingis merely throws a lacy cloth over her limited collection of dishes and cutlery, which are stored on a table—she has no cupboards—and goes outside to rinse every pot before using it. There's no sink in this kitchen; outside the Dutch door, a cold-water standpipe rises out of the ground next to a long, waist-high concrete "table" that overlooks the road; this is where the lambi are cleaned, the seasonings chopped, the dishes washed.

Since there are only four of us today, plus baby Bici, we sit together at a small table. Often, though, the kitchen is a confusion of people—friends, neighbors, relatives, kids, babies—and mealtime means perching inside or out, wherever there's available space, Dingis adamantly refusing to fill a bowl for herself or rest on a stool until everyone else has eaten.

After lunch, on the pretext of showing him something outside, Gennel grabs Steve and leads him well out of earshot. She wants our help in planning a surprise for her mother. "Since Ivan, I couldn't do anything on her birthday—not even a cake. And last year, she turn fifty. This year, I want to give her a surprise party." Her birthday, July sixteenth, is coming up fast. The party is set for the Saturday following the official day.

As they plot, Dingis is bouncing Bici on her hip in the kitchen, the baby obviously happy and not in the least missing her mom. Island babies are comfortable in other arms; only when she's put down for her nap is Bici not being coddled by someone—her nana, another relative, us, or teenage Lynn or her slightly older sister Desiann, who live with their dad in the next house up the road.

"You know how to plait hair?" Dingis asks me.

"No," I reply, and she swings her hip around, offering up Bici's head: "Here, try it."

Oh, no: I'd already been told, when we first cooed over how adorable she was, that Bici hates—despises—anyone fussing with her hair, so much so that they can style it only while she's sleeping to avoid her vexed howls.

"But she won't like it," I say.

"No, go ahead, tryyyy," says Dingis, in her irresistible musical voice.

Bici's hair is soft as cotton fluff. But like a mare who can sense a non-rider on her back, she instinctively knows I'm a plaiting novice. She squirms away from my tentative attempts to . . . to do nothing, actually, and empties her lungs in protest. Steve and her mom come rushing back inside.

. . .

Our island friends don't use recipes—I don't think I've ever heard the word cross Dingis's lips—or measuring utensils. Hands and fingers replace calibrated cups and spoons, with tongues used for fine-tuning. So replicating one of Dingis's dishes is a challenge, even when I've watched her make it first.

Not long after our welcome-back lunch, Steve goes to the hardware store and buys me a gift: a proper island swizzle stick like Dingis's. It may look like a wooden-handled wire whisk that's gone through a trash compactor, but I discover it's more convenient than and just as efficient as my electric wand-blender. I use it to make my own "creamed callaloo," as I call it. However, Steve, the in-house food critic, notes that it isn't quite right. "It tastes slimy," he says, ever the diplomat. So on our next trip up the hill, I take a container of leftover callaloo for Dingis and Gennel to critique.

Getting the judgment takes considerable prodding, though, and I realize they're reluctant to deliver a negative verdict.

"Too slippery," Dingis finally admits. "How many ochroes you use?"

"About ten or twelve," I tell her. I'd guessed the quantity of okra based on the bag I'd seen in her kitchen—but, unfortunately, I'd been involved with Bici when she chopped her ingredients and put everything in the pot.

She and Gennel laugh. "Two ochroes plenty," Dingis says. No wonder my callaloo is "slippery."

This very quality explains why Caribbean folk medicine calls for pregnant women to eat lots of ochroes—to help the baby slide out easily during delivery.

. . .

"Ahhnnnn, too many seasonings." Dwight is vigorously swinging his head from side to side in disbelief.

"Too many seasonings," echoes his partner Stevie, who frequently repeats what Dwight says, as if to make sure I've understood.

We're still anchored off Hog Island, and the two are sitting in *Receta*'s cockpit, having returned from a day's fishing. While they're busy hoovering up a batch of my chocolate chip cookies, I have been avidly recounting how I prepared the lambi they gave us yesterday—replicating BB's spice mix and technique, which had been so unpopular with Dingis—and describing the spicy, butter-drenched results. Dwight just looks mournful and keeps shaking his head. "Ahhnnnn, then you can't taste the lambi. Keep it simple." "Simple," says Stevie.

Rough or calm, rain or shine, Dwight goes to sea seven days a week—on Sundays, he has a different partner, since Stevie takes one day of rest—diving for lambi (which they sell to local stores), fish (directly to locals), and spiny lobster (to hotels and restaurants, in season). I can usually hear *Rake and Scrape*, their 17-foot open wooden boat, buzzing past *Receta* between 6:30 and 8:30 in the morning, depending on the tide, as they head for the gap in the reef and the open ocean beyond. *Rake and Scrape* is West Indian shorthand for taking on anything and everything, but these guys don't have time to take on anything more than the vagaries of the sea. Once they've cleaned their catch, piled it into the freezer, and readied the boat for the next day, darkness is falling.

Several times a week, in the late afternoon, the different-as-papayas-and-bananas duo takes a break on the way to shore after fishing. A regular routine has developed. "Ahhnnnn, you want lambi today?" Dwight calls as they maneuver *Rake and Scrape* alongside *Receta*. Or, "Ahhnnnn, bring a bucket," and he plops a fat fish or a lobster inside. He waves away all attempts at payment and, instead, we reciprocate with something from *Receta*'s oven. They both have a sweet tooth, and—especially since they never take time for lunch when they're on the water—can easily demolish a couple dozen cookies, the better part of a pan of brownies, six or eight muffins, or (the new favorite) a loaf of home-baked sourdough bread slathered with crunchy peanut butter.

My Steve, no slouch himself in the eating department—somewhat renowned for his intake, in fact—admiringly calls Dwight "the human vacuum." But the calories don't show. Thirty-one years old, he's tall and lean, with a washboard stomach and not an ounce of body fat. His sidekick Stevie, almost a year older, is also well muscled from hard physical work, but he's a shorter, more compact package, with only marginally more meat on his bones. My oven has been getting a real workout since we arrived in Grenada and the pair started visiting, helping to keep the temperature inside *Receta* hovering around a toasty 85°F (29°C). Steve has taken to calling it the "Easy-Bake Boat."

Dwight was raised by Dingis, and was Kellie's longtime fishing partner, albeit with a multi-year gap in the late 1990s while he recovered from a near-fatal encounter with the bends brought on by scuba diving for lambi and lobster. Consequently, Dwight now uses only his own lungs in the water—having gradually trained himself to make one breath last long enough to take him to depths of 60 feet to spear a fish or pick up as many as a dozen conch from the bottom before returning to the surface. But Dwight and Dingis have had a falling-out since we were last in Grenada. "He spit me out like a plum seed," Dingis says, spitting out the words to make the meaning clear. For his part, Dwight doesn't talk about it. Though they avoid each other, the connection between them is still alive, via Stevie: he regularly delivers a bag of lambi from Dwight's and his catch to her at the end of a day.

Despite his disapproval of my gussying up the seafood he gives us, Dwight wholeheartedly approves of my baking. "That cake gooooood," he says when I trot out a pan of freshly baked gingerbread. "Ahhnnnn, my chef." Or, after polishing off half a loaf of warm, buttered, homemade bread in a matter of minutes: "Ahhnnnn, you sure you not from Grenada?"

"See you tomorrow, please the Lord," he says each time they depart. And every time, I start planning what's coming out of the oven next.

. . .

The birthday party invitations have been delivered; Steve designed and printed them on board, following Gennel's wording exactly: "You are invited to a SURPRISE birthday party for Miss Evette Naryan," she wrote, giving her mother's formal name, which we've never heard anyone use, "on Saturday, July 21st at 2:00. Please walk with this invitation to her house in Lower Woburn." Gennel is quite certain that Dingis doesn't suspect a thing.

We've volunteered to take care of the cake for the big event, and Steve has been entrusted with placing the order. He's been given careful instructions by Gennel: order two cakes, a simply iced sheet-cake to serve forty, plus a small, round, fancily iced layer cake of the buttercream-ribbons-and-roses variety. He decides this assignment is best executed in person and, handily, the recommended bakery is right on our bus route to town.

"I wanted to be sure they did an extra-special job," he tells me afterward, explaining why he decided to schmooze the slender, attractive young woman who took his order. "I can't believe you work here and you're not fat," he told her. "Everything looks so wonderful, I'd be eating all the time." Before the young woman could respond, another woman, this one exceedingly well nourished, appeared from the back room—with an acre of apron spread across her substantial middle and a huge grin on her face—and said, "She just new here."

On the day of the party, we arrive at the house promptly at two—having already delivered Carib beer and soft drinks, as well as the two cakes (yes, they do look "extra-special"), and helped Desiann, Lynn and their father, Dannyboy, string party decorations. Just a handful of people are there, and all are involved in cooking, prepping, or blowing up the rest of the balloons. You would have sworn the party wasn't slated to start until six or seven. Dingis's friend, quiet Gail, who is a regular fixture around the house, is slowly sweeping outside, stirring up clouds of dust. In the kitchen, Shortman (although he's not particularly) is stirring a monster pot of pelau—a chicken-and-rice dish that's popular party food because it's easy to prepare, feeds a bunch of people, and makes a little meat go a long way. Stevie has just dropped off a big bag of lambi and has now headed home to shower and change out of his fishing clothes.

His sister and a friend slip oversized T-shirts over their party outfits and set to work on the long concrete "table" outside the kitchen, cleaning, pounding and chopping the contents of Stevie's bag to make "lambi water" (which, I discover well after dark when it's finally ready to be served, is a thick, wonderful conch chowder). I offer to help, and they hand me a knife to peel and cube potatoes. It's the only knife not in use, and it's more suitable for carving a roast. A cutting board is an unknown commodity in this, like many of the other West Indian kitchens I'm invited into, and cooks simply hold ingredients in one hand as they peel, slice and chop. I gamely set to it—under watchful eyes—but I am clearly making the Grenadians unhappy. Sugar—everyone here has a nickname—soon takes the knife from me. "I show you how to do it," he says. Shit. It's understandable that I can't plait hair or cook lambi or callaloo properly, but I can't even peel a potato to local standards?

Even a surprise party, it seems, operates on island time: GMT, or Grenada Maybe Time, as it's known here. When Gennel arrives home with the unsuspecting Dingis an hour later, only fifteen or so guests have gathered. "Don't worry, everybody else arrive jus' now," one of the girls tells me, using the classic island phrase that is more likely to mean sometime before sunrise than within the next ten minutes. But no matter: Dingis is so surprised that she refuses to get out of Gennel's car, not accustomed to being the center of attention and worried she's not dressed for a party.

Unlike the birthday gatherings we're used to, this one starts with the cake. After we've sung a rousing (despite our small numbers) "Happy Birthday," Dingis blows out the candles on the extravagantly decorated layer cake—the one that says HAPPY 51ST BIRTHDAY, DINGIS in pink-icing script surrounded by sugar pansies and roses planted in chocolate buttercream. The cake is then whisked away . . . and never reappears. (We later learn the fancy cake is served to family and close friends the next day; pieces are saved for Steve and me.) The other cake is served after sunset, after pelau and before lambi water, when the crowd is thick and the young kids are just starting to get sleepy. The darkness is warm and friendly, and the piping frogs lay down a plaintive background track for the reggae and the laughter, as Dingis recounts to yet another latecomer how surprised she was and how Ahhnnnn and Steve had to drag her from the jeep.

I've been dreading the cutting of the cake, however, because I fear it will signal the ritual of "sticking deh cake," which Dingis and Gennel had gleefully described to us weeks earlier, when discussing the cake that would accompany Bici's eventual christening. "It's done to raise money for deh baby," Dingis explained. Two people shove knives into the cake from opposite directions, and when they touch, the knife-wielders can kiss. Well, maybe: if we've understood them correctly, someone can "buy you off," as Dingis put it, and claim the kiss for him- or herself. ("Bidding for bussing," Steve called it afterward.)

"Someone can say, '$10 so Ahhnnnn can't kiss Steve,' and then someone else can say, '$20 so she can,'" Gennel chimed in. Both mother and daughter were now howling at full volume as, apparently, "sticking deh cake" involves much hilarity. It's also done at weddings, "and sometimes at birthdays," Dingis said, which is when my alarm bells started clanging. If this would happen at her birthday, I knew we foreigners would be front and center.

"Come, Ahhnnnn and Steve, come," the birthday girl insists. "Come stick deh cake."

We reluctantly move forward, and are each handed a blunt knife, which we dutifully shove into the cake from two corners.

But, thankfully (though Steve's not too sure), the other guests seem not to have planned anything further tonight. Steve and I share a kiss, and the party moves on.

. . .

"We met your friends Dwight and Stevie," Amanda on the sailboat *Adventure Bound* e-mailed us. Apparently, *Rake and Scrape* had approached them while they were anchored a few bays east of Hog Island, and Stevie had asked if they knew us. "Jim"— Amanda's husband—"went out diving for lambi with them for a day, and then I cooked it on the barbecue. I used your recipe. Another day we fed them lasagna. They are very much looking forward to your return."

We had left Grenada to explore elsewhere for a while, and clearly Amanda and Jim had raised the stakes while we were away. Homemade lasagna? My wonderful barbecued lambi, cooked with peppers, garlic and onions on top? She even used *my* recipe? I started worrying what the Easy-Bake Boat would have to turn out to keep the boys happy when we returned.

Dwight and Stevie spot *Receta* the very day we're back and swinging at anchor in our customary place off Hog Island. They clamber aboard to catch up, bringing along some carefully chosen lambi for us. They never give us the first ones they put their hands on: they pick through the slimy mound of, oh, maybe a couple of hundred cleaned conch in the bottom of their boat for the ones that are big enough to offer substantial meat but not so big as to be tough no matter how thoroughly they're tenderized—though I'm not sure either of us is enough of a lambi connoisseur to know the difference.

"We met Jim and Amanda," Dwight says. "Dey nice," adds Stevie.

"Jim afraid of lambi," Dwight says, launching into an account of their day fishing together. "Yeah, Jim afraid," says Stevie. Eventually, we translate this to mean Jim's reaction (exaggerated for effect, we're sure) to the slippery, gritty layer of conch goo in the bottom of the boat.

"So, uh, how did you like the barbecued lambi they made for you?" Steve asks in his shit-disturbing way, not letting on that Amanda used my recipe. "Too fancy," pronounces Dwight, with the usual shake of his head to emphasize his disapproval. Steve delightedly probes for specifics; after all, my recipe has only a few ingredients, and all but the splash of white wine are staples of Grenadian cooking. "What made it too fancy, Dwight?"

"The foil," Dwight says. Yes, the pepper-and-onion-topped lambi are wrapped in aluminum foil and then cooked on the grill. "Deh foil too fancy," echoes Stevie.

. . .

Along with fresh seafood, we regularly get lessons from them on island life, and the natural cycles of the island. "Cherry trees over there, you know," Dwight says one afternoon, waving toward the mainland side of the anchorage. "Sweet cherries over d'ere," confirms Stevie.

They are pointing to the green hills just behind a patch of sand with a couple of tall, waving coconut palms. When we first visited Grenada, a farm was located there, and we would pick our way from the tiny beach up a path hidden by tall grass to visit the farmer, Mr. Butters, and buy tomatoes, greens and sweet little melons. But Mr. Butters was forced to relocate when the government sold a broad swath of land behind that tiny beach, as well as all of adjacent Hog Island, for a hotel and golf course development.

Seemingly under the influence of GMT, the project appeared to be in a state of perpetual delay. Recently, however, work has actually begun—despite renewed outrage, since part of the land slated for development is a nature reserve, one of the last remaining habitats of the endangered Grenada dove. But the government's blind eye is unsurprising: it recently passed an amendment allowing it to sell off pieces of its national parks and other protected areas to developers.

Area residents, including Dwight and Stevie, worry that once the development starts, Hog Island—and the gap between Hog and the mainland that small boats like theirs use to get out to sea—will be closed to local use. Though all Grenada's beaches technically are public, in practice the law is sometimes abused. Calivigny Island, for instance, is where local families once went to swim, picnic, and play on the beach. A few years ago, the government sold it to French interests, and armed guards with dogs now "discourage" visitors. If you don't know enough or are unwilling to protest, you will be driven away.

The mainland where Mr. Butters once farmed has already been surveyed and staked and a dirt road put in, but it has not otherwise been cleared, and the old fields lie fallow and heavily overgrown. "We found a melon growing wild when we were walking there," another cruiser told us recently. Someone else described a lime tree, a vision of abundance, the fruit as thick on the ground as on the branches, just begging to be gathered up. And now cherries?

I report all this to our friends Chuck and Barb, whose boat, *Tusen Takk II,* is also anchored off Hog Island. "Do you want to go for a walk tomorrow?"

The next morning, in *Tusen Takk*'s dinghy, we head for the tiny patch of sand. Once we pull it well up on the beach and secure it to the low branch of a sea-almond tree, we head off on foot—from the sand to a muddy track, to open fields of tall grass where a few bony cows graze. We don't know exactly what West Indian cherries (also called Barbados cherries) look like, so we inspect every tree and bush—we're looking for a "bushy tree," according to my reference book. "Do you think these are them?" Barb asks, pulling down a branch with clusters of tiny red berries. Since none of us knows, and none of us is willing to risk a taste, I break off a clump to show Dwight and Stevie.

Farther along, we reach the rutted dirt road, which leads to a saddle between the hills and, from there, back to the beach. Along the way, we pass a stand of trees laden with fruits that, once again, none of us recognizes: hard, kiwi-like spheres with fuzzy, dusty-brown skin. When I pull off a couple to add to my backpack for Dwight and Stevie to ID, they ooze a milky, exceedingly sticky sap.

"Only deh birds eat dese," Stevie says that afternoon, as Dwight tosses the red berries overboard. "Maybe deh cherries finish." But the sapodillas—the kiwi-like fruits—are, they both agree, "very nice to eat." The ones I brought back aren't "full," Stevie explains—still a little small and hard yet for picking. "Once dey full, you can pick dem and put dem to ripe. Dey very sweet."

I only know sapodillas from a classic, if somewhat salacious, Trinidadian soca tune by Preacher, called "Market Vendor," whose lyrics repeat, *All she crave / Sapodillas and banana till she reach deh grave / Two sapodillas and a nine-inch banana / Wah she want, wah she want*. But a flip through my cookbooks yields recipes for sapodilla mousse, sapodilla sorbet, sapodilla ice cream and sapodilla pie. And one of my most trusted cookbook authors describes the flavor as resembling "pears infused with a rich maple syrup."

The sapodilla tree, native to the Caribbean and Central and South America, also has a well-chewed place in food history: the milky sapodilla sap that gummed up my hands and backpack led to the commercial production of chewing gum. In the 1860s, an American inventor named Thomas Adams was introduced to sapodilla sap, called chicle, by a deposed Mexican president-cum-exile in New York, who was trying to sell the idea of using it as a rubber substitute. After Adams attempted unsuccessfully to vulcanize it, he got the idea of using it as a base for gum, mixing it with sassafras and licorice flavorings and sugar, and patenting the idea in 1871. His "chicle gum" took off. By 1900, Philadelphia gum makers Frank and Henry Fleer had encased the gum in a hard sugar shell to make Chiclets. (In most of today's chewing gum, chicle has been replaced by synthetics.)

A few days later, we head back to the tiny beach and retrace our way to the grove of laden trees. Barb and I each fill a bag with the largest of the sapodillas within easy reach, the ones I think qualify as "full."

"Now we just have to put them to ripe," I tell her. Recently I've caught myself unconsciously slipping into island-speak. One day, I told Steve about someone who had "the sugar" (diabetes); another, about someone who died of "the pressure" (a stroke). He and the Grenadians may understand me, but my cruiser friends are giving me curious looks.

. . .

If *Adventure Bound* was offering more than cookies in exchange for seafood, obviously I have to follow suit to uphold the honor of the Easy-Bake Boat. I invite Dwight and Stevie to come back to *Receta* for pizza one evening after they've got the day's catch to shore. The pepperoni pie and the (admittedly riskier) eggplant, red pepper, onion and olive one are both big hits.

"My belly full," Dwight says after we finish, leaning back in the cockpit and patting his non-existent stomach. "Ahhnnnn born in General Hospital."

I've been given the ultimate compliment: I cook like I was born Grenadian. But I'm given no time to rest on my laurels—because now Steve opens his big mouth: "If you liked these, you should try her lobster pizza," he says.

. . .

"Ahhnnnn, bring the bucket." Dwight drops a thrashing two-and-a-half-pound lobster in it—a mighty big hint.

"I guess tomorrow is pizza night," I tell them.

Making lobster pizza from scratch requires a bit of a running start. First I have to cook and cool the big beast—well, okay, I make Steve do the nasty job of dropping it into the pot—then crack it open and pick it clean. Unlike its cold-water cousins, a Caribbean spiny lobster doesn't have big, meaty claws. Most of the eating is from the large tail, but it does have smaller, equally succulent pieces of meat in its antennae, legs and body—and I'm determined to mine every last bit. Next up is the scratch dough for the crust . . . and then I get to tackle sapodilla mousse for dessert. The fruit I put to ripe almost ten days ago finally is ready.

Dwight and Stevie are late for dinner, and they arrive smelling mightily of conch. They had a great day on the water, they explain, and it consequently took them longer than usual to clean the catch, get it bagged and in the freezer, and the boat ready for the next morning. As I slice pizza in the galley, Dwight catches a whiff and leans in from the companionway. "I can't wait. My mout' spring water," he says, and grabs the quickly proffered first piece.

Aside from a tiny bit of slivered onion as a counterpoint to the rich seafood, a few flecks of fresh tomato for color, and a blanket of creamy melted mozzarella, this pizza is all about extravagant chunks of lobster on a crisp, garlic-butter-brushed crust. It is a huge hit. Dwight is certain I am the first person to come up with this luxurious version of one of his favorite foods—in fact, I took the idea from Mac's Pizzeria on the island of Bequia—and we have a hard time convincing him otherwise. "But they couldn't have done it so fine," he says, finally admitting that maybe I'm not the world's only lobster-pizza-maker. "Ahhnnnn smart enough to cook it simple and keep the flavor. Ahhnnnn the best."

Then I bring out the sapodilla mousse. It has a delicate, somewhat pear-like taste—I don't pick up on those notes of maple syrup, though—and a delicate pale-pink color, the result of combining the purple-hued sapodilla pulp with an equal amount of whipped cream. Granted, the mousse is a bit texturally challenged: whipping heavy cream until it's stiff and then getting it to stay that way once you fold it into pureed sapodilla pulp is pretty well impossible on *Receta*, whose fridge just isn't as cold as a home model, especially when (thanks to the pizza in the oven) the ambient temperature is now in the high eighties. Still, I know that swirled into elegant stemware, topped with a twist of lime, and sided with crisp sugar cookies, it would have got raves at a Toronto dinner party.

It does not fly here, however. More specifically, it is a full-blown crash-and-burn. "Most West Indians eat fresh fruit without frills," advises one of my West Indian–authored cookbooks, "and it is not often that we make fancy desserts with them, preferring it [the fruit] just as nature produced it." I should have paid attention: Eat-everything-in-sight Dwight ignores the mousse after a single, tentative bite and focuses on the cookies. Stevie, more polite and tolerant, finishes his mousse, then remarks: "Sapodillas real nice if you just put them to ripe and eat them. Very sweet."

. . . LOBSTER PIZZA . . .

Down-to-earth comfort food and special-occasion dish rolled into one, lobster pizza is the ultimate crowd-pleaser—whether the crowd is Grenadian fishermen or North American cruisers.

2 tbsp	unsalted butter	25 mL
1	clove garlic, finely chopped	1
	Dough for one 14-inch (35 cm) pizza (recipe on next page)	
2 cups	cooked lobster meat, cut into large chunks	500 mL
¼ cup	finely slivered onion (scant)	50 mL
¼ cup	finely chopped tomato (scant)	50 mL
	Freshly ground black pepper	
2 cups	grated mozzarella cheese	500 mL
	Hot chili oil (optional)	
	Cornmeal (for dusting pan)	

1. Place butter and garlic in a small saucepan and melt over low heat. Set aside while you prepare dough (see next page).
2. Preheat oven to 400°F (200°C). Grease pizza pan or baking sheet well and dust with cornmeal. Stretch dough to fit pan.
3. Brush dough with garlic butter. Scatter lobster meat on top.
4. Sprinkle with onion, tomato and pepper, then top with grated cheese.
5. Bake for 20 to 30 minutes, or until crust is nicely browned and cheese has melted.
6. Serve with a drizzle of chili oil on top, if desired.

Makes 1 pizza.

· · · BOAT-FRIENDLY PIZZA DOUGH · · ·

This recipe comes from my friend and colleague Jane Rodmell's Best Summer Weekends Cookbook. *Jane had lakeside cottages in mind when she came up with this quick-and-easy crust, but it's ideal for a small boat galley, too.*

2 ½ to 3 cups	all-purpose or bread flour	625 to 750 mL
¾ tsp	salt	4 mL
1 tbsp	quick-rising or instant yeast (1 envelope)	15 mL
1 cup	water	250 mL
2 tbsp	olive oil	25 mL
	Cornmeal (for dusting pans)	

1. Toss 2 cups (500 mL) flour with salt and yeast in a large bowl.
2. Heat water and oil until hot (125°F/50°C). Briskly stir or beat the liquid into the flour mixture for about 2 minutes.
3. Stir in enough remaining flour to make a soft dough. Knead on lightly floured surface until smooth and elastic, about 4 minutes, adding more flour when the dough becomes sticky. (You may not need to use all the flour.)
4. Shape dough into a smooth ball, cover, and let rest 10 minutes. Divide dough in two if you want to make thin-crust pizzas.
5. Oil pizza pans or baking sheets well and dust with cornmeal. Stretch or roll dough to fit. Cover with toppings and bake in preheated 400°F (200°C) oven for 20 to 30 minutes until crust is browned and topping is piping hot.

Makes one 14-inch (35 cm) thick-crust pizza or two 12-inch (30 cm) thin-crust pizzas.

· · · CREAMED CALLALOO (OR SPINACH) · · · WITH COCONUT MILK

This version of Dingis's callaloo gets added richness from coconut milk. Fresh callaloo—the leaves of the dasheen bush—is difficult to find in North America but, luckily, spinach is an islander-approved substitute. (Don't use baby spinach; older, larger leaves are closer to the texture of callaloo.) We love this side dish paired with rice and simple grilled shrimp, fish or chicken.

1 tbsp	olive oil	15 mL
2	large cloves garlic, chopped	2
½	onion, chopped	½
1	green onion, chopped	1
½	cubanelle or small green bell pepper (or 2 seasoning peppers), chopped	½
1	small piece hot pepper, chopped	1
2	okra, cut into rounds (optional; see Tip, below)	1
1	large bunch callaloo or spinach (about 12 oz/375 g), washed and chopped, including stems	1
¾ cup	coconut milk	175 mL
	Salt and freshly ground black pepper	
	Freshly grated nutmeg	

1. Heat oil in a large sauté pan or frying pan with cover. Cook garlic, onion, green onion and peppers over medium heat until fragrant and tender but not brown.

2. Stir in okra (if using), then add callaloo or spinach; stir until wilted. Pour in coconut milk and season with salt, pepper and nutmeg.

3. Cover and cook over medium heat until greens are soft—20 to 30 minutes for callaloo; about 10 minutes for spinach—stirring occasionally.

4. Using a swizzle stick or electric wand or stick blender, roughly cream the mixture. It should still have a distinct texture, with bits of leaf. (Don't use a regular blender or a food processor, as it will puree the mixture too much.) Taste and adjust seasoning.

Makes 4 side-dish servings.

Tip:

- I frequently omit the okra—it's often difficult to buy just two! The greens are thick enough without it. (Alternatively, if you buy a bag of okra, you can use the rest in the Island Poppers recipe that follows.)

· · · ISLAND POPPERS · · ·

Since jalapeños aren't found in the eastern Caribbean, I experimented with okra to make the popular bar snack—and happily discovered that they lose much of their "slippery" texture once the seeds and ribs are removed. Although making them is a bit fiddly, they're worth the effort for a special occasion.

24	small to medium okra (approx)	24
1 ½ cups	grated mozzarella cheese	375 mL
¼ cup	mayonnaise	50 mL
1	green onion, chopped	1
¼ to ½	Scotch bonnet or other hot pepper, chopped (or to taste)	¼ to ½
	Angostura bitters	
½ cup	cornmeal	125 mL
½ cup	dry bread crumbs	125 mL
½ tsp	dried thyme leaves	2 mL
	Salt and freshly ground black pepper	
1	egg, beaten	1
	Vegetable oil (for deep frying)	

1. Remove tops from okra and slit lengthwise, leaving the two halves connected. (Don't worry if they separate—the filling will glue them back together.) Using a grapefruit spoon or a paring knife, scrape out seeds and ribs and discard.
2. With a fork, mix together cheese, mayonnaise, onion and hot pepper. Add a couple of shakes of the bitters and stir until thoroughly blended.
3. Fill each okra with the mixture, then push the halves

together. Refrigerate for at least half an hour.

4. Combine cornmeal, bread crumbs, thyme, salt and pepper. Dip the okra in the beaten egg and then roll in the crumb mixture. Chill at least 15 minutes.

5. In a pot or deep fryer, heat vegetable oil to 375°F (190°C). Fry the okra in batches until they are golden on all sides. Serve warm.

Makes 24.

Tips:

- The poppers can be fried a couple of hours ahead and rewarmed before serving in a 350°F (180°C) oven for about 5 minutes.
- If you like, serve the okra with a spicy tomato salsa or the Garlic–Cilantro Aïoli Dip in Chapter 4.

SEVEN

Rolling Rice and Drinking Jack Iron Rum

· · · CARRIACOU & PETITE MARTINIQUE · · ·

> . . . I want to apologize for yesterday and last Thursday. As you know when I am sober, I am a polite, kind, generous person. But when I am drunk, I turn into a horrible animal. For the sake of my family as well as yourselves, please do not serve me Jack Iron . . . I am witnessing this letter with the police to show my sincerity.
>
> *letter quoted by Edward (the "Minister of Rum") Hamilton,*
> *in* Rums of the Eastern Caribbean, *1997*

> OUR MOTTO: BEWARE OF MENTAL SLOVENLINESS
> *sign in front of the Dover Government School, Dover, Carriacou*

"WE'RE GOING TO TAKE the ferry to Carriacou to see a new boat launched," Steve tells Dingis and Gennel when we next walk up the hill.

"They does build boats nice," Gennel says, referring to the shipwrights on both Carriacou and tiny neighboring Petite Martinique, the two other main islands that make up the country of Grenada.

"Dey building us a new boat," Dingis chimes in, much to our surprise. We knew the old one had been destroyed by Ivan, but we'd heard no talk of a replacement.

The Grenadian government has compensated fishing families for their Ivan-incurred losses, Gennel explains, and they have commissioned a new, 19-foot boat from a Petite Martiniquian named Clyde. "He a young man, but he have a very good reputation," she says. "While you're on Carriacou, go to Petite Martinique and see how our boat comin'."

. . .

Carriacou, just 14 miles northeast of Grenada at their closest point, has the feel of a place time has forgotten and tourism has not yet found, the feel of the Caribbean before resorts sprouted like fallen coconuts after a rain.

A month before, *Receta* had stopped here on the way to Grenada, and we'd driven around the island with Leo Charles, a born-and-bred Kayak, as residents of the island are called. ("It's easier to say than Carriacouan," another local explained.) The national colors were everywhere—tree trunks and utility poles sporting bright bands of red, green and yellow as high as a man with a paintbrush could reach; roundabouts circled with red, green and yellow rocks; roadside walls decorated with bright rectangles of the Grenadian flag. Meanwhile, the island's goats and black-bellied sheep strolled the roads as if they owned them. Since the sheep aren't woolly, we mistook them for goats at first, until someone let us in on the secret: a goat's tail points up, a sheep's tail hangs down.

A functioning horn is more important on vehicles here than functioning locks (no one bothers to use them), as it is required equipment for encouraging livestock to move, as well as for sounding greetings and saying thanks. The island needs just one gas station—it has more goats than vehicles, we were informed several times—but the number of rum shops tops one hundred. People make their living as they've done since the 1800s: by boatbuilding and fishing, mostly. Smuggling, too—of everything from refrigerators to furniture, with an emphasis on wine, beer and spirits—has long been a respected occupation.

At a stop in Windward (located, unsurprisingly, on the island's windward east coast), we'd watched a group of men at work on a traditional 40-foot, white-cedar sailing sloop, being built from scratch by Bernard Compton for his older brother, fifty-three-year-old Cyril, "Uncle C." The *Margeta-O II* would be finished in just a couple more weeks, the men said, though even to Steve (an incurable optimist when it comes to deadlines) it still looked months away from the water. Uncle C would then use it for fishing, his livelihood, and racing; Carriacou is famous in the West Indies for its annual summer regatta, where the locally built workboats compete.

Windward is Carriacou's center of boatbuilding, a skill that arrived in the early nineteenth century with Glaswegian ship-wrights. (Successive waves of French, British and Scottish settled various parts of the island, though most of the residents are descended from slaves, and Carriacou is one of the few islands where they are able to trace their lineage back to a par-ticular West African tribe.) Boatbuilding techniques don't appear to have changed much in the last two hundred years. Uncle C's boat-in-progress was supported by old rum casks, and the usual sheaf of builder's drawings was nowhere to be found; instead, the men were working, they told us, from a 3-foot scale model they had constructed. Steve, who was invited to climb the wooden ladder onto the deck for a closer look, reported that even in its unfinished state, few modern computer-assisted designs could compete with the graceful lines of this boat, and certainly not with its traditional craftsmanship. "Come back for the launching," they told us before we drove away.

"When they finish a boat, there is a big celebration," Leo explained, back in the vehicle. "It's called a *saraca*. You can say 'party' or 'fete' or 'festival,' but *saraca* means a lot of people comes." I sensed Steve scheming, working out the timing for a return trip to Carriacou to coincide with the launch.

"They were just being polite," I told him later. "We'd be crashing a private affair." But Clemencia Alexander, who runs the sleepy Carriacou Museum, assured us we would be welcome. Everyone was welcome, she said. You don't need to be a relative, friend or even a casual acquaintance of anyone associated with a new boat to attend its launch party. Party-goers have always been relied on to provide the labor for the launch.

Clemencia—one of the twenty-three children of Carriacou's best-known citizen, the late Canute Caliste, whose charming naive paintings of island life grace the collections of notables including Queen Elizabeth II—was also the first person to mention the matter of The Goat. "They kill a goat on the boat, you know." She's not referring to present practices, I reassured myself, just to long-ago launches, when a goat sacrificed on the foredeck ensured a new boat would be butted toward fair winds. Because it was clear I was going to be present when the *Margeta-O II* slipped into the water.

"I told you we'd be welcome," Steve said to me. "We'll see you again in a few weeks," he told Clemencia.

. . .

The day before the boat launch, the less-than-two-hour ride on the Osprey ferry from St. George's to Hillsborough, Carriacou's main town, is nasty, against strong winds and steep seas. The crew is forced to hand out seasick bags almost as soon as we are beyond the lee of Grenada. At least Steve and I know from bitter experience on our own boat to remain above decks (where we can see the horizon, which has a stabilizing effect), thus giving us a better chance of arriving soaked with nothing worse than seawater.

"Deh rum revive you," says Bill Paterson, balling his fists and flexing his arms Popeye-style, having just delivered an eighth of Jack Iron rum to help us recover from the lumpy trip. The tall, dapper (if you ignore the turned-up pant legs and sockless feet) Paterson is the owner of one of those hundred-plus shops on the island that bear signs stating they are "licensed to sell spirituous liquors." We note, however, one Carriacou rum shop is "licensed to sell spiritual liquors," while another, on Grenada, offers "intoxicated liquors."

Paterson's shop, just down Hillsborough's main street from the ferry dock, seemingly lacks a name. Even the banner that hung out front when we tentatively peeked inside on our first visit to the island—"Bill Paterson," it proclaimed, just his name, nothing more—has disappeared now, revealing faded lettering underneath: CARRIACOU FARMER'S CO-OP DEPOT. This, coupled with the view through the open door—flats of eggs, newspapers, and a jar of tamarind balls on the counter; tins of corned beef on the shelf; and clothes for sale hanging from the ceiling—nicely disguise that this is a popular local watering hole.

Bill is also a justice of the peace and can usually be found working two phones and holding forth among patrons in the mostly open-air back room overlooking the sea. He had welcomed us the first time ("Please, you should call me Bill," he said, when I addressed him as Mr. Paterson), remembered us when we next returned, and now insists on buying us our restorative eighth of Jack Iron rum.

Jack Iron is breathtaking stuff; for a long time, its label showed a top-hatted skeleton and bore the warning "Keep clear from open flame!" "Its aficionados will tell you that you never have a headache the morning after drinking Jack," wrote island historian Frances Kay in her slim, hand-annotated 1966 book, *This—Is Carriacou*, which I'd bought from Clemencia at the museum. "They don't mention you quite likely have no head either." Exported from Trinidad in barrels for small distilleries to blend with their own rums, Jack Iron is distilled to formidable strength to maximize shipping efficiency; an alcohol content upward of 80 percent—160 proof—is not uncommon, though it varies from barrel to barrel. The stamp on the cask in Bill's back room today shows a mere 73 percent, 146 proof.

However, the "blending" step is skipped when Jack arrives in Carriacou, where it is dispensed as-is to rum-shop customers in "eighths"—small recycled medicine or pop bottles containing one-eighth of a regular-sized bottle of rum—and, unlike the locals, I need more than water to wash it down . . . especially since it's only eleven in the morning. Bill delivers a grapefruit-flavored soft-drink called Ting and lots of ice. "Ice melts quickly in Jack Iron," he says. More telling, ice cubes sink in it, a sure indicator that it's seriously overproof. "When you first see those frightened ice cubes huddling on the bottom of your glass, it shakes you," Frances Kay wrote.

"Guys need to drink a little rum to steady their heads," Leo Charles had said when he drove us around Carriacou, commenting on why an island with a total population of only five thousand required so many rum shops. By the time we leave Paterson's, Steve feels his head is most definitely steadier.

. . .

A large jug of Jack and an accompanying bottle of water are already in evidence when we arrive in Windward at nine the next morning for the boat launch. The *Margeta-O II* doesn't exactly look ready to hit the water. No one—not even the well-connected Bill Paterson—had been able to tell us what time the launch would get going, but the consensus was that we should be in Windward early. "You won't be bored," a woman in a local shop told our friends Chris and Yani, who had accompanied us from Grenada to see the launch. ("She also said something about the sacrifice of a goat," Yani worriedly reported.) But only a handful of other people are there as early as we are—and they are all still working on the boat. Among other things, her rudder still needs another troweling of epoxy and a final coat of paint, and the fanged snake that's meant to decorate the length of her topsides is only partially complete. Uncle C is looking nervous.

Things are much livelier, though, a few steps up the road, where preparations for the day's food are well under way. Three huge cauldrons, each supported on a tripod of rocks, are starting to bubble over open fires, tended by men with Gulliver-sized wooden stirring paddles called "turner sticks": pork and mutton seasoned the day before with "plenty onion, garlic, sive and thyme," and pigeon peas flavored with salt beef. (There's no goat meat anywhere in sight, and I'm not sure that's a good sign.) "When you taste the pea soup, you gonna run around deh island of Carriacou because it so niiiice," says one of the men busily stirring. Though the cooking area is clearly run by women, they smartly let the men do the heavy-duty paddling. While one woman tops and tails an entire crate of plantains, another caramelizes what is easily a couple pounds of demerara sugar over one of the fires; when the sugar is bubbling and burnt to a dark brown, she removes the pot—using pieces of cardboard as potholders—and spoons this "browning" into the cauldrons of pork and mutton. "Stir, Johnny, stir, stir stir," she orders, as he works the browning into the sizzling meat with his 4-foot paddle.

Over the next two hours, the crowd grows; the epoxy pots, paint and brushes disappear; the *Margeta-O II* is strung with pennants in the country's colors; and the boat's godchildren—it's a tradition that a new boat must have godchildren or godparents— begin to gather. Around noon, we know the launch finally is close to starting when the island's one Roman Catholic priest arrives. Father Mike de Verteuil has been on Carriacou only two days, a temporary replacement from Trinidad, and this is his first boat launch. "It's not something I learned in seminary," he admits quietly, before gamely hiking his white robes and climbing up the wooden ladder and onto the boat's deck.

Once the godchildren (some of them in fancy dress), Uncle C (in a long-sleeved white shirt and Yankees ball cap, still looking very serious), brother Bernard (the shipwright, with an omnipresent carpenter's pencil behind his ear), and the other men who helped build *Margeta-O II* are seated on the cabin top behind him, Father Mike begins: "*Margeta-O II* is a symbol of resurrection, of perseverance, of never giving up," he says, reminding the crowd that Uncle C's previous boat, the *Margeta-O,* had been destroyed by 2004's Hurricane Emily. "We come to ask God's blessing," he booms into the crowd, his robe billowing to leeward in the stiff breeze, making a crisp triangle of white against the brilliant sky. "Blessing on the hands of all who worked on this boat . . . Bless it with bountiful catches . . . Blessing that you will surround all who sail on it with protection . . ."

"Deh priest, he touching deh manchineel," the woman next to me tsk-tsks. Sure enough, a green branch of the poisonous tree is rubbing Father Mike's shoulder as he gestures heavenward. Island kids learn early not to brush against its leaves, or eat its green apples, or seek shelter under it during a rainstorm, for fear of getting the burning sap on their skin. On Columbus's second voyage, some of his men picked manchineel fruit and ate it, "but no sooner did they taste them than their faces swelled, growing so inflamed and painful that they almost went out of their minds," wrote Dr. Diego Álvarez Chanca, the expedition's physician. But Father Mike likely didn't learn any of this in seminary either: he got his priestly training in Halifax, Nova Scotia.

As a string band plays and a small choir of local ladies sings, Father Mike moves out from under the manchineel branches to sprinkle holy water on the *Margeta-O II* from bow to stern. Uncle C then throws open the boat's sliding hatch so the priest can sprinkle holy water below decks too. Not to place all their spiritual eggs in one basket, Uncle C and Bernard then similarly anoint her bow to stern with Jack Iron.

"On Carriacou, you do it even when you finish building a house," the woman next to me explains, now that the priest is safe from the manchineel and busy sipping a Carib beer he has accepted from Uncle C "And they will knock two times with a hammer"—on the boat's stern—"for good luck, and then they will dance the cake when they're done."

"Dancing the cake" is a very different island ritual than "sticking the cake." A woman appears with an elaborate cake—as fancy as the one at Dingis's birthday, but larger, an ocean of white icing decorated with big sky-blue buttercream roses, an outline of the sailboat, and its name. With the string band, the choir, and assorted friends and family behind her, she begins swirling and sashaying the cake around the boat. Another member of the procession sprinkles the ground with Pink Lady Champagne. "Libation, for the old ones," the helpful woman next to me now explains. This wetting of the ground with spirits (and sometimes water) to demonstrate respect and gratitude for one's forebears is a ritual with West African roots, still regularly practiced at feasts and festivals here. A man beats out the rhythm on an overturned bucket, and the hairs stand up on my arms as the procession circles twice and I catch the lyrics to one of the carefully chosen hymns. *He'll roll me, roll me, over the tide,* they sing. In this harbor surrounded by shallows, on an island whose name comes from the Carib word for "land surrounded by reefs," what better wish for those taking to sea in a new boat.

Small, napkin-wrapped pieces of dark, currant-studded spice cake are soon passing from hand to hand through the crowd. And Uncle C's face finally creases with a smile.

There's a pause in the action as a long, heavy sacrificial plank appears and is bent and nailed to the side of the freshly painted white hull. Soon, a hundred hands are braced against the boat. "Ease her down," someone shouts. The Jack Iron barrels that hold her upright are knocked out, and the *Margeta-O II* is laid over, plank side down, so that she rests on a series of round logs. Her 100-foot trip to the water's edge is ready to begin. With the aid of a block and tackle, they begin to pull and push her, grunting and straining as they lean into the work. "Heep,

heep," one of the women calls out each time they shove the boat forward a few inches. "Hurraaaaaaaay," the crowd responds.

Realizing it's going to be a long, slow trip, I wander back to the cooking area, where cauldrons of white rice and coo-coo— a golden, polenta-like cornmeal porridge—have followed the meat stews onto the fires.

"You want to roll rice?" a young woman asks me after the huge rice pot is wrestled from the fire to a shady spot across the way. A bunch of ladies have gathered there, holding empty plastic margarine containers. Without waiting for an answer, she thrusts one of the Glow Spread tubs into my hand. Another woman, stationed on an overturned bucket next to the pot, scoops a mound of soft, steaming white rice into my tub. Taking my cue from the others dancing around me, I start to shake and swirl the container. "Harder, harder, harder," the young woman who got me into this instructs, in competition with the soca tunes issuing from Volkswagen-sized speakers across the road. I pick up the pace very cautiously, as I envision my rice ricocheting out of the tub and splatting into the crowd. "Now, stop and look," my mentor commands. To my surprise, the rice has formed a perfect ball. She approves, and I tip it into a wooden tray that's quickly filling with similar balls, and hold out my container for another scoop. "Watch deh manchineel," another woman cautions. My rice-rolling exuberance has backed me into a tree and, like Father Mike before me, I am oblivious. Meanwhile, a turner stick has been thrust into the middle of the pot of coo-coo; when the stick can stand up on its own, the coo-coo will also be pronounced ready for rolling.

Rolling rice and coo-coo is traditional on Carriacou—you won't find it routinely done even on neighboring Grenada, nor on many other islands (except maybe Barbados)—with Glow

Spread tubs now standing in for the calabashes once used. The peach-sized balls are served at other festivities, too, such as weddings, tombstone feasts (which celebrate the life of the departed), and maroons (the traditional gatherings used to give thanks for a good harvest and bless the coming planting season with bountiful rain). I relinquish my container after a few balls, however, not wanting to slow the process—which I'm clearly doing, gyrating my rice at about half the speed of the others—and watch the many-hands-make-light-work axiom prove itself. The vats of rice and coo-coo are magically transformed into great pyramids of white and yellow balls.

More than an hour after the pushing started, the *Margeta-O II* finally floats free, having been pulled clear of shore at the very end by a speedboat from Petite Martinique that had been hovering all morning, waiting to do the job. Its crew is a little overzealous and pulls her too quickly—despite the yells of "Slow it down, slow it down"—slightly damaging her keel. But that will be fixed later, when they tow her to the commercial boatyard in Tyrrel Bay on the other side of the island, to step her mast. For now, she's beautiful, and as she shimmers at anchor under the crystalline sky, I suspect I'm not the only one with tears in my eyes.

But then bedlam ensues as the crowd begins to converge in the cooking area. "Don't worry, don't worry, take it easy, take it easy, d'ere plenty for everyone." Still, I feel really badly when someone takes me by the arm, ushers me forward, grabs a groaning plate—piled obscenely high with stewed mutton, stewed pork, pigeon pea soup (a stew, really), provision, and plump rice and coo-coo balls to absorb the rich sauces—and explains to the woman dishing things up: "Dis is for deh white lady." The supremely embarrassed white lady shares her plate with Steve.

On one of my trips back to check on the boat's progress, I had again found myself next to Father Mike in the crowd. As usual, I couldn't resist. "Have you heard anything about a goat, Father?" I asked obliquely.

"You mean a sacrifice?" he replied, too instantly. "I don't know anything about that—but maybe they're just not telling me."

Much to my relief, a goat never appears. We eventually learn that there was a goat—two, actually—but the goat part happened much earlier. The goats were killed, Uncle C tells us when we see him again a few months later, when the boat's keel was laid, their blood falling on the planks to ensure "the building go well and nobody get hurt. And for the old ones," he said, meaning his ancestors.

Soon, people begin dancing to the pounding, ear-splitting soca and slightly more mellow, though equally loud, reggae, selected and played relentlessly by a young DJ. He reigns under a little tent that shades a small store's worth of sound equipment—and a body-sized cooler full of beer.

Dark descending, ears sufficiently assaulted, and feeling we've seen—been—part of history in Carriacou, we catch a lift back to the other side of the island.

. . .

While she was being built, a red flag had hung from the *Margeta-O II*'s transom, and now we see that a red flag hangs from the half-planked skeleton of a wooden sailboat on the beach of Petite Martinique. "We're looking for a boatbuilder named Clyde," we call up to the guy on its deck, who wears a dust mask and wields an electric sander. He shakes his head and goes back to his work. On an island with only nine hundred residents, I hoped we might hit it lucky at the first unfinished boat.

An easy fifteen-minute ferry ride from Carriacou had deposited us on the main jetty of this less-than-a-mile-square island of fishermen and boatbuilders, whose name is pronounced "Pitty Martinique" or simply "PM." At the end of the jetty, a few arrowed signs point the way to the main road, the bank, the post office, a telephone, one beachfront restaurant, two supermarkets, a single guesthouse, and not much else. "We're looking for Clyde, the boatbuilder," we ask a woman on the main road. She's shepherding a group of preschool charges, the girls in green-checked gingham dresses, the boys in shirts of the same material, who are out serenading to raise money for a holiday party. *Mama in deh kitchen makin' johnnycake, / Christmas on deh way,* they sing, accompanying themselves on *shak-shaks,* maracas made from small pop bottles filled with seeds and stones.

"Oh, he jus' now pass by," the teacher says. "But we'll tell him you're looking for him."

Clyde finds us before we find him—not surprising, given that PM is the least visited (by a long shot) of Grenada's three main islands, and we stand out like grapes in a basket of mangoes. He's tall and slender, with shorts that sit low on his slim hips, flip-flops on his feet, and a killer smile.

When we pass the sailboat under construction on the beach for a second time as we walk toward his boatyard, I point to its red flag. "It means a new boat is being built," he says. "But it's also for the *mal yeux*." Mal yeux—it sounds like "mahl joe" when Clyde says it, and it's also spelled *mal jeux* and *maljoe*—is Creole for "bad eye," and the red flag is to ward off bad luck or mis-fortune caused by someone casting the evil eye. Houses under

construction on Carriacou and PM fly a red flag from the rooftop
for the same reason. "You need to ask an older person about it,"
says the twenty-something Clyde. In fact, an older person had
already told us about mal yeux—though she didn't use the word
and we didn't know enough to ask: months earlier, Dingis had
explained that the tiny band of red and black beads around Bici's
ankle was to counter "bad words." "Someone might say 'what a
fat baby,' and then she would get diarrhea and lose weight,"
Dingis said. A string of red-and-black jumbie seeds tied around
one's wrist or ankle is the adult equivalent, warding off both
mal yeux and jumbies, evil spirits. Keep a jumbie seed in a purse,
I'm told, and it will stay filled with money.

"Craziness," Dwight says, when I float the matter of red
flags and mal yeux by him when we're back at Hog Island on
Receta, and refuses to talk about it. And when Stevie says,
"Some people believe it keep harm away," Dwight snorts.
"Ahhhnnnn, if you believe in the Creator in here"—he pounds
his heart—"you don't need that stuff."

. . .

Two open fishing boats—not sailboats like Uncle C's; these will
use outboard engines—are under construction in Clyde's boatyard, framed but not yet planked. One is 34 feet long and the
other, about 17. Neither is the 19-footer commissioned by
Gennel and Dingis. A boat that size takes only three weeks start
to finish, Clyde assures us, "and I start their boat soon." Taking
in the laid-back nature of the boatyard, and the laid-back nature
of the clients at the other end, Steve and I are skeptical that we
will see this boat any time soon. (It turns out we're right: eight
months later the boat had not yet been delivered.)

As we run our hands along the smooth white-cedar ribs of the boats under way in the yard, admiring their lines, Clyde disappears—returning a couple minutes later with a bottle of wine he inexplicably wants to give us. We thank him profusely, but tell him to save it for the launching of his next boat. We notice, though, that it is a very nice French rosé—not the kind of bottle you'd expect to find kicking around a sawdusty back-yard boatyard on a petite Grenadian island. "It must be *bobol*," Steve whispers as we walk away. Smuggled goods.

On Petite Martinique, as on Carriacou, smuggling goes hand-in-hand with building well-found boats and sending skilled mariners to sea in them, the other seafaring traditions. "Carriacouans have been smuggling for hundreds of years. You don't expect us to stop now, do you?" a retired ship's captain told some visitors to the island a few years ago. Meanwhile, "Sam the Smuggler," as he's called (though I've changed his first name to protect the flow of duty-free goods) putt-putts by *Receta* most evenings when we're at anchor in Carriacou, a few cardboard cases visible in the bottom of his small wooden boat. "Need any wine?" he asks. He makes house calls, too, we recently heard, and, according to our unimpeachable local source, also offers fine French brandy at an excellent price.

The stuff comes via Martinique, French St. Martin, and St. Barts, all duty-free overseas departments of France (though not all the wine on offer here is French: South American bobol is also popular); if the smuggled goods arrive on one of the big freight boats, a small amount is declared, and the rest is apparently overlooked. Some also comes in at night, we're told, on smaller go-fast boats like those Clyde builds, then makes its way under cover of darkness into houses and supermarkets. Officials turn a blind eye, though occasionally there's a crackdown—

most often, one local notes dryly, just before a major holiday, such as Christmas, when the confiscated contraband can most easily find its way to another appreciative home.

The inimitable historian Frances Kay tells a story about a very strict customs official from Grenada who was sent to make a thorough search on Petite Martinique (which, she says, has a reputation for a "be-damned-to-you attitude"). "When he arrived, he found the entire population standing mournfully around an open grave. 'Who died?' he asked. 'Nobody,' came the matter-of-fact reply, 'we dug it for you.'" It would appear that island occupations, like boat launchings, are not on seminary curricula: Kay also recounts how a priest innocently blessed a boat, unaware that it belonged to a popular smuggler. The boat had been out of commission for half a year, being rebuilt. At the launch, the priest, like Father Mike, asked the Lord's blessing on everyone connected with the project: the builders, the family who owned the boat, the crew. But then he also included a blessing for its cargo. "A sigh of bliss went up from the spectators present, who had been deprived of their goodies for six months."

. . .

Quite unlike its lush sister Grenada, Carriacou is scrubby and dry, giving it an unkempt (perhaps even unloved) look at first glance. "Ten months drought, two months flood" is how Kayaks describe their weather. Without rivers or lakes—or any groundwater at all—Carriacou depends entirely on rainy-season downpours to fill cisterns. In contrast to the riotous abundance of the St. George's market, the main street of Hillsborough has just a handful of market stalls, with modest offerings, and the liveliest shopping mornings are the ones after the twice-weekly freight boat arrives from Grenada. By early summer, before the rains start, the local sive on market tables is spindly and browning at its tips, and the thyme that's tied to it is meager. Corn and pigeon peas are the main crops on Carriacou, with kitchen gardens yielding sweet potatoes, ginger and other tubers, seasoning peppers, some tomatoes and a few herbs. The climate and soil won't support the profusion of fruit trees, nor the spices, that flourish in the rain-forest conditions of Grenada; the nutmeg and mace, cinnamon and cloves, allspice and cocoa are all imported here.

Hillsborough's tiny fish market, a squat, open-faced cinderblock affair just off the main street, can be as discouraging as its market tables. Any time I've poked my head inside and asked if there is any fish, the women in the dim interior have given me a firm, "All finish." Until the day I go shopping with Leslie Ann Calliste.

We met Leslie Ann through her husband Godfrey, the caretaker of a place we'd rented on the island to stay ashore a few days on one of our visits. (We become so taken with Carriacou—where, without even trying, we easily slip into the routine of island life—that we visit five times in twelve months.) Leslie Ann and Godfrey are a young, hardworking, churchgoing couple with a blended family of three kids. Among other things, Leslie Ann is known for her baking: she sells pizzas and special-occasion cakes, the kind that are popular at island birthdays, weddings and boat launchings. However, with pizza already in my repertoire and not having a particular interest in buttercream swirls and roses, I ask her if she'll show me how to make a typical Kayak family dish for dinner. "Of course," she readily agrees. "We'll do fish with coo-coo and ochroes."

Mid-morning the next day, the fish market is as barren as ever when Leslie Ann and I pass, in town to do the shopping for the evening's meal. "Don't worry, fish will be coming soon," she says, heading to the stalls on the main street to help me select the okra, corn flour—"it's grown and ground here, you know"—green figs (the term commonly used in this part of the Caribbean for bananas, from the Creole *figue*), sive, and seasoning peppers we'll also need. Suddenly, very un-Carriacou-like, she takes off at a trot, and I can barely keep her jeans-clad backside and vigorously bouncing braids in sight as she barrels down the street. She had spotted the morning's catch being unloaded at the fish market, and on an island where nothing and no one ever moves quickly, this is apparently one time when speed counts.

Barracuda is "the fish of Carriacou," the islanders say, and when I catch up with Leslie Ann at the fish market, I can see the table inside is heaped with the long, silvery, impressively toothed predators. The shallow, abundant reefs surrounding the island provide the sort of hunting ground barracudas love; and some of the local fishermen, in turn, specialize in hunting them. (Their small boats are recognizable even from afar by the long wooden outriggers that hover like arched eyebrows above them.) Because barracuda can carry ciguatera, a particularly nasty (and occasionally fatal) form of food poisoning, it is a rarity on dinner tables on more northern Caribbean islands. But ciguatera is unknown on Carriacou (as well as Grenada and Petite Martinique), and so this is the place to eat the tender white-fleshed barracuda, a cross between mahi-mahi and swordfish in texture and taste.

But among the piles of barracuda this morning, Leslie Ann spots a single glistening red snapper. "Can we have that one, Mr. Hubbard?" she says, giving me a double thumbs-up and a wide smile to let me know we have really scored. Mr. Hubbard weighs the fish (an even 7 pounds), hands it over to Leslie Ann, and life slows down again.

In our kitchen that night, fat snapper fillets sizzle in a fry pan, having spent the afternoon marinating in "green seasoning" (a mixture of minced green herbs), a little bit of onion and lots of garlic. Before sliding them into the pan, Leslie Ann had dredged the fillets in flour, spiked with curry powder along with the usual salt and pepper. Meanwhile, the okra simmer with onion, garlic, seasoning pepper, and sive in a mixture of coconut milk and water, and the coo-coo plops and bubbles. Leslie Ann had poured the corn flour into boiling coconut milk a good hour earlier, and worked the lumps out as it cooked with the wooden turner stick she'd brought along. It's a smaller version of the ones wielded at the boat launch, but an alarmingly large tool nonetheless.

Okay, this isn't a boat launch or wedding feast—but it is a party of sorts. We've invited not just Godfrey and Leslie Ann, but also their kids to join us for dinner: seventeen-year-old Adrian; Callista, who's about fifteen; and Godson, who has just started elementary school and politely calls me "Miss"—a real gentleman. So I request party food. Which means, once again, I'm coached through that bit of culinary sleight of hand that tonight transforms molten coo-coo into tidy balls. Following Leslie Ann's lead, I again begin tentatively gyrating my small plastic bowl to set the hot cornmeal mush in motion. Like my last teacher, she encourages me to pick up the pace—but my first lump refuses to cooperate. "Let the wind go through it a bit," she advises; and, sure enough, after I let it cool for a minute, it rolls into a perfect ball. A couple dozen more and we'll be ready for dinner. "Move those hips, shake that arm, gyrate, gyrate," coaches Steve, impatient to get to the table.

Just before dinner, Leslie Ann lowers the fried fish fillets into the simmered ochroes, and adds a good lump of butter, a heaping tablespoon of that popular island cook's helper, dried chicken-noodle soup mix, and a little "seasoning." A quick glance at the label confirms my suspicions: *ve-tsin*, a.k.a. MSG.

As we sit at the big round table on the veranda, laden with wonderful-smelling food, none of our guests makes a move toward the serving dishes. A lightbulb goes on above my head: "Would one of you like to offer grace?" It's the question they've been waiting for, and Godfrey leaps quickly into the opening I've provided. After a chorus of "amens," Leslie Ann takes charge, filling plates, and then everyone digs in. The dense, satisfying coo-coo balls prove the perfect foil for the delicate snapper in its rich sauce of well-seasoned okra and creamy coconut. While we eat, Steve and I quiz the younger kids about school—shy Calli is a star in the classroom, while outgoing little Godson is already starting to shine as a runner—and Adrian about his job in construction.

Though we all do our part, when we finish eating there are still enough coo-coo balls to rack up for a game of pool, and I ask Leslie Ann if she'd like to take them home with her. "I'll fry them for breakfast," she says. She also scrapes out the bottom of the pot, where the coo-coo has burned into a dark crust. "You use the burned part to make coo-coo tea," she explains. We've learned that tea, in the West Indies, doesn't just mean a clear beverage steeped from leaves. When Dingis mixes cereal into baby Bici's milk, she calls it tea, and older West Indians sometimes use the word to refer generally to their first meal of the day, which comes before "breakfast." For coo-coo tea, Leslie Ann says, you boil the "bun-bun"—from "burn-burn"—with milk and spices, until the liquid thickens, and then you eat it hot, in the morning or for a snack.

. . .

When *Receta* stops at Carriacou again a couple of months later, I give Leslie Ann a call: "Why don't you bring the family out to the boat for dinner? Steve will pick you up at the jetty in our dinghy."

They arrive in two groups, Leslie Ann and Godfrey first, followed by the kids, Calli and Godson shepherded by big-brother Adrian. Steve gives them his patented, kid-pleasing amusement-park version of a dinghy ride, going fast, bouncing over waves, creating the (untrue) expectation that a head-to-toe soaking is imminent. On board, everyone wants a tour. "Miss, what's this?" Godson asks repeatedly, peppering us with smart questions. Adrian seems genuinely captivated by the thought of sailing—Steve later reports that he had a faraway, dreamy look in his eyes when they stood together on the bow. But poor Calli: the gentle rocking that I don't even notice anymore is enough to make her queasy and, refusing to leave early, she spends much of the evening with her head in her daddy's lap.

"Would you like to offer grace?" I immediately ask when it's time to eat. Now, without hesitation, Adrian begins, giving thanks not just for the food, but also for the friendship, and for this evening, the opportunity to be together.

But what was I thinking? Focusing on food that would be easy on the cook and enjoyable for the kids, and remembering Dwight and Stevie's reaction in Grenada, I decided to make pizza—remembering too late that this is Leslie Ann's specialty. It also dawns on me—also too late—that my boat-oven version can't measure up to a pro's.

"Miss," exclaims Godson, ever the gentleman. "This is the best food I ever had."

· · · PEPPER RUM · · ·

Though Jack Iron is the rum of choice on Carriacou for making this condiment, any ordinary rum—dark or white—will do the trick. A couple of shakes add spirit to soups, sauces, stews, omelettes, Bloody Marys, salad dressings, dips and marinades. (See the recipe that follows.)

6	fresh hot peppers (such as Scotch bonnet, habañero, Congo or bird peppers)	6
1	bay leaf	1
6	black peppercorns (approx)	6
1 to 2	whole allspice berries (optional)	1 to 2
1	sprig of dried thyme (optional)	1
2 cups	rum	500 mL

1. Cut a small slit in each pepper (so they don't float on top of the rum). Combine all ingredients in a glass jar or bottle. Let stand for 2 weeks.
2. Taste, and if the rum is hot enough for you, remove peppers and other seasonings. The longer you leave them in, the hotter it gets. Store at room temperature.

Makes about 2 cups (500 mL).

· · · LIME AND PEPPER RUM MARINADE · · ·

This marinade is excellent on flank or skirt steak and firm white fish such as mahi-mahi and marlin. The recipe makes enough for about 1 pound (500 g) of fish or meat.

1 tbsp	olive oil	15 mL
1 tbsp	lime juice	15 mL
1 tbsp	pepper rum	15 mL
½ tsp	ground cumin	2 mL
½ tsp	dried oregano	2 mL
1	large clove garlic, finely chopped	1
	Salt and freshly ground black pepper	

1. Combine all ingredients and rub marinade into fish or meat. Makes about ¼ cup (50 mL).

Tip:
- Flank and skirt steak will profit from several hours or overnight in the marinade; fish requires only 15 to 30 minutes.

· · · COCONUT CHIPS · · ·

Though coconut chips certainly aren't unique to Carriacou, I first came across the idea while we were staying there, when I thumbed through an old local cookbook I found: Rosamond Cameron's now out-of-print A Carriacou Cookbook: Island Flavours to Enjoy at Home. *These go extremely well with drinks, and make a nice change from potato chips.*

1	coconut	1
	Sea salt	

1. Preheat oven to 400°F (200°C). Drain liquid from coconut, crack shell, and remove meat. (See Tip with the recipe for Coconut Drops in Chapter 5.)
2. Using a vegetable peeler, shave coconut meat into thin strips.
3. Spread strips on nonstick or parchment-covered baking sheets. Bake in preheated oven for 10 minutes until light brown, stirring occasionally. (Watch carefully for burning.)
4. Remove from oven and sprinkle with salt. Cool and serve.

Makes a bunch.

· · · LESLIE ANN CALLISTE'S FISH · · ·
WITH OCHROES AND COO-COO BALLS

Invite some friends for a Carriacou-style meal, and get them involved in the "kitchen vibration." You'll definitely want extra hands when it comes to rolling coo-coo (recipe follows)—and cleaning up.

For the fish:

1 ½ lb	firm fish fillets or steaks (such as snapper, kingfish, grouper, mahi-mahi or marlin)	750 g
1	lime	1
3 tbsp	green seasoning (see recipe at the end of Chapter 9)	50 mL
½	small onion, chopped	½
2	cloves garlic, chopped	2
	Salt and freshly ground black pepper	
½ cup	all-purpose flour	125 mL
1 tbsp	curry powder	15 mL
2 tbsp	vegetable oil (approx; for frying)	25 mL
2 tbsp	chopped cilantro (for garnish)	25 mL

For the ochroes:

20	medium okra (approx)	20
2 tbsp	olive oil	25 mL
½	onion, chopped	½
2	cloves garlic, chopped	2
½	cubanelle or green bell pepper (or 2 seasoning peppers), chopped	½
2	green onions, chopped	2

2 tsp	white vinegar	10 mL
	Salt and freshly ground	
	black pepper	
¾ cup	coconut milk	175 mL
2 tbsp	butter	25 mL
1 heaping tbsp dried chicken-noodle soup mix		20 mL

1. Several hours ahead, season the fish: Cut the lime in half and squeeze the juice over the fillets or steaks, rubbing them with the cut surfaces. Rinse fish with fresh water, pat dry and place in a large pan. Rub with the green seasoning, chopped onion and garlic, and salt and pepper. Cover and refrigerate.

2. To make the ochroes: Wash and dry the okra thoroughly. Cut into ½" to ¾" (1 to 2 cm) rounds; you should have about 2 cups.

3. Heat the oil in a medium-sized pot and sauté onion, garlic, pepper and green onion until soft.

4. Stir in okra, sprinkle with vinegar and season with salt and pepper. Cook over medium-high heat for about 5 minutes, stirring frequently.

5. Add the coconut milk and 2 cups (500 mL) water. (If you have any of the coconut milk–water mixture left from making the coo-coo—see next page—use that for part of the water.) Simmer, uncovered, for about 20 minutes, stirring from time to time, until mixture has thickened and okra is tender.

6. While the okra is cooking, season the flour with the curry and some freshly ground black pepper. Dredge the fish in the seasoned flour.

7. In a large frying pan, heat the vegetable oil. Cook the fish, turning once, until it is golden brown on both sides and just

cooked through. Remove from pan and keep warm.

8. Just before serving, add butter and soup mix to okra, and taste for seasoning. Slide fish into mixture and simmer a couple more minutes to allow flavors to blend.

9. To serve, place fish and coo-coo balls (see next page) on plates and spoon okra on top. Sprinkle with chopped cilantro.

Makes 4 servings.

· · · COO-COO BALLS · · ·

Sure, you can serve the coo-coo straight from the pot—but turning it into balls is so much more fun.

½ cup	coconut milk	125 mL
¼	cubanelle or green bell pepper	
	(or 1 seasoning pepper), chopped	¼
1	clove garlic, chopped	1
½	small onion, chopped	½
3 cups	finely ground cornmeal	
	(see Tip, below)	750 mL
	Salt	

1. In a large pot, bring the coconut milk and about 6 cups (1.5 L) of salted water to a boil. Then remove about 2 cups (500 mL) of the hot liquid to a second pot or other container, and set aside.

2. Add the chopped seasonings to the main pot of boiling coconut milk and water. Stir in cornmeal all at once. Keep stirring and turning using a large wooden paddle or spoon, working out the lumps. When all the liquid has been absorbed, add more hot liquid from the second pot.

3. Lower heat to medium (cornmeal should still be bubbling), cover, and continue cooking for about 1 hour. Stir frequently and add more hot liquid if it seems dry. (Reserve any left-over liquid, and use it to cook the okra; see previous page.) The coo-coo is done when it pulls away from the sides of the pot. Taste and add salt if necessary. Remove from heat and allow to cool for about 5 minutes.

4. Scoop a scant ½ cup (125 mL) of hot coo-coo into a small plastic

bowl or margarine-type container. Shake the container vigorously for about 30 seconds—put your body into it!—until the lump forms a ball, then tip it onto a large tray or platter. Repeat with remaining coo-coo.

Serves 4.

Tips:
- The coo-coo will likely form a crust on the bottom of the pot as it cooks. Some West Indians maintain this is the best part.
- To shorten the cooking time, start with instant polenta instead of regular cornmeal. (It's sold in packages, often imported from Italy.) Follow the cooking directions on the box, adding the other ingredients for the coo-coo balls.
- Leftover coo-coo balls are delicious sliced and fried in a little butter and/or olive oil until the exterior is crispy.

EIGHT

Curry Tabanca

· · · TRINIDAD · · ·

You know you're a true Trini if … you think steak is a waste of good meat. You rather cut it up and stew it with some potatoes (or curry it and make some roti)…You know a "lime" is not necessarily a fruit …You have experienced "tabanca."

from "Trini Test," trinitribute.com

It is time for Bas to wake up and smell the curry.

from a letter to the editor of Trinidad's Daily Express,
September 14, 2007, about Basdeo Panday,
leader of Trinidad's opposition party

IF OUR FRIENDS ARE ANY INDICATION, quick goodbyes are not part of the Grenadian mindset. The local water taxi has been waiting patiently alongside *Receta* as Dingis gives each of us one more hug, and then Gennel gives each of us one more hug, and then baby Bici is held up for more kisses, and then Dannyboy, Lynn and Desiann take their turns. Island gatherings are rarely closed affairs even when they're not of boat-launch proportions, and people are accustomed to bringing a friend or two along. So Gennel has brought her friend Charmaine (and she's brought her kindergarten-aged son), but since we've only met her once before, she sticks to one quick hug.

Back from Carriacou, we'd invited our Lower Woburn friends to the boat for Sunday lunch before we headed to Trinidad—*Receta* at full capacity, everyone somehow squeezed around the table and managing to eat spaghetti and meatballs (a previously proven winner) without poking an elbow into someone else's plate.

You'd think from the farewells that we are leaving for the other side of the world, never to return, rather than temporarily relocating a mere 75 miles to the south. "We'll be back before Christmas," Steve promises. They'd taken our departure for Carriacou with equanimity—but Carriacou is like family, close and well known, no reason to fear for us there. (They took with equal equanimity our news that their boat was not yet under way on Petite Martinique.) The water-taxi driver revs his outboard—*Snack* can't handle this big a crowd—a polite reminder that it's time for our guests to climb in and get going. "We goin' to miss you," Dingis says. "If deh christening while you away, Dannyboy stand up for you in church." The date hasn't yet been set—christenings are apparently also governed by GMT—and Dannyboy, who will be one of Bici's godparents along with us, nods agreement.

With the leftovers I've packed for her to take along, Dingis is finally settled in the water taxi, Bici is handed down, and the others follow. Now cautions ensue—"Be careful, Trinidad dangerous, not like Grenada," "We see you soon, please God"—over the sound of the engine until finally, finally, the patient driver pulls away, with everyone—even baby Bici—still waving and blowing kisses.

The next time we are at Grenada's Point Salines International Airport, awaiting a flight for a visit home, we see a sign pointing the way to a WAVING GALLERY. There's also a notice saying it is permanently closed. "I can see why," Steve says. "It would be full to bursting. The entire population would be there. No one would ever leave it."

. . .

Though they've never been there, Dingis and company nailed it: Trinidad is, indeed, not like Grenada. Oil and natural gas rich, it is one of the most prosperous islands in the Caribbean, one of the few whose economy does not depend on tourism. But it is a country of cutlass-sharp contrasts. The booming oil economy has brought glittering high-rises, upmarket malls, lavish gated homes and stylish high-end restaurants—which serve to highlight the other side of the capital city, Port of Spain: the gritty, gang-riddled, drug-dealing neighborhoods and a sprawling waterfront shantytown (disarmingly known as "Sea Lots," making it sound like a prime waterfront development). Oil and gas account for about 40 percent of gross domestic product and 80 percent of exports, but only 5 percent of employment. The government—mired in mudslinging, endless rhetoric and blame-shifting based on old East Indian versus African political rivalries—has not been able to keep control of this rapid growth, and violent crime has soared. The papers blare headlines of kidnappings, cutlass slashings, shootings, armed robberies and revenge killings daily; almost four hundred murders occurred on the island in 2007, about the same number as in New Jersey, which has eight times the population. Crime is so pervasive that even we newcomers, with only a small circle of Trini friends and acquaintances, find it touches several people we know.

Still. We fall in love with Trinidad.

Coming from Grenada—depending on wind and fickle currents, the trip takes twelve to sixteen hours on a sailboat like *Receta*—the oil business is unmissable, greeting us 25 miles off Trinidad's north coast: an offshore-drilling platform is parked almost on the direct line between the two islands, glimmering like a fairyland at night. But, then, as we get close to the Boca de Monos (Mouth of the Monkeys), the slot of churning tidal water that forms the entrance to the Gulf of Paria, which separates Trinidad from neighboring Venezuela, another side of Trinidad shows its face: dramatic rugged cliffs rear up through a haze of misty-hot morning light, and seabirds wheel high overhead. Just 9 miles away, downtown Port of Spain is sweaty, grimy, traffic-clogged and, occasionally, urine-scented, but in Scotland Bay just inside the Boca de Monos, howler monkeys roar in the rain forest. And every day, while *Receta* is tied to a dock in the island's pleasure-boating center of Chaguaramas, flocks of orange-winged Amazon parrots wake me at first light with their squawking conversations. (As the fishermen were in the Dominican Republic, so the parrots are now my snooze-button-equipped alarm clock in Trinidad.) Shortly before sunset, they squawk by again, always in pairs, the afternoon sun highlighting their brilliant green plumage and orange-patched wings as they return to their roosts in the trees.

Trinidad, "land of oil and music," sing Trini icons David Rudder and Machel Montano in their recent anthem to what are probably the island's two most valuable commodities. Violent crime may be in your face daily, but so too is music: a petrochemical economy uses oil drums, and those drums gave birth to the only new acoustic musical instrument invented in the twentieth century, the steelpan—sometimes miscalled the steel drum, but never in Trinidad—which along with calypso and soca (calypso with a soul beat) put Trinidad on the world musical map. More contrasts: Trinidad is the business hub of the Caribbean, but "liming"—kicking back and relaxing with friends—is a firmly entrenched practice. The ad campaign for one of the local cell providers uses the tagline: "What time we limin' later?" The *Daily Express* newspaper has a weekly what's-on column called "D Lime Guide." One of our Trini dictionaries, three hundred pages devoted entirely to the unique and highly expressive linguistic possibilities of the two-island nation of TnT, Trinidad and Tobago (our other Trini dictionary is 990 pages plus), defines a lime—it's both noun and verb—as "an anywhere, any-event, pleasure-shared occasion," which, almost by definition, includes music, food and rum. "If you throw a tin pan down a staircase," an island saying goes, "a true Trini could discern some form of rhythm and a party would start."

Another beloved soca song, "Trini to de Bone" by Rudder and Ian Wiltshire, captures how passionate Trinidadians are about their island, despite its enormous problems: *Sweet, sweet TnT / Oh how I love up my country / Sweet, sweet TnT / Nowhere in this world I'd rather be* . . . The Trinis try to do everything they can to ensure that we will have a *tabanca* for it when we leave. (A tabanca is a state of acute lovesickness. "He still have a tabanca for Gennel," Dingis once said about one of her daughter's old boyfriends.) They want us to love their island as they do, in all its frenetic, multicultural, musical, food-obsessed glory.

. . .

"Honey," Miss Pat sings, one hand on her ample hip and the other rooting around on our friend Don's plate. "Pick up the shrimp with your fingers, honey, and suck the sauce off." She had emerged from her kitchen and spotted Don politely dissecting lunch with a knife and fork. Finding a fat shrimp in the pool of garlicky, pepper-flecked sauce in front of him, she picks it up, jockeys it toward his mouth, pops it in, and then licks her own fingers. Turning to me, she shrugs and says, "My fingers always in everybody's mout'."

As Dingis took us underwing in Grenada, Miss Pat orchestrates our care and feeding in Trinidad. She owns a tiny restaurant off the Savannah, Port of Spain's Central Park, where she spoils and scolds her devoted patrons in equal measure. "You call Mommy," she says one day, waggling her finger at me, after checking to make sure I have her restaurant, home, cell, and her husband's cell numbers, just in case Steve and I ever need any help while we're here. "Give me some sugar," she says to us another day, opening her arms for a hug when we get ready to leave after lunch.

Today, happy that Don is now properly appreciating her shrimp, she turns her attention to me. "Your belly full?" she asks disapprovingly. I've completely demolished the crispy fried kingfish steaks (note the plural) that dominated my plate, along with the sweet stewed lentils and pumpkin, and the spicy sautéed bodi beans (a foot-long version of green beans, with a bit more attitude), plus a sauce-slathered shrimp fingered from Don's plate. However, this means I've left a mountain of rice, a garden's worth of green salad and a heap of steamed provision. Even Steve, who can usually be relied on for help in such situations, has barely managed his own lunch.

According to our well-thumbed Trini dictionary, "big up we country" means to promote it, praise it, extol its virtues. But after time with Miss Pat, we can be forgiven for thinking it means something else.

. . .

We first met Pat Jones a few years earlier, following a lead from a Trinidadian soca celeb, Anslem "Who Let the Dogs Out?" Douglas, who was taking a break from music and running a Caribbean takeout food and grocery business near our Toronto home. But he merely told us we could find his friend Miss Pat "on Maraval Rd. around the corner from the Canadian High Commission"—no address, no restaurant name. Come to think of it, he didn't even say she had a restaurant, just that we had to try her cooking.

We found our way to the general neighborhood, pushed through the imposing smoked-glass doors of an office building, and greeted the equally imposing woman guarding the lobby desk with a cheery "good day." Her very un-Trini-like reception was chillier than the blessedly cool interior—until I explained we were trying to find "Miss Pat." Her standoffishness melted in a heartbeat, as she took my arm and accompanied us back outside; if we knew about Miss Pat, her attitude now said, then we were clearly deserving of her warmest attention. "You'll see deh bar," she told us, pointing precisely into the middle distance. "Go straight t'ru it, to deh back."

Two blocks farther, we very tentatively walked into the dim interior of Hereford's Recreation Club ("deh bar"), hesitating at its barred windows and the raucous voices rising from its four booths and five stools, all occupied by local men liming over a lunchtime rum. A formidable Rasta with graying dreadlocks that extended well below his knees presided behind the wood-paneled, Formica-topped bar. But no one paid us any mind as we headed "to deh back," down a narrow, whitewashed hallway thick with heat. The hallway led to a tiny kitchen, an invisible-unless-you-know-it's-there dining room, a seductive bowl of kingfish simmered in a tantalizing yellow-flecked sauce, and the start of our friendship with the irrepressible Miss Pat and her husband Pie . . . who, we discovered, was the tall man behind the bar with the calf-length dreads.

She's long since insisted we call her simply "Pat." "That 'Miss' is for old ladies," she scolds, though we were just following the lead of other (younger) customers, who use the title to show respect. But neither we nor any of the friends we bring to taste her cooking can break the habit. We've also learned that her motherly exterior hides the love-a-good-time personality of an unrepentant party girl, and wickedly funny routines worthy of a stand-up comic. (We're not sure whether she really checks her twenty-nine-year-old son's bedroom every night to make sure the two condoms on his dresser haven't disappeared but her telling makes for great theater.) The room we ate in on our first visit has given way to a slightly larger space, and though the gilt-framed clock and assortment of framed religious pictures are gone, the tiny glass pot of homemade pepper sauce on a pressed-glass saucer and the vase of artificial flowers on each table help it retain its feeling of dining in the parlor of a favorite aunt.

"Anything you want, darlin'," Miss Pat said when I asked after our first visit if we could return to watch her cook. It had taken only one lunch to convince us that Anslem hadn't been exaggerating when he said Miss Pat "have sweet hand," the highest praise a Trini can give—or get—when it comes to cooking. A couple days later, Steve and I had sweated away the morning in the one-window, un-air-conditioned, unvented, home-kitchen-sized space where she turned out upward of fifty lunches daily. The phone started ringing about ten o'clock, as locals—mostly professional types who work in the nearby office buildings—called to place their orders for one of the two, or at most three, main dishes she was cooking that day. By 1 p.m., she was completely out of food—as she always is.

Swathed in a full-length apron, an errant curl or two springing from her flowered headscarf, Miss Pat had chatted constantly as she slid from one battered pot to the next, stirring with an outsized metal spoon, then ladling a taste into a cast-iron palm and licking it off. The geera pork was found wanting, in need of "a pinch" of hot pepper, she said, tossing in a hefty spoonful of her homemade, seed-flecked, devastatingly hot orange pepper sauce. "That's a Trinidadian pinch," she gleefully explained, before following it with a blizzard of ground, roasted geera—cumin seed, a popular spice in East Indian cooking (as well as a component of curry powder). "My mother would tell me, 'Paaaattt'"—she drew out her name in the melodic Trini lilt, "I want to taste the geera."

East Indian influence is strong in Trinidadian cooking. As elsewhere in the Caribbean, indentured servants from India arrived here to fill the labor gap left on the sugar and cocoa plantations after full emancipation occurred in 1838. (Since working conditions—and the token wages—were still deplorable, many of the former slaves left the plantations, and the owners had to find a new source of workers. Indentured labor was essentially slavery dressed in new clothes, and most of the workers never made enough money to return to their homes.) But more than on other islands, East Indians poured into Trinidad between 1845 and 1917—an estimated surge of 144,000 workers before the system of indentured labor was abolished—bringing their spices and style of food along with their religion, language and traditions.

Despite its East Indian roots, however, Miss Pat's geera pork is definitely West Indian. She starts by caramelizing sugar in oil, to produce a rich color and a dark crust that seals in the sweetness of the meat, a technique that came to Trinidad (and the other Caribbean islands) with the Africans who preceded the East Indians. Satisfied that the geera pork now had sufficient kick, Miss Pat scooped a piece of curried kingfish from another pot, added a potato, ladled some sauce on top, and passed it to me for a mid-morning snack flavored with the rich butteriness of thickened coconut milk and the distinctive spicy grittiness of curry. Meanwhile, she handed Steve a napkin-wrapped piece of fried fish, just plucked from the oil. Double-dipping, she said—first in flour, then back in her lime-based marinade, then back in flour again—is what makes her fried fish "nice and flaky." She neglected to mention the crunchy, delectable exterior that I also discovered when Steve grudgingly offered up a taste. No wonder the regulars here call her "Sweet-Hand Pat."

"A sweet hand is when the cooking is so good you want to lick the plate," says Wendy Rahamut, who easily qualifies as Trinidad's foodie-in-chief. She's the cooking columnist for the *Trinidad Guardian,* one of the island's three dailies, host of the weekly TV cooking show *Caribbean Flavors,* editor-in-chief and publisher of the quarterly magazine *Caribbean Gourmet,* owner of the Wendy Rahamut School of Cooking, and author of three cookbooks, while keeping her own sweet hand in other pots as well. (When does the woman take time to lime?) "Three people can follow the same recipe and it comes out differently. You have to be able to taste—that's what gives someone a sweet hand." Or, as Miss Pat puts it, "You have to love the food."

. . .

The Port of Spain central market sprawls through, between and around two large buildings on the city's eastern fringe, backing onto the island's main highway on one side and a district that doesn't invite lingering on the other. A "maxi-taxi"—this island's name for its minivan buses—picks me up at the marina at 6:30 a.m. every Saturday, the city's main market day. If I'm not there early, I'm told, I'll miss the just-off-the-boat, Gulf of Paria shrimp.

The shrimp are in the first building, which is devoted to seafood and meat. I scoot past the fishmongers with their piles of carite, shark and redfish to a woman at the far end who sells only shrimp, hopeful that she'll still have some jumbos—though they're not called that, just heaped by size with a piece of soggy paper in front noting the price. The big guys are usually about TT$38 (a bit over US$6) a pound, a bargain to us North Americans, even if they still include their heads. "Make a broth out of them," advises Miss Pat, who makes shrimp-head soup sound like the food of seduction. "You sit next to your husband on the couch, eating your broth, and you reminisce, 'You remember the first time we kiss, honey?'"—she wriggles tight to Steve—"and you sit closer, and then . . ." ("What kind of romantic are you?" Steve complains, when he subsequently catches me decapitating my purchases and—gasp—throwing away the heads.)

The next building, and the area around it on three sides, is a sea of fruits and vegetables, changing from week to week, as things come into and go out of season. Something else that makes food "so much sweeter here," Wendy Rahamut says, is that ingredients "don't have to travel—they come from garden to market.

Every Saturday, I make it my mission to buy something new: a variety of mangoes called *doux doux,* from the Creole "sweet sweet" (and they are, although they're also small-small); *seim,* flat green snow-pea-like pods ("Very good in curries; would you like me to come home with you and cook them?" the shopper next to me says); *peewah,* which look like cute, golf-ball-sized coconuts (they're the fruit of a different palm tree) and are a popular Trini snack. Boiled in well-salted water, peeled and popped in our mouths, they remind us of roasted chestnuts.

Every week I buy my herbs—*cive* (as it's spelled here) and thyme (sold separately), parsley and *chadon beni* (a close relative to cilantro)—from the same Rastafarian farmer, who always welcomes me, though this market swims with shoppers, and commerce generally gets in the way of idle chat.

Outdoors, at the very back of the market, a long line snakes from one or two stands, signaling the presence of "doubles." Breakfast. A uniquely Trini fast food, doubles are a national addiction. Granted, it's difficult to understand their allure based on description alone. Essentially, doubles are a curried chick-pea sandwich on fried bread. But even I, the unwavering Ms. Cereal Topped with Fruit and Yogurt, eat them for breakfast whenever given the chance.

"Four, plenty peppah," the woman in front of me in line says. (Fair warning: unless you like things really hot, order your doubles with "slight peppah.") Doubles are constructed on the spot in a high-speed, well-choreographed piece of street theater. The doubles-maker slaps a square of paper into the palm of one hand and throws a round of *bara,* the East Indian–style, deep-fried bread, on top. In a blur of fingers and spoons, she (or he) then quickly tops the bara with warm, lightly curried *channa* (chickpeas), *kuchela* (a spicy green mango relish), and pepper sauce, finishing with a second piece of bara. In a final flourish, he (or she) gives the ends of the paper two quick twists, some-times even a spin, and passes the little package over, along with a completely inadequate napkin.

Doubles stands pop up like umbrellas during a rainy-season shower—and disappear just as quickly (and unpredictably) an hour or two later when the ingredients run out. Various doubles connoisseurs—which means just about every ordinary Trini—send us in several directions for the best: to the town of Curepe, close to the main campus of the University of the West Indies (makes sense, since doubles—cheap, filling and tasty—are ideal student food); to the highway exit ramp at Arima, halfway across the island (great road food too, as long as you never attempt to eat one in a moving vehicle); to the sidewalk in front of the Brooklyn Bar in downtown Port of Spain (yes, the bar is open at 7 a.m.); to the airport, where a stand is hidden around the side of the main terminal so returning Trinis can inhale a quick doubles along with their first lungfuls of island air, and departing ones can start to mourn what they'll miss while they're away. "A Trini offered me one of his doubles on the plane," our cruising friend Devi e-mailed us after she arrived in the United States to visit family. "Not quite as good as sex at 30,000 feet, but real close."

Although Trinis disagree about where to find the best doubles, they are pretty much united on the criteria that make one doubles better than the next. The bara have to be thin, freshly made, and actually melt in your mouth. The channa must have a soft, melting consistency too. And the whole thing

has to be balanced—with spiciness and heat, chickpeas and toppings, in every bite. Some Trinis swear by doubles early in the
morning, others claim they're nighttime food, the perfect post-
lime snack. Steve, on the other hand, whimpers for a stop at
whatever time he sees a vendor. "I have to eat a few to understand their finer points," he says, ordering two.

Eating this quintessential Trini street food, mind you, is not
as straightforward as tackling a hot dog on a bun. "Don't
attempt to eat doubles like a sandwich," one Trini acquaintance
lectures, after watching me in sloppy action—fingers gooey, a
trail of kuchela running down my wrist, curried chickpeas
splotching the sidewalk at my feet, the paper wrapper shaggy
from being inadvertently bitten along with the bara. A Trini
eats doubles, he demonstrates, by tearing off a neat piece of bara
and, with a deft little finger twist, using it as a scoop for some
of the channa and sauce.

Months later, when we are walking through the courtyard of
the public market in Kingstown, St. Vincent—150 miles north
of Trinidad—I spot the sign: DOUBLES. It brings on an instant
tabanca, and we beetle over and each order one. "Slight or plenty
peppah?" the doubles-maker asks, his voice confirming what we
already intuitively know. David and his partner Nicole are
Trinis, not Vincentians—or Vincys, as they're nicknamed—
who have relocated northward to be closer to his aging mother.
As I dribble channa and slop sauce in my usual fashion, Nicole
whispers in my ear: "You eat doubles like a Vincy." Obviously
not a good thing, not a good thing at all. Having already handed
me an extra piece of doubles paper to support my mess, David
now plops an additional bara on top to help me eat the remains—
properly, Trini style. Steve, neater and faster than I am, orders
a second. Of course. "To practice."

Frankly, I'm not much better with roti, the hubcap-sized, griddle-baked East Indian flatbreads filled with curry. At Patraj or Shiann's or Grace's, our favorite roti shops, my plate—the entire table, according to Steve—is a scene of destruction within seconds, as if someone has exploded a curry-filled bomb. Meanwhile, the roti in front of the Trini at the next table invariably remains a tidy package as he or she disassembles it bite by careful bite.

Buss-up-shut suits my eating style much better, since it's deconstructed before it even gets to me. The name is derived from "burst up shirt," because the flaky flatbread—the Trini version of the East Indian bread called *paratha roti*—is beaten with wooden paddles as it finishes baking on a flat griddle called a *tawa*, so it ends up looking like ragged strips of cloth. The torn bits of roti are used to scoop up the curries and relishes that are served alongside. Buss-up-shut and I get along extremely, dangerously well. (With butter rolled into this type of roti and the dough liberally brushed with oil as it bakes on the tawa, it's not precisely a low-fat, heart-healthy food.) When I eat buss-up, I look Trini. I feel Trini.

"We love our bellies," says Wendy Rahamut. "Everything here centers on food. It's our religion."

Curry is a key component of that religion. Peruse the choice of fillings at a roti stand and you'll see the Trinis curry everything—from chickpeas to chicken, pork to pumpkin, goat to green bananas, even liver. Curry's popularity comes thanks to the mid-nineteenth-century influx of East Indians. Trinidad's current million-plus population continues to reflect this part of its history: 40 percent Indian to 37.5 percent African; the next largest group, 20.5 percent, calls itself "mixed." Religious affiliation is split almost equally between Hindu, 22.5 percent, and

Roman Catholic, 26 percent, with no other religion getting higher than single-digit support.

Since the new arrivals couldn't make the curries they were accustomed to, they made ones built on local ingredients, explains Wendy, who is herself of East Indian ancestry. "They couldn't find fresh coriander—cilantro—here, for instance, so they used chadon beni." The saw-toothed, bladelike chadon beni—pronounced, and sometimes also spelled, "shadow benny"—is slightly more pungent, with a somewhat less "soapy" taste. The name is a corruption of the French *chardon béni*, or "blessed thistle." It's called *culantro* in some parts of the world, but "East Indians also call it *bandania*, which means 'bad coriander,' because it's a weed." We find it growing wild in the grass when we're hiking in the Trini countryside, and pick a big bag of it to use ourselves and share with friends. Steve and I much prefer it to cilantro. Curries, chadon beni sauce, geera pork, doubles, roti, buss-up-shut: "Here in Trinidad we've taken things from India and used them in entirely different ways," says Wendy. "We've made them our own."

. . .

I was sure fine cooks such as Miss Pat would blend and grind their own spices for curries. So I was surprised when she pulled a package of store-bought curry powder out of her pantry. She's not alone, Wendy told me, and commercial blends are found in the best Trini kitchens. "There's such a wonderful assortment available," she explained, admitting that she, too, prefers to buy. "Homemade ones are few and far between."

The heart of the island's curry-making business is Tunapuna, a busy commercial town with a large East Indian population, a short traffic-choked commute east of Port of Spain. "I grew up in New Jersey, and so am naturally wary of all emissions of an industrial nature," calypso singer-turned-journalist Daisann McLane once wrote. "But the first time I visited Tunapuna, I found myself thinking that I might consider moving to a factory town someday, as long as it smelled like this . . . simply by breathing, one was exposed to hazardous levels of piquant longing. To die in Tunapuna, I imagine, would be to die wondering what was for lunch."

Steve points our latest rental car toward Tunapuna, cranking up the air conditioning in an attempt to survive the ten congested, diesel-scented miles. The floor of this SdS—we have it for a week—is already well anointed with grease-stained paper bags, crumpled doubles wrappers, and the odd stray chickpea, an embarrassing testament to our newfound Trini-like snack habits.

The directions I'd been given deposit us in a dusty parking area in front of a nondescript, unsigned building. But we don't need a sign to tell us we're in the right place: even a block away, the air is full of curry. By the time we reach the parking lot, it's not merely an aroma, but a visible ocher haze. The building is home to Turban Brand Products, which produces almost a million pounds of curry each year. My mouth already "spring water," as Dwight would say, by the time we step inside.

Maybe that's why Nanak Hardit-Singh, director of the company, decides to invite us to taste the family's spices through his own cooking. But that comes later—after he's quickly whisked us away from the curry-dusted factory floor (the precise blends are a carefully guarded secret, and the actual production area is off limits to prying eyes), squeezed us into his air-conditioned office, and told us how his family came to be one of the island's two biggest competitors for the loyalty of

Trini cooks. (The other is Chief Brand Products.) Nanak's great-grandfather came to Trinidad from the Punjab in the nineteenth century—they were the first Sikhs on the island, he says—but it was his father who had the "divine intervention." Starting with small batches at home, he took the curry spices he knew from his East Indian heritage—coriander, cumin, turmeric, fenugreek, black cumin, celery seed, fennel—"and played with the proportions, making them to the palate of West Indians." He then began to sell the curry locally to cooks who were delighted not to have to blend and grind their own.

The biggest change his father made was to take down the heat, Nanak says—which seems completely counterintuitive, given that we've been left gasping by the Trini passion for hot pepper. It's not that Trinis don't want fire in their curry, he assures us. "Because peppers are so easily available here, they can be added after." No need to have dried chiles in the blend when incendiary fresh peppers and screamingly hot pepper sauce are in almost every Trini home. Turban's spices are sourced from a variety of countries, including India, Singapore, Grenada, Syria, Pakistan, Morocco, and Sarawak, Malaysia; very little comes from Trinidad itself. "The issue is not where it comes from, but what you do with it." Turban has six or seven different curry blends—all the same spices, but in different quantities and combinations.

Nanak has turned over day-to-day operations of the factory to two of his sons, Rishi and Reva. Rishi's house, a large two-story stone affair that radiates success, is next to the factory, and it serves as a kind of test lab for the family. "When can you come for a lime?" Nanak asks.

An offer we can't refuse. Even before we've cleaned up the SdS, we're back in Tunapuna, and Rishi, elbow-deep in

12 pounds of duck pieces in his long, open kitchen, is explaining the corporate creative process. "We limin' and we cookin' and we addin' spices. And we have ten other critics limin' with us who tell us what they think." The Turban curry blend that he's massaging into the duck was invented by his father at one of these limes, he says. "We like to cook, my father, myself, the whole family"—though he readily admits his father's kitchen talents outshine the rest.

All afternoon, friends and relatives keep arriving—some alerted ahead to the lime (a once-or-twice-a-week happening), others drawn in from the road by their noses. Two local cops drop in for a sip of Scotch and vow to return later when the food is ready. "I was on my way to the gym to work out," explains Reva's wife Fariyal, the latest arrival, "but I couldn't keep going."

Soon pots are bubbling not only on the gas range in the kitchen, but also on a no-nonsense stand-alone propane burner that has been set up in the laundry room to handle the overflow. I dart from one room to the next, trying to keep an eye on the six different dishes that are under way: two curry stews (rabbit and chicken), curry duck, chicken with *amchar masala*, split-pea dhal, and rice. Rishi caramelizes sugar until it's brown and bubbling and its sweetness has given way to a roasted caramel flavor, then stirs in 10 pounds of marinated rabbit— "the difference between a curry stew and a curry is that a curry stew uses caramelized sugar and a curry doesn't"—while Nanak sets to work on the amchar masala, another Trinidadian take on an East Indian spice blend, this one involving dry-roasting the spices first. He holds up a chicken's foot: "The length of the spurs tells you the age of the bird, which tells you this fowl is going to need to cook longer." The chicken and the duck are free-ranging "yardies," or "yard-fowl," and therefore leaner, he says.

A family friend arrives with green mangoes and cucumbers, and begins slicing them for "cutters," salty snacks served with drinks. They get their name, Fariyal tells me, because they "cut" the alcohol, and allow you to have another drink. Or two. The new arrival combines his sliced fruits with liberal amounts of salt, lime, finely diced Congo pepper, and chadon beni to make a chow. "A little hot," he warns me, as he passes the bowls around as finger food. Screechingly hot, actually, but they are an appetite-arousing pre-dinner snack, a taste-bud-awakening combo of salty, fruity, spicy, tart, sweet, hot and cold.

People keep arriving, bottles keep getting opened, the noise level rises, and the mouthwatering aromas keep getting stronger. Finally declaring the pots ready, Rishi says, "You want the meat on the bone. In Trinidad we like a little . . ."— he mimes a jaw workout. Warm roti have also appeared from somewhere—plain flatbreads, not stuffed packages—for scooping up the curries, and I count fourteen hungry people by the time we line up to fill our plates. "For sure a lime makes a lot of dirty dishes," someone says.

Back well after dark, too happily full to even consider a late-night doubles on the way, we stumble out of the SdS and into a stranger, a local woman. "You smell like curry," she says with a shy smile. But she's wrong. Actually, we *reek* of curry. Even after showers. Even the next day. A small price to pay.

· · · MISS PAT'S PEPPER SHRIMP · · ·

Don't even think about using a fork to eat these. Pick them up in your fingers and suck the sauce off the shell before peeling.

1 lb	large shrimp, deveined but with the shells left on	500 g
2	limes	2
2	large cloves garlic, chopped	2
1 tsp	paprika	5 mL
¼ tsp	cayenne pepper	1 mL
1 tsp	all-purpose seasoning (see Tips, below)	5 mL
1 tsp	freshly ground black pepper	5 mL
2 tbsp	olive oil	25 mL
½ cup	shrimp stock, fish stock, or fish bouillon (approx) (see Tips, below)	125 mL
1 ½ tsp	cornstarch	7 mL
	Salt	
2 tbsp	chopped parsley or chives (for garnish)	25 mL

1. Squeeze one of the limes into a bowl of water and add the shrimp. Let stand for 5 minutes, then drain and rinse with fresh water.

2. Season the shrimp with the chopped garlic, paprika, cayenne, all-purpose seasoning and pepper, tossing to coat well. Let stand for 15 to 20 minutes at room temperature, or longer in the fridge. Add juice of half the remaining lime just before you're ready to start cooking.

3. Heat oil in a large frying pan. Add the shrimp with their marinade, and cook for a couple minutes over medium-high heat. Then add all but about 2 tbsp (25 mL) of the stock or bouillon, and continue cooking, uncovered, until the shrimp are just cooked (about 3 to 5 minutes longer, depending on size).

4. Mix the remaining stock with the cornstarch, and stir just enough into the sauce to thicken it so that it coats the shrimp.

5. Taste and adjust seasoning with salt, pepper and additional lime juice. Sprinkle with chopped parsley or chives and serve.

Makes 2 to 3 servings.

Tips:

• To devein the shrimp without removing the shells, Miss Pat inserts a toothpick between two of the shell segments and pulls out the intestinal tract. Buying already-cleaned "zipperback" shrimp is much easier.

• Caribbean all-purpose seasoning is a blend of salt, herbs and spices, dehydrated garlic and onion, chili and, frequently, MSG. Look for brands from Jamaica or Trinidad in the spice racks of large supermarkets. Or you can substitute an MSG-free North American all-purpose seasoning, for a slightly different taste.

• Miss Pat saves the heads from her shrimp and makes stock, which she uses in the sauce. To make shrimp stock, put the heads (or tails and shells, if you're buying headless shrimp) in a pot with some chopped onion, celery and garlic, a bay leaf, a few sprigs of thyme, a few whole black peppercorns and salt. Cover with cold water, bring to a boil, reduce heat, and simmer for about 1 hour, skimming off any scum that rises to the top. Strain and refrigerate.

· · · GEERA PORK · · ·

*Although Steve loves everything Miss Pat cooks, he always has his
fingers crossed that she will have a pot of this on her stove. Fragrant
with geera—ground, roasted cumin seeds—and caramelized sugar,
this dish isn't shy about its flavor.*

2 tbsp	vegetable oil	25 mL
2 tbsp	demerara or brown sugar	25 mL
1 ½ lb	boneless pork, cut into cubes	750 g
1 tsp	kosher or sea salt	5 mL
4 tsp	ground roasted geera (see Tips, below)	20 mL
	Hot pepper sauce (to taste)	

1. Heat the oil in a large pot. Add the sugar. Cook, stirring
   frequently, until it is bubbling and dark brown and you can
   smell the caramel (about 3 to 4 minutes). Watch carefully, as
   it goes very quickly from golden to dark brown to too black
   (which will give the dish a burnt taste).

2. Carefully add the meat, sprinkle with salt and geera, and stir
   until the meat is coated in the caramelized sugar. Cook,
   uncovered, until the meat has released its juices and is very
   brown, stirring frequently (about 15 to 20 minutes).

3. Add 2 cups (500 mL) of hot water, pouring it in the side of
   the pot (not on top of the pork)—"so it doesn't take off the
   sweetness and the juice," Miss Pat says—and continue
   cooking for about 1 hour, partly covered, until the pork is
   tender and the sauce has cooked down. The finished dish
   should be fairly dry, not a stew, and the sauce should be very
   dark brown and coat the meat.

4. Stir in pepper sauce and additional salt and geera to taste; there should be sufficient geera to give the dish a slight grittiness. Continue to cook for a few minutes longer to blend flavors.

Makes 4 servings.

Tips:

- Packages of ground, roasted geera—cumin seed—are available in East Indian and West Indian food stores, or you can make your own: Place whole cumin seeds in a dry frying pan and toast over medium heat for a couple of minutes, until they begin to pop and darken and release their aroma. Remove from heat, cool, and then grind to a powder in a spice mill.
- Try this recipe with lamb instead of pork, leaving the pieces of bone in for flavor.

· · · STEWED LENTILS WITH PUMPKIN · · ·

West Indian pumpkin, or calabaẓa, has mottled green and beige skin and dense, brilliant-orange flesh. Its flavor is similar to butternut squash, which works well as a substitute. The "punkin," as Miss Pat calls it, softens almost into a sauce, giving a wonderful sweet edge to the seasoned lentils. The same treatment, she says, can be used with any sort of bean.

1 cup	lentils, picked over	250 mL
1	onion, chopped	1
2	cloves garlic, chopped	2
½	cubanelle or green bell pepper (or 2 seasoning peppers), seeded and chopped	½
1	green onion, chopped	1
½ lb	West Indian pumpkin or butternut squash, peeled and cubed	250 g
1 tsp	granulated sugar	5 mL
1 tsp	salt	5 mL
	Freshly ground black pepper	
1 tbsp	butter	15 mL
	Parsley, chives or green onion, finely chopped (optional, for garnish)	

1. Cover lentils with water. Add onion, garlic, pepper, green onion, pumpkin or squash, sugar and salt.
2. Bring to boil, reduce heat, cover, and simmer for 30 to 40 minutes until lentils are soft. If pot starts to become dry, add more hot water.
3. Taste, adding additional salt and pepper as needed. Just

before serving, stir in butter and garnish with chopped herbs if desired.

Makes 4 side-dish servings.

· · · CURRY STEW CHICKEN · · ·

"We don't want to rush it," Rishi Hardit-Singh warned. But since everyone was happily liming at his Tunapuna house, there wasn't much reason to rush the stew. The trick, he said, is to wait for the bubbling sugar in the pot to turn a deep dark brown before adding the chicken.

1	4- to 5-lb (2 to 2.2 kg) chicken, cut into pieces	1
½ cup	green seasoning (see Tips, below)	125 mL
2	onions, roughly chopped (divided)	2
3 tbsp	curry powder (see Tips, below)	50 mL
1 tbsp	garam masala (see Tips, below)	15 mL
¼ cup	vegetable oil	50 mL
3	cloves garlic, roughly chopped	3
1 tsp	fenugreek seeds (optional)	5 mL
½	Scotch bonnet or other hot pepper, finely chopped (or to taste)	½
¼ cup	demerara or brown sugar	50 mL
1	bay leaf	1
	Salt and freshly ground black pepper	

1. Toss the chicken pieces with the green seasoning and one of the chopped onions. Marinate in the refrigerator overnight.
2. Sprinkle curry powder and garam masala on chicken and mix well.
3. In a large pot, heat the oil. Add the remaining onion, garlic, fenugreek seeds (if using) and hot pepper, and cook for a couple of minutes until golden.

4. Add the sugar, and cook over medium-high heat, turning the mixture frequently with a wooden spoon.

5. When the mixture is bubbling, dark brown, and no longer sticks to the spoon (about 5 to 6 minutes), carefully add the chicken pieces with their marinade and stir until they are coated in the caramelized sugar mixture. Add the bay leaf and salt and pepper.

6. Lower heat and simmer, uncovered, for 20 to 30 minutes, then add 2 cups (500 mL) of hot water and continue to cook for another 20 to 30 minutes, until chicken is tender and sauce is thick. Skim fat off sauce and remove bay leaf. Taste and adjust seasoning. Serve hot with rice or roti.

Makes 6 servings.

Tips:

- Bottled green seasoning is available in stores that specialize in West Indian foods, but it's easy to make your own; see the recipe in Chapter 9.

- Though you can use any good-quality curry powder in this recipe, West Indian–style ones have a distinctive taste. (People who say they "don't like" curry often enjoy ones made with West Indian spice blends.) Look for Trinidadian brands such as Turban, Chief's, and Carib Herb in specialty food stores or supermarkets with a selection of West Indian foods.

- Garam masala is a curry-like East Indian spice blend. It's sold in places specializing in Indian foods, as well as other specialty food stores.

NINE

Feelin' Hot, Hot, Hot

··· TRINIDAD ···

My first experience with hot pepper was when Mama put it on my fingers to stop me from sucking them.

from an article on pepper, in Trinidad's Daily Express,

July 21, 2007 (no byline)

Always put a hot pepper in food that will be traveling at night; that way you ward off the spirits from entering your home.

from an article on Trinidadian superstitions, in Trinidad's

Guardian, *February 20, 2008 (no byline)*

"SING A LITTLE SOMETHING for them, darlin'," Miss Pat urges the young man in her kitchen who's wearing a *TnT Idol* tee. "This is Impulse and he sings calypso," she explains to Heather and me, who are in the kitchen with her, awaiting a promised lesson in making her pepper sauce.

Heather and her husband Don (who had tried to tackle Miss Pat's shrimp with cutlery), also from Toronto and longtime friends of ours, had set sail on *Asseance* the same year we left on our second trip to the Caribbean on *Receta*. Although we crossed paths briefly once or twice farther north, we've only really caught up to each other in Trinidad. Heather—outgoing, always talking—throws herself headlong into adventure; Don—quieter, more restrained—is only occasionally reluctant to follow. Since we introduced them to Miss Pat, they too have taken seriously to her cooking—and to her. For her part, Miss Pat adds them to the list of those to be spoiled and scolded. "You tired, baby? You so quiet," she says to Don, ruffling his hair affectionately; this, after dressing him down for his shrimp-eating technique not fifteen minutes earlier.

Impulse is happy to oblige Miss Pat, and launches into a calypso—something about love, I think—but, really, I can't focus on the lyrics when this cute guy is standing barely a foot away and singing straight into my eyes. About midway through the private performance, my self-consciousness ratchets even higher when Miss Pat tries to get me dancing. "Get you wining, you mean," says Heather, who is enjoying my embarrassment. Mercifully, Steve and Don are still in Miss P's dining room, polishing off the last pieces of geera pork, which she had prepared today on special request from Steve.

Wining is an extremely sexy dance move—all Trinis seem able to do it effortlessly, naturally—which means Miss Pat is, in fact, gyrating behind me, our bodies making contact, "winding" her waist and hips in a highly suggestive manner to Impulse's beat. I had lamented to her one day that I feared I would look the fool if we returned to Trinidad for Carnival because of my inability to dance even remotely like a Trini. "Don't worry, honey, the music will move you," she had said. She is now trying to prove her point. Unsuccessfully.

The mistake North Americans and Europeans make is that

they dance from the waist up, a Trini once told British writer Lucretia Stewart, "with their heads and shoulders, jiggling all over the place . . . with their brains, and expect their bodies to get the message."

Making "peppah" is more my sort of no-brainer, and a skill I don't need to have possessed from birth. The only trick appears to be devoting a blender solely to the cause. Otherwise, you risk serving tear-inducing coladas and sizzling-hot frozen daiquiris. Miss Pat puts in a handful of peppers and enough white vinegar "to run the blender," covers her mouth and nose with a kitchen towel, and sets it whirring. When she expanded her dining room a few years back, she also relocated and enlarged the kitchen, equipping it with a no-nonsense array of steam tables, a professional hood-topped stove and a sumo-sized exhaust fan. But even it is no match for Trini pepper. In seconds, the fumes rising from the blender force Heather and me to retreat, gasping and coughing, to the farthest corner.

Some culinary authorities call hot pepper the most important element in Caribbean seasoning. "Caribbean cooking is synonymous with hot peppers," says Wendy Rahamut. The Caribs used them long before Columbus arrived in the Caribbean, and they were unknown in Europe until he brought them back. "The land was found to produce much *ají,* which is the pepper of the inhabitants," he reported to his royal employers in 1493, calling it "more valuable" than the black peppercorns he was seeking. "They deem it very wholesome and eat nothing without it." As keen as his boss to believe they'd reached the Orient, Columbus's physician, Dr. Chanca, called it "Indian pepper," which started the misconception that the hot pepper is native to India. In fact, it first reached India a few decades later, via Portuguese explorers, who brought it from Brazil. Meanwhile, the peppers Columbus carried back to Spain didn't take off. They gained acceptance only after they were cultivated in India and then brought from there to Europe—thereby perpetuating the peppery confusion.

"Peppah" is never called "hot sauce" or even "hot pepper sauce" in Trinidad; that it's hot goes without saying. When she's making a full batch for the restaurant, Miss Pat uses about five hundred red, orange, yellow and green Congo peppers. These little lantern-shaped scorchers—rating about 300,000 units on the Scoville scale of pepper heat—are close relatives of Jamaica's Scotch bonnets and Mexico's habañeros, all *Capsicum chinense*. By comparison, a run-of-the-mill jalapeño is generally only 3,500 to 4,500 Scoville units; even the best Mexican jalapeño only measures about 8,000.

In the Port of Spain market, Congo peppers are sold in hundred-pepper sacks for people like Miss Pat, as well as loose for people like me. I point and ask before I buy, because the market vendors also sell similar-looking peppers that carry just a hint of heat. In Grenada, these are called "seasoning peppers," which nicely explains what they do. If I ask for "seasoning peppers" in Trinidad, however, I get a blank look. Here, they're "pimientos" or "pimentos." But if I ask for pimentos in Grenada, I get allspice. Shopping has its challenges.

Whatever they're called, seasoning peppers are a brilliant cook's helper—adding flavor (I've also heard them called "flavor peppers"), color, texture and just a little kick—and I've become hooked on having them in the galley. Occasionally, a rogue seasoning pepper packs a real wallop, and I can smell the heat when I cut it open. But I've been fooled, so just to be sure, I've learned to touch a teensy piece of every seasoning pepper to my tongue before adding it to the pot.

As Miss Pat's blender reduces the Congo peppers to a thick puree, she opens the lid and pops in more, one by one. Along the way, she adds two big globs of ordinary yellow mustard—the type used on ballpark hot dogs—and a Pat-sized pinch of salt. When the blender contains about as much sauce as it can handle, she adjusts the consistency and color with a bit more white vinegar and/or mustard. "It will get thicker as it stands, and hotter."

And that's it: no cooking, no preservatives, no additional ingredients. "You could add garlic if you like, or chadon beni—but never onion." Onion makes things go sour, she says, if they're not eaten right away.

Only a few cautious drops of Miss Pat's sauce are required to torch a sandwich or sear a meat dish. But underneath their pore-opening heat (that peppah gets you sweating and thus cools you off is one reason it's so popular in tropical climates), Congo peppers have a distinct fruitiness, giving a depth of flavor to the sauce. And, unlike some peppers, their incendiary attack on the mouth and tongue is short-lived; the burning disappears quickly, leaving behind a pleasant—some claim euphoric—glow. Still, the recycled rum bottles of peppah sauce that Heather and I take away from our lesson are likely to last us a long, long time.

. . .

Congo peppers are grown commercially a scant thirty-minute drive from Miss Pat's restaurant, high in the mountains of the Northern Range, in the area around a small village called Paramin, where the steep hillsides are a vertical checkerboard of garden plots. Paramin is also known for growing herbs—the area is called Trinidad's "herb basket"—and a cottage industry has grown up around them. Local entrepreneurs bottle the peppers into sauce and the herbs into "green seasoning," used for that critical, ubiquitous first step in Caribbean cooking: "seasoning up" the meat or fish to kick-start the flavor of the finished dish.

"Nothing is cooked without being seasoned a few hours ahead of time," unequivocally states Dominica-born Yolande Cools-Lartigue in *The Art of Caribbean Cooking*, first published in 1983 and still popular in island bookshops. "This is probably the essence of Caribbean cooking."

Dingis would certainly agree: "First you season it up," she always tells me, no matter what meat or seafood she's showing me how to prepare. Olive 'splained me the same thing in St. Martin, Moses and Neville seasoned up their crayfish before cooking them in the mountains of Dominica, Martin marinated our land crabs, and Leslie Ann and Godfrey, our Carriacou snapper. Miss Pat, meanwhile, made Steve and me stick our fingers in the seasoning bathing her raw kingfish "to take a taste," so we'd realize how important it was to the flavor of the finished dish.

"Seasoning it up" is a virtue born of necessity. The Africans who came to the West Indies as slaves not only introduced foods such as okra and callaloo, but also developed the cooking technique that's basic to Caribbean dishes. Fed as cheaply as possible—the stuff their masters disdained, the cuts they discarded, the dregs on the edge of going bad—they turned to herbs and spices to make this cast-off food taste good. Spices also have preservative properties, giving them usefulness beyond taste in hot, tropical climates.

In Trinidad, I've taken to bottled green seasoning with a passion. For island cooks, storebought seasoning is a timesaver; for me, it's a foolproof first step, both tenderizing and providing a fresh, herby foundation for the flavor. Even kitchen goddess Miss Pat uses prepared green seasoning that she buys directly from Paramin by the bucketful—although never on her fish; she wouldn't dream of not seasoning that, from scratch, herself. "Only Pat hand touches the fish," she says.

One of the popular brands on store shelves—so popular, it's often sold out at our closest mini-mart—is the straightfor-wardly named "Paramin Green Seasoning," made by a collective of women who, we've heard, farm their own herbs.

Time to rent another SdJ and head for the hills.

. . .

"We can't walk the fields on an empty stomach," says Steve, whose approach to life is becoming more Trini-like every day. "We're driving right by the Breakfast Shed. We need a quick stop."

In Steve's book, a trip to the Breakfast Shed is right up there with a doubles run as the perfect morning exercise. Home to a dozen or so women who all have "sweet hand," it opened about a half-century ago in the city's port area to feed the dockhands. These days, stevedores and suits eat breakfast side by side at the long communal tables, tackling mammoth bowls of steaming fish broth and whole fried fish. (No two eggs, toast and coffee here.) The cooks all prepare the same dishes, competing for clientele on the strength of their cooking. Each woman has her loyal followers, and Steve has become devoted to Charmaine. Her mother Stephanie used to be in charge—Steve was devoted to her, too—but she turned the business over to her daughter around the time the Breakfast Shed relocated (was moved by the government, under protest, actually) from a steamy, corrugated, full-of-personality canary-yellow tin shed to a bland, charmless (albeit cooler), concrete setup a half-mile away.

"Peppah you want?" Charmaine asks Steve this morning, and when he nods yes, she splashes some on his breakfast, stoking the fire of a dish that already goes by the name of *buljol*—Creole for "burn mouth," from the French *brûle gueule*—thanks to its liberal dose of diced Congo peppers. A salad of shredded saltfish and raw vegetables, buljol is a worthy rival for doubles as the breakfast choice of Trinis on the run, especially when it's stuffed into a "bake."

You've got to love cooks like Charmaine, who dish up oxy-morons like "fried bakes"—air-filled ovals of deep-fried deli-ciousness that have been nowhere near an oven. Order a "bake," and she slides a circle of dough into a heavy pot of bubbling oil on her propane-fired stove, and then fishes it out a few minutes later when it's puffed and golden. (If I'm feeling virtuous, I order a "roast bake," which hasn't been near an oven either, but is merely "roasted" in a thin layer of oil in a pot on the stovetop.) She splits it open, stuffs its still-steaming interior with buljol, anoints it with peppah, and wraps it in paper to go. But the interior of the pre-vious rental car (the one that went to Tunapuna) had suffered mightily when Steve, in a gross error of judgment, tried to eat a buljol-stuffed bake while practicing his opposite-side-of-the-road driving. This morning I steer him to a long table.

. . .

The current SdJ—a serious junker—can't take us all the way to Paramin. Then again, few cars could. "You have to park at the jeep stand in Maraval," according to our helpful friends in the office at the marina where *Receta* is docked. "A jeep will take you from there." I picture an unpaved track meandering through endless fields of herbs and peppers, and I assume travel by normal vehicle is impossible because of rainy-season mud.

The first clue that mud is not the issue comes when we pile into one of the jeeps, which have been fitted out as mini maxi-taxis, with two bench seats running lengthwise behind the driver. Swinging from the rearview mirror is a placard entitled the "Paramin Drivers' Prayer." "Heavenly Father, we ask your blessing as we drive the hills of Paramin," it begins. "Because the roads are steep and winding, we live with danger every day . . ."

Soon, the jeep is hanging almost vertically on a one-lane road that is more amusement-park ride than drivable surface. If the back door flies open, I fear Steve and I will spill out like cartoon characters and roll all the way back down the mountain to Maraval. The jeep hurtles upward, flinging itself around switch-backs, grinding through S-curves, careening past sheer dropoffs, and delivering all the thrills of a roller coaster at a fraction of the price: TT$3, about 50 cents, for the ten-minute ride from Maraval to Paramin. We're so high up that *corbeaux*—"carrion crows," big jet-black vultures—soar past at eye level.

We finally brake in front of Felix Boisson's postage-stamp-sized shop, home to the local post office, on the outskirts of Paramin. Behind it, past a house and down a flight of steps, is a whitewashed, one-story cinder-block building. Surrounded by a tangle of banana and breadfruit trees, it hangs off the side of the mountain above a jade valley: the home of the grandly named Paramin Women's Agro Processing Enterprise, a.k.a. the Paramin Women's Group.

"Welcome to our factory," says Veronica Romany, as we walk into an overgrown kitchen: homey oilcloth-covered table, home-style stove topped with big pots, a pair of sinks with a small window above them looking out on a hillside patterned into light- and dark-green cultivated squares, and the valley beyond. The room's centerpiece—the only equipment that makes it look even vaguely factory-like—is a freestanding, missile-shaped electric grinder. The place is aggressively pungent, an herb and onion combination that comes from thick bundles of sive and bales of "broadleaf," a variety of thyme with velvety, fleshy, spinach-sized leaves and a boosted-up smell.

"Besides me, all the other ladies in the group are farmers," Veronica says, "but they can't supply the factory with the quantity we need, so we also buy from other villagers." For its once-a-week production day, the group requires six hundred pounds of cive alone, but today's batch is a small one—the bottles of seasoning will be donated to a local fundraiser—and the herbs have come entirely from the garden of Martina Romany, who is quietly listening as the ebullient Veronica carries the conversational ball.

Like other Paramin women, Veronica and Martina used to make their own green seasoning at home, the way their grandmothers did. The business got its start with a government program that sent tutors to the village to teach cake decorating, basketry, upholstering, crocheting and other crafts. "But eventually we exhausted everything," and one of the tutors—out of desperation, I suspect—offered to teach the Paramin women how to give their green seasoning a shelf life. The tutor then encouraged them to apply for a grant to open a factory to produce it on a larger scale. They also began bottling their own pepper sauce, though it's since taken a backseat to green seasoning.

Veronica disappears to change into a plain white T-shirt ("so I can throw it in Clorox; I'm a mess at the end of the day") to top her ankle-length skirt, and she, Martina and Jean, a third "golden girl" (as they call themselves) tuck their hair under headscarves. Time for work. As Martina and Jean stem and wash broadleaf, Veronica stuffs armloads in the grinder. Soon, she is splattered with green bits—as is Steve, who is sticking his nose in close, under the guise of getting a good photo but just as interested in getting a good sniff. "When we grindin', people all up the road are smellin'," says Veronica approvingly. Each herb is ground separately—cive, small-leaved thyme ("French thyme"), pimentos and chadon beni follow the broadleaf—poured into a waist-high plastic barrel, then all stirred together into an electric-green slush. Once vinegar and salt are added, plus a little potassium sorbate for shelf life, the seasoning is transferred to pots and boiled briefly before bottling.

While they wait for it to come to a boil, the women take a break at the oilcloth-covered table, pouring Steve and me glasses of the homemade fruit wines they've brought along to sip after lunch. Like guavaberry liqueur and Saba Spice, banana wine and guava wine are something of an acquired taste, "but much more civilized," says Steve, since at least they're not eye-crossingly alcoholic. The women sell their home brews locally, along with homemade sweets, including the lurid-red preserved mango and other fruits that Trinis adore. "We make a living out of little t'ings like that," Veronica says. "There are so many t'ings you can do to make a bit of money that if a woman can't afford food, she must want to suffer."

Our walk through the village gardens is rained out by a sudden squall, and the women insist we come back the following week. "Only if you promise to let us help next time," Steve says.

Until then, I marinate my heart out. We bought several bottles of Paramin Green Seasoning at the end of our visit, but the golden girls also sent us away with a gift: a special hot seasoning they sometimes make on request, which includes

Paramin-grown Congo peppers. "Use it on fish," Martina says. Forget that: I slather it on *everything*.

. . .

The ride is no less hair-raising the second time we take a Paramin jeep to Felix Boisson's shop, and this driver also has the Paramin Drivers' Prayer prominently displayed. But when we arrive this time, the factory is dark. "The current is out," Veronica says, "so we can't use the grinder. It's a good time for a walk."

First, however, they must live up to their end of the promise: I join her and Martina in breaking the tough ends off the broadleaf stems and removing damaged leaves before tossing the stalks into the sink. This is a full production day, and the floor is carpeted with thick bundles of cive and thyme, delivered that morning by the farmers but picked the evening before. "You have to let the sun strike the plants before you pick," the quiet Martina says. "Then the leaves are soft and easy to stem," Veronica chimes in. "Otherwise the leaves break and you have to throw them away."

Steve's job is to heft bundles from floor to tabletop as the pile in front of us diminishes. As usual, I'm much slower than the others—but at least this work doesn't involve sharp implements. The golden girls use the time to talk. "That's what's kept us together all these years," Veronica says. "If I'm in tears because something frustrates me, I would leave here in a better mood. And if you have a problem and you talk here, you feel comfortable that someone won't take it outside."

Today, of course, the talk is casual. When I tell them how well my meals have been turning out with the help of their magic ingredient, Veronica recounts the story of someone— clearly not a Trini—who didn't realize green seasoning was for marinating. "She was using it as a sauce instead," she says with disbelief, while Martina chortles. I'm too embarrassed to admit I'm considering that myself. I tasted it straight out of the bottle, and know it would be terrific on grilled fish.

Leaving Martina to finish and the current to come back on, Veronica leads us on a tour—past Martina's house and garden (these "gardens" are much larger than the word makes them sound; they're actually fields), past the school, down to the river ("we used to bathe right there, around the bend; the village only got public water about a decade ago"), back up to (and through) the church (by far the grandest building in the village), past people working the steep hillsides. All the farming is done by hand, Veronica says, demonstrating how the cive is harvested. (You never take the whole cluster of stalks; while one hand holds part of the clump in place, the other hand "rocks" the other stalks out of the soil.) Human labor is cheaper than farm equipment, but even if the farmers could afford them, tractors and harvesters probably wouldn't be an option, given the precipitous slant of these fields.

. . .

Before we climb back on board *Receta* that afternoon, I deliver a requested bottle of green seasoning to my friend Roberta on another boat. "Thanks," she says. "I really like this stuff. Have you tried it as a sauce for fish?"

. . .

Steve can't understand why I'm worried. "You have people to dinner on *Receta* all the time," he says, as I fret about my miscalculation. I hadn't realized when I invited guests for dinner on Sunday evening that the day before was a public holiday, the start of Eid al-Fitr, or Festival of Fast Breaking, when Muslims celebrate the end of Ramadan. (About 6 percent of the Trini population is Muslim.) Nor had I realized that therefore the public market in Port of Spain would be shut tight on Saturday, and I would be forced to rely for my dinner party on puny supermarket shrimp, thin, pre-cut refrigerator-case fish, and imperfect produce picked days before.

Normally, I wouldn't be particularly concerned—I'd just make do and let the wine and conversation cover any short-comings in the food—but the guests include Miss Pat. "It's like cooking for Julia Child," I moan to Steve. And then there's Pie: he is a practicing Rastafarian and follows many of the dietary restrictions. "I do everything he doesn't do," Miss Pat had told us, running the list: "He doesn't drink, he doesn't eat meat, he doesn't eat shellfish, he doesn't use foul language." (Miss Pat, in fact, has helped further my linguistic education, adding a couple of choice anatomical Trini-isms to my vocabulary.) "And he doesn't smoke or use weed—but I don't do those either."

Pie does eat fish, however, and Miss Pat doesn't barbecue (at least not at the restaurant), so I settle on grilled skewers of supermarket shrimp and fish, marinated in Paramin green sea-soning first. (I don't dare serve it as a sauce though, and plan a garlic-lime butter instead.) Heather and Don, the other guests, will be bringing dessert and an hors d'oeuvre, and, for the rest of the dishes, I decide the safest course is to steer clear of any-thing local—except for a pre-dinner mango chow.

I've made chow many times since Rishi's lime in Tunapuna, not just with mangoes but also with *pomme cytheres*, or golden apples, as they're called on some islands. Like mangoes, they can be eaten both green and ripe, and the Trinis use them in all sorts of dishes to "stand in" when mangoes go out of season. But it's been a long time since I've tasted any chow but my own, and—since it only involves combining five ingredients in a bowl—I want to be sure I've got the balance right. I do a trial run.

"Enough lime? Enough salt?" I ask Steve. "But I think I put in too much pepper—it's really hot."

"Why don't you let Elizabeth and Meleen taste it?" he says. "They're in the office tonight."

The women who work at the front desk of the marina enjoy our gung-ho enthusiasm for their island, and happily offer suggestions when given half a chance. I've shown thanks for their help the way I always do, with something from *Receta*'s oven. But I've never had the nerve to try out something Trini on them. "Better them than Miss Pat," Steve says.

"Oh, toothpicks, what an interesting idea," Meleen says, as she and Elizabeth spear slices of mango from the bowl of chow. Trinis tend to take "finger food" a bit more literally than I do. "Very nice," they agree.

I know from hard experience with Dingis that I will need to probe to get anything beyond a compliment. "Enough lime?" I ask. "Enough salt? I know there's plenty of pepper."

"Not enough," Elizabeth says. "A Trini would put in more peppah." Meleen agrees. "But a Trini wouldn't put in as much chadon beni." Well, at least I got the lime and salt right.

. . .

Miss Pat, in a diaphanous top and clingy skirt, teeters along the dock toward *Receta* on a pair of glittery mules with kitten heels.

Oops. I'd neglected to mention that climbing on board *Receta* can be more than a bit inelegant, since I'd never seen her in anything other than sensible shoes and sedate clothing. Pie, who is such a quiet man that we don't really know him beyond what we've heard from Miss Pat—in the bar and restaurant downtown, he never says much more than a warm "Good afternoon"—swings easily aboard, looking like a well-dressed sailor in a print shirt, chinos and deck shoes, with his long dreads coiled out of the way on top of his head. Only later will we learn about his underwear . . .

Let the record show that from hors d'oeuvres to dessert, lots of food and drink disappear. The size of the shrimp and the thinness of the fish go unremarked, though Miss Pat notices that my supermarket-bought mangoes are riper than they ought to be for a chow. ("Ripe mangoes, what an interesting idea. And toothpicks!") There are only compliments, and many laughs, as Miss Pat and Heather compare notes on how quiet their husbands are; Steve, a non-contender in the quiet category, stirs the pot by suggesting that perhaps they can't get a word in edgewise. They then move on to discussing how much more organized they are than their men too. "I arrange all my bath towels and kitchen towels by color," Miss P says. "Me too," says Heather. "I arrange my pantry with the same type of cans all together and their labels neatly lined up and facing the same way," "Me too," says Heather. "And I arrange all Pie's Jockeys by color in his Jockey drawer." Heather, getting a look from Don, doesn't say anything. "Isn't it nice to have your underwear drawer discussed with strangers?" Steve asks. Pie, as good-natured as he is quiet, simply smiles.

Afterward, Pie and Miss Pat offer to drive Heather and Don around to the other side of the harbor, where their boat is moored. We walk them all to the car and exchange hugs all around. As they pull away, Steve puts his arm around me, and I sink against him with relief and pleasure that we've pulled off the evening successfully. Heather reports the next day that in the car, Miss Pat had a different take on the scene. "Look at that," she said. "They can't even wait until they're back on the boat to start their snuggling."

· · · MISS PAT'S PEPPER SAUCE · · ·

Take a tip from Miss Pat. Don't stick your nose too close to the blender or food processor: the fumes are knockout strength.

20	Scotch bonnet, Congo, bird or similar hot peppers (not jalapeños)	20
½ cup + 2 tbsp	white vinegar (approx)	155 mL
1 tbsp	yellow mustard (approx)	15 mL
	Salt	

1. Put about ⅓ of the peppers in a blender or food processor, and add about ¼ cup (50 mL) of the vinegar.
2. Process until the peppers are pureed, then add the rest, one or two at a time, along with another ¼ cup (50 mL) of the vinegar, the mustard and a good pinch of salt.
3. When all the peppers have been reduced to a smooth puree, adjust the consistency by adding the rest of the vinegar and/or more mustard. (The sauce will get thicker over time.) Taste cautiously, and add a bit more salt if you like.
4. Pour into a bottle and store in the refrigerator. It will last indefinitely.

Makes about 1 cup.

· · · SALTFISH BULJOL · · ·

Although the Trinis traditionally stuff this spicy salad inside a fried or roast bake and eat it as a breakfast sandwich, we think it makes a terrific cocktail-hour snack spooned on crispbread, crackers or one-bite coconut bakes. (The recipe follows.) It's meant to be quite pepper-hot— after all, the name comes from the Creole for "burn mouth"—but you can dial down the heat to suit, and offer pepper sauce on the side for those who want more.

½ lb	boneless, skinless salted cod	250 g
2 tbsp	fresh lime juice	30 mL
1	small onion, finely chopped	1
1	medium tomato, finely chopped	1
½	green bell pepper, seeded and finely chopped	½
¼ to ½	Scotch bonnet or other hot pepper, finely chopped (or to taste)	¼ to ½
2 tbsp	finely chopped chadon beni or cilantro	25 mL
1 tbsp	finely chopped celery leaves	15 mL
2 tbsp	olive oil	25 mL
1	clove garlic	1
	Freshly ground black pepper	
	Leaf lettuce (for garnish)	
½	avocado, pitted, peeled and sliced (optional; for garnish)	½

1. Cover salted cod with cold water and soak for about 12 hours in the refrigerator, changing water several times.
2. Place fish in a pot and cover with cold water. Bring to a boil,

turn off the heat, and allow the fish to cool in the liquid.
Drain fish and squeeze to get rid of excess water.

3. In a large bowl, shred the fish and squeeze lime over top. Mix
in the onion, tomato, peppers, chadon beni or cilantro, and
celery leaves.

4. In a small pan, heat the olive oil with the clove of garlic to
near bubbling, and cook until garlic is golden. Discard garlic.
Pour hot oil onto the salad and mix well.

5. Line a serving plate with lettuce and pile buljol on top.
Surround with sliced avocado (if using). Serve with crackers
or coconut bakes.

Makes 6 to 8 snack-size servings.

· · · ONE-BITE COCONUT BAKES · · ·

This is an hors d'oeuvre–sized, oven-baked version of the "roast" bakes Charmaine makes at the Breakfast Shed. Fill them with a spoonful of buljol or another seafood mixture, such as the one for the Cocktail Bites in Chapter 11. They are best eaten on the day they're made.

4 ½ cups	all-purpose or bread flour	1.125 L
2 tsp	instant yeast	10 mL
¾ tsp	salt	4 mL
1 tbsp	brown sugar	15 mL
⅛ tsp	cinnamon	0.5 mL
⅛ tsp	freshly grated nutmeg	0.5 mL
¼ cup	butter, margarine or shortening	50 mL
1 ½ cups	coconut milk	375 mL

1. Combine flour, yeast, salt, sugar and spices in a mixing bowl. Cut in butter or shortening until mixture resembles fine crumbs.

2. Heat coconut milk to about 120°F (50°C). Pour on top of flour mixture and stir to make a firm dough.

3. Turn dough out onto a floured surface, and knead lightly for 2 to 3 minutes until smooth. Place in a greased bowl, cover with a kitchen towel or plastic wrap, and allow dough to rest in a warm spot for about 20 minutes.

4. Preheat oven to 400°F (200°C). Pinch off small pieces of dough (about 1 heaping tbsp/20 mL), roll into smooth balls and place on greased baking sheets. Cover with a kitchen towel and let rise for 20 to 30 minutes.

5. Press balls with palm of hand to flatten slightly. Prick in center with a fork.

6. Bake in preheated oven for 12 to 15 minutes or until lightly golden.
7. Split in half and spoon in filling.

Makes 3 dozen one-bite bakes.

· · · GREEN SEASONING · · ·

Marinating meat or fish in green seasoning before cooking gives a dish a real underpinning of Caribbean flavor.

1 ½ cups	coarsely chopped green onions	375 mL
⅓ cup	coarsely chopped fresh parsley	75 mL
⅓ cup	coarsely chopped fresh thyme	75 mL
⅓ cup	coarsely chopped chadon beni or cilantro	75 mL
⅓ cup	coarsely chopped celery leaves	75 mL
4	cloves garlic, coarsely chopped	4
¼ cup	white vinegar (approx)	50 mL
1 tsp	salt	5 mL

1. Combine all ingredients in a food processor. Process until mixture is pureed.
2. Taste and add more salt if necessary. Blend in additional vinegar or water to give the seasoning a thick pouring consistency.
3. Store in a jar in the refrigerator.

Makes about 1 cup.

Tips:
- Add a bit of fresh hot pepper to the ingredients if you like.
- As a general rule, use about 2 tbsp (25 mL) of the seasoning for every pound (500 g) of meat.

· · · PLANTAIN-CRUSTED CHICKEN FINGERS · · ·
WITH GREEN SEASONING

Serve this tropical version of chicken fingers with mango chutney or chadon beni sauce (see the recipe in Chapter 12) for dipping.

1 lb	boneless chicken breasts or fillets	500 g
2 tbsp	green seasoning	
	(see recipe, previous page)	25 mL
½ cup	flour	125 mL
	Salt and freshly ground	
	black pepper	
2	eggs	2
1 ¼ cups	plantain chips, thoroughly crushed	
	(see Tips, below)	300 mL
	Vegetable oil (for shallow frying)	

1. Pound the chicken breasts or fillets to even thickness and cut into strips about 1 inch (2.5 cm) wide. Mix with green seasoning and set aside in refrigerator for several hours to marinate.
2. Season flour with salt and pepper. Beat egg.
3. Dip chicken strips into seasoned flour and then egg, and then dredge in crushed plantain chips.
4. Heat a couple of tablespoons (25 mL) of oil in large frying pan. Cook chicken in batches until golden on both sides, adding more oil to the pan as necessary. Drain on paper towels and serve hot.

Makes 2 dinner-size or 4 snack-size servings.

Tips:

- Plantain chips—like potato chips, except made with plantains—are sold in bags in North American supermarkets that specialize in Latin American or West Indian foods; you can also sometimes find them in bulk-food stores.

- If your green seasoning doesn't include hot pepper and you'd like to spice things up a bit, add a couple of pinches of cayenne to the flour.

- To cook in the oven: Preheat oven to 400°F (200°C). Coat a large shallow baking pan with a couple of tablespoons (25 mL) of oil and arrange chicken fingers in a single layer in the pan. Bake for 10 minutes, then turn fingers and cook 5 minutes or so longer, until they are golden on both sides and chicken is cooked through.

· · · MANGO CHOW · · ·

This is probably the all-time favorite snack on Receta. *It's quick to make, requires only five ingredients, and can be adapted to whatever fruit is in season. The recipe is meant to be only a general guideline: "Make it to your taste," the Trinis say.*

2	unripe or half-ripe mangoes, peeled and sliced (see Tips, below)	2
¼ cup	finely chopped chadon beni or cilantro	50 mL
¼ to ½	Scotch bonnet or other finely chopped hot pepper (preferably red, for color)	¼ to ½
2 tsp	coarse kosher or sea salt	10 mL
½	lime	½

1. Place mangoes in a serving bowl. Add some of each of the remaining ingredients and toss well.
2. Taste and adjust balance of hot/tart/salty/sweet by adding more of the ingredients as you please. Serve with toothpicks to accompany drinks.

Makes 4 to 6 snack-size servings.

Tips:
- While an authentic Trini chow uses completely unripe fruit, we like it with just a hint of sweetness and use mangoes that are about half ripe.
- Try the same technique with cucumbers, wedges of

mandarin orange (the Trinis use a similar fruit called "portugals" in season), pomme cytheres (also called golden apples) or any half-ripe crisp fruit such as pineapple, guavas, or even unripe peaches or tart green apples.

· · · TRINI-STYLE CURRY SHRIMP · · ·

The fresh, inexpensive shrimp available at Port of Spain's central market on Saturdays were impossible to resist. This easy dish became one of my favorite ways to use them.

1 tbsp	olive oil	15 mL
1	large clove garlic, finely chopped	1
1	green onion, chopped	1
1 tbsp	fresh ginger, finely chopped	15 mL
½	cubanelle or green bell pepper (or 2 seasoning peppers), finely chopped	½
¼ to ½	Scotch bonnet or other hot pepper, seeded and finely chopped (or to taste)	¼ to ½
1 tbsp	curry powder (preferably West Indian), mixed with a little water to make a paste	15 mL
1	tomato, chopped	1
½ cup	coconut milk	125 mL
1 lb	large shrimp, peeled and deveined	500 g
½ tsp	sea salt	2 mL
½ tsp	freshly ground black pepper	2 mL

1. Heat oil in a large frying pan. Add garlic, green onion, ginger and peppers, and cook for a couple of minutes until tender and fragrant.
2. Stir in curry paste and continue cooking for a couple minutes longer.

3. Add tomato and coconut milk. Simmer about 10 minutes until mixture thickens and reduces.

4. Toss shrimp with salt and pepper. Add to pan and cook until they are just done (about 5 to 8 minutes, depending on size.) Taste and adjust seasoning if necessary. Serve hot over basmati rice.

Makes 2 lavish servings.

TEN

Cramming for a Chocolate-Tasting Test

· · · TRINIDAD, TOBAGO & GRENADA · · ·

"Sa ki ni kako an solèy ka gadé pou lapli."
"Who have cocoa in deh sun have to look for rain."

> *West Indian proverb, used in Creole and English,*
> *which warns that people who have many possessions*
> *spend lots of time worrying about keeping them*

"DO NOT GET THE KEY WET," the woman at the car-rental place barks at us sternly. She's all big hair and bigger attitude, and her vehicles are the Trinidadian equivalent of our Odalismobiles in the DR. "The car will not start if you get the key wet."

It's rainy season in Trinidad; it pisses at least a couple times a day; it's almost impossible to move the key from pocket to car door without getting it wet. Everything is wet. And then there is the grinding sound—reminiscent of trying to shift gears without putting the clutch in—that occurs when the car is started up. "No problem," says Ms. Econo-Car, impatiently waving us off. "It's fine. Besides, I don't have any others." (Ms.

Econo-Car eventually reveals that if we expect a vehicle where everything works, we need to move up to a higher price bracket.)

We've chanced another of Ms. Econo-Car's SdJs so we can visit Darin Sukha at UWI, the University of the West Indies. ("Ooo eee," the Trinis say.) Darin has a PhD in food science and technology, and a surprisingly small waistline, considering his line of work.

Darin tastes chocolate for a living. Granted, I'm summarizing here, cutting to the part of his job that interests Steve and me the most, the part that compelled us to brave the heavy morning traffic through Port of Spain—in our eagerness, even skipping the requisite breakfast stop—and then crawl nine more miles down the highway to St. Augustine, the home of UWI. Darin trains others to taste chocolate too—putting them through a rigorous, life-changing (to hear him tell it) two-week course so they are fit for one of his tasting panels. "Where do I sign up?" Steve asks as soon as he hears this. Alas, this year's group has already been selected and trained, and the trials are in progress—though Darin assures Steve he'll give us a chance to do some tasting ourselves. To tantalize us, his assistant then breezes through the lab—it's a miniature version of Willy Wonka's factory—and opens Darin's refrigerator: it contains nothing but cocoa and chocolate in various forms.

Darin works for the Cocoa Research Unit at UWI, set up by British chocolate manufacturers in the 1930s. For the past thirteen years, he's been evaluating varieties of cocoa beans for their flavor. "All the stuff about yield, disease resistance, fat content and so on," he says, "wouldn't mean anything if the end product didn't taste good."

Meanwhile, he has ushered us out of the lab and into the staff room so we can have a cup of coffee while we talk. A coffee break? When Steve and I have bypassed doubles and buljol, and are slavering to get to the chocolate? "Eating chocolate utilizes all your senses," he explains unhurriedly, while our senses are engaging only with truly terrible instant coffee. "First, there's the look of the chocolate, then the sound it makes when you break off a piece." Good chocolate has a distinct *snap*. And then there's smell, and touch—which here refers to "the feel of the chocolate when you put it in your mouth. How does it melt?" The final sense, of course, is taste.

. . .

When I paid my first visit to the Cocoa Research Unit (CRU) only a few days earlier, I had no idea that tastings happened here. None of the Trinis I asked were aware of the sweet research happening on their island. But I'd read that UWI was home to the world's largest cocoa gene bank, and I was curious to see it. The usual way to bank plant genes is to dry or freeze their seeds, but cocoa seeds can't be preserved reliably this way. To maintain the genetic material, cocoa seeds have to be grown: so a cocoa gene bank consists of trees—eleven or twelve thousand of them in this case, representing some 2,300 varieties, on an island where cocoa isn't even a native species.

The trees are a good 10 miles down the road from UWI, near Trinidad's Piarco International Airport, "at the end of the runway," says CRU director David Butler cheerfully, implying that a low-flying jet could make a permanent withdrawal from his bank. Dr. Butler moved to Trinidad from Bristol, England, ten years ago to head the CRU, and he is the picture of the stereotypical expat professor relocated to the Tropics: pale, bearded, rumpled, and (despite temps consistently in the high eighties) dressed as if expecting a sudden chill. To explain how the gene bank started here, he needs to take me through the history of cocoa on Trinidad and its sister island Tobago. Chocolate 101.

Cocoa was among the "discoveries" Columbus brought back from Central and South America on his second voyage. The Spanish then introduced the bean, he says—specifically, a variety called Criollo—to Trinidad in the sixteenth century. Cocoa plantations flourished here until 1727, when a "blast"— it's not known exactly what, but likely a hurricane or disease— wiped out most of the cocoa trees. Afterward, the Criollo fields were replanted with Forastero, another variety of South American cocoa, and the two hybridized naturally over time to produce a new variety: Trinitario, named after its place of origin.

It was a marriage made in heaven. Criollo is "fine-flavored" cocoa; Forastero is "bulk cocoa," the trees hardy and high yielding but the beans decidedly lacking in flavor. (They're used for blending into run-of-the-mill candy.) Trinitario combined the best aspects of each, producing fine-flavored cocoa from robust, farmer-pleasing trees. "It turned out to be quite useful," Dr. Butler explains in his understated, very British way. In fact, by 1830, Trinidad and Tobago had become the world's third-largest cocoa producer.

But the sweet times melted away after 1920, in part because of a disease called witches' broom. (An easily spread fungus, it causes cocoa branches to shrivel into something appropriate only for Halloween.) The fall in worldwide market prices that accompanied increased supply after West Africa began commercially producing cocoa didn't help either, nor did the onset of the Great Depression. "I'm here thanks to that decline," Dr. Butler says. Looking for a fix, the British chocolate manufacturers set up the

CRU, and collecting expeditions set off to search farmers' fields and uncultivated rain forest for trees that were "productive" (lots of pods with lots of beans) and disease resistant. The species they brought back to UWI formed the start of the gene bank.

Dr. Butler offers to arrange a trip to the end of the runway with one of his cocoa breeders, and a trip to the lab to meet Darin and learn about the "flavor work." When the CRU and the gene bank were first established, the taste of the cocoa took a back seat. "But," says Dr. Butler, again understating with a vengeance, "there is increasing interest around the world now in factors that affect flavor."

. . .

It's like *terroir*, with wine, explains Michel Boccara, the French cocoa breeder who gets the nod to show us around the gene bank when Steve and I return in the SdJ. (Dr. Butler's teaching strategy appears to be that the hard-slogging part comes before the chocolate-reward part.) Although vintage plays no part in cocoa flavor, different varieties taste different when grown in different locations. "Soil and climate are important with cocoa. And if a chocolate is more than 75 percent cocoa, you really get the flavor of the terroir when you eat it." Terroir is part of the reason Trinidad cocoa is so highly regarded and is currently selling for twice the going rate on the world market.

Let's be frank here: in the rainy season, a cocoa gene bank is a bunch of trees surrounded by mud and infested with mosquitoes. And to non-scientists like Steve and me, one part of a cocoa gene bank looks pretty much the same as the next, give or take a few dozen bites. As we continue to slop and slap along the mucky paths, Michel is rattling off all sorts of fascinating tidbits—but once I've seen the first few hundred trees, I'd be happy to listen to him from the comfort (it's all relative) of the SdJ. We learn that small ants play a large part in cocoa tree pollination; that baksheesh and political fiefdoms are said to play a large part in the government end of the cocoa business; and that in Ghana (where he worked previously) the white pulp around the beans is used for jams and jellies and fermented to make an alcoholic drink. (It's not very good, he admits.) And on top of all that, he confesses that he doesn't taste cocoa anymore. "I tasted it every day for a month—6 a.m. and 6 p.m.—and then I said, 'No more cocoa.' It's very intense."

We've been forewarned.

. . .

Back in the staff room, the enthusiastic Darin—he has all the professorial chops of his boss, but with a sweet Trini accent and without the sweater—explains how people taste. "By association," he says. "We build up a mental library of flavors." His job is to channel people's associations within that library, helping them "deconstruct" the flavor. During his two-week training course, he gives his students flavor extremes—very smoky, say, or very acidic—to teach them to turn an impression into a numerical value. "Being on my panel changes the way you taste forever," he says, obviously not suffering his boss's problem of understatement.

Along with terroir, he stresses the effect of processing. "How the raw cocoa beans are fermented, dried, roasted and stored suppresses or expresses their genetic potential."

Finally, he decides we have been sufficiently briefed and leads us into the tasting room, a cross between a boardroom, a high-school science lab, and the dining room of a large family. Each of the nine or ten places at the long table is set with a white paper placemat, a glass of water, a miniature tasting spoon, a pencil and an evaluation sheet. A bowl of plain crackers graces the middle of the table, for cleansing the palate between samples.

The real tasters are served their samples in the form of "chocolate liquor," which sounds extremely promising—I'm happily imagining spoonfuls of melted high-quality dark chocolate mixed, say, with a fine aged dark rum—until Darin explains this means the roasted beans have simply been pulverized to turn them from solid to liquid; 100 percent pure cocoa, not even a granule of sugar. But he's going to start us off with some chocolate instead, he says, which is easier for newbie tasters to evaluate.

Self-consciously, I place the first piece in my mouth. "Well?" asks Darin. "What do you taste?" Uh, I just taste chocolate—nothing special—and I suddenly fear I am one of those people who, when it comes to tasting, "just don't get it," as Darin had earlier described the occasional failure trainee. But it turns out, my unexcited reaction isn't far off the mark: Darin has started us with chocolate made from "bulk" South American cocoa beans, to give us a basis for comparison with the samples made from the "fine-flavored" Trinitario beans that follow.

Our second piece is obviously superior, with a very distinctive fruity taste. But that's about as far as I can get, still feeling incredibly self-conscious and not knowing quite how to dissect the flavor. Sure, this sample rates higher on my personal yummy scale, but I'm not sure that's going to cut it with the trained tongue who's conducting the tasting. "An aroma of dried brown fruit," he helpfully suggests. "A raisiny note."

"This one tastes like it was barbecued," Steve says a couple of samples later. "With an overtone of barbecue lighter fluid, actually." Darin is decidedly pleased. "You'd be good at this," he says. Once again, I can sense the wheels in Steve's brain turning as he plots a return visit to Trinidad, figuring he's a shoo-in for acceptance in the next tasting course. Darin concocted these samples to use with cocoa farmers, who are invited to CRU for tastings, to show them how the way they process their beans affects the flavor. He made this batch of chocolate to demonstrate the negative results of quick-drying the beans with the help of a wood fire, instead of drying them naturally, slowly, in the sun. "I smoked them in a barbecue, and I used one of those fluid starters to light it," he confirms.

We move on to chocolates with "dirty-tasting" and "earthy-tasting" flavors—"there are certain off-flavors that no chocolate manufacturer wants"—before he pronounces us ready to graduate to the liquors. Frankly, I wouldn't mind being held back and practicing on more real chocolate. The liquors are served in shot glasses, wrapped in foil to keep them warm, since they're all tested at 122°F (50°C). He demonstrates how to dip in the tasting spoon, evaluate the sample in our mouths (and spit it out if we wish), and mark the score sheet. Only six samples are tasted per session, he says, because the palate gets too confused after that.

No kidding. We are expected to grade, on a scale of 0 to 10, the liquor's astringency, acidity, bitterness, fruity flavor, floral flavor, nutty flavor, cocoa flavor, raw/beany/green flavor, and other flavors. Not accustomed to the completely unsweetened intensity of pure cocoa, I find bitterness trumps everything else in each sample. Not so Steve, who is busy making trenchant observations about how one liquor makes his mouth pucker ("high astringency," Darin concurs) and another tastes "green."

(Darin nods approvingly: "That's the raw flavor.") Show-off.

Before we leave, Darin hands us a flyer, on request of his boss. "Chocolate lovers of the world unite!" its headline reads. "Help us save the trees you need." It seems that maintaining the CRU's "priceless natural resource"—those eleven to twelve thousand trees in the gene bank—and breeding new and improved varieties requires individual donations in addition to corporate and government support. So the CRU has launched a low-key (almost invisible) fundraising campaign, urging chocolate lovers to adopt a tree, "or even a whole plot." Sponsors receive a certificate with their tree's characteristics and origin, a map, and a color photograph of a pod from their plot—not quite as cute as a dolphin, manatee or panda. But, hey, you don't get a bar of dark chocolate when you adopt one of those.

.   .   .

With its good genetics and favorable terroir, you'd think the Trinidad and Tobago cocoa business would be sitting pretty these days. After all, the market for dark chocolate with a high cocoa content has boomed in recent years, with chocolate-makers now trumpeting the percentage of cocoa in their bars and rebranding them as small, good-for-you luxuries. Studies—some financed by chocolate manufacturers—have shown health benefits: cocoa can have high levels of antioxidant flavonoids, which can help fight heart disease and aging—plus it contains mood-elevating theobromine and serotonin, as well as phenylethylamine, "the love drug." If that wasn't enough to get us buying the good stuff, fine chocolate producers have begun to follow in the clever marketing footsteps of the coffee guys and to sell us on area-specific tastes: there is a growing trend toward "single-origin chocolates," made with beans from a single region, or even a single estate, with the provenance of the chocolate touted on the wrapper.

But even as the world price has soared for fine-flavored cocoa beans, leaping as much as 70 percent in one year, TnT's cocoa business hasn't recovered from the decline of the 1930s and 1940s. Though demand for TnT beans far outstrips supply and Trinbagonian cocoa commands a hefty premium, the glory days of the 1920s—when cocoa was king and cocoa farmers were considered people of the highest status—haven't returned.

"You have to blame oil," says Dr. Butler. The discovery of offshore oil in 1910 and the subsequent growth of Trinidad's oil business created new, lucrative, easier jobs; suddenly, the labor-intensive cocoa estates didn't have enough people willing to work. At the same time, the booming petrochemical-fueled economy made TnT one of the most prosperous countries in the Caribbean—so the government forgot about agriculture, and cocoa along with it.

The few cocoa farmers who are making a go of it have moved away from the old ways, Dr. Butler says, planting intensively (many more trees per acre) and mechanizing, for higher yields with fewer workers. "But the culture here doesn't lend itself to that; it doesn't fit the traditions of the island. Most of the old estates that operated on traditional lines have been abandoned. The farmers simply can't make ends meet."

. . .

"Can you tell us how to find the Cameron Estate?" I ask two women on the roadside. They confer: "You know where you pass the First and Last? It right past there." Not twenty minutes earlier, we had driven by the First and Last Parlour, a tiny rum shop on the road that cuts through Tobago's mountainous middle, between Bloody Bay on one coast and Roxborough on the other. I hadn't seen any sign for, or of, Cameron Estate—though I was pretty intent on the latest SdJ's brakes at the time, which were billowing out smoke signals to protest the endless series of downhill curves. "There is no sign," the women tell me. "Stop at the First and Last and ask."

His neighbor is away, the man at the First and Last says, but he will give him a message when he returns. I hand over a slip of paper with our cell number, fully expecting we will never hear from David Ross, the owner of Cameron Estate.

We had done as the Trinis do, and driven (after doubles) right onto the morning ferry that leaves from Port of Spain for Tobago. (The government-supported boat line has all the frills—reclining seats, big-screen films, air-conditioning, food and drink—and none of the stomach-somersaulting discomfort of its privately owned Grenada-to-Carriacou counterpart.) And, like the Trinis, we'd driven off the ferry and straight into a bowl of curried crab and dumplings at the other end. This is the national food of Tobago—and Store Bay, not far from where the ferry docks in Scarborough, is the place to eat it. Behind the beach is a row of stalls, each cook offering her version of the dish; I try Miss Esmie's, swayed by the row of cooking trophies on display, and Steve tries Miss Alma's, swayed by the size of her crabs and the fatness of her dumplings. We swap tastes and argue whose is better, in the end agreeing with both those who call it "the world's messiest dish" and those who focus on the "paroxysms of pleasure" it brings.

"Tobagonians are not a loud outspoken people," says one of the government-produced tourism brochures. "They'll tell you to go to Trinidad for that." The two islands are, in fact, as different as hot sauce and hot cocoa, having been thrown together by their British masters in 1888 simply as a matter of political convenience. (Together, they opted for independence from Britain in 1962, and became the Republic of Trinidad and Tobago in 1976.) Tobago is smaller (one-sixteenth the size of Trinidad), slower, quieter and more laid-back; Trinidadians come here to lime on the beaches and escape the hustle-bustle of their own island, flocking here in droves to recover after Carnival.

Though Tobagonians may not be outspoken, they are just as willing to go out of their way to help. David Ross calls us that evening, and we arrange a visit to Cameron Estate the next day. We'd heard that he was bringing the estate, part of Tobago's once-flourishing cocoa economy, back to life using traditional cocoa-farming techniques; that he was processing the beans the old way too, including the traditional polishing with bare feet, called "dancing the cocoa." But when we arrive, the estate has a shaggy, disheveled, neglected look: lush but overgrown, cocoa pods rotting on the trees, the cocoa-drying house ramshackle. "It all comes back to labor," he tells us. "When the oil boom came, everybody dropped their tools."

His accent, attitude and overall look immediately mark him as a Trinbagonian who has spent time in the States. He was born in New York, he confirms, and served in the U.S. military. "People didn't like me here when I returned—I was young, energetic and had the most land." It probably didn't help that he continued to wear his military fatigues—"they called me Soldier"—or that he evicted locals who had taken to squatting on the estate in his absence. His father had purchased it in the 1960s—"he was a ship's captain but farming was his thing"— and when he died, David inherited a cocoa plantation that couldn't sustain itself. To hear him tell it, he has been thwarted at every turn in his attempts not only to get the estate producing again, but also to turn it into an eco-tourist attraction: plagued by problems with workers, neighbors, the government cocoa board—and parrots.

Cocoa pods are a favorite food of the orange-winged Amazon parrot, and Tobago has an abundant parrot population. In fact, I'd heard that Tobagonians attribute the fecundity and rowdiness of these raucous birds to the beneficial effects of eating cocoa. Unfortunately, when I put the randy-parrot theory to Michel Boccara at the CRU, he shot it down: theobromine, the chemical responsible for the mood-elevating and stimulating effects of cocoa, is in the beans, but the parrots only eat the pulp. Party-pooper.

The government is doing little in the way of parrot population control, David complains, because "tourists love the birds." With more than two hundred different species on the 116-square-mile island, Tobago has the highest concentration of bird species anywhere in the world and, as a result, attracts a lot of bird-watchers. The government isn't going to jeopardize that. As Dr. Butler had put it, "You can't ask the hunters to come out. Tourists don't like people shooting at parrots."

David takes us upstairs in the estate's cocoa house and pushes open its peaked roof, built in sections, on rollers, to show us how the cocoa beans would have been exposed to the sun to dry. Workers continually monitored the sky for signs of rain so that the roof could be rolled closed before the beans got wet. He pulls up a square of floor to show us how the dried beans were shoveled down into the grader, a big, hand-turned metal drum that sorted them by allowing them to drop through holes of varying sizes. Though there's not a bean in the building—

plenty of bat droppings, though—we can easily picture the estate in operation.

Perhaps that will still come. "I think you sent blessing onto me," David e-mails us a few weeks later. "I'm going into a joint venture with a local guy, who is knowledgeable in cocoa, and an Italian company that sells high-end dark chocolates." One of his estate neighbors, meanwhile, has found a successful niche making specialty chocolates from his own crop of organic beans, pairing them with various rums, and offering tastings; and the Trinidad government is under renewed pressure to recognize the potential the country's cocoa offers, and to support the tradition of the small cocoa farmer. Maybe things are beginning to look up.

But we'll have to go elsewhere to see the cocoa danced.

. . .

Sagging under the weight of the bucket he's carrying in each hand, a lone farmer trudges along the road in the direction of Belmont Estate, two-thirds of the way up Grenada's east coast. "A good sign," I tell Steve as we follow him up the hill toward a barnlike wooden building. Scorching sunlight beams into the muted interior through the open door, illuminating a scene from another time: a smattering of farmers standing patiently with buckets of "wet cocoa," the white pulp still clinging to the raw beans, waiting their turn at a time-worn weigh scale. At a small table behind the scale, a woman records the weights—by hand—in an equally worn ledger. At the rear of the barn, another woman is removing the mace from freshly harvested nutmegs, methodically sorting it—by hand, one nutmeg at a time—into three different grades.

A wooden spindle near the door holds ragged, much-handled squares of cardboard with numbers inked on them, though the farmers who've come this morning to sell their cocoa beans to Belmont Estate haven't had to take numbers to establish their turn. However, in prime season, October to May, the line of waiting men would snake through the building, one of the farmers tells us, and it might take him most of the day to sell his beans.

The business of buying cocoa here is excruciatingly low tech. When a farmer's turn comes, he dumps his buckets one by one into a wooden trough, called a sifter, which allows any accumulated liquid from the pulp to drain off before the beans are weighed. While they're draining, a worker picks through them by hand to remove pieces of pod, twigs and other debris— anything that might inflate the weight. Using a piece of board, he then squeegees the beans into an old feed sack, and the farmer pours the next bucket into the trough. When a sack is full, the worker carries it to the scale and calls out the weight to the woman with the ledger. Once all the farmer's cocoa has been sifted and weighed, he is given a handwritten chit, which he then takes to the estate office to receive payment. "Next."

The buying price for wet cocoa today is EC$1.30 per pound (less than US$0.49), a farmer named Kenny tells me. "Dry cocoa pays more"—about EC$3.25/lb—"but you need facilities for that," he says. Kenny has only a few buckets of beans today, each weighing about 50 pounds, but during the height of the season, he says, he brings in more than 6,000 pounds of wet cocoa a month from 11 ½ acres. He manages the land, which is "in the mountains," for its Grenadian owner, a woman who lives in the United States. He and his workers pick the pods on Mondays and Tuesdays. On Wednesday morning, they crack them and remove the beans, which they then bring to the cocoa station.

"What about the rest of the week?" I ask. "That's when we work on the nutmeg, provision, *bluggoes*"—cooking bananas— "and plantains."

Before 2004's Hurricane Ivan, the Belmont station bought about 600,000 pounds of wet cocoa a year from Kenny and three hundred other farmers in the parishes of St. Patrick and St. Andrew. In 2005, it bought only 50,000 pounds. Compared with shallow-rooted nutmeg trees, though, "the cocoa trees come back quickly," Kenny explains. "They lost their leaves, but the trees remained." In 2007, however, Belmont still processed less than half of what it had three years earlier. The decrease can't be laid entirely at Ivan's feet; as in Trinidad, the larger problem is labor. "Someone working cocoa would make $35 (US$13.11) a day," one of the Belmont station's managers tells us, "while the government pays $50 a day for working on the roads"—clearing the fast-growing vegetation that threatens to overwhelm them—"and it's easier than cutting cocoa."

After the beans are weighed, they're fermented in the same building, using techniques that are much the same as they were in the 1800s, when cocoa became a major crop on this three-hundred-year-old estate. The fermenting "equipment" consists of a line of tallish wooden bins (like animal stalls in a barn, but with removable wooden slats across the front), a pile of old sacks, a bunch of banana leaves and a couple of shovels. The wet, pulp-coated cocoa beans are poured in, covered with leaves and sacks, and left to ferment for eight or nine days. During this time, the white pulp liquefies, the bitterness of the beans softens, and their flavor and color develop. Every two days, the beans are "turned," shoveled from one bin to another to ensure even fermentation.

A worker lifts a slat on one of the bins and gestures for us to put a hand close to the beans, which have lost their white pulp and turned a lovely chocolatey brown. It's as if I'm warming in front of a fire; no wonder this process is called "sweating the cocoa."

"It get so hot you have to wear boots or you burn your feet," Dingis had told us, explaining that her daddy fermented the family's cocoa himself. Mr. Mac and his workers would cut the pods from the trees—they attach directly to the trunk and branches via short, tough stems—using long-handled, curve-bladed cocoa knives. Dingis would help crack them open and then carry sacks of the pulp-covered beans on her head back to the house. "Deh liquid drip down on meh face," she says, wrinkling her nose at the memory. "Daddy put deh beans to sweat under deh house. He lay fig leaves"—banana leaves—"on deh ground, pile on deh beans, and cover all over with more fig leaves and cocoa sacks." Every couple of days, one of the family would shuffle through them with booted feet to turn them, or do the job with a wooden board.

After fermenting, the beans are put in the sun to dry—at Belmont, on wheeled flatbed wagons that ride on rails, which means they can quickly be rolled back under cover when rain threatens. Every half hour, the woman we'd earlier seen sorting mace slips off her sandals and climbs into the wagons to "walk the cocoa," methodically stirring the beans with her feet so they dry evenly in the sun. "Why don't we use a machine to do this?" a Belmont Estate worker asks a group of Grenadian school kids who have come to watch the process. When the kids don't respond, he explains: "Because they would dry too fast, which robs the flavor," an answer that Darin Sukha would approve. But then he continues: "But the main reason is that sunlight is free." Obviously, human labor comes cheap here too.

"We didn't have carts," Dingis said. "You know deh balisier I show you in deh country? We used deh tree"—not really a tree but, like its relative, the banana, a plant with a thick, fibrous stem—"to make mats, and then we spread deh beans on deh mats to dry." When it rained, they could drag the mats under the house. "Or we use galvanize. You could bend up deh ends of deh galvanize and pour deh beans into a bucket. You know how you tell when they dry? You rub them in your hands and they go, 'crip, crip.'"

Dingis's family didn't dance the cocoa; they polished the beans with their hands, she said, as Mr. Mac believed this was less likely to damage them.

I'd been hoping—finally—to see people dancing the cocoa at Belmont: the beans poured into a big "copper" (a pot maybe four feet in diameter), then a bit of water and two or three people added in. Following tradition, drums would be played, singing would start, and the workers would dance in the pot, the movement of their feet polishing the beans—a laborious process that could take as long as four hours. But, ironically, polishing is the one phase of the operation that's been mechanized here. We're not going to see anyone dance.

. . .

Just up the road from Belmont Estate is the Grenada Chocolate Company. "Good, you don't smell," Mott Green says to us almost as soon as we step into his small, two-story candy box of a factory in the village of Hermitage. A patchwork of tropical blue, pale green and hibiscus pink, it has stylized painted cocoa pods snaking across its veranda, and a garden of solar panels rising like flat-topped trees out front. I had forgotten— fortunately, it seems—to put on my usual body unguents and perfume in our crack-of-dawn hurry to leave *Receta,* and

Steve's token swipe of deodorant goes undetected. Because if Mott had caught a whiff of us, he wasn't going to let us get anywhere near his chocolate.

Mott is one of the three founders—two Americans, one Grenadian—of this small-scale, organic, fine-chocolate-making company, the first of its kind in the Caribbean. For starters, it is producing chocolate where the cocoa grows, a rarity in the islands (and in other cocoa-growing regions). In addition, Mott and his partners have—radically—brought cocoa farmers into the business: the small Grenada Organic Cocoa Farmers Cooperative (five members, five more pending) owns 20 percent of the company. Essentially, they've united both ends of the chocolate-making process, with the goal of turning cocoa farming into a less-marginal occupation while ensuring the quality of their main ingredient. Brilliant, and a concept that is now spreading to other Caribbean islands, such as St. Lucia, where the U.K. chocolatier Hotel Chocolat has also started working with local cocoa farmers, is bringing an old cocoa estate back to life, and hopes to have a chocolate factory running on it in a few years.

A lean, wiry, close-cropped, type double-A, speed-talking, full-of-nervous-energy ex–New Yorker, Mott tells us chocolate is very sensitive to picking up other scents and flavors. His employees aren't permitted to wear perfume, cologne, deodorant or insect repellent—a workplace rule, he admits, to which some people find it hard to adjust. This is the Tropics, after all, and people are bound to get a little ripe in the course of a day's work.

The man is constantly in motion as he talks: shoveling beans into the roaster; dashing outside to talk to someone on the road; pouring roasted beans onto a screened table to cool (first popping one in his mouth and crunching it—"I need to taste the cocoa to know when to stop the roast," he says, offering us each a bean); charging off to find a tool to loosen a hockey puck of cocoa from a cocoa-butter press; moving the cooled beans into the antique winnower (where they are shelled and cracked); having a stand-up confab with a sales rep from a packaging company who's come all the way from Trinidad for an appointment (apparently forgotten by Mott; three minutes later, she's on her way again)—before he rushes to his car and speeds off to meet an inspector who's making his annual visit to recertify the company's products as completely organic. Mott is not someone who needs chocolate for energy.

Meanwhile, we feel like kids in the proverbial candy store: there's chocolate in some form everywhere we turn, and with each breath we're inhaling its thick, mouthwatering scent. At first, I'm mesmerized by the *melangeur*, which looks like two steam rollers at work in a bathtub of molten chocolate. It first grinds the nibs, the shelled bits of cocoa bean, to a thick liquid—called the cocoa or chocolate liquor, the same stuff that forms the basis of Darin's tastings in Trinidad—and then regrinds the mixture with sugar into a luscious-looking paste. "It's starting to taste like chocolate at this point, but it's gritty," Mott says. But then I see the "dosing" machine, where one young local guy—just about everyone employed here comes from Hermitage, and the odd exception comes from the next village up the road—fills two-bar molds with a stream of dark chocolate. After he's filled the mold with a flourish, he taps it to settle the chocolate, weighs it, moves it to a wooden rack to harden, and picks up another two-bar mold. It's hard to believe the company has a container of seventy thousand chocolate bars, all made the same laborious way, ready to ship to the United States, its first exports.

Most of the machines here are either antiques that have been meticulously restored and converted to work on solar power, or contraptions that Mott and his partners have invented to fill their needs—like the Rube Goldbergian cocoa-butter press, which squeezes the fat from the liquor—we can see it dripping into a bowl beneath—leaving behind a hockey puck of cocoa powder. (The presses remove only 50 percent of the cocoa butter, which is why the cocoa powder made here is so rich.) Some of the cocoa butter is added back to enrich the chocolate; the rest is sold locally, a popular skin cream.

Mott and the CRU's Darin speak the same language. After explaining that the variety of Trinitario cocoa grown in Grenada—the same variety that's grown in Trinidad—tastes different here because the soil and climate are different, Mott describes the taste of his Grenadian cocoa as "more dry-fruit raisiny than fresh notes, a browner, more chocolatey flavor." And he concurs with Darin on the importance to flavor of the fermenting and drying processes—"as important to chocolate as how grapes are fermented is to wine." Though the Grenada Chocolate Company buys all the beans grown on three hundred certified-organic acres of Belmont Estate, which is one of the Cooperative's members, they are not fermented and dried there: the company has its own fermentary, about a mile away in the mountains north of Hermitage. The processes used are the traditional ones, same as at Belmont Estate—except that the beans go into a dehumidified storage area afterward.

No dancing the cocoa here either, however. In fact, Mott doesn't even polish the beans by machine, believing (like the folks at Belmont) that it simply makes them look pretty for export. And since he's in the business of making chocolate, not selling beans, he skips the polishing entirely. "Some people say it gets rid of insect eggs that become an issue in storage—there is a terrific problem with cocoa moths—but others, like me, say we have better roasting now to take care of that."

We have a wallet-debilitating weakness for the Grenada Chocolate Company's 71-percent-cocoa chocolate bar. Steve, who now considers himself an expert, if only slightly experienced, chocolate taster, tells Mott he thinks he's picked up on a change in flavor recently—a change for the better: "The chocolate seems richer, and the raisin taste more pronounced." As I gape—peeved that my husband's palate is more sensitive than mine—Mott agrees: after Ivan, he explains, they had to buy beans from Costa Rica to make up the shortfall, blending them with whatever Grenadian beans the hurricane had left behind. Now that more trees are bearing again, "we're weaning off the Costa Rican beans. The chocolate is better now because we're back to near 100-percent Grenadian cocoa."

Dingis, like many islanders, has never tasted real chocolate made from beans grown on her island. In Grenada—and the rest of the cocoa-growing West Indies—after the best-quality cocoa beans are sold, the ones left over are used locally to make cocoa balls or sticks, not chocolate. "We parch deh beans," she says—except it sounds like "patch," and I'm momentarily confused, until I remember that in St. Lucia we had seen an elderly woman roasting cocoa beans in an iron pot over an open fire. "Then we break away deh shells and let deh air carry away deh bits of straw"—winnowing them by hand by pouring them from one container to another. "Then we grind them in a mortar with spice [cinnamon], nutmeg and a bay leaf." The soft, unsweetened paste is then rolled by hand into balls, logs or sticks that harden as they sit. The result is gritty and bitter, and not meant to be eaten (or used) like chocolate. Instead, it's usually grated and boiled with water, sugar and milk to make cocoa tea, a popular morning drink and evening snack. To those of us accustomed to sweet, creamy hot chocolate, however, spiced cocoa tea takes some adjustment.

But maybe islanders feel the same about what *we* do to *their* cocoa. Steve brings Dingis a bar of Grenada Chocolate Company chocolate. "What do you think, Dingis?" he asks.

She tries a piece, puckers her face, and gives him a one-word response: "Bitter," she says, firmly refusing a second bite.

· · · SEARED TUNA · · ·
WITH A COCOA CRUST

We met Grenada-born Leslie-Ann Hyacinth on Carriacou, where she cooks at the Green Roof Inn, combining island ingredients with a natural surety for what tastes wonderful. (This is a different Leslie-Ann than our Carriacou pizza- and cake-baking friend.) She introduced us to the idea of using cocoa as the basis of a savory fish rub. When we next bought the wonderful just-caught yellowfin tuna that's usually available in the St. George's, Grenada, fish market (for the hard-to-believe equivalent of US$3 per lb/500 g), I concocted my own spice blend using the Grenada Chocolate Company's rich cocoa powder, as Leslie-Ann does.

4 tsp	pure cocoa powder	20 mL
¼ tsp	cayenne	1 mL
½ tsp	salt	2 mL
½ tsp	freshly ground black pepper	2 mL
½ tsp	cumin	2 mL
⅛ tsp	cinnamon	0.5 mL
⅛ tsp	mace	0.5 mL
1 tsp	demerara or brown sugar	5 mL
4 tsp	olive oil	20 mL
1 ½ lb	sushi-grade tuna, about	
	1 to 1 ½ inches (2.5 to 4 cm) thick	750 g

1. Combine cocoa, spices and sugar.
2. Rub fish with about 2 tsp (10 mL) of the oil. Sprinkle with the spice mixture on all sides, and rub to distribute evenly.
3. Heat a frying pan until it smokes. Add just enough of the remaining olive oil to cover the bottom of the pan. Using

tongs, carefully place tuna in pan and sear over high heat, about 20 seconds per side for rare.

4. Allow tuna to rest for a couple of minutes. Using a wet knife, cut into generous ¼-inch (5 mm) slices and serve.

Makes 4 servings.

Tips:

- The fish can also be cooked on the grill. Oil grill rack and preheat barbecue to very high—smoking hot. Grill tuna about 1 minute or so per side for rare.
- Try drizzling Passion Fruit–Ginger Sauce (recipe in Chapter 13) around the fish.
- The spice rub is good on other firm fish, too, such as mahi-mahi.

· · · GREEN ROOF INN'S · · · LOCAL-CHOCOLATE CAKE

At the Green Roof Inn on Carriacou, Leslie-Ann Hyacinth makes this dense, almost flourless chocolate cake with local cocoa balls (the type that Dingis uses to make cocoa tea). The same taste can be achieved by using chocolate with a high percentage of cocoa and melting it with spices. Because it's so rich, the cake should be served slightly warm. (Reheat briefly in microwave or oven if you bake it ahead.) It's fabulous with unsweetened whipped cream, or coconut or vanilla ice cream on the side.

¾ cup	butter	175 mL
1	bar (3 ½ oz / 100 g) high-quality 85-percent cocoa (approx) dark chocolate (see Tip, below)	100 g
1	bay leaf	1
½ tsp	ground cinnamon	2 mL
¼ tsp	freshly grated nutmeg	1 mL
1	vanilla pod, slit lengthwise and beans removed (or 1 ½ tsp/7 mL pure vanilla extract)	1
3 tbsp	high-quality cocoa powder	50 mL
2	eggs	2
1 cup	granulated sugar	250 mL
⅔ cup	all-purpose flour	150 mL

1. Preheat oven to 325°F (160°C) and line the bottom of an 8-inch (2 L) round cake pan with parchment paper.
2. In a medium-sized pot, combine butter, chocolate, spices, and vanilla beans or extract. Melt over low heat.

3. Stir in cocoa powder. Remove pot from heat and allow to cool. Remove bay leaf from cooled chocolate.

4. Whisk eggs and sugar into cooled chocolate mixture until smooth. Add flour, whisking until blended.

5. Pour batter into prepared pan and bake in preheated oven for 20 to 22 minutes until center is just set. For a firmer cake, bake 5 minutes longer.

6. Serve warm with softly whipped unsweetened cream or ice cream on the side.

Makes 8 to 10 servings.

Tip:

• Grenadian cocoa balls are available online. To use them in this recipe, omit the bay leaf, cinnamon and nutmeg, and replace the dark chocolate with 3 ½ oz (100 g) of cocoa balls.

· · · COCOA TEA · · ·

This spicy breakfast and nighttime drink is a grown-up's hot choco-late. "You have a cup and you sleep real well," a St. George's market lady told my friend Devi when she explained how to make it. Grenadian cocoa balls already contain spices, so you can omit them—but I add them for extra flavor, as some of the locals do.

I	cocoa ball (or 2 ½ tbsp/37 mL pure cocoa powder)	I
2 cups	water	500 mL
I	bay leaf	I
¼ tsp	freshly grated nutmeg	1 mL
I	cinnamon stick	I
I cup	evaporated or regular milk, heated	250 mL
2 tsp	sugar, or to taste	10 mL

1. Grate the cocoa ball or sprinkle the cocoa powder into the water. Add the spices and bring to a boil. Cover, reduce heat, and simmer for 5 minutes if using cocoa ball, about 10 minutes if using cocoa powder.
2. Strain the cocoa tea. Stir in warm milk and sugar. Taste, and sweeten more if desired.

Makes 2 servings.

Tips:
- Add another note of spice by sweetening the tea with vanilla sugar. (See the recipe in Chapter 16.)
- Grenadians sometimes use sweetened condensed milk in their cocoa tea instead of sugar.

ELEVEN

Snow on the Mountains, Christmas on the Way

· · · GRENADA, TRINIDAD, CARRIACOU · · · & THE GRENADINES

Bring out the mauby, ginger and ice.

Pour out the sorrel boiled up with spice.

It's Christmas! It's Christmas!

from UP! BEAT! drums *by Carver Milton Scobie, 1973*

"BRING A BUCKET," Dwight says as he and Stevie gently maneuver *Rake and Scrape* alongside *Receta* on an early December afternoon after our arrival back from Trinidad. "Do you want a fish?" While Steve is saying, "Great," Dwight is plopping an actively disgruntled 2-pound lobster into the bucket. He then adds a dinner-for-two fish—"a grass grouper, we call it." We're always concerned about taking away from their livelihood. And two offerings? But a glance into their boat reassures us they've had a very good day.

"When deh moon cut," says Stevie, allowing me to picture

perfectly the slice that hung like a hammock in last night's sky, "deh current not so strong and deh fishing good." They always make connections for us between the moon, tides, weather and the rest of the natural world—showing a sensitivity and an expressiveness that continue to surprise us. These are supposed to be rough-and-ready fishermen, after all, not literary types.

Recently, they stopped by and reported the fishing terrible, due to a combination of a particularly low tide and particularly rough seas. As the waves crashed and foamed against the jagged tops of the tide-exposed reefs protecting the Hog Island anchorage, Dwight said, "See, Steve, the reef cleaning its teeth." And then, pointing between the squall-blackened sky and the froth of whitecaps underneath, "It coffee and milk," Stevie said.

Despite the harshness of their livelihood (maybe in part because of the careful observation it demands), Dwight and Stevie can still see their island with the eyes of someone seeing it fresh, for the first time. "Look how beautiful it is," Dwight says, pointing to the late-afternoon light on the hills above Lower Woburn. "Why would I ever want to leave here?"

Now, with the guys lounging in the cockpit and powering through a platter of peanut-butter cookies, I return to the moon. "It will be full on December twenty-fourth," I say, anticipating that this will be the prelude to a quick refresher on the relationship between lambi and lunar cycles. I can't remember what they told me several full moons ago: is that when the lambi "bury in the sand" and are hard to find . . . or is it when "they walk on the sea bottom" and the pickings are easy? I'm hoping it's the latter: some lambi would be nice for Christmas Eve.

But Stevie surprises me. "Den we have beautiful moonlight for Christmas," he says with wistful anticipation in his voice.

Despite the absence of the cues we're accustomed to—the cold, the carols, the whiff of fresh-cut evergreen, the manufactured consumer madness—Christmas is definitely in the air. It was already officially in the steamy air of Trinidad weeks ago, when Miss Pat put her fruit to soak in rum for her black cake. ("Don't worry, darlin', I'll make you one when you come back for Carnival," she told Steve.) It gets its name from the caramelized-until-almost-black sugar that's added to the batter, along with copious currants, raisins and prunes. Deeply alcoholic thanks to generous amounts of brandy and rum, black cake is synonymous with Christmas in the Caribbean, and recipes are closely guarded secrets. Each family is certain theirs is the best, and they confirm it anew each year when they make their Christmas rounds and sample their neighbors' versions with a little glass of *ponche de crème,* the seriously overproof island version of eggnog.

Meanwhile, Steve—who generally avoids Christmas music like the plague—was organizing outings in Trinidad to hear it performed live. "There's a big difference," he snorted when I pointed out his double standard. "This is parang." Which, he might have added, is about as similar to the standard overdone carol as smooth, rich black cake is to the standard-issue fruitcake that also used to set his teeth on edge back home.

Parang is a traditional folk music that tells the Christmas story in Spanish, possibly introduced to Trinidad by Venezuelans imported to work on the cocoa estates in the late nineteenth century. In its purest contemporary form, parang is the Trini equivalent of "O Holy Night" on speed, a dozen or more *paranderos* singing and quick-strumming guitars, mandolins, distinctive small four-stringed cuatros, and box basses; it's "Away in a Manger" with maracas, claves and an up-tempo

Latin beat; it's fast, furious, festive. But the Trinis have also blended parang with soca, to create soca parang, with a soul-calypso-Latin beat, a more secular storyline, and lyrics mostly in English. (Think Santa and Frosty with their heat dialed to molten and suddenly endowed with island rhythm.) Traditionally, paranderos would move from house to house, serenading the inhabitants—the word *parang* derives from the Spanish *parranda*, meaning merry-making or out on the town— in exchange for food and drink. No guavaberry liqueur was involved here; plain rum, ponche de crème, and sorrel wine were traditional.

The door-to-door aspect has mostly given way to public per-formances: part concert, part dance, part food-and-drink-infused lime. *I don't want a manicou / Keep your callaloo / Ah want a piece ah pork for meh Christmas*, sings Scrunter in what is perhaps Trinidad's best-known (and most filled with double-entendre) soca parang song, "Piece ah Pork." Parang is cer-tainly many pig's feet away from the carol singalongs Steve so unfondly remembers from his childhood.

By November, the leaves of the poinsettias were already turning a festive red, enflaming full-size bushes and decorating the landscape as effectively as strings of colored lights. "And pretty soon you'll see snow on the mountains," Veronica had said in Paramin. We did a double take—but then caught on: the snow-on-the-mountain shrubs (*Euphorbia articulata*, also called snow poinsettia and Christmas bush) burst into luxuriant masses of tiny delicate white blossoms at this time of year, blan-keting hillsides in tropical snow. The golden girls were already at work on their Christmas specialties when we visited— Veronica, her ruby-red sorrel wine; Jean, her *pastelles:* rectan-gles of cornmeal dough stuffed with spiced meat, wrapped inside festive green banana leaves, pressed flat like perfect little padded envelopes, and tied closed with colored string. Like parang, pastelles point up the Spanish influence in Trinidad; they're similar to South American *hallacas,* Puerto Rican *pasteles* and Mexican *tamales.* Jean insisted on giving us a few to take home, some tied with red string and some with blue. They looked like Christmas packages, begging to be opened. "The ones with red string contain peppah," she warned.

"I guess we should wait until Christmas to eat them," I told Steve, but my voice lacked conviction. "Not a chance," he said. "What if *Receta*'s freezer has a meltdown and they spoil?" So we steamed them briefly over boiling water as Jean had said, and untied the blue-stringed ones first. Each bite combined the roasted-corn flavor of polenta, which had been given a hint of sweetness from its banana-leaf wrapper, with a sweet-and-savory richness from the mixture of minced meat, raisins, olives, capers and herbs (all the usual Paramin suspects: cive, thyme, pimentos, garlic and onion). The red-stringed ones were very different, substituting Paramin pepper heat for sweet—and equally popular on *Receta.*

. . .

Back in Grenada, Stevie's mention of Christmas moonlight, however, turns Dwight uncharacteristically melancholy. "My lady away for Christmas this year," he reminds us. Glenis is going to the United States to stay with relatives through the birth of her and Dwight's first child together. He usually lights up when his forthcoming son is mentioned, but not today. "That means no Christmas baking, no sorrel," he says mournfully, thinking (so like Dwight) of his stomach.

It's hard to imagine a drink that could look more like Christmas than sorrel. A glass of it gleams like an old-fashioned ruby-red tree ornament, like a jewel with light shining through it. Conveniently, the sorrel plant blooms just before the holiday. When the petals wither, the red sepals (the part of the plant that protects the seed) are left behind, becoming fleshy and succulent; and these are picked to make the drink. This sorrel, also called hibiscus, is not to be confused with either the showy, worn-behind-the-ear garden flower (it's a different species of the genus *Hibiscus*) or with common sorrel (a different family entirely), whose tangy, spinach-like leaves are destined for salads and soups. I'd already been thinking our own Caribbean Christmas wouldn't be complete without sorrel to drink, and I want to give making it a try.

The instructions from our fishermen friends are as succinct as usual. And as specific. "You just boil the sorrel," Dwight says. "Jus' boil deh sorrel," echoes Stevie.

"But I thought I had to remove some part of it first?"

"Ahhnnnn, no," Dwight replies emphatically. "You just boil it."

Stevie leaps in: "Dwight, no, you just boil deh red part. You pull out deh pod and deh seeds and t'row dem away. Unless you want to plant dem."

"No." Dwight again. "She buy it in the market already clean."

The problem is, I haven't yet seen any sorrel, cleaned or uncleaned, in the St. George's market.

"What time you go?" Dwight asks. I tell him we're usually there mid-morning. "Too late. I there at five-thirty. I bring you some sorrel tomorrow, please the Lord."

"I remind him," says Stevie.

. . .

Sorrel in the market isn't the only thing in Grenada heralding the arrival of the holiday season. In the countryside, the bamboo cannons are booming.

"Kimon goin' to show you how we buss'"—burst—"deh bamboo," Dingis says while we are visiting her father, Mr. Mac. Rural island boys apparently take to this seasonal ritual—which involves turning a stout length of bamboo into a 6-foot-long, kerosene-fueled Christmas cracker—as naturally as their northern counterparts do to throwing snowballs at passing cars. "You can hear deh loud blasts at night—boom, boom, boom— from all deh villages," Dingis says. "Dey mean Christmas on deh way. It very exciting—you'll see." And with that, eleven-year-old Kimon heads off with a couple of other village boys to get things ready.

By the time Dingis, Steve and I arrive at the bamboo-bussin' location, a hollow trunk of dry bamboo about 6 inches in diameter has been braced between cinder blocks at a slight upward tilt—a very efficient-looking cannon—and the boys are pouring a disconcertingly lavish amount of kerosene into the "ignition hole" they've bored near its lower end. Now they begin taking turns holding a lighted flambeau over the hole and, with mouth close to hole, blowing the flame into the bamboo to warm up the air inside and ignite the kerosene. As the hot air expands, the theory goes, it's noisily blown out the home-made cannon's barrel.

We lounge against a wall a few feet away, chatting, and wait. And wait some more. As the lighting and blowing continue, I am lulled into thinking this is a very overblown entertainment. And then suddenly, the thing goes—bloody booming like a giant firecracker exploding within arm's reach—and I leap into the air, caught unawares, much to everyone's delight.

Only afterward do I learn that bamboo-bussers sometimes have their eyebrows singed and hair restyled (or worse) when a "backfire" suddenly shoots out the ignition hole. Several successful booms later, our ears are ringing, but the boys are still intact.

. . .

My alarm clock right on time, Dwight and Stevie roar up on their way to sea, slowing down only long enough to pass me a bag of what look like shiny, waxy, unopened red rosebuds. "Ahhnnnn, here the sorrel. We see you later, please the Lord." I decide to tackle it right away, figuring they can critique my efforts when they stop by after fishing.

Sorrel is such a popular Christmas drink that it turned out to be easy to find a detailed recipe, or two, or three, or four, or five. Unfortunately, however, none of my cookbooks agree on which spices I should "boil deh sorrel" with, and even when they do agree on a spice, they certainly don't agree on the quantity. One recipe recommends six allspice berries; another, which starts with a third less sorrel, advises twelve; still another, none at all. Ten whole cloves, six cloves, half a teaspoon, or none? Almost all of them call for "spice" (cinnamon stick), but a few also suggest a bay leaf (or two), an inch of grated ginger (or more), or a strip (or so) of orange (or lime) peel. I decide to compromise—this isn't a recipe, it's a negotiation—and split the differences. I pour boiling water over sepals and spices, and allow the brew to steep for several hours, then strain it and sweeten with sugar.

Not one of the recipes warned me against boiling sorrel while wearing a white tee. By the time I've steeped, strained and bottled a couple of quarts, my countertop, stove, pots, assorted implements, and I are festively blotched with red. On the upside, the mulled spices have given *Receta* the smell of Christmas.

"This is good," says Dwight that afternoon. "Real good," says Stevie.

It *is* good—floral, fruity ("raspberry like," says Steve of the sensitive palate), gently spiced . . . and just a bit tart. Too tart to be authentically Grenadian, I eventually learn when I probe a bit deeper, and Dwight pours in a hefty additional slug of sugar syrup from the requested jug.

"It build up the blood, you know," he says. Whether that's folk medicine or simply folklore, no one would ever accuse this blood-red drink of looking anemic.

The sorrel can also be made into wine—Veronica does this—fermented to make an alcoholic liqueur (along the lines of guavaberry), or stewed into jam or jelly. Or one can simply take the advice of the St. George's market lady who sells me my next bag of sorrel. "It's very good mixed with rum, you know."

. . .

A couple of days before Christmas, we hike up the hill to deliver gifts to our Lower Woburn friends. After we exchange hugs and kisses hello as always, Steve reads the tags as he pulls the wrapped packages out of our duffel bag: "Gennel . . . Bici . . . Lynn . . . Desiann . . . Dannyboy . . . Oh, no, nothing here for Dingis," he jokes.

"That okay, it deh love that matters," she replies, and we are truly touched.

Hers, the largest and heaviest package, is at the very bottom: a pressure cooker, to replace the one that Ivan "mash up."

Though we don't know quiet Gail well, we have also

included a small gift for her, since she's usually part of the goings-on in this household. She's off on an errand when Steve pulls it out of the bag.

"Dis is deh first Christmas Gail have a present to open," Dingis says. Steve and I are speechless. What had been a casual gesture on our part turns out to have real meaning and, once again, we are sharply reminded of how hard life can be in "paradise." We count our blessings.

I've brought them some Christmas baking—a ginger cake, because I'd caught Dingis snacking approvingly on the one I'd made for Mr. Mac—and, proudly, a bottle of my sorrel.

The next day Dingis delivers me the ultimate Christmas present when she tells Steve: "Ahhnnnn boil sorrel better than most Grenadians." Hey, maybe I *was* born in General Hospital.

. . .

Receta's Christmas tree is hung over her cabin table with care, a 12-inch-high foldout of green, gold, silver and red metallic paper that we had bought in Grenada on our first voyage through the islands almost a decade earlier. You don't get any closer to an artificial tree than this—but my nod to fresh Christmas greenery comes from some small branches tucked under the canvas rain dodger that protects our cockpit, which waft a spicy fragrance whenever I pass and crush a leaf: a combo of nutmeg, cloves, black pepper and cinnamon.

We'd picked the leaves when we bused, hiked and ultimately hitched our way to Laura Land, a hilly area high above Grenada's southeast coast. This is where the Minor Spices Cooperative, and the Laura Herb and Spice Garden associated with it, are located. Farmers bring their cloves, cinnamon and other "minor" spices (meaning other than nutmegs) to the cooperative, which buys and processes them along the same lines as the stations for cocoa and nutmeg we've visited elsewhere on the island.

It wasn't until after we got off the bus at a crossroads with an arrowed sign that we realized there were still several uphill miles between us and the gardens. (This was shaping up to be a pretty convoluted excursion to buy a few packets of spices for holiday gifts.) As we started walking the road, climbing toward a ridge, the hillsides—vibrantly green again, now that we are almost a month into the rainy season—were sprinkled with middle-class houses, and hammers rang out from new construction. People waved and called "good afternoon." Everyone was out, busily sprucing up their homes—slapping a fresh coat of paint on exterior walls, laying out freshly washed curtains on bushes to dry; in the West Indies, a pre-Christmas freshening is the equivalent of my mother's annual spring cleaning. Just as we were walking up a good sweat, a Grenadian kindly gave us a ride in his jeep, dropping us at the end of the long, tree-lined side road leading to our destination. Curiously, with not a house in sight now, I caught the smell of Christmas baking.

It came from the trees: allspice, we learned once we finally reached the gardens. Though the dried berries are the part of the tree that's used as a spice, the fresh leaves echo their flavor when crushed—a sensuous blend of nutmeg, cinnamon, cloves and black pepper; some noses (no names mentioned) pick up a subtle ginger aroma as well. The combination of scents, and the name, sometimes leads the uninitiated to assume ground allspice is a spice mix, rather than a single spice. Jamaica has a monopoly on the world's supply, producing about 90 percent, but Grenada grows the remainder—most of it here, in Laura Land.

The tree is native only to the West Indies and Central

America, and was unknown in Europe until the Spanish (who discovered it growing in Jamaica) brought it home, where it immediately became popular. They called it *pimienta de Jamaica*—Jamaican pepper—because of its resemblance to black peppercorns, which is how it comes by its other name, *pimento*. Well before the conquistadores arrived, the Amerindians were using it as a seasoning and preservative. Père Labat, a French priest who was posted to the West Indies between 1693 and 1705 and meticulously recorded the events of his daily life, described in lavish detail a barbecue he organized for a buccaneer-style picnic in the woods of Martinique. (His memoirs reveal the priest was quite fond of food and drink.) Père Labat's barbecue featured a *"cochon boucanné,"* barbecued pig, prepared following the techniques of the Amerindians. We have the Arawaks to thank for barbecuing: they cooked their meat on a *barbacoa,* a latticework of green sticks above an open fire. "The belly of the pig must be filled with lime juice and plenty of salt and crushed pimento," Père Labat wrote. "For though pork is excellent and more tender in America than in any other country, these additions are necessary to make it really succulent." Additional calabashes of pimento—allspice—lime juice, pepper and salt were placed on the table, "and from there each guest mixes his gravy according to his taste."

Well, I'm not planning barbecued pig for Christmas, but I do need some dried allspice for baking, and for my sorrel, of course. This year's berries have already been harvested, according to the young woman who showed us around. They're picked when green, and then dried in the sun before being sold whole or ground to a powder. Though she generally lacked enthusiasm for this (or any other) spice, she was decidedly more excited—and forthcoming—about leaving the berries on the tree until they ripen. "When they ripe and turn red, then you can make wine," she said. "Sweeten water, add 1 ounce of yeast, put in the berries, and twenty-one days later, it's ready to drink."

It's equally unlikely we'll brew up the other beverage from the allspice tree: a medicinal tea steeped from the leaves—excellent, we're told, for taking care of colds and flu. But we haven't suffered from either of those ailments since we've been living in the islands. The leaves we picked along the roadside as we left the garden were destined only for sweet-smelling Christmas decor.

. . .

Given Dwight's reputation, Steve suggests the following tag for his edible gift: *DO NOT OPEN BEFORE CHRISTMAS*, it says, and, *WE'RE NOT KIDDING*. The afternoon of Christmas Eve, having taken possession of his package (and merely laughing at its tag), the human vacuum himself is watching me at work in the galley. He's meeting friends on Hog Island, and they're hoping to shoot a wild goat for Christmas dinner. Christmas means a break from fish as well as fishing, and wild meat—especially manicou—is popular, and in season. But Dwight is in no hurry to leave. Unfortunately. Because I—now completely adapted to GMT—am running seriously late. Heather and Don, also back at anchor behind Hog Island, are hosting a Christmas Eve gathering on *Asseance,* and I'm just starting to cut up lambi—a gift from Dwight and Stevie the day before—into minuscule bits to make fritters for the party. (Yes, the lambi are indeed out walking on the sea bottom now.)

Dwight's watchful eyes are making me nervous. "Ahhnnnn," he begins mournfully, and I know what's coming: either he doesn't approve of the way I'm handling the knife or he's spotted the stiffly beaten egg whites—definitely not part of Grenadian cooking—into which I'll be folding the lambi bits. But it's worse than that. "You didn't pong the lambi, like I tell you," he says, shaking his head with disappointment. I didn't think I had to—surely cutting it into minuscule bits would have the same effect. (It's what Bahamians do, after all, when they make a raw conch salad.)

"Ahhnnnn, no, it swell up when you cook it." Meaning the itty bits are going to get bigger, and my fritters are going to be tough.

Dwight finally off to the hunt, Steve is rhyming off a list: "Sorrel and rum? Sorrel wine? Our guavaberry collection? Saba Spice? Ginger beer?" He wants to take an appropriately festive drink to *Asseance*—though I suspect he's also trying to do some of his own Christmas housecleaning at the same time. *Receta*'s bottle collection, according to Steve, is threatening to sink the boat. "Whatever you like," I tell him. "Except there's no more ginger beer." Non-alcoholic ginger beer, ginger ale's spicy, extroverted cousin, used to be a made-only-at-Christmas treat, since ginger root is plentiful in kitchen gardens "come November-time," as a Kayak put it, giving this "root" beer time to develop its flavor before the holidays. Though commercially made ginger beer is available year-round now even in the smallest island shops, absolutely nothing beats homemade: deeply gingery—even peppery—especially when sweetened much less than Dwight and Stevie would approve. Steve finished off my homemade ginger beer weeks ago.

That night, on *Asseance*, nobody complains about a little toughness in the fritters, or anything else, for that matter. "To the luckiest people in the world," Steve says, raising a glass of sorrel in a holiday toast.

. . .

The last day of the year delivers another gift. Immediately after Christmas, we leave Grenada to sail north for a few weeks before shooting back down to Trinidad for Carnival. Our first stop is Carriacou, where we have unfinished business. Having watched the *Margeta-O II* being built, blessed, and baptized, it seems only right that we complete the circle: we've arranged for Uncle C to take us sailing on the last day of December— the day of Old Year's Night. Usually, Uncle C is out fishing on her—often for five or six days at a stretch—but when he's not, he takes passengers on day trips to nearby islands.

Six months after her launch, the *Margeta-O II* looks at the same time weathered and unfinished. The paint on her deck is already worn thin from salt and hard use; but beyond a portable cooler wedged on the side deck, no frills have been added since we saw her in the boatyard. A small wooden dinghy and an anchor occupy the foredeck. Passengers sit right on the aft deck, sliding to the upwind side on our backsides when the boat tacks. However, from the moment Uncle C gives the nod for his second-eldest son, Dean, and the other crew member, David, to raise the sails and release the *Margeta-O II* from her mooring off the beach in Windward, she starts to show us what a sweet, sweet boat she is.

"If we catch a barracuda, I get half and you get half," Uncle C says, as he silkily skins the channel markers and clears the reef, and Dean runs out a hundred feet of wire baited with a silver spoon. We are heading toward the island of Mayreau (part of another country, St. Vincent and the Grenadines, though no one fusses about formalities) and then on to the Tobago Cays (ditto), and the boat is slicing cleanly through the waves, keeping us dry, comfortable and in Uncle C's thrall. From his perch on a very low, three-legged stool, his legs curled under him, he controls the boat with a light finger on the tiller. "So easy a baby could do it," he says, though he doesn't offer to let us try and only rarely relinquishes the tiller even to his crew. "My brother"—Bernard, the shipwright—"put himself into this boat," he says, pounding his hand on his heart. "He said she something special to him."

Just as pleasurable as her speed and sea-kindly motion is the unerring skill with which Uncle C handles her—an easy, unassuming confidence that comes with sailing these reef-strewn waters for more than forty years. "I started as a boy, in a wooden sailing dinghy my mother gave me. I sank it several times, in big waves over reefs and t'ings like dat." Slow to start talking, he becomes more loquacious as the day progresses—helped along, perhaps, by our interest and, later in the day, a small glass or two from a jug in the cooler marked MAGIC ELIXIR.

Mayreau's Saltwhistle Bay is wall-to-wall fiberglass when we arrive, over-packed with anchored boats this time of year, leaving newcomers to jockey for space in the yachting equivalent of a parking lot. It's so crowded that, as we sail in, a fender-bender is in progress among three big charter boats, all with powerful engines to help them maneuver. But Uncle C nonchalantly threads the *Margeta-O II* through the crowd, under sail—he has no engine to assist him—and drops the hook in a prime position, so close to the beach that we have an easy swim to shore. The vacationers on the other boats drop what they're doing and stare in admiration at this anachronistic show of skill. And then they stare again a couple of hours later as we sail just as sweetly out.

"There are many routes through the reefs," says Uncle C, as we enter the Tobago Cays through a route definitely not advised by the guidebook we use on *Receta*. He shows us how he lines up the tip of one island with the notch in the end of another for a straight shot through the reef. The *Margeta-O II* has no electronic gizmos—no GPS, no depth sounder, no radar—to help fix a position or plot a course. At night, Uncle C uses the silhouettes of distant hills, and lights on distant houses. We also don't see a chart on board, but I suspect the picture in Uncle C's brain is at least as detailed as any we could buy. There's not even a compass in evidence, though when I ask, Uncle C says he's got one stowed below.

However, the most prominent feature below decks is a jumble of round, melon-sized boulders—ballast, to supplement the lead in her keel, melted down from old batteries. "How do you know how much ballast to add?" Steve had asked Bernard at the launch, expecting to hear a formula based on length, draft and weight. "Enough until she sits on her lines," he said. "How much does she weigh?" Steve asked. Bernard just gave him a look that said: Does it matter?

Besides the boulders peeking between the floorboards, there's not much else. The boat doesn't have a head, only a unisex bucket—though the guys just go off the bow or stern, depending on which way the wind is blowing; we suggest to Uncle C that if he wants to expand his day-charter business he might want to look into that. There's no galley either, and no electricity: only a couple of rough bunks and a two-burner propane cookstove with a big pot wired in place on top. And while Steve and I eat peanut-butter-and-mango-jam sandwiches and share cookies we've brought from *Receta*, the crew pre- pares their own lunch, cooking up a fish broth with potatoes, okra and small potfish they brought along from home.

We don't land a barracuda—or any fish—either coming or

going. But no matter: Uncle C's sun-creased face breaks into a smile as his wooden, engineless boat with rocks in her hold and stained second-hand canvas on her mast leaves a long, sleek, expensive modern fiberglass yacht in her wake. What better way to close out the year than seeing the yacht's open-mouthed skipper left fruitlessly tweaking his high-tech sails as the *Margeta-O II* blazes by.

· · · *RECETA*'S GINGER BEER · · ·

Don't wait until Christmas to try this drink. It packs a really peppery, almost hot, gingery punch, and it's less sweet than the bottled varieties. The most difficult part of making it is grating a full pound of ginger root.

Ginger beer concentrate:

8 cups	water	2 L
3	cloves	3
1	cinnamon stick	1
1	bay leaf	1
1 lb	fresh ginger root, peeled and grated	500 g
1 cup	lightly packed demerara or dark brown sugar	250 mL
2 tbsp	lime juice (½ large lime)	25 mL

For serving:

Soda water (club soda)
Lime
Coarse (large crystal) cane sugar (optional)
Sugar syrup (see the Tip with the Moonshine Punch recipe in Chapter 5)

1. In a medium-sized saucepan, bring 2 cups (500 mL) water to a boil with the spices. Remove from heat and leave to steep for about 30 minutes.
2. Add remaining 6 cups (1.5 L) water to the grated ginger. Leave to steep for about 30 minutes.
3. Remove spices from the boiled water and stir in sugar. Bring

to a boil, reduce heat and simmer just until sugar has thoroughly dissolved, stirring occasionally.

4. Strain ginger water, squeezing ginger until it is quite dry (to extract all the flavor), then discard.

5. Combine spiced sugar water, ginger water and lime juice. Allow mixture to settle (so sediment sinks to the bottom), then strain through a fine sieve, pour into bottles and refrigerate.

6. When ready to serve, rub the rim of the glass with a wedge of lime and dip into the coarse sugar (if desired). Add ice and ginger beer concentrate until glass is about two-thirds full. Top with soda water, add a squeeze of lime juice and stir. Taste for sweetness and add a bit of sugar syrup if you like.

Makes approximately 2 quarts (2 L) ginger beer concentrate.

Tips:
- Dandy Shandy: Combine equal parts of ginger beer concentrate and a light lager beer (such as Carib, brewed in Trinidad, Grenada and St. Kitts). Add a couple of dashes of Angostura bitters and serve.
- Dark and Stormy: This drink originated in Bermuda, where it is traditionally made with Gosling's Black Seal rum. Combine 2 oz (50 mL) of dark rum with 4 oz (125 mL) of ginger beer concentrate and a splash of soda. Serve with a wedge of lime to squeeze into the drink.

· · · CHOCOLATE-CRAMMED · · ·
CHRISTMAS COOKIES

Dwight's weakness for freshly baked cookies, especially ones involving chocolate, inspired me to include these in his edible Christmas gift. The undertone of coffee enhances the chocolate rush.

2 ½	bars (3 ½ oz / 100 g apiece) high-quality dark chocolate (cocoa content of 65 percent or higher), coarsely chopped	250 g
6 tbsp	unsalted butter	100 mL
3	eggs	3
1 ¼ cups	lightly packed demerara or dark brown sugar	300 mL
⅓ cup	granulated white sugar	75 mL
1 tbsp	instant coffee powder or 2 tsp / 10 mL instant espresso powder	15 mL
½ cup	all-purpose flour	125 mL
½ tsp	baking soda	2 mL
½ tsp	salt	2 mL
¾ cup	chopped pecans or walnuts	175 mL
1 ½ cups	semi-sweet chocolate chips	375 mL

1. In a medium-sized pot, melt dark chocolate and butter over low heat. Set aside to cool.
2. Beat eggs with both types of sugar and coffee or espresso powder.
3. In a separate bowl or on a piece of waxed paper, combine flour, baking soda, salt, nuts and chocolate chips.
4. Pour egg-and-sugar mixture into cooled chocolate. Stir in

dry ingredients. Refrigerate mixture until batter starts to get firm, about 45 to 60 minutes.

5. Preheat oven to 375°F (190°C). Drop batter by heaping tablespoonfuls onto parchment-lined baking sheets. Bake in preheated oven for 6 to 10 minutes,
until tops begin to crack and insides are still fudgy.

6. Cool on baking sheets for 10 minutes or until set, then transfer to racks.

Makes 3 dozen cookies.

· · · SEAFOOD-STUFFED · · ·
COCKTAIL BITES

They aren't traditional Caribbean Christmas fare by any stretch, but these cocktail-sized cream puffs make a great special-occasion hors d'oeuvre. You can vary the filling depending on what's at the market—or what the fishermen bring by.

Cocktail-sized cream puffs:

1 cup	water	250 mL
½ cup	butter	125 mL
¼ tsp	salt	1 mL
1 cup	flour	250 mL
4	eggs	4

Shrimp filling:

1 tbsp	olive oil	15 mL
2 tsp	curry powder	10 mL
⅓ cup	mayonnaise	75 mL
2 tsp	mango chutney	10 mL
1 tsp	grated lime zest	5 mL
2 tbsp	finely chopped chadon beni or cilantro	25 mL
Dash	hot pepper sauce (or to taste)	Dash
	Salt and freshly ground black pepper	
1 lb	cooked shrimp, peeled and chopped	500 g

Lobster filling:

1 tbsp	olive oil	15 mL

1 tsp	curry powder	5 mL
⅓ cup	mayonnaise	75 mL
1 tbsp	diced dried mango	15 mL
1 tsp	fresh lime juice	5 mL
1 tbsp	finely chopped chadon beni	
	or cilantro	15 mL
Dash	hot pepper sauce (or to taste)	Dash
	Salt and freshly ground	
	black pepper	
2 cups	chopped lobster meat	500 mL

To make the cream puffs:

1. Preheat oven to 425°F (220°C). Grease baking sheets or line with parchment paper. In a small, heavy saucepan, heat water, butter and salt to boiling. Reduce heat to medium and beat in flour until mixture pulls away from side of pan and forms a ball (about 1 minute).
2. Allow mixture to cool completely. Then beat in eggs one at a time.
3. Drop small spoonfuls (about 1 tbsp/15 mL) of mixture on prepared baking sheets. Bake in preheated oven for about 15 minutes, then prick each puff once with a skewer to allow steam to escape. Lower temperature to 350°F (180°C) and continue baking for 10 to 12 minutes, or until puffs are golden and dry. Cool completely.

To make the seafood filling:

1. In a small frying pan, heat the oil. Stir in curry powder and cook for a minute or two to release the flavor of the curry. Set aside to cool.
2. In a medium bowl, whisk together curry oil with all

ingredients except the seafood for one of the fillings. Season to taste. Fold in seafood. Refrigerate until serving time.

When ready to serve:
1. Slice cream puffs in half. Put a dollop of filling on the bottom half, and cover with top.

Makes about 4 dozen.

· · · LAMBI FRITTERS · · ·

Though not part of island tradition, beating the egg whites sepa-
rately and folding them in makes the fritters wonderfully light.
When I made a batch for Dwight and Stevie post-Christmas with
some lambi they brought us, the fritters met with unequivocal
approval—and a suggestion that they would be good with lobster.
The next time they dropped a lobster in our bucket, I proved them
right. (See Tip, below.) The fritters (called accras in the French
Antilles) are also delicious made with shrimp.

1 lb	cleaned and tenderized lambi, finely chopped	500 g
2	green onions, finely chopped	2
1 tbsp	chopped fresh thyme (or 1 tsp/ 5 mL dried thyme)	15 mL
1	clove garlic, finely chopped	1
¼ to ½	Scotch bonnet or other hot pepper, finely chopped (or to taste)	¼ to ½
½	small cubanelle or green bell pepper (or 2 seasoning peppers), finely chopped	½
1 tbsp	finely chopped chadon beni or cilantro	15 mL
1 tsp	grated lime zest	5 mL
2 tbsp	fresh lime juice	25 mL
1 ½ cups	all-purpose flour	375 mL
1 tbsp	baking powder	15 mL
1 tsp	salt	5 mL
	Freshly ground black pepper	

4	eggs, separated	4
¼ cup	white wine	50 mL
¼ cup	water	50 mL
	Vegetable oil (for deep frying)	
	Hot pepper sauce (to taste)	

1. Combine lambi with green onions, thyme, garlic, peppers, chadon beni or cilantro, and lime zest and juice.
2. Combine dry ingredients and stir into seafood mixture.
3. Beat egg yolks with wine and water and stir into seafood mixture to form a soft dough.
4. Heat 2 to 3 inches (5 to 8 cm) of oil to 375°F (190°C) in a deep fryer or pot.
5. Beat egg whites until they hold soft peaks. Stir about ⅓ of egg whites into seafood mixture to lighten it, then fold in the rest.
6. Drop batter by tablespoonfuls into hot oil and fry until golden brown on all sides, about 2 to 3 minutes.
7. Drain on paper towels. Serve hot with pepper sauce.

Makes about 2 ½ dozen.

Tip:
- To make lobster fritters, substitute the meat of a 2- to 2 ½-lb (1 to 1.25 kg) steamed lobster, finely chopped. For shrimp fritters, substitute 1 lb (500 g) of cooked shrimp, peeled and finely chopped.

TWELVE

All Ah We Is One

· · · TRINIDAD · · ·

Minister Wants Safe Sex for Carnival
> *headline in Trinidad's* Newsday, *reporting on*
> *Marlene McDonald, Minister of Community Development,*
> *Culture and Gender Affairs, February 1, 2008*

The person who is free of any mental illness may feel depressed from the lack of excitement and the cooling down period [after Carnival]. This type of depression is not a psychiatric syndrome. . . .
> *Trinidadian psychiatrist Dr. Dave Ameerali,*
> *on post-Carnival symptoms, in* Newsday, *February 7, 2008*

THE AIR AROUND PORT OF SPAIN'S Savannah is so heavy you can slice it with a cutlass. Smoke drifts overhead, carrying the scent of jerk chicken charring on barbecues, of corn soup and "boil corn" bubbling in big pots, of bake and shark frying in hot oil. People squeeze past us clutching Styrofoam cups of geera pork or chicken, or souse, an alcohol-absorbing, hangover-reducing concoction of animal feet (and assorted other parts) mixed with spices, lime and hot pepper. The crowd, thick and friendly, flows through the darkness, carrying us along in its embrace. And then the forward movement abruptly stops, as a stick taps a beat: One . . . two . . . one, two, three, four. The crowd shivers in anticipation, and we are suddenly surrounded—no, swallowed—by the sound of a steelpan orchestra, 120 players strong, warming up. We feel the music as much as hear it, pulsing inside us, lifting us up. "Are you enjoying your Carnival?" a stranger shouts over the wall of sound, before the crowd surges forward to another pan band and another tidal wave of music.

A couple of nights later, 15-foot-tall Moko Jumbies cavort in almost the same spot, and Blue Devils breathe fire into the darkness. Held back on chains by the Imps who are their keepers, frothing at their mouths when they're not belching flames from them, the horned beasts lunge frighteningly at passersby. "It's just part of Carnival," another stranger reassures. "Are you enjoying it?"

The Trinis modestly call their annual pre-Lenten bacchanal "the greatest show on Earth." The entire country comes together at Carnival time, differences are forgotten, politics are put on hold, business stops cold. Even crime takes a little holiday. The island is swept into a frenzy, and we newcomers struggle as best we can to hang on for the ride.

. . .

We'd been warned when we were in Trinidad before Christmas that coming back just for Carnival proper—the two days preceding Ash Wednesday—would be a grave mistake. Sure, we'd enjoy it, but it would be kind of like sex without foreplay, to use an analogy that the Trinis would approve. The Carnival season swings into high gear as soon as Christmas is over. And with Carnival falling in early February this year, the Trinis have a scant six weeks for the buildup. "People are vex," one Trini tells us, clearly conveying that he counts himself among them, "vex that Carnival is so early."

"You'll see," someone else promises, "not a lick of work will be done all of January."

By the time *Receta* arrives back in Trinidad a couple of weeks after New Year's, the daily papers are already reporting a dizzying array of events: limes at panyards and calypso tents, outdoor fetes with six or more live performers (and start times that are later than the hour I usually go to bed), and the early rounds of the competitions that will ultimately crown Carnival's king and queen, and the year's calypso and soca monarchs. The preliminary stages of Panorama, the hard-fought competition between pan bands, are soon to follow. "You can sleep after Carnival," Steve says, as we horse-trade over exactly how many late nights in a row I can manage. "You can sleep in the restaurant, on the floor in my old dining room," Miss Pat says, when I ask her advice on which events I shouldn't skip. "That way, you can get a few hours' rest rather than waste time going back to *Receta*." Grossly underestimating the Trini stamina for partying at Carnival time, I decline her invitation, not realizing that we'll get stuck in bumper-to-bumper traffic jams at two in the morning, as people continue to arrive at fetes that last until sunrise.

Eager-as-a-puppy Steve is insistent, however, that we can't just be spectators but have to "play *mas*," masquerading ourselves. But I'm worried that by *playing* mas we'll miss *seeing* mas—specifically, its euphoric climax, Carnival Tuesday's day-long parade featuring tens of thousands of extravagantly (albeit often scantily) costumed masqueraders chipping and wining through the streets of Port of Spain in themed mas bands. We compromise: we'll watch Tuesday's "pretty mas" and play "dirty mas" on J'ouvert Monday. *J'ouvert*—pronounced "joo-vay," a contraction of the French *jour ouvert*—means daybreak, and it is when each year's Carnival officially begins. An American who has been in Trinidad for seven years has a wistful longing in his voice when he describes J'ouvert. "It is incredibly freeing, an incredible release."

Carnival is a license to "play yourself," to ignore what others might think, to let barriers fall. "What happens at Carnival stays at Carnival," our taxi-service-owning friend Jesse says, and it's a mantra we hear repeated by others in the weeks to come.

We sign up with a J'ouvert band, and order our costumes.

. . .

The roots of the island's Carnival lie in both African festivals and European masquerade balls. As they had back home, the French and British upper class in eighteenth-century Trinidad engaged in extravagant feasting and other debaucheries before the deprivations of Lent; the word *Carnival* comes from the Latin *carne vale*, meaning "farewell to the flesh." Although slaves were forbidden from dancing and drumming or engaging in their own religious practices the rest of the year, they could get away with it in the permissive few days before Lent. The slaves also took this opportunity to mimic and mock the pre-Lenten celebrations of their masters. In the process, a cast of traditional Carnival characters developed: human donkeys called Burrokeets, Midnight Robbers, Fancy Sailors, big-breasted Dame Lorraines with exaggerated backsides, Blue

Devils and ones called Jab Jabs, and Moko Jumbies—spirits on sky-high stilts.

Some Trinis lament that these characters have been overwhelmed in recent years by "bikinis and beads," that the meaning in the mas, the masquerade, is slowly being lost—though there are still a few "mas men" whose bands tell multichaptered stories through elaborate themed costumes. For that matter, some lament a general deterioration of Carnival: its commercialization, with the price of tickets and costumes rocketing beyond the range of ordinary people (some take loans to buy costumes and participate in a mas band); shoddy workmanship (some of the big mas bands now outsource much of their costume-making to countries such as China); the stretching of the Carnival season; the erosion of calypso music, which traditionally carries social and political messages in double- or triple-edged lyrics; and the level of licentiousness in public view on the streets. But we weren't here in the good old days, and to our unjaundiced eyes, it is still something wondrous. And we can't get enough.

. . .

"Why we don't commission studies to find ways to harness the Carnival energy into other areas?" a newspaper columnist asks in the morning *Guardian*, writing in dialect, as is her shtick. "What is it about Carnival that does drive we so? Anybody ever ask the question in a systematic way so that we could apply that to, say, secondary school dropout rates? . . . How come we could design them big big costume and put 200 pounds of fiberglass and nylon to balance perfect on a man back but we can't engineer a good road that ent go mash up every rainy season?"

She's got a point: one of the contenders for this year's Carnival King is costumed with an undulating silver fan spreading from his body like a peacock's tail: 38 feet tall, 44 feet wide, twenty thousand individually folded pieces of silver cloth, the whole fabric/foil/fiberglass/aluminum/steel construction weighing 400 pounds, supported only by his body and two wheels. As he dances onstage, the fan spills forward in a silver waterfall that makes the audience gasp and cheer. And he only places second, trumped by a black-and-orange, six-legged, spiral-headed creature—part insect, part apocalypse—played by a completely invisible human walking backward on tall stilts that shoot orange smoke. (Some bands do indeed still put meaning in the mas: this obscene animal—called "Pandemic Rage"—symbolizes the evilness we have unleashed by abusing our planet.) Separate children's events parallel the adult ones, and the costumes are even more staggering, given the size of the bodies that support them. A jellyfish with glistening translucent tentacles completely engulfs the costume's young wearer; a swarm of antennae-waving worker bees surrounds the enormous iridescent wings of a sequin-striped queen bee who's barely eight years old; a stunning beaked bird wears a 12-foot-wide skirt made of hundreds of sequined orange cloth "feathers." And the children's costumes are not allowed to have wheels.

In comparison, the J'ouvert costume I've ordered is positively Spartan: just a flaming-orange tank top with the name of our band across the front and a gauzy matching tie-dyed wrap bottom. I discover only after it's delivered that it's sized and styled for someone with Carnival in her blood. "Nice," leers Steve, when I try it on. "Forget it," I snarl back. The top is circulation-stoppingly tight; the bottom is so teensy it leaves one entire thigh exposed from the hip down—even though I'd followed local advice and ordered a size larger than I usually require. Luckily, I still have a few days to make some modesty modifications.

. . .

The Ministry of Health starts running ads in the papers. "Noise can be DEAFENING around Carnival time," it warns. "Stay well away from speaker boxes, music trucks, steelbands . . ."

Impossible. Who are they kidding? Steve and I have been unwittingly turned into pan jumbies, and we are helpless to stay away. We have become wired on the heart-pulsing, yet impossibly sweet sound of the large steelpan bands. "Large" is an official category: in 2008 it included bands with 95 to 120 players, many of them playing more than one pan; a single bass pan player can be responsible for as many as twelve. A steelband has no other instruments besides pans, except in its "engine room," the assemblage of percussion instruments—scraped, shook and struck—that drives the beat.

Our addiction started in the panyards where the bands rehearse, and became serious on "the drag," the area beyond the Savannah grandstand, where they warm up for the semi-finals of the Panorama competition. "This is where the real energy is, where the real supporters are, not in the seats inside," a stranger tells us with an approving nod. But we help fill the seats inside too—and, not content to watch on TV or listen on the radio, we even travel several hours "to sout'"—to San Fernando, the island's second-largest, and more southern, city—to see the finals live. Here, the bands ratchet up their high-voltage playing even higher, in one last ecstatic, frenzied performance. "D'ere's fire in deh pan," the jumbies around us say, and we are close enough to feel the heat—flaunting government warnings about our eardrums by taking third-row seats. Steve's beloved Trinidad All Stars lose the large-band crown, getting 480 points to Phase II Pan Groove's 481. "One point!" he moans, over and over, as crushed as if he's been a lifelong supporter.

But he's not alone. Steelpan and Panorama are such an important, passion-raising national institution that, in the same way I can remember exactly where I was and what I was doing—arithmetic, in my sixth-grade class—when I heard John F. Kennedy was shot, Trinis can tell you where they were and what they were doing when they heard the All Stars play "Curry Tabanca," their 1987 Panorama song—and, twenty-one years later, they're still talking with disbelief about the band not winning.

. . .

This being Trinidad, no one goes hungry or thirsty at these events. At Panorama, people arrived with coffin-sized coolers, some of them on wheels, and set up complete cocktail-mixing stations next to their seats. At another event, the woman next to me dished up full hot meals for her family, with a dark, fragrant chicken pelau as the entree. Luckily for the peckish and unprepared, food and drinks are sold everywhere—from the panyards to the Savannah grandstand; from peppery pineapple chow to (one stall only) stewed horse.

Among the most popular late-night offerings is steaming-hot corn soup. Served in tall Styrofoam cups, it's an energy drink and full meal in one, packed with chunks of corn on the cob (to be eaten with one's fingers, once they're cool enough to handle), solid corn-flour dumplings, and sweet cubes of pumpkin and other vegetables. The vendors often have plastic squeeze-bottles of pepper sauce and chadon beni sauce at their stations, allowing us to personalize our servings. I take to this soup with a vengeance, as if it were being served at a chilly late-fall football game instead of on a sweaty, sultry tropical night. I even regularly try to bargain extra dumplings from Steve's cup . . . with precious little success.

"Why don't you make your own?" he says. "Then you can have as many dumplings in it as you want." Seeking a little verbal direction from Miss Pat first ("of course I make an excellent corn soup, darlin'"), I take on the challenge. My dumplings puff up like duvets, the broth is orange from too much pumpkin, and the whole thing is so porridgy from too many split peas that we can almost eat it with a fork. It's certainly not Trini, but that doesn't stop us from finishing every last bit. "Maybe you should try again," Steve suggests.

. . .

Pages of Carnival tips have begun appearing in the papers. A list of dos and don'ts advises me to carry condoms, "just in case." When we picked up our J'ouvert costumes, we discovered each of our bags contained half a dozen of them and, hating to be wasteful, I bring them along on our next visit to Miss Pat. She quickly distributes them to her patrons—"You want a condom? Here, have two"—telling us a big box had been sent to the bar a few days earlier, but they're gone: she and Pie handed one out with every beer. Apparently, 66,000 will be distributed free before Carnival ends, in an attempt to thwart the well-documented "Carnival Baby" effect—the annual 15-percent spike in the birth rate nine months later—as well as the spread of HIV/AIDS. The island's adult prevalence rate is disturbingly high: 3.2 percent, compared to 0.3 percent in Canada and 0.6 percent in the United States.

"DO walk with vex money," the list of tips continues. Miss Pat explains: "That's in case you get vexed at the man you come with, then you are free to leave on your own." She advises shoving some vex money under the insole of one of my runners and leaving it there for the duration of Carnival. "And you know to come here, honey, if you need money or any other help."

But vex money is low on my list of Carnival concerns. I'm more worried that Steve and I haven't mastered chipping, the shuffling step done for hours on end to the soca beat during Carnival parades. I've accepted that pelvis-grinding wining is simply beyond the capabilities of a middle-aged woman who didn't get it in her mother's milk, and even further beyond her rhythmically challenged husband. But we simply can't partic-ipate in Carnival without knowing how to chip. "Don't worry, when you hear the music it will move you," Elizabeth at the marina tells us. We've been hearing the music incessantly for weeks—the year's Carnival songs are so all-pervasive that they even dance through my dreams at night now, until exhaustion shuts them down—and I'm still not moving even remotely like a Trini. Meanwhile, when I (reluctantly) raise the subject with Miss Pat, she gives a little shake of her hips and brushes off my concern. "It will come naturally once you're on the road." No one seems to think chipping is some-thing that has to be taught.

But chubby Thompson, who mans the gatehouse at a marine complex across the harbor from our dock, takes pity and offers an impromptu lesson. "One part of the body at a time," he says, breaking the step down for us. "First, get the knees going, don't worry about anything else." Following him, we start our knees flexing back and forth, as if we're warming up lazily for a run. "Okay, now keep the knees going and move your feet—don't lift them up, shuffle forward. That's the way. Now put a little hip into it—side to side, right—and you can add your arms and shoulders." He chips across the parking lot with an agility, grace, rhythm and style that belie his considerable, tightly uniformed bulk. We inelegantly follow. "You got it."

Not precisely, but we certainly have a start. Pleased as two kids who've just got their training wheels, we chip our way back toward *Receta* along the grassy edge of the main road. We'd been warned when we first arrived in Trinidad not to walk this stretch at night, but it's broad daylight and, besides, after several months off and on here, we firmly believe what David Rudder sings about his island: *You could get a beach and the sun, but the heat really come from we* . . . We've yet to be hassled anywhere in Trinidad, by anyone.

This morning, however, a disreputable-looking man—torn shirt, dirty trousers, long, matted dreads, and body language that signals a chip on his shoulder—approaches from across a field. He starts calling; I pick up my pace; he keeps heading our way. A confrontation is inevitable, and I clutch my backpack tighter. Soon the man is close enough that we can make out what he's yelling: "Put your hips into it! Slide your feet along the ground! Listen to the beat and you'll get it." He demonstrates a little chip, flashes a huge smile and then heads back across the field. Feeling exceedingly guilty about suspecting the worst, we wave our thanks and swivel our hips homeward.

. . .

Sunrise, Monday morning: J'ouvert. I'm slathered head to toe in thick mud the color of coffee with cream, and thick paint, applied indiscriminately by several hands; I'm a walking, talking, chipping Jackson Pollock. I've got a Carib in my hand and a nice, solid crust forming on my body; you can no longer tell where my skimpy costume ends and my skin begins.

Our J'ouvert band, one of the smaller ones (a mere four hundred strong, including perhaps four dozen "yachties"), had convened at our mas camp at 4 a.m. After breakfast, our first order of business in the predawn darkness was to swab on a base coat of mud, then paint, before we fell in behind our music truck (a flatbed transport with a towering wall of speakers and a DJ) and its trailer, which holds barrels of yet more mud and paint.

"Hieronymous Bosch would have felt at home playing J'ouvert," a government publication says. "It's a . . . celebration of the darker side of human life." Most people playing "dirty mas" are paint and mud smeared, but J'ouvert is when strange creatures that can't endure the light of day are said to prowl the streets, and basically anything goes. There are grotesque costumes, satirical ones lampooning well-known people, and occasional roving bands of "oil men," who look like they have been dipped head to toe in used motor oil; they carry cans with a supply for lubricating others, and we give them a wide berth. We hear one band uses melted chocolate instead of mud, which occasions a round of whining-puppy noises from Steve.

A stranger from another band chips by from the opposite direction, catches my eye, and softly caresses the length of my arm—leaving it brilliant ink blue. Another stranger sees me with a double handful of fresh paint from our well-stocked trailer and wants to hold hands. As the sky lightens and dawn breaks, and we dance through the Woodbrook section of Port of Spain, we become progressively dirtier, progressively freer about anointing others, and—I like to think—progressively more proficient at our chipping. I understand completely why Carnival is called an occasion for release. I feel not just like a kid again, but like the kid I never was.

. . .

"I met Ken 'Professor' Philmore the other night," I proudly tell Miss Pat. "And he gave me a big hug and kiss." The Professor is a Trini celeb—a Panorama-winning pan arranger, conductor and player—and for a new pan jumbie, the encounter was like getting my sugar from a piece of Hollywood eye-candy. I'd recognized him at the bar at the Panorama finals, and gone over to say congratulations on his win, with the Laventille Sound Specialists in the medium-band category. His very warm response was a very pleasant surprise, and I'd been bragging about it for days.

Miss Pat neatly deflates my middle-aged ego. The Professor sometimes patronizes Pie's bar, she says. "He kiss and hug *everybody*, honey. Especially when he been drinking." Pie, standing nearby, gently smiles his agreement.

. . .

Crisis on the Queen's Park Savannah: Carnival isn't over, and there is an acute coconut shortage.

At any time of year, you'll find at least two or three trucks filled with green coconuts parked around this 260-acre greenspace in the middle of Port of Spain. The vendors stand by, cutlasses at the ready, to serve up refreshment to the cricket players, runners, walkers, lovers and limers who use the Savannah's playing fields, paths and tree-shaded benches at all times of day and well into the night. Holding a nut in one hand—if you're lucky, he'll have pulled it from a cooler—the vendor will give it a few deft thwacks with his long blade, slicing just enough off the top to open a hole for drinking. Once you've slurped out the refreshing water—a young nut holds about two cups, sometimes more—you hand the empty shell back to the vendor, who attacks it with his cutlass once again. Now he cuts it in half and then hacks off a small wedge to serve as a spoon for scooping out the soft, tasty jelly lining the inside. (As the coconut matures, the jelly layer thickens and hardens into the white coconut meat.) "Cold water, slight jelly coconut, and doubles will fix anything," a Trini will tell you.

Given its reputation for curing hangovers, lowering blood pressure and generally improving health, coconut water is extremely popular at Carnival time. Not to be confused with coconut milk (which is made by grating and squeezing the white meat in water to extract its oil and flavor compounds), clear coconut water is almost entirely fat-free, low in calories and excellent for rehydration—better, even, than sports drinks. It replenishes electrolytes (coconut water has the same electrolyte balance as blood, and in the Pacific during World War II it was given intravenously to wounded soldiers as an emergency substitute for plasma), and is high in minerals such as potassium. A cup of coconut water provides more potassium than a banana. And—at least before it's been thwacked by a cutlass—the water is completely sterile.

Although there were no coconuts in the Caribbean when Columbus passed through, they showed a rabbit-like proficiency at spreading themselves once they were introduced to the New World by other explorers a few years later. Discovered by

Europeans when Vasco de Gama reached the Indian Ocean in 1497, the coconut was quickly identified as an excellent source of drinking water. Because the nuts float, they can drift on open seas to other areas to propagate. About four months after a nut falls off the tree, one of its three seeds germinates, and the seedling (which pushes out through one of the soft eyes) sustains itself on the now-spongy inside. If you're ever lost and hungry, a Trini hiking guide tells us, look for a germinated coconut on the ground. That spongy interior, which he calls "coconut bread," is nutritious and surprisingly palatable. It's been calculated that there is one coconut palm for every five people on the planet. The trees are prolific too—they bear year-round, each one producing 50 to 100 coconuts on average, with some yielding significantly more. (No wonder we're warned not to stand under them.)

Given all that, you'd think there would be plenty of coconuts in Trinidad for Carnival. The problem is, the green nuts can't be stockpiled: coconut water starts to ferment soon after a nut is picked.

The snow-cone vendors, on the other hand, are still well supplied. But shaved ice topped with lurid, tooth-achingly sweet syrup is not on anyone's health-improvement plan. "With milk?" the snow-cone man behind the Savannah grandstand asks, and when I give him the nod, he swirls on a viscous sugary stream of sweetened condensed milk. Like coconut water, however, a snow cone seems enormously restorative at Carnival time: the high dose of sugar jolts my system into wakefulness and the icy base is seriously thirst-quenching. Besides, they're such fun.

. . .

On Carnival Tuesday, wave after wave of costumed revelers flows through the streets, the music of one mas band—the big ones boast upward of 3,500 participants—barely fading before the next is in earshot. I count the trailer trucks required to support one popular band: nine 40-foot sound trucks, each bearing a wall of speakers and its own DJ; ten equally long bar trucks; three food and snack trucks; a couple of miscellaneous supply trucks; an ambulance; and (bringing up the rear) a flatbed "wee-wee truck" (yes, that's what it's called), carrying eight "D-Johns" and giving new meaning to the term "porta-potty." And then there are the sponsors, the security details, the swag bags. Bands such as this will gross more than TT$10 million during Carnival. Mas has indeed become big business.

The flow of ecstatically gyrating masqueraders continues hour after hour, each band a different theme, each a sea of feathers, glitter, sequins, sparkles, spandex and beads. An extraordinary sight—but in the end, an overwhelming blur, and not what I'll remember as the heart of this hedonistic time. What I *will* remember is the way Carnival opened up to let us outsiders in. "Are you enjoying your Carnival?" people said. They didn't ask if we were enjoying theirs.

. . .

Ash Wednesday is for recuperation. But even after all that action and all those late nights, the partying doesn't stop cold; it just switches to a lower key. Those who can take yet more time off swarm to Tobago to lime on the beach for a few days. It's impossible to score a hotel room, a ticket on the inter-island ferry, or a seat on one of the puddle-jumper flights unless you've planned way ahead. Closer to home, people gather at nearby rivers, to chill in the water and cook curry duck—the de rigueur dish for river limes—or they head to Maracas Beach, on Trinidad's north coast, the island's most popular stretch of sand. The food that's de rigueur there is the bake and shark, the superlative, primo, ultimate, unbeatable fried-fish sandwich: sizzling deep-fried shark stuffed into a hot-out-of-the-oil bake, and dressed with enough toppings—pepper sauce, garlic sauce, chadon beni sauce, assorted sliced veggies and unripe fruits—to satisfy the most hardcore of the self-pro-claimed "condiment-crazy" Trinis. But even though Maracas is barely 10 miles from the Savannah, getting there requires braving the North Coast Road—a sequence of climbing curves canopied by stands of bamboo and umbrella-like samaan trees, just one lane in each direction. Even at the best of times, it can be slow-going; the day after Carnival, it's at a standstill, clogged bumper to bumper.

But Miss Pat, who has begun phasing herself out of the grueling daily routine of her restaurant (much to the dismay of her regulars, including us), issues a closer-to-home post-Carnival invitation. "I bought some corn, honey. Come for corn soup. Tell Heather and Don, and bring the other friends you play mas with. We'll have a party."

Wonderful. "But, Pat, I have to watch you make the soup."

"No problem, honey. Come early."

When we arrive, however, she tells me I'm the one making the soup. So while Steve and our friends tear into the pre-lunch snacks she's laid out in her old dining room behind Pie's bar, I'm in the kitchen chopping carrots and celery, pumpkin and pimentos, cive and thyme. "Put the stems in the pot too, honey, to get more flavor." Meanwhile, the ears of corn have "pressured" (island corn is generally tougher than the sweet corn we're used to, and it needs a session in the pressure cooker before being added to the soup), and the split peas have boiled until they burst. Miss Pat coaches me through the dumpling dough, making me eyeball the correct quantities of flour and cornmeal without measuring—"you don't want it too yellow"—and watching me mix in water with my hands to make a stiff dough and then knead it into submission. After the football-sized mound rests, she demonstrates how to turn it into dumplings. "One, two," she says, breaking off a marble-sized hunk and giving it two quick rolls between her palms before pitching it in the pot. At the very end, we throw in a Pat-sized pinch of her pepper sauce as well.

Even Pie, who leaves the bar briefly for a bowl, gives "my" soup his smile of approval. The dessert, however, is all Miss Pat: she's baked two moist, rich, alcoholic Christmas black cakes, as she had months ago promised Steve. And when we leave, she sends each couple home with a big wedge of leftover cake. "Sprinkle it with rum every few days and it will last a year," she says.

"Only if you don't eat it," says Steve.

Ours is gone within the week.

Heather and Don show more restraint. When we meet up with *Asseance* in Carriacou four months later, they generously share the piece of Miss P's cake they still have left. It's as delicious as it was in February—though decidedly higher octane. "I only did what Miss Pat told us to," Heather protests, as fumes waft from our plates. The cake has had more than a dozen supplementary dousings of rum.

. . .

It's time for us to leave Trinidad, to explore the islands a bit farther north, with stops on the way to see our friends in Grenada and Carriacou, of course. The day before we pull away from the marina that now feels like home, I head to Port of Spain's central market one last time. In the fish building, I see a vendor with *cascadura* or *cascadoux*, a prehistoric river fish with large scales interlocking like armor. If you eat cascadura, the Trinis say, you will return to end your days in Trinidad. I don't have time to deal with an armor-plated fish today, but I hope that simply seeing a cascadura counts for something— at least guaranteeing us a return trip. For Steve and I have fallen hard for this island.

The next afternoon, after hugs from Elizabeth, Meleen and our other friends at the marina's front desk, we slip our lines and motor out through the Boca de Monos, but only as far as Scotland Bay, where we anchor overnight. By the time we've finished bowls of Miss Pat-perfect, *Receta*-made corn soup, the howler monkeys are in full voice. I lie on the settee and read the day's newspapers (now that Carnival is over, crime and politics have stolen the headlines back), Steve listens to the finals of the Stanford 20/20 cricket match (we can imagine the jubilation ashore when Trinidad hammers Jamaica), and a bat swoops through the cabin toward our fruit basket, looking for its own taste of Trinidad tonight.

My cellphone rings suddenly, unexpectedly. Cells usually don't work in Scotland Bay because the high cliffs block the signals. It's Miss Pat. Pie is watching the cricket on TV, she tells me, but she was thinking of us.

"I know you're leaving in the morning, and I wanted to tell you I love you, and stay safe," she says.

Hearing my response, she gives me one final scolding.

"When you say goodbye, it means forever. So don't say goodbye; say 'I'll see you soon.'"

Immediately after we hang up, the cell signal disappears, completely, and for good. *I'll see you soon* are the last words I hear from this lovely island.

· · · CARNIVAL CORN SOUP · · ·

Don't be put off by the long ingredients list: This hearty, meal-in-a-bowl soup will feed a crowd of hungry limers. For true Trini authenticity, serve scorching hot in Styrofoam cups. And put on a steelpan CD.

For the soup:

1 cup	dry split peas	250 mL
2 to 3	cloves garlic, chopped	2 to 3
4 to 5 ears	corn, chopped into ¾- to 1-inch (2 to 2.5 cm) rounds	4 to 5
2 to 3	carrots, peeled and chopped	2 to 3
1 lb	West Indian pumpkin or butternut squash, cubed	500 g
2	bunches green onions, chopped	2
2 to 3	sprigs fresh parsley, chopped	2 to 3
2 to 3	branches fresh thyme, chopped (or 2 to 3 tsp/10 to 15 mL dried thyme)	2 to 3
1	stalk celery, with leaves, chopped	1
1	red pepper, chopped	1
¼ cup	demerara or brown sugar	50 mL
1	can (12 oz/355 mL) kernel corn, including juice (or kernels from 2 additional ears of corn)	1
3 to 4 tbsp	butter or margarine (optional)	50 to 65 mL
1 cup	coconut milk	250 mL
	Salt and freshly ground black pepper	
	Hot pepper sauce	

For the dumplings:

1 ½ cups	white flour (approx)	375 mL
½ cup	corn flour or finely ground cornmeal (approx)	125 mL
1 tbsp	salt	15 mL
4 tsp	demerara or granulated white or brown sugar	20 mL

1. Rinse and pick over the split peas to remove any debris. Put peas in a large pot with about 10 cups (2.5 L) of salted water. Bring to a boil, lower heat to medium, cover and cook until split peas burst (about 30 minutes).

2. Add the chopped ears of corn (but not the extra kernels) and the other fresh vegetables and herbs, and about 1 tsp (5 mL) each of salt and pepper. Raise heat to return pot to a gentle boil, cover and continue cooking for about 30 minutes.

3. While the soup simmers, make the dumplings: In a bowl, stir enough corn flour or cornmeal into flour to make a very pale yellow mixture. Mix in salt and sugar. Add enough water to make a stiff dough that holds together. Knead with the heel of your hand until smooth (about 5 minutes). Cover with a damp tea towel and leave to rest for about 30 minutes.

4. Add sugar and canned kernel corn and juice, or fresh corn kernels, to pot. Stir in butter or margarine (if using). If soup is too thick, add hot water to thin. Return soup to a gentle boil.

5. When soup is again at a boil, break off marble-sized pieces of dumpling dough, give each piece a couple of quick rolls between your palms to turn it into a 2-inch (5 cm) rope, and toss into the pot.

6. Add coconut milk. Continue cooking until carrots are soft, dumplings are cooked through, and soup is nicely thickened,

about 30 minutes.

7. Taste and adjust seasoning. Add pepper sauce and serve hot.

Makes 10 servings.

Tip:

- Since the soup thickens as it stands, leftover soup will likely need to be thinned with a little water when reheated.

· · · CHADON BENI SAUCE · · ·

Trinis love this sauce swirled in corn soup (see previous recipe), on bake and shark (Trinidad's version of a fishwich), and with jerked or barbecued chicken. Try it with the Plantain-Crusted Chicken Fingers in Chapter 9 or the Lambi Fritters in Chapter 11.

1 cup	fresh chadon beni or cilantro	250 mL
1 tbsp	fresh thyme leaves	15 mL
2	cloves garlic	2
¼ to ½	hot pepper (or to taste)	¼ to ½
2 tbsp	white wine vinegar	25 mL
½ cup	olive oil	125 mL
	Salt and freshly ground black pepper	

1. In a food processor, pulse chadon beni or cilantro, thyme, garlic and hot pepper until finally chopped.
2. Add vinegar and process to combine.
3. Slowly add the oil and process until a thick puree forms. Season to taste and store in the refrigerator.

Makes about 1 cup (250 mL).

· · · WENDY'S · · ·
SPICY SMOKED HERRING SPREAD

"Never believe you need that 'little something' extra to make your dish taste great," says cookbook author Wendy Rahamut. She was talking about stewed chicken—but the advice applies just as well to this simple appetizer from her book Modern Caribbean Cuisine *(Interlink Books). Even though I invariably fiddle recipes, this one defies fiddling. It's always popular—although it often leaves people guessing what the main ingredient is.*

1	smoked herring fillet (about 1 oz/30 g)	1
½ cup	cream cheese	125 mL
⅓ cup	mayonnaise	75 mL
1 tsp	hot pepper sauce (or to taste)	5 mL
1 tsp	fresh lime juice	5 mL
½ cup	chopped fresh herbs (parsley, chives, basil)	125 mL

1. Soak the herring in hot water for 20 minutes. Rinse and pick out the bones.
2. Place in a food processor and chop finely. Add the rest of the ingredients and process to a thick paste. (On the boat, I just mash everything together with a fork.) Refrigerate until ready to use.
3. Serve accompanied by crackers, toast rounds or raw vegetables, and sprinkled with additional herbs.

Makes about 1 cup (250 mL).

· · · TASSA CHICKEN · · ·

East Indian tassa drumming accompanies street parades during the Muslim festival of Hosay. But in true Trini fusion style, East Indian and West Indian have blended, and tassa drums— traditionally made of clay with goatskin heads—can be spotted at Carnival festivities, too.

Tassa is an appropriate name for this fusion dish, which layers Trini flavor on a traditional East Indian curry recipe. It was developed by one of the sweet hands in the kitchen at Allyson Hennessy and Rosemary Hezekiah's Port of Spain restaurant, Veni Mangé.

4	bone-in chicken quarters (about 3 lb/1.5 kg)	4
8	cloves garlic, finely chopped	8
	Kosher or sea salt and freshly ground black pepper	
2 tbsp	vegetable oil	25 mL
3 tbsp	West Indian curry powder (see Tips with the Curry Stew Chicken recipe in Chapter 8)	50 mL
2	onions, cut in eighths	2
4	medium tomatoes, cut in eighths	4
1 cup	coconut milk	250 mL
2 tbsp	raisins	25 mL
½ cup	whole peanuts	125 mL
½ cup	sweet mango chutney	125 mL
1 tbsp	tomato paste	25 mL

1. Cut the chicken into pieces at the joints, and season with the garlic, salt and pepper. Set aside for at least 1 hour.

2. Heat the oil in a large pot, add the curry and cook for about 2 minutes over medium heat, stirring to avoid burning.

3. Add the chicken pieces, and stir well to coat them with the curry mixture.

4. Add the onions, tomatoes and coconut milk. Bring to a boil, then lower the heat and simmer, uncovered, stirring occasionally, for 40 to 50 minutes until chicken is tender and sauce has thickened.

5. Stir in the raisins, nuts, chutney and tomato paste; cook for a couple minutes more to blend flavors and heat through. Serve over rice.

Makes 4 servings.

· · · WATERCRESS & AVOCADO SALAD · · ·
WITH SPICY SHRIMP

One Saturday, I toted home peppery watercress and a perfectly ripe avocado from the Port of Spain market, along with my usual fresh shrimp and weekly supply of herbs. When I served the salad I concocted from my haul, it occasioned a chant of "write it down, write it down now," from Steve, to ensure I'd be able to make it the same way again.

For the shrimp:

1 lb	large shrimp, with shells, deveined	500 g
6	peppercorns	6
1	bay leaf	1
1 tsp	salt	5 mL
4	slices of fresh ginger	4
3 tbsp	mayonnaise	50 mL
3 tbsp	yogurt	50 mL
1 tsp	hot pepper sauce (or to taste)	5 mL
1 tsp	grated lime zest	5 mL
1 tbsp	fresh lime juice	15 mL

For the salad:

1	bunch watercress, chopped	1
1	avocado, pitted, peeled and cubed	1
1	cucumber, peeled, seeded and cubed (about 1 cup/250 mL)	1
2 tbsp	chopped chadon beni or cilantro	25 mL
2 tbsp	chopped green onion	25 mL

For the vinaigrette:

½	small clove garlic	½
1 tbsp	fresh lime juice	15 mL
2 tbsp	olive oil	25 mL
	Salt and freshly ground black pepper	

1. Put 4 cups (1 L) of water in a large saucepan and add peppercorns, bay leaf, salt and ginger. Bring to a boil, reduce heat, cover, and simmer 5 minutes. Return to boil, then add shrimp. Cook until just done (2 to 5 minutes, depending on size). Drain, and allow to cool, then remove shells and spices.

2. Combine mayo and yogurt with pepper sauce and lime zest and juice. Fold in cooled shrimp.

3. To make the vinaigrette, mash garlic with a little salt. Add lime juice and then whisk in olive oil. Season to taste.

4. When ready to serve, toss watercress, avocado, cucumber and half the herbs with just enough vinaigrette to lightly coat. (You may not need all the vinaigrette.) Arrange the salad on a platter, pile the shrimp on top and sprinkle with the remaining herbs. Serve with crusty bread.

Makes 3 to 4 servings.

In Search of Passion

· · · GRENADA & ST. LUCIA · · ·

"It's good for the back." This phrase is used to describe any food
considered to be a male aphrodisiac.

Harriet Nelson, Harriet's Tobago Cookery Book, *2004*

PARTY ICE, SEAMOSS, AND FUNERAL SERVICES

sign in front of a business in rural St. Vincent

"MY HUSBAND LOVES SEAMOSS," I chirp brightly to the
man who opens the door of the small white frame house along
Grenada's Maurice Bishop Highway. (All the country's prime
ministers qualify to have a road named after them, even those
who were unelected; Bishop took control of the country via
coup in 1979.) Before we left for Trinidad, we had passed the
little house several times on the local bus, and I'd taken note of
its hand-painted, wobbly-lettered sign: CLEANED FISH, LAMBI
AND SEAMOSS FOR SALE. Now, back on the island, I'd insisted
we make a special trip there.

The man in the doorway gives Steve an undisguised

pitying look before telling me there's no seamoss to be had right now. "My brother is the one who collects it from the sea"—we can see scuba tanks in the open trunk of a vehicle in the drive—"and he won't have more till next week." Steve, meanwhile, gives me an undisguised look that tells me I'm in big trouble. For seamoss—a type of seaweed—is reputed to be a potent aphrodisiac, the island version of Viagra; in fact, Marvelous Marva's, a lunch spot on the hill above the market in St. George's, makes a seamoss drink its owner calls "Stay Up." Steve is more than slightly taken aback at my apparent public aspersion on his, well, you know.

But, really, *really,* I didn't mean to insinuate that he needed any help in that department. It's just that the drink is yummy—like an outrageously thick, rich, old-fashioned vanilla milkshake, spiced with nutmeg and cinnamon, and with a slight ocean tang—and I want to try making it myself. Really, it's not that we need it. But, well, it couldn't hurt, could it?

A couple of days earlier, planning ahead, when Dwight and Stevie stopped by *Receta* on their way back from fishing, I had asked them how one goes about turning a handful of dried seaweed into a drink. I didn't have the nerve to inquire outright about its effect on their sex lives, however, and Steve certainly wasn't helping me by asking any leading questions. "It give you energy," Dwight volunteered—a euphemism, I figured, if ever there was.

"You soak it," Stevie said between brownies, that afternoon's offering from the oven.

I could see this wasn't going to be any easier than my past attempts to extract information from them. "How long do you soak it, Stevie?" I asked.

"Overnight. Then you cook it."

"How long do I cook it?"

"Until it look different."

"Put a nice piece of spice in it," Dwight chimed in helpfully. "And cloves. And just a little milk to give it flavor."

Clearly, more specific instructions were called for. And of course, I still had to get some seamoss.

. . .

The road along St. Lucia's western coast wends into the mountains on its way to Laborie, a rural fishing village at the island's southern end. Past the rough-edged town of Soufriere, it climbs through rain forest that supported rich cocoa and coffee plantations in the eighteenth and early nineteenth centuries and is now dotted with resorts. Seaward, the Pitons erupt out of the ocean, two massive volcanic cones that were sacred ground for the island's first inhabitants, who believed the twin peaks brought them one step closer to heaven. The Pitons received their fifteen minutes of fame a few years ago when Oprah declared they were one place everyone should see before they die. Approaching from offshore, they make St. Lucia unmistakable; when you're anchored between them, they brood overhead—astonishingly immense, and beautiful in a looming, hulking, jaggy-toothed sort of way.

Beyond the Pitons, the road slowly unwinds to sea level until it reaches Laborie, whose palm-fringed beach is well beyond the range of most island visitors. A jumble of houses with narrow verandas hugs the road that passes through the village, and our rental—late model, shiny, undented, smooth-running (a rarity for us)—is immediately marked as belonging to strangers.

In the Caribbean, seamoss (or Irish moss, as it's sometimes called, especially in Jamaica) has been used to make "energy" drinks at least since the early nineteenth century. Most seamoss is harvested from the wild, gathered from reefs and rocks by divers, like the one who advertises on the highway in Grenada, or by foragers, who simply cut it off reefs exposed at low tide. But overharvesting has taken its toll, and in an attempt to conserve the dwindling resource and still meet demand, a few enterprising St. Lucians have started to farm it—apparently, the first West Indians to do so—and I'd heard that one of the farmers lives in Laborie. "I don't have an address or a phone number," I'd warned our friends Julie and Barry, whom we'd convinced to come along on the drive. "Just a name: Phillip Simeon." In my usual optimistic—Steve would say deluded—way, I'm expecting a big sign that says SIMEON SEAMOSS FARM. He's once again muttering about goat cheese and red herrings.

We cruise from one end of tiny Laborie to the other, and of course there is no sign—nor is there any sign of seaweed, other than a stray clump or two washed onto the beach. But the first person I ask near the dock used by the local fishermen's co-op knows "deh seamoss man" and directs us to his house, a skinny, two-story gingerbreaded affair that backs onto the ocean at the opposite edge of town.

When he appears from behind the house, Phillip Simeon is wearing shorts and a T-shirt that reads, *I'm really excited to be here*—and he immediately sets about proving it. He is consumed by his passion for seamoss, and once he starts talking about it, there's no stopping him . . . though he's a bit wary at the same time, almost as if he suspects we plan to steal his secrets and take up seamoss farming ourselves. (Later on, he won't let me fully read—let alone take away—some printed directions for preparing the seamoss.) He walks us through the little garden at the rear of the house, where fat, frilly tangles of rubbery seaweed dry on chicken wire, the translucent reddish-brown clumps turning a pinkish-gold as they stiffen in the sun.

Of the hundreds of varieties in the Caribbean, only two are cultivated in St. Lucia: *Gracilaria* and *Eucheuma*, which are both types of red algae. Traditionally, seamoss is bleached in the sun before it's dried, usually by sweating it under sheets of clear plastic, Phillip tells us, which turns it a pale tan. But he doesn't like that step—"it removes some of the minerals," he says, and weakens its energy-building effects—so he skips the bleaching. Once it's thoroughly dried, his harvest is ready for market or (in his longer-range plans) for bottling into drinks. A carbohydrate in the seamoss—agar or carrageenan, depending on the variety—dissolves in hot water and becomes gelatinous when cooled, giving the drink its body. One unappreciative foreigner likened it to drinking banana cake batter.

A gate at the back of Phillip's garden opens onto the beach, which is strewn with coconuts and coconut fronds, long stalks of bamboo, pieces of Styrofoam, old tires and other flotsam and jetsam—most obviously, a heap of empty plastic bleach jugs, motor-oil containers and pop bottles. "They're floats for the farm," he says.

Meanwhile, he's thrust a sheaf of dog-eared papers into my hands: a laboratory report on the properties of seamoss (it's apparently rich in protein, magnesium, calcium, potassium and iodine), plus a business plan for his farm. "We used to be able to harvest ten or twelve bags of wild seamoss from the rocks in fifteen minutes, and then all of a sudden it was declining," he explains as he walks us down the beach. "I wanted to protect the natural resource so I started to farm it." No doubt, environmental protection was coupled with fears of his livelihood disappearing, and he also surely saw a business opportunity. "But I need more money to really get it going," he says, warming to his audience. "Things will really take off once we get people in Europe and America familiar with the benefits of seamoss."

That's my cue: "What about its reputation as an aphrodisiac, Mr. Simeon?" I ask, ignoring Steve, who I can sense doing an eye-roll behind me.

"People say it good for the sex drive," he replies. "I'm afraid to drink it every day because my wife is away." She's an American, he later explains, currently working in the United States. He's forty-nine, and credits his product with keeping him "flexible" and—that euphemism again—"full of energy." "I challenged an eighteen-year-old to a race. I won." Not just a seamoss farmer, but a natural pitchman to boot.

After ten minutes of leisurely walking, we reach the far end of the beach. "There it is," he says, pointing beyond an open wooden fishing boat named *No Excuses* to an empty patch of water about a hundred yards offshore. Above the surface, a seamoss farm isn't much to look at: just a few of those plastic-bottle buoys balancing on the waves. Since the engine isn't working on his boat, Phillip says, he can't take us out to the farm. But he's determined to show us a sample of his crop, so he'll just swim out and harvest a bit. He strips off his shorts and dives into the ocean clad in his *I'm really excited to be here* T-shirt—and an itty-bitty thong. Julie and I get a glimpse of great legs and an even better backside before he disappears under water. We're really excited to be here too, Phillip.

About five minutes later, he wades back onto the beach with a length of polypropylene rope bulging with seamoss. But bulging seamoss isn't what captures Julie's and my attention: Phillip's soaking tee is now doing a wholly inadequate job of covering up his itty-bitty soaking thong, which is hardly covering anything at all. We attempt to steal glances without him, or our husbands, noticing. (Fat chance.) This guy is forty-nine? Just two years younger than Steve? He's a poster boy for his product. ("You were visibly drooling," Steve says afterward, while Barry later reports that Julie continued to make occasional reference to Phillip's tightly muscled butt.)

Suffice to say, Julie and I have difficulty keeping our eyes on Phillip's demonstration of how he "plants" a new crop: braiding small bits of seamoss between strands of rope. The ropes will then go back into the ocean and be hung from the buoys, where they will grow "super big," ready for harvest in a couple of months.

Again, I cut to the chase: "Can I buy some of your seamoss, please?"

. . .

The Caribbean offers a long menu of items that supposedly put "lead in deh pencil." Not all these "man foods," as they're also known, are quite as appealing, however, as a cold glass of seamoss. The aroma of the bark of the *bois bandé*, or mountain spice tree, for instance, has been likened to floor polish and ammonia. But bois bandé (Creole for "hard wood") is so highly regarded that, despite the vile smell, easily accessible trees are regularly stripped bare of their bark. In Castries, St. Lucia's capital, an entrepreneur has set up shop just outside the lavish produce market to capitalize on those who have post-shopping activities in mind: EC$3.50 (about $1.25) buys a shot of rum infused with bois bandé. To make sure potential customers are well aware of his product's efficacy, he's painted STAMINA AND COCK STAN on the front of his stall, the words accompanied by a primitive drawing of a rooster. Rural St. Lucian rum shops sometimes have a bois bandé drink available for special customers: *en bas kontwen*, it's called in Creole, the name describing where it's kept: under the counter.

Some truth does perhaps underlie bois bandé's reputation. "This infusion . . . is powerful but dangerous," warn the authors of *Caribbean Spice Island Plants*, a scholarly tome published by the University of Oxford in association with Grenada's Forestry Department. "There are stories . . . where men have overdosed and their penis had to be iced to bring down the erection. There are other cases when they were hospitalized." Steve, no surprise, refuses to fork over $3.50 to give it a try.

Goat water—also known as "mannish water"—resides firmly among the tastier, and subtler, aphrodisiacs. "Water" or "waters" is the West Indian term for a whole class of soups. While the name conjures up thin (and somewhat unappetizing-sounding) drinks, they are actually hearty chowders, like the lambi water at Dingis's birthday party—closer to a stew than a broth. Perhaps because of the restorative nature of a hot, hearty, nutrition-packed bowl of soup (particularly after a night of rum drinking), "waters" are reputed to have a positive effect on sagging masculine libidos. They are traditionally weekend food—likely because Friday is traditionally a night for liming at the local rum shop, as well as because Saturday is the traditional day for using up leftovers before going all-out for Sunday lunch. But their popularity isn't limited to men seeking an "energy" boost. In St. Kitts and Nevis, where goat water is a national institution, we lined up on Saturdays with parents and kids of all ages for brimming bowls of the clove-scented soup packed with breadfruit, onions, peppers, dumplings and tender pieces of goat meat. Afterward, though, we felt like nothing more strenuous than a long nap.

. . .

I don't tackle Phillip Simeon's dried seamoss right away, still not exactly sure how to prepare it. In the meantime, I encourage Steve to order the drink whenever opportunity presents, so I can take advantage of his talents as a taste-tester. (Really. Honest.)

"You know about this?" asks the young man who sells him an unlabeled bottle of a very cinnamony homemade seamoss drink in a restaurant in Vieux Fort, about twenty minutes down the road from Laborie.

"Yes," Steve replies. "Do you think it works?"

"Well . . ." Obviously not wanting to suggest he might need such assistance, the young man shrugs and smiles. "I like the flavor," he says, echoing the standard line we're fed up and down the island chain by men who admit they drink it.

The best seamoss drink Steve tastes was whipped up by Gill, at the Breakfast Shed in Port of Spain: a spice-flecked, densely creamy concoction that Gill explains gets its flavor from "seasonings"—how helpful—although he does allow that it contains a shot of cola syrup. Though it "doesn't look as nice," he says he prefers the local Trinidadian seamoss to the imported

St. Lucian stuff because "it stronger."

As usual, I can't resist: "My husband just finished the big glass you gave him. Am I going to be in trouble?"

"You don't need to worry," he replies with a deep laugh. "It's just going to make him"—he takes a long pause here—"fit."

In the interest of husbandly fitness, I finally decide to ask Dingis for help. I show her my precious, grapefruit-sized clump of Phillip's seaweed, which is dusted with a coating of white sea salt and feels like the springy dried lichens that served as landscaping for my brother's toy trains. "Listen to me," she says, "you have to soak it first. Put half deh seamoss in a bowl with water. It fresh, so squeeze a lime into deh water, then put in deh lime skins too."

At home, "freshness" is prized in foodstuffs; in the Caribbean, I'm learning, it has a somewhat different meaning. "Ahhhnnnn, wash the fish in lime to cut the freshness," Dwight tells me. Before cooking, meat likewise needs to have its "freshness" tamed, and lime (or vinegar or sour oranges when limes aren't in season) is the standard way to cut a strong, fresh-killed flavor. As one Grenadian cook told me, aged beef here means the cow was killed in the morning and sold that afternoon. On the flip side, this lime wash is also a holdover from the past, when slaves were given cast-off food and the citrus helped defeat the unpleasant flavor and surface bacteria of meat or fish that was past its prime.

"It swell up nice overnight," Dingis continues, referring— of course she was—to the seaweed. Next day, "wash it up clean and put it on deh fire to boil with two bwa den [bay] leaves, a little nutmeg, and spice," she says, indicating the length of her index finger for the piece of cinnamon that should go into the pot. "Let deh seamoss boil till it get soft."

That evening, I follow her instructions and set the seamoss to soak in a large bowl. Scarcely fifteen minutes later, I casually glance in the bowl—and see it has "swell up" alarmingly, already to the brim and now threatening to colonize the rest of the kitchen, like some sci-fi blob. "It looks like a lab experiment gone terribly wrong," observes Steve encouragingly. I pour the swollen mess into an even larger bowl, add a bit more water, and hope for the best.

The next morning, the seamoss is fat and slippery, and the bowl is mostly dry. I dutifully "wash it up clean"—though it doesn't look at all dirty—cover it with fresh water in my biggest pot, and start it cooking. Ten minutes later, I have a viscous beige sludge, which when chilled becomes beige Jell-O. Now it's time to turn it into a drink. "Swizzle it," Dingis had said the previous day, rolling an imaginary swizzle stick between her palms. (Gill at the Breakfast Shed used a blender.) "Then add milk." Fresh milk is almost unheard of here: when children drink milk, it's the powdered or non-refrigerated UHT type; when "milk" is mixed with seamoss or used in cocoa tea, it's sweetened condensed or evaporated milk, which Dingis and others simply call "Carnation."

Much to my delight, the result is delicious—particularly when we add a bit of dark rum, to make what our old friend rum guru Ed Hamilton, founder of the Ministry of Rum, calls a seamoss cocktail. "If you're thinking milk, seaweed, nutmeg, cinnamon, rum, how good can that be?—just try it. It makes a great low-cholesterol replacement for eggnog during the holiday season." Funny, I don't recall Ed mentioning fitness, energy, or "good for the sex drive."

. . .

"Peanuts," says Greta Joseph when we give up guessing.

We're sitting on her couch, admiring her family photo albums and sipping tall glasses of her icy seamoss—which is far better than my own, and even giving Gill's some serious competition. Beyond the usual nutmeg and spice, we'd been trying to identify the mysterious extra something.

"Peanuts, and a tiny bit of rum—for flavor," she adds, not wanting us to think she put it in for any other reason.

Like Phillip Simeon, Greta farms seamoss—but she and a few other women she's recruited turn their harvest into bottled "energy drinks." Vita Moss is the brand, and the label shows a cartoon figure with bulging arm muscles—picture a clean-shaven, tattoo-free Popeye in his early years—holding up an inexpertly Photoshopped image of seamoss and nutmegs with ocean behind. When I called out of the blue to ask about her drinks, Greta had offered to show us her seamoss farm and her style of farming.

We found our way to the village of Praslin on St. Lucia's rugged east coast—diagonally across the island from Phillip Simeon in Laborie—and down a muddy path off the main road to her large, well-built house, the equivalent in this village to a mansion on a street of bungalows. She met us at the door with a winning gap-toothed smile and a hug hello. Petite and slender, she reminds me of a dancer, floating along barefoot in a long flowing skirt and loose crinkly top. She's certainly not dressed for farming, and I notice that her six-burner stove is full of pots; perhaps I misunderstood her suggestion on the phone? It wouldn't be surprising, given that English, the official language on St. Lucia, is heavily inflected with Creole, particularly away from the larger, more touristed centers. When I pronounce "Praslin" the way it looks, no one

in Praslin understands me; in Creole, it's "P'walin," with the
r and s gone missing.

Slowly, of course, things become clear, unfolding in their
own sweet island way. Yes, we are going out to her farm, but
first we must finish our seamoss drinks, listen to some Creole
music and have lunch, Greta says. There is no refusing (not that
we want to, but this is unexpected, and we don't want to
impose), and soon Steve and I are sitting at her dining room
table while she dishes up heaping plates of fried flying fish,
stewed red beans, cabbage salad, and a week's worth of carbs:
giant squares of cheesy macaroni pie and slabs of provision—
boiled yam, plantain, green banana and dasheen. Her husband,
a taciturn man who has just arrived home from his banana
fields, doesn't eat with us, disappearing with his plate onto the
porch; her teenage son and a couple of other village kids eat
after we've finished, so our plates and forks can be rinsed and
passed along.

"I usually bone deh fish but I didn't today," Greta explains
after she says a blessing and begins to pull hers apart with her
fingers. Underneath its crisp thyme-flavored skin, the flesh is
white and sweet; but flying fish have teensy bones, and lots of
them. I offer up my own silent prayer—please, Lord, don't let
me choke on a bone in P'walin—but the bigger problem is the
volume of food on my plate. I silently gesture my difficulty to
Steve, hoping to slide some carbs across to him while petite
Greta is already reloading her plate in the kitchen.
Unacceptable, he signals back. He's having enough trouble
himself. I must clean my own plate.

I do. I feel like I am going to explode. And then Greta insists
we have another glass of her seamoss—a nice, light milkshake
finisher.

Greta started farming seamoss in the early '90s, inspired—
like the Paramin women with their green seasoning—by a gov-
ernment-sponsored workshop. Her husband attended too, but
thought it was fiddly work and went back to his bananas. "I
was deh first woman. I had to learn how to swim, and people
made fun of me, saying I soak my bum-bum in deh water." A
determined go-getter, she brought seven more women into
what became the Praslin Seamoss Farmers Association. Helped
by foreign-aid agencies (again, like the women in Paramin),
they built a "processing plant" and began to produce bottled
seamoss drinks, including ones flavored with passion fruit,
guava, ginger, sorrel and (the one we tried) peanuts. But
they're still having trouble getting the business off the ground,
Greta says, hampered by labels whose expiry dates smear off;
a shortage of bottles, which are shipped from Trinidad; and,
now, not enough "covers" (bottle tops), which means it's
impossible at the moment to find Vita Moss in any island store.

Like Phillip Simeon, she readily reels off evidence of its
value as a health drink, telling stories of how it "gave back
energy" to the St. Lucia cricket team after they'd been training hard. Her own hair was breaking off, she says, until she
started treating it with seamoss gel. Like Phillip, she's a poster
child for her product: lithe and fit, "and very attractive," adds
Steve, getting even.

The sun has disappeared behind threatening clouds and the
water is an angry brown by the time we've piled into a local
fishing boat and are heading toward the outer edge of Praslin
Bay, where the seamoss "fields" are located. Islands enclose the
bay, and reefs break the waves almost all the way across its
mouth. Still, it's windy, rough and spitting cold rain by the time
we arrive at the stakes marking Greta's farm, the farthest from

shore. She'd changed into a knee-length denim skirt and added a cute straw hat before we left the house, but she now carefully lays them on one of the boat's wooden-board seats and, without hesitation, slips over the side in her crinkly blouse and the short, checked, flannel jammy bottoms that were underneath her skirt. One of the neighborhood kids, perhaps eleven or twelve years old, has come along and he hops in to help; within minutes, he's shivering noticeably in the chest-deep water.

Greta pulls up a rope that's encased in seamoss, making it easily a foot in diameter, and slips it over her shoulders—like a high-style, living evening wrap; a flamboyant boa, dark gold, edged with red. "Now I'm harvesting," she says, twisting off great clumps of seaweed. As she stuffs handfuls into the coarse crocus bag that floats alongside her, I attempt to hold the big sack upright and open in the water from my perch inside the boat. But it's a struggle: wet seamoss is surprisingly heavy, and I realize that the stole she had effortlessly lifted onto her shoulders probably weighed a good hundred pounds, that her underwater farming requires both strength and dexterity. "Now I'm planting," she says, twisting tiny pieces of algae back into the strands of rope, much as Phillip had demonstrated—except she is being slapped by waves as she does it. The bits of "planted" seamoss will double in size in six weeks and the rope will be ready for harvesting again in three months, she explains after wriggling back on board.

Back on shore, Steve takes one end of the full crocus bag and helps Greta carry it to the house. "Careful with that," calls out a local guy liming with his friends by the roadside, "or you'll have ten more children."

. . .

I once questioned a woman I met in the Bahamas about whether she believed in the efficacy of a locally touted aphrodisiac, the gelatinous wormlike strand that's part of a conch's innards. She smiled and said, "Anything you believe can work, can work."

Passion fruit, I'm convinced, falls into that category, though it certainly wasn't named for an ability to incite desire. The Spanish, who came upon the passion fruit vine in South America, thought the shape of the flowers and the arrangement of their parts evoked the Crucifixion, and therefore named the plant for the passion of Christ. No doubt looking for a stamp of approval from a higher authority on their brutal colonizing and converting, they were passionate to spot religious symbolism wherever they could; although one might be willing to accept that the petals bear a vague resemblance to a crown of thorns, it's quite a stretch to see the styles as an image of Christ on the cross and the stamens as wounds. On top of that, the shape of the fruit itself is said to evoke the tears of Christ—though the passion fruit I see are always as round as tennis balls. It's a lot easier to think of passion fruit in terms of romance.

"If you want some passion—I mean extra passion—we have passion fruit juice today," says the young woman behind the counter at Leo's, a popular lunch spot in Castries, St. Lucia's capital. Although other St. Lucians might say passion fruit "cut your nature"—meaning it reverses the good work done by seamoss, bois bandé, or mannish water—Steve and I choose to ignore that advice. Passion fruit juice marries the sweetness of pineapple with just a touch of citrus astringency (not a bad combo for a relationship), and we choose it whenever it's on offer. (On Dominica, an herbalist tells us that a tea made from passion fruit leaves and flowers "improves a woman's mood when she has her period"; not a bad thing for a relationship either.)

When I send him to shore for fresh bread one day, Steve returns with a bagful of passion fruit—they're very light, and not just the shape but also the size of tennis balls, with smooth, yellow, pale-green, and sometimes rose-colored skin—which the woman at the waterfront produce stand had convinced him to buy. Steve is a sucker for market ladies and is always returning with some unexpected fruit or vegetable that I have to figure out how to use; for the record, at least in this instance, he had the requested loaves too.

I'd never been inside a passion fruit straight off the tree before, and when I cut the first one open, a floral fragrance floods the boat, as alluring as any Valentine's Day bouquet. Some people are happy to dig right in with a spoon, but I'm less than enamored of the mass of small black seeds in the gelatinous yellow-orange pulp. The fruits are also known as *granadillas* in the Spanish-speaking Caribbean and *granadille* in the French, from the Latin *granatum*, "having many seeds." So I scoop the pulp into a bowl, mix it with water, and then push the mixture through a sieve to extract the juice. With just a squeeze of lime to point up the flavor and a tiny bit of sugar to soften the acidity, it's ready to drink.

If orange juice is called liquid sunshine, then passion fruit juice is surely liquid sunset, gloriously colored, unmistakably tropical. It's also completely seductive—even before we add some rum. And if it doesn't do anything for your love life, it's still an excellent source of Vitamin C. And much, much simpler than seamoss.

· · · *RECETA'S* PASSION PUNCH · · ·

Easier than seamoss, and just as romantic . . .

⅓ to ½ cup	dark rum	75 to 125 mL
1 cup	passion fruit nectar	
	(see Tips, below)	250 mL
2 tbsp	fresh lime juice	25 mL
2 dashes	Angostura bitters	2 dashes
½	fresh pineapple slice (or other	
	tropical fruit for garnish)	½

1. Combine rum, passion fruit nectar, lime juice and bitters.
2. Fill two tall glasses with ice. Pour in punch and garnish each glass with a piece of the pineapple slice.

Makes 2 drinks.

Tips:

- Passion fruit nectar—sometimes sold under its Spanish name, chinola, maracuyá or granadilla—is available in some supermarkets; look for it with the bottled and canned juices, as well as in the freezer case. (It's also sold online.)
- If you find fresh passion fruit, here's how to prepare your own: Cut 4 passion fruit in half and scoop flesh into a bowl or pitcher. Add 1 cup (250 mL) water and mix well. Let stand about 10 minutes and then strain into a bottle or jar, pressing as much juice from flesh as possible. Sweeten to taste with sugar syrup (see the Tip following the Moonshine Punch recipe in Chapter 5), then use in punch as above.

· · · GRILLED FISH · · ·
WITH PASSION FRUIT—GINGER SAUCE

Once I started making passion fruit juice, it seemed a shame not to work it into dinner too. Steve was passionate about this sauce on grilled fresh mahi-mahi (called dorado or dolphinfish in the English-speaking Caribbean).

| 2 | firm white fish steaks, 6 to 8 oz (175 to 250 g) apiece (such as mahi-mahi, halibut, kingfish or grouper) | 2 |

For the marinade:

2 tbsp	lime juice	25 mL
2 tbsp	olive oil	25 mL
1	clove garlic, finely chopped	1
2 tsp	finely chopped fresh ginger root	10 mL
	Salt and freshly ground black pepper	

For the sauce:

2 tbsp	butter	25 mL
1 tbsp	finely chopped garlic	15 mL
2 tbsp	finely chopped fresh ginger root	25 mL
1 tbsp	flour	15 mL
2 tbsp	coconut milk powder	25 mL
½ cup	passion fruit nectar (see Tips, previous page)	125 mL
¼ cup	water	50 mL
1 tbsp	rum (optional)	15 mL

| ¼ tsp | turmeric | 1 mL |
| Sugar (to taste) |

1. Preheat barbecue to high and oil grill rack. Combine marinade ingredients and rub into fish. Allow to stand while you make the sauce.
2. Melt butter in a small frying pan. Add garlic and ginger; sauté until fragrant but not brown.
3. Stir in flour and coconut milk powder and cook, stirring, until lightly colored.
4. Add passion fruit, water, rum and turmeric; cook, stirring, until sauce has thickened. If too thick, thin with additional water.
5. Taste and sweeten as necessary. Keep sauce warm.
6. Grill fish over medium-high heat until just opaque throughout. Serve with passion fruit sauce and rice.

Makes 2 servings.

Tip:
- For a different taste, replace the passion fruit nectar and water with ¾ cup (175 mL) of mango nectar.

· · · MANGO & PINEAPPLE GAZPACHO · · ·

We first encountered cold mango gazpacho in a Marigot, St. Martin, restaurant, where we had dinner with Yani and Chris from the sailboat Magus. *The next time mango season rolled around, Yani, a trained chef, invented this version, which we pronounced the most sensual soup we've tasted. Serve it as a starter for a romantic dinner, with a heart-shaped drizzle of cream.*

4 cups	chopped ripe mango	1 L
4 cups	chopped ripe pineapple	1 L
1 tbsp	chopped onion	15 mL
2 tbsp	chopped red bell pepper	25 mL
2 tbsp	chopped green bell pepper	25 mL
1 tbsp	chopped chadon beni or cilantro (plus additional for garnish)	
1	lime, juiced	1
	Salt and freshly ground black pepper	
	Crème fraîche, sour cream or yogurt (optional; for garnish)	

1. In a food processor or blender, combine (in batches, if necessary) fruit, onion, peppers, chadon beni or cilantro, and half the lime juice. Puree until smooth. Thin with a little water if necessary to obtain soup consistency.
2. Cover and chill at least 4 hours. Taste and add more lime juice if desired. Serve cold, garnished with a sprig of chadon beni or cilantro and a drizzle of cream or yogurt.

Makes 6 servings.

FOURTEEN

Barks That Bite

· · · ST. LUCIA & TRINIDAD · · ·

I want you to be sure & remember to have in the bath-room, when I
arrive, a bottle of Scotch whisky, a lemon, some crushed sugar, & a
bottle of Angostura bitters. Ever since I have been in London I have
taken in a wine-glass what is called a cock-tail . . . before breakfast,
before dinner, & just before going to bed. . . . To it I attribute the fact
that up to this day my digestion has been wonderful—simply perfect.

Mark Twain, from a letter to his wife in 1874

THE PLACE TO SHOP FOR SPICES on St. Lucia is the
hundred-year-old market in Castries. It sprawls just back from
the harborfront in a photogenic mishmash of outdoor stands,
covered buildings, and crowded, warren-like passageways,
and its market women—by and large, only the fishmongers
and butchers are male—don't leave commerce to chance.

"Do you need something from me, sweetheart?" one market
lady sings out as we wander past. Farther into the market's
heart, along a crammed corridor lined with stalls whose cooks
turn out some of the island's best local lunches, another woman

calls: "Do you want something to eat, darlin'?" I'm never entirely certain whom these ladies are addressing, Steve or me.

"Mahngoes, try my mahngoes," someone else cries.

"St. Lucians love deh mahngoes," she continues, when we pause in front of her. From late spring until about mid-summer, the tables are heaped with evocatively named varieties: mango pon (Creole for "bridge mango," though no one can tell us how they come by this name), mango blé (with dark, bluish-purple skin), mango blan (white inside a mostly green skin), mango kayenn ("cayenne mango," big and fleshy, with red patches on yellow skin when ripe), mango lonng (small and kidney-shaped, with lots of long strings in its flesh), and mango tin kwenm (or "ti crème," also small, and creamy sweet). "But all mahngoes sweet," she says, "except if young girls climb deh mahngo tree. 'Doan climb dat tree,' their mother say, 'or you make deh mahngoes sour.'" We don't just have a mango for breakfast but— like true connoisseurs—we have a Ceylon or a Julie, a Graham or a palwi, a cayenne or a blue. St. Lucia has more than 100 identified varieties.

"What are these?" I ask a market lady one morning, when I'm not sure which variety is in front of her. "Dey mahngoes," she answers. Dumb tourist.

At least she can't fault us for being out of step with the seasonal rhythm of island food. We smoothly switched to sour oranges and the warty orange-sized island lemons when limes weren't in season; snapped up spiky-skinned green soursops to make juice when passion fruit were scarce; and slid right into drinking "tambran"—tamarind—juice just as soon as it started appearing on the chalkboard menus at the market lunch stalls.

Tamarind trees grow well on most Caribbean islands, extremely tolerant of strong winds (sometimes planted as windbreaks, tamarind trees can even weather a hurricane), almost any kind of soil, and a lack of rainfall. In fact, they require a dry period for the fruit to develop. Native to Africa, the tall, supple, feathery-leaved tambran was introduced to the West Indies probably sometime in the sixteenth century and became widely distributed. On Carriacou, Bequia and Grenada, we plucked our own tamarind pods from wild trees as we hiked.

Like the local kids, we crack the lumpy, thin-shelled, brittle-brown pods and pull out the sticky, pulp-covered seeds to suck. In taste and texture, they remind me of dates, although much, much sharper. The pulp has been described as ranging from "sweet and mildly sour" to "sweet and very sour." The sourness is due to tartaric acid, which doesn't disappear as it does in other fruits when the sugar content rises during ripening. Then, like the kids, we spit out the naked seeds, aiming at each other as they do.

Though the local women add a significant quantity of sugar to their tamarind juice, it still has a thirst-quenching tartness. "If you making juice for you and your husband," the woman behind the counter at one of the lunch stalls tells me, "use just a couple pods or it will be too sour." But the market ladies only sell large bags of easily two or three dozen pods. And so after turning some into juice—shelling the seeds, covering them with boiling water, "beating" off the pulp with a fork, and then straining the sludgy brown liquid—I attempt to use up the rest by making tamarind balls, the popular island candy that's a tongue-confusing combo of tart fruit, sugar, salt and hot pepper. It had seemed a simple, if sticky, job when I asked in the market and followed up by consulting an island cookbook, but I somehow end up with a gooey mess that steadfastly refuses to form balls. Kitchen disaster being the mother of invention, I finally decide to throw in a little roasted cumin and some chopped chadon beni, and call it tamarind chutney. It proves excellent with chicken—despite its taffy-like consistency and unsubtle tendency to weld itself to our teeth and hang from our forks (and mouths) in sticky strings. Note to self: Do not serve this to guests. Steve, ever supportive, suggests I try again.

· · ·

Tamarind is rumored to be an ingredient in the complex—and very secret—formula of an essential island ingredient: "bitters." In the West Indies, the generic term "bitters" refers exclusively to Angostura Aromatic Bitters, made in Port of Spain, Trinidad, and sold in small glass bottles that are instantly recognizable on store shelves because their labels are too big. Angostura bitters—an infusion of gentian root (the only named flavoring) and other unspecified aromatic herbs, barks, buds, fruits and roots in a 45% alcohol solution—are still used in the Caribbean for their original purpose, curing intestinal complaints. But assorted West Indian cooks have also revealed that they are an essential ingredient in their rum punch, lemonade, seamoss, or ponche de crème. At a beach cook-up on Carriacou's White Island, we ate barbecued chicken, ripe plantains roasted black in their skins, and whole potfish smeared with butter seasoned (by one of the group, who was from Trinidad) with a copious amount of garlic and Angostura bitters, then cooked in foil over the open fire until the skin crisped. "And I can't imagine ice cream without bitters," says Glenn Davis.

Glenn is a bit biased, mind you, as he's the (now-retired) hospitality manager for the House of Angostura, "one of two companies outside England that has a Royal Warrant of

Appointment to her Majesty, the Queen of England," he says proudly. "Wherever the Queen goes, we have to make sure there are bitters." He swears by bitters himself for medicinal purposes—"when I have an upset stomach, I take it like a shot of rum"—and, of course, he uses bitters in his rum.

"You know the recipe?" he asks. "*One part sour/Two parts sweet/Three parts strong/Four parts weak/Five drops of bitters and nutmeg spice/Serve well chilled with lots of ice.* But we never put in four parts of weak. My mother said, 'Four parts weak for foreigners.'"

Dr. Johann Siegert, the surgeon-general of Simón Bolivar's army, developed the formula for Amargo Aromático, his aromatic bitters, in 1824 to improve the appetite and digestion of the soldiers under his care in the town of Angostura, Venezuela. Angostura was an important trading port, and as ships arrived from around the world, their sailors, complaining of seasickness and other stomach ailments, learned the "restorative qualities" of Dr. Siegert's remedy. Word spread, and soon the doctor had resigned his army commission to concentrate on the manufacture of his bitters. His sons moved the company to Trinidad after their father's death, because of Venezuela's ongoing political unrest.

Dr. Siegert was a frugal man, and frugality became corporate policy; consequently, when someone ordered a batch of wrong-size labels for the bitters bottles early on, there wasn't a chance they were going to be wasted. ("Angostura never throws anything away," Davis says. "They don't spend a bad cent here.") The mistake was accidentally continued when more labels were ordered—everyone thought someone else was correcting the problem, or so the story goes, chalking it up to the laid-back Trini nature—until the point that the oversized label became the brand's identifying hallmark.

The House of Angostura is more obsessed with secrecy than the CIA. Glenn shows us around, but we don't go near the "secret room," where the ingredients for a batch of bitters are weighed. Even employees are allowed in only one at a time, he explains, and only five living people are said to know the entire formulation. The "botanicals" come into the country under code—"not even Customs knows what they are," he claims—and the "spent" herbs are taken away at night to a secret destination to be burned. But we get the sense that the secrecy, like the ill-fitting label, is continued as marketing hype, since someone intent on industrial espionage could easily have the contents scientifically analyzed. "It's not like it's worth a lot," admits Davis, "so they leave us to our little adventure." The big moneymaker for the House of Angostura has long been rum.

Corporate secrecy extends even to reluctance to talk about what's not in Angostura bitters. But one ingredient that it definitely doesn't include is angostura bark. "It can be poisonous, and we don't want to confuse people into thinking bitters might contain something poisonous."

. . .

Though other sources beg to differ about angostura bark's toxic nature, the women who specialize in spices in the Castries market don't have it for sale. But they do have several other barks on their tables, banded into thick bundles. The warm, sweet aroma of cinnamon is instantly recognizable, drifting from a table where a woman is rolling pieces into long quills. When the cinnamon trees are harvested once a year, the bark is carefully peeled from the branches. Its outer layer is cut away with a sharp knife, and the inner layer is "put to dry" in the sun. The bark begins to curl naturally, and then is rolled and pressed by hand to complete the process.

"A kind of cinnamon has been found," wrote Dr. Diego Álvarez Chanca, the physician on Columbus's second voyage, "though it is true that it is not so fine as the cinnamon we know at home. This may be because we do not know the right season to gather it, or possibly there are better trees in the land. . . ."

Once again, this was just wishful thinking on the doctor's part: Cinnamon trees are native only to Asia. Though the New World disappointed Columbus and his followers for failing to deliver the cinnamon, cloves, nutmeg, and other spices they coveted, when the Europeans began to colonize the West Indies, they brought the spices of the East Indies with them, and the imports flourished in the tropical climate and rich volcanic soils. The variety of cinnamon that grows in the West Indies—and for that matter, much of the spice sold as ground cinnamon in North America—is cassia, which has a coarser bark and a stronger, more pungent flavor, compared with the more-noticeable sweetness of true cinnamon; it's also a more reddish brown.

You can't be on St. Lucia, Dominica, Grenada, St. Vincent, or any of the other volcanic, rain-forested Caribbean islands for very long without someone scraping the bark of a tall, evergreen tree and asking you to sniff. Cinnamon trees, members of the laurel family, grow more than 30 feet high in the wild, but are trained to grow shorter and denser when cultivated. The leaves, too, carry a pronounced cinnamon flavor, and they're sometimes used to make a "stimulating" bush tea.

. . .

Next to the bundles of cinnamon on the market tables in Castries are ones that consist of darker, more slender quills, with a snake-skin-like pattern of brown and tan. This is mauby, the bark of small indigenous woodland trees, *Colubrina elliptica* and *Colubrina arborescens*, used to make an extremely popular West Indian drink. We first encountered it in Dingis's kitchen years ago, when she was steeping mauby bark for Kellie's nightly tea. It's widely believed to have strong medicinal benefits.

"The old-timers tell you it cool deh system," says my mauby-loving Trini friend Marlon. This ubiquitous phrase is used up and down the island chain, along with its partner "cleans deh system," to cover off unspecific health benefits of various natural remedies. ("Good for cooling," says Dingis, about soursop juice. "Cools deh system," another Grenadian tells us, about tea made from soursop leaves. "Cools out your body," a Dominican says about citronella bay tea.)

More specifically, mauby is reputed to reduce high blood pressure, lower cholesterol, counteract arthritis and—what a surprise—be an effective aphrodisiac. The only item on this list to have more than anecdotal proof, however, is its ability to control hypertension. A 2005 study at the University of the West Indies Faculty of Medical Sciences investigated the effects of coconut water and mauby—alone and together—and the results showed a significant reduction of hypertension, especially when the two are combined.

"Sometimes one needs to acquire a taste for it," advises one of my Caribbean cookbooks. Count us in that group. I've tried any number of homemade and commercial mauby brews—sold out of bottles, buckets, pitchers, and bubbling soda-fountain machines—and each time I have to give up after two sips. Steve, who will eat or drink almost anything, is revolted by the stuff.

The overwhelming initial flavor is that of licorice, followed by a lingering, shiver-inducing bitterness. Mauby is also sold as a bottled concentrate to be mixed with water. The Trinidadian brand Matouk's, the market leader, sells enough of the concentrate to mix 25 million liters of mauby drink a year. It must be good. For someone.

Maybe I just need to make my own. A market woman sells me one of her already-prepared small plastic bags containing everything I need to brew a big batch: about a half-dozen short pieces of tightly curled mauby bark, a bay leaf, an inch-long piece of cinnamon, a whole star anise and a bunch of fennel seeds. I boil up the whole shebang with water, then let it steep at room temperature until it's cold. Chill, sweeten, add ice, pour, and . . . ick.

"Mauby Fizzz," which had been described to me as "licorice-flavored soda pop," appears to be the only form of mauby I still haven't tried. I buy a bottle (it's made in Trinidad, by Pepsi) and—Marlon had stressed that mauby has to be drunk icy-cold—stick it in the depths of the fridge surrounded by my soda of choice, Diet Coke; it's the one back-home habit I haven't been able to leave behind, and I get nervous if my supply slips below half a dozen.

But island supply systems are finicky, and on a day when I'm hot, tired and really feel like swilling a soda, my Diet Coke runs out, leaving only the Fizzz. The first swallow is what I expect: a licoricey, root-beer-like sweetness that gives way to rough medicinal bitterness when it hits the back of my mouth. But on the second swallow, the one-two punch reminds me of eating real Dutch licorice. And by the third swallow, geez, it's not so bad. Learning to love mauby, it seems, requires a little deprivation—and carbonation—first.

. . .

"Cloves are the new goat cheese," Steve moans with a sigh. *Receta*'s spice cupboard already has several bags of them, and I've dragged him back to the Castries market to buy more. I'm hoping the purchase of yet one more bag of cloves will finally lead the way to a grove of ready-for-harvesting clove trees.

Cloves are the dried unopened flowers of yet another tall evergreen; the buds are picked by hand when they're fully grown, but before the petals have opened, and then they are set to dry in the sun. When they resemble small rusty nails, they're ready to be used. (The name comes from the Latin *clavus*, for nail.) Despite the abundant bags of the spice in the markets of Grenada (the Caribbean's largest producer, though the crop took a hit from Ivan), St. Lucia, St. Vincent, St. Martin, Martinique and Guadeloupe, I've yet to set eyes on a clove-bearing tree.

In the sixteenth century, the Portuguese had the monopoly on cloves, having discovered the Moluccas, the Spice Islands. They were prized for medicinal uses as well as for their scent and flavor; eugenol, the main constituent of clove oil, has proven anesthetic properties, which is why cloves have long been a home remedy for dental pain. The Portuguese and then the Dutch, who took control of the Moluccas in the seventeenth century, kept a tight rein to ensure themselves a clove monopoly. But that was finally broken by the French in the late eighteenth century, when a diplomat managed to smuggle some seedlings into the French colonies of Mauritius and Réunion; from there, clove seedlings crossed to the French Caribbean, and spread. You couldn't prove it by me.

"I have clove trees," said Lyton Lamontagne, owner of Fond Doux Estate, a small working cocoa plantation near the village of Soufriere, at St. Lucia's southern end. I was ready to leap out of my seat and suggest we go immediately for a look when he continued, "but they're not bearing yet. It takes ten years before a clove tree starts to bear"—and up to twenty years before it's producing fully. Unlike cocoa, he explained, cloves have never been an estate crop on St. Lucia. "I planted mine"—he has twenty young clove trees—"because I realized there were very few in the country now."

At the Minor Spices Cooperative and Laura Spice Garden in Grenada, their one clove tree was lost in Hurricane Ivan; in Martinique, they blamed Hurricane Dean for the absence of clove trees. In the botanic gardens of Kingstown, St. Vincent, we were shown a dead tree trunk when I asked about cloves. "So pretty when it's in bloom," Dingis had said when her brother pointed to a tall, cloveless clove tree on the mountainside behind her father's house.

Now I've bet my chips on Maggie, the woman behind the table laden with cloves and other spices near the food stalls in the Castries market, sure she is going to tell me where I can see cloves growing.

"I never seen a clove tree," Maggie says. "Dey say dey up in deh forest."

Seeing my disappointment, she tries to distract me with some ground ginger. "Use it to make *tablette*," she says, using the Creole name for coconut candy. Though the shapes and names vary—it's also commonly called "sugar cake"—each island has a version, either rolled into balls, dropped into mounds, or spread in a pan and cut into squares. A similar coconut candy, called *tooloom*, includes both sugar and molasses, and is probably one of the oldest island sweets, made by West Africans working the sugar plantations.

I need to buy a coconut, Maggie explains, and grate it. Then mix it with two rum bottles of water, brown sugar and some of the ginger—she indicates the amount on her little finger, and I guess it's about a teaspoon. Add one large or two small bay leaves—she gives me a gift of a small bag—and cook until the mixture gets thick and golden brown. Then form it into balls.

"I'll let you know how they turn out when we come to the market next week," I tell her as we leave. The ever-helpful Steve adds: "And she'll bring you some to taste so you can tell her if they're right." Nothing like a little pressure.

. . .

Maggie is at her table when we return to the market, more than a week later. I pull out a Ziploc bag of irregular walnut-sized balls and hand it to her. She is surprised, and then laughs out loud—delighted. "It's tablette," she says, waving the bag at the neighboring market ladies. "She made tablette." I'm guessing tablette isn't really up there on the normal list of tourist must-dos. It had taken forever for the mixture to cook down to anything that approached ball-rolling consistency, and the mocha-colored spheres I ended up with are decidedly fragile—and over-the-top sweet, in a maple-sugar candy kind of way. I insist Maggie try one on the spot to tell me whether it tastes the way it should. (This is the built-in hazard of making something you've never seen nor tasted: We didn't like my sugary candy much, but maybe what I've produced is nothing like genuine St. Lucian tablette.) "It right," Maggie assures me.

And with that, she carefully tucks the bag of my tablette out of sight, without offering to share with her neighbors. I interpret this to mean I really have passed the island candymaking test.

Now, about that clove tree.

··· DO-IT-YOURSELF LLB ···
(LEMON LIME BITTERS)

The House of Angostura bottles a thirst-quenching, non-alcoholic car-
bonated drink called "LLB"—Lemon Lime Bitters—that's reminis-
cent of a lemon-lime soda, but with an adult edge, thanks to a healthy
dose of Angostura bitters. After trying a few homemade lemon, lime
and bitters drinks (Angostura itself puts out a recipe), we mixed up
the following and found it mimicked the bottled version very well.

10 to 12 dashes	Angostura Aromatic Bitters	10 to 12 dashes
2 cups	lemonade	500 mL
1 cup	soda water (club soda)	250 mL
2 tbsp	fresh lime juice	30 mL
2	slices of lemon or lime (for garnish)	

1. Shake the bitters onto the insides of two tall glasses.
2. Add ice and swirl until the glasses are evenly coated.
3. Add half the lemonade, soda water and lime juice to each glass. Stir and garnish with the lemon or lime.

Makes 2 tall drinks.

· · · SOURSOP COLADA · · ·

Soursop has creamy, custardy flesh and a potent flavor that's reminiscent of pineapple and vanilla—a combination that makes it a splendid substitute for the piña in a colada. Fresh soursop can sometimes be found in North American markets that have a Caribbean or Latin clientele. Or look for bottled or canned soursop nectar or juice; it's often labeled guanabana, *the Spanish name for the fruit.*

1 cup	soursop juice	
	(see Tips, below)	250 mL
½ cup	dark rum	125 mL
3 tbsp	cream of coconut	50 mL
	Angostura bitters	
	Nutmeg	

1. In a blender, combine juice, rum and cream of coconut with ice. Whirl until thick and well blended.
2. Pour into two glasses. Add a shake or two of Angostura bitters to each glass and grate a little nutmeg on top.

Makes 2 drinks.

Tips:
- To make juice from a fresh soursop: When the soursop is ripe—soft to the touch—cut in half, scrape pulp from the skin with a knife, and put pulp and seeds into a bowl. Add 3 cups (750 mL) water (for a 2- to 2 ½-lb/1 to 1.25 kg soursop) and stir for about 3 minutes with a fork, until the liquid becomes thick. Allow to stand for about 10 minutes and then stir again. Strain, squeezing out as much liquid from pulp as

possible. Discard pulp and seeds. Proceed with recipe as above. (To drink the juice straight, dilute with more water and sweeten to taste with sugar syrup. Add a couple of shakes of bitters if desired.)

- If you're starting with a fresh soursop, set aside a couple of small wedges to garnish the drinks.

· · · PICKLED CHRISTOPHENE · · ·
COCKTAIL CUBES

I got the idea of using the versatile christophene (chayote) as a cocktail snack from chef Orlando Satchell, who makes a version to accompany drinks at St. Lucia's Ladera Resort.

2 tbsp	white wine vinegar	25 mL
1 tbsp	lime juice	15 mL
½ cup	water	125 mL
1	clove garlic, chopped	1
½	small onion, chopped	½
¼ tsp	black peppercorns	1 mL
¼ tsp	mustard seeds	1 mL
1	bay leaf	1
1 tsp	kosher or sea salt	5 mL
1	large christophene (chayote), peeled, seed removed, and cut into ½- to ¾-inch (1 to 2 cm) cubes	1
¼ to ½	Scotch bonnet or other hot pepper, preferably red (for color), chopped (or to taste)	¼ to ½
1 tbsp	finely chopped chadon beni or cilantro	15 mL
1 tbsp	finely chopped parsley	15 mL

1. In a small pot, combine vinegar, lime juice, water, garlic, onion, peppercorns, mustard seeds, bay leaf and salt. Bring to a boil, reduce heat and simmer for 10 minutes.
2. Put christophene cubes in a non-reactive container and strain vinegar mixture over top. Cover and set aside until cool,

stirring occasionally, then refrigerate for several hours or longer, to allow cubes to pickle.

3. When ready to serve, drain off liquid. Add hot pepper, chadon beni or cilantro, and parsley to the cubes; stir to combine. Serve with toothpicks alongside other cocktail snacks, such as salted nuts and olives.

Makes 1 cup (250 mL).

· · · ISLAND TABBOULEH · · ·

The Castries, St. Lucia market inspired this twist on the classic Middle Eastern bulgur, tomato and parsley salad.

½ cup	bulgur	125 mL
¾ cup	boiling water	175 mL
3 tbsp	olive oil, divided	50 mL
1 tsp	curry	5 mL
1 tbsp	fresh lime juice	15 mL
2 tsp	grated ginger	10 mL
	Salt and freshly ground black pepper	
¼ cup	chopped christophene (chayote)	50 mL
2 tbsp	chopped chadon beni or cilantro	25 mL
2 tbsp	chopped chives or green onion	25 mL
¼ to ½	Scotch bonnet or other hot pepper, chopped (or to taste)	¼ to ½
1	mango, peeled and chopped	1

1. Cover bulgur with boiling water. Set aside, covered, for about 20 minutes, until water is absorbed and bulgur has softened.
2. Heat 1 tbsp (15 mL) of the oil in a small frying pan. Add curry and cook, stirring, for a minute or two to release the flavor. Set aside to cool.
3. Combine remaining oil with lime juice, ginger, and salt and pepper. Whisk in cooled curry oil.
4. Toss bulgur with a fork. Add christophene (chayote), herbs and hot pepper; toss salad with about 3 tbsp (50 mL) of the dressing. Refrigerate until serving time.

5. When ready to serve, gently mix in mango. Add a little more dressing if desired.

Makes 4 servings.

· · · ICY PEANUT CREAM · · ·

We were introduced to this treat—a frozen version of peanut punch, a popular island drink—at the Saturday market in Soufriere, St. Lucia, where it's sold in small plastic bags. Like the locals, we ripped a corner off the bag with our teeth and sucked out the contents. When we make it ourselves, we forgo authenticity and serve it in individual dishes, with spoons.

¾ cup	smooth peanut butter	175 mL
¾ cup	sweetened condensed milk	175 mL
1 ¾ cups	milk	425 mL
1 tsp	vanilla extract	5 mL
¼ tsp	freshly grated nutmeg	1 mL

1. Whisk all ingredients together and freeze overnight.
2. When ready to serve, soften at room temperature for about 10 minutes. Scoop small balls of the frozen cream into bowls and grate a little additional fresh nutmeg on top.

Makes 6 servings.

Tips:
- Serve the Icy Peanut Cream with the Grenadian Banana Bread in Chapter 1 or the Local-Chocolate Cake in Chapter 10.
- Turn the frozen cream into a cocktail: Put a scoop of it in the blender. Add 1 ½ oz (45 mL) of dark rum and 1 tbsp (15 mL) of a chocolate- or almond-flavored cream liqueur. Blend until smooth.

FIFTEEN

Dog Sauce and Rhum

· · · ST. MARTIN, MARTINIQUE · · · & MARIE-GALANTE

Indeed, the whole secret of Creole cooking is to be found in its spices, and in the way the ingredients are marinaded [sic] before cooking, lending our food its incomparable bouquet of aromas.

Babette de Rozières, the Guadeloupean chef of acclaimed
Parisian restaurant La Table de Babette, in her cookbook Creole

ANNY BOISSARD FIRST GOT US HOOKED on the Creole cooking of the French Antilles—though, God knows, we didn't suspect when we first set eyes on her that she was the one actually turning out the superlative *accras de morue* (codfish fritters), *crabe farci* (stuffed crab back), *colombo de cabri* (a kind of goat curry) and *poisson frit* (fried fish). She was wearing a pristine, chic white sheath with cutout shoulders that hugged her lithe figure, not exactly work attire if your work involves flames shooting from sauté pans and hot oil splattering from pots. Her stylish, close-cropped gray hair was streaked boldly with blonde, and from head to well-shod toe, she certainly exuded good taste—but in fashion, not food.

We had wandered into Cas' Anny Two, a small, breezy restaurant with an unassuming, almost unnoticeable facade, in Marigot, on the French side of St. Martin, not expecting much, simply needing lunch. But the accras we started with were light, almost lacy, and completely irresistible, delivering the sharp bite of saltfish and the zing of pepper inside a crunchy, deep-fried batter shell. The colombo de cabri I ordered was fall-off-the-bone tender, and its curry sauce—creamier and milder than its Trini counterparts—was richly fragrant with a subtle hit of heat. For those who wanted fire, an entire Scotch bonnet pepper was delivered to the table, presented like a piece of art: all by itself on a white plate, with an elegant little silver knife laid alongside. Steve's whole red snapper—rubbed with lime juice, fresh thyme and garlic, quickly stove-top grilled, and then finished with an uncooked tomato, onion, garlic, and hot pepper vinaigrette-like topping—was a candidate, he said, for "best fish ever."

Georges, the middle-aged man who served us, said that, yes, the beautifully dressed Anny was indeed doing the cooking here. We surmised the gorgeous cook was also his wife. *Mais non.* She turned out to be his sixty-nine-year-old mother. Anny came to St. Martin from Martinique, Georges told us, and to Martinique from her birthplace, France.

One day before the lunch rush started, Anny (fashionably dressed that morning in brilliant yellow capris and a long, high-style T-shirt) showed us her kitchen, as petite and well put-together as she was. She had learned to cook from her mother, she said—"I like to eat, and I have the palate, the *saveur*"— and sang the praises of the fresh ingredients available in the islands: "fresh crab, fish, lobster, conch, seasonings, produce." The French Anny spoke, like her cooking, was strongly

Creole—a term that comes with confusing historical baggage.

When referring to people, the word has been used over the centuries to describe the descendants of European settlers (usually French or Spanish) in the New World—as well as the descendants of mixed African and European blood. Generally, in the Caribbean it now refers to people of mixed descent, and this mixing is at the heart of Creole food. Creole cooking is fusion food, a melting pot of ingredients and techniques. Much of Caribbean cooking is therefore to some extent Creole—but the word has become most firmly connected to the cuisine of those islands with a strong French influence.

One story explaining the invention of French-Caribbean accras—those delicate fritters of Anny's—is likely more fiction than fact, but it nevertheless captures the fusion that is Creole cooking. A French plantation owner in Guadeloupe, so the tale goes, employed a cook from the Normandy region of France. Relocated to the West Indies, she couldn't find apples to make her customary apple fritters. Savory fritters were part of the culinary heritage of an African woman working in the plantation's kitchen, and she suggested substituting readily available saltfish for the apples. The result satisfied neither cook, however—until a third woman in the kitchen, this one from India, suggested adding some of the cive and peppers she was chopping to the fritters. The French/African/East Indian result was a hit, and became a much-loved standard of Creole cooking.

Anny's colombo, too, demonstrates the waves of culinary influence on the French islands. Colombo refers both to a spice blend that's a close cousin to curry and to the traditional stew that's made with it—taking its name from the capital and chief port of Sri Lanka. After slavery was abolished, Sri Lankans were among the East Indians who came to the French islands between 1852 and 1865 to work as indentured servants on the sugar plantations. As had the East Indians in Trinidad, they brought their seasonings with them, and the Sri Lankan spice blends became known by their place of origin.

When I asked Olive, my 'splain-me-everything market woman in Marigot, if I could buy some colombo, she treated my request with her usual suspicion. "You know how to make chicken curry?" she asked.

"Yes," I replied.

"Okay, you do the same thing, except you use the colombo instead of curry," she said, handing over the little plastic bag. "And make sure you serve it with rice." Based on the result, and on Anny's tender, flavorful goat, we thought "colombo" translated as "gentle curry." Until we got to Martinique.

. . .

Like French St. Martin, Martinique is an overseas department of France, separated from its French sibling to the north, Guadeloupe, by the formerly British-owned Dominica. *Receta* is anchored at Le Marin, a well-developed pleasure-boating area on Martinique's south coast, and my trusty translator has rudely forsaken me for the marine stores—leaving me to tackle the small market by myself. (I'm the interpreter on the Spanish islands, Steve gets the job on the French ones.) "Do you make your own colombo?" I ask a market woman in badly fractured French as I buy a small bag of the burnt-orange powder. "*Poulet et viande*," she answers. Chicken and meat.

"Well, at least I know what she uses it for," I tell the snickering Steve afterward. Her colombo turns out to be powered by pepper, both *piment* (hot pepper) and *poivre* (black peppercorns),

so different from Anny's and Olive's that I'm left confused—
will the real colombo please stand up?—and wanting others to
compare. The next batch, I promise—I'm not above bribery—
will be used to colombo Steve's favorite meat: goat. And so, with
my translator once again happily in tow, we visit the modest marketplace in the nearby town of Ste. Anne, where Monique sells
me her take on the spice blend. This one replaces the bite of
pepper with one of cloves. *Vive la différence.*

Finalement, at the big store Le Monde des Épices—Spice
World—on the industrial outskirts of Fort de France,
Martinique's capital, I learn that colombo is generally built on
a base of four spices: turmeric, which is called *curcuma* in the
French islands, from its scientific name, *Curcuma longa,* coriander, dried garlic, and piment (hot pepper). But then, depending
on the place and the maker, any number of other spices are
added to the blend: perhaps cumin, mustard seed, black pepper,
fenugreek, clove, cinnamon, and even tamarind. "No, no, the
spices aren't from here," says the harried manager we corner in
Spice World. Hurricane Dean destroyed a lot of the island's spice
trees in 2007, she says, and, in any case, their colombo is blended
in France, to their specifications, and then imported in bulk.

. . .

Even with my pathetically basic French, I have no trouble
understanding the label on the jar: *Sauce Chien.* Dog Sauce.
Sure, I'll be buying some of that. How appetizing. But the
bright green sauce on Monique's and her neighbors' market
tables looks decidedly vegetarian; in fact, it looks like a more
textured version of Paramin green seasoning. "Maybe it's
meant to be served with dog," Steve suggests in his usual helpful

fashion. "*Petit poodle, le plat du jour.*" No, Monique says. It's meant to be served with *poisson*, fish. Just serve it straight out of the jar, at room temperature. She, like Steve, is completely unhelpful about where the dog comes in: Sauce Chien is made with herbs—mostly cive, with a bit of parsley, thyme, fresh hot pepper and shallots—steeped in vinegar, oil and lime. And when I check the Martiniquais cookbook I bought at Le Monde des Épices, I discover it pulls its punches and translates Sauce Chien as "Creole Sauce." Whatever we call it, its herby cive-and-thyme flavor is indeed fabulous on grilled fish—and roasted chicken too. One island's green seasoning is another island's green sauce. And the golden girls in Paramin had laughed.

Much later, I read that the dog in the dog sauce comes from the make of knife once commonly used to chop its ingredients. Chien knives have a little outline of a dog etched into their blades right above the handle, the company's trademark. (The word "Chien" is stamped across the dog's side.) Then again, a Guadeloupean chef claims it comes from the West Indian French phrase *C'est chien*, used to describe something that tastes delicious. And another source says it's because the sauce has a little bite. And . . . *ça suffit!*

. . .

How can you go wrong with an SdJ that's the pleasing color of pistachio ice cream? Besides, we've learned the trick of car rentals on a French island. Everything—except restaurants, *naturellement*—closes down promptly at noon for the French lunch hour, which usually lasts at least two and a half hours. Arrange to pick up an SdJ just before the rental place closes for lunch and, if you're lucky, they'll tell you not to return it until three the next afternoon. Schmooze the staff as Steve does, and they'll likely agree that you can pick up your one-day rental well before noon, and if you don't get it back until four or so the next day, well, *c'est la vie*. Or, from the renter's point of view, *voilà:* a one-day car rental magically turns into a day and a half.

The only problem with our economy-sized pistachio Twingo is that its space doesn't expand like the rental period. Four people, plus far too many bottles of rum, plus copious bags of groceries (chèvre, pâté, baguettes and other critical alcohol-absorbing supplies), make for one very crowded car.

Our old friend the Minister of Rum is partly—no, almost completely—to blame. We met Ed Hamilton in the late '90s, when he was making a career of sailing the Caribbean, tasting rums, and proselytizing about them to anyone who would stand still long enough to taste and listen. (He had a collection of some sixty types of Caribbean rum on his sailboat, as well as boxes of his self-published rum guidebook, to aid him in his work.) Eventually, the Minister became frustrated that the people he converted to the gospel of good rum couldn't buy some of his favorites—particularly French *rhum agricole*—anywhere except in the islands. Ed kept the Ministry of Rum going via the Internet and continued to work for it part-time, but branched into a new line of work, distributing the products of two Martiniquais distilleries in North America. When we wrote to tell him we were in Martinique, the Minister e-mailed us back from the United States, where business demands he now spend most of his time. "Sales are growing," he said. "I ship my thousandth case next month. Hope all's well in Martinique—I wish I was in the islands."

"We owe it to Ed," Steve says. "We need to visit his distilleries." Martinique has eleven rhumeries—more than any other Caribbean island—strewn across its 400-plus square miles; they all invite visitors for a look, and a taste; and they are all handily mapped on "La Route des Rhums." Steve wants to see how many stops a couple of stretched days of Twingo rental will allow.

Rhum agricole is made from fresh sugar-cane juice, rather than molasses, and it comes almost exclusively from the French islands (though Trinidad's House of Angostura recently started bottling a rhum agricole–style spirit called 10 Cane). In the French islands, molasses-based rum is called *rhum industriel,* the name quite aptly describing what the Martiniquais and Guadeloupeans think of it; most of it is exported, as they refuse to drink it themselves. In rhum agricole, the taste of the cane comes through quite clearly—especially in the unaged white rums—and one rhumerie's spirits can have a noticeably different flavor from another's.

Martinique's rhum agricole is the only product of any sort in the French Caribbean to have a French AOC designation, an *appellation d'origine contrôlée.* This certification, marked on the bottle, attests that the rhum uses ingredients from a particular, carefully defined geographic area and that it is produced in a traditional manner. The same certification is granted, in France, to geographic regions for specific agricultural products such as wines (Bordeaux, Burgundy and Champagne, for instance), cheeses (Roquefort, Comté, and more than three dozen others), poultry (Bresse hens) and spirits (such as Cognac and Armagnac). If a product is aged, the aging must occur at least partially in the region where it is made, and also must be done according to traditional methods. In the case of Martiniquais *rhum vieux,* aged rum, this means aging in 650-liter wooden barrels for at least three years, although many are aged much longer. None of the rhum agricole from rival Guadeloupe has been awarded an AOC.

. . .

Habitation La Favorite, founded in 1842, sits squarely in the middle of Martinique. When the Twingo arrives and four of us tumble out like eager circus clowns—Barb and Chuck from *Tusen Takk II* have joined us on the Route des Rhums—the factory is in full operation, and the air is rich with the sweet smell of cane. As we enter the old brick building, we are instantly transported back in time. Roaring furnaces burn crushed sugar-cane stalks, called *bagasse,* to produce steam to power the nineteenth-century engine that operates the cane crusher. Its antique innards are in open view, big cogwheels turning slowly through a vat of cooling black oil, pistons belching steam, the air sticky with the flying fibers of ground cane.

There is no official tour here, no railings or glass windows behind which we must stand to watch, no keep-the-tourists-safe INTERDIT signs restricting our access. We are more than welcome to stroll and pause where we wish, and the workers actually seem pleased at our presence. The man stoking the boilers opens one of its furnace doors, so we can see the flames and feel the intensity of the heat—and watch sparks come showering out . . . in the midst of a floor strewn with bits of fire-feeding cane. Another worker invites us to stick a finger in the fermented cane juice on its way to the copper distillation column, a working work of art. The distiller himself gestures for us to dip our fingers again for a taste, this time into the transparent sight-glass where he monitors the alcohol content of the nascent rhum with a hydrometer, and signals that Steve and Chuck must take photos of him with Barb and me. It's not a language gap that necessitates gestures here—it's just difficult to hear any language over the clanking, grinding and belching of the machines.

Still another employee beckons us into the aging warehouse, where oak barrels are stacked to the over 30-foot-high roof, and the name LA FAVORITE is spelled out in raised bricks set into the floor. This is where the angels take a sip. As the rhum ages, acquiring color and aroma from the oak barrels, some of it evaporates—which improves the flavor of the remaining rum—and this lost alcohol is traditionally called "the angels' share." The smell of the warehouse is a blend of oak, rhum, must and time. We know the Minister of Rum chose to import La Favorite because of its taste, but we can be forgiven for thinking it was also because of the rhumerie's archaic beauty.

The Minister's other favored rhumerie, La Distillerie Neisson, is a comparative child, born in 1931. Here, La Favorite's gritty Industrial Revolution tableaux are replaced by the kind of machines that get guys like Steve (okay, all guys) drooling: giant, polished, pristine working models in richly painted iron and steel, and gleaming copper and brass, an Erector Set come to life. Here, too, a steam engine crushes the cane—though it is quiet when we arrive shortly before noon. The bar in the tasting room, on the other hand, is a hive of activity, as the distillery's workers begin to stroll in, one or two at a time, to mix themselves a pre-lunch drink.

White rhum agricole rests for a minimum of three months before it is reduced with spring water to selling strength (50-percent or 55-percent alcohol) and bottled, and though it tastes pleasantly of cane, it is still very much a strong, rough-edged spirit. The Martiniquais and the Guadeloupeans like to mix it into a little punch, a *petit punch*—or *ti punch*, as it's known in Creole—to cushion its kick. After the Minister of Rum mixed us our first ti punch in *Receta*'s galley when we met in Grenada in the late 1990s—Ed had arrived at our boat bearing the necessary ingredients and equipment; the man is a traveling cocktail bar—Steve adopted it as *Receta*'s house drink.

A ti punch changes names depending on the time of day it's consumed. When downed before dawn, say, on the way to work, it's called a *décollage*, a liftoff. But ti punch is more than just a drink; it's a ceremony. Its ingredients are simple, but each drink is mixed individually, just so. In the Neisson tasting room, each worker pours a bit of sugar-cane syrup into a small, special ti punch glass: short, squat, and bearing the name of the distillery whose rhum it will soon contain. He then adds a squeeze of fresh lime and a generous pour of rhum agricole. The mixing must be done with a *lélé*—a natural swizzle stick made from a twig with five branches that grow perpendicular to the stem; the twig, from a tree called the *bois lélé* or swizzle-stick tree, is cleaned of its bark and smoothed, and the branches are trimmed into short "spokes." The lélé is inserted into the glass and rolled vigorously back and forth a couple of times between the palms to blend the ingredients. *Glace*—ice—isn't customary. The workers mix ti punches for us visitors, too, and toasts of *salut!* and *santé!* echo all around, before they disperse for lunch. "You gotta love the job perks here," says Steve.

. . .

In the soft late-afternoon sunlight, two oxen wait placidly by a river, yoked to an open-sided wooden cart. An older man, in rubber boots, hefts bundles of sugar cane into it, while a woman in a broad straw hat stoops to gather more cut cane into bundles, tying the stalks together with sugar-cane leaves. Other oxen plod along the roads, taking loads of cane to the rhumeries. The cane harvest is in full swing on Marie-Galante, an island that is virtually covered in sugar, famous for its rum, and seemingly caught in the nineteenth century.

An SdJ can easily circumnavigate tiny, pastoral Marie-Galante in a day—it's only 9 miles wide, and 61 square miles all together. Named by Columbus in honor of the *Maria Galanda*, the flagship on his second voyage, Marie-Galante is, like Martinique, part of France. Politically, it's a dependency of Guadeloupe, and located slightly to the southeast of that island, about midway between it and Dominica. But unlike Martinique and Guadeloupe—unlike most Caribbean islands, for that matter—Marie-Galante's economy remains firmly based on agriculture, with most of its residents involved in raising cane or making rum. Its round shape and almost flat surface make it well suited for sugar, and give it the nickname "La Grande Galette"—the Big Pancake. Though the Martiniquais might argue Marie-Galante's claim that it produces the best rum in the world, and though it lacks an AOC designation, it does have one undeniable distinction: it's the only French island with special permission by law to market rhum with an alcohol content of up to 59 percent.

As the SdJ rounds a bend on a cane-strewn road, Rhumerie Bellevue comes into view, the white sails of a stone windmill circling languidly next to the old buildings. More than a hundred of these windmills once dotted Marie-Galante, providing power to turn the stones that crushed the cane. Almost all of the seventy remaining ones stand in ruins—victims of time, and hurricanes—and even the one or two that still function, like Bellevue's, are kept operating only for heritage purposes; diesel now provides the power for the crushing.

In 1830, Marie-Galante had 105 sugar mills, half of them powered by wind, the rest by oxen. But only three rhumeries and one (large) *sucrerie*—sugar refinery—still operate. The decline in the sugar economy is reflected in the decline in population: only about 13,000 now, less than half what it was in 1950.

"The island is changing, unfortunately—but not too fast," says a worker at Distillerie Poisson, where much of the cane being fed into the crusher has been cut by hand. Hand-cut cane is distinctive, because it's cut with a diagonal slash, and the stalks are long; machine-cut cane is shorter, with a horizontal bottom. The product of Distillerie Poisson is called Rhum du Père Labat, named after the food- and drink-loving French priest. (The good priest is pictured on the label of the rhum vieux.) Along with saving souls and recording seventeenth-century life, he also advanced rum production in the French islands, introducing new machines to press the cane and improve distillation processes. In the rhumerie biz, he's something of a hero. On Martinique, he's immortalized in rum-making terminology: the boilers are called *les chaudières Père Labat*, the windmills—long gone—*la tour du Père Labat*, and the standard method of distillation, *type Père Labat*.

That night, in the Maria Galanda restaurant in Grand Bourg (the island's main town, as the name suggests, in whose *très petit* harbor *Receta* is anchored), we appropriately order ti punches before dinner. The owner doesn't bring us drinks, however. She sets down empty glasses, emblazoned with the logo of Marie-Galante's Distillerie Bielle, and tiny espresso-sized spoons and a saucer of lime wedges. And then she returns with a small bottle of Rhum Agricole Bielle, and another of cane syrup, and leaves them on the table. We, like everyone else, are expected to mix our own. As they say in French, "*Chacun prépare sa propre mort.*" Every one prepares his own death.

· · · CREOLE FISH · · ·
IN THE STYLE OF CAS' ANNY

The fish gets a double hit of flavor: first, from an herb rub before it's grilled, then from the uncooked topping spooned on just before serving. Anny uses small red snappers (a whole fish per person), "grilling" them in a super-hot stovetop ridged grill pan, but you can do them on the barbecue if you prefer.

4	whole small fish, such as red snapper (less than 1 lb/500 g apiece)	4

For the rub:

1	lime	1
2	cloves garlic, finely chopped	2
2 tsp	coarse kosher or sea salt	10 mL
2 tbsp	finely chopped fresh thyme	25 mL
1	green onion, finely chopped	1

For the topping:

1	small onion, finely chopped	1
1	green onion, finely chopped	1
¼ to ½	hot pepper, finely chopped (or to taste)	¼ to ½
1	small tomato, seeded and finely chopped	1
2	cloves garlic, finely chopped	2
1 tbsp	olive oil	15 mL
½	lime	½
	Salt (to taste)	

1. Rinse and dry fish. Cut lime in half and rub on both sides of fish, squeezing on the juice as you do so. If you're cooking the fish on the barbecue, cut several diagonal slits on each side.

2. Combine the remaining ingredients for the rub in a small bowl. Rub into fish and set aside for about 30 minutes.

3. To make the topping, combine onion, green onion, hot pepper, tomato, garlic and olive oil. Add 2 tsp (10 mL) lime juice. Taste and adjust flavor as desired with additional hot pepper, lime juice and salt.

4. Oil stovetop pan or barbecue rack. (A fish-grilling rack or fish basket is best to prevent sticking.) Preheat barbecue, if using. Cook fish over high heat for about 5 minutes per side, or until it is just opaque. (Time will depend on thickness of the fish.)

5. Remove from heat and spoon some topping on each fish.

Makes 4 servings.

Tip:
- This recipe also works well with firm fish steaks, such as dorado (mahi-mahi), halibut, kingfish or grouper. Reduce the salt in the rub to 1 tsp (5 mL), and check for doneness after 3 minutes per side.

· · · POUDRE DE COLOMBO · · ·
(COLOMBO POWDER)

When my supply of market-bought colombo runs low and I'm far from Martinique or Guadeloupe, I make my own Creole curry spice blend. Roasting and grinding the spices yourself gives the mix a real intensity. Use it to make Colombo Almonds (next page) or Colombo Shrimp (substituting colombo for the curry in the Trini-Style Curry Shrimp recipe in Chapter 9).

¼ cup	whole cumin seeds	50 mL
2 tbsp	whole coriander seeds	25 mL
2 tbsp	whole mustard seeds	25 mL
1 tbsp	fenugreek seeds	15 mL
1 tbsp	cloves	15 mL
2 tbsp	freshly ground cinnamon stick	25 mL
2 tbsp	freshly ground dried ginger root	25 mL
⅓ cup	turmeric	75 mL
1 tbsp	whole black peppercorns	15 mL
1–2	whole dried hot peppers	1–2

1. Toast the cumin, coriander, mustard, fenugreek and cloves in a dry pan until the mustard begins to pop.
2. Cool mixture slightly, then combine with remaining ingredients in a mortar (or spice grinder) and grind into a powder. Store in a tightly closed jar.

Makes about 1 ¼ cups (300 mL).

· · · COLOMBO ALMONDS · · ·

Use your homemade colombo (previous page) or a store-bought curry powder to make this spicy twist on plain salted nuts. Try it with other nuts, too. We like it with cashews, or a combination of cashews, almonds and pecans.

2 tbsp	butter	25 mL
1 tbsp	colombo (see recipe, previous page) or other good-quality curry powder	15 mL
½ tsp	hot pepper sauce (less if it's a truly fiery one, such as Miss Pat's)	2 mL
3 cups	unblanched whole almonds	750 mL
	Salt	
½ cup	slivered dried mango	125 mL

1. Preheat oven to 300°F (150°C). In a small saucepan over low heat, melt butter, stir in colombo or curry powder, and cook for a minute or two. Remove from heat and add pepper sauce.
2. Put nuts in a large bowl, pour on spiced butter, and toss to mix well.
3. Spread nuts on baking sheets and bake in preheated oven for 20 minutes, stirring occasionally. (Keep a close eye on them so they don't burn.) Remove from oven and sprinkle with salt, then transfer to trays lined with paper towels to cool.
4. When nuts are completely cooled, mix in the slivered dried mango. Store in tightly covered containers. Allow flavor to develop overnight before serving.

Makes a generous 3 cups (750 mL).

· · · SAUCE CHIEN · · ·

Despite the name, we love this Creole sauce. Its fresh, herby taste complements simply grilled fish, steak and chicken.

4	green onions	4
¼ cup	parsley	50 mL
3	cloves garlic	3
¼ to ½	Scotch bonnet or other hot pepper (or to taste)	¼ to ½
½	lime, juiced	½
1 tbsp	white-wine vinegar	15 mL
2 tbsp	olive oil	25 mL
¼ cup	boiling water	50 mL
	Salt and freshly ground black pepper	

1. In the bowl of a food processor, combine onions, parsley, garlic and hot pepper; pulse to finely chop. (Or finely chop by hand and mix well.)
2. Stir in lime juice, vinegar and oil. Pour boiling water over top, cover the bowl and let stand until mixture has completely cooled. Season to taste.
3. Store sauce in refrigerator. Serve at room temperature with grilled meat or fish.

Makes about 1 cup (250 mL).

· · · ONE-BITE TI PUNCH TARTS · · ·

Steve and I disagree over which of us came up with the idea of islandizing old-fashioned pecan pie into a petit dessert with the flavor of a ti punch. We agree, however, that the little tarts are irresistible. Santé!

½ cup	lightly packed demerara or cane sugar	125 mL
1 tbsp	butter, melted	15 mL
½ cup	cane syrup (see Tips, below)	125 mL
½ tsp	vanilla extract (or the vanilla beans scraped from 1 pod)	2 mL
2	eggs, beaten	2
2 tbsp	rhum agricole (see Tips, below) or white rum	25 mL
	Pastry for a 1-crust pie (half of the Pastelillo Pastry recipe in Chapter 3) or 24 frozen mini tart shells, thawed	
1 scant cup	small pecan halves (or large halves, coarsely chopped)	250 mL
½	lime	½

1. Preheat oven to 425°F (220°C).
2. Combine sugar, butter, cane syrup, vanilla, eggs and rum in a bowl; lightly beat (with spatula or spoon) until smooth.
3. If using pastry, roll out about ⅛ inch (3 mm) thick and cut 3-inch (8 cm) (approx) circles. Line 24 mini-muffin cups with the circles. Or arrange mini-tart shells on a baking sheet.

4. In each cup or tart shell, place two or three small pecan halves. Top each with approximately 1 tbsp (15 mL) of filling mixture.
5. Bake in preheated oven for 8 to 10 minutes, or until crust is golden and filling is puffed and set.
6. Allow to cool in pans 30 minutes, then remove to rack.
7. Just before serving, peel and slice the lime thinly and divide the slices into small (about ¼-inch/5 mm) segments. Place a segment on top of each tart.

Makes about 24.

Tips:

- Rhum agricole, made from sugar cane juice, has a distinctive taste. It's available in some U.S. liquor stores, or you can substitute another white rum.
- Cane syrup, made from cane juice that has been boiled down to the consistency of maple syrup, is available in some specialty food stores. Look for *"sirop de canne"* imported from France or the French Caribbean. You can substitute corn syrup, although the tarts will lose something of their ti punch taste.
- For a ti punch pie: Scatter 2 cups (500 mL) of pecans in an unbaked pie shell, and pour in double the filling. Bake at 425°F (220°C) for 10 minutes, then lower heat to 350°F (180°C) and bake an additional 25 to 30 minutes.

SIXTEEN

The Torments of Love

· · · GUADELOUPE · · ·
& THE ISLANDS OF THE SAINTS

The feast of cooking takes place annually the Saturday closest to the
August 10 anniversary date of [the cooks'] patron saint: Saint Laurent,
a priest who was burned on the grill . . .

from Antilles Découvertes *maga*ℨ*ine, 2007*

"WE GREW TO LOATHE POINTE-À-PITRE," Patrick Leigh
Fermor said of Guadeloupe's main city in *The Traveller's Tree*,
his now-classic account of island-hopping through the
Caribbean in the 1940s. "The general impression is one of aban-
donment and decay." After just a short time, he wrote, "Pointe-
à-Pitre had become as hateful to us as a plague-town." Some
sixty years later, Steve and I are having a similar reaction (well,
perhaps not quite so violent), finding it very hard to fall in love
with this city—or with Guadeloupe in general, for that matter,
though we really try.

The island is shaped like a butterfly, its two wings hinged
together in the center by a narrow isthmus, through which flows

the Rivière Salée (a "sluggish limb of sea," Fermor called it). *Receta* is anchored between the wings, just off Pointe-à-Pitre, at the south end of the island where the saltwater river begins. "At the ass end of the butterfly," Steve notes, with no small amount of irony. Day and night, a smoky haze obscures the butterfly's western wing, a constant stream of boats—pleasure craft, Jet Skis, ferries, container ships, tugboats—bounces us with their wake, and garbage burns on shore just upwind. We're left itchy-eyed, runny-nosed, irritated, and constantly grabbing for breakables before they crash to the cabin floor. The Caribs, who inhabited Guadeloupe when Columbus arrived in 1493, called it "Karukera," meaning "island of beautiful waters." But you sure couldn't prove it by us.

Those uncooperative Caribs resisted Spanish attempts to settle the island, and Spain abandoned its claim to Guadeloupe in 1604, making room for the French, who arrived in 1635 and didn't mess around. They wiped out the Caribs and brought in slaves to do the work of planting sugar cane and building the first sugar mill. The African and the French influences blended into a Creole culture, which remains the island's defining characteristic. Since 1946, it has been an overseas department of France, which puts it on the same political footing as Martinique.

Guadeloupe is reputed to have the best Creole food in the Caribbean. Its master cooks, called *cuisinières*, have their own association, more than three hundred cooks strong, with Lawrence, the grilled saint, as their patron. They call themselves "professionals of the mouth," and they have their own festival, the Fête des Cuisinières, or Festival of the Women Cooks, during which they prepare their Creole specialties for a huge public feast. The cooks first banded together in 1916, to form an "insurance association," the Association Le Cuistot Mutuelle, to provide medical care and funerals for their members; a year later, they created a fete to give them a happier reason to get together.

Unfortunately, when the cooks will be parading their towers of *oassous* (crayfish), *crabes farcis* (stuffed crab backs), *fricassée de chatrous* (octopus fricassee), *colombo de poulet* and *colombo de cabri* (chicken and goat colombos) and *boudins créoles* (blood sausages) through the streets of Pointe-à-Pitre on the way to the cathedral to get the food blessed before the feasting and dancing begin, *Receta* will be far from Guadeloupe. The Fête des Cuisinières is in August, the middle of hurricane season, and the butterfly island sits squarely in the middle of the hurricane highway.

Which is why we are determined to try some of the cuisinières' cooking now, several months before the festival. So far, it's not looking easy.

. . .

Our guidebook describes Pointe-à-Pitre as "bursting with life and color." "Oozing is more like it," Steve says, as we follow an unspectacular walking tour laid out in a recent tourist board brochure. With occasional exceptions, the old Creole buildings look unloved, and it is hard to credit the city with much architectural charm. I haul Steve off toward the Musée l'Herminier, housed in an 1873 building that was once home to the Chambre d'Agriculture, thinking its collections might hold some interest. Behind lovely wrought-iron gates, its tall louvered doors are locked tight on both stories, the verandas smeared with graffiti—a regular sight in Pointe-à-Pitre, and something we're unused to seeing elsewhere in the Caribbean. Maybe we were lucky: the museum had been open when Fermor stopped here in the '40s: "There was nobody there," he wrote. "The door was wide open, all the glass was broken, and everything was coated with the dust of decades."

A few blocks away, the flower market is sparse, even though it's Friday, the second-biggest market day of the week; the few arrangements on offer are decidedly non-tropical, bland distant cousins of the wildly exuberant bouquets we see in Dominica and Trinidad. On the waterfront, the handicraft market consists of a few stalls of beach towels and T-shirts. Adding insult to injury, the banks and the tourism office are closed—on an ordinary Friday, during ordinary business hours. Yesterday, however, was a French national holiday (VE day), and this coming Monday is a religious feast day, another holiday—so why bother opening on the days in between?

Meanwhile, the phone numbers I have for the association of the cuisinières all prove to be out of service, there are no listings in the phone book, and anyone we ask for help just gives a Gallic shrug.

"They won't even help me—and I live here," Steven Lee tells us sympathetically in perfect, unaccented English. The words come slowly, though, with occasional pauses between them. He's been speaking French daily for so long that he has to dredge up English vocabulary from the depths of his memory. He moved to Guadeloupe from San Francisco twenty years ago "for love"—his wife is Guadeloupean—and he now owns four Délifrance café-bakery franchises. The one in Pointe-à-Pitre, where we meet him, serves not just the usual espressos, croissants and baguette sandwiches, but full lunches, prepared by a Creole cook.

"Asking me where to eat Creole food in Guadeloupe is like asking me where to eat Chinese food in San Francisco," says Lee. "Too many excellent choices, and every Creole cook does it differently." We've already had a couple of good (if unspectacular) meals in the city—but we want to try a master cook: a traditional, real-deal original. Of course, he knows the cuisinières—"when their festival is on, it takes away all my business"—but he can't offer up any contact names, numbers or other help. Besides, we're unlikely to find them cooking in restaurants, he says. "Most of them are retired now. They're just trying to pass the tradition on to a younger generation before they die out."

In fact, he says, the grande dame of the cuisinières, Violetta Chaville, passed away a few years ago at the age of ninety-four. Which certainly explains why we have been unsuccessful in finding the acclaimed Creole restaurant called Chez Violetta.

At least we can console ourselves in the Marché Central and the waterfront Marché de la Darse while we try to find a master cook. The displays of fish and produce look like they have been prepared by food stylists. The combo packs—my name for the assortments of vegetables and herbs sold together so shoppers can buy exactly what they need to make a dish—are arranged like bouquets, more attractive, in fact, than the ones in the flower market: a thin curve of orange pumpkin backed by a fan of green cive and a pretty wedge of crinkly cabbage, with a few red piments providing flower-like accents to one side.

Beyond the fish and behind the produce, the covered section of the Marché de la Darse is devoted to spices. Madras-wrapped baskets overflowing with dried buds and seeds sit in front of bottles of spiced rums and colored potions. The label on one reads *Sirop de Pied de Cheval*—Horse-Hoof Syrup. "What does one do with it?" I ask the woman at the stall (or some approximation of that, given my French has improved only marginally since Martinique). "Aphrodisiac," she tells me, reaching for the bottle. "*No, no, merci,*" I quickly reply—before Steve can.

The centerpiece of most of the spice stalls is a pyramid consisting of thick bundles of long, slender vanilla pods. The market women are quick to thrust a bundle under the noses of passersby, knowing that a whiff of the dark (almost-black), moist (almost-sticky) pods is the prelude to a sale (almost guaranteed). Each bundle has upward of twenty pods—or beans, as they're commonly known in North America, though the beans are really inside the pod—making for a powerful, mouthwatering vanilla aroma. Guadeloupe is on the list of the world's top producers of the spice, in fourteenth or fifteenth place, depending on the year. Its annual yield of about 8 tonnes is a far cry, though, from the 6,200 tonnes produced by first-place Madagascar, which supplies about 59 percent of the world market.

Early attempts to introduce the vanilla vine to other tropical areas from its native Mexico, where it was cultivated by the Aztecs, met with no success; the flowers simply wouldn't bear fruit. But finally, in the nineteenth century, a Belgian botanist noticed that only one species of bee and one hummingbird pollinate vanilla flowers—and they live only in Mexico. As a result, most vanilla has to be hand-pollinated, which is part of the reason it is the world's second most costly spice—albeit a distant second behind real saffron (not the turmeric that goes by that name in the English-speaking Caribbean). Vanilla is pricey even in Guadeloupe (one of the big bundles of pods costs 10 euros, about US$14), though it still works out to just a fraction of the $2 or more I pay per pod in Toronto.

The other reason for vanilla's high price is that the pods can't simply be picked and sold. Straight off the vine, they're odorless and tasteless. Like cocoa beans, they have to be fermented to develop their flavor and dark brown color, a process that takes several weeks and involves alternately "sweating" the beans under heavy blankets or in airtight boxes and drying them in the sun. The pods are then set aside to age for a month or more, after which they are still supple, tender and moist but with fully developed aroma. (If a vanilla pod feels dry and leathery, and doesn't exude a powerful fragrance, it shouldn't be purchased.) You just have to wonder how the Aztecs first figured this out: "Hey, I think I'll tuck this tasteless green pod under my blankie at night for a few weeks, and then put it away for a couple of months, and see what happens."

I notice some of the pods in the bundle I've selected have a powdery white dust on them, and at first I assume it's mold, and not a good thing. In fact, it's a very good thing: vanillin, a white, crystalline substance that develops during the fermenting process and is responsible for the flavor and perfume of the spice. Vanilla's flavor, like that of cocoa, is strongly affected by *terroir*. But we don't have any other beans to compare with these Guadeloupean ones. I just know their fragrance lingers deliciously after I've touched them, and I want to keep licking my fingers.

"Where on Guadeloupe do they come from?" Steve asks the woman from whom I buy my pods. She produces a map from under her madras-covered table and circles her finger around the mountains of Basse Terre, the island's western wing. The two halves of Guadeloupe appear to have been named by a perverse Frenchman: Basse Terre, meaning "Low Land," is high and mountainous, and the larger of the two wings; Grand Terre, meaning "Large Land," is the smaller wing, and mostly low and flat.

"*Où est le rental car place?*" I ask Steve.

. . .

The Shitbox du Jour we acquire on the outskirts of Pointe-à-Pitre—a decidedly unsporty little Fiat—gets the prize for the car rental with the lowest return on investment ever. But we can't blame the SdJ.

Our destination is a vanilla plantation, located near Pointe-Noir, on the far edge of the butterfly's western wing. On other islands, someone had occasionally pointed out a shiny-leaved vanilla vine entwined around a tree—vanilla seems to have a particular affinity for cocoa trees—but never with even a single pod, because it either wasn't being pollinated or had recently been picked. And though we frequently spot small harvests of nutmegs or mace, cocoa or coffee beans drying in front of rural homes, we've yet to see even one vanilla bean in the process of being transformed from green to almost black.

When they want vanilla flavor, most West Indians use much cheaper "essence"—vanilla extract, which is commercially produced even on islands where the beans don't grow, using imported beans. (The beans are crushed and steeped in a solution of at least 35-percent alcohol for several months.) Or West Indian cooks turn to another spice entirely: the tonka bean, the seed of a tall, native rain-forest tree. The toffee-colored, almond-shaped, inch-and-a-half-long tonka bean is inside a thin, dark shell patterned like a peanut shell, but flatter. Break open the shell and the bean releases an unusual, potent, mouth-watering scent that's a combination of vanilla and almond.

Tonka bean is becoming a trendy spice in Europe, but it's not approved for food use in the United States or Canada. In fact, the first time I bought tonka beans, the woman selling them sensed my ignorance and warned: "Too much of she bad for deh healt'." The tonka bean's oil contains coumarin—toxic and liver-damaging in large doses. (It's an anticoagulant, and synthetic derivatives are used in rat poison and in blood-thinning drugs such as Coumadin.) But the beans are sold in West Indian markets from Tobago (where tonka is added to cocoa balls) northward, and island cooks like Dingis and Leslie Ann Calliste recommend a small amount—about half a bean—grated into cake batter. It does indeed add a luscious, nutty vanilla note.

Guadeloupe, however, is the first Caribbean island we've encountered with a vanilla plantation. Steve had called yesterday to confirm it was open to the public, since it's a couple of hours' drive from *Receta*. Yes, the man who answered the phone assured him, we could come and see it the very next morning.

From Pointe-Noir, signs for the CASA DE VANILLE lead us out of town, up the hills, and to . . . a deserted shack. Less than a shack, actually: more like an out-of-business fruit stand. There is no one and nothing around—in particular, no vines bearing slender green pods twisting around the trees—though a pile of brochures on the counter confirms we've found the right place. Luckily, we have a cellphone: "*Bonjour*," Steve says in his best schmoozing voice to the woman who picks up the phone at the other end. And in perfectly serviceable, if somewhat inelegant, French, he explains we're the people who called yesterday and we've arrived to see the plantation. "I will come at three," the woman says brusquely. Since it's not yet 10 a.m., Steve politely explains that the gentleman he spoke to yesterday had said specifically to come this morning and, gee, *s'il vous plait*, would it be possible to make it a little earlier because . . . *slam*. She hangs up on him. Did I mention the Guadaloupeans were making it hard to love their island?

We decide to console ourselves with a stop at a restored coffee plantation nearby that likewise invites visitors. (Coffee remains one of Guadeloupe's small export crops.) It offers perilously little to see, however, despite the 7 euros (more than US$10) per person admission: a few scrawny, beanless trees, a smattering of dilapidated old photos, a display of antique coffee-making equipment, and slim-to-non-existent signage. The coffee they serve us afterward is similarly lackluster—though, admittedly, we have had excellent Guadeloupean coffee elsewhere.

Fearful of stopping anywhere now, we lunch in the car on roadside *accras* (the crisp fritters, well laced with hot pepper and grease, are the highlight of our day so far) and loop the long way back toward Pointe-à-Pitre, following the coast. In the town of Sainte-Rose we pull over briefly for a cold coconut water, to help wash away the taste of fried food, bad coffee, unpleasant people and overhyped sights. We're also quite toasty: the quirk of this particular SdJ is that the air conditioner appears to work—well, the fan part does—but it fails to produce cold air. The woman at the stand hacks open a green coconut and passes it over without a smile; we have never yet been handed a coconut without at least a smile. We each take a long slurp: lukewarm and—worse—sour, a sure sign that the nut has been off the tree too long. "If this were Trinidad, she'd be drummed off the Savannah," Steve says in disgust.

. . .

We're parked in the SdJ, baking at the side of the road, and Steve, having ascertained that Rony Théophile at the other end speaks a bit of English, has passed me the cellphone. "It is not true," huffs a deep, throaty voice. "We are not all elderly. We have different generations. And we have males too—though not so many."

We have finally reached the vice president of the cuisinières association—who is, in fact, one of those few males—thanks to an employee at a branch of the Syndicat d'Initiative (Tourist Office), who had surprised us late yesterday, first with her OUVERT sign and then with her initiative, digging out a binder, turning all its pages, and eventually scrawling three phone numbers on a piece of paper. One of them worked. Now we're cooking.

Rony Théophile insists the association of cuisinières is going strong—"there are 375 persons"—and that in addition to the main fete in Pointe-à-Pitre, they put on a "party" somewhere on the island every weekend in August. "Our purpose is to share the culture of Guadeloupe with other people." He means its cooking, of course, but also the traditional Creole dress of the island's women: full madras skirts on top of multiple white petticoats, topped with a white blouse and a madras shawl. As Creole cooking is fusion food, this is fusion fashion. The inexpensive, colorful cotton fabric is named for Madras, a textile-producing city in southeast India, and East Indian indentured servants brought it with them when they came to Guadeloupe in the nineteenth century. The freed slaves adapted it for their own clothing, combining African styles with the French fashion trends of the time, which they knew from the clothes of the plantation owners.

Though it's only festival dress now, when Patrick Leigh Fermor was in Pointe-à-Pitre in the 1940s, this attire was still worn on the streets by older women. "Ravishing clothes," he wrote, complemented by "a load of gold jewelry." The pièce de résistance was a madras headdress, whose projecting points conveyed a language of love: one point meant a woman was available; two, that she was committed to someone; three, that she was happily married; four, that she was married but possibly open to other interest. The cuisinières wear a version of the costume for their fete, with new madras fabrics chosen each year and new aprons designed with a cooking motif that often includes St. Lawrence on the grill. In fact, Théophile is in the middle of planning the costumes for this year's fete—"it's not easy, you know"—could I call him back in a few days? But I'm not letting go of him quite yet: surely it's possible to taste the cooking of one of those 375 persons without waiting for the fete? Well, yes, he allows, there is Mme Jeanne . . .

That evening, we squash back into the hot SdJ, in one last attempt to salvage something from the dispiriting, vanilla-less day, and a half-hour later, we are seated on the *terrasse* of Mme Jeanne's homey La Nouvelle Table Créole. With its home-made-looking table decorations and its servers who look like volunteers rather than employees, it reminds me of a small-town community hall on the day of the annual strawberry social. A friendly, casually dressed woman of about our age brings us complimentary aperitifs—ti punches, of course—and informs us that dinner is "*poisson*." No choice, just fried fish. "No *chatrou?*" I ask, having hoped to taste something more distinctly Creole, like stewed octopus. Unfortunately, no. I brace for one last Guadeloupean letdown.

But no. First, unbidden, she brings us a plate of accras, light, crispy, and properly greasy, and salad. She then puts a whole fried parrotfish in front of Steve, accompanied by creamy slabs of baked layered vegetables including christophene and potato. But she sets a very different plate in front of me: the same slabs are there, but the centerpiece is chatrou et lambie, octopus and conch, prepared Creole style, in a thick sauce of tomatoes, garlic, onions, parsley, thyme and the ubiquitous cive. After Steve and I swap tastes and clean our plates—Mme Jeanne's cooking is superb, albeit decidedly rich—we ask if we can thank the cook.

A woman with the round, wrinkled face of an apple doll appears, dressed in a long, brilliantly colored dress—a madras-like plaid, but a heavier, richer fabric—and heavy gold jewelry. Clearly, Mme Jeanne tips the demographic of the cuisinières toward the elderly end. She didn't want to disappoint, she tells me (with Steve translating), and even though she didn't have a lot of chatrou on hand and had to combine it with lambie, she wanted to give me a taste.

Meanwhile, another of the friendly women who work here tells us that Mme Jeanne was in Paris last week, cooking for a thousand people. "Creole?" I ask. "All Creole," they answer in unison.

Since she is clearly such an expert, it would be a shame not to return to my colombo conundrum—especially since I've noticed the market ladies generally have a curry powder for sale alongside the colombo. Why should I choose one over another? Steve (reluctantly) translates. The women confer, discuss—obviously, this isn't a straightforward matter—and finally pronounce the verdict: colombo is hotter. "Definitely hotter," says the one woman, while Mme Jeanne agrees with a shake of her head. And perhaps we'd like to come back for her special breakfast banquet the next morning? she asks. Then we could try her hot goat and pork, *cabri et cochon*.

Alas, we're returning the SdJ tonight, and following the lead of Patrick Fermor and his friends in the morning. After exploring "the dwindling charms" of Pointe-à-Pitre, they "determined there and then to make a getaway." Quit while you're ahead. We'll set sail at dawn for Les Îles des Saintes, the Islands of the Saints.

. . .

These eight tiny volcanic dots—only two of them inhabited, and with a total population of just three thousand—demonstrate how islands that are close physically and joined politically can be worlds apart. Named by Columbus when he arrived here around All Saints' Day in 1493, the Saints are a dependency of Guadeloupe and sit a scant five miles south of the bottom of Basse Terre. Unlike Guadeloupe, however, these islands—particularly the largest, Terre de Haut—are steep and dry, with poor soil. Sugar couldn't be grown on a large scale and, as a result, a plantation economy never developed, and slaves were never brought in. The few Santois of African ancestry immigrated here in the twentieth century. Instead, the Saints were settled by fishermen from Brittany and Normandy. The British never seemed to take the Saints seriously, however. Under the Treaty of Paris in 1763, the British traded the Saints (and Guadeloupe) to France in exchange for Canada. Although they came under British rule again after Admiral Rodney bested France's Comte de Grasse in 1782 in the famous Battle of the Saints, the British once more gave them back to France, under the Treaty of Vienna in 1816.

As we get our first glance of Terre de Haut, we wonder what the British were thinking. In the sparkling-blue main harbor where we anchor *Receta*, brightly painted hand-built wooden boats are tied to moorings; called *santoises*, they are mostly fitted out with outboards now in place of the sails they once used. Le Bourg, the main town, still feels like a Mediterranean fishing village—at least until the first ferries arrive and disgorge hordes of daytrippers from Guadeloupe bound for the island's stunning beaches. But if we squint away the souvenir shops and the underdressed scooter-riding tourists, we can still catch images of traditional Santois life. In the open doorway of a wooden house on the main street, a man with weatherbeaten olive skin sits mending a fishnet, which is blue, with orange buoys, just as Santois nets have been for generations. A scooter belches by with a just-caught *dorade* (dorado, dolphinfish, or mahi-mahi) slung in front of the driver's feet, and at the shaded tables that serve as the outdoor fish market, a fisherman bends over a wooden block and reduces another dorade into steaks with his *machette*. And in a back-street kitchen, a plump, ruddy-cheeked, apron-clad woman who looks like she's from rural France rolls out *pâte brisée* for tarts. Unlike a Bretonne farmwife, however, Mme Therese Dabriou is using a rum bottle as her rolling pin.

Ah, these resourceful island women. On Saba, when their men went to sea, they brewed up a killer liqueur and made lace to console themselves. Here, they invented a tart and called it *tourment d'amour*—the "torment of love."

I figured I'd cut to the chase and save us the trouble (and calories) of eating inferior tarts. "Who makes the best tourments d'amour on the island?" I asked Yves at his shop on the main street, where he sells his own line of clothing and paints portraits of boats. "Mme Dabriou," he replied without hesitation, drawing a little map to show us how to find her.

Though the Santoise originally baked the tourments for their own lonely pleasure, tart-making has turned into a business. Every afternoon, just before the ferries start reloading their passengers to return to Pointe-à-Pitre, the women converge on the town's main dock, carrying madras-lined wicker baskets of small, warm tarts filled with a confiture of coconut, the traditional filling, or other fruit, topped with a light, almost custardy cake. The daytrippers snap them up.

Mme Dabriou is completely unfazed by two strangers dropping into her pastry-scented kitchen unannounced. So, too, are the overweight pooches that snooze under the counter where rows of tarts cool. One of them snores loudly; the other merely opens one eye and then resumes his nap. Another big table is dusted with flour and strewn with scraps of dough. We'd like to buy some tourments, we tell her. "Which type?" she asks. She has *coco* (coconut), *goyave* (guava), and . . . does she say *"ananas"* (pineapple) or *"banane"*? Poor Steve: Mme Dabriou's French is not easy for him, her diction made *plus difficile* by several missing teeth. Regardless, we want a couple of each flavor. As she carefully piles the warm tarts in a bag, Steve asks her how many she makes in a day. *"Beaucoup,"* she replies, walking over to her big beast of a range, unhooking the bungee cord that holds its oven door closed, and giving us a look inside: two long racks of tarts, easily four dozen, with four dozen more already cooling, and more underway on her table.

She started making tourments as a girl, says Mme Dabriou, following in her mother's and grandmother's footsteps. And, yes, we are welcome to return to watch her work. Not tomorrow, though; she's heading for the day to Guadeloupe. Which leaves us free to concentrate on the best boudin in Les Saintes.

. . .

When it comes to plate appeal, boudin has nothing going for it: plump, little (okay, I'll say it) turd-like sausages in unappetizing colors (mostly pasty white and pooled-blood red). They look like they will explode (okay, I'll say it) like an infected pimple if you poke them. Even arranged on a bed of colorful crudités, they ain't pretty.

Boudin is a Creole specialty, traditionally made from cooked pork blood and fat. Unlike tourments, they're not unique to the Saints, or even to the other French islands; on the Spanish-speaking islands, they're *morcillas;* on the English-speaking ones, they're black pudding, or simply pudding, and often paired with souse. But French-Creole cooks have taken the boudin concept and extended it to seafood.

"I'm entitled to more of the lambi boudin," I argue persuasively, "since I'm not eating the porkie one." I had reluctantly agreed to share a *boudin assiette*—a boudin plate—as a first course at dinner, sure that those rude little jobs wouldn't appeal. I can't get my born-Jewish, raised-kosher head around even a taste of the traditional pork-blood one, but the assortment includes lambi, crab and fish boudin—and they, to my surprise, are wonderful, each clearly conveying the distinct flavor of its main ingredient. The seafood is ground with soft bread and seasonings, and then the smooth, herb-flecked mass is stuffed into lengths of pork intestine, tied off into links, and steamed. The lambi contains some real pepper heat along with its hints of parsley, cive, onion, garlic, thyme, and a spice we can't put our fingers on. Steve relents and concedes all but a mouthful. "But we have to buy some to eat on board."

Samuel makes the boudins, the owner of the restaurant says, and we can look for him in the morning, by the fish market beyond the church, at the table with the parasol. Since Mme Dabriou was exactly what I expected the Santoise queen of tarts to look like, I fully expect Samuel to be a weathered old Breton fisherman, with a craggy face and well-worn trousers, gaining a little extra income by turning some of the morning's catch into strings of boudins.

In his well-fitting T-shirt and jeans, Samuel looks like a young, hip student at some European university. He stands under a large, faded-gray sun umbrella, behind a table clad in blue oilcloth with a tropical print. In a covered metal pot, his boudins keep warm in a steaming water bath, because passersby are buying them not only to take home for lunch and dinner, but also to eat on the spot, an early-morning snack. He snips off a few links of each type for us with his scissors and tells us the fish boudins today are made from *thon*, tuna. And he is happy to reveal the source of the one flavor that eluded us: a little *girofle*—clove.

. . .

When we arrive back in Mme Dabriou's kitchen the next morning at nine, the first batch of tarts is already in the oven, and a fresh rum-bottle-rolled batch of pâte brisée covers the tabletop. Talking all the while, as Steve furiously attempts to translate, she begins to line a heap of empty 3-inch fluted metal tartlet tins. She grabs a tin, slides it under the dough, presses down with the heel of her hand on the fluted edge and, *voilà*, a tart shell. On to the next.

The monster range has a pressure cooker and two big pots on top: the guava, coconut, and (yes) banana confitures. A layer of the confiture goes into each shell first, followed by the rich, custardy batter that will form the tart's light, sponge-cake-like filling. *Crème genoise*, she calls it, and "it must only be added right before it goes into the oven." She picks up a gargantuan whisk and gives the crème a good frothing before she spoons it into each tart.

Late that afternoon, we spot Mme Dabriou down by the dock, chatting on a bench with several other women, all with their big wicker baskets on their laps. "This morning's tarts were *délicieux*," Steve says. In fact, they were sublime fresh out of the oven.

Mme Dabriou lifts up her napkin to show him the inside of her basket. "All gone," she says.

"Ours are all gone too," Steve replies sadly.

· · · VANILLA SUGAR · · ·

A couple of vanilla pods from my Guadeloupean bundle were imme-
diately earmarked for a jar of sugar. Fragrant vanilla sugar can be
used instead of regular granulated sugar in almost any sweet recipe.
It's wonderful in baking—try it in the Ginger Spice Cookies in
Chapter 1 or the Torments of Love tart at the end of this chapter—
as well as in puddings, sweet sauces and drinks.

1	vanilla pod	1
2 cups	granulated sugar	500 mL

1. Split the vanilla pod lengthwise and scrape the beans from the inside into the sugar and stir to distribute. Bury the split pod in the sugar.
2. Store in an airtight container for at least 1 week before using.

Makes 2 cups (500 mL).

Tip:
- For vanilla rum, split a vanilla pod lengthwise and place it in a bottle of rum. Allow it to stand for at least 1 week before using.

· · · STEVE'S CREOLE CHATROU · · ·

I was off the boat the first time Dwight and Stevie dropped an octopus into Receta's *bucket, so Steve took charge in the galley. The dish he concocted was such a success—I think even Mme Jeanne would have approved—that he remains the cook whenever we're lucky enough to have chatrou on the menu. Even people who don't think they like octopus happily devour it prepared Steve's way. The dish can also be made with squid.*

2 lb	octopus or squid, cleaned, tenderized and cut into bite-sized pieces	1 kg
2	limes	2
¼ cup	olive oil	50 mL
1 tsp	chopped fresh thyme (or ½ tsp/2 mL) dried thyme	5 mL
1 tbsp	chopped chadon beni or cilantro	15 mL
1	green onion, chopped	1
1	small onion, chopped	1
2 to 3	cloves garlic, chopped	2 to 3
2	ripe tomatoes, chopped	2
½	cubanelle or small green pepper (or 2 seasoning peppers), chopped	½
¼ to ½	hot pepper, finely chopped (or to taste)	¼ to ½
	Salt and freshly ground black pepper	

1. Squeeze the juice of 1 lime over the octopus or squid and set aside.

2. Heat oil in a large heavy saucepan. Sauté octopus or squid in oil for about 5 minutes over medium-high heat, stirring constantly.

3. Add thyme, cilantro, onions, 2 cloves of chopped garlic, tomatoes and peppers; continue stirring and cooking for a couple of minutes more.

4. Season with salt and pepper and add enough water to partially cover the octopus or squid. Cover pot and simmer for 30 to 40 minutes.

5. Remove cover and cook for 5 to 10 minutes more, until the sauce thickens and the octopus or squid is tender. Taste and adjust seasoning, adding the juice of the remaining lime and more garlic and hot pepper if necessary to give the stew sufficient bite. Serve hot over rice.

Makes 6 servings.

Tip:
- Steve likes to use *Receta*'s pressure cooker to make this dish—it reduces the cooking time and thus helps keep the galley cool.

· · · TORMENTS OF LOVE · · ·

Since I lack a collection of tartlet tins like Mme Dabriou's, my
version of the Îles des Saintes specialty uses a muffin pan or ready-
made frozen tart shells. Though pâte brisée or pâte sablée is the
traditional base for these tarts, you can substitute your favorite pie
or tart pastry if you're starting from scratch. They're best eaten on
the day they're made.

12	frozen tart shells, thawed, or 12 muffin cups lined with pastry (such as the pastry with the Chicken Coconut Pastelillos recipe in Chapter 3)	12
¼ cup	coconut jam (recipe follows), or other thick tropical fruit jam such as guava or pineapple (approx)	50 mL
1 cup	pastry cream (recipe follows)	250 mL

For cake topping:

1	extra-large egg	1
3 tbsp	brown sugar	45 mL
2 ½ tbsp	flour	35 mL
1 tsp	lemon zest	5 mL
½ tsp	vanilla extract	2 mL

1. Preheat oven to 375°F (190°C). To make the cake topping,
   beat the egg with the brown sugar until the mixture
   thickens, then gently stir in flour, lemon zest and vanilla.
2. Spread about ¾ tsp (4 mL) of jam in the bottom of each tart

shell or pastry-lined muffin cup.

3. Top the jam with 1 heaping tablespoon (20 mL) of the pastry cream, leaving a little space for the cake topping.
4. Cover the pastry cream with a layer of cake topping.
5. Bake in preheated oven for 15 to 18 minutes until golden.

Makes 12 tarts.

· · · PASTRY CREAM · · ·

The cream can be made a few days ahead and refrigerated until using.

⅓ cup	granulated sugar	75 mL
1 tbsp	flour	15 mL
1 tbsp	cornstarch	15 mL
1	egg	1
1 cup	light cream	250 mL
1 tsp	vanilla extract	5 mL
1 ½ tsp	butter	7 mL

1. Combine sugar, flour and cornstarch in a small saucepan.
2. In a small bowl, whisk together egg and cream. Add to dry ingredients and cook over medium heat, whisking to keep lump-free, until mixture comes to a boil and is thickened (about 10 minutes).
3. Remove from heat and stir in vanilla and butter.
4. Cover and cool completely before using.

Makes 1 cup (250 mL).

· · · COCONUT JAM · · ·

This recipe makes enough for two batches of tarts—or try the jam spread on toast or scones. It will keep indefinitely in the refrigerator.

1 cup	packed grated fresh coconut	250 mL
½ cup	lightly packed brown sugar	125 mL
½ cup	water	125 mL
3 tbsp	rum	45 mL
½ tsp	ground cinnamon	2 mL

1. Place all ingredients in a heavy saucepan and cook 30 to 40 minutes over low heat, stirring occasionally, until mixture has a thick, jam-like consistency.
2. Cool and store in a covered container in the refrigerator.

Makes about ½ cup (125 mL).

SEVENTEEN

Lunch with Moses

· · · GRENADA & DOMINICA · · ·

IT IS AN OFFENSE TO SWITCH CHICKEN PARTS INTO DIFFERENT CHICKEN
PART BOXES. ANYONE FOUND DOING SO WILL BE ASKED TO LEAVE THE
COMPOUND OR BE PROSECUTED.

> *sign in a supermarket in Roseau, Dominica,*
> *a couple of aisles over from the medicinal bush teas*

SEACAT IS THE WEST INDIAN term for octopus, we learn
from Dwight and Stevie, who sometimes have one, or several,
in the bottom of their boat after a day's fishing. A prize catch,
it's useful even beyond the money it brings when they sell it to
locals who pound it tender and turn it into stew. "Lobsta 'fraid
of seacat," Dwight says, as if this explains everything.

When my Steve eventually spends a day helping in their
boat—and in the water, watching Dwight in action—the
meaning becomes clear. "He uses a hooked stick to pull the seacat
from its den between rocks or coral," Steve tells me afterward.
"The hole is just about invisible—I don't know how the hell he
spots it—and then Stevie quickly cleans the seacat over the side

407

of the boat, keeping it whole but somehow turning it inside out to remove the innards. I don't know how he does that either.

"Next he winds the deceased octopus onto the end of the stick, knotting a leg or two to tie it on. Dwight dives to the bottom with this seacat kebab and pokes it deep into another hole. Unbelievable: out scuttles a huge lobster, trying to escape the octopus." One seacat, double the catch.

Also courtesy of the seacat, Dwight and Stevie have brought me little gifts: perfect, hard-to-find, reticulated cowrie helmet shells, stippled black and tan on the outside but smooth as ivory and colored like a sunset when they're turned over. The seacat eats mollusks and crustaceans—which explains why a lobster would want to give it a wide berth—and once it has extracted the meat, it neatly deposits the shells outside its hole. "It like his garden," Dwight says, and it shows him where to look for seacat. Silly me: when the Beatles sang about an octopus's garden, I thought it was some trippy fantasy thing.

But why is an octopus called a seacat? Dwight gives a how-could-she-be-so-dumb head-shake. It's like I'm asking why a goat is called a goat. Ever the diplomat, Stevie volunteers that "maybe just because it so agile and move like a cat." An octopus is indeed a quick and stealthy hunter—camouflaging itself by changing color to blend with its environment, then unfurling its long legs (the word comes from the Greek *octo*, meaning eight; and *pous*, feet) to grab unsuspecting prey. The suckers help it hang on. To finish the job, the seacat bites into dinner with its tough beak and paralyzes it with nerve poison before sucking out the flesh. Although octopus is *le poulpe* in French, the cat analogy continues in the French Antilles, where it's a *chatou* or *chatrou* in Creole—from the French *chat d'eau*, or "water cat."

Seacat is also the name of the animated man with the short, bouncing dreadlocks who rents us a mooring for *Receta* in front of his house, just south of Roseau, when we return to Dominica. Being called Seacat is pretty much a given when you were christened Octavius at birth and you live in a part of the world where everyone carries at least one nickname.

"No problem. I can take you to Moses for lunch," says Seacat, who is a friend of both our crayfish-hunting friend Moses and his father. Moses Sr. offers simple "Ital" meals to those who can find their way (or, in the case of outsiders, be led) to his paradisiacal but well-off-the-beaten-path property. No relation to Italian cuisine, Ital (pronounced "eye-tal," from the word *vital*) refers to the type of cooking practiced by Rastafarians, who believe people should eat only natural, pure, unprocessed food. They avoid alcohol, prepared foods and chemicals and preservatives—including salt. Meat and shellfish are also shunned, and strict adherents eat only fish smaller than 12 inches. Some of the Rasta dietary laws are similar to the ones followed by observant Jews: pork and shellfish, for instance, are particularly discouraged because they are scavengers. Pure Ital cooking relies for its flavor almost completely on fresh vegetables, herbs and spices.

Seacat suggests that we hike while Moses prepares lunch. But Steve knows I won't be content just to taste Moses' cooking. "No problem," Seacat says. He says he will take a nap while we spend time in the kitchen.

· · ·

VICTORIA FALLS RASTARANT, reads the sign at the top of the path, hand-painted in the Rasta colors, green, red and gold. A new, open-sided structure with tables and benches has sprouted about 100 feet beyond Moses' simple wooden house, which we remember from our brief visit with Moses Jr. almost a year ago. Moses' son Israel comes out to greet us, quickly recognizing us from the night of the crayfish cook-up. His father is down by the river, he says.

We follow the path through tall grass to the edge of the White River, to find Moses emerging from the dense rain forest with a bucket of yams he's just dug up. He's an intimidating sight: wearing only a pair of dirty knee-length Tommy Hilfiger denim shorts, carrying a long, curving cutlass, missing teeth and a finger, matted dreads hanging below his waist, a full dread-locked beard. To a Rastafarian, dreads signify the Lion of Judah, and with Moses the resemblance is striking. But in distinct counterpoint to his appearance, he is gentle, well spoken and welcoming. He must have a bath in the river, he says, before we can start cooking.

Seacat wanders off for his nap, leaving us back at the Rastarant with Israel, who is lounging on one of the benches, smoking a healthy spliff. Like bush rum, ganja isn't legal in Dominica, but officials seem to turn a blind eye. Even employers in the tourism sector have been known to countenance Rastas who toke during working hours, because it's part of their religious practice.

Also a very gentle man—in his early twenties, I estimate—Israel asks us about our travels since last year, and recalls how good the crayfish broth was the last time we ate together. "Today, the food will be very different." Rastafarianism urges followers to move toward a simple, nonviolent way of living in harmony with nature, using what it provides both to nourish and to heal. Rasta practice echoes Hippocrates: "Let your food be your medicine and your medicine be your food." Everything that goes into lunch today will come straight from Moses' land.

Returned from the river, wearing the same shorts but his dreads now piled on his head and wrapped in a green towel, Moses ambles to a large bush behind the house, a calabash bowl in hand. "These are *boukousou,* peas," he explains, as I join him. Together we pluck the half-moon-shaped, bright-green pods— more like snow peas than the regular green pea pods of North American gardens—leaving behind the "soft" ones whose peas are not yet fully developed. He then sets me to work shelling them into another calabash while he peels one of the yams he harvested earlier and starts a pot of water boiling in the narrow enclosed kitchen behind the open-sided eating area.

At one end of the dirt-floored kitchen, an open fire burns on top of a waist-high wooden structure whose bottom is layered in dirt and ash. In its center, three large, round river rocks form a tripod, and the boiling pot balances on top; split pieces of wood protrude from between the rocks, allowing Moses to control the fire's heat. Lit only by natural light, the kitchen is dim, except in front of the windows and doors— which are simply open rectangles in bare-wood walls, offering views of tangled green punctuated by one or two tall coconut palms. Nothing in this kitchen could be called an appliance, or a convenience. Aside from a couple of metal pots and utensils, there is little, in fact, to connect this space with a kitchen as we know it. Wash water is carried from the river in buckets; drinking water, from a nearby spring. To rinse the peeled yam, Moses scoops water out of a bucket with a calabash and then pours it into another gourd. The used water gets tipped out one window, onto a section of galvanized roofing, from where it runs back into the soil. "You can wash the peas and add them to the pot now," he says, cleaning its lid with a scrubbie that's a piece of coconut husk.

When he begins peeling a green papaya and small, red-skinned sweet potatoes, I offer to take over. "I think it is faster if I do it," he says gently. How does he know that I will be painfully slow—if not downright dangerous—peeling and cubing hard vegetables in my hands without a cutting board, using his long-bladed folding knife? Surely my reputation with sharp objects in Lower Woburn hasn't spread upisland to the rain forests of Dominica?

And so I wander over to Israel, who is grating the coconut his father also brought back from his earlier foraging. "Can I help?" He passes over the grater—a large rectangle of old metal that has been heavily perforated to create an efficient, knuckle-destroying surface—watches me work for about a minute, and then joins in again beside me on the big-enough-for-four-hands grater, no doubt realizing (we both do) that the chore will take much too long in my hands alone. When a chunk of coconut gets too small and I'm in danger of adding bits of shredded skin to the shredded coconut, I follow Israel's lead and—in the time-honored manner of cooks everywhere—pop it in my mouth, or throw it to the dogs waiting outside the door.

Moses slices five green plantains from a stalk on the ground and shows me the easiest way to peel them. He cuts off the ends and deeply slits the skin along the plantain's entire length before passing it to me to push off the stiff peel with my thumbs. With the exception of the plantains, he has left a thin pattern of peel on all the vegetables. "It is very nourishable, and very good for the digestion," he says, moving a gnarled hand over his board-flat belly. Then he thickly slices the plantains into yet another calabash, which I empty into the pot.

. . .

The calabashes in Moses' household are another link with the natural world, and their use continues a tradition that dates back to the island's pre-Columbian Amerindians. Gourds from the calabash tree, hard enough when dry that they can even be used to boil water, were also used by Moses' African ancestors. *Dey washin', dey eatin', dey badin', dey drinkin' in ah calabash,* sings Trinidad's Mighty Killer in his 1950 calypso entitled "In a Calabash." In St. Lucia, the calabash is the national tree. Calabashes are also called *boleys, borries, boolies, bolees, borees* and *couis.*

In the Dominican Republic, where we first saw them growing, they're *calabasos.* Walking home from lunch one day in Luperón with two other couples, we had passed a heavily leafed tree that had strange fruits—like watermelons, except with smooth, solid-green, unpatterned skin—hanging directly from its branches. "*Qué tipo de arbol es ese?*" I asked the man on whose property it grew, and before we knew what was happening, he had sent his son up the tree to pick one, and his daughter to get plastic chairs so we could sit comfortably outside his house for a lesson on the calabaso.

After sawing it open, he scraped the inside of the two halves to remove the dense, seed-filled white pulp, using a knife and a piece of glass from a broken bottle. You don't eat a calabaso, he explained, as he tossed aside the copious innards. ("He have more guts dan ah calabash," the Trinis say of someone ballsy.) He continued scraping the walls of the gourd with the glass until the inside surfaces were clean and smooth. Once it dried, he explained, it would be ready to hold food or drink, one half serving as a bowl, the other as its lid. "It's a poor person's utensil, called a *jiguero*" our friend Jaime had said, "used in *el campo*," the rural countryside. Some trees produce smaller, perfectly round calabasos, which can be cut in half to create two matching meal-size bowls. Carriacou-based boating friends have a set of a dozen of these, which they use as durable, stackable, inexpensive, easily replaced, enviro-friendly picnic-ware.

Our Luperón calabaso instructor sent his daughter into the house to retrieve a finished jiguero to show us. "You can carve designs into it with a knife." And then he handed the newly scraped-clean calabaso to Steve and me, the dried jiguero to one of the other couples, and another whole calabaso, just picked from the tree, to the third couple. How could we not have calabasos in our homes? he said.

Two years later, I'm still using our gift calabaso on board as a fruit bowl, and still promising myself that I will get around to edging it with a design.

. . .

With the longest-cooking vegetables in the pot, Moses tells me to take one of the larger calabashes from the basket on the wooden "counter" next to the fire and follow him outside. "We are going to the garden for greens." As we walk through the large cultivated plot that he has carved out of the surrounding bush, he plucks a bit of this and a bit of that—several handfuls of spinach and cabbage leaves, purple basil, parsley, both cilantro and its kissing cousin chadon beni, feathery fennel tops, a few stalks of sive, a seasoning pepper and some fiery red and green bird peppers—and piles everything in my bowl. The hot peppers will be served separately, but the rest gets chopped and added to the pot—along with some fresh leaves Moses had brought back earlier from a shrub near the river; when he crushes them in his hands, the smell is instantly recognizable as black pepper. Having never seen any part of the plant but its peppercorns before, we had no idea the leaves carry the same flavor.

Moses' mother taught him to cook. "She said it best if everything cooks in one pot." Steve agrees wholeheartedly—but his motive is to reduce the cleanup required after dinner. Here, the reason is neither time nor effort, but reflects an overall Ital philosophy. "Each element combines its goodness in the pot."

He takes the bowl of coconut Israel and I grated, adds some water, and works his hands through it, squeezing fistfuls to extract the milk, which he then pours into the pot. "Almost done. We now give it a second boiling."

Moses tastes the stew just once, using the same technique that Dingis, Miss Pat, and all the other island cooks I've seen in action use to taste their cooking: by pouring some from the stirring spoon into a palm and slurping it from there. (Unfortunately, my palms lack the necessary toughening that comes with practice: every time I've been invited to follow suit, I feel my hand burning and instinctively toss the contents into my mouth, scorching it as well.) He declares the stew ready and dishes it out, passing us each a heaping calabash bowl and a spoon carved from a polished piece of coconut shell. At the table, he demonstrates how we should put a whole hot bird pepper into the bowl and mash it around with the back of the spoon to release its heat.

The rich, creamy stew is a revelation: each element maintains its distinctiveness—you can taste the individual flavors of the vegetables and herbs—but the dish is much more than just the sum of its parts. The freshness of each ingredient gives it real depth of flavor, and the combination of textures, tastes and colors is extraordinary. I also only now realize that although the cooking process seemed very casual and off the cuff—almost haphazard—the vegetables actually went into the pot in a precise order at precise times—the only timer being the one in Moses' head—so that each is now perfectly cooked, al dente tender. I also now understand why Moses Jr. had told us his father made him repeat a dish over and over until he consistently got it right.

As we eat, Moses talks about his self-sufficient way of life. If breadfruit were in season, he says, he would have included it in the stew and served it with a slice of avocado alongside, since both those trees also grow on his land. "That is our bread and our butter." He also explains that he presses milk from the rows of soybeans in his garden and "sours" it to make tofu. And he tells us that he delivered his own sons, and has now taught Moses Jr. how: he and a "Canadian lady" have just had their first baby together, he says, and Moses Jr. did the delivery himself. "Her mother came down from Canada for the birth," he adds, leaving me to imagine one of my urban First World friends watching her daughter give birth to her first child in this isolated mountain setting, well beyond easy reach of hospital or doctor. Moses Sr. was called in to advise when she went into labor, but he assured them everything was fine, that they just needed to relax and wait. He was proven right a few hours later, when around midnight, a healthy baby was born to a healthy mom.

This gives me my opening: years ago, Dingis had told me that Gennel's placenta was buried under a tall coconut palm on their property, and I had long wondered whether this was a common custom. "Yes," Moses says, "you dig a hole and put the navel and afterbirth in it. In five years, the child can drink from his own tree." Reference to where one's "navel string" is buried—especially in Trinidad—conveys a strong attachment to place. *Meh navel string so deep,* sings Denyse Plummer in the refrain of Christophe Grant's beloved calypso "Nah Leaving," whose verses list the reasons a Trini won't leave the island. *It's here where conceive me . . . is here I go dead!* The reference can be used with sarcasm too, as our Trini dictionary points out: "Wha happen? Yuh navel string bury in deh rum shop?"

As we get ready to leave, Moses touches his right fist to mine, then places it over his heart in the traditional Rastafarian greeting. "Bones of my bones, heart of my heart," he says. "Now we are friends."

Later that night, I begin to long for more of Moses' stew. And so I am forced to recreate it a few days later in *Receta*'s galley. Though my vegetables are fresh, they did have a stop or two between ground, bush or tree and my pot. And I do cheat . . . a tiny bit. "What's this?" asks Steve accusingly. "You didn't grate a coconut? You'll lose your island-cook license." I confess: my coconut milk came powdered, out of a package, out of the cupboard. None of that stops us from eating every bite of the dish we christen "Moses' Ital Stew."

. . .

Only one thing was lacking in Moses' private Garden of Eden: a clove tree. Of course, I'd asked. "Like a dog with a goat cheese," Steve had said under his breath, as Moses shook his head no, pointing out a (podless, unsurprisingly) vanilla vine instead.

On our way back to *Receta* late that afternoon, Seacat is again in his hyper-energetic mode, refreshed by his long nap. (He hadn't even awakened for his calabash of stew until the rest of us were almost finished.) As we pass a beautiful piece of land— "another beautiful piece of land," Steve corrects—Seacat tells us its owner has been selling it off bit by bit for upscale houses because he can't make a living from it as a "plantation," growing bananas, grapefruit, coconuts, coffee and other crops. Dominica's economy depends heavily on agriculture, with bananas the principal crop, which makes it highly vulnerable to international political and economic developments, and climatic events such as hurricanes. Between 1988 and 1999, the country's banana exports declined 62 percent.

Almost as an afterthought, Seacat adds, "He has clove trees too." Clove trees? And we're driving by? Seeing a way to rid himself of another of my obsessions, Steve gets the words out before I can: "Seacat, can you turn around? We have to stop."

The owners—he, working in a field of pumpkins; she, husking coffee beans in front of the house—are delighted to have a visit from their friend Seacat. As he explains our interest in cloves, she points to a wizened, scantily leafed tree nearby: "That one used to bear cloves, before Hurricane Dean." I'm hardly surprised that I've missed out yet again. But before the woman can say another word, Seacat is striding purposefully across the property and up a small hill, to a tall, skinny tree that holds its branches close and is covered—completely, densely, gaily festooned—with exquisite reddish-pink flower buds: a clove tree just about ready for harvesting. At last. When the buds turn bright red, the couple will pick them, still unopened, and set them to dry in the sun. After a couple of days, they will have shrunk to about a third their size, taking on the familiar shape and dark brown color of dried cloves. This one tree looks like it will yield enough to keep an entire village in cloves until the next harvest.

. . .

On the way to visit Moses Sr., we had stopped at another piece of land, whose young owners were in the process of taming its rain-forest wildness into their own tropical garden of fruits and flowers, and were eager to show off their efforts to Seacat and his friends. "Have some cocoa beans," one of them urged, twisting a cocoa pod from one of their trees and breaking it open so we could pop the slippery, pulp-covered beans into our mouths. "We ate hundreds when we were kids," the other one said.

Off another tree, they pulled a couple of bizarrely beautiful, shiny, pinkish-red pear-shaped fruits—each with a plump, inch-and-a-half-long, olive-green comma seemingly glued vertically to its bottom. "Have you tried cashew fruit?" The generous cashew tree serves up two snacks: not only the rich, buttery nuts, but also crisp "cashew apples," vaguely reminiscent of a tart, chalky Granny Smith. The green comma—which Seacat had removed before handing over the apple—is the shell that contains a single cashew nut. (Botanically, the cashew apple isn't a fruit but a pedicle, the swollen stalk of the flower, which produces the nut.)

Seacat carefully pried open one of the green shells. "Don't worry, Seacat won't give you anything poisonous," he said, as he cautiously flicked out half the raw nut with the tip of his penknife. The shell contains a toxic oil—the cashew tree is a relative of poison ivy—which can cause a reaction serious enough to kill a person. This is why cashews are always sold shelled, and always roasted; heat destroys any toxic residue on the nut. "You can't breathe in the smoke when you roast them," one of the young men said, meanwhile pulling up the sleeve of his T-shirt to show us a raised cashew-shaped mark on his upper arm. It was the result of a childhood prank, he told us, when another kid cracked open a cashew shell straight from the tree and "branded" him by pressing half the green comma—with its toxic oil—against his skin. His cashew tattoo led into more stories about popular kids' torments involving island plants. "When girls were bathin' in the river, the boys would go upstream and tear up a callaloo leaf into little pieces, and let them float down the river. When the pieces reach the girls . . ." He began flinging his limbs and scratching wildly. Callaloo leaves contain calcium oxalate crystals, which can cause much the same itchy, needles-in-the-skin feeling as raw fiberglass or stinging nettles (and which is why callaloo should never be eaten without being thoroughly cooked, as I learned from an ugly first-hand experience years ago). "The girls never realize we the ones who do it." Boys, whatever the culture, will be boys.

Dingis was the first West Indian—but certainly not the last—to tell us about a popular kids' prank using a large, smooth seed called a donkey eye. They're also quite aptly known as "hamburger beans," because they look like two halves of a golden bun with a strip of dark patty sandwiched in between. "We find donkey eyes up in deh mountains where we gather nutmegs," she said. "When we come down and reach deh road, we rub a donkey eye on deh pitch and then press it on someone's arm." The seed gets extremely hot, and the sur- prised victim is certain to yelp—much to the perpetrator's glee.

"We used to have fun with wild eggplant leaves too," a Trini acquaintance told us. "We'd put down pieces of the leaves and cover them with other leaves, then we'd get our friends to chase us. Of course, we knew where the eggplant leaves were and could avoid them. But our friends would run over them. Ow, ow, ow." The kids were all barefoot, of course—and wild egg- plant leaves are covered with fine thorns. Ouch. Nasty.

. . .

Things grow so prolifically in Dominica that the markets here feel different. In addition to the ever-present heaps of gnarled root vegetables, the always-available wedges of massive pumpkins, and the bundles of sive and thyme that you can bank on buying in every West Indian market whatever the time of year, the markets in Dominica always burst with greens. Vendors thrust lavish bouquets of watercress and spinach at passersby, the leaves still sparkling with droplets from the morning showers.

A burly policeman stops us as we're leaving the market in Roseau one Saturday. "Do you know how to use that?" he asks officiously, pointing to the big bunch of watercress poking from my bag. I'm sure I'm going to be chastised—maybe even arrested—for purchasing something I don't know how to prepare properly. (Shades of Olive, in St. Martin.) The local watercress is peppery, tough-stemmed stuff—much stronger in taste and texture than its North American counterpart. "I stir-fried it, sir, the last time I bought it." Though cooking it isn't exactly illegal, Corporal Thomas advises me to try it in a salad—tossing it with just a bit of chopped onion and grated garlic, dressing it with just a little oil and salt, and letting the peppery bite carry the flavor—and, before waving us on our way, he insists on writing his name and phone number in my notebook. You never know, he says, when we might need some assistance (or cooking advice) from the police.

Trinidadians may call their rain-forest flowers by alluring names like "sexy pink" and "hot lips," but Dominicans continue the seduction in the marketplace—where tall stalks of sensual blooms beckon shoppers alongside more prosaic produce. Our crab-catching mentor Martin Carrierre had brought a massive armload to *Receta* as a gift—flaming stalks of torch ginger; orange-and-purple bird of paradise; over-bright heliconia, the floral equivalent of fresh-faced girls painted heavily with makeup—dipping them in the sea to remove any insects before handing them to me. They were so extravagantly tall, and so heavy, that a vase on the table in *Receta*'s cabin was out of the question; they required a bucket, on the cockpit sole.

Dominica's biggest market is in Roseau, but the one in Portsmouth, the island's second-largest town, also bustles on Saturday mornings—and is every bit as lush, green and full of flowers—spilling onto the nearby streets from the crowded inside area. Outside is where most of the action is, the market ladies offering up fat heads of just-picked leaf lettuce and nosegays of parsley, basil, rosemary and oregano, plus other, purely medicinal herbs. ("For worms," I'm told, when I point at one mysterious bunch.) A pickup truck heaped with green coconuts attracts a line of people waiting to fill the bottles they've brought from home with the sweet water as the vendor slices open the nuts. A lambi shell is blown to signal that the boats are in and the catch has arrived. A dozen feet from the beach where their pirogues are dragged up on shore, fishermen carve thick slices off 50-pound carcasses of fresh-caught yellow-fin tuna and sell it for a mere $2.50 a pound. But inside, on a barbecue, is where Steve finds his new favorite snack. "Brilliant," he says, taking a bite from what at first appears to be a toasted hot-dog bun. "Much healthier than a hot dog, and just as much fun to eat." Closer inspection reveals the "bun" is a whole plantain that was roasted over the coals, then slit down the middle like a hot-dog roll to hold a spicy saltfish salad reminiscent of Trinidadian buljol.

We never see them again, however, after we leave Dominica, and Steve begins making noises about starting his own chain of hot-plantain concessions. "I'm sure they'd be a hit at the ballpark."

. . .

On the outside fringe of the Roseau market, an herbalist diagnoses and prescribes from behind a table laden with rows of brown paper bags of dried herbs. While I listen, she offers suggestions for everything from glaucoma to an enlarged prostate to "the pressure." Dominica has more centenarians per capita than most other countries, and Dominicans will tell you "bush medicine" is part of the reason why. Even the island's supermarkets offer a wide assortment of medicinal bush teas, "tested and approved by the Produce Chemist Laboratory of the Government of Dominica." The rain forest is "both pantry and pharmacy," as one of Moses' friends puts it, and other Dominicans routinely offer us advice on how to shop in it as they do. A tea made from soursop leaves helps solve sleeping problems; wild raspberry increases milk flow in breast-feeding women. Sometimes the local name for the herb reveals its medicinal purpose: besides "worm grass," there's "man better man," which we know as the depression-lifting St. John's wort. "Always take medication before six," we're told. After six, "the dew settles on the leaves," apparently diluting the medicinal effect. I pick up suggestions for several personal concerns: a tea made from sage helps get rid of gray hair (it's also a cough tonic), and one made from small-leafed thyme and used as a face wash keeps the skin from breaking out. But the only bush medicine whose efficacy I can vouch for first-hand is the stomach-settling effect of tea made from ginger root, and the soothing restfulness that comes from one made with lemongrass leaves.

"You should go see Sexy Bones," Heather on *Asseance* e-mails me when our boats are several islands apart. "He gave me herbs to make a tea for Don when he had a bad cough." The cough went away soon afterward—"though I suppose it might have gone away on its own anyway," she admits.

Sexy Bones—I'm left to imagine how he got his name, since anyone I ask claims not to know—is a well-known herbalist and bush doctor. He's also a Carib, or Kalinago, one of the three thousand remaining descendants of the island's indigenous people. They live mostly in the Carib Territory, a reserve on the east coast of Dominica established about a century ago, and they constitute the largest extant group of Caribs anywhere, electing their own chief and dealing as a separate entity with the Dominican government.

The territory is known for its poverty—Dominica is one of the poorest islands in the eastern Caribbean, with 39 percent of the population living below the poverty line (meaning an annual income of less than US$1,300), and the Caribs are the poorest of the island's poor. ("If you have any clothing you don't need, you can give it to me," Martin Carrierre had told us. "I bring it to the Carib Territory.") Dominica was the primary location for the filming of *Pirates of the Caribbean: Dead Man's Chest*, and it was a short-term windfall for some of the Caribs, who not only were paid for their on-screen appearances, but also were given big bucks to cut their hair, which is traditionally worn long, into the short bobs of the filmmakers' vision. Controversy erupted, however, over their portrayal in the film as cannibals. As early as the beginning of the eighteenth century, this widespread belief about the Carib diet had been revealed as untrue. "I repeat that though the Caribs do *boucan*"—barbecue—"the limbs of enemies they have slain," wrote the food-loving priest Père Labat in his meticulous observations of island life, "it is only done to preserve the memory of the fight and rouse them to future vengeance and not with any idea of eating them."

Augustine Auguiste, a full-blooded Carib (albeit one who lives outside the reserve) who has aspirations of being the country's first Carib prime minister, says the poverty in the territory is in part the result of historical job discrimination, as well as the inability of the Caribs to secure loans because they can't individually own their land. Unlike the Carib chief, Auguiste (who is currently the elected head of a three-village council at the very north end of the island) wasn't bothered by the portrayal of his people in the film—he himself served as driver to Johnny Depp's hairdresser, a position of serious importance, given the hair and beard coiffing Jack Sparrow required—and believes *Pirates* and similar filmmaking ventures benefit the island's people directly, rather than just putting money in government coffers. Filmwork aside, the Caribs work at keeping their traditional ways alive—among other things, the men still hollow out *gommier* trees for dugout canoes and the women weave local grasses into intricate and distinctive two-color, double-layer waterproof baskets. But this doesn't bring much income, especially on an island where the tourist industry is decidedly underdeveloped. Dominica gets just 65,000 visitors a year, compared with much smaller St.Martin/St. Maarten's one million.

Some of the best bush doctors also come from the Carib Territory. They reportedly use more than three hundred herbs for medicinal purposes, adjusting their choice of plants to suit both the illness and the specific patient, and their healing potions are generally revealed only to others chosen to take on the profession. Sexy Bones, we're told, is among those highly regarded for his expertise.

When he appears out of a hillside shack half hidden by rain-forest growth, I tell him that his treatment of Don's cough had been successful (leaving out Heather's it-might-have-gone-away-on-its-own suspicions, of course). "Can you put together some herbs for me?" Steve asks, seeing a respectable opportunity to add a little more to the local economy. "You don't have a cough," I whisper. But Dr. Bones—I really don't know what to call him, "Sexy" seeming a bit familiar—has apparently realized this himself. He tells us to wait, disappears up the hillside, and soon returns with an assortment of some twenty herbs—I recognize only rosemary and chadon beni—and puts them into my cupped palms. "Make a tea for him," he says. "Good for strength, including brain power."

Back on board, I brew up the whole mess, sweeten it with a little sugar and hand Steve a big mug. I'm convinced he's stronger afterward. Maybe even smarter.

· · · MOSES' ITAL STEW · · ·

Even though we don't pick, pluck and dig the ingredients ourselves, we love this stew for a wonderful-tasting, one-pot vegetarian dinner. Sugar snap peas or snow peas stand in for Moses' boukousou, and I add salt and a bit of bouillon cube in deference to taste buds not reared on Ital cooking.

The stew is immensely flexible, so don't fret if you don't have all the ingredients. What's important is a mix of colors, textures and tastes. I've substituted green pigeon peas for the snap or snow peas, carrot for the plantain, and christophene for the yam or white potatoes.

½ lb	West Indian yam (or regular white potatoes) peeled and cut into ½- to 1-inch (1 to 2.5 cm) cubes	250 g
½ lb	sweet potatoes, peeled and cut into ½- to 1-inch (1 to 2.5 cm) cubes	250 g
1	green plantain, peeled, cut into 1-inch (2.5 cm) slices, and slices cut in half	1
1 cup	sugar snap peas or snow peas, cut on diagonal into thirds	250 mL
½	cubanelle or green bell pepper (or 2 seasoning peppers), chopped	½
2 ½ cups	baby spinach leaves	625 mL
1	green onion, chopped	1
½	vegetable bouillon cube	½

½ cup	chopped fresh herbs	
	(see Tips, below)	125 mL
1 cup	coconut milk	250 mL
	Salt and freshly ground black pepper	
	Fresh hot peppers or hot pepper sauce	

1. In a large pot, bring yam or white potatoes to a boil in 4 cups (1 L) water and cook, uncovered, for about 10 minutes if using yam, 5 minutes if using white potatoes.
2. Add sweet potatoes and plantain, and continue cooking for 5 minutes longer.
3. Stir bouillon cube into broth to dissolve. Add peas and cubanelle or seasoning peppers, and continue cooking until all vegetables are just al dente (about 5 minutes more).
4. Add spinach, green onion, herbs and coconut milk; cook about 5 minutes more to combine flavors. Season to taste.
5. Mash a few of the yam and/or potato cubes into the broth to thicken. Serve in deep bowls, accompanied by the hot pepper or pepper sauce. (Those who like it hot should add a whole hot pepper to the bowl and bruise it gently with a spoon to release its heat.)

Makes 3 to 4 servings.

· · · THE POLICE OFFICER'S · · ·
WATERCRESS SALAD

The watercress grown in Dominica has real bite. For Corporal Edward Thomas's salad, use the most peppery cress you can find.

1	bunch watercress	1
1	small clove garlic	1
2 tbsp	chopped sweet onion	25 mL
2 tbsp	olive oil	25 mL
1 tbsp	red wine vinegar	15 mL
	Salt	

1. Wash and chop watercress, including stems.
2. Grate garlic on top and sprinkle with onion.
3. Whisk together oil, vinegar and salt; toss with salad.

Makes 4 servings.

· · · GINGER TEA · · ·

West Indians maintain ginger tea can fix everything from motion sickness to morning sickness, sore muscles to sore throats. It also settles indigestion, and inhaling its fragrant steam is said to relieve head colds. On top of that, it just plain tastes good.

1	piece (2 inches/5 cm)	
	fresh ginger root	1
4 cups	boiling water	1 L
	Honey (to taste)	
	Fresh lemon or lime juice (to taste)	

1. Peel and grate the ginger, and put it in a teapot.
2. Add boiling water and allow to steep for 5 minutes.
3. Strain into cups, sweeten to taste with honey, and add a squeeze of lemon or lime juice if you like.

Makes 4 cups.

Tip:
• The tea is also good chilled and served over ice.

EIGHTEEN

Back to the Isle of Spice

· · · GRENADA · · ·

I wake up on mornings and before I stretch,
Is fry bake by doubles meh nostrils done ketch,
And there for my view, / An ocean so blue
I'm going nowhere (nowhere);
Hummingbirds and blackbirds that sing in the trees,
Chaconia and spices that waft in the breeze . . .

from "Nah Leaving, " *composed by Christophe Grant,*
sung by Denyse Plummer

EVERYONE IS BREATHLESS at the house on the hill in Lower
Woburn this afternoon—Steve and I, because we ran the last
stretch up the steep road and even steeper drive to escape the
sudden onslaught of a squall; and Dingis and Gennel, because
they're trying to fill us in on everything that has happened since
they last saw us, all at once, in the first two minutes after we
hug hello. Both of them talk at the same time—high volume,
full speed, completely forgetting (or ignoring) that we're not
Grenadian and I have trouble when the conversation starts

scudding over my head as fast as the afternoon storm clouds. In one long, unbroken, wonderful deluge, they slide from Dingis's daddy's health ("He doin' good, thank deh Lord; how's your dad?"), to Bici's first birthday party, to the new pressure cooker ("I made pork, so you see how good it works"), to the birth of Dwight's son, Akel, to a sudden spike in crime, to Dannyboy standing up for us at the (yes, it finally happened) christening ("We'll go to the church office, so you can sign the book"), to the party afterward ("We miss you"), to the state of the various things growing on their property.

"The pigeon peas come ripe while you gone," Dingis says. "I save some for you." She opens her chest freezer and pulls out a big bag of the pale yellow-green peas, probably the Caribbean's (and most definitely Grenada's) favorite legume. Silver-green pigeon-pea bushes line the lower edge of the hillside behind their house, and Dingis had long lamented that *Receta* had never been anchored in Grenada when the peas were ready for picking and shelling. They're available canned and dried year-round, but any island cook will tell you that they taste best when fresh. The bedlam continues, as she and Gennel now simultaneously tell me how to prepare the popular dish of peas and rice, vehemently disagreeing on the main steps before they even get to the details. "Pressure the peas," Gennel says. "Listen to me," Dingis says, at almost the same moment, "you don't need to pressure the peas . . ."

When they have me well confused, they move on to pigeon pea soup, which includes salt meat for flavor, along with dumplings and provision. We'd tried some in Tobago; thinking that we were freshly arrived foreigners, the woman who took our order at the restaurant felt it necessary to explain carefully that the soup didn't actually contain pigeon meat. The *pigeon* part of the name apparently comes from Barbados, where the peas were once used for pigeon food. Pigeon peas are also called congo peas, or gungo or goongoo peas, names that reveal their African roots: they arrived and spread throughout the islands with the slave trade.

Finally, content that I'm properly educated on how to use my pigeon peas, Dingis pulls out a small plastic bag that contains maybe a couple of ounces of a yellow-brown powder. "I save *asham* for you too." She opens the bag, spills some of the powder onto our palms and tells us to lap it up from there. It's a sweet made from local corn, she explains, roasted and then ground with sugar, and it's traditionally eaten on All Saints' Day, when families go to cemeteries to visit the graves of beloved relatives. (It became associated with the departed perhaps because of its connection to the funeral phrase "from ashes to ashes, dust to dust.") "It's just like pulverized Corn Pops," Steve says, nailing the taste exactly. Dingis insists I tuck the asham into my bag and take it along—surely a lifetime supply for us. I mean, how much cereal dust can a person lick off her palms?

"Look," Dingis says, leading me to the back door and pointing out into the misty rain. "God has returned you safely to Grenada while two breadfruit still on deh tree. Dey fulllllll, so we can make an oildown." Finally, we can accept the invitation she had first issued almost a decade ago now, when we regretfully had to head homeward before the breadfruit were ready.

Simply put, oildown, or oildong, is a hearty meat-and-vegetable stew made with coconut milk, but that description completely fails to capture its heart. Dingis had previously shown us her oildown pot—as tall as Bici, and almost as big around as a trash can. Clearly, it's not a stew you'd make for an ordinary family dinner, unless your immediate family numbers a dozen plus. Oildown is an excuse to bring a group of people together—usually, outdoors around a fire—and the party begins with the cooking. In fact, the gathering loses its liveliness by the time everyone eats, since rich, filling oildown creates an overwhelming desire for a post-meal nap.

The dish takes its name from the "boiling down" of the vegetables and meat in coconut milk, until the liquid is absorbed and all that remains is the coconut's rich oil in the bottom of the pot—the "oil down," in other words. "You come early and help," Dingis says, after we set a day for the event. I then offer to do the shopping for the ingredients and bring them along. "No, no, we do it," she all-too-quickly replies, and Gennel leaps in to agree. "No problem, no problem, I drive Mommy to the Food Fair." Beyond their desire to have us as their guests, I suspect she and Dingis simply don't trust me to buy the right stuff . . . especially since I had mentioned casually that I could bring some of my ample stock of dehydrated coconut milk powder. Dingis had given me a horrified look. (After all this time, Ahhnnnn still doesn't get it?) "I grate my own coconut for the oildown," she said, clearly appalled. "It much better—you get all the oil." What? Use a shortcut and sacrifice quality? Spend money on store-bought coconut powder when there are coconuts right here, free for the picking? What was I thinking?

Dingis leads us down to the kitchen so Steve can have a heaping plate of her pork, pressure-cooked into extreme tenderness. Without saying anything, I focus on the provision—sweet potato, plantain and dasheen—but Dingis instantly remembers I don't eat pork, and assures me she will use salt beef in the oildown instead of the salted pig snout that is otherwise her meat of choice. "How come your provision tastes so much better than my provision?" I ask her. Although provision is called "blue food" in Tobago because dasheen usually has a blueish-purple cast when cooked, Dingis's tubers are creamy-white, with a satisfying, earthy, almost nutty taste. "Everyone tell Mommy that," Gennel says. "Everyone ask how come her provision so white." Dingis shrugs off the compliments and says it's simply because she washes the vegetables with lime before cooking—but then admits she didn't have any limes, so she skipped that step today. Just another island kitchen mystery.

At the back of the kitchen area, a three-foot stalk laden with hands of short, fat bananas hangs from the rafters. "Deh secret figs," Dingis says, marveling that we have returned to Grenada just as they too were ready to be picked from her tree, and taking it as another reason to give thanks to the heavens. These are archetypal bananas—completely smooth and unblemished, the ones at the top of the stalk still green, those at the bottom silky yellow—such complete perfection that if I hadn't known better, I would have sworn they were plastic. She cuts a hand of half-green ones from the stalk and hands it to me. Secret figs—also known as "rock figs"—are a sweet banana whose name is a folk derivation of the French *sucre*, sugar, or *sucré*, sweet, and the French-Creole *figue*, meaning banana. "But it takes them so long to ripen, it like a secret," says Dingis. "Hang them on deh boat until dey ready."

Later, hanging in our cockpit from the stainless-steel frame that supports our solar panels, the secret figs are a tropical Calder mobile, set against a brilliant blue background of sea and sky, shining in the sun, casting eerie shadows on the cockpit sole in starlight.

. . .

The Canadian ensign that flies from *Receta*'s stern is showing all too clearly that we've been traveling for two years, its edges tattered, its red maple leaf sun-and-salt-faded to a dull orange. When Dwight and Stevie stop at *Receta* to welcome us back, its sorry state does not escape Dwight's keen eyes. "We were just about to dig out the new one we have stowed below," Steve tells them.

"No, Steve," Dwight says, with the shake of his head we know so well. "You don't want a new one. This one shows you've gone many miles. You've earned this one."

In our travels farther up the island chain, we'd managed to find a few much-needed (and unavailable in Grenada) replacement parts for Dwight's spear gun, and when Steve brings those out, we can see his pleasure. It reminds Dwight, though, of some unfinished business. "When are you comin' fishing with us?" he asks Steve.

They'd been trying for months to get him to join them at sea for a day, but Steve has been reluctant. "I won't be able to keep up," he tells them.

"I think it 'cause you 'fraid of lambi, like Jim."

Obviously, Dwight has pressed the right button. Steve says they should plan on his company on the next calm day.

Meanwhile, I've offered congratulations to Dwight on his and Glenis's new son. "How's he doing?"

"He troublesome," Dwight says proudly. "He bad, Steve, bad. He mischievous."

"Just like his daddy," says Steve.

"Just like his daddy," echoes Stevie.

. . .

"Did you eat your figs yet?" Dingis asks a few days later.

They're solidly yellow now, but I had given one a gentle squeeze that morning and it still seemed too solidly hard to be ready for eating. "No," I tell her. "They don't seem ripe enough yet."

"Listen to me, eat them or they will fall," she says, the warning note strong in her voice.

I don't ask any questions, but figure we'll try them the next morning for breakfast.

But when we climb back onto *Receta* late that afternoon, we learn the real secret of the secret figs. Swinging in *Receta*'s cockpit is a strange postmodern sculpture . . . made of banana peels. Underneath it, bare bananas lie scattered on the cockpit sole. The figs have fallen. Now I understand what Dingis meant: when secret figs are ready for eating, they apparently peel themselves. We wipe off a bit of grit and give the self-peelers a try. They don't just look like the archetypal banana, they taste like it too. *Sucré*, indeed.

. . .

"Well, they invited me back again," Steve reports, completely spent after eight hours on the water with Dwight and Stevie. "These guys are in another league entirely," he says, blown away by seeing first-hand what they do every day, and with such unassuming nonchalance. "I looked for the gills in Dwight's neck—the man has to be part fish—and his eyes are incredible. It doesn't even look like he takes a breath before he slips below the surface—and the next thing you know, he's down 30 or 40 feet and has a fish on the end of his spear. Meanwhile, not only can't I get nearly that deep, I haven't even spotted anything huntable yet. And when he dives for lambi, he brings up a half-dozen in each hand. I could barely pick up two in one hand from the bottom of the boat."

For his part, Stevie has to follow his diver and position the boat precisely in the right spot each time Dwight surfaces, so he can deposit the catch onboard; a miscalculation is more than lost time or lost catch—it could mean serious injury or death for the diver.

"It was a pretty calm day," says Steve. "The seas were only 2 to 4 feet. I can't imagine what it must be like in rough water or when it's raining, but I know I don't want to be there."

Dwight is also a human GPS, Steve reports. When he surfaces from a dive, he takes bearings on shore and then stores them in his head. "On the way out, we're pounding along at full throttle, downwind and downwave, me concentrating on not crushing any vertebrae as we occasionally get airborne off a 4-foot wave and then slam into the next one, when suddenly Dwight says, 'Stevie, stop.' Keep in mind we're more than a half-mile off shore, in 25 or 30 feet of water, and it's not like there's a sign that says 'Dive Here.' Dwight adjusts his mask, takes his hooked stick, slips over the side, and is instantly below the surface. 'What's he doing?' I asked Stevie, who nonchalantly gave a one-word response: 'Seacat.' And a moment later an arm and stick pop out of the water with a nice octopus writhing around it. 'How did he know it was there?' I asked, totally amazed. 'Oh, he see it yesterday and decide to come back and get it.' Huh???"

Steve had managed only an hour and a half in the water before he was exhausted, with barely the strength to flop back on board—Dwight, meanwhile, took one fifteen-minute break all day—and spent the rest of the time helping Stevie "process" the catch. "Each time he surfaced, Dwight would reach high and dump five or six conch from each hand into my arms as I leaned over; it was all I could do to balance them long enough to get my arms back in-board. I can imagine the abuse I would have taken if I'd dropped one back into the depths—though, come to think of it, there was never an argument or harsh word between them, or even a loud order."

The boat was almost knee-deep in conch (and the bilge under the floorboards full of fish) by the end of the day, but even after the lambi were removed, the shells stayed in the boat until it was quite close to shore. "You never put the shells back in the water where you get them, because the other lambi will leave," Dwight had explained to us.

Removing a lambi from its shell is another one of those how-did-someone-first-figure-this-out things. Steve helped Stevie by pounding a hole into the shell with a rock hammer at a particular spot between the back two rows of spires, so that Stevie could insert his knife in exactly the right place to sever the attaching tendon and pull out the lambi and clean it. Steve was too slow to handle the extraction-and-cleaning part. He also figured it was another foreigner-with-a-knife problem: Stevie feared he might slice his thumb off while sawing his way through a tough, slippery lambi.

Nevertheless, Steve arrived home covered beard-to-dive-booties in conch carnage. Even his glasses were splattered with bits of lambi, as well as fish scales.

"I think they've accepted me in a new way," he says once he's recovered. Another local guy, whose cousin is Dwight and Stevie's partner—the one who handles selling the catch to supermarkets and restaurants—saw Steve on shore a couple of days afterward, once again helping to clean the boat and lugging buckets of lambi and fish up the hill to the freezer. "He called me over and handed me three monster avocados he'd just picked off his tree. 'You okay, man,' he said. 'You cool, you cool.'"

. . .

Dingis, who had cleaned dozens of lambi a day herself for many years, and Stevie had both told us that once in a very great while they find a pearl in the mantle of a lambi. Conch pearls are extremely rare—one estimate says you have to clean ten thousand lambi to find a single one—and, consequently, they are valuable.

"Gennel, bring deh big pearl," Dingis says one day, and Gennel returns with a small square of paper that Dingis carefully unfolds: inside is a luminous pinkish pearl the size of a large green pea. The internal structure of a conch pearl is unlike that of other pearls, with some having a distinctive flame pattern across the surface. "Here, I want you to have it." We know this is a heartfelt gesture, but it feels completely wrong to accept. "You found it, you must keep it for luck," I say.

Dingis believes in luck as well as in the Lord—she has to— so she understands why we have said no. But she is not to be thwarted. "Gennel, bring deh bottle." And this time Gennel returns with an unusual long-necked, bulbous-bottomed green-glass bottle. The glass is bubbled, and clearly old, and it has to be filled to stand upright on its own. It's marked with a formula that's meaningless to us: $E F$—$square root of C P$. "Daddy found this on deh beach by Industry, up in deh country, years ago. I want you to have it."

Knowing we can't refuse a second time, we accept the gift with pleasure.

Dingis, like others we've met in the Caribbean, has shown

us the meaning of generosity. From one end of the island neck-lace to the other, we've encountered people who (by our North American standards) have little yet nonetheless insist on giving of what they have—from the heart, without expecting anything in return. Each time it happens, we are taken aback. The Dominican stranger who poured an armload of limes into my bag along the road just outside of Luperón, *un regalo*, a gift. The Trinidadian who brought Steve a bag of fresh, fragrant bay leaves because he had just "trimmed a tree" by his house in the mountains. Even Stevie, making a special trip to *Receta* on a rare day off, just to bring us a fresh-picked lettuce from his lov-ingly tended hillside garden.

And we are equally amazed by the way people who can't afford to lose even a single dollar (whatever the currency) are willing to trust strangers. It's hard to imagine the guy behind the fish counter at a Toronto market encouraging two unknown customers to go ahead, take his lobster, even though they don't have any cash on them at the time, trusting that they'd find him the next day and pay up, as the fishermen in Luperón somehow knew we would. Or that the owner of a North American marine business would tell two strangers who stumbled on his store, with only a few dollars in their pockets, and found precisely the replacement prop they desperately needed for their outboard, to take it along without paying. But the owner of a store on Union Island trusted that we'd meet him on the beach by our anchorage where he was taking his family to swim the next day, and pay him then.

The Trini customs officer who brings me a sack of pomme cytheres from his garden, and a container of his wife's home-made chutney to try. The strangers, like Greta, who insist we share a meal. The people who cook for us and with us, who go out of their way to take us places and teach us things—to share their island, even when there's nothing in it for them. "Do unto others," the golden rule says. In some places, it hasn't been forgotten.

. . .

Oildown day. Four breadfruit wait on the concrete table outside Dingis's kitchen. To my Steve's relief, Stevie had got the job of climbing a spindly tree near the breadfruit tree, which offered the best angle for knocking the lime-green cannonballs to the ground with a long stick. From this perch, Stevie had seen two additional breadfruit hiding among the tree's long-lobed leaves, much to Dingis's delight. She now begins to attack them one by one with her cutlass, deftly cutting each into quarters and then switching to a somewhat smaller (but still impressive) knife to peel and core the pieces. "We used to play like this when I was a girl," she says, cutting a rough, silver-dollar-sized circle from a thick slice of breadfruit skin. She takes a kitchen match, breaks off the head, and inserts it through the center of the circle, instantly creating a top. A quick spin with her fingers and it whirls at great length around the table as well as any fancy, store-bought model.

Inspired by our pleasure in the homemade toy, Dingis leaves the breadfruit and wanders among the vegetation growing between the house and the road, returning with a pumpkin stem and a leaf from the secret-fig tree. "When I young, we used to make flutes out of these." She cuts off a 6-inch section of the pumpkin stem and blows it like a whistle to demonstrate. Then she tears off a small piece of fig leaf, rolls it up like a cigar, and gives it a shrill toot. Later, after the oildown prep has been completed and the pot is on the fire, she shows us how she and her brothers played "win' ball cricket," which uses a tennis ball—a "wind ball"—instead of the traditional leather cricket ball. Dingis makes her bat the way rural kids did: by trimming up a dry frond from a coconut palm. "I good, you know," she says, as she demonstrates the proper cricket swing. Then she winds up and hurls a grapefruit to Stevie to show us her prowess as a bowler.

Stevie was also in charge of harvesting a couple of mature coconuts, and he is now prying out their meat with a screwdriver. (Always barefoot when he's working with Dwight, today he's wearing a pair of bubble-gum pink Crocs, which somehow suit him perfectly.) I offer to do the grating, and he passes over a rusted box grater. But I'm scarcely five minutes into the job when—what a surprise—Dingis orders him to take over, telling me she's afraid I'll grate my knuckles. If I was working with a "cutlass grater," like the one she uses in "deh country"—consisting of a full-length cutlass whose working edge has been sliced at quarter-inch intervals and then bent up to form seriously sharp teeth—I could understand her concern. But this box grater is about as dangerous as . . . the small, very dull knife I'm now handed instead, and with which I'm asked to "chip up" the seasoning.

After two years of offering to help in island kitchens, by now I almost expect this to happen, and I've long since accepted it, without taking it personally. We all still get involved in "the kitchen vibration," as our Dominican friend Martin Carrierre would say, and a sweet, very Caribbean scene unfolds: Stevie and me working side by side at the table overlooking the road; he, gradually becoming speckled with grated coconut from black beard to pink Crocs; and I, sawing through sive and hacking dully at onions. Dingis, meanwhile, boils salt beef and saltfish in the kitchen to remove some of the salt before these go into the oildown pot, while keeping an eye out to make sure everyone else's efforts adhere to her standards. "Smash the garlic before you chop it, for more flavor," she calls to me through the Dutch door. Gennel is sent in search of green figs, the cooking figs on Dingis's trees having been deemed too small yet for picking, and Steve is put in charge of Bici. "Shake your locks," Dingis calls, and the child wriggles in Steve's arms, setting her plaits into wild motion. When everything is almost ready, Stevie starts a wood fire burning in a cleared area behind the house, arranging cinder blocks around it to support the giant pot. And then we layer all the ingredients in the pot: raw chicken legs first, then saltfish, salt beef, and smoked herrings. The seasonings I've chipped up are strewn on top, followed by the provision—chunks of breadfruit, peeled green figs and chopped yam—a good handful of chopped okra and some chopped callaloo. The coconut milk Stevie has made by soaking the grated coconut meat in water and then squeezing it through his hands—just as Moses did, and Martin taught me—is now poured on top of everything.

"Oildown has to have saffron," Dingis says, handing me a big bag of ground turmeric to sprinkle in the pot. "And, listen to me, if you have a bruise, you grate some saffron"—fresh turmeric root is usually on the market tables in St. George's (it looks like a skinnier, more orange-red version of ginger root)— "mix it with salt, put it on a piece of cloth, and tie it on your bruise." A friend on another boat told me one of their recent guests had twisted an ankle, and their Grenadian friends had suggested exactly the same saffron-root poultice to ease the sprain. Such medicinal uses of the spice have been studied, and tests have shown it to have anti-inflammatory and antiseptic properties among other positive effects. In fact, turmeric has long been a popular herbal remedy in India—and Johnson & Johnson even makes turmeric-treated Band-Aids for the Indian market.

The pot is now set over the fire to get it boiling, while Dingis and I return to the kitchen to make the dumplings. After my lessons from Martin in Dominica and Miss Pat in Trinidad, I think I'm well prepared—but, of course, one island's (let alone one cook's) dumplings are not the same as another's. Into Dingis's big bowl goes only hard white "counter flour," salt, and water—which makes a globby, heavy, resistant mass. "Knead it haaaardd," Dingis says, and she joins me with a hand in the bowl. I knead and turn, knead and turn, knead and turn—but this dough is stubborn and unyielding, and it takes all my hand and arm strength to get it to cooperate. When it's finally smooth and pliable enough to get Dingis's approval, she starts to roll walnut-size hunks between her palms to form smooth balls. I join in, and once we've converted all the dough to smooth walnuts, I assume we're done. But, no—now we again roll each walnut between our palms, this time converting the balls to fat ropes. We stir these into the now-boiling pot, and then lay whole callaloo leaves across the surface, forming an inner lid.

After the oildown has been boiling on the fire for an hour or so, Stevie takes a taste, pouring it into his palm first, of course. "More salt?" he asks, dipping again, and offering the spoon round for second opinions. (Of course, other friends have joined the gathering by this point.) This time, I wait until I think the spoonful has cooled sufficiently and offer up my palm. "Plenty salt," everyone agrees.

Then Dingis and Gennel dish the oildown into bowls and onto plates, making sure each serving has a bit of everything: chicken, beef, fish, breadfruit, yam, figs, dumplings and callaloo. The ingredients have taken on a complex, smoky flavor—from both the smoked herrings and the fire itself—and a silken richness from their coating of golden, reduced-to-a-thick-oil coconut-milk sauce. This is serious comfort food, deeply satisfying—heaven, for a carb lover. Even one-year-old Bici gives it a big, three-toothed laugh of approval, when I feed her spoonfuls of mashed provision and small bits of soft chicken and fish, all bathed in the coconutty sauce.

. . .

A few days later, when we climb the hill again to say thanks, Dingis and Gennel hand each of us a small, wrapped box. They know that soon we'll be leaving and, this time, it will be a while before they see us again. "So you remember Grenada," Dingis says, "and so you don't forget us." As if we ever could.

One at a time, we slowly open our boxes. Necklaces from the Isle of Spice. Each has been locally made, and very carefully chosen. Lynn and Desiann, the girls up the road, had also gone along on the shopping trip, Gennel says, to consult on the choices. Steve's consists of shark's teeth wrapped in copper wire and hung with beads on a black cord. When he puts it on, it looks so much a part of him that it's as if he's been wearing it for years. Mine is delicate, strung with tiny shells. Hanging in the middle is a larger, cream-colored cowrie, which is a fairly common beach find. But the top layers of this one have been sanded away to reveal a teardrop of lavender-blue inner shell. It's the color of farewell, the color of the Caribbean sky just after sunset.

And just before dawn.

"When you comin' back?" asks Dingis.

· · · DINGIS'S OILDOWN · · ·

You need access to a Caribbean market to make this dish—it's not
oildown without provision and callaloo—as well as a big pot and
several pairs of hands to help.

1 lb	salt beef or salt pork	500 g
½ lb	boneless saltfish	250 g
¼ lb	smoked herrings	125 g
3 to 4 lb	chicken pieces (thighs, drumsticks, wings)	1.5 to 2 kg
2	onions, chopped	2
4	cloves garlic, chopped	4
1	cubanelle or green bell pepper (or 4 to 6 seasoning peppers), chopped	1
1	bunch green onions, chopped	1
3	stalks fresh thyme	3
1	breadfruit, quartered, peeled, cored and cut into thick slices	1
3	green plantains, cut in half crosswise, peeled and cut in half lengthwise	3
2 lb	yam, peeled and cubed	1 kg
10 to 12	okra, cut into 1-inch (2.5 cm) rounds	10 to 12
2	bunches callaloo leaves, one bunch chopped, the other left whole	1
10 cups	coconut milk	2.5 L
2 tbsp	turmeric	25 mL
	Salt	

For the dumplings:

2 cups	flour	500 mL
1 tsp	salt	5 mL

1. In a saucepan, boil the salt meat in water to cover for about 20 minutes, changing water halfway through cooking time to eliminate some of the salt. Or soak meat about 12 hours in the refrigerator, changing the water several times. Drain and cut into small pieces. Do the same with the saltfish.

2. Layer the ingredients in a large pot in the following order: chicken, salt meat, saltfish, smoked herrings, onions, garlic, pepper, green onions, thyme, breadfruit, plantains, yam, okra and chopped callaloo. Pour in coconut milk and sprinkle with turmeric.

3. Cover pot, bring to a boil, and then continue cooking over medium heat.

4. Meanwhile, make the dumplings: Combine flour and salt. Gradually add enough water to make a very stiff dough. Knead until it turns into a smooth mass. Break off pieces and roll between palms into balls the size of large marbles. Then roll each ball between palms into a short fat rope. Add dumplings to pot. Lay the whole callaloo leaves on the surface and cover the pot.

5. Oildown is done when all the ingredients are tender and the coconut milk has "boiled down" into a thick sauce (about 1 hour). Taste and add salt if necessary. Serve on plates or in bowls, making sure each person gets some of every ingredient.

Makes 10 to 12 servings.

· · · GRENADA-STYLE · · ·
GINGER PEANUTS

*Each time we go to the market in St. George's, we stop at a little
stand around the corner that sells several types of freshly roasted
peanuts, including ones that have been caramelized with bits of fresh
ginger. Steve insisted I come up with a version we could make on
board ourselves, for those times we're far from Grenada and have a
tabanca for these sweet, gingery nuts.*

1 cup	raw peanuts, without skins	250 mL
½ cup	granulated sugar	125 mL
2 tbsp + 1 tsp water		30 mL
2 tbsp	finely chopped fresh ginger root	15 mL
	Salt	

1. Combine peanuts, sugar, water and ginger in a frying pan.
   Cook over medium heat, stirring constantly, until nuts are
   coated in golden-brown syrup and starting to brown themselves, about 10 minutes.
2. Scrape nuts onto a tray covered with greased foil. Sprinkle
   very lightly with salt. Allow to cool and break into small
   pieces.

Makes about 1 cup.

Tip:
- You can never make enough of these—they're great for
  gift-giving. Try the recipe with almonds too.

· · · RUGELACH · · ·
WITH AN ISLAND TWIST

Making these rich, flaky little crescent-shaped rollups reminds me of the importance of carrying on kitchen traditions. For me, the smell of rugelach baking and the taste of them fresh out of the oven are inextricably linked with my mother, and the kitchen of the house I grew up in. This is her recipe—I've merely islandized the fillings to reflect a bit of me.

For the dough:

1 lb	butter, at room temperature	500 g
1 lb	cream cheese, at room temperature	500 g
4 cups	flour	1 L

For the filling:
- Combination #1: guava, mango, pineapple or nutmeg jam; plus chopped walnuts or pecans
- Combination #2: toasted, grated coconut and grated dark chocolate
- Combination #3: granulated sugar spiced with a little cinnamon, nutmeg and cloves; plus chopped walnuts or pecans

1. Cream the butter and cream cheese thoroughly, until the mixture is light and fluffy.
2. Gradually blend in the flour. Gather dough into a ball and wrap in plastic. Chill at least several hours.
3. Preheat oven to 350°F (180°C). Line baking sheets with parchment paper.

4. Break off a piece of dough a little smaller than a tennis ball and roll it out thinly into a circle with the diameter of a pie plate. Spread and/or sprinkle it with one of the filling combinations.

5. Cut the circle of dough into 10 or 12 thin wedges and roll each one up, starting at the wide end. Curve slightly to form a crescent shape. Repeat with remaining dough.

6. Bake on parchment-lined cookie sheets for 25 to 30 minutes, until just starting to brown. Remove rugelach to racks to cool.

Makes about 72 small rugelach.

Afterword

AS I WRITE THIS, almost a year after the events in the last
chapter, *Receta* is still in the eastern Caribbean, currently
floating at anchor off St. Lucia. On our cockpit table, a
soursop, a few passion fruit, and a half-dozen figs ripen in a
still-undecorated calabash bowl, the one I was given in the
Dominican Republic. A branch of fresh bay leaves hangs
drying in a covered corner of the cockpit. But the process is
advancing slowly: there's no sun this morning; in fact, it's
pissing rain—a driving cold (comparatively speaking)
downpour—even though we're still not out of the dry season.
All *Receta*'s hatches and ports are dogged down tight.

Below decks, Curious George still sits in his customary
corner, and Ramón T. Ratón scowls from across the way: my
Haitian chicken, now overflowing with jumbie seeds and
donkey eyes in addition to its shells, is encroaching on his space.
He vex. Meanwhile, Steve lounges and guzzles tamarind juice
as an antidote to the steamy heat. The stove is going, and the
closed-up main cabin is not only hot and humid, but also filled
with acrid smoke. Deciding to burn sugar in oil to start a big

pot of lamb geera was a colossal mistake on a rainy day. However, *Asseance* is anchored across the bay, and Heather and Don have invited us to a sunset gathering.

Unfortunately, I reason with Steve, my promised contribution can't be properly made without spattering fat and billowing smoke at the start. All complaints are silenced, however, once the aroma of caramelizing lamb and roasted cumin kicks in.

It's been more than three years since we moved back on board *Receta* and started our Spice Necklace journey. When we first began cruising the Caribbean, a peripatetic long-term sailor told us that eventually it becomes impossible to return to land-based life. "I think three years is the point of no return," he said. "You just don't fit in anymore."

Still, we're not yet ready to turn into CLODs—the acronym in our boating world for "Cruisers Living on Dirt"—and we hope a short stretch on land each year will help us avoid that fate for a while longer. There's much still left uneaten . . . and undone. This spring, I finally convinced myself I could play "pretty mas," chipping and wining through Port of Spain on Carnival Tuesday. (Though I begged to differ, Miss Pat didn't think my bikini-and-beads costume was too skimpy at all.) Next season, I think we'll point *Receta* west, to explore the western Caribbean. We hear the cruising is interesting there . . . and, fingers crossed, the cooking.

When we're off the boat, Steve has to remind me to slow down on city sidewalks, and he has to leave me notes on the kitchen counter. "Take time to lime," they say. When we're living on *Receta*, our island friends help us connect with a much slower, simpler and consequently more satisfying—for us—way of life. They help me keep my "sweet hand" in practice too.

"We are what we eat," the old maxim says. When we

devoured black cake with Miss Pat and oildown with Dingis, sipped sorrel with Dwight and Stevie, or shared a bowl of curry crab, or crayfish broth, or lambi water with other island friends, along with the taste, we absorbed history, culture and traditions.

And began adding them to our own. Geera pork has turned irrevocably into geera lamb on *Receta*. Leslie-Ann Hyacinth's chocolate cake, its flour replaced by matzoh cake meal, is now traditional at Passover, the dessert I contribute to my brother's Seder table. Chivo guisado in the style of La Madonna, as interpreted by La Ana, is what Steve requests for his birthday dinner. We add something of ourselves as we move traditions forward.

"Ahhnnnn, you have enough to write a book," Dwight said one day when he and Stevie stopped by *Receta* at Hog Island and tasted the Easy-Bake Boat's latest creations. And, unprompted, he offered his usual and oh-so-island advice of how I needed to go about it. "Just keep it simple," he said.

"Like what you tell me about cooking," I replied.

"Just like cooking," he agreed.

"Just like cooking," echoed Stevie.

Acknowledgments

AS OUR FRIENDS IN TRINIDAD SAY, "One hand don't clap." So let me "big up" my editors, Amy Black at Doubleday Canada and Jenna Johnson at Houghton Mifflin Harcourt, for all their bang-on advice and careful attention as they shepherded this book toward publication. And I'm much indebted to the production, publicity, marketing and sales teams at both companies for capturing and conveying its spirit. Thanks, too, to Doubleday Canada publisher Maya Mavjee for her enthusiasm for the project from the start, and to my splendid agent, Jackie Kaiser, at Westwood Creative Artists for her always wise counsel. I'm also grateful to Bill Sertl and Barry Estabrook at the late, lamented *Gourmet* for their story assignments, which first led Steve and me to some of our island friends.

And a heartfelt thank you, a heaping helping of sugar, to all the wonderful people in the islands who welcomed us, fed us, taught us and befriended us, especially Dingis Naryan, Gennel Narine, Dwight Allen and Stevie Bruno in Grenada; Sweet-Hand Patricia and Maurice Jones in Trinidad; and Leslie Ann and Godfrey Calliste and family in Carriacou. Big hugs as well to Sharon Rose James and Jesse James, juggler, magician, eater extraordinaire and champion of all things Trini, who drove us everywhere even though we drove him crazy. I look forward to bussing a lime with all of you.

Rosa and Bruce Van Sant smoothed the way for us in the Dominican Republic, Martin Carrierre guided us in Dominica, and Canadian sailors Carolyn and Rick O'Brien introduced us around Carriacou. In Trinidad, the inexhaustible Wendy Rahamut and Veni Mangé's Roses Hezekiah and Allyson Hennessy dished information and fabulous food. In Toronto, home economist Jill Snider enthusiastically tested many of my recipes; John Warren kept business in order while we were away; Tracy and Peter Jones gave us bed and board whenever we arrived back; and Christina Hartling offered assurance and support throughout the writing process.

To our cruising friends who graciously allowed me to include them in the book: Amanda and Jim Grant on *Adventure Bound*, Roberta and Tito Figueroa on *Alleluia!*, Devi and Hunter Sharp on *Arctic Tern*, Heather Mackey and Don Mockford on *Asseance*, Julie Grm and Barry Burge on *Imagine*, Yani and Chris Wilder on *Magus*, and Barb and Chuck Shipley on *Tusen Takk II*. Thanks for letting me press-gang you into exploring with us, even when you didn't realize what you were in for.

I greatly appreciate the musicians and composers who gave me permission to quote lyrics from songs I love: Christophe Grant ("After the Storm" and "Nah Leaving"); Barnet Henry, a.k.a. Preacher ("Market Vendor"); Machel Montano, David Rudder and Kernal Roberts ("Oil and Music," Masuso Publisher); and David Rudder and Ian Wiltshire ("Trini to de Bone"). And to the pannists of Trinidad, your sweet music lifted me up from start to finish.

And, finally, this book wouldn't exist without my husband, Steve Manley, who read and commented on multiple drafts of the manuscript, ate and commented on multiple versions of the recipes, fed me great lines ("This is going to be a really bad day, Billy"), designed my website (and took the photos: www.spicenecklace.com) and is my partner in every adventure.

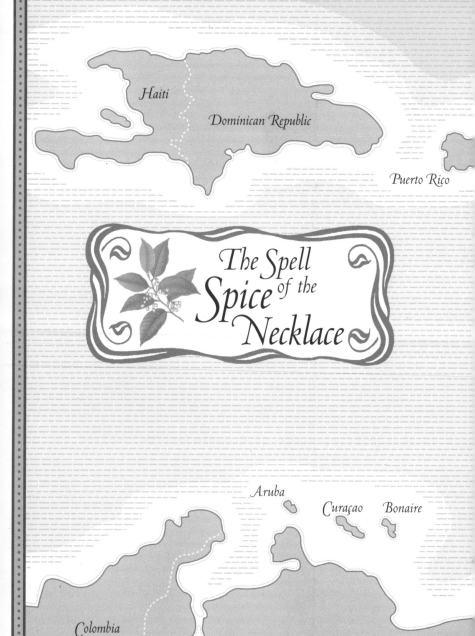

The Spell
of the
Spice
Necklace

INTIMATE
BEHAVIOUR
DESMOND
MORRIS

RANDOM HOUSE
New York

CONTENTS

ACKNOWLEDGMENTS

Although in the past no books have been devoted specifically to the subject of *Intimate Behaviour*, I have been greatly helped by a large number of papers and volumes on associated topics and on special aspects of the problem. These I gratefully acknowledge, and details concerning them can be found in the bibliography on pages 249–53. As I have been writing for a general audience, I have not included specific references to these works in the text, but a chapter-by-chapter guide is given on pages 245–8.

In addition, I would like to express my debt to my scientific colleagues and, above all, to my personal intimates, from whom I have learned so much. In particular, I would like to thank my wife Ramona, my publisher Tom Maschler and my assistant Trisha Pike. Without their help these pages could not have been written.

INTRODUCTION

To be intimate means to be close, and I must make it clear at the outset that I am treating this literally. In my terms, then, the act of intimacy occurs whenever two individuals come into bodily contact. It is the nature of this contact, whether it be a handshake or a copulation, a pat on the back or a slap in the face, a manicure or a surgical operation, that this book is about. Something special happens when two people touch one another physically, and it is this something that I have set out to study.

My method has been that of the zoologist trained in ethology, that is, in the observation and analysis of animal behaviour. I have limited myself, in this case, to the human animal, and have given myself the task of observing what people do — not what people say, or even what they say they do, but what they actually do.

The method is simple enough — merely to use one's eyes — but the task is not as easy as it sounds. The reason is that, despite the self-discipline, words persist in filtering through and preconceived ideas repeatedly get in the way. It is hard for an adult human being to look at a piece of human behaviour as if he were seeing it for the very first time, but that is what the ethologist must attempt to do if he is to bring new understanding to the subject. The more familiar and commonplace the behaviour, of course, the worse the problem becomes; in addition, the more intimate the behaviour, the more emotionally charged it becomes, not only for the performers, but also for the observer.

Perhaps this is why, despite their importance and interest, so few studies have been made of commonplace human intimacies. It is far more comfortable to study something as remote from human involvement as, say, the territorial scent-marking behaviour of the giant panda, or the food-burying behaviour of the green acouchi, than it is to tackle scientifically and objectively something as 'well known' as the human embrace, the mother's kiss or the lover's caress. But in a social environment that is ever more crowded and impersonal, it is becoming increasingly important to reconsider the value of close personal relationships, before we are driven to ask the forlorn question, 'Whatever happened to love?' Biologists are often wary of using this word 'love', as if it reflected no more than some kind of culturally inspired romanticism. But love is a biological fact. The subjective, emotional rewards and agonies associated with it may be deep and mysterious, and difficult to deal with scientifically, but the outward signs of love — the actions of loving — are readily observable, and there is no reason why they should not be examined like any other type of behaviour.

It has sometimes been said that to explain love is to explain it away, but this is quite unjustified. In a way, it is an insult to love, implying that, like an ageing, cosmetic-caked face, it cannot stand scrutiny under a bright light. But there is nothing illusory about the powerful process of the formation of strong bonds of attachment between one individual and another. This is something we share with thousands of other animal species — in our parent-offspring relationships, our sexual relationships and our closest friendships.

Our intimate encounters involve verbal, visual and even olfactory elements, but, above all, loving means touching and body contact. We often talk about the way we talk, and we frequently try to see the way we see, but for some reason we have rarely touched on the way we touch. Perhaps touch is so basic — it has been called the mother of senses — that we tend to take it for granted. Unhappily, and almost without our noticing it, we have gradually become less and less touchful, more and more distant, and physical untouchability has been accompanied by emotional remoteness. It is as if the modern urbanite has put on a suit of emotional armour and, with a velvet hand inside an iron glove, is beginning to feel trapped and alienated from the feelings of even his nearest companions.

It is time to take a closer look at this situation. In doing so, I shall endeavour to keep my opinions to myself, and to describe human behaviour as seen through the objective eyes of a zoologist. The facts, I trust, will speak for themselves, and will speak loudly enough for the reader to form his own conclusions.

1

THE ROOTS OF INTIMACY

As an adult human being, you can communicate with me in a variety of ways. I can read what you write, listen to the words you speak, hear your laughter and your cries, look at the expressions on your face, watch the actions you perform, smell the scent you wear and feel your embrace. In ordinary speech we might refer to these interactions as 'making contact', or 'keeping in touch', and yet only the last one on the list involves bodily contact. All the others operate at a distance. The use of words like 'contact' and 'touch' to cover such activities as writing, vocalization and visual signalling is, when considered objectively, strange and rather revealing. It is as if we are automatically accepting that bodily contact is the most basic form of communication.

There are further examples of this. For instance, we often refer to 'gripping experiences', 'touching scenes' or 'hurt feelings', and we talk of a speaker who 'holds his audience'. In none of these cases is there an actual physical grip, touch, feel or hold, but this does not seem to matter. The use of physical-contact metaphors provides a satisfying way of expressing the various emotions involved in the different contexts.

The explanation is simple enough. In early childhood, before we could speak or write, body contact was a dominant theme. Direct physical interaction with the mother was all-important and it left its mark. Still earlier, inside the womb, before we could see or smell, leave alone speak or write, it was an even more powerful element in our lives. If we are to understand the many curious and often strongly inhibited ways in which we make physical contact with one another as adults, then we must start by returning to our earliest beginnings, when we were no more than embryos inside our mothers' bodies. It is the intimacies of the womb, which we hardly ever consider, that will help us to understand the intimacies of childhood, which we tend to ignore because we take them so much for granted, and it is the intimacies of childhood, re-examined and seen afresh, that will help us to explain the intimacies of adult life, which so often confuse, puzzle and even embarrass us.

The very first impressions we receive as living beings must be sensations of intimate body contact, as we float snugly inside the protective wall of the maternal uterus. The major input to the developing nervous system at this stage therefore takes the form of varying sensations of touch, pressure and movement. The entire skin surface of the unborn child is bathed in the warm uterine liquid of the mother. As the child grows and its swelling body presses harder against the mother's tissues, the soft embrace of the enveloping bag of the womb becomes gradually stronger, hugging tighter with each passing week. In addition, throughout this period the growing baby is subjected to the varying pressure of the rhythmic breathing of the maternal lungs, and to a gentle, regular swaying motion whenever the mother walks.

Towards the end of pregnancy, in the last three months before birth, the baby is also capable of hearing. There is still nothing to see, taste or smell, but things that go bump in the night of the womb can be clearly detected. If a loud, sharp noise is made near to the mother's belly, it startles the baby inside and makes it jump. The movement can easily be recorded by sensitive instruments and may even be strong enough for the mother to feel it herself. This means that during this period before birth the baby is undoubtedly capable of hearing the steady thump of the maternal heartbeat, 72 times every minute.

It will become imprinted as the major sound-signal of life in the womb.

These, then, are our first real experiences of life – floating in a warm fluid, curling inside a total embrace, swaying to the undulations of the moving body and hearing the beat of the pulsing heart. Our prolonged exposure to these sensations in the absence of other, competing stimuli leaves a lasting impression on our brains, an impression that spells security, comfort and passivity.

This intra-uterine bliss is then rudely and rapidly shattered by what must be one of the most traumatic experiences in our entire lives – the act of being born. The uterus, in a matter of hours, is transformed from a cosy nest into a straining, squeezing sac of muscle, the largest and most powerful muscle in the whole human body, athlete's arms included. The lazy embrace that became a snug hug now becomes a crushing constriction. The newly delivered baby displays, not a happy, welcoming grin, but the strained, tightly contorted facial expressions of a desperate torture victim. Its cries, which are such sweet music to the anxiously waiting parents, are in reality nothing short of the wild screams of blind panic, as it is exposed to the sudden loss of intimate body contact.

At the moment of birth the baby appears floppy, like soft, wet rubber, but almost at once it makes a gasping action and takes its first breath. Then, five to six seconds later, it starts to cry. Its head, legs and arms begin to move about with increasing intensity and for the next thirty minutes it continues to protest in irregular outbursts of limb-thrashing, grasping, grimacing and screaming, after which it usually subsides exhausted into a long sleep.

The drama is over for the moment, but when the baby re-awakens it is going to need a great deal of maternal care, contact and intimacy to compensate it for the lost comforts of the womb. These post-uterine substitutes are provided by the mother, or those who are helping her, in a number of ways. The most obvious one is the replacement of the embrace of the womb by the embrace of the mother's arms. The ideal maternal embrace enfolds the baby, bringing as much of its body surface into contact with the mother as is possible without restricting breathing. There is a great difference between embracing the baby and merely holding it. An awkward adult who holds the infant with a minimum of contact will soon discover how dramatically this reduces the comforting value of the action. The maternal chest, arms and hands must do their best to re-create the total engulfment of the lost womb.

Sometimes the embrace alone is not enough. Other womb-like elements have to be added. Without knowing quite why, the mother starts to rock her child gently from side to side. This has a strong soothing effect, but if it fails she may get up and start slowly walking back and forth with the baby cradled in her arms. From time to time she may joggle it up and down briefly. All these intimacies have a comforting influence on a restless or crying child, and they do so, it seems, because of the way they copy certain of the rhythms experienced earlier by the unborn baby. The most obvious guess is that they succeed by re-creating the gentle swaying motions felt inside the womb whenever the mother walked about during her pregnancy. But there is a catch to this. The speed is wrong. The rate of rocking is considerably slower than the rate of normal walk-ing. Furthermore, 'walking the baby' is also done at a pace that is much slower than an average walk of the ordinary kind.

Experiments were carried out recently to ascertain the ideal rocking speed for a cradle. At very low or very high speeds the movements had little or no soothing effect, but when the mechanically operated cradle was set at between sixty and seventy rocks per minute there was a striking change, the babies under observation immediately becoming much calmer and crying much less. Although mothers vary somewhat in the speed at which they rock their babies when they hold them in their arms, the typical maternal rocking rate is much the same as that in the experiments, and the pace when 'walking the baby' is also in that region. An average walking rate under ordinary circumstances, however, usually exceeds a hundred paces per minute.

It seems, therefore, that although these comforting actions may well soothe by virtue of the way they copy the swaying motions felt inside the womb, the speed at which they are carried out requires some other explanation. There are two rhythmic experiences available to the unborn child, apart from the mother's walking: the steady rise and fall of her chest as she breathes, and the steady thump of her heartbeat. The breathing rate is much too slow to be considered, being roughly between ten and fourteen respirations per minute, but the heartbeat speed, at 72 beats per minute, looks like the ideal candidate. It appears as if this rhythm, whether heard or felt, is the vital comforter, reminding the baby vividly of the lost paradise of the womb.

There are two other pieces of evidence that support this view. First, the recorded heartbeat sound, if played experimentally to babies at the correct speed, also has a calming effect, even without any rocking or swaying movement. If the same sound is played faster, at over a hundred beats per minute — that is, at the speed of normal walking — it immediately ceases to have any calming effect. Second, as I reported in *The Naked Ape*, careful observations have revealed that the vast majority of mothers hold their babies in such a way that their infants' heads are pressed to the left breast, close to the maternal heart. Even though these mothers are unaware of what they are doing, they are nevertheless successfully placing their babies' ears as close as possible to the source of the heartbeat sound. This applies to both right-handed and left-handed mothers, so that the heartbeat explanation appears to be the only one that fits.

Clearly this is susceptible to commercial exploitation by anyone who takes the trouble to manufacture a cradle that can be mechanically rocked at heartbeat speed, or that is equipped with a small machine that plays a non-stop amplified recording of the normal heartbeat sound. A de luxe model incorporating both devices would no doubt be even more effective, and many a harassed mother could simply switch on and relax as it automatically and relentlessly calmed her baby to sleep, just as her washing machine so efficiently deals with the baby's dirty clothing.

Inevitably it is only a matter of time before such machines do appear on the market, and undoubtedly they will do a great deal to assist the busy mother of modern times, but there is an inherent danger in their use if it becomes excessive. It is true that mechanical calming is better than no calming, both for the mother's nerves and for the baby's well-being, and where demands on the mother's time are so heavy that she has no other choice, then mechanical calming will certainly be advantageous. But old-fashioned maternal calming is always going to be better than its mechanical replacement. There are two reasons for this. First, the mother does more than the machine could ever do. Her comforting actions are more complex and contain special features that we have yet to discuss. Second, the intimate interaction between mother and child that occurs whenever she comforts it by carrying, embracing and rocking it provides the important foundation for the strong bond of attachment that will soon grow between them. True, during its first months after birth the baby will respond positively to any friendly adult. It accepts any intimacies from any individual who offers them, regardless of who they are. After a year has passed, however, the child will have learned its own mother and will have started to reject intimacies from strangers. This change is known to occur around the fifth month in most babies, but it does not happen overnight and there is great variability from child to child. It is therefore difficult to predict with certainty the exact moment at which the infant will begin to respond selectively to its own mother. It is a critical time, because the strength and quality of the later bond of attachment will depend on the richness and intensity of the body-contact behaviour that occurs between mother and infant at just this threshold phase.

Obviously, excessive use of mechanical mothers during this

vital stage could be dangerous. Some mothers imagine that it is the provision of food and other similar rewards that make the baby become attached to them, but this is not so. Observations of deprived children and careful experiments with monkeys have shown conclusively that it is instead the tender intimacies with the soft body of the mother which are vital in producing the essential bond of attachment that will be so important for successful social behaviour in later life. It is virtually impossible to give too much body-loving and contact during these critical early months, and the mother who ignores this fact will suffer for it later, as will her child. It is difficult to comprehend the warped tradition which says that it is better to leave a small baby to cry so that it does not 'get the better of you', which is encountered all too often in our civilized cultures.

To counterbalance this statement, however, it must be added that when the child is older, the situation changes. It then becomes possible for the mother to be over-protective and to hold her child back just when it should be striking out and becoming more independent. The worst twist that can happen is for a mother to be under-protective, strict and disciplinary with a tiny infant, and *then* over-protective and clinging with an older child. This completely reverses the natural order of bond development, and sadly it is a sequence that is frequently observed today. If an older child, or adolescent, 'rebels', this twisted pattern of rearing is very likely to be found lurking in the background. Unfortunately, by the time this happens it is a little late in the day to correct the early damage that has been done.

The natural sequence I have described here—love first, freedom later—is basic not only to man, but also to all the other higher primates. Monkey mothers and ape mothers keep up the body-contact intimacies non-stop from the moment of birth for many weeks. They are greatly aided, of course, by the fact that baby monkeys and apes are strong enough to cling to them for long periods of time without assistance. In the great apes, such as the gorilla, the babies may take a few days to get started as active clingers, but after that, despite their weight, they manage it with remarkable tenacity. The smaller monkeys cling from the moment of birth, and I have even seen one half-born baby clutching tightly with its hands to the body of its mother during delivery, while the rear part of it was still inside the womb.

The human baby is much less athletic. Its arms are weaker and its short-toed feet are clingless. It therefore poses a much greater problem for the human mother. Throughout the early months it is she who must perform all the physical actions that serve to keep her and her baby in bodily contact. Only a few fragments of the infant's ancestral clinging pattern remain, rudimentary reminders of its ancient, evolutionary past, and even these are of no practical use today. They last for little more than two months after birth and are known as the grasp reflex and the Moro reflex.

The grasp reflex arrives early, the sixth-month-old foetus already having a strong grip. At birth, stimulation of the palm results in a tight clasping of the hand, and the grasp is strong enough for an adult to lift the whole weight of the baby's body in this way. Unlike the young monkey, however, this clinging cannot be sustained for any length of time.

The Moro reflex can be demonstrated by sharply and swiftly lowering the baby through a short distance – as if it were being dropped – while supporting it under its back. The infant's arms quickly fling outwards, with the hands opening and the fingers spreading wide. Then the arms come together again, as if groping for an embrace to steady itself. Here we can see clearly the ghost of the ancestral primate clinging action that is employed so effectively by every healthy young monkey. Recent studies have shown this even more clearly. If the baby feels itself dropping down while at the same time its hands are held and allowed to grasp, its reaction is not first to fling its arms wide before making the embracing action, but simply to go straight into the tight clinging response. This is precisely what a startled young monkey would do if it were grasping lightly on to the fur of its resting mother, who then suddenly leapt up in alarm. The infant monkey would instantly tighten its grip in this way, ready to be carried off rapidly by the mother to safety. The human baby, until it is eight weeks old, still has enough of the monkey left in it to show us a remnant of this response.

From the human mother's point of view, however, these 'monkey' reactions are of no more than academic interest. They may intrigue zoologists, but they do nothing in practical terms to lighten the parental burden. How, then, can she deal with the situation? There are several alternatives. In most so-called primitive cultures, the baby is almost constantly in touch with the mother's body during its early months. When the mother is resting, the baby is held all the time, either by herself or by someone else. When she sleeps, it shares her bed. When she works or moves about, it is carried strapped firmly to her body. In this way she manages to provide the almost non-stop contact typical of other primates. But modern mothers cannot always go to such lengths.

An alternative is to swathe the unheld baby in a sheath of clothes. If the mother cannot offer the baby the snug embrace of her arms or close contact with her body, day and night, hour after hour, she can at least provide it with the snug embrace of a wrapping of smooth, soft clothing, as an aid to replacing the lost engulfment of the womb. We usually think of clothing the baby merely as an act of keeping it warm, but there is more to it than this. The embrace of the material, as it wraps around and makes contact with the body surface of the infant, is equally important. Whether this wrapping should be loose or firm, however, remains a hotly debated point. Cultures vary considerably in their attitude towards the ideal tightness of this post-natal cloth-womb.

In the Western world today, tight swaddling is generally frowned upon, and the baby, even when new-born, is wrapped only lightly, so that it can move its body and limbs freely if it feels so inclined. Experts have expressed the fear that 'it might cramp the child's spirit' to wrap it more firmly. The vast majority of Western readers would instantly agree with this comment, but it does bear looking at more closely. The ancient Greeks and Romans swaddled their babies, yet even the most fanatical anti-swaddler would have to admit that there were quite a few uncramped spirits among their number. British babies, up to the end of the eighteenth century, were swaddled, and many Russian, Yugoslav, Mexican, Lapp, Japanese and American Indian babies are still swaddled at the present day. Recently the matter was examined scientifically, with both swaddled and unswaddled babies checked for discomfort by sets of sensitive instruments. The conclusions were that swaddling did in fact make the babies less fretful, as was shown by reduced heartbeat rate, breathing rate and crying frequency. Sleep, on the other hand, was increased. Presumably this is because the tight wrapping is more reminiscent of the tight womb-hug experienced by the advanced foetus during the final weeks of its gestation.

If this appears to be entirely in favour of the swaddlers, it should nevertheless be remembered that even the bulkiest, most belly-swelling foetus is never so tightly hugged by the womb that it cannot manage occasional kicks and struggles. Any mother who has felt these movements inside her will be aware that she is not 'swaddling' her unborn infant to the point of total immobility. A moderately close swaddling after birth is therefore probably more natural than the really tight binding that is applied in some cultures. Furthermore, swaddlers tend to prolong unnecessarily the close wrapping of their infants, well beyond the point where it is advisable. It may be helpful during the earliest weeks, but if it is extended over a period of months it may start to interfere with the healthy growing processes of muscular and postural development. Just as the foetus has to leave the real womb, so the new-born must soon leave the cloth-womb, if it is not to become 'overdue' at its next stage of maturation. We normally speak of babies being premature or overdue only in relation to the moment of their birth, but it is useful to apply this same concept to the later stages of childhood development as well. At each phase, from infancy to adolescence, there are relevant forms of intimacy, of bodily contact and caring, that should occur between parent and child if the offspring is to pass through the various stages successfully. If the intimacy offered by the parent at any particular stage is either too advanced or too retarded for that particular stage, then trouble may ensue later.

Up to this point we have been looking at some of the ways in which the mother helps her baby to relive some of its womb-time intimacies, but it would be wrong to give the impression that comforts during the early post-birth phase are no more than prolongations of foetal comforts. Such extensions provide only one part of the picture. Other interactions are taking place at the same time. The baby stage has its own, new forms of comfort to be added. They include fondling, kissing and stroking by the mother, and the cleaning of the baby's body surface with gentle, tactile manipulations such as rubbing, wiping and other mild frictions. Also, there is more to the embrace than merely embracing. In addition to offering the overall enveloping pressure of her arms, the mother frequently does something else. She pats the baby rhythmically with one of her hands. This patting action is restricted largely to one region of the baby's body, namely the back. It is delivered at a characteristic speed, and with a characteristic strength, neither too weak nor too strong. To call it a 'burping' action is misleading. It is a much more widespread and basic response of the mother's, and is not limited to that one specific form of infantile discomfort. Whenever the baby seems to need a little extra comforting, the mother embellishes her simple embrace by the addition of back-patting. Frequently she adds swaying or rocking movements at the same time, and often coos or croons softly with her mouth held near to the baby's head. The importance of these early comforting actions is considerable, for, as we shall see later, they reappear in many forms, sometimes obvious, sometimes heavily disguised, in the various intimacies of adult human life. They are so automatic to the mother that they are seldom thought about or discussed, with the result that the transformed roles they play in later life are usually over-looked.

In origin, the patting action is what students of animal behaviour refer to as an intention movement. This can best be illustrated by giving an animal example. When a bird is about to fly, it bobs its head as part of the action of taking off. During evolution this head-bobbing may become exaggerated as a signal to other birds that it is about to depart. It may perform vigorous, repeated head-bobs for some time before actually taking off, giving its companions the warning message that it is about to leave and enabling them to be ready to accompany it. In other words, it signals its intention to fly, and the head-bobbing is referred to as an intention movement. Patting by human mothers appears to have evolved as a special contact signal in a similar way, being a repeated intention movement of tight clinging. Each pat of the mother's hand says, 'See, this is how I will cling tightly to you to protect you from danger, so relax, there is nothing to worry about.' Each pat repeats the signal and helps to soothe the baby. But there is more to it than this. Again, the example of the bird can help. If the bird is mildly alarmed, but not sufficiently to fly away, it can alert its companions simply by giving a few mild head-bobs, but without actually taking off. In other words, the intention-movement signal can be given by itself, without being carried through into the full action of flight. This is what has happened with the human patting action. The hand pats the back, then stops, then pats again, then stops again. It is not carried through into the full danger-protection clinging action. So the message from the mother to the baby reads not only 'Don't worry, I will cling to you like this if danger threatens,' but also 'Don't worry, there is no danger, or I would be clinging to you tighter than this.' The repeated patting is therefore doubly soothing.

The signal of the softly cooing or humming voice soothes in

another way. Again, an animal illustration may help. When certain fish are in an aggressive mood, they indicate this by lowering the head-end of the body and raising the tail-end. If the same fish are signalling that they are definitely not aggressive, they do the exact opposite, that is, they raise the head and lower the tail. The soft cooing of the mother works on this same antithesis principle. Loud, harsh sounds are alarm signals for our species, as they are for many others. Screams, shouts, snarls and roars are widespread mammalian messages of pain, danger, fear and aggression. By employing tonal qualities which are the antithesis of these sounds, the human mother can, as it were, signal the opposite of these messages, namely, that all is well. She may use verbal messages in her cooing and crooning, but the words are, of course, of little importance. It is the soft, sweet, smooth tonal qualities of the cooing that transmit the vital, comforting signal to the infant.

Another important new, post-womb pattern of intimacy is the presentation of the nipple (or bottle-teat) for sucking by the baby. Its mouth experiences the intrusion of a soft, warm, rubbery shape from which it can squeeze a sweet, warm liquid. Its mouth senses the warmth, its tongue tastes the sweetness, and its lips feel the softness. Another very basic comfort – a primary intimacy – has been added to its life. Again, it is one that will reappear in many disguises later, in adult contexts.

These, then, are the most important intimacies of the baby phase of the human species. The mother embraces her offspring, carries, rocks, pats, fondles, kisses, strokes, cleans and suckles it, and coos, hums and croons to it. The baby's only really positive contact action at this early stage is to suck, but it does have two vital signals that act as invitations to intimacy and encourage the mother to perform her close-contact actions. These signals are crying and smiling. Crying initiates contact and smiling helps to maintain it. Crying says 'come here' and smiling says 'please stay'.

The act of crying is sometimes misunderstood. Because it is used when the baby is hungry, uncomfortable or in pain, it is assumed that these are the only messages it carries. If a baby cries, a mother often automatically concludes that one of these three problems must exist, but this is not necessarily the case. The message says only 'come here'; it does not say why. If a baby is well fed, comfortable and in no pain, it may still cry, simply to initiate intimate contact with the mother. If the mother feeds it, makes sure there is no discomfort, and then puts it down again, it may immediately restart its crying signal. All this means, in a healthy baby, is that it has not had its quota of intimate bodily contact, and it will go on protesting until it gets it. In the early months the demand is high, and the baby is fortunate in having a powerful attraction-signal in its happy smile, to reward the mother for her labours.

Amongst primates, the smile of the human baby is unique. Monkey and ape babies do not have it. They simply do not need it, because they are strong enough to cling on to their mother's fur and stay close to her in this way by virtue of their own actions. The human baby cannot do this and somehow has to make itself more appealing to the mother. The smile has been evolution's answer to the problem.

Crying and smiling are both backed up by secondary signals. Human crying starts out in a monkey-like way. When a baby monkey cries, it produces a series of rhythmic screaming sounds, but sheds no tears. During the first few weeks after birth, the human baby cries in the same tearless way, but after this initial period, weeping is added to the vocal signal. Later, in adult life, the weeping can occur separately, by itself, as a silent signal, but for the infant it is essentially a combined act. For some reason, man's uniqueness as a weeping primate has seldom been commented on, but clearly it must have some specific significance for our species. Primarily it is, of course, a visual signal and is enhanced by the hairlessness of our cheeks, on which tears can glisten and trickle so conspicuously. But another clue comes from the mother's response, which is usually to 'dry the eyes' of her infant. This entails a gentle wiping away of the tears from the skin of the face—a soothing act of intimate body contact. Perhaps this is an important secondary function of the dramatically increased secretion of the lachrymal glands that so often floods the face of the young human animal.

If this seems far-fetched, it is worth remembering that the human mother, as in many other species, has a strong basic urge to clean the body of her offspring. When it wets itself with urine, she dries it, and it is almost as if copious tears have evolved as a kind of 'substitute urine' serving to stimulate a similar intimate response at times of emotional distress. Unlike urine, tears do not help to remove waste products from the body. At low levels of secretion they clean and protect the eyes, but during full weeping their only function appears to be that of transmitting social signals, and they then justify a purely behavioural interpretation. As with smiling, the encouragement of intimacy seems to be their main business.

Smiling is supported by the secondary signals of babbling and reaching. The infant grins, gurgles and stretches out its arms towards its mother in an intention movement of clinging to her, inviting her to pick it up. The mother's response is to reciprocate. She smiles back, 'babbles' to the baby, and reaches out her own arms to touch it or lift it. Like weeping, the smiling complex does not appear until about the second month after birth. In fact, the first month could well be called the 'monkey phase', the specifically human signals appearing only after these first few weeks have passed.

As the baby moves on into its third and fourth months, new patterns of body contact begin to appear. The early 'monkey' actions of the grasp reflex and the Moro reflex disappear and are replaced by more sophisticated forms of *directed* grasping and clinging. In the case of the primitive grasp reflex, the baby's hand automatically took hold of any object pressed into it, but now the new, selective grasping becomes a positive action in which the infant co-ordinates its eyes and its hands, reaching out for and grabbing a particular object that catches its attention. Frequently this is part of the mother's body, especially her hair. Directed grasping of this kind is usually perfected by the fifth month of life.

In a similar way, the automatic, undirected clinging movements of the Moro reflex make way for orientated hugging in which the baby clings specifically to the mother's body, adjusting its movements to her position. Directed clinging is normally established by the sixth month.

Leaving the baby stage behind and passing on to the later period of childhood, it becomes obvious that there is a steady decline in the extent of primary bodily intimacy. The need for security, which extensive body contact with the parent has satisfied so well, meets a growing competitor, namely the need for independent action, for discovering the world, for exploring the environment. Clearly this cannot be done from the encompassing circle of the mother's arms. The infant must strike out. Primary intimacy must suffer. But the world is still a frightening place, and some form of indirect, remote-control intimacy is needed to maintain the sense of security and safety while independence is asserting itself. Tactile communication has to give way to increasingly sensitive visual communication. The baby has to replace the confining, hampering security of the embrace and the cuddle with the less restricting device of exchanged facial expressions. The shared hug makes way for the shared smile, the shared laugh, and all the other subtle facial postures of which the human being is capable. The smiling face, which earlier was an invitation to an embrace, now replaces it. The smile, in effect, becomes itself a symbolic embrace, operating at a distance. This enables the infant to function more freely and yet, at a glance, to re-establish emotional 'contact' with the mother.

The next great phase of development arrives when the child begins to speak. In the third year of life, with the acquisition of a basic vocabulary, verbal 'contact' is added to the visual. Now the child and its mother can express their 'feelings' towards one another in words.

As this phase progresses, the early, primary intimacies of

direct body contact are inevitably restricted still further. It becomes babyish to be cuddled. The strongly growing need for exploration, independence and separate, individual identity increasingly dampens down the urge to be held and fondled. If parents over-express these primary body contacts at this stage, the child does not feel protected, but mauled. Being held now becomes being held back, and the parents have to adjust to the new situation.

For all this, body contact does not disappear completely. In times of pain, shock, fear or panic, the embrace will still be welcomed or sought, and even at less dramatic moments some contact will still occur. There are considerable changes, however, in the form which it takes. The all-embracing hugs shrink to small fragments of their former selves. The semi-embrace, the arm around the shoulder, the pat on the head and the hand clasp begin to appear.

The irony of this phase of later childhood is that, with all the stresses that exploration brings, there is still a great inner need for the comfort of bodily contact and intimacy. This need is not so much reduced as suppressed. Tactile intimacy spells infancy and has to be relegated to the past, but the environment still demands it. The conflict that results from this situation is resolved by the introduction of new forms of contact that provide the required bodily intimacy without giving the impression of being babyish.

The first sign of these disguised intimacies appears early and takes us almost back to the baby stage. It starts in the second half of the first year of life and has to do with the use of what have been called 'transitional objects'. These are, in effect, inanimate mother-substitutes. There are three common ones: a favourite sucking-bottle, a soft toy and a piece of soft material, usually a shawl or a particular piece of bedding. In the early baby phase they were experienced by the infant as part of the intimate contacts it had with its mother. They were not preferred to the mother then, of course, but were nevertheless strongly associated with her bodily presence. In her absence they become substitutes for her, and many children will refuse to go to sleep without their comforting proximity. The shawl or the soft toy has to be in the cot at bedtime, or there is trouble. And the demands are quite specific—it has to be *the* toy or *the* shawl. Similar but unfamiliar ones will not do.

At this stage the objects are employed only when the mother herself is not available, which is why they become so important at bedtime, when contact with the mother is being broken. But then, as the child grows, a change takes place. Now, as the infant becomes more independent of the mother, the favourite objects become more, rather than less, important as comforters. Some mothers misinterpret this and imagine that the infant is feeling unnaturally insecure for some reason. If the child becomes desperate for contact with its 'Teddy', or 'shawly' or 'cuddly'—these objects always seem to acquire a special nickname—the mother may look upon it as a backward step. In fact, it is just the reverse. What the child is doing, in effect, is saying, 'I want body contact with my mother, but that would be too babyish. I am too independent for that now. Instead I will make contact with this object, which will make me feel secure without throwing me back into my mother's arms.' As one authority has put it, the transitional object 'is reminiscent of the pleasurable aspects of mother, is a substitute for mother, but is also a defense against re-envelopment by mother'.

As the infant grows older and the years pass, the comforter may persist with remarkable tenacity, surviving in some cases even into middle childhood. In rare cases it may last into adulthood. We are all familiar with the nubile girl sprawled on her bed clutching her giant Teddy bear. I say 'rare cases', but that requires qualification. It is certainly rare for us to retain an obsession for precisely the same transitional object that we employed in infancy. For most of us the nature of the act would become too transparent. Instead, we find substitutes for the substitutes—sophisticated adult substitutes for the childish mother-body substitutes. When the baby-shawl becomes transformed into a fur coat we treat it with more respect.

Another form of disguised intimacy in the growing child is found embedded in the development of rough-and-tumble play. If it is babyish to embrace and cuddle but the need is still there, then the problem can be solved by embracing the parent in such a way that the body contact involved does not look like an embrace. The loving hug becomes a mock-aggressive bear-hug. The embrace becomes a wrestling-match. In play-fighting with the parent, the child can once again relive the close intimacy of babyhood whilst hiding behind the mask of aggressive adulthood.

This device is so successful that mock body-fighting with the parent can be seen even in later adolescence. Still later, between adults, it is usually restricted to a friendly punch on the arm or thump on the back. Admittedly, the play-fighting of childhood involves more than merely disguised intimacy. There is a great deal of body-testing as well as body-touching, of exploring new physical possibilities as well as reliving old ones. But the old ones are certainly there and they are important – much more so than is usually recognized.

With the arrival of puberty, a new problem asserts itself. Bodily contact with the parent is now further curtailed. Fathers find that their daughters suddenly become less playful. Sons become body-shy with their mothers. In the post-baby phase, the need for independent action began to express itself, but now, at puberty, the need intensifies and introduces a powerful new demand: privacy.

If the baby's message was 'hold me tight', and the child's was 'put me down', that of the adolescent is 'leave me alone'. One psycho-analyst has described the way in which, at puberty, 'The young person tends to isolate himself; from this time on, he will live with the members of his family as though with strangers.' This statement makes its point, of course, by over-emphasis. Adolescents do not go around kissing strangers, but they do continue to kiss their parents. True, the actions have now become more formalized—the smacking kiss has become a peck on the cheek—but brief intimacies do still take place. As with adults, however, they are at this stage largely limited to greetings, farewells, celebrations and disasters. In fact, the adolescent is already adult—sometimes super-adult—as far as his or her family intimacies are concerned. With unconscious ingenuity, loving parents overcome this problem in a variety of ways. A typical example is the 'clothing-adjustment' pattern. If they cannot perform a direct loving touch, they can nevertheless make body contact by disguising it as 'let me straighten your tie' or 'let me brush your coat'. If the reply is 'stop fussing, mother' or 'I can do it myself', then this means that the adolescent has, equally unconsciously, seen through the trick.

When post-adolescence arrives and the young adult moves outside the family, then—from the point of view of body intimacy—it is as if a second birth has been experienced, the womb of the family being abandoned as was the womb of the mother two decades before. The primary sequence of changing intimacies—'hold me tight/put me down/leave me alone'—now goes back to the beginning again. The young lovers, like the baby, say 'hold me tight'. Occasionally they will even call one another 'baby' as they say it. For the first time since baby-hood, intimacies are once again extensive. As before, the body-contact signals begin to weave their magic and a power-ful bond of attachment starts to form. To emphasize the strength of this attachment, the message 'hold me tight' becomes amplified by the words 'and never let me go'. Once the pair-formation is completed, however, and the lovers have set themselves up as a new two-piece family unit, the second babyhood phase is over. The new intimacy sequence moves relentlessly on, copying the first, primary one. The second babyhood gives way to the second childhood. (This is the true second childhood, and is not to be confused with the senility phase, which appears much later and has sometimes been mistakenly referred to as the second childhood.)

Now the enveloping intimacies of courtship begin to weaken. In extreme cases, one or both members of the new pair start to feel trapped, their independence of action threatened. It is normal enough, but it feels unnatural and so they decide it was all a mistake and split up. The 'put me down' of the second childhood is replaced by the 'leave me alone' of the second puberty, and the primary family separation of adolescence becomes the secondary family separation of divorce. But if divorce creates a second adolescence, then what is this neo-adolescent doing alone, without a lover? So, after the divorce, each of the ex-pair members finds a new lover, goes through the second babyhood stage once more, remarries and, with a crash, is back at the second childhood. To their astonishment, the process has repeated itself.

This description may be a cynical over-simplification, but it helps to make the point. For the lucky ones, and even today there are many of them, the second adolescence never comes. They accept the conversion of the second babyhood into the second childhood. Augmented with the new intimacies of sex and the shared intimacies of parenthood, the pair-bond survives.

In later life the loss of the parental factor is softened by the arrival of new intimacies with the grandchildren, until eventually the third and final babyhood appears on the scene with the approach of senility and the helplessness of old age. This third run-through of the intimacy sequence is short-lived. There is no third childhood, at least in earthly terms. We end as babies, snugly tucked in our coffins, which are softly padded and draped—just like the cradles of our first babyhood. From the rock of the cradle we have passed on to the rock of ages.

For many, it is difficult to contemplate the third great intimacy-sequence ending there. They refuse to accept that the third babyhood does not continue into a third childhood, to be found in heaven. There the condition is ideal and permanent, and there is no fear of being over-mothered, for God the Father has no wife.

In tracing these patterns of intimacy from the womb to the tomb, I have dwelt at greater length on the early phases of life, passing more swiftly over the later stages of adulthood. With the roots of intimacy exposed in this way, we can now look more closely at adult behaviour in the chapters that follow.

2

INVITATIONS TO SEXUAL INTIMACY

Every human body is constantly sending out signals to its social companions. Some of these signals invite intimate contact and others repel it. Unless we are accidentally thrown against someone's body, we never touch one another until we have first carefully read the signs. Our brains, however, are so beautifully tuned in to the delicate business of assessing these invitation signals that we can often sum up a social situation in a split second. If we unexpectedly spot a loved one amongst a crowd of strangers, we can be embracing them within a few moments of setting eyes on them. This does not imply carelessness; it simply means that the computers inside our skulls are brilliant at making rapid, almost instantaneous calculations concerning the appearance and mood of all the many individuals we encounter during our waking hours. The hundreds of separate signals coming from the details of their shape, size, colour, sound, smell, posture, movement and expression, crowd at lightning speed into our specialized sense organs, the social computer whirrs into action, and out comes the answer, to touch or not to touch.

As babies, our small size and our helplessness act as powerful stimuli encouraging adults to reach out and make friendly contact with us. The flat face, the large eyes, the clumsy movements, the short limbs and the generally rounded contours, all contribute to our touch-appeal. Add to this the broad smile and the alarm signal of crying and screaming, and the human infant is clearly a massive invitation to intimacy.

If, as adults, we send out similar signals of helplessness or pain, as, for instance, when we are sick or the victims of an accident, we provoke a pseudo-parental response of much the same kind. Also, when we are performing the first tentative body contact, in the form of shaking hands, we nearly always accompany it with a smiling facial expression.

These are the basic invitations to intimacy; but, with sexual maturity, the human animal moves into a whole new sphere of contact signals — the signals of sex appeal — which serve to encourage a male and female to start touching one another with more than mere friendliness in mind.

Some of the sex signals are universal and apply to all adult human beings; others are cultural variations on these biological themes. Some concern our adult appearances as males and females, and others have to do with our adult behaviour — our postures, gestures and actions. The simplest way to survey them is to make a tour of the human body, pausing briefly at each of the main points of interest in turn.

The crotch. Since we are dealing with sexual signals, it is logical to start with the primary genital region, and work our way outwards. The crotch is the major taboo zone, and this is not merely because it is the site of the external reproductive organs. Packed into this one small area of the body are all the main taboo subjects: urination, defecation, copulation, fellation, ejaculation, masturbation and menstruation. With this array of activities it is little wonder that it has always been the most concealed area of the human body. To expose it directly to view as a visual invitation to intimacy is much too strong a sexual signal to be employed as a preliminary device, before a relationship has progressed through the earlier stages of body contact. Ironically, by the time that a relationship has reached the more advanced phase of genital intimacy, it is usually too late for visual displaying, so that the first experience of the partner's genitals is normally tactile. The act of looking directly at the genitals of the opposite sex therefore plays a comparatively small role in modern human courtship. There is, nevertheless, considerable interest in this region of the body, and if direct exposure of the genitals is not possible, alternatives can still be found.

The first is to employ articles of clothing which underline the nature of the organs hidden beneath them. For the female this means wearing trousers, shorts or bathing costumes which are one size too small for comfort, but which, by their tightness, cut into the genital cleft and thereby reveal its shape to the attentive male eye. This is an exclusively modern development, but the male equivalent has a longer history. For a period of nearly two hundred years (from roughly 1408 to 1575) many European male genitals were indirectly displayed in all their glory by the wearing of a codpiece. This began life in a modest way as a front flap which formed a small pouch at the fork of the extremely tight trousers, or hose, worn by the males of the day. The hose were, in fact, so tight that they had little choice. 'Cod' is an old word for scrotum, hence the name 'codpiece'. As the years passed, it grew dramatically in size until it became a blatant phallus-piece, rather than a mere scrotum-piece, and gave the impression that the wearer was the possessor of a permanently erect penis. To emphasize the point further, it was often differently coloured from the surrounding material, and even decorated with gold and jewels. Eventually the codpiece went so far that it began to become something of a joke, so that when Rabelais described the one worn by his hero, he was able to comment that 'For the codpiece sixteen yards of material was required. The shape was that of a triumphal arch, most elegant and secured by two gold rings fastened to enamel buttons, each the size of an orange and set with heavy emeralds. The codpiece protruded forward as much as three feet.'

Today such extravagant penile displays are missing from the world of fashion, but an echo can still be found, for the young male of the 1960s and 1970s has once again started to wear his 'hose' too tight. Like the modern female, he squeezes himself into closely fitting jeans and bathing costumes, in which he is forced to change the resting position of his penis. Unlike the older males, who still fill the generation gap between their legs with a loosely hanging penis beneath their slacker slacks, the younger male of today walks with his penis in the upright position. Held firmly in its vertical posture by the snugly clinging material, it presents a mild but distinctly visible genital bulge to the interested female eye. In this way the young male's costume once again permits him to display a pseudo-erection and, as with the earlier codpiece, this has surprisingly happened without any undue criticism from puritan quarters. It remains to be seen whether the codpiece itself will make a come-back in the years ahead, and how far the trend will have to go before this male embellishment once again becomes so sexually obtrusive that it falls into disrepute.

Other modern costume-genital displays are of a frankly exotic nature and not in wide use. They include female bathing costumes and panties trimmed with fur in the pubic area, or with lace-up fronts which imitate the shape of the genitals. Another form of indirect genital display that has, without comment, survived the passage of time is the Scotsman's sporran, a symbolic genital pouch worn in the scrotal region and frequently covered with symbolic pubic hair.

A less direct way of transmitting visual genital signals is to use some other part of the body as a 'genital-echo', or copy. This enables a primary sexual message to be transmitted, whilst keeping the real genitals completely obscured. There are several ways in which this is done and to understand them we must look again at the anatomy of the female sex organs. For purposes of symbolism, they consist of an orifice—the vagina—and paired flaps of skin—the minor and major labia. If these are covered up, then any other body organs or details that resemble them in some way are likely to become employed as 'genital-echoes', for signalling purposes.

As orifice-substitutes, candidates available are the navel, the mouth, the nostrils and the ears. All have mild taboos associated with them. It is impolite to pick the nose or clean the ear with a finger in a public place. This contrasts with a cleaning action such as wiping the forehead, or rubbing the eyes, which we permit without comment. The mouth is frequently covered for some reason, if not with a veil, at least when we are yawning, gasping or giggling. The navel is even more taboo, having frequently been air-brushed out of photographs completely in past decades, to protect our eyes from its suggestive shape. Of these four types of 'aperture', only the mouth and the navel appear to have been specifically employed as genital-orifice substitutes.

The mouth is by far the most important of these, and transmits a great deal of pseudo-genital signalling during amorous encounters. I suggested in *The Naked Ape* that the unique development of everted lips in our species may well be part of this story, their fleshy pink surfaces having developed as a labial mimic at the biological, rather than the purely cultural, level. Like the true labia, they become redder and more swollen with sexual arousal, and like them they surround a centrally placed orifice. Since the earliest historical times, the lip signals of the female have been heightened by the application of artificial colouring. Lipstick is today a major cosmetic industry and, although the colours vary from fad to fad, they always return before long to something in the pink-red range, thereby copying the flushing of the labia during the advanced stages of sexual arousal. This is not, of course, a conscious imitation of the genital signals; it is merely 'sexy' or 'attractive', with no further questions asked.

The lips of the adult female are typically slightly larger and fleshier than those of the male, which is what one would expect if they are playing a symbolic role, and this size difference has sometimes been exaggerated by spreading the lipstick over a wider area than the lips themselves. This also mimics the enlargement they undergo when sexually engorged with blood.

Many authors and poets have seen the lips and mouth as a

powerfully erotic region of the body, with the male tongue inserting itself, penis-like, into the female mouth during deep kissing. It has also been suggested that the structure of the lips of a particular female reflects the structure of the (as yet unseen) genitals below. A woman with fleshy lips is supposed to be the possessor of fleshy labia; one with tight, thin lips to have tight, thin genitals. Where this is in fact the case, it does not, of course, reflect the precision of the body-mimicry, but merely the overall somatotype of the female in question.

The navel has excited far less comment than the mouth, but some curious things have been happening to it in recent years which reveal that it does have a distinct role to play as a genital-echo. Not only was it painted out of early photographs, but its exposure was also expressly forbidden by the original 'Hollywood Code', so that harem dancing-girls in pre-war films were always obliged to appear with ornamental navel-covers of some kind. No real explanation was ever given for this taboo, except for the lame excuse that the exposure of the navel might start children asking what it was for and thereby precipitate an awkward 'facts of life' interlude for the parent. In adult contexts, however, this is clearly nonsensical, and the true reason was obviously that the navel is strongly reminiscent of a 'secret orifice'. Since harem girls are likely, at the drop of a veil, to start wriggling their abdomens about in an Eastern belly-dance, with the result that this pseudo-orifice starts gaping, stretching and writhing in a sexually inviting manner, Hollywood decided that this indelicate piece of anatomy would have to be masked. Ironically, as we started to move into the second half of the twentieth century and the grip of the Hollywood Code was beginning to relax in the West, the Arab world, with its new-found republican spirit, set about reversing the trend. Egyptian belly-dancers were officially informed that it was improper and undignified to expose the navel during their 'traditional folklore' performances. In future, their new government insisted, the midriff would be suitably covered by some kind of light cloth. And so, as the

European and American navels fought their way back, in the cinemas and on the beaches, the blind orifices of North Africa retreated into a new obscurity.

Since their reappearance, the naked navels of the Western world have undergone a curious modification. They have started to change shape. In pictorial representations, the old-fashioned circular aperture is tending to give way to a more elongated, vertical slit. Investigating this odd phenomenon, I discovered that contemporary models and actresses are six times more likely to display a vertical navel than a circular one, when compared with the artist's models of yesterday. A brief survey of two hundred paintings and sculptures showing female nudes, and selected at random from the whole range of art history, revealed a proportion of 92 per cent of round navels to 8 per cent of vertical ones. A similar analysis of pictures of modern photographic models and film actresses shows a striking change: now the proportion of vertical ones has risen to 46 per cent. This is only partly due to the fact that the girls have become generally much slimmer, for although it is true that a fat, sagging female cannot offer the contemplator of navels a vertical slit, it is equally true that a skinny female need not do so either. Modigliani's slender girls display navels that are quite as round as those of Renoir's plump models. Furthermore, two young girls of the 1970s with similar figures can easily display the two distinct navel shapes.

How this change has come about, and whether it has been unconsciously arrived at or knowingly encouraged by modern photographers, is not entirely clear. It appears to have something to do with a subtle alteration in the trunk posture of the displaying model, possibly partly connected with an exaggerated intake of breath. The ultimate significance of the new navel shape is, however, reasonably certain. The classical round navel, in its symbolic orifice role, is rather too reminiscent of the anus. By becoming a more oval, vertical slit, it automatically assumes a much more genital shape, and its quality as a sexual symbol is immensely increased. This, apparently, is what has been happening since the Western navel came out into the open and began to operate more overtly as an erotic signalling device.

The buttocks. Leaving the crotch and its substitute echoes and passing round to the back of the pelvic region, we come to the paired, fleshy hemispheres of the buttocks. These are more pronounced in the female than the male and are a uniquely human feature, being absent in other species of primates. If a human female were to bend down and present her buttocks visually to a male, as if she were adopting the typical primate invitation-to-copulation posture, her genitals would be seen framed by the two hemispheres of smooth flesh. This association makes them an important sexual signal for our species, and one that probably has a very ancient biological origin. It is our equivalent of the 'sexual swellings' of other species. The difference is that, in our case, the condition is permanent. In other species the swellings rise and fall with the menstrual cycle, reaching their maximum size when the female is sexually receptive, around the time of ovulation. Naturally, as the human female is sexually receptive at virtually all times, her sexual 'swellings' remain permanently 'inflated'. As our early ancestors became more upright in their standing posture, the genitals came to be displayed more from the front than the rear, but the buttocks still retained their sexual significance. Even though copulation itself became an increasingly frontal affair, the female could still send out sexual signals by emphasizing her rump in some way. Today, if a girl slightly increases the undulations of her buttocks when she walks, it acts as a powerful erotic signal to the male. If she adopts a posture in which they are 'accidentally' protruded a little more than usual, this has the same effect. Sometimes, as in the famous 'bottoms up' cancan dance posture, the full version of the ancient primate rump-presentation display is still to be seen, and jokes about the man who wants to slap or caress the bottom of the girl who has innocently bent down to pick up a dropped object are commonplace.

From earlier days, there are two buttock phenomena that deserve comment. The first is the natural condition known as 'steatopygia', and the second is the artificial device of the bustle. Literally, steatopygia means fat-rumped, and refers to a remarkably pronounced protuberance of the buttocks found amongst certain human cultures, notably the Bushmen of Southern Africa. It has been suggested that this is a case of fat-storage similar to that of the camel's hump, but since it is much more exaggerated in females than males, it seems more likely that it is a specialization of the sexual signals that emanate from this region of the body. It looks as if the Bushman females went further in the development of this signal than other races. It is even possible that this condition was typical of most of our early ancestors, but that later on it was reduced in favour of a more athletically adaptable compromise in the shape of the less ambitious female buttocks we see around us today. Certainly the Bushmen were once much more common than they are now, and owned much of Africa before the later Negro expansion.

It is also curious that so many prehistoric female figurines, from Europe and elsewhere, frequently show a similar condition, with huge protruding buttocks which are completely out of proportion with the general obesity of the bodies depicted. There are only two explanations. Either prehistoric women were endowed with huge rumps, sending out massive sexual signals to their males, or the prehistoric sculptors were so obsessed with the erotic nature of buttocks that, like many cartoonists of the present day, they permitted themselves a considerable degree of artistic licence. Either way, the prehistoric buttocks reigned supreme. Then, strangely, in region after region, as the art forms advanced, the big-buttocked females began to disappear. In the prehistoric art of every locality where they occur, they are always the earliest figures to be found. Then they are gone, and more slender females move in to take their place. Unless fat-rumped females really were common in earlier days and then gradually died out, the reason for this widespread change in prehistoric art remains a mystery. The male interest in female buttocks survived, but with a few exceptions they now became reduced to the natural proportions we observe on the cinema screens of the twentieth century. The dancing girls depicted on the murals of ancient Egypt could easily find work in a modern night-club and, had Venus de Milo lived, she would have had a hip measurement of no more than 38 inches.

The exceptions to this rule are intriguing, since, in a sense, they demonstrate a throw-back to prehistoric times and show man's revived interest in gross exaggeration of the female rump region. Here we move from the fleshy phenomenon of steatopygia to the artificial device of the bustle. The effect is the same in both cases—namely, a vast enlargement of the buttock region—but with the bustle this was done by inserting thick padding, or some kind of framework, beneath the female costume. In origin it was a sort of crinoline-in-retreat. The habit of padding the hips all round the pelvic region occurred frequently in European fashions, and all that was needed to permit a new rump-display to appear on the scene was to remove the padding at the front and sides of the body. This made the creation of the bustle a 'reduction' rather than an exaggeration and permitted its introduction into high fashion to take place without undue comment. Having arrived nega-tively in this way, it managed to avoid its obvious sexual implications. The hooped and padded bustle of the 1870s vanished after a few years, but returned in triumph in an even more exaggerated form in the 1880s. Now it became a great shelf sticking out at the back, kept in place by wire netting and steel springs, and created an impression that even a tired Bushman would have responded to. By the 1890s, however, this too was gone, and the increasingly athletic female of the twentieth century has never wished to reinstate it. Instead, the enlarged buttocks of modern times have been confined to rarely used 'bottom-falsies', to provocative 'come-hither' posturing and to the drawing-boards of the cartoonists.

The legs. Moving downwards from the pelvic region, the female legs have also been the subject of considerable male interest as sexual signalling devices. Anatomically, the outsides of the female thighs have a greater fat deposit than in the male, and at certain periods a plump leg has therefore been an erotic one. At other times, the mere exposure of leg flesh has been sufficient to transmit sexual signals. Needless to say, the higher the exposure goes, the more stimulating it becomes, for the simple reason that it then approaches more closely the primary genital zone. Artificial aids to the legs have included 'calf-falsies', to be worn under opaque stockings, but these have been as rarely used as 'bottom-falsies'. High-heeled shoes have been much more commonly adopted, the tilt of the foot supposedly enhancing the leg contour and also increasing the apparent length of the legs, which relates to the fact that elongation of the limbs is a characteristic of adolescent maturing. 'Legginess' equals sexual maturity, and therefore sexiness.

The feet themselves have often been squeezed into shoes which are much too tight for them, a tendency that results from the fact that the foot of the adult female is slightly smaller than that of the adult male. It therefore follows that to increase this difference a little will make the female foot more feminine, as a sexual signal to the male. The petite foot has often been praised by male admirers, and many a female has suffered tortures to obtain it. Byron's words sum up the traditional masculine attitude, when he writes of 'feet so small and sylph-like, suggesting the more perfect symmetry of the fair forms which terminate so well'. This view of the female foot is reflected in the perennial story of Cinderella—a tale that can be traced back at least two thousand years—where her ugly sisters have feet too big to fit into the tiny glass slipper. Only the beautiful heroine has small enough feet to win the heart of the Prince.

In China the trend towards small female feet was once taken to horrifying lengths, young girls often having to undergo such tight binding that they suffered serious deformity. The bound foot, or 'golden lily', which looked so attractive in its tiny decorated shoe, had more the appearance of a deformed pig's trotter when it was viewed unshod. So important was this painful practice that a girl's commercial value was measured by the smallness of her feet, her shoes being displayed to establish her worth during the bartering over bride-price. The modern woman whose 'feet are killing her' is merely echoing in a mild way this ancient phenomenon. The official reason given to explain the custom of the 'golden lilies' was that it showed that the female in question did not need to work – because she was so crippled that she could not. But her husband did not need to work either, yet his feet remained uncrushed, so that the exaggerated sex-difference element provides a more basic explanation. This rule applies in many other cases as well. A particular distortion, or exaggeration, is officially performed for reasons of 'high fashion' or status, but the deeper explanation is that the modification in question in some way emphasizes a female (or male) biological characteristic. The artificial tightening of the female waist is another case in point.

In addition to their anatomy, the posture of the legs is capable of transmitting sexual signals. In many cultures, girls are told that it is improper to stand or sit with the legs wide apart. To do this is to 'open' the genitals, and even if they are not visible, the message remains fundamentally the same. With the advent of female trousers and the disappearance of strict codes of etiquette, the legs-apart posture has become much more common in recent years, and is used with increasing frequency by model girls in advertisements. What was once a too-powerful signal has now become merely challenging; what was shocking is now no more than tantalizing. But nevertheless, a girl in a skirt still obeys the old rules. To expose the opened crotch, clad only in panties, remains too strong an invitation signal in most cases.

The traditionally 'polite girl' therefore keeps her legs together, but there is a danger, also, if she goes too far in this direction and presses them too tightly against one another. If she does this, or crosses them so vigorously that her thighs are squeezed together, she begins to 'protest too much' and thereby makes a new kind of sexual comment. As with all puritan statements, she reveals that she has sex very much on her mind. In fact, the girl who tries to protect her genitals unduly draws almost as much attention to them as the one who exposes them to view. Similarly, if a skirt rides up slightly when a girl sits down and exposes more leg than she intended, she only enhances the sexuality of the situation by making attempts to tug it down again. The only non-sexual signal is the one that avoids both extremes.

For the male, the opening of the legs carries much the same signal as with the female, because here, too, it says 'I am exposing my genitals to you.' Sitting with the legs wide apart is the gesture of a dominant, confident male (unless, of course, he is so fat that he cannot get them together).

The belly. Moving up above the genital region now, we come to the belly, which has two characteristic shapes: flat and 'pot'. Lovers tend to be flat-bellied, while pot-bellies are most commonly seen in starving children and overfed men. The adult female is less likely to become pot-bellied than the adult male, even if she becomes equally overweight. This is because, as a female, her tissues are hungrier for fat in the thigh and hip region than around the belly. If a male and female go far enough, of course, they will both end up with much the same spheroid shape, but at milder levels of overeating the difference in fat-distribution is marked. Many comparatively skinny men manage to develop moderate-sized pot-bellies in middle and old age. What is the explanation for this?

Sometimes a visual joke says more than the artist intended or even understood. A cartoon of a pot-bellied, middle-aged man standing on a beach shows him being approached by a beautiful young girl in a bikini. As she comes near, he spots her and starts to contract his sagging stomach, so that when she is abreast of him his chest is swollen out and his belly held tightly in. As she passes by, the stomach slowly begins to sag again until, as she disappears in the distance, it is completely back to its gross, original shape. This joke was clearly intended to reflect a conscious control of the man's body contour – and his sexual image – but what it also depicts is something that happens unconsciously and semi-permanently, as part of the male human sexual display. For sexual excitement, or pro-longed sexual interest, has the automatic effect of tightening up the stomach muscles. Regardless of individual variations, this is revealed in the general difference in the body contour of young males and old males. Young males are more sexually potent than older ones, and their general body shape goes in more as it goes down. They have the typical masculine display shape of our species, with broadened shoulders, expanded chests, and narrow hips. The flat belly is part of this general body-tapering. The older male tends towards sagging, rounded shoulders, flattened chest, and heavier hips. The swollen belly again is part of this now *inverted* tapering of the body contour. With this shape, the older male says plainly, 'I am past the pair-formation stage.'

In modern times, older males, who have made youthfulness and sexual potency into high-status cults, struggle desperately to stem the tide of this almost inevitable contour inversion. They diet ruthlessly, they indulge in physical training, they sometimes even wear tight corsets, and they consciously hold in their loosening stomach muscles as best they can. It would, of course, be much simpler if they could keep on falling in love over and over again. Belly-wise, they would find that an affair is as good as a diet and a corset combined, and that the physical exercise comes built-in. Under the influence of their passionate emotions, their stomach muscles would automati-cally contract and stay contracted, for by the act of falling in love they would be genuinely and biologically returning to a youthful condition, and their body would do its best to match their mood. Many men do, of course, take steps in this direction from time to time, but unless the process is a more or less continuous one, irreversible contour inversion will have started to take its toll, and their body success will be limited. Needless to say, such steps also play havoc with the older male's true biological role, which is by now that of the parental head of an established family unit.

The situation has not always been like this. Long ago, before the miracles of modern medicine stretched out our lives to such an unnatural extent, most older males soon vanished beneath the turf. To judge by our primate body weight and various other features of our life cycle, the natural life-span for man is probably somewhere between forty and fifty years, no more. Beyond that everything is a bonus. Also, in previous historical periods, a dominant, ageing male has often maintained his status more by his social power than by his youthfulness. An attractive young female has frequently been bought rather than wooed. A fat lord, or a fat master of the harem, cared little about his gross shape or the anti-sexual signals he transmitted. In the harem, this situation gave birth to the phenomenon of belly-dancing. Originally this consisted of the performance of pelvic thrusts by the female on the podgy, incapacitated form of her lord and master. Unable to make the thrusting movements himself, he had to be serviced by trained girls who would be able to take over the masculine role in the encounter, inserting his immobile penis into their vaginas, and then undulating and jolting their pelvises to stimulate it to a climax, in what amounted to little more than an act of fertile masturbation. The clever and varied movements developed by such females to arouse their fat, dominant males formed the basis of the famous Eastern belly-dance and, as a visual preliminary, this became more and more elaborate, until it grew into the display we see so often today in nightclubs and cabarets.

For the modern male, sexual conquests with no thought given to the masculine invitation signals are largely limited to brief visits to prostitutes. For his long-term relationships, he now has to rely much more heavily on his personal sexual appeal. In this respect he has returned to a much more natural situation for the human species, but at the same time his life-span has been artificially elongated. It is this situation that has led to the new concern about 'youthfulness and vigour' for the male who, as he leaves his twenties behind, inevitably starts to feel the decline of his sexual powers. Coasting to a natural death at forty, this would not have posed such a problem, leaving just enough time to rear the offspring and be off. But now, with something more like half a century confronting the post-parental male, the problem has become acute, and we have all the diet books, health farms and other paraphernalia of contemporary life to prove it.

The waist. Here we return again to the sexual-signalling world of the female. The waist is narrower in the female than the male, or appears to be so because of her widened, child-bearing hips and her swollen, rounded breasts. Narrowness of waist has therefore become an important female sexual signal, available for artificial exaggerations of the type we have met before. The signal can be made more powerful directly or indirectly, either by tightening the waist or by enlarging the bust and hips. The maximum signal can be transmitted by doing both at once. Busts can be magnified by holding or pushing them up with tight clothing, by padding them out, or by cosmetic surgery. The hips can be enlarged by padding or by the wearing of stiff clothing that curves out from the body. The waist itself can be reduced by tight lacing or the wearing of a belt.

Female waist corsets have a long and sometimes unhappy history. In previous eras they have occasionally become so severe that they have damaged the rib and lung development of young girls and interfered with their healthy respiration. In late Victorian times, an attractive girl was one whose waist measurement in inches was the same as her age at her last birthday. To achieve this goal many young ladies were forced to sleep in their tightly laced corsets, as well as wear them throughout the day. In historical periods when the crinoline was fashionable, the restrictions on the waist could be eased considerably, because, of course, any waist looked small by comparison with the enormous apparent hip width provided by the huge skirts.

Twentieth-century waists have suffered much less from the artificial compressions of the corset, and frequently have been completely free of them, relying instead on the 'compressions' of a rigid diet. The average British woman of today has a waist measurement of $27\frac{3}{4}$ inches. The model girl Twiggy, the typical *Playboy* 'playmate' and the average Miss World all have a 24-inch waist. Modern female athletes, making more masculine demands on their bodies, tend towards a 29-inch waist.

These figures acquire more meaning when they are related to the bust and hip measurements, thereby revealing the 'waist indentation' factor that transmits the essential female contour signal. Twiggy ($30\frac{1}{2}$–24–33) and Miss World (36–24–36) now part company, the latter sending out a much more powerful waist signal.

There is a further waist factor that requires comment. Indentation comes from both above and below, and one can be greater than the other. Miss World is perfectly balanced – from both bust to waist and hip to waist, she indents by 12 inches. The average British female, however (37–$27\frac{3}{4}$–39), goes in more from hip to waist than she does from bust to waist. The fact that her hips are two inches larger than her bust gives her what is called a 2-inch 'drop'. This is common in the average female of other Western countries as well. In Italy it is also 2 inches; in Germany and Switzerland it is $2\frac{3}{8}$ inches; in Sweden and France, $3\frac{1}{8}$ inches.

These figures show a marked and significant difference from the *Playboy* 'playmate', a typical example being 37–24–35: in other words, a 2-inch 'rise', rather than a 'drop'. That she is referred to as being 'big-bosomed' is therefore not merely a reflection of her breast size. Her bust measurement is exactly the same as that of the average British female. Her apparent 'bustiness' is more the result of the fact that, although her bust measurement is no bigger, both her waist and hip measurements are roughly four inches smaller, giving her a top-heavy contour which magnetically draws attention to her breasts. To find such an unusual female is not easy. Since, for the purposes of the magazine, the girl is to be photographed with her breasts naked, the problem is a strictly biological one – artificial aids cannot help her. To consider this more fully, we can now leave the waist behind and concentrate more specifically on the chest region.

The breasts. The adult female of the human species is unique amongst primates in possessing a pair of swollen, hemispherical mammary glands. These remain protuberant and swollen even when she is not producing milk and are clearly more than a mere feeding device. I have suggested that, in their shape, they can better be thought of as another mimic of a primary sexual zone; in other words, as biologically developed copies of the hemispherical buttocks. This gives the female a powerful sexual signal when she is standing vertically, in the uniquely human posture, and facing a male.

There are two other echoes of the basic buttock shape, but they are less powerful than the breast signals. One is the smooth, rounded shoulder of the female, which, if it is 'only just' exposed by the pulling down of a blouse or sweater, presents a suitably curved hemisphere of flesh. This is a common erotic device in periods of low-cut dresses. The other echo is found in the smooth, rounded knees of the female, which, when the legs are bent and pressed together, present another pair of feminine hemispheres to the eyes of the male. Again, knees have frequently been referred to in an erotic context. As with the shoulders, they make their greatest impact when they are 'only just' exposed by the skirt. If the whole leg is visible, some of their impact is lost because they then become merely the rounded ends of the thighs, rather than a pair of hemispheres in their own right. But these are much milder buttock-echoes, and it is with the breasts that the major impact is achieved.

It is important to distinguish here between the childhood reaction to the female breast and the adult sexual one. Most men see their interest in the female bosom as purely sexual. By contrast, some scientific theorists have viewed it as purely infantile. Both views are one-eyed, because both factors are operating. The male lover who kisses the nipple of his female's breast may well be harking back to the pleasures of infancy, rather than kissing a pseudo-buttock, but the amorous male who ogles or fondles a female's breasts may well be responding primarily to their hemispherical buttock shape, rather than reliving the feeling of his mother's breast with his infantile hand. To the tiny hand of an infant, the mother's breast is too vast an object to be cupped or clasped in the palm, but to the adult hand it presents a rounded surface remarkably reminiscent of the buttock hemisphere. Visually the same is true, a pair of breasts offering an image that is much closer to that of a pair of buttocks than to the looming shape seen at close quarters by a baby being suckled.

This sexual significance of the female breasts is therefore of primary importance to our species, and although this is not the whole story, it plays a major role in society's perennial preoccupation with the feminine bosom. For the early English Puritans it meant flattening the breasts completely with a tight bodice. In seventeenth-century Spain, the measures taken were even more severe, young ladies having lead plates pressed into their swelling bosoms in an attempt to prevent their development. Such steps do not, of course, indicate a lack of interest in the female breast, which could only be demonstrated by completely ignoring it. Rather, they show acceptance of the fact that sexual signals do come from this region and, for cultural reasons, have to be stopped.

A much more widespread and frequent tendency has been for the breasts to be emphasized in some way. This emphasis has nearly always been to make them not so much larger as more upstanding. In other words, the tendency has been to improve their hemispherical, pseudo-buttock appearance. They are pushed up by tight dresses, so that they bulge above them, or they are pushed together to make the cleavage between them more like that between the real buttocks, or they are clasped in stretched brassières so that they protrude forward instead of sagging down. At some points in history, even greater attention has been paid to the problem, an ancient Indian love manual advising that 'Continuous treatment with antimony and rice water will cause the breasts of a young girl to become large and prominent so that they will steal the heart of the connoisseur as a robber steals gold.'

In a few primitive cultures, however, sagging or drooping breasts do find favour, and young girls are encouraged to pull at them regularly in order to hasten their downward turn. Also, nearer home, the small-breasted, or even flat-chested, female has her ardent followers, and these exceptions to the general rule require explanation. The social anthropologist would probably merely put them down to 'cultural variations' and leave the matter there. Every culture and every period has its own special standards of beauty, he would say, and virtually anything goes, providing it becomes the accepted fashion for a particular tribe or society. There is no basic biological theme with variations, but merely a wide range of equally valid alternatives, and each one must be looked at on its own merits. But to take such a view is to beg the fundamental issue of why the adult male and female human animals have evolved so many different body details, differences which are typical for our species as a whole. The typical female *does* have swollen breasts which are lacking in the male, she *does* display them regardless of the presence or absence of milk production for her offspring, and other species of primate *do* lack this prominent visual feature. They do therefore present a basic biological theme for *Homo sapiens,* variations from which must be viewed as unusual and requiring special explanation, rather than simply as equally valid cultural alternatives that require none, except to say that they are 'differing tribal customs'.

To understand the exceptions, it helps to look at the 'life cycle' of a typical female breast. In the child it starts out as no more than a nipple on a flat chest. Then, at puberty, it swells into a breast-bud. At this stage the swelling points straight forward. As it grows and becomes heavier, its weight begins to pull it down, its underside becoming slightly more curved than its upper surface. The nipples, however, still project straight out in front. This is the condition of the older teenage girl. Then, as she moves into her twenties and the breast continues to swell, it slowly begins to turn downwards until, in middle age, a full-breasted female shows a marked sag if she does not employ some artificial booster device. There are, then, three basic stages: small for the immature girl, pointed and protuberant for the young adult, and drooping for the older adult.

Viewed in this light, the cultural variations begin to make more sense. If, for some reason, immature girls are thought of as sexually appealing, then small breasts will be favoured. If older women are preferred, then drooping breasts will be in fashion. For the vast majority, the intermediate stage will be preferred, since it represents the true phase of first sexual activity in the human female. Under-developed females will imitate the pointed, protuberant condition by padding their small bosoms, the older ones who wish to give the impression of being in the first bloom of sexual life will imitate it by adding an artificial upthrust.

In cases where pseudo-immature girls are preferred, there are several possible explanations. For the male living in a sexually repressed, puritan culture, flattening the female breast helps to damp down the strong sexual signal. For the male who has a strong inclination to play the 'father' role to a 'daughter' bride, the little-girl look of small breasts will be appealing. For the latent homosexual, small breasts give a more boyish look, which will be strongly attractive. Going to the other extreme, in societies where the maternal role of the female has become culturally much more important than the sexual one, the sagging breasts of the older female will be more appealing, even in younger girls. The latter must then 'age' their breasts by pulling at them to make them hang down.

For the majority of human beings, however, the maximum breast-appeal will come at the point where the hemispheres have reached their fullest protrusion *before* becoming so large that they begin to droop downwards. This explains the dilemma of the *Playboy* photographer, for as one breast quality (increased size) grows, the other (non-droop) diminishes. To take a picture of a super-breast, he has to search for a rare girl who has retained the firmness of her young breast past the point where it has already swollen to a full adult size. It is interesting that this limits him to a narrow age range in the late teens. Clearly this is the most vital point in the life cycle for this type of sexual signalling, and is the phase which older females are attempting to imitate and artificially prolong with their various breast-supporting techniques.

The super-breast effect is indirectly enhanced by selecting girls with modest-sized waists and hips. Here we come back to the question of the more general change in female body contour that occurs with age. Tests have shown that the average adult female puts on three pounds in weight every five years. The small proportion of this that goes on the breasts is what continues to pull them down as the years pass. The hips and thighs get an unfair share of this increase, giving the middle-aged female her characteristic 'hippy' (in the old sense) appearance. This is what accounts for the 'drop' mentioned earlier—the slightly larger size of hip than bust measurement. In some parts of the world, especially the Mediterranean region, this change can occur with startling rapidity as girls pass through their twenties. At one moment they are slim and slender and then, almost overnight, they start swelling out in the pelvic region, to assume the typical 'maternal' shape of the older woman. In other regions the change is more gradual, but the basic trend is the same. Not until very old age is there a reversal, when the body starts to shrink again.

To many Western women who wish to stay young-looking, this natural biological tendency of the species presents a severe challenge and demands the constant agonies of diet control. It is not merely that they are fighting gluttony, they are fighting nature as well. They must not merely eat 'normally', they must deliberately undereat, if they are to retain their girlish figures. The situation has not always been as extreme as it is today. In the past, a plumply rounded adult female figure has been perfectly acceptable sexually. There is nothing unfeminine about ample curves. They do, however, signal the maternal rather than the virginal phase, and the modern woman, under the influence of the contemporary youth-cult, wishes to remain a flesh-virgin, even while she copulates and bears children.

That the plump curves of the adult female are essentially linked to the maternal, rather than the courting, phase of life, is borne out by the fact that for every seven pounds a married woman with a child puts on, an unmarried woman only gains two pounds. The moral of this is that if a female wishes to remain girl-shaped, she should retain girl-status. Being un-married, regardless of age, means that, biologically speaking, she is still displaying to a potential mate and therefore tends to stay the shape that has evolved to fit such a context. Once she becomes married, she begins to slip into the more 'comfort-able' maternal shape, and her body contour starts to signal this new condition.

Although this trend is viewed by most modern women as merely a nuisance, it is too basic to be an accident. In biological terms it must have some value. One reason often given for it is that the plump, broad-hipped woman is a better child-bearer, but there seems to be little evidence to support this, especially as most of the added pelvic width consists not of a broader spacing of the bones that surround the birth-passage, but of heavy layers of fat. (The average human female body contains 28 per cent fat, the average male only 15 per cent.) There is another, more sexual explanation that seems to make better sense. The slender-girl shape is the one men enjoy visually—stare at, touch lightly, kiss, and fall in love with. The fuller, more womanly shape is the one they spend years copulating with. Perhaps, then, what happens is that the ideal visual shape changes to become the ideal tactile body, the 'dancing gazelle' becoming a cushion of 'pneumatic bliss'. Such a change would certainly explain the difference between the bony fashion model, who is to be seen but not touched, and the full-bodied female, who is to be embraced and hugged, and has already completed her biological task of attracting and becoming bonded with an adult male.

I am dealing here, of course, with extremes. In the case of the average female, the girlish body is not so bony as to be unpleasant to copulate with, and the womanly body is not so full as to be uneasy on the eye. The change is only a minor one, and both stages are successful in both a visual and a tactile sense. What has gone wrong is that modern society has swallowed the romantic myth that young lovers stay dreamily in love for ever, year in and year out, with the maximum intensity of the pair-formation stage lasting permanently, even after the pair has become fully bonded. Instead of accepting that the state of being crazily 'in love' must inevitably mature into a condition of deep but less violent 'loving', the married couple struggle to maintain the breathless ardour of their first contacts, and the physical contours that went with them. When, as must happen, they sense the initial intensity slackening, they imagine that something must have gone wrong and feel let down. In retrospect, those early Hollywood movies may have a lot to answer for.

Body skin. For both sexes and in all cultures, a smooth, clean, disease-free skin has a major sexual significance. Wrinkles, dirt and skin diseases are always anti-erotic. (The deliberately

scarred or tattooed skin that occurs in some cultures is a different matter and adds to rather than detracts from the owner's sex
appeal.)

In addition, the female body and limb skin is less hairy than
that of the male, so that she not only attempts to increase its
smoothness by the use of oils, lotions and massage, but also
depilates it in a variety of ways, to exaggerate the sexual
difference. Depilation has been used in many cultures and for
thousands of years. It was practised, not only by certain
'primitive' tribes, but also in particular by the ancient Greeks,
where women went so far as to remove much of the pubic
hair as well, this being done either by tugging the hairs out
manually – 'myrtle bunches pulled out by the hand', to quote
one classical author – or by singeing them off with a burning
lamp or hot ashes.

In modern times, females have depilated themselves with
electric or safety razors and, more recently, by chemical
means. Beauty experts claim that 80 per cent of women in
Britain are the possessors of 'unwanted' body hair, which,
although far more sparse and light than the male equivalent,
nevertheless makes them feel a shade too masculine for comfort. In addition to shaving and the application of hair-
dissolving creams, lotions and aerosol sprays, the beauty
advisers recommend several other alternatives, such as waxing,
rubbing, plucking and electrolysis. Waxing involves heating
a special wax until it can be applied to the skin as a soft mould
which then hardens. Once it is firm, it is stripped away,
pulling the small body hairs with it. This is essentially the same
device as that used from early times by Arab women, except
that in their case they used a thick syrup of equal parts of water
and sugar, with lemon juice added. This was poured on to the
offending skin and allowed to harden, then ripped off in a
similar way.

At first sight it is surprising that modern males, so many of
whom daily endure a long struggle to depilate their stubble-
strewn faces, have never risked experimenting with anything

beyond the traditional razor shave. At second sight, however, a hidden factor emerges. This is not cowardice, or lack of initiative, but the result of a paradoxical desire to appear bearded even when beardless. Shaving always leaves a masculine blue sheen to the lower face, a tell-tale ghost of the beard that was. If, with some new technique, the adult male beard could be banished for ever, so would that virile blue sheen, and the treated face would begin to look too feminine to please its owner. Instead, by the time he dies, the average clean-shaven man will have spent well over two thousand hours scraping and rubbing at his face—a high price to pay for so contradictory a signal.

During the intense phases of pre-copulatory and copulatory activity, the whole of the body-skin surface of both the male and the female undergoes considerable change in textural quality. It glows with heat and, at the point of orgasm, there may be profuse sweating. In erotically posed photographs, models are sometimes shown displaying these conditions as visual signals. The skin may be oiled or greased to make it shine, or sprayed with water to give the impression of profuse sweating. In such cases the water is not meant to be consciously thought of as sweat, the water is plainly water and the model can often be seen to be rising from a pool or a bath to prove it. It would be too direct a comment to make the skin look obviously sweaty. Instead, the dampened surface makes its impact by unconscious association. The same is true of the habit of using a high level of red in printing colour pictures. This gives the girl's skin an erotic, flushed appearance, as though she is sexually overheated, and is a commonly used device in many magazines. Editorial requests to 'have the red brought up' do not, however, go so far that the viewer becomes consciously aware of what is being done.

Products have recently been marketed to produce an erotic skin glow artificially on a more private basis. Lovers can now cover themselves with various strange substances that make them look (and feel) as though they are in an advanced arousal condition before they have even begun to perform pre-copulatory contacts. For example, 'Love Foam' comes in aerosol cans. When it is sprayed on it looks rather like shaving cream, but when rubbed into the skin, according to the manufacturers, it makes the body 'take on a magical glow'. For even more exotic tastes, there is a substance which goes by the colourful name of 'Orgy Butter'. Called 'The Luxury Lubricant', it is advertised as 'A bold, red warm body rub ... Gives a slippery, sensual effect. Works into the skin with rubbing, providing an after-glow.' Here, quite clearly, are the vital arousal signals – red/slippery/glow – once again mimicking the vaso-dilation and sweating of the real arousal state of the human body skin.

The shoulders. The rounded female shoulder has already been mentioned, but the larger male shoulder also deserves a comment. Width of shoulders becomes an important secondary sexual characteristic that starts to develop at puberty. The shoulders of the male adolescent widen out more extensively than those of the female, and by the time the young adult stage is reached the male is decidedly more broad-shouldered than his female companion. Like the other contour differences, this one has also been exaggerated artificially in various ways. Throughout history, male clothing has repeatedly involved an extra padding of the shoulder region, making it appear even larger as a masculine signal. The extreme situation is reached with the military epaulet, which not only makes the shoulders appear wider but also makes them much more angular. In this way they provide a double contrast with the narrower and more rounded shoulders of the female, and completely lose their hemispherical visual quality.

The jaw. There are several important sexual differences in the head region, and the first of these concerns the jaw and chin. The average human male has a slightly heavier jaw and chin region than the average female. For some reason this fact is seldom commented on, and yet it remains the one certain give-away clue in the case of an otherwise perfectly disguised male transvestite or female impersonator. Such men can pad out their body contours, depilate all visible areas of skin, cover their faces in heavy make-up, have wax injections to give themselves artificial breasts, and generally present such an alluring female appearance that occasionally a sailor in a foreign port has found himself, rather late in the transaction, involved with a 'female' prostitute who is not all that 'she' at first seemed to be. But even the very best of transvestites can do nothing about his jaw and chin, short of major surgery. Unless, by chance, he happens to be an abnormally small-jawed male, he will always present a tell-tale, heavy-jowled appearance to a discerning eye.

In some races, especially in the Far East, the extra heaviness of the male jaw and chin is less pronounced, and it is significant that in these same races there is typically a much less marked beard growth. It seems as if there is a connection between these two features. Jutting the jaw forward, by either sex, is an aggressive act—an intention movement of thrusting forward into the attack. It is the opposite of the submissive lowering of the head that occurs during a meek bowing action. The male, by having a more powerful jaw, is, so to speak, performing a permanent assertive jut. That this is important as a masculine trait is borne out by the fact that males who have receding chins are sometimes sneered at as 'chinless wonders', implying that they lack the normal male assertiveness.

Since one of the most obvious masculine characteristics of our species is the possession of a beard, it seems highly probable that this evolved in company with the more jutting jaw, the heavier bony structure providing a better base for the hairs, and the two features together producing a maximum virile jut. The peculiar chin of our species is important here. Unlike other primates, we have an outward protuberance of bone in the chin region, a protuberance which anatomists have now decided has no internal mechanical function. In the past, many theories have been put forward to explain this unique human feature, relating it to special properties of the jaw muscles and the tongue, but all of these arguments have recently been demolished. Instead, our chin jut is now accepted as primarily a signal feature and, as such, it must be seen as one that underlies the assertive jutting of the male beard.

The cheeks. Moving up the face and avoiding the mouth, which was dealt with earlier, we come to the cheeks. Here the most important signal is the blush, a reddening of the skin caused by vaso-congestion. This always starts in the cheek region, where it is most obvious, and may then spread to cover the whole of the face, the neck and, in some cases, the upper part of the trunk. Blushing is more common in females than males, and in young females than older ones. Accompanying the reddening there is a turgidity of the skin which takes on a surface glow that is visible even in a Negro blush. Blushing occurs in all human races and even in the deaf/blind, so that it appears to be a basic biological characteristic of the species. Darwin devoted a whole chapter to the subject of blushing and concluded that it reflected shyness, shame, or modesty, and indicated 'self-attention to personal appearance'. Its sexual significance is illustrated by the fact that the records show that girls who blushed freely when being offered for sale in ancient slave-markets for use in harems fetched higher prices than those that did not. As an invitation to intimacy, whether desired or not, the blush seems to have been a powerful signal.

The eyes. The most important of human sense organs, these not only see all the various signals we have been examining, but also transmit some on their own account. We all make and break eye contacts repeatedly during face-to-face encounters, looking at people to check their changing moods and then looking away to avoid the threat of staring at them. Between lovers, however, the stare can become more prolonged without being disconcerting or aggressive. Lovers 'gaze deeply into one another's eyes' for a particular reason. Under the influence of strong emotions of a pleasant kind, our pupils dilate to an unusual degree, the small dark spot in the centre of the eye becoming a great black disc. Unconsciously, this transmits a powerful signal to the loved one, indicating the intensity of the love felt by the dilator. This fact has only recently been studied scientifically, but it has been known for centuries, Italian beauties of earlier days having placed drops of belladonna into their eyes in order to create the effect artificially. In modern times a similar device has been used by advertisers, who, using black ink instead of belladonna, have touched up photographs of model girls, enlarging their pupils to make them more appealing.

Another change that takes place in the eyes when emotions run high is a slight increase in tear production. In an intensely loving condition this does not usually go to the extreme of producing tears that actually start to run from the eye, but merely gives the eye surface an increased glistening quality. These are the shining eyes of love, and combine with the pupil dilation to leave no doubt about the condition of the signaller.

Eye movements of various kinds also invite intimacy. Apart from the well-known wink, the rolling of the eyes is also reported to be a direct invitation to copulation in certain cultures. A demure dropping of the eyes also transmits its message in the female, while a slight narrowing of them can indicate interest on the part of a male. When making a first encounter, the holding of a glance slightly longer than is usual can also make an impact, acting as a hint, so to speak, of the deep gazing that may develop later.

A wide-eyed, or magnified, stare is sometimes employed by a female inviting intimacy, and associated with this is the feminine device of fluttering the eyelashes or batting the eyelids. The word 'bat' used in this connection is a modification of 'bate', which means a beating of wings, and, in our culture at least, is a decidedly non-masculine action, so much so that it is sometimes used by a male when he is mockingly imitating a female gesture. Perhaps because eyelash movements of this kind are so essentially feminine, a great deal of lash exaggeration is practised by females at the present time. This began with the use of mascara, to make the eyelashes look heavier and more conspicuous, then moved on to eyelash curlers, and finally, in the 1960s, culminated with the development of sets of long artificial lashes which were added to the real ones. Today, one company alone offers no less than fifteen different styles of artificial eyelashes, including 'Wispy-tipped Starry Lashes' that 'open up eyes' and 'Raggedy Lashes' that 'enlarge small eyes'. These are fixed to the upper eyelids, as are such exotic concoctions as 'Cluster-lashes', 'Natural-fluff Lashes' and 'Super-sweepers'. For the lower eyelid, there are 'Winged Under-lashes' to 'widen, brighten eyes'. As in so many other parts of the body, when the female has something that sends out an important feminine signal, she makes the most of it. This new trend to exaggerate the eyelash region would certainly provide a feast for an amorous male Trobriander, who, as an important part of his love-making, regularly bites off the lashes of his loved one. Luckily for the latter, eyelashes grow remarkably quickly, each one only lasting for three to five months even in the unbitten condition.

The eyebrows. Above the eyes the human animal possesses two unique patches of hair at the bottom of an otherwise hairless forehead. The eyebrows were once thought to operate as devices for stopping the sweat running down into the eyes, but their basic function is that of signalling changing moods. They are raised in fear and surprise and lowered in anger, knitted together in anxiety and cocked in a questioning glance. At the moment of a friendly acknowledgment they are flicked quickly once up and down.

The eyebrows of the female are less thick and bushy than those of the male, so, once again, they are available for exaggeration to make a female condition more feminine. They have frequently been plucked to make them thinner, and in the 1930s they were reduced to a mere pencil line. Even this extreme was exceeded in earlier days, however, Japanese brides once going so far as to shave them off altogether at the time of their marriage.

The sexual nature of this comparatively trivial modification to the female appearance is well illustrated by the fact that, in 1933, a girl who applied for a post as a nurse in a London hospital was warned by the matron that, amongst other things, she would not be permitted to continue plucking her eyebrows. A complaint was made, her case was taken up, and the London County Council was urged to give the matron an official rebuke, but the request was refused. The hospital patients were therefore spared the undue stimulation of a sensuously plucked eyebrow, and unmodified female shapes continued to glide through the long white corridors.

The face. Before leaving the facial region, it is worth taking a last glance at it as a whole, rather than as a set of smaller details. It is, without any doubt, the most expressive region of the entire human body, capable of transmitting incredibly varied and subtle emotional messages by means of its complex expressions. By contracting and relaxing the special muscles, particularly those around the mouth and eyes, we can signal everything from joy and surprise to sadness and anger. As a device for inviting intimacy, this is of major importance. A face that is soft and smiling, or alert and excited, attracts us strongly. One that is forlorn and helpless, or in agony, may also stimulate us to approach and console. A tense, hard or grumpy face has the opposite effect. This is common enough knowledge, but there is an interesting long-term effect that operates on the human face, and which deserves brief comment.

Where facial expressions are concerned, we can speak of an 'on-face' and an 'off-face'. The on-face is the one we use during social encounters. We speak of 'putting on a happy face', or 'putting a good face on it', and we try to avoid 'losing face' in public. If we want to appear friendly, we adopt a soft, smiling expression. Alternatively, we set our faces into a grim or pompous look to cope with more serious occasions. When we are alone and unseen, however, we let our faces go off-duty. When this happens they arrange themselves into the posture typical of our overall long-term mood. The basically anxiety-ridden man, who tried his best to look happy at the party, now tenses up his solitary face, revealing his true emotional condition, but revealing it, of course, to no one but himself. (Unless he catches sight of himself in a mirror, even he may not be aware of it.) The basically happy and contented man, who tried his best to look sad and serious at the funeral, now relaxes his solitary face, with his lips softened and the furrows in his brow smoothed out.

Most of us change our long-term moods from time to time, so that our facial muscles do not experience prolonged exposure to one particular off-face condition. We may feel depressed in the morning but happy again by the evening, and in our solitary moments our facial postures will vary accordingly. For individuals who live in a state of more or less permanent private anxiety, depression or anger, the situation is different. For them, there is a danger that their off-faces will become completely set. In such instances, the facial musculature seems to become moulded in one basic expression. The crease lines on the forehead, around the mouth and at the side of the nose become almost permanent.

Such people find it hard to switch to the appropriate on-face during social encounters. The anxious person still looks anxious even when smiling a greeting. The grumpy man still looks grumpy even when laughing at a joke. The set of the muscles somehow survives and the on-face becomes superimposed on the off-face, rather than replacing it. In this way, facial expressions can tell us something about a person's past as well as his present emotional condition.

It is not clear how long these off-face wrinkles will last after there has been a fundamental change in a way of life.

If someone who has been anxious and worried all his life suddenly achieves a contented condition, the wrinkles will not vanish overnight. If the person in question is elderly when this welcome change occurs, they may never fade. Certainly, in all such cases there will be a period of time when the old set-face will be lingering on despite the fact that its message is no longer relevant, but I know of no studies in which the length of this period has been measured.

These comments also apply, incidentally, to the general body posture of the human being. There are slumped bodies and alert bodies, stiffly tense bodies and softly lithe ones. Again, we are capable of changing our body-muscle tensions to match our social moods and occasions, but, as with the face, a prolonged, extreme condition can give us a set posture that is difficult to shake off even when we want to. Rounded shoulders can develop into a permanent hunch that even winning a million cannot straighten out, and a tense stiff-legged walk can become a companion for life.

The hair. Finally we reach man's crowning glory, his densely packed mop of roughly 100,000 head-hairs. In some races these are woolly or frizzy, in others they hang down long and straight, or flow in the wind. They grow at a rate of nearly five inches a year, and each one lasts up to six years before it falls out and is replaced. This means that the average uncut head of straight hair would reach down to the hips, and must have given an unbarbered, primitive human being an extraordinary appearance, when compared with any other species of primate. While our body hair became stunted and almost invisible at a distance, our head hair ran amok.

Apart from the fact that older males, but not older females, tend to become bald in many cases, there is no sex difference in the head hair. Biologically, both men and women are long-haired, and this characteristic has developed as a species recognition signal, rather than a sexual one. Culturally, however, it has frequently been modified as a gender signal. Sometimes men have worn longer hair than women, but usually the reverse has been the case. In recent centuries, masculine hair has been cropped basically as an anti-parasite device, aggressive army sergeants referring to long male hairs as 'louse-ladders'. Women have nearly always maintained a moderate hair length; it is the men who have fluctuated wildly from one extreme to the other. In the past this has sometimes led to the wearing of huge, drooping male wigs, a practice still seen today in the case of British judges. In general, however, the longer locks of recent times have become so firmly associated with the female sex that for a man to wear his hair in anything remotely approaching its natural length has been quite wrongly viewed as essentially feminine. During the last decade this situation has changed dramatically amongst young males, and hair length seems once again to be re-establishing itself in its truly non-sexual role. It is perhaps ironic that, although it is modern hygiene that has made this so much less of a parasite risk, it is the anti-hygiene hippie movement that has taken the lead.

Cleaning, grooming, washing and oiling the hair has always been an important accompaniment to its cultural use as a sexual signal. Ancient urbanites, like their modern counterparts, were prepared to go to great lengths to obtain the desired effect. The oldest known hair tonic consisted of 'Paws of a dog, one part; kernels of dates, one part; hoof of a donkey, one part. Cook thoroughly with oil and anoint.' Today, glistening, gleaming, swishing hair remains almost every girl's ideal and, as the advertisers repeatedly tell us, hair that is 'dull and lifeless' ruins its owner's chances of inviting intimacy.

In this grand tour of the signalling human body the different parts have been taken one by one, but there is still the whole person to be considered. The isolated parts are displayed not singly but all at once, in a general combination and in a specific context. It is the tremendously varied way in which they can combine with one another, and the great range of contexts in which they can be presented, that makes social interaction so complex and so fascinating. Every time we enter a room, or walk down a street, we are transmitting a mass of signals, some purely biological and others culturally modified, and we are always unconsciously aware of this fact and adjusting them in a hundred subtle ways as we move through our many kinds of social encounter. Nearly always we are striving to send out a balanced set of signals, some attracting intimacy, others repelling it. Just occasionally we go much further in one direction or the other, either displaying our invitations blatantly, or presenting ourselves in a hostile, rejecting manner to those around us.

Throughout this chapter, in surveying the various visual invitations to sexual intimacy, I have tended to dwell on extremes. I have selected the most vivid examples in order to underline the points I have been making. Codpieces, corsets and epaulets may seem remote from the ordinary signals of sex appeal used by the average adult of today, but they nevertheless help to draw our attention to the less exaggerated devices—the tight trousers, the belts and the padded shoulders—that are more widely and less obviously employed. Similarly, belly-dancing may be no more than an exotic form of entertainment, but again its inclusion in this survey helps us to appreciate the less extreme dance movements used nightly by hundreds of thousands of ordinary girls at parties and discotheques.

Whether, as adults, we go to great lengths to improve and display our visual signals of sex appeal, or whether we treat the whole business in a more off-hand manner, whether we resort to artificial aids (and there are few of us who do not employ *some*), or whether we scorn them and prefer a more 'natural' approach, we are all of us constantly transmitting a complex set of visual signals to our companions. Many of these signals inevitably have to do with our adult sexual qualities, and even when we are totally unaware of what we are doing, we never stop 'reading the signs'. In this way we prepare ourselves for a major social step—the step that leads us to initiate the first tentative contact with a potential sexual partner and carries us over a vital threshold into the whole complex world of sexual intimacy itself.

3

SEXUAL INTIMACY

In discovering his personal identity, the growing child must reject the soft embrace of his mother's arms. At last, as a young adult, he stands alone. As a baby, his trust in his mother was unlimited, his intimacy total. Now, in maturity, both his relationships with other adults and his intimacies with them are severely limited. Like them, he keeps his distance. Blind trust is replaced by alert manœuvring, dependency by inter-dependency. The gentle intimacies of infancy that gave way to the joyful games of childhood have become the tough social transactions of adulthood.

There is no denying the excitement. There are things to explore, goals to achieve and status to be raised. But where did all the loving go? Loving was an act of giving, giving oneself without question to another person, but adult relationships are not like that ...

Up to this point my words could apply as much to a growing monkey as to a growing human. The pattern is the same. But now comes a difference. If the monkey is a male, it will never again, as an adult, know the total intimacy of a loving bond. Until the day it dies, it will continue to exist in the loveless world of rivalries and partnerships, of competition and co-operation. If it is a female, it will eventually regain the loving condition, as a mother with an infant of its own, but like the male it will know no such bond with another adult monkey. Close friendships, yes; partnerships, yes; brief sexual encounters, yes; but total intimacy, no.

For the adult human, however, there is such a possibility. He is capable of forming a powerful and lasting bond of attachment for a member of the opposite sex that is much more than a mere partnership. To say that 'marriage is a partnership', as is so often done, is to insult it, and to completely misunderstand the true nature of a bond of love. A mother and her baby are not 'partners'. The baby does not trust the mother because she feeds and protects him; he loves her because she is who she is, not because of what she does. In a partnership one merely exchanges favours; the partner does not give for the sake of giving. But between a pair of adult human lovers there develops a relationship like that between mother and child. A total trust develops and, with it, a total bodily intimacy. There is no 'give and take' in true loving, only giving. The fact that it is 'two-way giving' obscures this, but the 'two-way receiving' that inevitably results from it is not a condition of the giving, as it is in a partnership; it is simply a pleasing adjunct to it.

For the cautious, calculating adult, the entry into such a relationship appears a hazardous affair. The resistance to 'letting go' and trusting is enormous. It breaks all the rules of bargaining and dealing that he is so used to in all his other adult relationships. Without some help from the lower centres of his brain, his higher centres would never permit it. But in our species that help is forthcoming and, often against all reason, we fall in love. For some, the natural process is suppressed, and if they do enter into a state of marriage or its equivalent, they do so as if it were a business transaction: you rear child, I earn money. This 'baby-buying', or 'status-buying', has sadly become commonplace in our crowded human zoos, but it is fraught with dangers. The mated pair are held together, not by internal bonds of attachment, but by the external pressures of social convention. This means that the couple's natural potential for falling in love still lies waiting inside their brains and can leap into action without warning at any time, to create a true bond somewhere outside their official one.

For the lucky ones this sequence does not take place. As young adults, they find themselves falling in love uncontrollably and forming a true bond of attachment. The process is a gradual one, although it does not always appear to be. 'Love at first sight' is a popular concept. It is, however, usually a retrospective judgment. What occurs is not 'total trust at first sight', but 'powerful attraction at first sight'. The progress from first attraction to final trust is nearly always a long and complex sequence of gradually increasing intimacies, and it is this sequence that we must now examine.

To do so, the simplest method is to take a pair of 'typical lovers', as seen in our Western culture, and follow them through the process of pair-formation from first glimpse to ultimate copulation. In doing this we must always remember that there is in reality no such thing as the 'typical lover', any more than there is the 'average citizen' or 'man in the street'. But it helps if we start out by trying to imagine one, and then, afterwards, consider the variations.

All animal courtship patterns are organized in a typical sequence, and the course taken by a human love affair is no exception. For convenience we can divide the human sequence up into twelve stages, and see what happens as each threshold is successfully passed. The twelve (obviously over-simplified) stages are these.

1. *Eye to body*. The most common form of social 'contact' is to look at people from a distance. In a fraction of a second it is possible to sum up the physical qualities of another adult, labelling them and grading them mentally in the process. The eyes feed the brain with immediate information concerning the sex, size, shape, age, colouring, status and mood of the other person. Simultaneously a grading takes place on a scale from extreme attractiveness to extreme repulsiveness. If the signs indicate that the individual in view is an attractive member of

the opposite sex, then we are ready to move on to the next phase in the sequence.

2. *Eye to eye.* While we view others, they view us. From time to time this means that our eyes meet, and when this happens the usual reaction is to look away quickly and break the eye 'contact'. This will not happen, of course, if we have recognized one another as previous acquaintances. In such cases, the moment of recognition leads instantly to mutual greeting signals, such as sudden smiling, raising of the eyebrows, changes in body posture, movements of the arms and eventually vocalizations. If, on the other hand, we have locked eyes with a stranger, then the rapid looking away is the typical reaction, as if to avoid the temporary invasion of privacy. If one of the two strangers does continue to stare after eye contact has been made, the other may become acutely embarrassed and even angry. If it is possible to move away to avoid the staring eyes, this will soon be done, even though there was no element of aggression in the facial expressions or gestures accompanying the stare. This is because to perform prolonged staring is in itself an act of aggression between unfamiliar adults. The result is that two strangers normally watch one another in turn, rather than simultaneously. If, then, one finds the other attractive, he or she may add a slight smile to the next meeting of glances. If the response is returned, so is the smile, and further, more intimate contact may ensue. If the response is not returned, a blank look in reply to a friendly smile will usually stop any further development.

3. *Voice to voice.* Assuming there is no third party to make introductions, the next stage involves vocal contact between the male and female strangers. Invariably the initial comments will concern trivia. It is rare at this stage to make any direct reference to the true mood of the speakers. This small-talk permits the reception of a further set of signals, this time to the ear instead of the eye. Dialect, tone of voice, accent, mode of verbal thinking and use of vocabulary permit a whole new range of units of information to be fed into the brain.

Maintaining this communication at the level of irrelevant small-talk enables either side to retreat from further involvement, should the new signals prove unattractive despite the promise of the earlier, visual signals.

4. *Hand to hand.* The previous three stages can all occur in seconds, or they may take months, with one potential partner silently admiring the other from a distance, not daring to make vocal contact. This new stage, the hand to hand, may also take place quickly, in the form of the introduction handshake, or it is likely to be delayed for some considerable time. If the formalized, non-sexual handshake does not come into operation, then the first actual body contact to occur is likely to be disguised as an act of 'supporting aid', 'body protection' or 'directional guidance'. This is usually performed by the male towards the female and consists of holding her arm or hand to help her cross a street, or climb over an obstruction. If she is about to walk into an obstacle or danger spot, then the hand of the male can quickly take the opportunity to reach out swiftly and take her arm to alter her course or check her movement. If she slips or trips, a supporting action with the hands may also facilitate the first body contact. Again, the use of acts which are irrelevant to the true mood of the encounter is important. If the body of the girl has been touched by the man in the act of assisting her in some way, either partner can still withdraw from further involvement without loss of face. The girl can thank the man for his help and leave him, without being forced into a position where she has to deliver a direct rebuff. Both parties may be well aware that a behaviour sequence is just beginning, and that it is one that may lead eventually to greater intimacies, but neither as yet does anything which openly states this fact, so that there is still time for one to back out without hurting the other's feelings. Only when the growing relationship has been openly declared will the action of hand-holding or arm-holding become prolonged in duration. It then ceases to be a 'supportive' or 'guiding' act and becomes an undisguised intimacy.

5. *Arm to shoulder.* Up to this point the bodies have not come into close contact. When they do so, another important threshold has been passed. Whether sitting, standing or walking, physical contact down the side of the body indicates a great advance in the relationship from its earlier hesitant touchings. The earliest method employed is the shoulder embrace, usually with the man's arm placed around the girl's shoulders to draw the two partners together. This is the simplest introduction to trunk contact because it is already used in other contexts between mere friends as an act of non-sexual companionship. It is therefore the smallest next step to take, and the least likely to meet rebuff. Walking together in this posture can be given the air of slight ambiguity, half way between close friendship and love.

6. *Arm to waist.* A slight advance on the last stage occurs with the wrapping of the arm around the waist. This is something the man will not have done to other men, no matter how friendly, so that it becomes more of a direct statement of amorous intimacy. Furthermore, his hand will now be in much closer proximity to the genital region of the female.

7. *Mouth to mouth.* Kissing on the mouth, combined with the full frontal embrace, is a major step forward. For the first time there is a strong chance of physiological arousal, if the action is prolonged or repeated. The female may experience genital secretions and the male's penis may start to become erect.

8. *Hand to head.* As an extension of the last stage, the hands begin to caress the partner's head. Fingers stroke the face, neck and hair. Hands clasp the nape and the side of the head.

9. *Hand to body.* In the post-kissing phase, the hands begin to explore the partner's body, squeezing, fondling and stroking. The major advance here is the manipulation by the male of the female's breasts. Further physiological arousal occurs with these acts and reaches such a pitch that, for many young females, this is a point at which a temporary halt is called. Further developments mean increasing difficulty in breaking off the pattern without continuing to completion, and if the

bond of attachment has not reached a sufficient level of mutual trust, more advanced sexual intimacies are postponed.

10. *Mouth to breast.* Here the threshold is passed in which the interactions become strictly private. For most couples this will also have applied to the last stage, especially where breast manipulations are concerned, but advanced kissing and body-fondling does occur frequently in public places under certain circumstances. Such actions may cause reactions of disapproval in other members of the public, but it is rare in most countries for serious steps to be taken against the embracing couple. With the advance to breast-kissing, however, the situation is entirely different, if only because it involves the exposure of the female breast. Mouth-to-breast contacts are the last of the pre-genital intimacies and are the prelude to actions which are concerned not merely with arousal, but with arousal to climax.

11. *Hand to genitals.* If the manual exploration of the partner's body continues, it inevitably arrives at the genital region. After tentative caressing of the partner's genitals, the actions soon develop into gentle, rhythmic rubbing that simulates the rhythm of pelvic thrusting. The male repeatedly strokes the labia or clitoris of the female and may insert his finger or fingers into the vagina, imitating the action of the penis. Manual stimulation of this kind can soon lead to orgasm for either sex, and is a common form of culmination in advanced pre-copulatory encounters between lovers.

12. *Genitals to genitals.* Finally, the stage of full copulation is reached and, if the female is a virgin, the first irreversible act of the entire sequence occurs with the rupture of the hymen. There is also, for the first time, the possibility of another irreversible act, namely that of fertilization. This irreversibility puts this concluding act in the sequence on to an entirely new plane. Each stage will have served to tighten the bond of attachment a little more, but, in a biological sense, this final copulatory action is clearly related to a phase where the earlier intimacies will already have done their job of cementing the bond, so that the pair will want to stay together after the sex

drive has been reduced by the consummation of orgasm. If this bonding has failed, the female is liable to find herself pregnant in the absence of a stable family unit.

These then are twelve typical stages in the pair-formation process of a young male and female. To some extent they are, of course, culturally determined, but to a much greater extent they are determined by the anatomy and sexual physiology common to all members of our species. The variations imposed by cultural traditions and conventions, and by the personal peculiarities of certain unusual individuals, will alter this major sequence in a number of ways, and these can now be considered against the background of the typical sequence through which we have just passed.

The variations take three main forms: a reduction of the sequence, an alteration in the order of the acts and an elaboration of the pattern.

The most extreme form of reduction is forcible mating, or rape. Here the first stage runs as quickly as is physically possible to the last stage, with all the intervening phases condensed to the absolute minimum. After eye-to-body contact has been made by the male, he simply attacks the female, omitting all arousal stages, and goes as rapidly to genital-to-genital contact as her resistance will allow. The non-genital body contacts are limited purely to those necessary to overpower her and strip her genital region of clothing.

Viewed objectively, rape in the human species lacks two important ingredients: pair-formation and sexual arousal. The rapist male, by omitting all the intermediate stages of the sexual sequence, clearly does not allow a bond of attachment to grow between himself and the female in question. This is obvious enough, but it is relevant in biological terms, because our species does require this personal attachment to develop, as a means of safeguarding the successful rearing of the off-spring that may result from the copulation. There are other species, with little or no parental responsibilities, where, in theory, rape would create no problems. That it is rare is due, amongst other things, to the physical difficulty of achieving the goal of rape. A man without a pair of grasping hands and verbalized threats would find it virtually impossible, and this is a dual advantage which other species lack. Even where animal rape does seem to occur, appearances can be deceptive. For example, carnivores can, and most carnivore species do, grab their females by the scruff of the neck with their jaws during the act of mating, as if to prevent their mates from escaping, but there is still the problem of successfully inserting the penis into the vagina of a writhing female form. If the female is unresponsive, the male stands little chance. The truth is that the superficially savage act of neck-gripping in male carnivores is a rather specialized movement. Although it looks like the act of a rapist male, it is in fact the carnivore equivalent of a gentle parental embrace in our own species. The bite is strongly inhibited, so that the teeth do not harm the female. This is the pattern of behaviour a parent carnivore employs towards its young when carrying them from place to place. The male is, in effect, treating the female like a cub or a kitten, and if she is sexually responsive to him, she reacts like one, going limp in his jaws as she once did when being protectively transported by her mother in early life.

For the human male animal, rape is comparatively easy. If physical force is not enough, he can add threats of death or injury. Alternatively he can contrive to render the female unconscious or semi-unconscious, or can enlist the aid of other males to hold her still. If the absence of the female's sexual arousal makes penis insertion difficult or painful, he can always resort to the use of some alternative form of lubrication to replace the missing natural secretions.

For the female in question these proceedings are, to say the least, both unsatisfying and unsatisfactory, and, to say the most, may result in severe trauma and psychological damage. Only in cases of rape where the partners are already known to one another and where the female has a strong masochistic streak is there any chance at all of an emotional attachment developing as a result of this violent reduction of the normal sexual sequence of our species.

I have gone into this question of rape at some length because it bears a close relationship to another form of sexual reduction which is much more widespread and important in our culture. To contrast it with the violent rape we have been discussing, we might call it 'economic rape'. Unlike the violent kind, it occurs, not in derelict building-sites or damp hedgerows, but in decorously draped boudoirs and cosy bedrooms. It is the loveless mating act of the marriage of economic convenience, the act of couples who marry and copulate with only the barest hint of a true bond of attachment.

In past centuries, the parentally controlled status marriage was commonplace. Today it is becoming increasingly rare, but the psychological scar it left on the children it spawned is more lasting. As growing, developing witnesses to this loveless relationship, the offspring of the match were themselves in danger of becoming sexually crippled, so that they were incapable of expressing the full amatory sequence typical of our species. Their sexual anatomy was in perfect working order; their physiological arousal mechanisms were operating efficiently; but their ability to relate these biological features to a deep and lasting bond of attachment will have been stunted by the atmosphere in which they matured. They, in turn, will find it difficult to make successful pair-bonds, but social pressures will encourage them to try, and once again the next generation of children will suffer. Such a reverberation is difficult to eliminate, and the untold damage caused by past cultural interferences with the natural human process of falling deeply in love is still with us today, even though the parentally controlled marriage is fading into history.

The pattern of 'economic rape' is not, of course, as extreme as that of violent rape, in the way in which it condenses the full twelve-stage sequence. Superficially it may appear very similar to the full pattern, with the partners 'going through the motions' of the different stages, one by one, until copulation is reached. But if we examine the actions in detail we find that they are all reduced in intensity, duration and frequency.

Take first the classic case of the young couple who are pushed together to satisfy the economic or status relationship of their two families. In earlier centuries, their pre-marital courtship might typically involve no more than a few abbreviated embraces and kisses, following prolonged verbal exchanges. Then, with little knowledge of one another's bodies or sexual emotions, they are thrust together into a marriage bed. The bride is advised that nasty but necessary things will have to be done to her by her bridegroom in order to ensure the future population of the nation, and that while this is going on, she is to 'lie still and think of England'. The male is given rudimentary instruction concerning female anatomy and told to be gentle with his bride because she will bleed when he penetrates her. With this information the young couple perform their sexual duties as simply and quickly as possible, with a minimum of pleasure and a minimum of pair-bonding. For the female, there is rarely if ever an orgasm. For the male, there is an unresponsive object in his bed, which happens to be his wife, but which sexually is little more than an object, the vagina of which he uses like a hand to masturbate his penis. In their public, social lives the young couple will, naturally, be provided with a set of rules enabling them to simulate a loving relationship. Each of the public intimacies, severely restricted in the form it can take, is precisely described and defined by the books of polite etiquette, so that it will become almost impossible to tell the true loving couple from the false. Almost, but not quite, and for the children it will be painfully easy, for they have not yet had their heads crammed with detailed rules of conduct, and they will intuitively detect the degree of lovingness or lovelessness in their parents' relationship. And so the damage will go on.

If this description seems bizarre today, in the latter half of the twentieth century, then this is not because such marriages no longer occur, but rather because they are less blatantly organized than they once were. A much greater show of loving is put on nowadays to mask such relationships, but a show it remains nevertheless. Parents are less involved than they were, which also disguises the pattern. Now it is one or both members of the pair who set out themselves to construct an economically based marriage. Behind her wedding veil the bride's lips are moving, but she is not overcome with emotion; she is busy calculating her alimony rating. The man at her side with a faraway expression on his face is not lost in a romantic dream, he is working out the impact his socially efficient bride will have on his business colleagues. Admittedly, the brides no longer lie still and think of wherever-it-is on their wedding nights. Instead, they check their orgasm frequencies against the national average for their age group, educational level, and racial and urban background. If they fall below the required level, they employ a firm of private investigators to find out where the husband is relocating the additional 1·7 orgasms per week that they should be getting. Meanwhile the husbands are trying to estimate how many early evening drinks they can consume before running the risk of alcoholically impairing their ability to achieve an insertable erection later that night. All too often it is these that are the sweet mysteries of life in modern urbania.

In looking at reductions in the sexual sequence, we have progressed from rape, to the parentally controlled marriage of the past, to the so-called 'bitch/bastard' marriage of modern times. The obsession with orgasm frequency in the last of these is an important new development that appears to lead us away from the reduction and compression of the full sexual sequence that we were discussing. Indeed, it looks like a swing in the other direction, towards elaboration rather than reduction. But the matter is not quite so simple. Basically, what has happened in the new 'sexual freedom' is that the later stages have been given much greater emphasis. The elaboration of the sequence has all been concentrated at one end of it—the copulatory end. The earlier courtship patterns, so important for pair-formation, instead of being elaborated, have been reduced and simplified. It is worth trying to discover the way this has come about.

In earlier centuries, the courtship stages were prolonged in time, but severely restricted in intensity. Insistence on obeying formal rules of procedure, down to the last detail, reduced their emotional impact. Then, after marriage, the later pre-copulatory and copulatory patterns were strongly curtailed by ignorance and anti-erotic propaganda. The males solved this problem with brothels and mistresses. The females, by and large, did not solve it. In the first half of the present century the situation changed. Parental control was loosened and serious attempts were made at sexual education, with the publication of books on 'married love'. The result was that young couples were much freer to search for a partner that suited them and to indulge in less formalized courtship activities. The phenomenon of the chaperone vanished. The rules of conduct for body contact were relaxed, so that virtually all stages of the sexual intimacy sequence were permitted, excluding only the final, genital ones. These pre-marital activities were, however, still expected to cover a considerable period of time. Eventually, when marriage did take place, the couple were able to take to their mating bed with a much greater knowledge of one another's bodies and emotional personalities. Efficient contraception had appeared on the scene, combining with the new sexual knowledge to make marital pleasures less restricted and more satisfying.

During this phase there was a tendency for young couples, before marriage, to indulge in prolonged 'petting sessions'. The idea that they were now allowed to go so far, but no further, seemed good in theory, but was difficult in practice. The reason is obvious enough. Unlike the young couples of earlier days, they were now permitted to go past the first stages of courtship—the ones which helped to form a bond of attachment, but which did not produce strong physiological arousal of the sex organs—and on into the stages which were really concerned with pre-copulatory stimulation. The half-way mark between the two is the act of the mouth-to-mouth kiss. Simply performed this is a pleasant bonding act, but energetically repeated it is also the starting point of pre-copulatory arousal.

This led to a new type of crisis for the young lovers. Prolonged petting resulted in prolonged erections for the males and prolonged sexual secretions for the females. One of three things then happened: they broke off the sequence in accordance with 'official ruling' and remained intensely frustrated, or they continued by non-copulatory means to achieve mutual orgasm, or they broke the rules and copulated. If they used the second method and masturbated or fondled one another to orgasm, and if they continued to do this over a long pre-marital period, there was always the danger that this pattern of climax would begin to assume too great a significance in their sexual relationship, making for difficulties when, eventually, they were able to complete the act of copulation after marriage. If they chose the third alternative and broke the rules, there was the problem of guilt and secrecy. Nevertheless, despite these difficulties, the prolonged pre-marital phase was strongly conducive to the formation of a powerful bond of attachment, so that it had a great deal to commend it over the previous situation, when the couple were severely restricted in their actions.

Moving on now to more recent times, a new change has occurred. Although official attitudes may still be the same, they are less strictly enforced. With further improvements in contraception, virginity has lost its significance for many young girls. The non-copulation rule that was once reluctantly broken is now commonly ignored. Virginity, far from being prized, has almost become a stigma, an indication of some kind of sexual inadequacy. Pre-marital copulation is an accepted pattern by the young lovers, if not by their parents. The result of this development, which is more widespread than some people like to admit, is that the lovers no longer experience the intense 'petting frustrations' of their predecessors, nor are they in danger of becoming fixated on masturbatory activities. Instead, their courtship grows naturally, and without undue postponement, into the full twelve-stage sexual sequence.

Assuming the existence of adequate venereal hygiene and efficient, readily available contraception, what, if any, is the danger of this new situation? The answer, as some have seen it, is the 'tyranny of the orgasm', the need created by the social pressures of the new permissive convention to achieve maximum copulatory performance. This is seen as a threat to the person who truly falls in love, but who is incapable of sufficiently impressive orgasmic achievements.

There is something curiously short-sighted about this criticism. Earlier I did mention the obsession with orgasm frequency, but that was in connection with the loveless marriage, the modern equivalent of the economic or status marriage. There, as I pointed out, the female may feel she has failed if her sexual athleticism is below standard, because she is concerned, even in matters of sex, with the business of status. But if two young people are in love today, they will laugh at the desperate athleticism of the copulating non-lovers. For them, as for true lovers at all points in history, a fleeting touch on the cheek from the one they adore will be worth more than six hours in thirty-seven positions with someone they do not. This has always been so, but for these new lovers there is the added advantage that, circumstances permitting, they are no longer restricted to a mere cheek touch. They can do anything they wish with one another's bodies, as much *or* as little as they wish. If the powerful bond of attachment has formed, then it will be the quality of the sexual behaviour that counts, not its mere quantity. For them, the new conventions simply permit, they do not insist, as some critics seem to think.

Another point which the critics seem to miss is that when a couple have started to fall in love, they will not want to omit the earlier stages of the sexual sequence. They will not give up holding hands merely because they are permitted to copulate.

Furthermore, they are not the ones who will be likely to have much trouble in quite naturally enjoying maximum orgasmic pleasure when they reach the final stages of the sequence. The emotional intensity of their personal relationship will ensure this, and they will happily reach climax after climax without having to resort to the contorted wrestlers' postures of the ubiquitous modern sex manuals.

Perhaps the greatest danger that the permissive young lovers face today is an economic one, for they still inhabit a complex, economically structured society, and it was no accident that economics came to figure so largely in the marriages of yesterday. Previously this aspect was safeguarded by all the rigid restrictions placed on early sexual behaviour. Sexual intimacy suffered, but social status was ensured and organized. Now the social status of the young pair has become a problem, as sexual intimacy blossoms. How can a pair of seventeen-year-old lovers, who are fully sexually mature, who have developed a powerful bond of attachment, and who are enjoying a full sexual life, set up home in our modern economy? Either they have to wait in a kind of social limbo, or they have to 'drop out' of the accepted social pattern. The choice is not an easy one, and the problem has yet to be solved.

We arrived at this discussion by considering the ways in which the sexual sequence becomes reduced from its full expression. We must now leave the young lovers, fully expressing it, but enduring considerable social problems in so doing, and return to the reductions once more. What of the sexually active non-lover? We have dealt with the rapist and the sexually inhibited marriage partners who reduced their copulatory stages to a child-spawning minimum, but what about the loveless sexual athletes of today? How do they reduce the sexual sequence of the typical lovers? For them, the later genital stages are not expressed as the culmination of a pattern, but as a replacement for it. In earlier times this was precisely what occurred when a man visited a prostitute. There was no holding of hands, no cuddling or murmuring of sweet nothings, merely a quick business transaction and then straight to direct genital contact. What we might call 'commercial rape'. In previous generations this was often a young man's first introduction to copulation, but today such professional services are hardly necessary. Instead they are replaced by what is referred to as 'sleeping around'. In such cases there is frequently a massive reduction in the early stages of the sequence, just as there was with the visit to the prostitute. The situation is summed up by the girl in the cartoon who says 'Boys simply don't want to kiss any more', as she returns late at night to her room in an obvious post-copulatory condition, exhausted and with her clothes dishevelled, but with her make-up still neatly intact.

The result of this type of reduction is to provide the maximum of copulatory activity with the minimum of pair-bond development. As a status device this may permit repeated ego-boosting, but as a source of intense pleasure it degrades sexual activity to the level of something like urinating. It is not surprising, therefore, that for the 'permissive', non-loving copulator some elaboration of the consummatory act becomes desirable. If it has lost its emotional intensity along with its powerful bond of personal attachment, then it must be given some increased physical intensity as a compensation. This is where the illustrated sexual manuals come on the scene, and it is worth analysing some of them to see what they recommend.

A sample taken at random from the large number now on sale included a combined total of several hundred photographs, each showing a young naked couple in the act of 'making love'. Of these illustrations, no more than 4 per cent showed any of the first eight stages in my twelve-stage sequence described earlier. By contrast, 82 per cent showed full copulation, each book including between thirty and fifty posture variations. This means that the vast majority of all the various sexual intimacies were illustrated as the final stage of genital/genital contact, and clearly demonstrates the great emphasis placed on this concluding element of the sequence.

Whereas previous censorship limited the illustration of amorous activities to the earlier stages, the removal of this censorship, instead of enriching the situation, has simply had the effect of shifting concentration from one end of the scale to the other. The implied message is that the act of copulation should be made as complex and varied as possible, and forget about the rest. Many of the postures shown are obviously uncomfortable, if not actually painful to maintain for any length of time, except possibly for trained circus acrobats. Their inclusion can only reflect a desperate search for copulatory novelty as a means to obtaining further arousal. The emphasis is no longer on loving, but on sexual athletics.

There is, of course, nothing harmful about these patterns as amusing and playful additions to sexual behaviour, but if obsession with them replaces and excludes the personal emotional aspects of the interaction between the male and female involved, then their ultimate effect is to decrease the true value of the relationship. They may elaborate one element of the sexual sequence, but over all they reduce it.

Young lovers who *need* these copulation variations, rather than merely play with them in an exploratory fashion from time to time, are perhaps not young lovers at all. At a later point, when they have passed right through the intense pair-formation stage of their lives, and have arrived at the more mellow pair-maintenance phase, they may well find that some embellishments and novel additions to their sexual activities will provide a valuable way to re-heighten intensity, but if as young lovers they are truly in love it is surprising if this will be necessary.

Needless to say, this does not mean that any of these sexual intimacies, no matter how contrived or unusual, should be condemned or suppressed. Providing they are performed voluntarily in private by adults and cause no physical harm, there is no biological reason why they should be outlawed or attacked by society. In certain countries this is still, however, the case. One example concerns oral/genital contacts, which I omitted from my earlier twelve-stage list. The reason why they were not included is because they do not represent a clear-cut stage in the progress from first encounter between the lovers to final copulation. In the vast majority of cases they appear only after the first copulations have occurred, as a further embellishment of the genital intimacies. Later, when copulation has become a regular feature of a relationship, they are frequently included as a standard pre-copulatory pattern, and evidence from ancient art and history indicates that they have long been so employed.

Modern American surveys indicate that today oral/genital contacts are used by about half of all married couples as part of their pre-copulatory activities. The application of the male mouth to the female genitals was recorded in 54 per cent of cases, that of female mouth to male genitals in 49 per cent. Although this is well below the figures for the other pre-copulatory patterns in my twelve-stage list (mouth to mouth, hand to breast, mouth to breast, and hand to genitals all occur in over 90 per cent of cases), an average of roughly 50 per cent of the population for mouth-to-genital contact can hardly justify calling this activity 'abnormal'. Yet despite this, and despite the fact that it occurs widely in other mammalian species, it is often regarded as an 'unnatural' intimacy. It is condemned by the Judeo-Christian religious codes, even between married partners, and in many places it is not only considered immoral but is also illegal. It is surprising to find that, right into the second half of the twentieth century, this has been the case in almost all the states in the United States of America. To be more specific, in only Kentucky and South Carolina can an American married couple privately engage in any kind of oral/genital contact without breaking the law. This means that in recent times 50 per cent of all other Americans have, technically speaking, been sexual law-breakers at some time in their married lives. In the states where it is outlawed, the act is rated as a felony everywhere except in New York, where it is classified as a mere 'misdemeanor'. In the states of

Illinois, Wisconsin, Mississippi and Ohio, the law has applied a curious kind of sexual inequality, the act being legal when the husband makes oral contact with his wife's genitals, but a felony when she performs a similar intimacy with him.

These strange legal restrictions have seldom been applied in practice and have been rendered nonsensical in recent years, during which open sale and advertisement of flavoured vaginal douches has been permitted in America, but they do appear from time to time in divorce cases, where oral/genital acts have been cited as factors contributing to 'mental cruelty' in marriage. It has also been pointed out that, in theory, these laws could lead to instances of blackmail. Biologically, as I have already pointed out, there is no case against mouth-to-genital contacts. On the contrary, if they heighten the emotional intensity of pre-copulatory activities, they will merely serve to tighten the bonds of attachment between the mated pair and thereby strengthen the married condition which is so vigorously protected in so many other ways by the Church and the laws of the land.

If we examine the exact form which this type of intimacy takes in the human species, it is possible to detect a difference between man and the other mammals that employ mouth-to-genital contacts. Usually, in other species, the action begins as sniffing and nuzzling and then extends into licking. Rhythmic friction is less common. The significance of the act lies in the acquisition of detailed information concerning the state of the partner's genitals. Unlike man, other mammalian species only come into full sexual condition at certain times of the year, or at certain restricted phases of the menstrual cycle, and it is important for the partner, especially the male, to know as much as possible about the precise state of arousal before attempting copulation. The application of the nose and tongue to the genital region provides valuable clues concerning odour, taste and texture. The actual stimulation of the partner by these contacts is probably of secondary importance.

In man, the situation is reversed, the stimulation element

becoming more important. The mouth is employed to arouse the partner rather than to learn about his or her sexual condition. It is for this reason that, in man, rhythmic friction takes on a more important role than mere touching or licking, the female using her mouth as a pseudo-vagina and simulating the actions of pelvic thrusting by movements of her neck. The male may also use his tongue as a pseudo-penis, but he is more likely to employ clitoral stimulation, using rhythmic tongue pressure. Again, he will imitate the repeated massage of the female organ that occurs during the pelvic thrusting of copulation itself. The great advantage to the male of this form of mimic-copulation is that he can provide prolonged stimulation for the female without himself becoming orgasmically satiated. In this way he can compensate for the longer time the average female takes to reach the orgasmic level.

This last fact no doubt explains why the extensive use of this type of sexual intimacy is more common amongst males than females. A contrast, however, has been found in the portrayal of these acts in 'blue movies'. A recent study of the history of films of this type made over the past half-century reveals that here the female action is portrayed much more frequently than the male. There is a special reason for this. These films have traditionally been made for use at all-male gatherings, or 'stag-parties', and are often referred to as 'stag movies'. Such occasions have little to do with love, being concerned instead with sex as a status device. If male status is involved, the historians of blue movies have pointed out that it 'belittles' the man to show him in a subordinate posture to the female, but enhances his feelings of dominance to portray him in the superior role of being 'served' by the female. Here we are back to basic animal behaviour and the postures of inferior submissions. When kneeling and bowing are performed as submissive acts, their biological significance lies in the lowering of the inferior's body in front of the superior. It is significant that the slang expression for oral/genital contact in man is 'going down' on the partner. In order to apply the mouth to the genitals, the active partner must considerably lower his or her body in relation to that of the passive one. This applies in any position, but is particularly clear when the act is performed with the passive partner standing. The active male or female must then kneel or crouch in front of the standing body to apply the mouth to the genital region, thus entailing the adoption of an almost medieval posture of servility. It is little wonder, then, that the performance of this act by the female to the male appeals so strongly to the status sex gatherings of males at stag-parties. Between lovers in private, of course, the situation is entirely different. Unless the encounter is one of loveless sexual gratification, the act will be one of giving pleasure and not of status-boosting, and will show no such bias. Because of the time-lag difference in reaching orgasm that exists between the sexes, it will then, as we have already seen, become more commonly extended as a male action rather than a female one.

In considering variations in the basic sexual sequence, we have so far been dealing with some of the ways in which it has been reduced and elaborated, but I also mentioned a third possibility, namely shifts in the order of appearance of the acts. Clearly these are many, and the fixed sequence I outlined is often altered in some way. As it stands, it is no more than a rough guide to the general trend which the various actions follow, from the moment of the first encounter to the final pattern of copulation. It remains a true picture of the average sequence of events, but the formalization of certain specific elements will have a marked effect on the order in which they follow one another in many cases. Some examples will clarify this.

The first three acts listed were: eye to body, eye to eye, and voice to voice. These pre-tactile 'contacts' rarely change position in the sequence. Today, exceptions can occur in instances where the initial encounter takes place over the telephone, and one sometimes hears someone say, 'It's pleasant to meet after having spoken on the phone so often.' This implies that vocal exchanges on the telephone do not by themselves constitute a 'meeting'. Combined with eye contact, however, they do. The phrase 'we met last year' need not signify any tactile contact, but merely a combination of visual and verbal exchanges. Nevertheless, a 'meeting' does usually include at least the minimal body contact of the handshake. To 'meet someone' it does seem important to have displayed some degree of physical touching. Since, in modern life, we encounter so many strangers, it is not surprising to find that this initial touching is rigidly stylized in form. A more variable type of body contact would involve too great an intimacy at such an early stage in the time-scale of the sequence of a developing relationship.

Because it has become so formalized, the handshake can frequently jump almost to the front of the whole sequence. A third party says simply, 'Here is someone I want you to meet'; and, within seconds of making eye contact, skin contact has taken place, the two hands immediately stretching out and joining. The action may even occur slightly before verbal contact has been made.

This basic rule, that the more formalized a contact action becomes, the more it can jump forward in the sequence, is also particularly well illustrated by the mouth-to-mouth kiss. Although, strictly speaking, this is the first of the pre-copulatory arousal actions, and should belong to the second half of the sequence rather than the first, it often jumps forward in time by virtue of the accepted convention of the 'goodnight kiss' between young lovers. It is significant that the first kiss usually takes place as an act of farewell. The device employed here, which enables the kiss, combined with a full frontal embrace, to jump ahead of the less intimate semi-embraces of arm-around-shoulder and arm-around-waist, and possibly even hand-holding, is the way in which it borrows 'innocence' from the non-sexual kissing of family greetings and farewells. The young couple, having met and talked for some hours, may, at the moment of parting, go straight into a brief, formal embrace-and-kiss, even though they have not touched one another's bodies previously in any way. This contrasts sharply with the situation where a man visits a prostitute, when the kiss may drop back in the sequence to a point where genital contact has already been made, or where kissing may even be totally omitted.

It will have become obvious that, in discussing these sexual variations, I have been thinking primarily of modern 'civilized' societies. In other cultures and tribes the patterns vary to a certain extent, but the general principles of a sequence of escalating intimacy still apply. An American survey of nearly two hundred different human cultures revealed that 'unless social conditioning imposes inhibitions upon active foreplay it is very likely to occur'. Nearly all the arousal actions occur in most societies, but sometimes they take a slightly different form. The nose, for example, occasionally takes over from the mouth as a contact organ, nose-rubbing or -pressing replacing mouth-kissing. In certain tribes, mutual nose-and-face-pressing appears at the point where, more usually, mouth-to-face or mouth-to-mouth contacts would occur. In others, mouth-to-mouth and nose-to-nose contacts are performed simultaneously. Some males employ nose-rubbing rather than lip contact, to stimulate the female breasts. In other tribes, kissing takes the form of placing the lips close to the partner's face and inhaling. In still others, it is more a question of reciprocal lip- and tongue-sucking. These variations of detail are interesting in their own right, but to over-emphasize their importance, as has sometimes been done in the past, is to obscure the fact that, in more general terms, there is a great similarity in the courtship and pre-copulatory patterns of all human beings.

Having looked at the sequence of human sexual intimacies, we now come to the question of their frequency. I have gone on record as saying that man is the sexiest of all the primates, a comment which has met with some criticism. The biological evidence, however, is irrefutable, and the argument that the high level of sexual activity observed in certain quarters today is the artifical product of civilized life is nonsensical. If anything, it is the remarkably *low* level of sexual activity in certain other quarters that can best be ascribed to the artificiality of modern living. As anyone who has been under severe stress will know, anxiety is a powerful anti-sexual influence, and, since there is a great deal of stress involved in the high-pressure existence of our modern urban communities, the fact that so much sexual behaviour still occurs is a remarkable testimony to the sexuality of our species.

Let me be more specific. If I put my statement in a slightly different way, namely that man is *potentially* the sexiest of all the primates, then there can be no argument. In the first place, other primates are limited in their sexual activities to a brief section of the female's monthly sexual cycle. At these times her external sexual organs undergo a change that in most species is clearly visible to the male. This makes her sexually attractive to him. At other times she will have little or no appeal for him. In the human species the active phase is extended throughout almost the whole of the monthly cycle, more or less tripling the time when the female will be appealing to the male. Already, in this respect alone, the human animal has three times the sexual potential of his near relatives, the monkeys and apes.

Secondly, the female human remains both sexually appealing and responsive during most of her period of pregnancy, when other primates are not. Also, she becomes sexually active again much sooner after giving birth than do the other species. Finally, the average human animal of modern times can expect to enjoy roughly half a century of active sexual life, a range that few other mammals can match.

Not only is there this enormous potential for sexual activity, but in the vast majority of cases it is fully realized, so that I see no reason to modify my original statement. Most human beings express themselves sexually by finding partners and indulging in frequent sexual interactions, but even those who do not, or who are temporarily sexually isolated, do not normally become inactive. For them, it is typically the case that masturbation at fairly high frequency will be employed to compensate for the absence of a mate.

Above all, the human sexual pattern is complex. It involves not only vigorous copulation, but also all the gentle subtleties of courtship and the intense arousal actions of pre-copulatory behaviour. In other words, it not only occurs with high frequency over a long period of years, and with few interruptions from 'dead periods' in female reproductive cycles, but, when it does occur, it is prolonged and elaborate. This enlargement of the sexual life of the species is achieved by the addition to its primate inheritance of a great variety of sexual body contacts and intimacies, of the kind we have been discussing. Here the contrast with other species is striking and, to clarify this point, it is worth pausing to look at the way in which monkeys and apes perform sexually.

Monkeys do not form deep bonds of attachment to their mates and there is little courtship or pre-copulatory behaviour. During the few days of her monthly cycle when she is in full sexual condition, the female approaches the male or is approached by him, she turns her rump towards him, crouching down slightly with the front end of her body, he mounts her from behind, inserts his penis, makes a few quick pelvic thrusts, ejaculates, dismounts, and they move apart again. The whole encounter is usually over in a few seconds. A number of examples will give a clear idea of the widespread occurrence of this extreme brevity. In the bonnet monkey, the male makes only 5 to 30 pelvic thrusts. In the howler monkey, the figure is 8 to 28 thrusts, with an average of 17, taking 22 seconds, with a preceding 10 seconds for 'body adjustment'. The rhesus monkey performs 2 to 8 pelvic thrusts, lasting a total of no more than 3 or 4 seconds. Baboons, in one report, made up to 15 pelvic thrusts, lasting for a total of 7–8 seconds; in another report, an average of 6 thrusts, lasting 8–20 seconds; in a third, 5 to 10 thrusts, lasting 10–15 seconds. Two reports for chimpanzees give the average male performance as 4 to 8 thrusts, with a maximum of 15 in one instance, and 6 to 20 thrusts in a total copulating time of 7–10 seconds in another.

These details plainly indicate that our hairier relatives do not linger at the business of mating. To be fair, however, they do perform these 'instant copulations' with a very high frequency during the short period of days while the female is in sexual condition. In some species, remounting occurs within a few minutes, and may be repeated a number of times in quick succession. In the South African baboon, for instance, there are usually from 3 to 6 mountings one after the other, with only two-minute intervals between them. In the rhesus monkey this figure rises, and there may be from 5 to 25 mountings with intervals of only a minute or so between each. It seems as if the male only ejaculates after the final mounting, which is more vigorous and intense, so that here the pattern does appear to be more complex. In all these cases, however, the mating activity differs markedly from that of the human animal.

In the human species, not only is there more sexual foreplay, but the act of copulation itself takes longer. In the pre-copulatory phase, over 50 per cent of human couples spend longer than ten minutes indulging in a wide variety of arousal techniques. After this, pelvic thrusting for the male could, in most cases, lead to ejaculation in only a few minutes, but typically he prolongs this phase. He does so because, unlike the monkeys, his female is able to experience a sexual climax, similar to his own in emotional intensity, but she usually takes from ten to twenty minutes to do so. This means that, for an ordinary human couple, the whole pattern, including both foreplay and copulation, takes roughly half an hour, which is more than a hundred times as long as for the typical monkey pair. Again, to be fair to the monkeys, they will be likely to repeat their brief encounter much sooner than the human pair, but against this must be set the fact that the female monkey will be receptive only for the few days of her period of heat.

To compare the situation for the female monkey and the female human, the former comes into heat as ovulation time approaches and stays in heat for nearly a week. During this time, copulation neither arouses nor exhausts her sexually. She remains permanently aroused during the whole mating period. For the human female it is as if each mating pattern is a short period of heat, now unrelated to the time of ovulation, but related instead to the pre-copulatory stimulations of the male. She has, in effect, become a mate-responder, rather than an ovulation-responder. Her physiological arousal is geared to the shared sexual intimacies with her male, rather than to the rigidly fixed sequence of the monthly cycle of ovulation and menstruation. This vital step, which represents a fundamental change in the usual primate sexual system, leads inevitably to a far greater degree and complexity of body contact between the mated pair and forms the basis of human sexual intimacy.

This leads us to the question of the origins of the more complex human sexual acts. What are the sources of all the additional body contacts? Since monkeys do little more than mount and copulate, the act of mounting, making rhythmic pelvic thrusts and ejaculating is virtually all we share with them. So from where do we derive all the gentle, hesitant touchings and hand-holdings of the courtship period, and all the passionate arousal actions of sexual foreplay? The answer seems to be that in almost all cases they can be traced back to the intimacies of the mother-infant relationship that were described earlier. Hardly any of them appear to be 'new' actions, specifically evolved in connection with sexuality itself. In terms of the behaviour involved, falling in love looks very much like a return to infancy.

In tracing the way in which the primary embrace of our earliest years gradually becomes restricted as we mature, we watched the decline and fall of close body intimacy. Now, as we observe the young lovers, we see the whole process put into reverse. The first actions in the sexual sequence are virtually identical with those of any other kind of adult social interaction. Then, little by little, the hands of the behavioural clock start to turn backwards. The formal handshake and small-talk of the first introduction grow back into the protective hand-holding of childhood. The young lovers now walk hand in hand, as each once did with his or her parent. As their bodies come closer together with increasing trust, we soon witness the welcome return of the intimate frontal embrace, with the two heads touching and kissing. As the relationship deepens, we travel still further back, to the earlier days of gentle caresses. The hands once again fondle the face, the hair and the body of the loved one. At last, the lovers are naked again and, for the first time since they were tiny babies, the most private parts of their bodies experience the intimate touch of another's hands. And, as their movements travel backwards in time, so too do their voices, the words spoken becoming less important than the soft tonal quality with which they are delivered. Frequently even the phrases used become infantile, as a new kind of 'baby talk' develops. A wave of shared security envelops the young couple and, as in babyhood, the hurly-burly of the outside world has little meaning. The dreamy expression of a girl in love is not the alert face of an active child; it is the almost blank face of a satisfied baby.

This return to intimacy, so beautiful to those who are experiencing it, is often belittled by those who are not. The epigrams tell the story: 'The first sigh of love is the last of wisdom'; 'Love is a sickness full of woes'; 'Love is blind'; 'We are easily duped by what we love'; 'Love's a malady without a cure'; ''Tis impossible to love and to be wise'; 'Lovers are fools, but nature makes them so'. Even in the scientific literature, the term 'regressive behaviour' takes on the flavour of an insult, instead of an impartial, objective description of what is taking place. Of course, to behave in an infantile manner in certain adult contexts is an inefficient way of coping with a situation, but here, in the case of young lovers forming a deep bond of personal attachment, it is exactly the opposite. Extensive, intimate body contacts are the very best way of developing such a bond, and those who resist them because they are 'babyish' or infantile will be the losers.

When courtship advances to the stage of pre-copulatory behaviour, the infantile patterns do not fade. Instead they grow still younger, and the clock ticks backwards to the sucking at the mother's breast. The simple kiss, in which lips are gently pressed to the lover's mouth or cheek, becomes a vigorous, moving pressure. With muscular actions of their lips and tongues, the partners work on one another's mouths as if to draw milk from them. They suck and squeeze rhythmically with their lips, explore and lick with their tongues, like hungry babies. This active kissing is no longer confined to the partner's mouth. It seeks other sites, as if searching for the long-lost mother's nipple. In its quest it travels everywhere, discovering the pseudo-nipples of the ear-lobes, the toes, the clitoris and the penis, and, of course, the lover's nipples themselves.

Earlier, I mentioned the reward these actions bring from the knowledge of the sexual pleasure they give, but clearly that was only part of the story. There is also this more direct reward of re-experiencing the strongly gratifying oral contact of the suckling interaction in infancy. The effect is heightened where the pseudo-breast can be made to produce pseudo-milk. This can be obtained from the increased salivation of the lover's mouth, from the increased sexual secretions of the female's genitals and from the seminal fluid of the male's penis. If the mouthing of the penis by the female is prolonged until ejaculation occurs, it is as if the action has finally succeeded in starting the 'milk-flow' from this pseudo-breast, a similarity which was recognized as long ago as the seventeenth century, when the slang expression 'milking' for this activity first came into common usage.

Even when the pre-copulatory patterns are terminated and copulation itself begins, the infantile actions do not completely disappear. For the mating monkeys, the only body contacts, apart from actual genital interaction, are the mechanical holding actions by the male's hands and feet. He grips the female's body, not as an amorous intimacy, but to steady himself while he makes the rapid pelvic thrusts. Such graspings also occur between the human partners, but in addition there are many contacts that have no 'body adjustment' function. The hands clasp or hold the partner, not for mechanical reasons of thrust facilitation, but as tactile signals of intimacy.

Turning again to the illustrated sexual manuals discussed earlier, and taking only the cases where the male and female were shown actually copulating, it is possible to score the frequency of these non-genital contacts that accompany the pelvic thrusting. In no less than 74 per cent of the copulation postures depicted, the hand (or hands) of one partner clasps or touches some part of the other's body, in a 'non-steadying' way. In addition, there are many embracing acts, kissing acts and non-kissing head-to-head contacts; also a number of hand-to-head and hand-to-hand contacts. All these actions are basically embraces, partial embraces or fragments of embraces. They indicate that, for the human animal, copulation consists of the adult primate mating act *plus* the returned infantile embracing act. The latter pervades the whole sexual sequence from its earliest courtship stages right through to its final moments. The human animal does not merely copulate with a set of genitals belonging to a member of the opposite sex; it 'makes love' – a significant phrase – to a complete and special individual. This is why, in our species, all stages of the sequence, including copulation, can serve to enhance the pair-bonding process, and why, presumably, the female evolved an extended period of sexual receptivity, stretching far beyond the limits of the ovulation period. It could even be said that we now perform the mating act, not so much to fertilize an egg as to fertilize a relationship. There is no reproductive danger in this, for even the small proportion of mating acts that do happen to coincide with the time of ovulation will still be sufficient to produce an adequate number of offspring, and there are more than three thousand million of us alive today to prove the point.

4

SOCIAL INTIMACY

To study human sexual intimacy is to witness the rebirth of lavish bodily contact between adults, replacing the lost intimacies of infancy. To study human social intimacy is, by contrast, to observe the restraint of cautious, inhibited contact, as the conflicting demands of closeness and privacy, of dependence and independence, do battle inside our brains.

We all feel overcrowded from time to time, and overexposed to the prying eyes and minds of others. The monkish idea of shutting ourselves away from it all becomes appealing. But for most of us a few hours will do, and the idea of lifelong monastic solitude is appalling. For man is a social animal, and the ordinary healthy human being finds prolonged isolation a severe punishment. Short of physical torture or death, solitary confinement is the worst agony that can be inflicted on a prisoner. He is driven eventually, in near-madness, to talk into his lavatory pan so that he can enjoy the echo of his voice coming back to him. It is the nearest thing to a social response he can get.

A shy single person living in a big city can find him- or herself in almost the same situation. For such people, if they have left the intimacies of home behind and are now existing by themselves in a small room or apartment, the loneliness can soon become intolerable. Too timid to make friends, they may ultimately prefer death by suicide to prolonged lack of close human contact. Such is the basic need for intimacy. For intimacy breeds understanding, and most of us, unlike the solitary monk, do want to be understood, at least by a few people.

It is not a question of being understood rationally or intellectually. It is a matter of being understood emotionally, and in that respect a single intimate body contact will do more than all the beautiful words in the dictionary. The ability that physical feelings have to transmit emotional feelings is truly astonishing. Perhaps it is their strength that is also their weakness. In tracing the sequence of intimacies that occur through life, from birth to death, we saw the way in which the two phases of massive body contact were also the two phases of powerful social bonding, first between parent and child and second between lovers. All the indications are that it is impossible to be lavish and uninhibited with one's body-to-body contacts and not become strongly bonded with the object of one's attentions. An intuitive understanding of this is perhaps what inhibits us so strongly from indulging in the pure pleasure of more widespread bodily intimacies. It is not enough to say that it is unconventional to hug and embrace one's business colleagues, for example. That does not explain how the convention of 'keeping oneself to oneself' or 'keeping one's distance' arose in the first place. We have to look deeper than that to understand the extraordinary lengths we go to to avoid touching one another in ordinary day-to-day affairs outside the close family circle.

Part of the answer has to do with the great overcrowding we experience in our modern urban communities. We encounter so many people in streets and buildings every day that we simply cannot embark on intimacies with them, or all social organization would come to a halt. Ironically this overcrowding situation has two completely incompatible effects on us. On the one hand it stresses us and makes us feel tense and insecure, and on the other hand it makes us cut down on the very exchanges of intimacies which would relieve this stress and tension.

Another part of the answer has to do with sex. It is not merely that we cannot afford the time or energy to start setting up the endless social bonds that would result from widespread indulgence in extensive body intimacies. There is also the problem that, between adults, body intimacy spells sex. This is an unhappy confusion, but it is not hard to see how it has arisen. Since copulation, short of artificial insemination, is impossible without body intimacy, it has become in some respects synonymous with it. To indulge in the mating act, even the most 'untouchable' adult has to touch and be touched. At almost all other times he can avoid it if he wishes to, but then he cannot. Some Victorians went as far as they could to reduce contact by wearing nightgowns with small slits in the front, but even they had to make contact to the extent of inserting a penis into a vagina if they were to populate their world with children. And so it came to be that, in the year 1889, the expression 'to be intimate' became a euphemism for having sexual intercourse. During the present century it has become increasingly difficult for any adult, of either sex and with either sex, to indulge in intimate body contact without giving the impression that there is a sexual element involved in what is taking place.

It would be wrong to give the idea that this is an entirely new trend. The problem, of course, has always been there, and adult intimacies have always been curtailed to some extent to avoid sexual implications. But one gets a distinct impression that the situation has tightened up more in recent years. We no longer seem to be quite so free at falling on one another's necks in joy, or weeping copiously in one another's arms. The basic urge to touch one another remains, however, and it is intriguing to study how we go about this in our day-to-day affairs outside the bosom of the family.

The answer is that we formalize it. We take the uninhibited intimacies of infancy and we reduce them to fragments. Each fragment becomes stylized and rigidified until it fits into a neat category. We set up rules of etiquette (a word taken from the

French and meaning, literally, a label) and we train the members of our cultures to abide by them. No training is necessary where an embrace is concerned. This, as we have seen, is an inborn biological act that we share with all our primate relatives. But an embrace contains many elements, and which particular fragment we are to use at which particular social moment, and in what rigidly stylized form, is something that our genetical make-up cannot help us with. For the animal, there is either behaviour or no behaviour, but for us there is either behaviour or misbehaviour, good behaviour or bad behaviour, and the rules are complex. This does not mean, however, that we cannot study them biologically. No matter how culturally determined they may be, or how culturally variable, we can still understand them better if we view them as pieces of primate behaviour. This is because we can nearly always trace them back to their biological origins.

Before surveying the whole scene, let me give a single detailed example to illustrate what I mean. I will use an action that does not appear to have received much attention in the past, namely the pat on the back. You may think that this is too trivial a piece of behaviour to be of much interest, but it is dangerous to dismiss small actions in this way. Every twitch, every scratch, every stroke and every pat has the potential of changing a person's whole life, or even a nation's. The warm caress that was withheld at the vital moment when it was desperately needed can easily be the act, or rather the non-act, that finally destroys a relationship. The simple failure to return a smile, between two great rulers, can in the same way lead to war and destruction. So it is unwise to sneer at a 'mere' pat on the back. These little actions are the stuff that emotional life is made of.

If you have ever had a close personal relationship with a chimpanzee, you will know that back-patting is not a uniquely human activity. If your ape is particularly glad to see you, he is likely to come up, embrace you, press his lips warmly and wetly to the side of your neck, and then start rhythmically patting you on the back with his hands. It is a strange sensation, because in one way it is so human and yet in another it is subtly different. The kiss is not quite like a human kiss. I can best describe it as being more of a soft-open-mouth-press. And the patting is both lighter and faster than human back-patting, with the two ape hands alternating rhythmically. Nevertheless, the actions of embracing, kissing and patting are basically the same in the two species, and the social signals they transmit appear to be identical. We can therefore start out with a reasonable guess that back-patting is a biological feature of the human animal.

I have already, in the first chapter, explained the probable origin of the activity, as a repeated intention movement of clinging that says, 'I will cling to you like this if necessary, but at the moment it is not, so relax, all is well.' In infancy we only get patted as an embellishment of the embrace, but later on the friendly pat may be executed by itself, without any embracing. The patter's arm simply reaches out towards the companion and contact is made with the hand alone. Already, with this change, the process of formalization has started to take place. Seeing only an embraceless pat would make it impossible to guess its true origin. Another change occurs at the same time: the area of the body patted becomes less restricted. A baby is patted almost exclusively on the back, but an older child is patted almost anywhere, not only on the back but also on the shoulder, the arm, the hand, the cheek, the top of the head, the back of the head, the stomach, the buttocks, the thighs, the knees and the legs. The message of the pat also becomes extended. The comforting signal 'all is well' becomes the congratulatory signal 'all is *very* well' or 'you have done well'. Since the brain that has done well is housed inside the skull, it is natural that the pat on the head should be the action that comes to typify the congratulatory message. In fact, this particular form of the action becomes so strongly associated with childhood con-gratualtion that it has to be abandoned later on when patting occurs between adults, because it then acquires the flavour of condescension.

Other changes also occur as we move from the context adult-pats-child to adult-pats-adult. In addition to the head, certain other areas now become taboo. Patting on the back, shoulder and arm is still unhampered, but patting the back of the hand, the cheek, the knee or the thigh begins to acquire a slightly sexual flavour, and patting on the buttocks a strongly sexual flavour. The situation is highly variable, however, and there are many exceptions to this rule. Handback-patting and thigh-patting between two women, for example, may occur without any hint of sexuality being involved. Also it is possible, by comic over-exaggeration, to pat almost any part of the body without causing offence. The patter then makes joking remarks, as he pats his victim on the head or cheek, such as 'there, there, little man', indicating that the contact he is making is not sexual but mock-parental, and is not to be taken seriously. There is an element of offensiveness involved, of course, but it has nothing to do with the breaking of sexual taboos on touching certain areas in certain ways.

To complicate matters further, there is an intriguing exception to this last exception. It works like this. One adult, say a male, wishes to make sexual body contact with another, say a female. He knows she will not accept a direct, undisguised contact, which she would find distasteful. He knows, in fact, that she finds him sexually unattractive in general, but his urge to touch her is strong enough to ignore the disencouraging signals she transmits to him. His strategy therefore becomes one of pretending to behave like a mock-parent. He makes a great joke of patting her on the knee and calling her a funny little girl. He hopes that she will accept the contact as a joke action, even though the true reward he is getting is sexual. Unhappily for him he is not usually good enough at concealing other sexual signals, especially from his facial expressions, and the girl in question can normally see through the device and respond in an appropriately negative way.

The least sexually loaded patting action is the primary pat on the back. This somehow manages to retain its original quality and may often be observed between complete strangers, in contexts of either condolence or congratulation. Two specific situations which illustrate this are the road accident and the sportsman's moment of triumph. Following a road accident, if one of those involved is sitting slumped by the roadside in a state of numbed shock, he will soon be approached closely by one of the helpers who arrive on the scene. Typically, the helper will peer closely at the shocked person and ask some quite nonsensical question, such as 'Are you all right?', when clearly he is not. Almost immediately the helper realizes how meaningless his words are in such a situation, and reverts instead to the more powerful and basic communication pattern of direct body contact. The most likely form that this contact will take is a comforting, gentle patting on the back of the victim. The same response can be observed, but with much more vigour, when a sportsman has just achieved some sort of athletic triumph. As he returns cheerfully from the field or arena, his fans will compete with one another to get close enough to pat him warmly on the back as he passes by.

We have already come a long way from the primary situation of the mother lovingly patting her tiny baby, but there is still further to go, for amongst adults the action of patting has extended its range even beyond the tactile. The basic touch signal has, in two important contexts, become a sound signal and a visual signal. Both human clapping, when an audience applauds a performer, and human waving, during greetings and farewells, have been derived from the primary patting action. Let us take clapping first.

For years I was puzzled by the widespread use of hand-clapping as a method of rewarding a performer. The sharp slapping of one hand against another seemed an almost aggressive action, as did the harsh sound it produced. Yet clearly it was the exact opposite of aggressive in its effect on the happy performer. For centuries, actors have craved the applause of a sea of clapping hands, and have devised many a 'trap to catch a clap', thereby giving the English language its word 'claptrap'.

To understand the potent reward of hand-clapping, we must search for its origins in childhood. Careful studies of infants in the second half of the first year of life reveal that at this age a hand-clap may often be given as part of the greeting towards the mother, when she returns to her baby after a brief absence. The action may be performed either just before, or instead of, reaching out with its arms towards the mother. It appears at about the same time as the act of holding on to the mother with the arms. It is as if the baby, seeing the mother approaching, makes a movement in which the arms are brought out and round as if to hold her. But her body is not there yet to be held, and so the arms continue in the arc of embracing until the hands meet with a clap. At this stage the clap is performed, as it were, from the arm, not from the wrist as in the adult version of hand-clapping.

Detailed observations have indicated that this occurs where there is no evidence of the mother's having taught a clapping response previously. The baby clap, in other words, can best be interpreted as the audible culmination of a vacuum-embracing of the mother. The rhythmically repeated clapping-from-the-wrist that develops later can then be seen clearly as a kind of vacuum-patting added to the vacuum-embrace. When we applaud a performer, we are, in effect, patting him on the back from a distance. It is inconvenient or impossible for us to all rush up and actually make physical contact with him, giving him a real pat to show our approval, so instead we stay in our seats and repeatedly pat him in vacuo. If you test this by clapping your hands as though you were applauding, you will find that you do not bring both hands together with equal force. One tends to take the role of the performer's back and the other does the vigorous vacuum back-patting on it. It is true that both hands move, but one makes a much stronger action than the other. In nine people out of ten it is the right hand, with the palm facing half-downwards, that takes the patting role, and the left hand, with the palm facing half-upwards, that takes the role of the back to be patted.

Occasionally one gets an unexpected glimpse, even in the adult world, of the basic relationship that exists between the primary embrace and the action of hand-clapping. When the first Russian cosmonaut returned in triumph to Moscow and stood in Red Square with the Russian leaders, a vast crowd filed past paying homage, reaching up and clapping their hands to him as they went by. A film of the event clearly shows one man in the crowd so overcome with emotion that he keeps on interrupting his prolonged hand-clapping with vacuum embraces. He claps his outstretched hands, embraces the air in front of him and hugs it to him, then reaches out, claps again and embraces again. When the power of the emotion breaks down the formalization of the conventional pattern in this way, it provides us with an eloquent confirmation of the origins of the adult act.

Russia happens to provide us with another interesting variation in hand-clapping. In that country it is usual for the performers to clap the audience as the audience claps them. This does not mean, as has sometimes been cynically suggested, that Russian performers are so narcissistic that they even applaud their own performances. They are simply returning the audience's formalized embrace, as they would do if they met them body to body. In the West we lack this convention, although a variant of it can sometimes be seen in the wide-stretched arms of the performer seeking applause at the end of an act. Circus performers and acrobats are particularly prone to adopt this posture. At the completion of a difficult stunt, they stand proudly poised, face the audience, and fling their arms out wide. The audience immediately breaks into ringing applause. The opening of the arms in this way is an example of an intention movement of embracing. The arms are positioned ready to embrace the audience, but do not go on to consummate the act in vacuo. Some cabaret singers who specialize in highly emotional songs use much the same action whilst actually singing, arousing emotion in the audience by offering them an imploring invitation to embrace as an accompaniment to the imploring words of the song.

Hand-clapping is also used occasionally as an act of summoning a servant. In the harem fantasy, it is the signal that says 'bring on the dancing girls'. In these cases the clapping is not the typical fast, rhythmically repeated action of the applause pattern, but simply one or two hard slaps of one hand against the other. In this respect it is much more like the infant clapping that was performed as a greeting to the mother. The message is also similar. The infant's request, 'come closer', to the mother, becomes the adult's demand for the same thing from the servant.

I said earlier that the basic touch signal of patting has been extended both as a sound signal, which we have been examining, and as a visual signal, in the form of waving. Like clapping, waving is usually taken for granted, but it, too, has some unexpected elements, and it is worth analysing in detail.

To start with, it seems obvious that we wave when greeting or saying goodbye because, from a distance, it makes us more conspicuous. This is true, but it is not the whole answer. If you watch people who are really desperate to make themselves conspicuous, say when hailing a taxi, or when trying to make visual contact with a person in a crowd who has not yet spotted them, they do not wave in the usual, conventional manner. Instead, they raise one arm stiffly, straight up, and start swinging it from side to side, moving it from the shoulder. Under even greater pressure, they may raise and wave both arms in this way at the same time. This is the action that makes for maximum conspicuousness at a distance. It is not, however, the way we wave to one another when we are already in visual contact. If we are waving goodbye to someone, or if we are waving a greeting to someone who has already seen us but is still out of reach, we do not normally wave our arms. We raise the arm, but what we wave is the hand. We do it in one of three ways. One is to wave it up and down, with the fingers pointing away from us. When the hand is in the up position, the palm faces outwards; when in the down position, the palm faces downwards. Here again is the ubiquitous patting action. The greeting arm reaches out to embrace and pat, but, as with the clapping, the intervening distance forces us to perform the action in vacuo. The difference is that whereas in hand-clapping the long-distance embrace-and-pat is elaborated into a sound signal, here it is modified into a visual signal. The arm goes upward instead of forward, as it would in a true contact embrace, because this increases the visibility of the action. Otherwise there is little difference.

A second form of hand-waving reveals a further modification towards visibility. Instead of moving the hand up and down, it is waved from side to side, with the palm kept in the out-facing position. The speed is much the same, but the action is now one step further removed from the primary patting motion. It is significant that this form of waving is favoured more by adults than by children, who seem to prefer the primitive up-and-down version.

The third type of hand-wave is one that will not be familiar to most Western readers. I have myself observed it only in Italy, but apparently it also occurs in Spain, China, India, Pakistan, Burma, Malaysia, East Africa, Nigeria, and amongst gypsies. (This is, to say the least of it, a most curious distribution, for which I can as yet find no explanation.) It is reminiscent of a hand-beckoning action, but one only has to see it performed as a goodbye signal to realize that this is not what it is. Like the first form of hand-waving I mentioned, it is an up-and-down action, but this time the hand starts out palm uppermost (as in a begging posture) and is then moved repeatedly upwards towards the body of the waver. Again, it is basically a patting movement, and in true back-patting one often sees the hand adopt this position, with the fingers pointing upwards on the back, when the embracing arm has the elbow in a low position.

Two rather specialized waves are related to this last one. They are the Papal wave and the British royal wave. In both cases, for some reason, they are performed neither from the shoulder, as in the conspicuous arm-wave, nor from the wrist, as in the usual patting-wave. Instead they are done from the elbow. The Pope normally uses both arms at once and brings his hands and forearms slowly, rhythmically and repeatedly towards himself, palms uppermost, making a series of embracing intention movements. But it is not as simple as that, because his arms do not bend directly towards his chest. He does not hug the crowd to his bosom. Instead, the arc the arms perform is half-inward and half-upward, as though his action is a compromise, embracing the crowds partly towards himself and partly towards the heavens above, where one day they presumably all hope to be welcomed.

The British royal wave is also typically stiff from the elbow, but is normally one-handed and with the fingers pointing straight up. The palm faces inwards towards the royal body, emphasizing the embracing nature of the action, and the forearm is slowly and rhythmically rotated, with the emphasis on the inward part of the rotation. In this way the Queen, in a highly stylized manner, embraces her subjects and reassures them with a rather formal pat on the back.

As in the case of clapping, one is sometimes lucky enough to see the formality of waving break down under emotional pressure in a revealing way, laying bare its basic origins. A specific instance of greeting will illustrate this. At a small airport where I was making observations of waving behaviour, there is a balcony from which friends and relatives can watch the new arrivals descend from the incoming aircraft and walk across the tarmac to the customs entrance. This entrance is just beneath the balcony, so that although the new arrivals cannot touch the excited figures waving frantically to them from above, they do come very close before finally disappearing into the airport building. This, then, is the setting, and the action usually takes place as follows. After the aircraft doors open and the passengers start piling out, there is a great deal of distant eye-scanning from both the arrivals and the greeters. If one makes eye contact before the other, he normally starts vigorous arm-waving, moving the arm from the shoulder in the maximum-conspicuousness manner. After mutual eye contact has been made, then both sides tend to adopt the arm-raised hand-wave action. This goes on for some time, but it is a long walk to the building and after a while they usually break off. Their waving and smiling urges have become temporarily exhausted (like the person being photographed who, as time passes, finds it hard to maintain a natural smile for the lens-fiddling cameraman), but they do not wish to appear 'ungreetful', so both sides now take a sudden interest in other aspects of the airport scene. The new arrival glances round to survey the landscape of the airfield, or re-arranges that suddenly awkward piece of hand-luggage that is mysteriously slipping from his grip. The greeters for their part start to exchange comments about the appearance of the new arrival. Then, as the latter comes nearer and his facial details can be made out more clearly, both sides start up the vigorous hand-waving and smiling again until the arrivals have disappeared into the building below. Half an hour later, with customs inspection over, the first body contact is made, with handshakes, embraces, pattings, hugs and kisses.

This is the basic story. Naturally, there are many minor variations, and on one occasion the pattern was exceeded in a most revealing way. A man was returning to the bosom of his family after a long spell abroad. From the moment he stepped off the aircraft both he and his group of family greeters exploded into an orgy of arm- and hand-waving. As he reached the building and saw the details of their faces clearly above him, he found the convention of hand-waving inadequate for his emotional needs. With tears in his eyes and his mouth shaping unheard words of love, he had to do something with his arm that would better express the enormous intensity of his feelings at being reunited with his family. At this moment, as I watched, I saw his hand actions change. The ordinary waving movements ceased and were replaced by a perfect miming of a passionate series of back-pattings. The arm was now held out towards the family group, rather than raised upward, which foreshortened it and reduced its conspicuousness. The hand curled round sideways and made vigorous, rapid patting actions in mid-air. The power of his emotions was so strong that all the secondary, conventionalized modifications of the primary embrace-and-pat actions, which help to improve the signal quality of this pattern from a distance by making it more clearly visible, were abandoned in the heat of the moment, and the original primary behaviour was once again laid bare.

The intensity of this encounter was confirmed by the tactile greeting behaviour that followed the customs interlude. When the man emerged into the body of the airport, he was embraced, hugged, kissed and patted with such vigour by all fourteen members of his family that, by the time they had finished, he was emotionally exhausted, his face flooded with tears, his body shaking. At one point a woman who appeared to be his mother augmented her embrace with vigorous face-kneading, taking both the man's cheeks in her hands and grappling with them as though she were in her kitchen kneading soft dough. While this was going on, the man's hands were embracing her and patting her back at high intensity. However, after about the tenth passionate greeting, it seemed as if the emotional exhaustion of the occasion was beginning to tell on him. As this occurred, his patting actions changed significantly. Once again, a signal convention was breaking down under emotional pressure, and once again the origins of a formalized pattern were being laid bare. Whereas, before, the waving had reverted to vacuum-air-patting, this time it went one stage further back to its original source. The repeated patting gave way to brief, repeated clinging actions.

Each pat became a tightening of the hand contact, a sort of clinging squeeze, that was repeatedly relaxed and then tightened again. Here, without doubt, was the original clinging intention movement. This was the 'ancestral' pattern, the one from which all the others had descended by a process of signal specialization: to a tactile signal by modification to on-off patting, to a sound signal by using the other palm as the more noisily patted object in the act of hand-clapping, and to a visual signal by patting in mid-air with a raised arm in the act of hand-waving. Such are the ramifications that occur with our so-called 'trivial' acts of human intimacy.

In following this one small human-contact action through all its various developments, I have tried to show how it is possible to see old familiar activities in a new light. The need that we, as adults, have to make body contact with one another is basic and powerful, but, as we have seen, it is rarely fully expressed. Instead, it appears in fragmented, modified or disguised forms in many of the signs, gestures and signals we make to one another in our daily lives. Often the true meaning of the actions is hidden from us and we have to trace them back to their origins to understand them fully. In the examples I have just been describing, the primary contact action frequently became remote, operating at a distance, but there are also many ways in which we do still make actual body contact with one another, and it is interesting to survey these and see what forms they take. To do this it will help to go back for a moment to the primary embrace itself. This is not commonly seen today between adults in public, but it still does occur from time to time and it is worth studying the situations in which it appears.

The full embrace. If we make careful observations of as many full embraces as possible, then it soon becomes clear that between adults this action falls into three distinct categories. The biggest group, as we might expect, consists of amorous contact between lovers. This accounts for about two-thirds of all public embraces today. The remaining third can be split up into the two types that we can call the 'relatives' reunion' and the 'sportsman's triumph'.

Young lovers perform the full embrace, not only when they meet and part, but also frequently during the times they are together. Amongst older couples, after marriage, it is rare to see a full embrace in public unless one partner is going away for some time, or returning from a separation of at least some days. At other times, if the embrace occurs at all, it will be publicly expressed merely as a token contact of a rather mild kind.

Between adult relatives, such as brothers and sisters, or parents and their adult children, the passionate embrace is even less common. It does occur with remarkable predictability, however, whenever there has been some major disaster from which one of the relatives has escaped. If he or she has been hijacked, kidnapped, taken captive, or trapped by some upheaval of nature, then you can be sure that the 'relatives' reunion' that follows safe delivery and return will exhibit full embraces of the most intense kind. Under such circumstances the action may even extend to close friends of either sex, who would normally give only a handshake or a kiss on the cheek. Such is the emotional intensity of the situation that the passionate embracing of a man by a man, or a woman by a woman, or a man-*friend* by a woman-*friend*, creates no difficulties with regard to sexual taboos. At a lower emotional intensity there would be more of a problem, but at moments of high drama the taboos are forgotten. In triumph, relief or despair it is acceptable even for two adult males in our culture to hug and kiss one another, but if, in a less dramatic situation, they were to perform a mere fragment of an embrace such as holding hands, or pressing cheek to cheek, they would immediately create a homosexual impression.

This difference is significant and requires explanation. It tells us something about the way in which basic body contacts are fragmented and formalized. To begin with, the full embrace is natural between parent and baby, and therefore also between parent and older child, even though it becomes less frequent. Between adults it is typical of lovers and mates. Other adults who, for a variety of reasons, feel the urge to embrace one another, must therefore somehow make it clear that there is no sexual element in their contact. This they do by employing some formalized fragment of the full embrace, a fragment which by conventional agreement is non-sexual. A man, for example, can put his arm around another man's shoulder without running any risk of sexual misinterpretation, either by his contact partner, or by others who see him perform the action. If, however, he were to perform other simple fragments, such as, say, kissing the man's ear, a sexual connotation would immediately be placed upon the act.

The situation is entirely different when two men are seen employing the full embrace, complete with hugging and kissing, in a situation of great triumph, disaster or reunion. No sexual interpretation is made here because it is recognized that the response is not formalized, but basic. The onlookers recognize the situation as being one where the usual conventions are overpowered by the intensity of the emotions involved. They know, intuitively, that what they are witnessing is the return to the primary, pre-sexual embrace of infancy, with all the layers of later, adult stylization stripped away, and they accept the contact as being perfectly natural. In fact, if two male homosexuals wished to make body contact in public without arousing the usual heterosexual hostility or curiosity, they would do better to indulge in a wild hug rather than a gentle kiss.

By studying the various formal fragments of the basic embrace, we should therefore be able to see how convention has pigeon-holed them into different categories, so that each one now signals something quite specific about the nature of the relationship between the 'contacters'.

Before doing this, however, there is still the third category of the full embrace to be mentioned, namely the 'sportsman's triumph'. The embrace of two men following a major disaster has been with us for a long time, but the passionate hugging of football players after a goal has been scored is something comparatively recent. How is it that this occasion has suddenly been elevated to the ranks of a major emotional experience? To find the answer we have to go much further afield than the football pitch. We do, in fact, have to go back many hundreds of years.

Two thousand years ago, when the world was less crowded and the relationships between members of a community were more clearly defined, the full embrace was much more commonly used as an ordinary form of greeting between equals. The embrace-and-kiss was employed between men and men as well as between women and women and between non-amorous men and women. In ancient Persia it was even common for men of equal rank to kiss one another on the mouth, reserving the kiss on the cheek for someone of slightly inferior status. It was more usual in other places, however, for the cheek kiss to be employed between equals. This situation persisted for many centuries, and was still to be found in medieval England, where valiant knights would kiss and embrace one another at times when their modern equivalents would do no more than nod and shake an outstretched hand.

Towards the end of the seventeenth century the situation in England began to change, and the non-sexual greeting embrace went into a rapid decline. This began in the towns and slowly spread to the country, as we know from a line in Congreve's *The Way of the World*: 'You think you're in the country, where great lubberly brothers slabber and kiss one another when they meet. 'Tis not the fashion here; 'tis not indeed dear brother.'

Social life in the cities was becoming more crowded and personal relationships more complex and confusing, and with the arrival of the nineteenth century further restrictions were imposed. Now even the elaborate bowing and curtsying that had survived through the eighteenth century became more and more limited to formal occasions and lost their everyday role. By the 1830s that minimal body contact, the handshake, had arrived, and it has been with us ever since.

Similar trends were taking place elsewhere, but not always to the same extent. The Latin countries tended to restrict their body contacts far less than the British, and, even into the twentieth century, friendly embraces between adult males remained far more acceptable. They do so to this day, and this is where we return to the case of the 'footballer's hug'. Football, which began as a British sport, spread rapidly in the present century to many parts of the world. In Latin countries it became especially popular, and before long international matches of great emotional intensity were being played. When Latin teams visited England, the passionate embracing of their members, following a successful goal, was at first met with astonishment and derision, but the excellence of their playing soon changed all that. As the years passed, the 'Well done, old chap' of the British players when one of their members scored began to seem almost churlish. Back-patting gave way to mild embracing, and mild embracing grew into wild hugging, until today spectators have become quite accustomed to seeing a goal-scorer almost submerged beneath a dense cluster of passionately hugging congratulators.

In this one specific context, then, we have gone full circle back to the times of medieval knights and the ancient world beyond. It remains to be seen whether this trend will extend to other spheres. It may do so, but there is one limitation we must bear in mind. The players embracing on their football field are in a strictly non-sexual context. Their roles are clearly defined and their physical masculinity is being strongly demonstrated by the toughness of the game they are playing. In a social situation of a less clearly defined type, the situation would be different, and the usual restrictions of our complex society will probably then continue to apply. Only in spheres where the expression of powerful emotions is part of the ordinary stock-in-trade, such as the acting profession, can we expect to

find major exceptions. If the rest of us find the social embracings of actors and actresses somewhat excessive, we must
remember three things. Not only are they trained to show
passions easily, but they are also put under severe emotional
strain by the nature of their work and, in addition, theirs
happens to be a particularly insecure occupation. They need
all the mutual reassurance they can get.

Leaving the full embrace now, we can start to look at its
less intense forms of expression. So far we have been dealing
with the maximal frontal embrace, in which the two partners
are pressed close together with the sides of their heads in
contact and their arms wrapped tightly around one another's
bodies. When this action is performed at a lower intensity,
there are usually three major changes. The bodies now make
contact side to side instead of face to face; only one arm is
wrapped around the partner's body instead of two; and the
heads are usually apart instead of touching. My observations
reveal that, between adults in public, a partial embrace of this
type is six times as likely to occur as a full embrace.★

The shoulder embrace. The most common form of partial
embrace is the shoulder embrace, in which one person wraps
an arm around his partner so that the hand comes to rest on his
far shoulder. This is twice as common as any other form of
partial embrace.

The first difference to emerge, when comparing this with
the full frontal embrace, is that it is predominantly a masculine act. Whereas the full embrace was given more or less
equally by males and females, the shoulder embrace is five
times more likely to be performed by a male than by a
female. The reason is simple enough: men are taller than
women, and women will always have to look up to them
physically, no matter what their attitudes may be in other
respects. The consequence of this anatomical difference is

★ This, and other similar quantitative statements, are based on personal observations backed up by a detailed analysis of 10,000 photographs taken at random from
a wide variety of recent news magazines and newspapers.

that certain body contacts are much easier for men than for women, and the shoulder embrace is one of these.

This fact gives the shoulder embrace a special quality. Since, when it is performed between a man and a woman, it is nearly always done by the man, this means that there is nothing effeminate about it. This in turn means that it is also available for use between males in casual, friendly situations, without giving any sexual flavour to the contact. About one in four shoulder embraces do, in fact, occur between males, and this is the only form of body embrace that does occur commonly in an all-male context. The difference with the full frontal embrace is striking. There, if two males were involved, the situation was typically one of high drama, or intense emotion, but here the context can be much more relaxed, the usual scene being one of team-mates, 'old pals' or 'buddies'.

This 'safely masculine' rule does not apply to other types of partial embrace, such as putting the arm around the partner's waist. Since this is easier for either sex to do and since it also brings the hand closer to the genital region, it is rarely if ever employed between males.

If we now move still further away from the full embrace, shifting our attention from partial embraces to mere fragments of the complete act, we find similar differences. Some embrace fragments have a non-sexual quality and can be used freely between males, while others retain a more amorous flavour and are largely restricted to use between lovers and mates.

The hand-on-shoulder. A common action is placing one hand on the partner's shoulder, without involving any actual embrace. This is a simple reduction of the shoulder embrace and, as we might expect, is employed in similar contexts. Being slightly less intimate, it is even more common between males. Whereas only one in four of the shoulder embraces was done between two males, here the figure is one in three.

The arm-link. If we watch the embrace disintegrate still further, to a mere linking of arms, then the situation shows a striking change. Here, instead of increasing, the figure for males sinks to one in twelve, and we have to ask the question why, with an even less intimate form of body contact, men should become so much less inclined to link arms with other men rather than with women. The answer is that this action is basically feminine. When it occurs between males and females, it is five times more likely to be done by a female to a male than the other way around. This exactly reverses the position we found in the shoulder embrace, and means that if this contact is to be made between members of the same sex, it is going to have an effeminate quality. This leads to a prediction that if it is going to occur between friends of the same sex, it should occur more between women than between men, and observations do, in fact, bear this out.

If we look for cases where one man does link his arm through that of another, then we find that they fall into two categories: the Latin and the elderly. Latin males, with their culturally freer body contacts, often do it, and in non-Latin Western countries it can also be observed as the support-seeking act of an elderly male who is past the sexually potent phase of life.

The hand-in-hand. Continuing our anatomical progress away from the full embrace, via the shoulder embrace, the hand-on-shoulder and the arm-in-arm, we come finally to the hand-in-hand (not to be confused with the handshake, which is discussed separately later). Although this is a more remote form of contact than the last three, with the two bodies usually kept separate from one another, it does have something in common with the full embrace that the others do not. It is a mutual act. I can place my hand on your shoulder, for example, without you doing anything, but if I hold your hand, you are also going to be holding mine. Since it occurs frequently between a male and a female, and since they are always *both* doing it, it acquires neither a masculine nor a feminine quality, but rather a heterosexual one. This makes it, in effect, like a tiny version of the full embrace, and it is not surprising, therefore, to find that it is seldom used today between two males in public.

This was not always the case. Back in the days when the full embrace was freely employed between men, they could also be seen holding hands as an act of non-sexual friendship. To give one example, on an occasion when two medieval monarchs met, it is recorded that they 'took each other by the hand, when the king of France led the king of England to his tent; the four dukes took each other by the hand and followed them.' Before long this custom faded and 'leading by the hand' became restricted to use between males and females. In modern times the action has become modified in two different directions. On formal occasions, such as when a male escorts a female into a banquet, or down the aisle of a church, it has grown into the more reassuring arm-link. On less formal occasions it has changed into the typical hand-holding of mutually grasped palms. And sometimes, when greater intimacy is required, a couple can be seen to perform both acts at the same time.

Despite this general trend, there are certain specialized occasions when males in our modern world do still hold hands. One example is the multiple hand-holding that occurs when a whole group of people are joining hands with one another to do such things as sing community songs, or take curtain calls in the theatre. Even here the tendency is to alternate the positions of the males and females, so that each person is flanked by members of the opposite sex, but if the numbers are not equal, or if it is too difficult to jostle everyone into the correct positionings, then it is permissible to hold hands with your own sex. This is because you are not in any sense forming a pair with them. The very size of the group eliminates the potential sexual flavour of the hand-holding.

Another highly stylized version of hand-holding that can occur between males is for one of them to take the other's hand in his own and raise it high in the air as a sign of victory.

Although this originates from the world of boxing, it is perhaps more frequently met with today between pairs of male politicians, who appear to fantasize imaginary boxing-gloves on the hands of their victorious colleagues. The hand-holding is permissible in this context because of the primarily aggressive nature of the arm-raising gesture. In its more original form, prior to the hand-holding embellishment, this movement of holding the raised fist aloft was undoubtedly a winning fighter's signal that he was still capable of hitting, at a stage when his rival was not. It is the frozen intention movement of delivering an overarm blow and is the same gesture that has been adopted as the modern communist salute. Studies of fighting behaviour between young children have revealed that this form of hitting, bringing the arm downwards from above, is very basic to our species and does not have to be learned. So it is interesting to see that the modern boxer still uses the intention movement of this action as a victory gesture, even though, in his actual fighting, he no longer employs it, but uses instead highly stylized and 'un-natural' frontal punches. It is also intriguing to notice how, in more informal fighting, such as that which occurs during street rioting, both the police and the rioters revert largely to the more primitive form of overarm hitting.

Returning now to the question of males holding hands in public, there is one final special context in which this occurs. It concerns priests, and especially those of high rank in the Catholic Church. The Pope, for instance, can frequently be seen to hold hands with his followers, both male and female, and this exception illustrates the way in which a well-known public figure can set himself outside normal conventions. The Pope's image is so totally non-sexual that he can perform a whole variety of fragmented intimacies with perfect strangers, intimacies which ordinary citizens could never contemplate. Who else, for example, could reach out and hold the cheeks of a beautiful girl in a completely non-sexual way? The Pope is, in fact, able to behave very much like the 'holy father' that he is called, and can confidently make intimate body contacts with adult strangers in the same way as a real father would do with his real children. By adopting the role of a super-father, the pontiff can strip away the body-contact restrictions that others must use, and return to the more natural and primary intimacies typical of the early parent-offspring phase. If he still appears more inhibited with his followers than a real father would be with his children, this is not due to the sexual confusion that restricts the rest of us, but simply to the fact that, in the face of a family of 500 million children, he has to conserve his strength.

Up to this point we have been moving away from the full embrace by travelling, as it were, across the shoulders and down the arm to the hand, and in that direction we can go no further. Instead, we can look at what other parts of the body come into contact with one another during the full embrace, and see if there, too, there are sources of useful fragments that can be employed in day-to-day encounters.

The pressing together of the trunks and legs during the full frontal embrace does not appear to be a very rich source and it is not hard to see why. For adults to touch one another in these regions, in public, brings them too close to the forbidden sexual zones. But there is another important contact region involved in the full embrace, and that is the head. At high intensities, the sides of the heads are pressed together, caressed with the hands or touched with the lips, and from these actions we do find the development of three important fragments that are widely used in everyday life. They can be labelled as the head-to-head contact, the hand-to-head contact and the kiss.

The head contacts. Touching the partner's head with the hand, and putting the two heads together, are both specialities of young lovers. This is especially true of the former. Hand-to-head contacts are four times as common between young lovers as between older married couples. Head-to-head contacts are twice as common with young lovers, and in both cases this contrasts with an intimacy such as the shoulder embrace, which is more common between the older couples.

Males rarely employ these head contacts with other males. When men 'put their heads together', they do not usually do it literally, the function being to indulge in intimate conversation rather than true body intimacy. If a male hand touches a male head, it usually does so for one of three special reasons: giving first aid, bestowing a blessing or delivering an attack. If a male (or a female) encounters an accident victim, the helplessness of the wounded person transmits strong infantile signals that are hard to resist. Photographs of the victims of assassination attempts, for example, nearly always show someone cradling the victim's head in their hands. Medically this is a somewhat dubious procedure, but medical logic has no place here. This is not a trained act of assistance; it is a more basic response related to the primary parental care of a helpless child. It is much too difficult for an untrained person to pause and make a reasoned assessment of the physical injuries the victim has sustained before taking first-aid action. Instead, he will reach out and touch or lift as a primary act of comfort, with no thought to the further damage he may be causing. It is too painful to stand by and coldly calculate the best steps to be taken. The urge to make comforting body contact is overpowering, but we have to face the fact that it can sometimes prove fatal. Once, as a small boy, ignorant of what was happening, I watched a man killed in this way. Following an accident, his injured body was cradled in the loving arms of anxious helpers who lifted him into a car to drive him away. The loving act destroyed his life by pressing his splintered ribs through his lungs. Had he been 'callously' left lying where he was until a stretcher arrived, he might have lived. Such is the power of the urge to make body contact when tragedy strikes, and this applies to males and females equally, for disaster knows no sex.

The bestowing of priestly blessings is equally sexless, as in the laying on of hands of a bishop in ordination or confirmation. Here we are back again to a copy of the primary parent-child relationship.

The delivering of an attack by the hand of one male to the head of another requires little comment in itself, but it does provide one possible source of inter-male intimacy. If a man feels the friendly urge to touch another man's head but is inhibited about making it a friendly caress, he can employ the simple device of mock aggression. Instead of fondling his partner's head, which would have too strong a sexual flavour, he can deliver a playful 'pretend-attack', such as ruffling the hair or squeezing the neck in a mock-grasp. Just as play-fighting helped the parent to prolong intimacies with his growing children, so many a fragment of play-assault can be observed between male friends, enabling them to be both manly and intimate at one and the same time.

The kiss. This brings us to the last of the important derivatives of the primary embrace, namely the kiss, an action with an intriguing and complex history. If you feel that a kiss is a simple enough act, think for a moment about the many ways in which you do it, even in today's supposedly informal society. You kiss your lover on the lips, an old friend of the opposite sex on the cheek, an infant on the top of the head; if a child hurts a finger, you kiss it 'to make it better'; if you are about to face danger, you kiss a mascot 'to bring you luck'; if you are a gambler, you kiss the dice before you roll them; if you are the best man at a wedding, you kiss the bride; if you are religious, you kiss the bishop's ring as a sign of respect, or the Bible when taking an oath; if you are bidding someone farewell and they are already out of reach, you kiss your own hand and blow the kiss towards them. No, the kiss is not a simple matter, and to understand it we must once again turn back the clock.

The most sensitive areas of skin on the human body are the tips of the fingers, the clitoris, the tip of the penis, the tongue and the lips. It is not surprising, therefore, that the lips should be used a great deal in intimate body contacts. Their role begins in the act of sucking at the mother's breast, which provides a major tactile reward in addition to the reward of obtaining milk. This has been proved by studying the behaviour of unfortunate babies who have been born with an abnormal, blocked oesophagus, and who have to be fed by artificial means. It was observed that if they were given rubber teats to suck, this helped to calm them down and stopped them crying. Since they had never taken any food through the mouth, the reward of having a teat between the lips could have nothing to do with the pleasures of the milk supply that normally results from such an action. It had to be a case of contact for contact's sake. So the touching of something soft with the mouth is an important and primary intimacy in its own right.

As the child grows and exchanges head-to-head contacts with the mother, feeling her lips pressed to his skin and his to hers, it is easy to see how this early mouth contact can develop into a potent act of friendly greeting. In the embrace of childhood, the usual position for the lips when touching the parent will be the cheek or the side of the head. As I have already mentioned, in ancient times, when the full embrace was given more freely between adults of either sex, the kiss on the cheek was the usual form of mouth contact employed between equals. This was, in a sense, the primitive greeting kiss taken straight from childhood with little modification, and it has persisted through the centuries right down to the present day. In our culture, male and female friends and relatives still kiss in this way when meeting or parting, and the act can be performed without any sexual implication whatever. The same is true of adult females with adult females. Between adult males the situation varies considerably from country to country, with France, for example, remaining much closer to the ancient system than England.

Direct mouth-to-mouth kissing has taken a different course. At various times and in various places it has been employed to some extent as a non-sexual greeting between close friends, but the joining of two body orifices in this way has usually seemed to be an act of too great an intimacy even for close friends, and generally speaking it has become more and more restricted to contacts between lovers and mates.

Since the female breasts are sexual signals as well as feeding devices, the kissing of a female breast by an adult male has also become totally sexual in context, despite the similarity of the act to the primitive action of sucking at the breast in infancy. Needless to say, kissing of the genitals is also exclusively sexual, and so indeed is the kissing of many other parts of the body, especially the trunk, thighs and ears. Certain specific parts of the body, however, have been formally set aside for a special kind of non-sexual kissing — what we might call the subordinate kiss, or the kiss of reverence. This differs categorically from both the friendly kiss and the sexual kiss, and to understand it we must look at the way in which a subordinate human being presents himself in front of a dominant.

It is well known from studies of animal behaviour that one way to appease the wrath of a dominant animal is to make yourself seem smaller and therefore less threatening to him. If you threaten him less, then he is less likely to see you as a challenge to his superiority and therefore less likely to take damaging action against you. He will simply ignore you as being beneath him, both metaphorically and literally, which, if you happen to be the weaker animal, is precisely what you want (at least for the moment). And so we see all manner of cringings and crouchings, grovellings and hunchings-up, downcast eyes and lowered heads, in a wide variety of animal species.

It is the same with man. Where there are no formalities, the response takes the animal form of cringing low on the ground, but in many situations the response of the inferior man has become highly stylized, and these stylizations have varied considerably from place to place and from time to time. This does not put them outside the realm of a biological analysis, however, for they all, without exception, still reveal basic features that clearly relate them to the submissive behaviour of other species of animals.

The most extreme form of submissive body-lowering ever seen in man is full prostration, in which the whole body lies flat on the ground, face down. You simply cannot get any lower than that without an act of burial. The dominant, on the other hand, can, and often did, enhance the lowering effect by viewing it from a raised platform or throne. This total act of servility was common and widespread in the ancient kingdoms, performed by prisoners to their captors, slaves to their masters, and servants to their rulers. Between it and the act of standing fully erect, there is a whole range of formalized submissions, and we can scan them briefly in ascending order.

Next to the full prostration comes the kowtow of the Eastern world, in which the body does not lie, but kneels down and then bends the trunk low until the forehead is touching the ground. Coming one stage up from this is the full kneel, with both knees on the ground, but without the forward bending of the body. This, too, was frequently used in the ancient world when confronting an overlord, but by medieval times it had already risen to the half-kneel, with only one knee lowered to the ground. Men were then specifically instructed to reserve the full kneel for God, who by this time had to be given a little more respect than the rulers of the day. In modern times it is rare for us to kneel to any man at any time, except on certain state occasions in the presence of royalty, but worshippers in church have not changed the ancient full-kneel custom to this day, God having maintained his dominant status rather more successfully than modern rulers.

Coming one stage further up, we reach the curtsy (or courtesy), which was no more than an intention movement of the half-kneel. One leg was drawn back slightly, as if its knee was going to go down and touch the ground, and then both knees started to bend, but neither reached ground level. The body was not bowed forward. Up until the time of

Shakespeare both men and women made the curtsy. In this respect, at least, there was equality between the sexes. The male bow had not yet appeared. With the arrival of the curtsy, the act of servility was further reduced, and the half-kneel started to fade from the scene, being given only to royalty.

In the seventeenth century the sexes split up, the men now bowing from the waist while the women retained the curtsy. Both actions lowered the body in front of the dominant individual, but in entirely different ways. From that day to this the situation has remained much the same, except that the extent of the actions has been reduced. The flowery male bowing of the Restoration period gave way to the much simpler and stiffer bow of Victorian times, and the curtsy dwindled to little more than a bob down and up. Today, except in the presence of powerful rulers or royalty, the curtsy is rarely given by women, and the male bow, if given at all, is seldom more than a mere lowering and raising of the head.

The one exception to this rule occurs at the end of a theatrical performance, when, for some reason, the performers slip back several centuries and indulge in deep bows and elaborate curtsies. It is amusing that here we sometimes also see an entirely new trend, with female performers bowing deeply as if they were males. It looks as if this return to sexual equality in the act of subordination is mirroring the new trend towards female equality in all other matters, but if this is the case, the males can at least claim that it was the females who changed to the male action, rather than that the males had to return to their medieval curtsying. It is just possible that there is another reason altogether for the actresses' bow which has nothing to do with the masculinizing of the modern female in our culture. It may instead have to do with the precise opposite, dating back to the earlier times of play-acting, when all the actors were male, and half the men were feminized to play the female roles. Perhaps the modern actress when she bows is by force of tradition merely imitating her male transvestite predecessors. Even allowing for the persistence of ancient traditions, however, this explanation appears improbable. It seems much more likely that she feels she is joining the men.

All the bowing and scraping of yesterday's everyday greetings has now been almost universally replaced by the far more forthright and upstanding handshake. In this act, at last, there is no lowering of the body. We greet erect and, in so doing, have travelled the full distance from flat prostration. Today all men are not only 'born equal', but are still considered to be so, in greetings at least, when they are fully adult.

I have gone into these formalities of greeting at some length, despite the fact that, until we reach the handshake, they do not in themselves involve the intimacies of body contact. This digression was necessary because of their importance in relation to the kiss of reverence. I began by saying that, in ancient times, two equals kissed one another on the cheek, that is, at equal body height. But for an inferior to kiss a superior in this way would have been unthinkable. If he was to show his friendship by a touch of the lips, then that touch had to be performed at a level low enough to match his inferiority. For the lowest subordinates this meant the act of kissing the dominant one's foot. For an abject prisoner even this was too good, and he was forced to kiss the ground near the dominant shoe. In modern times these actions are rare, rulers not being what they once were, but even now the ruler of Ethiopia, for example, may find himself accorded this honour by one of his subjects in a public place. And slang phrases such as 'kiss the dirt', 'bite the dust' and 'boot-licker' are still with us to remind us of the humiliations of yesterday.

For those of slightly less inferiority, it was permissible to kiss the hem of a garment, or to kiss the knee of the dominant individual. A bishop, for instance, was permitted to kiss the Pope's knee, but a lesser mortal had to be content with kissing the cross embroidered on his right shoe.

Coming one step further up the body, we arrive at the kiss

on the hand. This, too, was performed to many a dominant male, but today, apart from high-ranking priests, we reserve it entirely as a mark of respect to a lady, and even then only in certain countries and on certain occasions.

There were therefore four points on the body which were licensed, so to speak, for non-sexual kissing: the cheek, for friendly equality; the hand, for deep respect; the knee, for humble submission; and the foot, for grovelling servility. The action of touching with the lips was the same in each case, but the lower the point of its application, the lower was the expression of relative status. Despite all the pomp and ritual, nothing could be closer to a sequence of typical animal appeasement gestures. When stripped in this way of the fussy details of cultural variation and viewed as a whole, even the most courtly of human behaviour patterns come remarkably close to the patterns of animal behaviour we see all around us.

Earlier I listed a number of forms of modern kissing, some of which I may not appear to have explained: for example, kissing the dice before rolling them, kissing a lucky mascot, or a hurt finger to make it well. These and other similar actions, all of which are basically concerned with bringing good luck, are related to the kiss of reverence I have been describing. It is impossible to kiss God, the most dominant one of all, and so worshippers have to make do with symbols of God, such as crosses, Bibles, and similar objects. Since kissing them symbolizes kissing God, the act brings good luck simply because it appeases God. Any lucky mascot, therefore, is being treated as a holy relic. It may be odd to think of a gambler in Las Vegas kissing God when he blows on his dice during a crap game, but that is in effect what he is doing, just as when he crosses his fingers for good luck he is doing no more and no less than making a reverential sign of the cross to protect him from God's wrath. When we kiss our hands in farewell and blow a kiss to our departing friends, we are performing another ancient act, for in earlier days it was more servile to kiss one's own hand than the hand of the dominant person. The hand-kiss at the modern airport is the only survivor of this custom, even though it is now distance rather than servility that makes us perform the movement.

The handshake. With that farewell kiss, we leave the world of the fragmented embrace, with all its complexities, and come to the last of the adult body contacts that is important enough to be examined in detail, namely the handshake. I have already mentioned that this did not gain wide usage until about a hundred and fifty years ago, but its precursor, the hand-clasp, was employed long before that. In ancient Rome it was used as a pledge of honour, and this was to remain its primary function for nearly two thousand years. In medieval times, for instance, a man might kneel and clasp hands with his superior as an act of swearing allegiance to him. The addition of a shaking movement to the clasping hands is mentioned as early as the sixteenth century. The phrase 'they shook hands and swore brothers' appears in Shakespeare's *As You Like It*, where again the function is the binding of an agreement.

In the early part of the nineteenth century the situation changed. Although the handshake was still employed after the making of a promise or a contract, as an act of sealing it, it was now for the first time used in ordinary greetings. The cause of this change was the industrial revolution and the massive expansion of the middle classes, forcing an ever widening wedge between the aristocracy and the peasants. These new middlemen, with their businesses and their trades, were for ever 'doing deals' and 'making agreements', and sealing them with the inevitable handshakings. Dealing and trading was becoming the new way of life, and social relationships began more and more to revolve around them. In this way the contractual handshake invaded the social occasion. Its message became the bartering one of 'I offer you an exchange of friendly greeting'. Gradually it ousted the other forms of greeting until today it has become universally used as the principal act performed, not only when meeting equals, but also when meeting both subordinates and superiors. Whereas once we would have had a wide range of alternatives to suit each type of social encounter, today we have merely this one. What a president does to a farm worker is now the same as what a farm worker does to a president—they both offer a hand, clasp it and shake it, both smiling as they do so. Furthermore, when a president meets another president, or a farm worker meets another farm worker, they will behave in precisely the same way. In terms of body intimacies, times have certainly changed. But if the ubiquitous handshake has simplified matters in one way, it has complicated them in another. We may know that it is the thing to do, but when precisely do we do it? Who offers the hand to whom?

Modern books of etiquette are full of conflicting advice, clearly indicating the confusion that exists. One tells us that a man never holds out his hand to a woman for a handshake, while another informs us that in many parts of the world it is the man who takes the initiative. One tells us that a younger man should never offer his hand to an older one, while another advises that, whenever we are in doubt, we should offer the hand, rather than risk hurting someone's feelings. One authority insists that a woman should rise to shake hands, another that she should remain seated. Further complications exist in respect of whether we are hosts or guests, male hosts offering their hands to female guests, but male guests waiting for a female hand to be offered to them. There are also separate rules for business and social occasions. One book goes so far as to say that 'There are no rules as to when to shake hands,' but clearly this is a statement of despair, the truth being that there are in fact far too many rules.

Obviously there is some hidden complication in the superficially simple act of handshaking which we must unravel if we are to understand these confusions. To do this we must look back at the origins of the act. If we go back as far as our animal relatives, we find that a subordinate chimpanzee will often appease a dominant one by reaching out towards it with a limp hand, as if making a begging gesture. If the action is returned, the two animals briefly touch hands in a contact that looks remarkably like an abbreviated handshake. The initial signal reads, 'See, I am just a harmless beggar who dare not attack you,' and the reply is, 'I will not attack you either.' Developing into a friendly gesture between equals, the message then becomes simply, 'I will not hurt you, I am your friend.' In other words, the chimpanzee hand-offering can be done either by a subordinate to a dominant, as a submissive act, or by a dominant to a subordinate, as a reassuring one, or it can be performed between equals as an act of friendship. Nevertheless, in this respect, it is fundamentally an appeasement gesture and, translated into the modern terms of the etiquette books, we would expect more emphasis to be placed on the inferior individual offering the hand first, to the superior.

Advancing now to the ancient human hand-clasp, we can see this in a similar light. Specifically, the offering of an empty hand revealed that there was no weapon in it, which would explain why we always use the right, or weapon hand. Showing the hand in this way could be done either submissively, by a weaker to a stronger, or reassuringly, by a stronger to a weaker, as in the chimpanzee case. Developed into a strong, mutual hand-clasp, it became a vigorous pact-making device with two men accepting one another, momentarily at least, as equals. Essentially, however, it remains an act in which neither performer is asserting his dominance but, regardless of his relative status, is temporarily displaying himself as harmless.

This is one likely origin for the modern handshake, but there is another that confuses the picture. One of the important greeting acts of a male to a female was the kissing of the hand. To do this, the man took her offered hand in his before applying his lips to it. As this action became more stylized, the actual kissing element declined in intensity to a point where the

mouth only approached the back of the lady's hand and stopped
before making contact, the lips then forming a kiss in mid-air.
Becoming even more fossilized, the act then sometimes occurred
as a mere holding and raising of the lady's hand, accompanied
by a slight bow of the head towards it. In this modified form it
is little more or less than a weak handshake, but with the
vigorous pumping action omitted. One writer has seen this as
the sole source of the modern handshake: 'As a contact
salutation the handshake would appear to be a late derivative of
the "face-kiss", with the "hand-kiss" as a connecting link.' In
this respect, offering the hand is essentially the act of asserted
dominance towards a subordinate, and therefore differs
fundamentally from the display of the male-pact handshake.

The truth appears to be that both the hand-clasp theory and
the hand-kiss theory are correct, and that this double origin
is the cause of all the confusion in the modern etiquette books.
The point is that we do not today shake hands for a single
reason only. We do it as a greeting, as a farewell, to make a
pact, to seal a bargain, to congratulate, to accept a challenge,
to give thanks, to commiserate, to make up after a squabble
and to wish one another luck. There are two elements here.
In some cases it symbolizes a friendly bond, in others merely
that we are friendly at the moment of shaking. If I shake hands
with a man when I am introduced to him for the first time, it
is merely a courtesy and says nothing about our past or even
our future relationship.

To put it another way, we can say that the modern handshake is a double act masquerading as a single one. The
'pact handshake' and the 'greeting handshake' have different
origins and different functions, but because they have come to
have the same form, we think of them both simply as the
'friendly handshake'. Hence all the confusion. Up to early
Victorian times there was no problem. Then there was the
pact handshake for males with males which said 'it's a deal',
and the hand-kiss for males with females which said 'it's an
honour to meet you'. But when the Victorians increasingly

began to mix business with social life, the two became blended and muddled together. The vigorous pact handshake became softened and weakened, while the gentle clasping of the lady's hand in the already abbreviated hand-kiss became strengthened.

Although we accept this happily enough today, there was some resistance to it in nineteenth-century France, where the greeting shake was referred to as 'the American handshake', and frowned upon when it was done between visiting males and unmarried French girls. The reason for this was not so much the body contact involved, but simply that the French were still interpreting the handshake in its old masculine role. The visiting males were then seen to be 'making a pact' and establishing a bond of friendship with young girls they had only just met, which was considered highly improper. The foreign visitors, of course, thought that they were doing no more than offering a polite salutation.

This brings us back to the misunderstandings and confusions of the etiquette books. The big problem is who offers the hand to whom. Is it an insult to fail to offer the hand first and therefore to appear to be unfriendly, or to offer it first and therefore to appear to be demanding a modified hand-kiss? Careful observation of social occasions reveals that the confused greeters tend to solve the problem by watching for tiny clues. They look for the slightest sign of an intention movement of raising the arm on the part of the other person, and then try to make the contact appear to be simultaneous. Contributing to their confusion is the fact that with most other salutations the subordinate acts first to show his respect. The private salutes the officer before the officer salutes the private. In earlier days, it was always the junior who bowed first to the senior. But with kissing the hand it was different. The lady had to offer her hand first. No respectful male would grab it first without waiting for a sign from her. Because the hand-kiss is involved in the origin of handshake greetings, this rule still applies in most cases. The man waits for the woman to offer her hand for shaking, as if she were still offering it to be kissed. However, not to offer the hand to her first, now that the kissing has vanished from the act, is tantamount to saying that he is the officer and she the private, and that she must make the first sign of salute. Hence all the warnings and mumblings of the etiquette experts.

The other origin of the handshake, concerning the making of pacts, further confuses the situation. The weaker male usually offers his hand first here, to show his eagerness to the stronger one. In a contest, it is usually the weaker loser who offers his hand to the stronger winner in the act of congratulation, to show that, despite his defeat, the bond of friendship is reconfirmed. So, for an eager young business man to greet a senior colleague with an outstretched hand may be looked upon either as brashness ('you may kiss my hand'), or as humility ('you are the winner'). Again, as with the social occasions, the problem is usually solved by watching for small intention clues and trying to contrive a simultaneous act.

Given its complicated past and its confused present, one might expect to see the handshake on the decline in the increasingly informal world of today, and in certain contexts this appears to be the case. Social greetings are becoming increasingly verbal. Around the middle of the present century, the etiquette experts announced that 'Handshaking on introductions between men is nowadays on the wane in Great Britain.' Despite this, it is still much more common for a male/male shake to occur, rather than a male/female shake or a female/female shake. My observations suggest that two-thirds of all handshaking is done between males; in the remaining third, shaking between the sexes is three times as common as between females. These figures fit well with the history of the action, for men have inherited the handshake as a pact device and then added to it the greeting function, giving the all-male pattern double value, so to speak. Women with men have inherited it from the hand-kiss, but have not yet taken an equal role in business, so are poor on pact handshakes. And women with women never did hand-kiss, so are poor on both, and come at the bottom of the hand-shaking league.

A final point about this particular form of body contact, which may seem obvious but is significant nevertheless, is that lovers do not do it. Nor, in most countries, do married couples. Ask an Englishman who has been married for, say, twelve years when he last greeted his wife by shaking hands with her, and the answer is more likely to be twelve years than twelve days. This is, without any doubt, the least amorous of all friendly body contacts. In all the other cases mentioned in this chapter, from the full embrace to the kiss, there has always been a strong sexual element. They have all originated from the same primary source and they have all been performed more between lovers and mates than between adults in any other roles. When performed between males there have, in most cases, been special circumstances which make this possible. The handshake, by contrast, stemming originally not from a tender embrace but from a masculine act of pact-making, has avoided these difficulties. Even the later involvement of the hand-kiss in its history has not created any problems, because this was already a formalized, de-sexed kiss of reverence before it became incorporated. Strong men have therefore been able to shake one another's hands until they are blue in the palms without running the slightest risk of creating an amorous impression. The very act of shaking the clasped hands up and down in mid-air that typifies the action helps to make it more brusque and less gentle, and distinguishes it clearly, even at a distance, from the lovers' act of holding hands.

In this chapter we have looked at the way adults behave towards one another in public and we have seen how the all-enveloping, uninhibited intimacies of infancy have become restricted, pigeon-holed and labelled. It can be argued that this has taken place because adults need greater independence of action and greater mobility than infants, and that more extensive body contacts would limit them in this respect. That would explain the reduction in the amount of time actually spent touching, but not the reduction of the intimacy of the touches that do still occur. It can be argued that it has taken place because adults do not need so much body contact; but if that is so, then why do they spend so much of their time indulging in second-hand intimacy in books, films, plays and television, and why is it that popular songs cry out the message hour after hour? It can be argued that our untouchability has to do with status, with not wishing to be touched by our inferiors and not daring to touch our superiors; but if this is so, then why are we not more intimate with our equals? It can be argued that we do not wish to have our intimate actions confused with those of lovers; but how does this explain the fact that lovers themselves, in public, restrict their intimacies so much more than they do in private?

All these arguments give partial answers, but there is something missing. This hidden factor seems to be the powerful bonding effect that close body intimacies have on those who perform them. We cannot be close physically without becoming 'close' emotionally. In our busy modern lives, we hold back from such involvements, even though we may need them. Our relationships are too profuse, too vague, too complex, and often too insincere for us to be able to risk the primitive bonding processes of body intimacy. In the ruthless world of business, we can dismiss a girl with whom we have only shaken hands, or we can betray a colleague with whom we have done no more than rest a hand on a shoulder; but what if the body contacts had been greater? What if, without any sexual involvement, we had experienced greater intimacies with them? Then, without a doubt, we would have seen our tough determination soften, and our competitiveness dwindle, when the moments for brutal decisions came. And if we dare not expose ourselves to these dangers, to these powerful reciprocal involvements that know no logic, then we certainly do not want to be reminded of them by seeing them flaunted in public by others. So the young lovers can keep to themselves and do it in private, and in case they ignore our request we will make it law. We will make it a crime to be intimate in public. And so it is that, even to this day, in certain sophisticated, civilized countries it remains a crime to kiss in public. A tender act of touching becomes immoral and illegal. A gentle intimacy becomes legally equated with an act of theft. So hide it away quickly, lest the rest of us see what we are missing!

It has sometimes been said that if only all the tight-lipped defenders of public morals would embrace one another lovingly, caress one another's faces, and kiss one another's cheeks, they might suddenly feel it was time to go home and leave the rest of society to go about its friendly, loving business without having to endure their desperate envy. But it is pointless to despise them, for society stitches its own strait-jacket. The teeming zoo in which we live is not the ideal setting for public intimacies. It suffers from people pollution; we bump into one another and apologize, when we should be reaching out to touch; we collide headlong and curse, when we should be embracing and laughing. There are strangers everywhere and so we hold ourselves back. There seems to be no alternative. Our only compensation is to indulge more heavily in private intimacies, but this we frequently fail to do. It seems as if our public restraint can spread to infect our conduct even in the bosom of our families. For many, the solution is to indulge in second-hand intimacies by spending the evening hours avidly watching the abandoned touchings and embracings of the professionals on our television or cinema screens, listening to endless words of love in our popular songs, or reading them in our novels and magazines. For some, there are other, more heavily disguised alternatives, as we shall see on the pages that follow.

5

SPECIALIZED INTIMACY

By studying the behaviour of infants and lovers, it becomes clear that the degree of physical intimacy that exists between two human animals relates to the degree of trust between them. The crowded conditions of modern life surround us with strangers whom we do not trust, at least not fully, and we go to great pains to keep our distance from them. The intricate avoidance patterns of any busy street bear witness to this. But the frenzy of urban living creates stress, and stress breeds anxiety and feelings of insecurity. Intimacy calms these feelings, and so, paradoxically, the more we are forced to keep apart, the more we need to make body contact. If our loved ones are loving enough, then the supply of intimacy they offer will suffice, and we can go out to face the world at arm's length. But supposing they are not; supposing we have failed as adults to form close bonds with either friends or lovers, and have no children; what do we do then? Or supposing we have formed these bonds successfully, but then they have broken down, or become fossilized into the remoteness of indifference, with the 'loving' embrace and kiss becoming as formalized as a public handshake; what then? The answer for many is simply to grouse and bear it, but there *are* solutions, and one of these is the device of employing professional touchers, a measure which helps to some extent to compensate for the shortcomings of the amateur and amatory touchers who are failing to supply us with our much-needed quota of body intimacy.

Who are these professional touchers? The answer is that they are virtually any strangers or semi-strangers who, under the pretext of providing us with some specialist service, are required to touch our bodies. This pretext is necessary because, of course, we do not like to admit that we are insecure and need the comforting touch of another human body. That would be 'soft', immature, regressive; it would assail our image of ourselves as self-controlled, independent adults. And so we must get our dose of intimacy in some disguised form.

One of the most popular and widespread methods is being ill. Nothing serious, of course, merely some mild sickness that will stimulate in others the urge to perform comforting acts in intimacy. The majority of people imagine that when they fall prey to some minor ailment, they have simply been unlucky in accidentally encountering a hostile virus, bacterium, or some other form of parasite. If they come down with a nasty bout of influenza, for instance, they feel it could have happened to anyone — anyone who, like them, has been shopping in busy stores, standing on tightly packed buses, or jamming themselves into stuffy corners at overcrowded parties, where coughs and sneezes can be heard incessantly wafting their eager pathogens through the air. The facts, however, do not support this view. Even at the height of a flu epidemic, there are still many people — equally exposed to the infection — who do not succumb. How is it that *they* manage to avoid taking to their sick-beds? How, in particular, does the medical profession manage to remain so remarkably healthy? They, more than anyone, are massively exposed to infection all day and every day, but they do not seem to become proportionally sick.

Minor ailments, therefore, do not appear to be entirely a matter of unlucky accident. In a modern city there are hostile microbes everywhere. Almost every day, and in almost every place we walk and breathe, we are exposed to sufficient of them to bring us down with some sort of infection. If we defeat them, it is not so much that we manage to avoid them, as that our bodies are equipped with a highly efficient defence system which slaughters them by the million, week in and week out. If we succumb, it is not so much that we have been accidently exposed to them, as that we have, for some reason, lowered our body defences. One way we do this (apart from excessive hygiene!) is to let ourselves become overstressed and overstrained by the pressures of urban life. In our weakened condition, we soon fall prey to one or other of the wide selection of unfriendly microbes that fill the world around us. Luckily for us, the disease is its own cure, for, in putting us to bed, it provides us with the very comfort we were lacking before. We might call this the 'instant-baby' syndrome.

The man who is feeling 'poorly' begins to look weak and helpless and starts to transmit powerful pseudo-infantile signals to his wife. She responds automatically as an 'instant-parent' and begins to mother him, insisting on tucking him up in his bed (cot) and bringing him soup, hot drinks and medicine (baby food). Her tone of voice becomes softer (the maternal coo) and she fusses over him, feeling his forehead and performing other intimacies of a kind that were missing before, when he was fit and well but equally in need of them. The curative effect of this comfort behaviour works wonders and he is soon back in action again, facing the hostile world outside.

This description does not imply malingering. It is essential for the patient to be truly and visibly sick in order to stimulate fully the necessary pseudo-parental care. This accounts for the high frequency of strongly debilitating, but comparatively pain-free, minor ailments in cases of emotionally induced illness. It is important, not only to be sick, but to be seen to be sick.

To some, these comments will seem cynical, but that is not my intention. If the stress of life demands that we shall obtain increased comfort and intimacy from our closest companions, and forces us once again to sink into the warm embrace of the soft bedding of our 'cots', then this is a valuable social mechanism and must not be sneered at.

It is, indeed, so useful a device that it has come to support a major industry. Despite all the impressive technological advances of modern medicine and our so-called conquest of the environment, we still get sick at an astonishingly high rate. The majority of the victims do not see the inside of a hospital ward. They may be out-patients, pharmacy clients, or merely self-treating in the home. They suffer from a great variety of common ailments such as coughs, colds, influenza, headaches, allergies, backaches, tonsillitis, laryngitis, stomach-aches, ulcers, diarrhoea, skin rashes, and the like. The fashions change from generation to generation — once it was 'the vapours', now it is 'a virus' — but basically the list remains much the same. In terms of simple frequency of occurrence, these cases account for the vast majority of present-day illnesses.

In Britain, for example, over 500 million pharmaceutical purchases are made every year to treat minor illnesses, which works out at roughly ten ailments per year, per head of the population. Some 100 million pounds is spent annually on these products. Over two-thirds of all illnesses are not serious enough to involve the services of a doctor.

The reason for this situation is simple enough. All the time, our populations are increasing in size and our communities becoming more and more overcrowded and overstressed. The larger numbers of people involved means that there is more and more money available for medical research, which finds better and better cures. In the meantime, however, the populations have grown again, the social stresses have become greater and the susceptibility to disease has increased. There-fore more medical research is needed, and so on, neck and neck, into an imaginary, disease-free future that will never come.

But suppose for a moment that I am being pessimistic; suppose that some medical miracle has eventually appeared on the scene and defeated and exterminated all the parasites. Will we then finally have arrived at a condition where the downtrodden, emotionally bruised urbanite can no longer collapse with impunity into the comforting arms of his sick-bed? The chances are more than remote that this miracle will ever happen, but even if it did there are still several alternatives open to the would-be 'instant-baby'. These are already in frequent use. In the absence of suitable viruses or bacteria, he can always have a 'nervous breakdown'. Minor mental illnesses have the advantage that they can operate in the absence of acquired microbes, and they are equally effective as comfort-producers. Indeed, they are so effective that even a murderer can plead 'temporary insanity' as an excuse for his actions and have his sentence modified on the grounds of 'diminished responsibility'—again being treated as if he were a 'temporary infant'. Pleading that he was suffering from a cold in the head at the time of the murder would provide less comfort to him, so there is clearly a lot to be said for the power of mental breakdown as a survival device when stress becomes extreme. The main disadvantage here is that many of the milder versions of mental illness are lacking in the external symptoms necessary to provoke the much-needed comforting reactions. The emotionally bruised individual is driven to extremes to produce the required response. Internal agonizing is not enough, but after a good bout of screaming hysterics, his collapsed body stands a very high chance of feeling itself snugly enveloped in the embracing arms of an earnest comforter. If the breakdown is more violent, he may instead find himself encased in forcibly restraining arms, but even then all is not lost, for he will have succeeded, albeit in a desperate way, in making some kind of intimate body contact with another human being. Only if he loses control completely will he fail and find himself condemned to the solitary self-embrace imposed by the canvas sleeves of a strait-jacket.

A second alternative in the absence of foreign parasites is

the use of the patient's own endogenous microbes, the ones that he has been carrying on his body all his life. To explain how this works, we must take a close look, in fact a microscopic look, at the surfaces of our bodies.

Many people seem to imagine that *all* microbes are nasty and that they automatically mean disease or dirt, but this is not true. As any bacteriologist will testify, this is nothing more than the modern myth of the new hygiene religion, the religion whose aerosol prayers keep its worshippers 'free from all known germs', whose holy water is antiseptic solution, and whose god is totally sterile. Of course, there *are* vicious, deadly germs that we do well to destroy as ruthlessly as possible. There is no denying that. But what about the 'germs' whose main activity in life is killing off other germs? Do we really want to kill all known germs?

The fact is that we are each of us protected by a vast army of friendly microbes that do not hinder us but, on the contrary, actively help us to keep healthy. On our healthy, clean skin there is an average of five million of them to every square centimetre. Ordinary saliva, spat from the mouth, contains between ten million and 1,000 million bacteria in every cubic centimetre. Every time we defecate we lose 100,000 million microbes, but their numbers are soon made up again inside the body. This is the normal condition of the adult human animal. If we managed to live 'germ-free' of our own microbes all our lives, we would be at a grave disadvantage. Amongst other things, we would be less resistant to the foreign, and really vicious, microbes that we would encounter from time to time. We know this from careful experiments with germ-free laboratory animals. Our natural load of body microbes is therefore of great value to us, but now comes the catch. We have to pay a price for their good services, for even they can get out of hand when we become unduly stressed. Some of our diseases are caused, not by acquiring infections from others, but by a sudden eruption and 'overcrowding' of our own 'normal' microbes. The usual measures of public hygiene that assist in cutting down cross-infection from one person to another cannot help in such cases: we do not 'catch' the diseases; we carry the makings of them ourselves all the time. This is particularly true of many of the alimentary upsets so common in the emotionally stressed patient. If we have 'stomach trouble' we put it down to 'something bad' that we ate, but it is amazing what a healthy, happy person can devour and get away with. Probably nearly all the mild stomach and intestinal upsets we suffer from are due instead to emotional disturbances resulting from failures to adjust to the stresses and strains of modern living. To remind ourselves of this we have only to watch a natural history film of a flock of healthy vultures on the plains of Africa, gobbling down the putrid flesh of a decaying carcass, an event which is more likely to turn our own stomachs, rather than those of the birds concerned.

A third alternative for the human individual in need of comfort is a more drastic one. Failing mental illness or endogenous illness, he can, with a little agitated carelessness, become dramatically accident-prone. If he trips over and breaks an ankle, he will soon be able to curse that he is 'as helpless as a baby', and in no time at all find himself helped and supported just like one. But surely accidents are accidental? Of course they can be, but nevertheless it is surprising how much people vary in their susceptibility to 'accidental' injuries. In a recent hospital investigation into the emotional backgrounds of disease patients, a number of accident patients were used as a control group, because it was assumed that they must be in their hospital beds 'by accident', in both senses of the word. Results showed that this was far from being the case, the accident victims proving to be, if anything, more emotionally disturbed than the disease patients.

Our stressed urban comfort-seeker, therefore, has several ways in which he can become suitably helpless and promote calming intimacies from those who attend him. There is a considerable advantage in being mildly ill from time to time, and if the advantage cannot be gained in one way, there is always another open. This method of increasing adult intimacies does, however, have its drawbacks. In all cases it involves the sick individual in the adoption of a submissive role. To obtain the comforting attention that his ailment provokes, he is forced to become genuinely inferior, either physically or mentally, to his comforters. This was not so with the young lovers, who went 'soft' on a reciprocal basis that did not lower their social status. Furthermore, the patient's comfort-bath soon grows cold when he regains his health and strength, and the tender intimacies of those who have been caring for him cease abruptly. The reward was temporary, and the only way to prolong it is to become a chronic invalid who, as the saying goes, 'enjoys bad health'. Apart from prolonging the inferior status, this also introduces a new danger, that of ailment escalation. The comforting fire that has been lit may get out of control and burn down the house. Even when used as a short-term measure, there is always the risk of long-term damage to the organism, as ulcer-sufferers know to their cost. But for many who find the tensions of modern living hard to bear, the risk is worth it. Temporary respite is better than no respite. If they are lucky, it gives them time to recharge their emotional batteries, and in so doing it can be said, in biological terms, to have considerable survival value in today's crowded human communities.

Although much of the comfort obtained in this way is provided by the close companions of the patient, whose intimacy quotient becomes dramatically increased in most cases, the phenomenon of 'going sick' also provides the additional reward of obtaining the intimate attentions of a group of people who are comparative strangers—the members of the medical profession. Doctors are 'licensed to touch', and to do so with a degree of intimacy forbidden between most adults. Intuitively aware of this important element in their work, they know well the curative value of the 'bedside manner'. The reassurance of the softly spoken word, the confident touch of the hand that takes the pulse, or taps the chest, or turns the head to examine eyes and mouth, these are the body-contact actions that, for some, are better than a hundred pills.

Sometimes a doctor will order the removal of a patient to a hospital bed on emotional grounds alone. For an individual whose source of stress lies solely in the outside world, such a move is unnecessary. By staying at home and taking to his bed, he escapes the tension that is damaging him. But if the tension lies in the home itself, there is no such escape. If the emotional pressures are coming from inside the family unit, then even his bedroom may not provide the necessary hiding-place, where he can curl up and find the comfort he needs so badly. Then the only solution is the hospital cot, and pray God for short visiting hours.

The medical solution for the adult intimacy-seeker is, as we have seen, a mixed blessing, and he would clearly do better to look elsewhere. If he is religious, he can perhaps enjoy an unmixed blessing from the hands of a priest, but, failing that, there are several other soothing contacts he can enjoy.

There is the whole lush world of body conditioning and beautifying to indulge in, where an army of professional touchers is waiting to rub, slap, stroke, smooth and pluck almost any part of your body you wish to indicate. This is like a kind of 'healthy medicine', the unpleasant stigma of sickness being replaced by a mood that is predominantly athletic or cosmetic. Or so it seems; but once again there is a powerful element of body-contact-for-contact's-sake underlying all these activities. To be massaged from head to toe by a young masseuse is, for a man, almost as intimate a procedure as if he were to make love to her. In some ways it is more so, since by the time she has finished she will have made active body contact with nearly every part of his body, applying to each section of it in turn a rich variety of pressures, touches and tactile rhythms. Herein, we might dare to say, lies the rub, for the interaction, although it involves no direct sexual contact, is far too close for some men's comfort.

Perhaps it would be more correct to say that it is too close for the comfort of Western society. Privately, the massaged body would no doubt enjoy itself greatly, but the public image of the massage parlour is, in our culture, not what it might be. One trend has been to reduce the imagined eroticism of the activity by introducing sexual segregation, so that men massage men and women massage women. Even this step has failed to give this intrinsically harmless form of soothing body contact a widespread acceptance in modern society. In removing the heterosexual contact, the way was inevitably paved for dark murmurings about the homosexual element. Only intensely athletic males can, with ease, overcome this slur. For the boxer or the wrestler there is no problem. Like the triumphant foot-ballers who could embrace passionately in public without criticism, because of their obviously aggressive, masculine role, the prize-fighter can luxuriate on his massage table without any adverse comment. In theory, the rest of the adult popula-tion could follow his lead and do so without the slightest sexual involvement, regardless of the sexes involved, but in practice this plainly has not happened, and so, for the unmassaged majority, we must look elsewhere for adult body intimacies.

One way in which the problem has been solved is to multiply the numbers involved and to eliminate the atmosphere of an intimate 'pair'. This is done in many gymnasiums and health farms, where groups of people gather to indulge in a variety of exercises which may include a great variety of body contacts without creating the flavour of two 'consenting adults in private'. Another method is to replace the human masseur or masseuse with a strictly sexless machine that embraces them, not with loving arms, but with an impersonal canvas belt which then proceeds to be mechanically intimate with them.

A more commonly employed solution is to restrict the body contacts to the less private parts of the human body. Here we move into the totally acceptable world of hairdressers and beauty experts, pausing only to cast a last sympathetic glance at the massage world, where some practitioners have attempted a similar restriction by coyly advertising that they provide only 'arm and leg massage'.

Since, in Western society, we all expose our heads to one another's public gaze, the hairdresser is automatically excused the stigma of increased nudity during the course of his professional body contacts. What he or she handles, we all see. Nevertheless, touching the head, as we saw in an earlier chapter, is normally reserved for only the closest of intimates and particularly characterizes the amorous contacts of young lovers. Between adult strangers it is almost taboo, and so the hairdresser, in the guise of a cosmetician, can fill an important gap for a contact-starved adult. This does not mean that the cosmetic role is unimportant, but merely that there is more to hairdressing than meets the mirror's eye.

Head-grooming, in the dual cosmetic/intimate role, has been with us for thousands of years. If we care to include our primate ancestors, we can safely put the figure at millions of years. The detailed and tender fingering that can be seen in any zoo monkey-house, as one monkey or ape works lovingly over the head-hair of its companion, leaves little doubt about the intimacy factor involved. Cleansing alone cannot account for the relaxed ecstasy of the primate groomee. And so it is with us, except that we, of course, cannot extend the interaction over our whole bodies like the furry monkey or ape. Where we cover our naked skins with clothing, we must rely on the deft, delicate touch of the tailor's fingers as he adjusts our new garments, to rekindle—faintly, very faintly—the long-lost sensation of intimate body-grooming.

For the monkey, hair-grooming by another is an act of social bonding, so it is not surprising to find that in earlier periods of our history the professional hairdresser was a rarity. Hair was groomed by close intimates, rather than by comparative strangers. In the days when we lived in small tribes this was, of course, inevitable, since everyone in the social group knew everyone else on a personal basis. Later, when the urban revolution came and we found ourselves increasingly surrounded by strangers, the tendency was to restrict hair-dressing and its associated activities to interactions between close personal contacts. Much later, with the increasingly complex coiffure that appeared after the Middle Ages, more expert attention was needed by the high-ranking members of society, and the professional hairdresser began to make his mark. At first, where ladies were concerned, his intimate operations were confined to the privacy of his clients' homes, but, gradually, more efficient public salons were opened and ladies of fashion began to flock to their doors. Even so, it was not until the second half of the last century that this became a common practice. Then the rush was on. In 1851 there were already 2,338 hairdressers operating in London, but fifty years later, in 1901, this figure had shot up to no less than 7,771, a dramatic rise that far outstripped the general increase in the city's population. Part of the reason for this change was undoubtedly economic, but perhaps, too, there was another factor, for the Victorian female was severely restricted in the other ways in which she could make adult body contacts. The rules of conduct were so tightened during this period that the caress of the hairdresser's hands must have provided a welcome intimacy in an era of such rigid restraint. Not only did more and more women venture forth, but they did so with increasing frequency. In the present century the pattern has spread out from the great cities and down to the smallest towns, involving almost the entire female population.

Aware that their modern clients craved more intimacy than the mere dressing of the hair could offer, this new army of professional touchers expanded the nature of their activities. Wherever there was exposed skin, they applied their delicate attentions. Manicures became popular. The 'facial' appeared on the scene. Mud-packs were applied, wrinkles smoothed and caressed, soft skin 'toned-up', the latest style of make-up demonstrated by a professional hand. 'Beauty', cried *Vogue* in 1923, 'is a full-time job.' There is no denying that the primary motive was visual, but the increased tactile intimacies involved in obtaining the desired visual effect were also undoubtedly of great importance. To visit a modern beauty parlour is nothing if not a touching experience.

By comparison, the modern male is poorly supplied with intimacies of this kind. Some men indulge in manicure and scalp massage, and a few still have their faces shaved occasionally, but for most the visit to the barber's is a quick snip-snip and home again to wash the hair themselves. It is interesting that the barber does his best to increase the intimacy of this simple snipping by employing a ritual device. If you are a male, the next time you visit your barber, listen to the snipping sound of his scissors and you will find that for every hair-snip there are a number of 'air-snips', the scissors snapping together rapidly in mid-air before closing in for the next actual cut. There is no mechanical function to these air-snips, but they create the impression of great activity in the proximity of the scalp and thereby effectively increase the impression of 'contact-complexity'.

For all that, the intimacy involved is a remarkably limited one, and it is surprising that today's males should accept such restrictions. Perhaps with the return of longer male hair-styles we shall witness some changes. So far, it must be admitted, there is little sign of any general increase, rather the reverse. If anything, long male hair now means that there is a rapid decline even in the simple snip-snip, with the hair-washing still done largely in the home. Only in the more sophisticated urban centres is there any indication that the new hair-styles are leading to greater barbering activities, and it remains to be seen whether this development will spread. But the fashion is new and, if it survives, it will take some time for it to regain the widespread respectability it once had. There is an unjustified stigma of 'effeminacy' attached to it by the older males in the population, who have still not woken up to the fact that their close-cropped styles arose primarily as anti-louse devices and that to insist on all males retaining such styles in a post-lousy era is the height of irrationality. As long as this slur persists, there will be a reluctance on the part of many of the younger males to continue their trend to its logical conclusion and once again luxuriate in more elaborate tonsorial intimacies.

Just about the only 'cosmetic' intimacy that the modern male enjoys more than the female is the use of a public shoe-shine and, as a trade, even that has been losing ground of late. In most big cities now it has become little more than a curiosity, found only at one or two special points. Apart from the oral-genital contacts discussed earlier, this is probably the only time in a modern man's life when he will see other human beings going on their knees before him to perform an act of body contact, and it is certainly the only time it will happen in public. (The shoe-shop attendant avoids the posture by sitting and leaning forward.) The kneeling posture of the shoe-shine creates such a striking impression of servility that this feature has perhaps been his undoing. In the past, a man could more easily accept a display of humility of this kind, so that the humble intimacy performed was doubly rewarding, but with a growing respect for human equality such an overt submissive-ness becomes almost embarrassing. A symbolic kissing of our feet is too much for us, and the shoe-shine is fast becoming a vanishing breed. It is not that we have ceased to be responsive to humiliating services – that would be too congratulatory a thought – but rather that we no longer wish to be *seen* to be so responsive to them.

In this survey of professional touchers, we have so far covered the doctor, the nurse, the masseur, the gymnastics and health-and-beauty instructors, the hairdresser, the tailor, the mani-curist, the beautician, the make-up specialist, the barber, the shoe-shine and the shoe-shop attendant. To this list we could add many other related occupations such as those of the wig-maker, the hatter, the chiropodist, the dentist, the surgeon, the gynaecologist and a whole variety of medical and semi-medical specialists. Of these, few warrant special comment. The dentist usually causes too much stress for his oral intimacies to provide any contact reward. The surgeon, whose body intimacies go so very much deeper than those of even the most passionate lover, also has little impact on us emotionally, thanks to the use of anaesthetics.

The actions that must take place during a gynaecologist's examination of a patient are so similar, at a descriptive level, to the hand-to-genital contacts of a lover that here, too, paradoxically, there is no comfort in the intimacy. Embarrassment is reduced today by an intensely professional atmosphere, with both sides strictly on their guard against any misinterpretation of the anatomically sexual contact. Whereas holding a woman patient's hand while taking her pulse may provide the secondary benefits of soothing bodily intimacy, touching her genitals is inevitably *so* intimate that the emotional barriers clamp down immediately and no such benefits are possible.

In the past, the special nature of genital examinations has caused endless trouble for well-meaning gynaecologists. Extraordinary anti-intimacy procedures have been insisted on. Three hundred years ago he was even, on occasion, required to crawl into the pregnant woman's bedroom on his hands and knees to perform the examination, so that she would be unable to see the owner of the fingers which were to touch her so privately. At a later date, he was forced to work in a darkened room, or to deliver a baby by groping beneath the bedclothes. A seventeenth-century etching shows him sitting at the foot of the labour bed with the sheet tucked into his collar like a napkin, so that he is unable to see what his hands are doing, an anti-intimacy device that made cutting the umbilical cord a particularly hazardous operation.

Despite these bizarre precautions, the male midwife was for ever under fire, and just over two hundred years ago a learned textbook on the theory and practice of midwifery was openly condemned as 'the most bawdy, indecent and shameful book which the press ever brought into the world'. Needless to say, it was usually the men who complained and always the women who suffered. For centuries the sexual nature of the intimacies involved in assisting at the birth of a child stood in

the way of efficient medical attention. Usually, properly qualified men were banished altogether from the labour bed, and the
duties were performed by unskilled and often highly super-
stitious female midwives. (The word 'midwife' means simply
'with-the-wife', and makes no reference to the sex of the person
concerned, although today we automatically think of it as
indicating a woman, a fact that reflects this early ban on men.)
As a result of this, an enormous number of women died in
childbirth and many thousands of children succumbed at birth
or in the first month of life. A large number of these cases were
due entirely to the anti-intimacy rules that prevented skilled
aid from being provided.

Here, then, is an instance of the sexual taboos on bodily
contact creating a major social disaster and influencing the
whole course of history. Year after year was to pass, and
countless human miseries were to be heaped one on top of the
other, before sanity prevailed and science was able to sweep
away the ancient prejudices. Only by obeying the strictest
possible code of conduct has the profession gradually been
able to eliminate these early stupidities. Even so, the echoes of
ancient fears can still be felt, and the modern gynaecological
examination remains comfortless in the sphere of bodily
contact.

There is only one area of social activity where sexual contacts do not suffer in this way, and that is the theatrical profession. Actors and actresses, including ballet dancers, opera
singers and photographic models, all enjoy a professional life
where they are widely licensed to touch one another in a sexual
manner. In their performances they kiss and fondle, embrace
and stroke, as the director demands. If it is in the script, it is
within the social 'law', and the actor or actress can, during his
or her working day, enjoy many bodily-contact comforts. For
such an insecure profession this is undoubtedly a major benefit,
although the extremes sometimes demanded can lead to
difficulties. It is hard to pretend to make love to someone, even
a professional colleague, time and time again, without the basic

emotional reactions beginning to creep into the relationship, and this often happens, to the detriment of other intimate relationships in the 'real' world outside. If sexual intimacies are mimicked well enough, it is not easy to suppress the true biological responses which normally accompany them.

Another hazardous contact reward for the stars who dazzle us in the entertainment world is the physical acclaim of their more ardent followers. In public places they may find themselves hemmed in by eager fans, desperate to touch their idols. At a mild level this can provide a pleasant emotional reward, but occasionally it can lead to bruises and even injury. The powerful urge to touch the bodies of certain star musicians and singers—and even some of the more glamorous politicians—has recently reached staggering proportions. For the groupie girls who follow the more famous pop stars, there are literally no holds barred. Perhaps the most intimate example is that of the 'plaster-casters', groupies who persuade their pop idols to permit them to take plaster casts of their erect genitals, so that these effigies can be touched later at leisure, after their gods have departed.

In dealing with these interactions between pop stars and their fans, we have moved away from the situation in which touching is an inherent part of the professional activity itself. A masseur or a hairdresser *has* to touch his client or he cannot perform his task, but a singer does not have to touch or be touched in order to perform his songs. The fact that his special role in society makes him more touch-worthy is a secondary factor. A similar condition applies in other spheres, an obvious example being the police.

It is not the policeman's job to touch people, but he is nevertheless licensed to do so with much greater freedom than the rest of us. He can lay hands on us in a way we would resent in a member of the general public. He can take a child's hand in the street without causing comment. In a crowd he can push against us to keep us back, and we accept his contact role with equal ease. If he manhandles us when we are violent, again we are less likely to lash out wildly at him than we are at someone else who treats us in a similar manner. Only at the extremes of violence, where his own restraint breaks down and he begins to behave, under intense provocation, like a uniformed thug, do we fully disinhibit our reactions to him. Then, by contrast, our fury knows no bounds, as recent riot-scenes have testified all too often. It is as if, having given him a limited licence to touch us, we find abuse of that licence particularly unacceptable, as when a choir-master behaves improperly with a choirboy, or a schoolmaster with a pupil. The result is that, if driven to repeated breakdown in restraint, the police rapidly become dubbed as hated men and violently persecuted whenever angry crowds gather. Only in countries such as Great Britain, where the police are deliberately sent out into the streets completely unarmed, have there been any signs at all of slight restraints being applied on both sides during the worst civil rioting of recent years. It is as if the fact that both sides are forced to indulge in the greater body intimacy of hand-to-hand grappling, rather than the remoter savageries of overhead club- and stick-beating, or the totally remote brutalities of firearms, has some kind of restraining influence on the hostilities. There is nothing inherently less vicious about such encounters; even without weapons, eyes can be gouged out and genitals kicked in, but such cruelties are extremely rare. When compared with the cracked and bleeding skulls of other riot-scenes, the hand-to-hand battles of London and other British cities begin to look almost civilized, and it is ironic that they do so by returning to the more intimate forms of pre-civilized, pre-weapon combat.

There is a well-known film-sequence cliché in which two tough and otherwise admirable men set about one another with their fists to settle some long-standing quarrel. A sophisticated movie audience knows full well that, if the two men both begin to lose, each beating the other into total physical exhaustion, they are about to witness the birth of a great new friendship. As the two bruised hulks sprawl weakly on the ground, sure enough, one pair of cracked and bleeding lips spits out a loose tooth, and grins admiringly at his equally beaten opponent. In no time at all, our heroes are helping one another up and crawling to the bar (there is usually one nearby) to share a reviving drink. After this we can be sure that nothing will ever separate them again, and that they will become indomitable partners in righting all wrongs, until, at the end of the film, one of them will die bravely saving the life of the other, breathing his last gasp cradled in the loving arms of the man whose face he once succeeded in beating to a pulp.

The moral of this highly coloured story is, of course, that a warm enemy is better than a cold friend, and it bears some investigation in terms of the body intimacies involved. It is almost as if any form of intimacy, even violent intimacy, providing it is performed on a sufficiently personal basis, can produce a bond of attachment between two antagonists. Needless to say, it is dangerous to generalize, and it can certainly not be offered as a general excuse for violence, but to ignore the phenomenon completely because it frightens us is equally unwise.

The difficulty is that impersonal violence has in recent times reached such a horrific scale that an almost total taboo has descended on the subject. For the sexually permissive society, violence, all violence, regardless of scale or context, has become the new philosophical restriction. In the broad context in which it is intended, the creed that we should 'make love not war' is unassailable, but the message underlying the ritualized film fight may perhaps lead us to consider a possible exception to this general rule. Clearly I am not thinking of anything as savage as the brawl I described above. I am imagining instead a situation in which certain people have so suppressed their aggressiveness that, even under intense provocation, they will 'not so much as lay a finger on' their partners' bodies. To take non-violence to such an extreme in every instance can create a new form of anti-intimacy. Let me give an example.

If, unavoidably, two individuals have grown cold towards

one another, for whatever reason, the relationship can finally freeze to death in an atmosphere of hypocritical restraint. The thin hard smile of inhibited anger can cut sharp as any knife. Sometimes, under such conditions, an explosion into a flaming row, accompanied with mild but nevertheless aggressive inter- action, can clear the air like a long-awaited thunderstorm, and release the damaging tension. Perhaps for the first time in months, a bickering couple actually take one another in their arms and, even though it is to shake the partner violently by the shoulders rather than to embrace lovingly, the result is the feel of the first truly meant body contact in ages. It is, of course, a desperate situation to have arrived at, when to touch at all means to touch in this hostile way, and it may very well fail. But just occasionally it may succeed, and to ignore this fact because it is out of step with the current cultural mood is to disregard another facet of the powerful emotional impact that body intimacy can have on the bonds of attachment between two human beings.

A related pattern of behaviour is the rough-and-tumble play of children, or the 'horse-play' or 'rough-housing' that can sometimes be observed between friendly adults. Again, the body contacts involved make their emotional impact, and they do so because they are accompanied by the unspoken message, 'Even though I am being aggressive, you can see that I am not *really* aggressive.' The message is a subtle one, however, and play-fighting at any age can become a delicately balanced interaction. The man who playfully slaps a companion on the back can easily reverse the signal, so that it becomes, 'Even though I am pretending to be only playfully aggressive, you can tell by the way I am doing it that I am not.' He uses the slap because it has become formalized as an accepted play-fighting pattern, but by his accompanying actions and by the hardness of the slap it becomes instantly apparent to his com- panion that he has twisted the message back to front.

A similar complexity exists in the case of the bickering couple mentioned above. If, under extreme provocation, the action is no more than a mild slap on the cheek, or the shaking of the partner's shoulders, then the message reads, 'Although you have made me want to kick your teeth in, this is all I am doing to you.' But if the provocation is less than extreme, then even the most moderate of aggressive contacts transmits a signal that is merely surly and unpleasant.

The subtle dangers of play-fighting can sometimes be observed very clearly when two boys start idly wrestling on a street-corner. At first they both obey the conventions of playful aggression. Each body-push and arm-lock is performed with exactly the right intensity—strong enough to make it forceful, but not so strong that it becomes truly violent. If this delicate balance is accidentally upset and one of them is hurt, the mood changes. Now he retaliates more powerfully and, if the situation is badly handled, a real fight can slowly grow out of the playful one. The changes that signal this are difficult to analyse, because even the playful wrestling may look real enough. Usually the tell-tale signs begin to show in the facial expressions, which, instead of being relaxed and smiling, or exaggeratedly mock-savage, become hard and set, often with accompanying changes in pallor and flushing.

Where professional wrestlers are concerned, a mimic of this change-over can be seen. The 'villain' deliberately fouls the 'hero', who then becomes expansively outraged, protesting to the referee and demanding sympathy from the crowd. Lunging wildly at his opponent, he appears to switch from the conventional combat techniques to uncontrolled violence, returning foul for foul, and the audience roars its approval. But here, even the 'uncontrolled' aggression is itself formalized, and the audience, joining in the game, knows this perfectly well. Should one wrestler genuinely hurt a rival, the bout is immediately called off and, instead of 'savage reprisals', ill-concealed concern is shown on all sides.

Leaving this dangerous subject, we can turn now to the safer and more tender intimacies of the dance-floor. As a sphere of activity in which there are professionals who are licensed to touch, dancing offers limited possibilities. True, the adult who is seeking some form of body contact can achieve it by using the services of a dancing instructor, and a male dancer can, in certain localities, visit a dance-hall which supplies professional dancing partners at a set fee per dance, but the world of social dancing is today largely one for the amateur. At parties, discotheques, dance-halls and ballrooms, adults who are strangers to one another can come together and move around the room in an intimate frontal embrace. Individuals who are already friendly can also use the situation to escalate a non-touching relationship into a touching one. The special role that social dancing plays in our society is that it permits, in its special context, a sudden and dramatic increase in body intimacy in a way that would be impossible elsewhere. If the same full frontal embrace were performed between strangers, or partial strangers, outside the context of the dance floor, the impact would be entirely different. Dancing, so to speak, devalues the significance of the embrace, lowering its threshold to a point where it can lightly be indulged in without fear of rebuff. Having permitted it to occur, it then gives a chance for it to work its powerful magic. If the magic fails to work, the formalities of the situation also permit retreat without ignominy.

Like so many other aspects of body intimacy, dancing has a long history stretching back into our animal past. In behaviour terms, its basic ingredient is the repeated intention movement. If we look at the dancing displays of various birds, we find that the rhythmic movements they perform are mostly made up of movements that start to go one way, then stop and go another, then stop again and repeat the first action, and so on. Turning from side to side, twisting back and forth, or bobbing up and down, the bird displays vigorously in front of its mate. It is in a state of conflict, one urge pulling it forward and another holding it back. During the course of evolution, the rhythm of these intention movements becomes fixed and the display becomes a ritual.

The form the ritual takes varies from species to species and in each case becomes characteristic of their particular sexual preliminaries.

Most of our dance movements have originated in the same way, but in us they have not evolved into a fixed form. Instead, they have been culturally developed and are highly variable. Many of the actions of human dancers are no more than intention movements of going somewhere, only instead of carrying the action through, we check it, move back or round, and start again. In earlier centuries, many dances were like little parades, with the couple demurely holding hands and stepping round the floor, pausing every so often, turning round, and then going on again, to the rhythm of the music. Because the pattern was essentially one of going on a journey, it also frequently included mock-greetings towards the partner, with formal bowings and curtsyings, as though the two dancers had just met. In both folk-dancing and the courtly ballrooms, there was typically an intricate weaving round and round and in and out of other pairs on the floor, or arena. The body intimacies involved in such performances were so strictly limited that they gave rise to no sexual problems. They simply permitted a general social intermingling. The fact that the leading of the female by the male, around and around the floor, was so formalized, stopped any awkward questions about where he was really supposed to be leading her, or for what purpose.

The situation changed dramatically at the beginning of the last century, as a new dance craze swept across Europe. The waltz had arrived. For the first time the dancing couple embraced as they moved, a public intimacy that immediately created widespread scandal and concern. Such a major advance required a subterfuge, and it is one we have met before. When discussing the first way in which a simple hand-to-hand contact can be effected, I mentioned that a much used trick is the intimacy-disguised-as-aid. The hand that reaches out does so ostensibly to support or steady the other person, to guide them or to prevent them from falling. In this way it can cross the vital threshold of making body contact without causing alarm. So it was with the waltz. At the very beginning of its history it was an incredibly rapid and athletic dance, so that the partners were forced to clutch at one another's bodies to prevent themselves from spinning apart. This was the 'supporting' device and, once it had enabled the waltz to gain an entrance into the ballroom, it was then only a matter of slowing down the speed of the performance to convert these actions of mutual physical aid into the more tender intimacies of a true frontal embrace.

The older generation, who had not known such delights, were outraged. The waltz, which today seems quaintly old-fashioned, was, in its early years, described as 'polluting' and 'the most degenerate dance that the last or present century can see'. The early Victorian author of *The Ladies' Pocket-Book of Etiquette* devoted ten pages to an all-out attack on this abominable new public intimacy. Among her comments: 'Ask any mother ... can she consent to commit her daughter promiscuously to the arms of each waltzer? Ask the lover ... could he endure the sight of the adopted of his heart ... reclining in the arms of another? ... Ask the husband ... will you suffer your wife to be half-embraced by every puppy who turns on his heel or his toe?' The attacks persisted and, less than a hundred years ago, an American dancing-master in Philadelphia pronounced the waltz immoral because it involved the hugging of a lady by a gentleman she might not previously have met. But the battle was gradually lost, and the wicked waltz reigned supreme, bringing in its wake a whole variety of dances involving the full frontal embrace. These, in their turn, caused further scandalized mutterings.

The importation of the tango from South America in 1912 was again greeted with outrage. Because this dance included 'suggestive lateral movement of the hips', which reminded the hawk-eyed guardians of morals of the actions of copulation, it was instantly dubbed as depraved.

No sooner was that battle lost than the Jazz Age burst upon the scene, and the frantic dancing-teachers of the 1920s called urgent meetings to discuss this new threat to their respectability. They issued strong official protests about this new craze, pointing out that all the jazz dances had originated in Negro brothels.

Perhaps the most extraordinary attack on jazz dancing came in a newspaper report which claimed that 'The dance, and the music, with its abominable rhythm and copulative beat, was imported from Central Africa by a gang of Bolshevists in America, their aim being to strike at Christian civilization throughout the world.' Perhaps this puts into true perspective the recent claims that the current wave of student revolt, dropping-out and drug-taking is also a 'Red plot'.

Since its early days, jazz has given birth to several lusty offspring, and each in turn has caused the inevitable raised eyebrows as the dancers have taken to the floor with more and more variations of the public embrace. In the 'forties it was jitterbugging and in the 'fifties rock-and-roll, but then something strange happened. For some reason that it is perhaps still too early to understand, the couples separated. With the 'sixties, the dancing embrace went into a rapid decline. Now only the older, more staid couples clung to one another as they rotated around the floor. The younger dancers pulled apart from one another and danced more or less on the spot where they stood. It began with the twist and before long involved a confusingly large number of alternatives such as the hitch-hiker, the shake, the monkey and the frug. More and more styles were specified until eventually, as the decade drew to a close, the situation became so confused that they all merged into one more or less nameless amalgam, and became simply the dance that was danced to 'pop'. All had the same important feature—no touching. Presumably the significance of this change lies in the marked increase in sexual permissiveness. If young Victorian couples were not allowed to enjoy extensive private intimacies, then the embrace of the waltz had great meaning for them, but if matters are freer today, then who cares about a specially 'licensed' context for a mere standing embrace? It is as if the young dancers of today are publicly stating, 'We don't need it, we have the real thing.'

This brings us to the end of this brief survey of the way in which we, as adults, find specialized methods of indulging in bodily intimacy. All through the chapter, from doctors to dancers, there has always been something other than pure contact involved. At no point has there been touching merely for touching's sake. In every case there has been some excuse that provides us with a licence to touch or be touched. And yet, frequently, there is the distinct impression that it is the contact that is more important than the official activity. Perhaps one day, as the stresses of modern living increase, we shall see the appearance of an undisguised professional toucher, who will sell embraces like beads. Or perhaps to buy his wares will always be too great an admission of failure on our part, a failure to achieve the longed-for intimacies with a family unit of our own.

Whatever happens, we can always fall back on that perpetual substitute for body intimacy, namely verbal intimacy. Instead of exchanging embraces we can exchange comforting words. We can smile and talk about the weather. It is a poor substitute where emotional interchanges are concerned, but it is better than total emotional isolation. And if we still yearn after a more direct form of contact, there are other alternatives open to us: we can touch some non-human animal, or an inanimate object, using it as a stand-in for the human body we would really like to approach, or, if there is no other solution, we can always touch ourselves. The ways in which we employ animals, objects and our own bodies as substitutes for human intimates are discussed in the next three chapters.

6

SUBSTITUTES FOR INTIMACY

In the adult human world, a world full of stress and strangers, we reach out to our loved ones for comfort. If, through their indifference or through their preoccupation with the complexities of modern living, they fail to respond, we are in danger of becoming starved of the primary reassurance of bodily contact. If, through the moralizing of a warped minority, they have become inhibited in their intimacies and have been driven to accept the view that indulgence in the tactile pleasures of the body is somehow sinful and wicked, then, even in the midst of our nearest and dearest, we are liable to become touch-hungry and body-lonely. We are, however, an ingenious species, and if we are denied something we badly want or need, our resourcefulness soon urges us on to find a substitute to replace it.

If we cannot find love inside the family, we soon start looking for it outside. The ignored wife takes a lover; the husband, a mistress. Body intimacies reblossom. Unhappily, these particular substitutes do not always add to the surviving intimacies of family life; they compete with them, and perhaps eventually replace them altogether, causing varying degrees of social havoc as they do so. A less damaging alternative was the one discussed in the last chapter – the use of contacts with specialists who are licensed to touch. These have the great advantage that they do not usually compete with the relationships inside the family unit. The extensive intimacies of the masseur, providing they are applied with a strict professionalism, cannot be cited as grounds for divorce. But even a professional toucher, no matter how valid his official excuse for touching may be, is still a physiologically functional adult being, and as such is inevitably seen as a potential sexual threat. The 'seeing' of this threat is seldom spoken of openly, except occasionally in jest. Instead, society quietly imposes more and more restrictions on the nature and context of the specialist intimacies. To begin with, they are rarely admitted to exist. One goes dancing, not to touch, but 'for fun'. One goes to the doctor because of a virus, not because one needs comfort. One goes to a hairdresser to have the hair styled, not to have the head caressed. These official functions are, of course, all perfectly valid and important. They have to be so in order to mask the fact that something else is going on at the same time, namely the seeking of friendly body contact. The moment they cease to be important, this unfulfilled need becomes too obvious, and some basic questions about our way of life start demanding answers we would rather not be forced to consider.

Unconsciously, however, we are all aware of the game that is being played, and so, indirectly, we tie the hands that we would have caress us. We do this by applying conventions and codes of conduct that reduce our sexual fears. Usually we do not say why. We simply accept the abstract rules of good etiquette, and tell one another that certain things are 'not done' or 'not nice'. It is rude to point, leave alone touch. It is impolite to show one's feelings.

So where do we turn? The answer is as soft and cuddly as the kitten in your lap. We turn, in fact, to other species. If those humans closest to us cannot supply us with what we want, and if it is too dangerous to seek intimacies with strangers, then we can make tracks to the nearest pet shop and, for a small sum, buy ourselves a piece of animal intimacy. For pets are innocent; they cause no questions and they ask no questions. They lick our hands, they rub softly up against our legs, they curl up to sleep on our thighs, and they nuzzle us. We can cuddle them, stroke them, pat them, carry them like babies, tickle them behind the ears, and even kiss them.

If this seems trivial, consider the scale of the operation. In the United States, more than 5,000 million dollars is spent on pets every year. In Britain the annual figure is 100 million pounds. In West Germany it is 600 million Deutsche marks. In France, a few years ago it was 125 million new francs, and estimates already indicate that this figure has by now doubled. Trivial is not the word for figures such as these.

The most important pets are cats and dogs. In the United States there are 90 million of them. Puppies and kittens are born there at the rate of 10,000 every hour. There are over 16 million dogs in France, eight million in West Germany and five million in Britain. Precise information on cats is not available, but there are certainly as many cats as dogs and probably more.

Putting these figures together, one can say that, at a rough guess, there are approximately 150 million cats and dogs in these four countries alone. Making another rough guess, let us say that each owner of one of these animals strokes, pats or caresses it, on the average, three times a day — or about 1,000 times a year. This adds up to a total of 150,000 million intimate body contacts per year. What is astonishing about this figure is that it represents for Americans, Frenchmen, Germans and Englishmen, intimacies performed not with other Americans, Frenchmen, Germans, or Englishmen, but with alien species belonging to the order Carnivora. Viewed in this way, the phenomenon looks even less trivial.

As we have already seen, we pat one another on the back when we embrace, and we stroke one another's hair and skin when we are lovers, or parents with children. But clearly we do not get enough, and those thousands of millions of animal caresses are there to prove it. Blocked in our human contacts by our cultural restrictions, we redirect our intimacies towards our adoring pets, our substitutes for love.

This situation has led to violent criticism from some quarters. Dubbed 'petishism' by one author, it has been condemned as reflecting a decadent failure of modern, civilized human beings to communicate intimately with one another. In particular it has been stressed that more money is usually forthcoming to support the prevention of cruelty to animals than to prevent cruelty to children. The answers given in support of modern pet-keeping are rejected as illogical and hypocritical. The argument that it teaches us the ways of animal life is considered nonsensical, in view of the gross anthropomorphism of the relationship in almost every case. The pets are humanized – they are seen as furry people, not real animals at all. The argument that animals are innocent and helpless and need our aid is seen as hopelessly one-sided in an era of battered babies and napalmed peasants. How is it that, in this enlightened age, we can have permitted a million children to be killed or wounded in Vietnam, while our cats and dogs have been provided with expert and immediate attention whenever they have needed it? How is it that in the twentieth century we can have licensed our adult males to murder 100 million members of their own species in warfare, while we have spent more millions on stuffing food into our luxuriating pet animals? How is it, to sum up, that we have come to be kinder to other species than to our own?

These are strong arguments and they cannot be dismissed lightly, but they contain a vital flaw. The answer, put very simply, is the old one that two wrongs do not make a right. Undeniably, it is monstrous to cuddle a pet and ignore a child, and it is true that in extreme cases this does happen. But to use this as an argument for not cuddling a pet is a folly. It is doubtful if, even in extreme cases, the pet 'steals' the caress from the child. If, for some neurotic reason, the child is not receiving love from the parent, it is doubtful whether the absence of a cuddlesome pet would help to improve the situation. In almost every case, a pet animal is being used either as an additional source of intimacy, or as a substitute for intimacies that are already lacking for some reason. To say that more caring for animals is actively causing less caring for other humans seems to be totally unjustified.

Imagine for a moment that a freak disease exterminated all pet animals tomorrow, and effectively eliminated all those millions of tender intimacies that would have occurred between them and their owners. Where would all that loving go? Would it magically be re-redirected, back on to other human companions? The answer, sadly, is that it would probably not. All that would happen is that millions of people, some of them lonely and incapable for a variety of reasons of enjoying any real human intimacies, would be robbed of a major form of tender body contact. The old lady who lived alone with her cats would hardly start stroking the postman. The man who fondly patted his dog would be unlikely to pat his teenage son more in its absence.

It is true that in an ideal society we should not need these substitutes or additional outlets for our intimacies, but to suggest banning them because of this is to attempt to cure the symptom and not the cause of the trouble. And even in the ideally loving and body-free society, we would probably always have plenty of intimacy to spare for our animal companions, not because we would then need such contacts, but simply because they would give us additional pleasures that would in no way compete with our human relationships.

A final word in defence of pets: if we are capable of tenderness towards animals it does at least reveal that we are capable of such tenderness. But, the answer comes back, even the commandants of concentration camps were kind to their dogs, so what does that prove? It proves, in short, that even the most monstrous of human beings is capable of some kind of tenderness, and the fact that its juxtaposition to callous brutality in this particular case offends us so deeply, and makes the brutality even more horrific, must not blind us to this fact. It serves as a constant reminder that the human animal, when not warped by what must paradoxically be called the savageries of civilization, is fundamentally endowed with a great potential for tenderness and intimacy. If witnessing the gentle, friendly touching that occurs between pet-owners and their pets does no more than bring home to us that man is basically a loving, intimate animal, then this alone is a valuable lesson to learn and relearn, all the more so in a world that grows yearly more impersonal and cold-hearted. When, under pressure, men become merciless, it is then that we need all the evidence we can muster to prove that this need not be so — that this is not the natural condition of man. If our capacity to love our pet animals serves to demonstrate one facet of this, then well-meaning critics must think twice about launching an attack on it, no matter how unreasonable it may seem when viewed from certain angles.

This said, what of the nature of the animal intimacies themselves? Why, for example, do we pat a dog and stroke a cat, but rarely stroke a dog or pat a cat? Why does one kind of animal draw forth one type of intimacy and another another? To answer this we have to look at the anatomy of the animals concerned. In their roles as pets they are, of course, acting as stand-ins for human companions, and their bodies are therefore substitutes for human bodies. Anatomically, however, there are striking disparities. The stiff legs of a dog cannot embrace us. We cannot fling our arms around a cat. Even the largest cat is no bigger than a human baby, and its body is soft and pliable. We therefore adjust our actions accordingly.

First, the dog. As our loving companion, we want to embrace him, but because his legs make this difficult, we isolate the patting element from the embrace-and-pat complex and apply it direct. Reaching out, we pat the animal's back, or perhaps its head or flanks. In a typical large dog, the back is broad and firm and a suitable substitute for the human back which we are patting by proxy.

The cat is a different matter. Being smaller and softer to the touch, it does not feel right as a back-substitute to be vigorously patted. Its soft, silky fur is more like human head-hair to the touch. We tend to stroke a loved one's hair, and so it follows that we tend to stroke a cat. As the dog was a back-substitute, so the cat is a hair-substitute. In fact, we often treat a cat as though its whole body is a stand-in for a silky-haired human head.

Extending this argument, it might be thought that patting is something we automatically do to all canines, and that stroking is an action for all felines, but it is not as simple as this. It has much more to do with the typical body quality of the domestic dog and the domestic cat. Anyone who has enjoyed the exotic luxuries of body intimacies with a tame cheetah, lion or tiger will know that there the pattern changes. Although they are true felines, they have broad, firm backs more reminiscent of the domestic dog than of the family cat. Like the typical dog, the hair is also coarser. The result is that they are patted, not stroked. By contrast, a tiny lap-dog with long flowing hair is stroked and caressed more like a cat.

Moving up the scale in size, the horse-lover is also a patter, but there is a subtle change. The original human back — where the patting began, so to speak — was a vertical surface, but the back of a horse is horizontal and therefore less satisfying as a site for the substitute action. The horse's neck, however, comes to the rescue, being both the right height and, what is more, providing the ideal vertical surface, and it is here that the majority of horse-pattings are delivered. In this respect, the horse goes one better than the dog, whose neck is generally too small to be of much use in this respect. Again, the horse's height makes it ideal for head contacts which, in the dog, force us to lower ourselves to his level, or raise him up in our arms. And so many a horse-lover can be seen with her head pressed to her animal's neck or face, while her arm embraces and her hand pats the firm, warm flesh.

For many people a pet is not merely a substitute companion, but more specifically a substitute for a child. Here the size of the animal becomes important. Domestic cats are no problem, but the typical dog is too large, and so certain types have been progressively reduced in size by selective breeding until they have been successfully scaled down to human baby proportions. Then they, like cats and various other creatures such as rabbits and monkeys, can be scooped up in their owner's pseudo-parental arms without undue exertion. This is by far the most popular form of body contact to occur, where pet animals are concerned. An analysis of a large number of photographs depicting owners in contact with their pets reveals that the act of holding the animal in the arms, as if it were an infant, accounts for 50 per cent of all cases. Patting is the next most common action (11 per cent), followed by the semi-embrace, in which one arm is wrapped around the animal (7 per cent), followed closely by the pressing of the cheek to the pet's body, usually in the region of its head. Another intimacy that appears with rather surprising frequency is the mouth-to-mouth kiss (5 per cent), the species involved ranging from the budgerigar to the whale. The whale, one might think, leaves something to be desired as an animal intimate. Captain Ahab would certainly have been startled at the idea of a girl kissing one on the mouth, but the recent trend in oceanarium displays has changed all that. Both tame whales and their smaller relatives, the dolphins, have become front-line favourites in recent years, and since their bulbous, swollen foreheads give a baby-like shape to their heads, they create a strong urge in their human companions to pat, tickle and caress them when they protrude their apparently grinning faces from the sides of their pools.

Birds that are hand-tame, such as parrots, budgerigars and doves, are frequently brought up to the face and held against the cheek, where the soft smoothness of their plumage can be felt against the skin. The intimacy is often elaborated with mouth-to-mouth feeding of morsels of food. Because of their small size, which rules out embracing and patting, the hand intimacies are limited to finger-stroking and gentle tickling 'behind the ear'.

If we move further away on the evolutionary scale, the

possibilities for intimacies decline rapidly. For most people, reptiles, amphibians, fish and insects are singularly unrewarding to the touch. The tortoise, with its smooth, hard shell, rates an occasional pat on the back, but its scalier relatives lack the essential qualities for friendly body contact. Perhaps the only exceptions worth mentioning are the giant constricting snakes. When suitably tamed, pythons, for example, can provide their owners with something that even the cats and dogs cannot offer – an all-enveloping embrace. Wrapping their strong coils around their human companions' bodies, tightening and relaxing their muscles, undulating their many ribs, and flickering their gentle tongues across their owners' skins, they create a sensuous impact that has to be felt to be believed. However, because of their difficult feeding habits and the bad press they have received ever since the fracas in Eden, not to mention our horror of their smaller and highly poisonous relatives, the big snakes have never enjoyed wide popularity as close intimates, even for the most embrace-hungry of humans.

Fish-touching, if we draw a discreet veil over the treacherous human intimacy of trout-tickling, is virtually non-existent. Perhaps the only exception here is the voluptuous hand-kissing sometimes performed by tame giant carp when sticking their gaping heads out of water as they beg for food. These fish can gape and gulp with such energy at the edge of a carp pond that even a passing bird may be coerced into a brief act of intimacy. There is an extraordinary photograph in existence which shows a small finch, its beak full of luscious insects for its hungry nestlings, pausing in front of the inviting gape of a tame carp's mouth and impulsively ramming its precious catch down the wide open throat of the fish. If a bird can be attracted in this way to make a thoroughly unnatural body contact, then it is little wonder that human visitors to carp-ponds react in much the same way.

Up to this point we have considered only friendly and parental intimacies, but for some humans the contacts go further and include full sexual interaction. These cases are rare, but they have a long and ancient history, references to them being scattered throughout art and literature from the earliest times. They take two main forms. Either a human male copulates with an animal, usually a domesticated farm animal, or masturbation occurs. In the latter case, a natural tendency on the part of a particular species to lick or suck is directed towards the human genitals, either male or female, as a device for producing sexual arousal. It says a lot for the degree of alienation and body-contact frustration that must exist in human societies that such aberrant intimacies occur at all. However, when we remember the millions of lesser intimacies, in the form of cuddlings, kissings and strokings, that take place in our modern cultures between pet-owners and their vast army of pets, it is not so surprising that, in a small minority of cases, greater intimacies such as these do occasionally arise.

In surveying the whole question of human-animal contacts, mention has so far been made only of pets and farm animals, but there are two other spheres of interaction that deserve some comment. Human-controlled animals exist not only in private homes and on farms; they are also found in large numbers in zoos and research laboratories. Here, too, frequent contacts occur and they are not always ones that meet with general approval.

Visitors to zoos not only want to see the captive creatures held there; they also want to hold the captive creatures seen there. The urge to touch is so strong that it constitutes a constant hazard for the zoo authorities. The first-aid department register of any major zoological gardens bears witness to this. For every sprained ankle or cut finger, there is a bitten hand or a scratched face. Sometimes the injuries sustained by the eager animal-gropers are serious, but they are seldom caused by carelessness on the part of the zoo staff. Two examples will suffice to illustrate this. The first concerns a woman who arrived at the first-aid department of a major zoo, holding her screaming child, who had a badly mauled hand. While it was being treated, it emerged that he had begged to be allowed to touch the body of the zoo's adult male gorilla. Complying with his wish, the woman had lifted him laboriously over the safety barrier, past the large warning sign indicating that the animal was extremely dangerous, and had thrust him forwards so that he could push his arms around the edge of the protective armoured glass screen and through the bars into the cage. The gorilla, misinterpreting this friendly act, had promptly sunk its teeth into the boy's hand. Unrepentant, the woman now presented herself, outraged, to the helpless zoo authorities.

The second case concerns the tragic affair of the 'tiger-toucher', an elderly gentleman who repeatedly clambered over the barrier at the same zoo's big cat house in order to caress one particular tigress. Removed, protesting, time and again by the zoo staff, he finally leapt over the barrier in such desperation that he broke a leg and was removed to a hospital bed. During his absence the tigress in question was dispatched to another zoo for breeding purposes. On his return to health, the man went straight back to the cage, only to find it occupied by a strange leopard. Furious at this, he marched across to the zoo office and demanded to know what they had done with his wife. At first the authorities were nonplussed by this extraordinary accusation, but after quiet questioning it emerged that the unhappy man had recently lost his real wife, after a lifetime of close companionship, and had since transferred all his emotional attachments to the tigress in question. Because the animal had, in his mind, become the embodiment of his late mate, it was only natural that he should want to continue to make intimate contact with her body in its new form, even at considerable risk to life and limb.

If these examples seem outlandish, it is worth remembering that they are only extremes of actions which, at a more moderate level, are occurring in zoos throughout the world in large numbers every day. When the urge to touch another human being is blocked, either by personal tragedy or by cultural taboo, it will nearly always find a way of expressing itself, no matter what the consequences. One is inescapably reminded here of the pathetic cases of child-molesters who are arrested for supposedly sexual assaults on infants. Unable to make proper contact with adults, they turn to children who are innocent of the strictness of adult taboos. Frequently all that such men want is some kind of gentle, friendly body intimacy, but always the cry for blood goes up and the actions are interpreted as inevitably sexually motivated. This they may of course be, but it is by no means inevitable, and many a harmless old man has suffered heavily as a result. Needless to say, the children in such cases always suffer too, not from the original intimacies, which even in the specifically sexual cases they probably did not understand, but from the parental panic that follows and, above all, from the trauma of the court proceedings through which they are shamefully dragged.

Returning to the animal situation and leaving the zoo gates behind us, we come now to the fourth major category of man-animal contacts, namely those that exist in the world of science. Millions of laboratory animals are bred and killed annually in the course of medical research, and the contacts that occur between research workers and their experimental subjects have given rise to much heated debate. To the scientist, the interaction is a totally objective one. He admits to no emotional bond, either positive or negative, either loving or hating, with the animals he must handle while carrying out his investigations. The decision is simple enough: if he can reduce human suffering by sacrificing the lives of laboratory animals, he sees no other choice. He would avoid it if he could, but he cannot, and he refuses to place the lives of animals on a higher plane than the lives of fellow humans. That, briefly, is his case, but it is frequently and vociferously contested.

The opponents have been many, and their general attitude can best be summed up in the words of George Bernard Shaw, who said that 'If you cannot attain knowledge without torturing a dog, you must do without knowledge.' A more moderate view is expressed by those who feel that many animal experiments are pointless and that the results they obtain are worthless in any humanitarian sense, doing no more than satisfy the idle curiosity of the academic world. Surprisingly enough, such a view was voiced by the great Charles Darwin himself, in a letter to another famous zoologist, in which he said, 'Physiological experiment on animals is justifiable for real investigation, but not for mere damnable and detestable curiosity.' More recently, it has been pointed out by a respected experimental psychologist that 'One consequence of the obsessively behaviouristic and mechanistic approach is the apparent callousness of much of the experimental work carried out on the lower animals, often without any worthwhile aim.'

It is certainly true that the number of licensed animal experiments performed each year has risen sharply as the twentieth century has grown older. In Britain the figure for 1910 was 95,000; by 1945 it had exceeded 1,000,000; more recently, in 1969, it was in the region of 5,500,000, involving 600 separate research establishments. The vast scale of the operation has started to cause comment in political circles. One member of the British Parliament, speaking in 1971, protested: 'I know that the object is to preserve human life; but it does make me wonder whether a human race that can take such morally degrading practices in its stride is really worth preserving.'

It is important to separate two distinct elements in these and other criticisms of the large-scale use of animals for research. First, there is the extreme, anthropomorphic element, which sees the animals as symbolic people and therefore dislikes the idea of causing them pain for whatever purpose. Second, there is the humanitarian element, which sees animals as *similar* to people, in that they are capable in their own ways of feeling fear, pain and distress, and dislikes the idea that they should be caused any unnecessary suffering at human hands. This second element accepts, however, that it is necessary to cause some degree of suffering, but only if it is kept to an absolute minimum and only if the research is directly aimed at reducing a greater suffering.

The research scientist responds to these two criticisms in the following way. To the first critic he says, 'Tell that to the mother of a thalidomide baby.' If more extensive animal experimentation had been carried out, she might have had a normal child. Or he may say, 'Tell that to the mother whose child died of diphtheria.' Only a few years ago this disease killed thousands of children annually, but now, thanks to the development of a vaccine developed entirely by experiments on living animals, it has practically disappeared. Or he may say, 'Ask the mother of a polio child how she feels about the fact that it costs the life of an experimental monkey for every three doses of the polio vaccine that could have saved her child.'

In other words, what the out-and-out anti-vivisectionist is proclaiming is that it is better for a child to die or suffer agonies than for living animals to be used for experimental research. Whilst this may reflect an admirable concern for the welfare of animals, it also reveals a startlingly callous attitude towards human children. This putting of animals before people takes us back again to the pet-keeping situation, but here there is an important difference. Where pets were concerned, it was perfectly possible to be kind both to pets and to people. One did not automatically exclude the other, and the anti-pet argument to the contrary was shown to be false. But here the situation does demand that in order to be kind to the child it is unhappily necessary to be unkind to the experimental animal. We simply cannot have it both ways. An unpleasant choice has to be made.

To the second and more moderate critic, the research scientist says, 'I agree; animal suffering must be kept to a minimum, but there are problems.' A great deal of detailed study has been made in recent years of ways in which experimental procedures can be made less painful for the animal subjects, and everything is done to devise tests which use fewer animals, which cause them the minimum of distress and, where possible, replace them altogether. On this basis we might expect to see the number of laboratory animals killed annually declining steadily. As the figures I quoted show, however, this is not the case. The research scientist's answer is that this does not mean that more wasteful methods are being used, but rather that research programmes are becoming increasingly extensive and investigating more and more ways of alleviating human suffering. Furthermore, he will point out that one of the great problems with research is that it is impossible to limit it to areas which are directly and obviously connected with specific forms of suffering. Many of the greatest and ultimately most beneficial discoveries are made as a result of animal experiments in 'pure' rather than 'applied' research. To say that an animal experiment must not be done because, at the moment, it has no obvious application in such spheres as medicine or psychiatry is to stifle the whole progress of scientific understanding.

This is the point at which some of the least emotional and most educated critics begin to get worried. How far, to use Darwin's words, does 'real investigation' have to go before it becomes 'mere damnable and detestable curiosity'? This involves a much more difficult and delicate argument. Reading some of the scientific journals, especially those concerned with experimental psychology, it is difficult to escape the conclusion that many research workers in recent times have, by any reasonable standards, gone too far. By so doing they are endangering the public acceptance of scientific endeavour as a whole, and many authorities believe that it is high time that a drastic revision was made of the direction that many research projects are taking. If this is not done there may be a large-scale public backlash that will, in the long run, do untold harm to scientific progress.

Having made these general points, it now remains to ask why the man/animal contacts that occur in the laboratory should cause so much heated debate and concern. The obvious — too obvious — answer is that, even when we accept that it is justified and necessary, we do not like the idea of a man causing pain to the animal he handles. But what about the man who finds mice in his kitchen, or the slum-dweller who finds rats in his bedroom, and beats them to death with a stick or condemns them to a slow and painful death by putting down poison? He does not receive our criticism, only our sympathy. There are no protection societies formed to protect the wild rats and mice that infest our dwelling-places, and yet these are the same species that are used in the laboratory experiments which cause so much comment. Killing a wild rat is approved of because it may spread disease, but killing a laboratory rat is disapproved of, even though its death may also help to prevent the spread of disease, via the agency of scientific discovery.

How can we explain this inconsistency? Clearly it has little to do — whatever we may say — with our objective concern for the welfare of rats, wild or tame. If we really cared about the laboratory rat for its own sake, as an exciting form of animal life, we would not treat its wild counterpart so brutally. No, what is happening is that we are responding in a much more complex and subtle way than we imagine. We respond to the wild rat in a very basic way as an invader of our private territory, and we feel justified in defending that territory with any means at our disposal. No treatment is too harsh for a dangerous intruder. But what of the tame white rat in the laboratory? Is this not the creature whose ancestors brought the great plague into our midst? Certainly it is, but now it appears in a new role, and we must understand what that role is if we are to understand the strong emotions its experimental death causes in us.

To start with, the white rat is no longer a pest, but a servant of man. He is gently handled, well fed, well housed and cared for in every possible way. The attitude of his human companion is that of a doctor tending a patient before an operation. Then he is experimentally infected with cancer. Later he is killed by the same hands that cared for him. Except for the cancer element, this sequence could also apply to the relationship between a farmer and his domestic stock. He cares for them, then kills them. Yet we do not complain about the behaviour of the average farmer towards his animals, any more than we complain about the man who poisons a wild rat in his kitchen. Where does this leave us? The laboratory sequence involves tender handling, then causing pain, then killing. The farm sequence involves tender handling, then killing. The pest sequence involves causing pain and killing. In other words, we do not object to killing after caring, or to killing after causing pain, but we do object to causing pain after caring. The symbolic role that the white rat plays in the research laboratory is that of the humble and faithful servant who is loved by his master until, one day, without warning or provocation, this loving master starts to torture his servant and does so, not for the servant's own good, but for the benefit of the master himself. This is the allegory of betrayal that causes all the trouble.

The critics of animal experiments will hotly deny this, claiming that it is the rat they are thinking about and not this symbolic relationship, but unless they are full-time vegetarians who literally would not swat a fly, they are deluding themselves. If ever they have received any kind of medical aid, they are hypocrites. If, however, they are honest, they will admit that it is the *betrayal of intimacy* inherent in the symbolic man-rat relationship that really concerns them.

Now it should become clear why I have gone at some length into a pattern of human behaviour that, at first sight, does not appear to have any close connection with the subject of this book. The whole essence of the experimentalist's dilemma is that, to allay fears, he must emphasize over and over again how well he treats his laboratory animals: how gently he handles them, how relaxed and contented they are in their hygienic cages where they await the important part they have to play in his research. It is the contrast between this tender intimacy and what he then proceeds to do to them that is the crux of the passionate antagonism he arouses in his critics. For, as we have seen throughout this book, intimacy means trust, and the symbolic rat-servant is made to trust his master totally, only then to be subjected to pain and disease at his gentle, caring hands. If this betrayal of intimacy occurs only occasionally and for very special reasons, then most of the critics can reluctantly accept it, but when it takes place millions of times every year, then they begin to get the creepy feeling that they belong to a nation of emotional traitors. If a man can inflict deliberate pain on an animal that trusted him and which, a moment before, he was handling so gently and carefully, then how can he be trusted in his human relationships? How, when in all other respects of his social life he behaves in a perfectly reasonable and friendly way, can we ever be sure again that reasonable friendliness is any true guide to the nature of the members of the society in which we live? How can he behave so well towards his real children, when he constantly double-crosses his symbolic laboratory 'children'? These are the fears that run unspoken through the minds of his critics.

There is a similarity here to the case mentioned earlier of the concentration camp commandant who was kind and gentle to his pet dogs, whilst brutally torturing his prisoners. There, the kindness to his animals reminded us that even such a monstrous human being was not totally devoid of tender feelings. Here, the position is reversed, with a man who is capable of being kind to his fellow men nevertheless being able to spend his working days inflicting pain on his experimental animals. It is the contrast that frightens us. If we see a friendly-looking soldier patting his dog on the head, we cannot help wondering whether he, too, would be capable of gassing helpless human victims. If we see a friendly-looking father playing lovingly with his children, we cannot help wondering whether, beneath the surface, he is capable of cruel experiments. We begin to lose our sense of values. Our faith in the bonding power of body intimacies begins to waver, and we rebel against what we call the callousness of science.

We know perfectly well that this rebellion is unjustified because of the immense benefits that scientific research has brought us, but it hits so hard at our basic concepts of what gentle, caring intimacy means that we cannot help it. We still rush to the pharmacy when we get sick and quickly swallow our pills and tablets, but we try not to think of the trusting, betrayed animals who suffered to give us these anti-biotic blessings.

If the situation is bad for the general public, what must it be like for the experimentalist? The answer is that it is not bad at all, for the simple reason that he has trained himself specifically not to see his relationship with his animals as a symbolic one. In applying a ruthlessly objective approach to his subject, he overcomes the emotional difficulty. If he handles his animals with gentle care, he does it to make them better subjects for experimental procedure, not to satisfy his emotional needs for substitute body intimacy like the ardent pet-keeper. This often requires considerable restraint and self-discipline, because, of course, even the most intellectually controlled act of body contact can begin to work its basic magic and start to form bonds of attachment. It is not unknown for a large laboratory to house, in a corner cage, a fat, lop-eared rabbit that has become the departmental mascot, a pampered pet that no one would dream of using for an experiment, because it has slipped into a totally different role.

For the non-scientist it is difficult to make these rigid distinctions. For him, all animals belong in Disneyland. If, through the modern educational media of film and television, he broadens his horizons and begins at last to forget the toy-animal images of his childhood, he does so not at the deft hands of experimentalists, but in the company of naturalists, whose basic approach is that of the observer, rather than the manipulator, of animal life.

The plight of the serious experimentalist therefore remains unsolved. Like the surgeon who operates to save his patients' lives, he strives to improve our lot, but unlike the surgeon he gets little thanks for it. Like the surgeon, he remains strictly objective and unemotional throughout his operations. In either case, emotional involvement would be damaging. For the surgeon this is less obvious, for he must put on a bedside manner outside the operating theatre. Once inside, however, he treats the bodies of his patients as coldly and objectively as the experimentalist, carving them up like a master chef performing with a choice joint of meat. If this were not so, we would all suffer for it in the long run. If the experimentalist became emotionally involved with his animals and treated them all like beloved pets, he would soon be incapable of carrying on his arduous research projects that bring us so much widespread relief from disease and agony. He would be driven to drink by the enormity of what he was doing. Likewise, if the surgeon allowed himself to become emotionally aroused by the plight of his patients, his knife might waver as it sliced, and vital damage would be done. If hospital patients could hear the conversations that take place in many operating theatres, they would probably be horrified by the sometimes jocular, sometimes matter-of-fact tones, but their response would be misguided. The terrible intimacy of entering another person's body with a sharp instrument demands a dramatic switching-off of the emotional impact of the act. If the action is performed as a piece of desperate, loving care, then the patient's next piece of body intimacy is liable to be at the cold hands of an undertaker.

In this chapter we have been looking at the use of living substitutes for human bodies in a contact-hungry world. Where the contacts have been loving, as with cuddly pets, the intimacies involved have caused considerable pleasure; where they have been strictly non-loving, as with experimental animals, they have caused considerable displeasure. In sum total they account for a vast number of tactile interactions, and animals are clearly of great importance to us in this respect. We have been considering mostly cases of adult human activity; but pet-keeping is also a significant pattern for the older child, when it starts to imitate its parents by showing intense pseudo-parental care for small animals, cuddling them, carrying them, nursing them and caring for them as if they were totally dependent infants. Since cats and dogs are often already stamped as the pseudo-infants of the real parents in the family group, the young pseudo-parents frequently become more devoted to other species of a type that adults normally scorn, such as rabbits, guinea-pigs and tortoises. These species, being uncontaminated by parental involvements, then provide a separate and more private world for the substitute intimacies of the juvenile pseudo-parents.

For younger children the problem is solved by the use of toy animals—substitutes for the substitutes for love. These are cared for and loved exactly as though they were living beings, and the attachment to a favourite Mickey Mouse or Teddy bear is as passionate and powerful as that of any older child to a favourite rabbit or, later, to an adored pony. For many girls the attachment to a large cuddly toy animal survives right into adulthood, and a newspaper photograph of recent hijack victims shows a teenage girl returning to safety 'still clutching the Teddy bear that comforted her through her ordeal in the desert'. When we are badly in need of some kind of reassuring body contact, even an inanimate object will do, and this is the subject of the next chapter.

7

OBJECT INTIMACY

On a hoarding in Zurich, Switzerland, there is a large poster showing a man's head reproduced twice, one beside the other. The heads are identical except for one detail: between the lips of one there is a cigarette; between the lips of the other there is instead a baby's dummy, or pacifier. It is assumed that the message is obvious, since not a single word accompanies the picture. Without realizing it, the designers of this poster have said far more about the importance of smoking than they intended. In one simple visual statement they have explained why so many thousands of people are prepared to risk a painful death, coughing and spewing as their lungs clog with cancerous cells.

The poster is, of course, supposed to put adult smokers to shame by making them feel immature and babyish, but it can also be read backwards. If the man with the dummy in his mouth is gaining some comfort from it, just like a baby, then all that is wrong with that part of the picture is that it looks so infantile. Now switch to the other head—here the problem is solved. Like the dummy, the cigarette gives comfort, too, and in one stroke the babyish element is gone. Seen this way, it might almost be an advertisement to encourage smoking in those who have not yet discovered the basic comfort of this activity. Smoke a cigarette and you can be pacified without feeling immature!

Even if we do not perversely twist the well-intended message in this way, it nevertheless provides us with a valuable clue concerning the world-wide smoking problem that faces society today. It is a problem that has been dealt with recently for the first time. A large-scale campaign to alert smokers to the dangers of filling the lungs with carcinogenic smoke has been undertaken in many countries. Cigarette promotions have been banned on television in several major areas, and there has been endless discussion of how to discourage children from taking up the habit. Gruesome films are shown of pathetic hospital patients in the advanced stages of lung cancer. Some smokers have responded intelligently and given up, but many others have become so alarmed that instead they have been forced to light up an extra cigarette to calm their shattered nerves. In other words, although the problem is at last being dealt with, it is by no means solved. Simply to tell people they must not do something because it is harmful may be a wise step to take, but it is also a short-term one. It is like using war to solve the population problem. War kills millions, but as soon as it is over there is a post-war birth bulge and the population growth goes soaring on again. Similarly, every time there is an anti-smoking scare, thousands of people stop smoking, but after the scare is over, the shares of the cigarette companies start to soar again.

The great error of the anti-smoking campaigners is that they rarely stop and ask the basic question: why do people want to smoke in the first place? They seem to think it has something to do with drug addiction — with the habit-forming effects of nicotine. There is an element of this, certainly, but it is by no means the most important factor operating. Many people do not even inhale their smoke and can be absorbing only minute amounts of the drug, so that the causes of their addiction to cigarettes must be sought elsewhere. The answer clearly lies in the act of oral intimacy involved in holding the object between the lips, as the Zurich poster so beautifully demonstrates, and this answer almost certainly applies as the basic explanation for the full inhalers as well. Until this aspect of smoking is properly investigated, there will be little long-term hope of eliminating it from our stressed, comfort-seeking cultures.

What we are plainly dealing with here is a case of an inanimate object being used as a substitute for a real intimacy with another human being. In examining this phenomenon, we are moving one step further away from the original source — namely, intimacy with intimates. The first step away took us to intimacy with semi-strangers (the professional touchers), the second step took us to intimacy with live substitutes (pet animals), and now the third step takes us into the world of dummies — objects with a hidden intimacy factor. There are many of them besides the cigarette, but it helps to start with this one because it leads us naturally back to the start of the whole story, at the point where a distraught mother jams a rubber substitute for her nipple into the mouth of her screaming infant.

The baby's dummy, sometimes called a pacifier or a comforter, is usually described as a 'blind' nipple, since, unlike the teat of a feeding-bottle, it has no hole in it. The description is a little misleading because no mother can boast such a huge bulbous nipple as that found on the average commercial dummy. This is a super-nipple, milkless, but with a greatly magnified tactile quality. At its outer end there is a flat disc to simulate the mother's breast and to stop the rubber super-nipple being sucked right into the mouth.

Dummies of this sort have been in use for centuries, but not so long ago they fell into disrepute because they were considered a dangerous source of infection. More recently they have started to make a come-back, and today they are recommended in many cases by medical authorities. Babies given dummies in their early months are much less likely to become thumb-suckers (the obvious alternative if no nipple is available to give comfort when comfort is needed). Also, it is no longer believed that dummies deform the mouth or damage the developing teeth, and recent experiments have shown the experts what many mothers knew already, namely that dummies do have a really dramatic calming effect upon a distressed infant. 'Non-nutritive sucking', as it is officially termed, was studied carefully in a large number of babies and their responses recorded. It was found that after only thirty seconds with the dummy in the mouth, crying was reduced to one-fifth of its previous level, and agitated hand and foot movements to one-half. It was also pointed out that, even without active sucking, the presence of the super-nipple between the baby's lips has a calming effect. If a baby is half asleep and has stopped sucking, the removal of the dummy can easily start it crying again.

All this adds up to the fact that having something between the lips is a comforting experience for the human animal, since it spells reassuring contact with the primary protector, the mother. It is a powerful form of symbolic intimacy, and when we look at an old man sucking contentedly on the stem of his pipe, it becomes abundantly clear that it is one that stays with us all our lives.

The important thing for the adult 'sucker' is that he should not appear to be doing what he is doing; hence the message of the Zurich poster. The use of a baby's dummy by a stressed adult would probably be as calming as anything else, if only it did not carry the 'infantile' stigma. Since it does, however, he is forced to adopt disguised dummies of various kinds. The cigarette, in this respect at least, is ideal, because it is so totally adult. Being prohibited for children means that it is not only non-infantile, but also non-childlike, and therefore completely removed in context from the baby-sucking that is its true origin. The object feels soft between the lips and the smoke warms it, which makes it even more like the genuine mother's nipple than a rubber dummy. Furthermore, the sensation of something being sucked out of the end of it and drawn down the throat adds to the illusion. A new symbolic equation is set up: warm inhaled smoke equals mother's warm milk.

Many smokers, when putting a cigarette to their mouths,

or when taking it away, let their fingers fall on the outsides of their lips, simulating in this way the touch of the mother's breast. Some put the cigarette between their lips and leave it there for long periods of time, only drawing on it occasionally. When they do this, the non-drawing moments are similar to those of the half-asleep baby who still held the dummy in its mouth after it had stopped sucking on it. Other smokers, when they take the cigarette from the mouth, continue to fondle it between their fingers, even though it would be easy to put it down on an ashtray or some other surface. Deeply stained 'nicotine fingers' bear silent testimony to this urge to hold on to the comforting tobacco-nipple, even when it is not in oral use.

Variations on this theme include the businessman's super-nipple, the cigar, the tip of which is suitably rounded and smooth where it touches the mouth. With quiet ceremony this smooth 'blind' nipple is pierced and snipped with special gadgets, to ease the comforting flow of warming smoke-milk. For some, the soft touch of the cigarette or cigar is sacrificed to increased smoothness in the form of a cigarette-holder, a cigar-holder or a pipe. Here the tongue can play with a surface as smooth and slippery as a nipple of flesh or a teat of rubber. It is surprising that some device has not been used that is both soft and slippery — say a rubber holder — but perhaps this would not be sufficiently disguised, and would begin to look too much like the real thing to maintain its adult respectability. It would certainly make it more difficult for pipe-smokers to employ one of their favourite devices, namely sucking an empty pipe. That is already getting dangerously close to the obvious, and a rubber pipe-stem would be the final give-away.

The enormous amount of tobacco-smoking that takes place around the world today bears evidence to the vast demand that exists for comforting acts of symbolic intimacy. If the damaging side-effects of this pattern of behaviour are to be eradicated, it will be necessary either to de-stress the population to the appropriate degree, or to provide alternatives. Since there is no sign of any great or immediate hope for the former, the solution will have to be the latter. Plastic cigarettes have been suggested and even tried, but there seems little hope for them. The suggestion is valid enough in itself, but it overlooks the important factors of the warmth and true 'suckability' of real cigarettes. Also, it fails to provide any official excuse for the action. There must be a disguise of some kind if the activity is to be readily acceptable. It is true that many people suck the ends of pencils, pens, matchsticks, and the tips of the side-pieces of spectacles, but all these objects have other 'official' functions. A plastic cigarette would fail in this respect and would therefore appear too much like the baby's dummy in the Zurich poster. Some other solution will have to be found, and it looks very much as though this will have to come from the cigarette manufacturers themselves, in the form of a synthetic or herbal tobacco that does not damage the lungs. Research is already progressing in this direction, and perhaps the most valuable contribution made by the recent lung-cancer scares and propaganda campaigns will be to force a drastic speeding up in these investigations. Bearing in mind the deep significance of smoking, as I have outlined it here, this is probably the only long-term way in which these campaigns will be able to help.

Those people who have given up smoking, or who have attempted to give it up, complain that they start getting fatter soon after they abandon their non-nutritional tobacco-nipples. This immediately gives a clue about certain kinds of feeding. A great deal of the nibbling and food-sucking we do is primarily concerned with symbolic oral intimacies, rather than true adult food-intake. The cigarette-hungry ex-smoker, when in sudden need of added comfort, grabs a sweet food morsel and stuffs it into his nipple-empty mouth. Sucking candies and sweets is yet another of our disguised breast-feeding substitutes. For most of us it is the pattern of behaviour that fills the gap between the dummies of infancy and the cigarettes of adulthood. The confectionery shop is the world of the child. Too old for rubber pacifiers, he takes to sucking gob-stoppers and bulls-eyes, lollipops and sticks of seaside rock. They may rot the teeth, but they help to replace the lost comfort. As adults we largely turn our backs on these delights, but many a young lover still brings to his 'sweetheart' the comforting gift of a box of assorted chocolate nipples. And many a bored housewife dips into a box of soothing candies. A trick sometimes used to give these objects adult respectability is to fill them with anti-childish alcohol and pop them into our mouths in the form of 'liqueur chocolates'.

Although these food objects do not last as long as nipples, they do have the important qualities of softness and sweetness to help them in their symbolic role. One special form over-comes this drawback of being short-lived, and that is chewing-gum. Chewing-gum consists of an elastic substance known as chicle gum, sweetened and flavoured. (One part of chicle gum to three parts of sugar, warmed and kneaded together and flavoured with cloves and cinnamon, wintergreen or pepper-mint.) It can be chewed for hour after hour and is advertised as something to 'calm your nerves and help you concentrate'. Symbolically, it is nothing short of a rubbery, detachable nipple. Because of its special properties it should enjoy enor-mous success, but it is badly hindered by the conspicuous jaw movements that accompany its use. These cause no problem for the chewer, but for those near him they create the impres-sion that he is incessantly eating. Since he never swallows the 'food' in his mouth, this conveys the feeling that the object in his mouth is in some way unpleasant, like a tough piece of gristle, and as he becomes soothed, his observers become irritated. The result has been that, in many social settings, chewing a piece of gum has become looked upon as a 'dirty habit', and the activity has therefore remained a restricted one.

Since mother's milk is a warm, sweet liquid, it is not sur-prising that adults employ a variety of warm, sweet drinks to soothe themselves at moments of tension or boredom. The millions of gallons of tea, coffee, drinking-chocolate and cocoa that are consumed annually have little to do with the real demands of thirst, but again thirst is there to provide the vital official excuse. The cups and mugs from which we sip these milk-substitutes so eagerly also provide a pleasantly smooth, slippery surface to press against our comfort-seeking lips, and the outcry when modern 'disposability' demands the use of non-smooth, non-slippery paper cups is easy to understand.

Once more, it is interesting to see the way we avoid the obvious: we drink tea hot, but milk cold. To drink hot milk is too overtly babyish. Only invalids drink hot milk, but that is permissible because, as we have already seen, the invalid has given up the adult struggle and has become an 'instant-baby' in other ways as well, so for him one more baby pattern makes no difference.

Apart from cold milk, or milk-shakes, which significantly are usually sucked through a straw, there are many other types of cold, sweet drink that we employ as comforters. They are nearly always advertised as thirst-quenchers, but in this respect they always fall far short of simple, plain water. They do, however, provide that vital sweet taste, and the increasingly acceptable habit of drinking them straight from the bottle helps to improve their symbolic value. The bottles in question have therefore shrunk in size from the traditional dimensions down to something remarkably close to that of the baby's bottle. In fact, if someone were to emulate the Zurich cigarette poster and show a man drinking from a cola or lemonade bottle with a rubber teat on it, the game would be up.

Many other objects, such as the stems of plants, or the beads of a necklace worn around the neck, are often brought up to the lips in fleeting moments of self-comfort, but enough has been said now to show that the oral intimacies of infancy remain an important part of our adult lives, even outside the more obvious spheres of friendly or sexual kissing, and we can move on to consider other parts of the adult body.

Another basic form of contact in babyhood is the pressing of the cheek against the mother's body when resting. Cheek-pressing with soft substitute objects is rare amongst adult males, but it remains fairly common with females. Many advertisements for soft bedding, blankets and linen display a serenely smiling female hugging to her body the cuddly product, her head tilted to one side and her cheek pressed lovingly to the smooth surface of the cloth. This is particularly common with blanket advertisements, to the extent that it is almost the only pose employed, despite the obvious fact that, once on the bed, the blanket will be prevented from making such a contact by the intervention of the inevitable bed-sheets.

Fur coat advertisements follow a similar course, frequently showing the fur collar turned up, or pushed up with the hands, so that its ultra-soft surface caresses the wearer's cheeks. Fur rugs offer a more extensive contact surface, like a giant maternal body flattened out on the floor or bed.

Perhaps the most widespread and common form of soft cheek contact, and one that is employed by both males and females, is the use of a down-filled pillow when sleeping at night. The caress of this tender pillow-breast provides a major soothing element at the end of the day, helping to calm us into a condition where we are prepared at last to sink into a deep slumber and give up the adult battle of the day. Great subtlety has been employed by pillow manufacturers in producing exactly the right balance between springiness and softness, and at any large bedding store it is possible to select a new pillow from a wide range of slightly varying tactile qualities. For many adults, one particular pillow, or pillow 'strength', becomes extremely important as an aid to falling asleep, and if they are faced (in both senses of the word) with the wrong type of pillow when trying to sleep in a strange bed, at a hotel or in a friend's house, they may find it difficult to drift off into a peaceful sleep as quickly as they can at home. This phenomenon is much more pronounced in the case of 'home-lovers' who travel little and who, over a period of years, become fixated on a specific pillow quality, such as resilience, thickness or sagginess.

A similar development occurs with the rest of the bed. In addition to sensitive pillow responses, adults come to prefer a particular softness or hardness in the mattress beneath them, and a certain lightness or heaviness, a looseness or a tight 'tucked-in-ness' in the bedding that covers them, as they settle down to the vitally important nocturnal bed-embrace that will envelop them for a total of one-third of their entire lives.

In 1970 a new type of bed appeared on the market in America—the 'waterbed'. Essentially, this is a vinyl mattress filled with water. Lying on it, the sleeper sinks gently into its liquid embrace as if returning to a semi-womb. A thermostat and heating element inside it keeps the water at an appropriately soothing temperature. In the second half of 1970, over 15,000 of these beds were sold, and the demand soon outstripped the supply. The advertisers encouraged their prospective buyers with significant phrases such as 'Live and love in liquid luxury' and 'You can make them rock-and-roll you to sleep'. The only hazard, to use a gynaecological expression, is rupturing the membrane. Accidentally puncturing a waterbed is almost as messy and comfortless as being born. Perhaps this slight but nagging fear will, in the end, keep most of us wrapped in the safer embrace of our old-fashioned cloth-beds.

Examined objectively, our sleeping habits, with our soft pillows, bedding and mattresses, begin to take on a special significance. They are more than a device for acquiring dream-time, in order for our computer-brains to sort out and file away the confusing bombardment of new thoughts from the past day, and much more than the mere act of obtaining physical rest for the exertions of the new day that is coming. They represent also a massive, world-wide indulgence in abandoning ourselves to the comforting intimacy of an inanimate envelopment that is part cloth-womb and part cloth-mother embrace.

Even during our waking hours we do not entirely reject these primal delights, as the modern furniture industry can demonstrate so clearly. 'Easy' chairs and sofas, of a voluptuous softness and bed-like snugness unknown in previous centuries, have become the almost inevitable centre-piece of every drawing-room, sitting-room and lounge. There, at the end of the hard working day, we sink gratefully into the soft intimacy of our favourite piece of soft furniture, whose 'arms' may not actually embrace us, but whose yielding surfaces nevertheless provide great body comfort. Cuddled snugly on the symbolic laps of our chair-mothers, we then settle down with child-like security to view at a safe distance the chaos of the harsh adult world outside, as symbolically portrayed on our television screens or between the covers of our novels.

If, in describing the act of watching television from the soft comfort of an easy chair in this way, as an infantile act similar to looking out of a window while safely held on a mother's lap, I appear to be condemning it, I hasten to add that this is not my intention. On the contrary, it is an added advantage to this now world-wide pattern of behaviour. In addition to providing entertainment and education, the act of watching television can, as I have shown, provide a vitally important soothing element in our stressful adult world. The glass screen that covers the pictures we watch traps them safely inside the television box where they cannot harm us. This helps to compensate for the fact that our chair-mothers only provide one of the two vital security factors that the real mother gives to her infant. The real mother provides both the intimacy of soft body contact *and* protection against the outside world. Our chair-mothers provide only the soft contact – they cannot protect us. But this is where the inpenetrable glass surface of the television screen comes to our rescue, compensating for the missing protection by safely walling us off from the adult dramas unfolding inside the box. The symbolic equation is therefore simple enough: real mother that protects and comforts = screen that protects + chair-mother that comforts.

Viewing our home life in this way, it is not surprising to find that when we travel or go on a vacation most of us prefer to stay in hotels which simulate in almost every way the conditions we once knew in the nursery. As in our infancy, everything is done for us and we do not need to lift a finger. Our food is prepared by the chef-mother, served to us by the waitress-mother, and our beds are made and our rooms cleaned by the maid-mother. At the best hotels, the use of room service can take us back virtually to the cradle, with our baby-crying replaced by the simple act of pressing the wall-button or lifting the house-phone. And frequently one of the first things that people do when they become rich is to introduce these nursery conditions into their own homes by employing personal staff-mothers. Also, as I pointed out in an earlier chapter, the sick-bed and the hospital provide a similar condition for the invalid who has temporarily given up the adult struggle completely.

Sometimes we indulge ourselves briefly in the even more basic luxury of a return to a womb-like condition by the act of taking a hot bath. It is no accident that nearly all of us prefer to do this at womb-temperature, floating blissfully in our mock-amniotic fluid and feeling beautifully secure inside the curving walls of our bath-wombs, with the bathroom door safely locked against the adult world outside. Sooner or later, however, we are forced to remove the cervical bath-plug and reluctantly face the trauma of a new birth. As if knowing of our fears at this dreaded moment, the towel manufacturers compete to provide us with the softest embrace they can produce. As one towelling advertisement puts it, 'Our towels just hug you dry!'; and the girl in the accompanying picture is shown clutching the object in question ecstatically to her body and face, as if her very life depended on it.

When this towel-hugging girl finally gets dressed, she need not fear that these tender intimacies will cease. Advertisers of body clothing—underwear, sweaters, skirts, and the rest—all promise her similar rewards. Those brief panties are much more, it seems, than a matter of mere modesty, for we learn that they also offer you a 'bare hug' which 'gently, caressingly ... stretches to follow every curve of your body'. And those tights — they are 'silky soft and sensual' and 'hug you snugly from top to toe', not to mention those stockings which 'embrace your legs in a gentle, lingering caress', or those jersey dresses with that 'clinging feeling'. The lucky girl can therefore walk about fully dressed and apparently alone, but symbolically clad in a whole mass of caressing, embracing, hugging cloth-lover intimacies. If all the clothing advertisements put together had a cumulative effect, it would be surprising if she could perform the simple act of crossing a room without experiencing a multiple orgasm. Luckily for her real lovers, however, the impact of her assorted cloth-lovers is much milder, in most cases, than the advertisers would have us believe. Nevertheless, mild though it may be, it is still a genuine and important part of the body reward of wearing the soft and comfortable clothing of today.

This intimacy between clothing and wearer is more than a one-way affair. Not only do the clothes embrace the wearer — in addition, the wearer also embraces the clothes. This is, after all, a fair return for all that snug hugging and gentle caressing. The favourite way of repaying the compliment is to thrust one or both hands deep into some suitable fold of cloth. Napoleon's characteristic pose, with one hand inserted into his jacket, immediately comes to mind, but today the most widespread version is the hands-in-pockets action. Pockets are officially there to carry small objects, and if we put a hand into one, it is supposedly in the process of taking something out. But the vast majority of hand-in-pocket poses have nothing to do with object-retrieving. Instead, they are prolonged contact actions in which we, so to speak, hold hands with our pockets. Schoolboys and soldiers are often ordered to 'take your hands out of your pockets', with no explanation given other than that it is slovenly or untidy. The truth is, of course, that the posture indicates that they have relaxed into a symbolic act of intimacy, and this conflicts with their official roles as attentive, subordinate males. For males who are not restricted in this way, there are several alternatives open, and the choice made in any particular instance follows a rather curious rule. It is this: the higher up the body the hand/clothing contact is made, the more assertive it is. The most assertive of all is the grasping of the lapels. Coming a close second is the thumbs-in-waistcoat action. Next is the Napoleonic hand-in-jacket-front posture. Further down there is the hands-in-jacket-side-pockets pose, and further still the very common hands-in-trouser-pockets. Going any lower, with a hands-grasp-trouser-legs action, becomes appropriately low on the assertiveness scale.

The reason for this rule seems to be that the higher up the hand goes in making the contact, the more it adopts what amounts to an intention movement of striking a blow. Whenever a real blow is struck, it must be preceded by a raising of the hitting arm, prior to lashing out at the opponent. As we have already seen, this action becomes frozen as a formal signal in the case of the raised fist of the communist salute. The firm grasping of the lapels goes a long way towards this — as far, in fact, as a hand-to-clothing contact can go — and it is natural therefore that this should be the most truculent message of the various alternatives. Along with the thumbs-in-waistcoat posture, it has become almost a caricature of assertiveness, and a serious dominant male today is much more likely to adopt the lower-level hands-in-jacket-side-pocket posture when he finds himself displayed in a public place. This latter action is particularly favoured by tycoons, generals, admirals and political leaders, and it also became a cliché posture for the big-time gangsters of the roaring 'twenties. Such men are much more reluctant to adopt the lower-level posture of hands-in-trouser-pockets, at least when they are in a context that demands the assertion of their dominant rights.

An intriguing exception to the above rule is the thumbs-hooked-in-belt posture. Although this occurs rather low down on the body, it conveys a decidedly truculent flavour. It is popular with 'he-men', cowboys, pseudo-cowboys and mock-aggressive girls. Its assertive qualities appear to stem not only from a quick-on-the-draw intention movement, but also from the fact that it has become the modern, waistcoatless version of the old-fashioned thumbs-in-waistcoat posture. Sometimes the whole hand is slipped beneath the belt, or into the top of the trousers, but it then immediately loses much of its aggressiveness and fits more suitably on to the scale outlined above.

In addition to these actions, there are many small ways in which the hands perform minor intimacies with different parts of the clothing. All of them appear under stress, and many of them seem to represent symbolic versions of grooming acts that we would like someone else to be applying to our bodies to soothe us. Men can frequently be seen adjusting their cuff-links or smoothing their ties. President Kennedy frequently fingered his central jacket button at moments of public stress. Winston Churchill was often pictured at times of tension with his hand pressed flatly against the lower part of his jacket, as if engaged in a fragmentary self-embrace.

With the female sex, bracelets and necklaces come in for a great deal of handling and fingering at moments of strain, just as nuns no doubt obtain soothing comfort from the physical actions of telling their beads. At other times, the smooth caress of lipstick on lips, or powder-puff on cheeks, will provide a reassuring sensation of touch for a nervous female taking time off from a stressful social engagement. At more private moments, the repeated combing or brushing of hair, far beyond the demands of 'hair adjustment', can also have a marked calming effect, playing the role of a self-directed lover's caress.

In some instances, the act of making contact with a companion is performed indirectly, through an intermediate object of some kind, as when we clink our glasses together in making a toast, instead of making direct skin contact. A classic example can be found in any old Victorian scrap-book where a family group photograph has been taken. Typically, the mother sits in a central chair, with the latest addition to the large family nestled on her lap. Her husband, whose natural inclination is to put his arm around her shoulder, is too inhibited to do this in so public a situation and instead embraces the back of the chair in which she is sitting. The modern version of this can often be seen when two friends sit together informally and one stretches his arm along the back of the sofa they are sharing, aiming it in the direction of the other's back. Similarly, if a person is sitting alone in a chair, he may embrace the arms of it lovingly while talking animatedly to a companion in a chair opposite. Occasionally, additional chair-comfort is obtained by the use of a rocking-chair—another favourite action of President Kennedy's when under stress. The rocking comfort, needless to say, relates directly back to the rocking of the cradle or the mother's arms.

Finally we come to those objects that provide, quite specifically, substitutions for sexual intimacies. At the mildest level there are the photographs of loved ones, or the 'pin-ups' of those we would like to make love to, which can be kissed and touched in the unavoidable absence of the real thing. The use of life-size 'pillow-posters' is a new trend in the direction, it now being possible to buy a pillow-slip imprinted with a picture of the face of a favourite film star, to fit over the pillow that graces your bed. Then, at bedtime, you can lie cheek to cheek with the adored one, and fall gently asleep in this surrogate, cloth embrace.

Moving on to copulation itself, it was claimed during World War II that enemy soldiers (it is always enemy soldiers) at the front line were supplied with inflatable rubber dummy-females, complete with sexual orifices, for purposes of relieving sexual tensions. Whether this was merely propaganda to show how sex-starved and badly off the enemy were, or whether it actually happened, I have not been able to ascertain.

Inanimate substitutes for the male penis have, by contrast, a long and factual history, and even rate a mention in the Old

Testament. Usually called dildoes, but also referred to as godemiches, consolateurs, bijoux indiscrets and dil-dols, they were known even before biblical times, and appear in ancient Babylonian sculptures dating from hundreds of years before Christ. In ancient Greece they had the name 'olisbos', meaning 'slippery bull', and they were apparently particularly popular amongst the Turkish harems. As the centuries passed, their use spread to practically every land in the world. Their popularity waxed and waned, apparently reaching a peak in the eighteenth century, when they were sold openly in London, a phenomenon not encountered again until the second half of the present century. Great care and skill is said to have been put into their manufacture 'so as to enhance realism in a coition fantasy'. In the 1970s they are now on sale in several versions in the 'sex shops' of a number of Western countries. Those that are not purchased by males out of sheer curiosity are used by lesbians or by solitary females for the purpose of masturbation.

Two forms of mechanically operated dildo have also appeared in recent times. One sort was of a highly technical nature, designed especially for an American research investigation into the nature of human copulation. Devised by radio-physicists, electrically powered, made of plastic with the optical properties of plate glass, equipped with cold-light illumination to facilitate intra-vaginal film-making, and fitted with masturbator-operated controls for varying both speed and depth of thrust, this was, by any standards, a truly remarkable instrument, a sensitive and tireless dummy lover, the sex-surrogate to end all sex-surrogates. A less ambitious and much less expensive mechanical device, and one that has gained widespread popularity in recent years, is the comparatively simple 'vibrator', or 'vibro massager'. It is a small, smooth-surfaced, battery-operated, plastic object, long and thin, with a rounded tip, the original and official function of which was localized muscle massage. It soon found a new and more sexual function as a gently vibrating masturbation dildo, and since it could be bought in its official role as a simple massage machine, had the added advantage that it could be obtained without undue embarrassment by purchasers who would have hesitated to acquire the more obvious forms of sexual equipment. Even in the outspoken underground press, the charade is maintained. A typical advertisement reads: 'Personal Massagers – penetrating, stimulating massager. Throbs away aches and frustrating pains. 7 in. long by 1½ in. Standard batteries included.' The coyness employed in this advertisement is completely out of step with the rest of the text of underground papers, where the bluntest and most uninhibited forms of sexual comment are to be found. Once again we see the operation of the rule we have met so many times before, namely that adult intimacies require some sort of disguise, either to ourselves or to others, to obscure the real purpose of what is going on.

A most unusual and ingenious form of sex-surrogate sometimes used by females in Japan is the rin-no-tama, also known as the watama or ben-wa. This consists of two hollow balls, roughly the size of pigeon's eggs, which are inserted into the vagina. Originally made of leaf brass, but nowadays probably of plastic, one ball is empty and the other contains a small quantity of quicksilver (mercury). The empty ball is inserted first and pushed up to the end of the vagina, next to the cervix. The second is then placed against it and the opening of the vagina plugged with paper or cotton. Thus equipped, and with no embarrassing outward signs of her peculiar condition, the female proceeds to amuse herself with apparent innocence by swinging on a swing or rocking in a rocking-chair. The rhythmic back-and-forth motions then produce shifting pressures inside the vagina which simulate the thrusting of a male penis. Although, as a sexual 'toy', the rin-no-tama has the great advantage of permitting private enjoyment in public, it has not achieved the widespread popularity of the ubiquitous vibrator, presumably because, unlike the latter, it lacks a non-sexual, 'official' function.

Toys themselves, of completely non-sexual types, should also, incidentally, be a medium where tactile rewards are made available to us through inanimate objects. The possibilities are enormous, but few are attempted and even fewer succeed. When they do appear, they are usually presented as some kind of athletic exercise. The trampoline was one. The main reward here was the strange sensation of being embraced by the springy surface, flung into the air and then embraced again in a new posture. But the whole process had to be carried out under the cover of a highly muscular and sporting atmosphere, which ruled it out for many people. The short-lived hula-hoop was another case, combining the rotating embrace of the hoop around the performer's waist with an undulating action of the hips. Its appeal, however, was strictly limited and did not survive past the novelty stage.

The art world has several times attempted to present intimacy objects to an intimacy-hungry world, but with little success. In 1942 the Museum of Modern Art in New York exhibited for the first time a new type of sculpture called 'handies' or hand sculpture. They consisted of small, smoothly rounded pieces of polished wood in abstract shapes that would fit comfortably into the human hand and could be squeezed and turned this way and that to vary the tactile sensation. The artist who created them stressed that they were meant to be felt rather than looked at, and suggested that they would make an excellent substitute for cigarettes, chewing-gum or doodling for those who tend to be fidgety in committee meetings. Unhappily, it was not to be, and handies have hardly been heard of since. Once again, the message was too obvious, no committee member wishing it to be known that he was so obviously in need of a little comforting pseudo-body contact.

More recently, in the 1960s, certain artists have attempted more ambitious assaults on the bodies of art-lovers by creating 'environmental sculptures'. These have taken many forms, some of which have included a kind of play-space into which the visitor walks, there to be assailed by a series of varying tactile impressions as he passes through tubes, tunnels and passageways, walled and hung with a wide variety of textures and substances. Again, success has been short-lived and great possibilities have been wasted.

A final example neatly sums up the whole situation. One particular artist devised a simulated copulation capsule, into which the 'art-lover' was placed and wired up in various ways. The capsule was then shut and the machine switched on, with the idea of producing a massive sensory experience. At an art institute, the creator of this machine delivered a lecture about his concepts to an engrossed audience, who listened with interest as he explained that, owing to technical hitches, he had now devised a much simpler version of the machine, in which he had great faith. The modified device consisted basically of a large vertical sheet of rubber, or some such material, with a small hole at genital height, through which a male art-lover could insert his penis. For the female art-lover there was a similar vertical sheet, with a penis-shape protruding through it. In serious tones he then explained that, in addition to its simplicity, this new exhibit had the advantage that it could be used simultaneously by a male and female art-lover, with one standing on each side of it.

The absurdity of this story brings us back inevitably to the inherent absurdity of many of the examples given in the present chapter. It *is* absurd that an adult human being should have to coat his lungs with carcinogens in order to enjoy a crude substitute of the pleasures he once knew at his mother's breast, or when a baby's bottle was held to his lips. And it *is* absurd that grown men should endlessly have to mouth a disembodied, rubberized nipple in the form of chewing-gum, or that adult females should have to use a plastic massager instead of a live penis to achieve sexual gratification. But although these actions may seem absurd, pathetic or even downright repulsive to some, to many they are the only solution that seems to be available, and it must always be borne in mind that any intimacy, no matter how far removed it becomes from the real thing, is still better than the frightening loneliness of no intimacy at all. In other words, we must stop attacking the symptoms and take a closer look instead at the causes of the problem. If only we can become more intimate with our 'intimates', then we should need less and less in the way of substitutes for intimacy. In the meantime, almost any dummy-touch is better than no touch.

8

SELF-INTIMACY

The woman standing on the railway platform, about to board a train, is horrified. Her husband has just asked her if she remembered to lock the kitchen door and she has realized that she did not. What does she do? Before uttering a word, her mouth drops open and she clasps a palm to one of her cheeks. Even as she starts to speak, the hand stays there, pressed against the side of her face. Then, after a few moments, it descends, and the next phase of the behaviour sequence begins. We will not follow it further, however; instead we will concentrate on that hand, for it is the clue to a whole new world of body intimacies — intimacies with oneself.

In her fleeting moment of horror, the woman on the platform gave herself the instantaneous self-comfort of a swift caress — the clasping of a cheek. Her sudden feeling of emotional distress drove her, unconsciously, to provide the soothing contact which, under other circumstances, a loved one's hand might have offered, or which, long ago, her parents would have provided when she was a tiny, hurt child. Now, in place of a lover's or a mother's hand reaching out to touch her cheek, it is her own hand that flies up to make the contact. It does so automatically, unthinkingly, and without hesitation. In performing this act, her cheek has remained *her* cheek, but her hand has symbolically become someone else's — the lover's or the mother's.

Self-contacts of this kind are a form of body intimacy that

we hardly recognize as such, and yet they are fundamentally the same as the others discussed in previous chapters. They may appear to be 'one-person' acts, but in truth they are unconscious mimes of two-person acts, with part of the body being used to perform the contact movement of the imaginary companion. They are, in other words, pseudo-interpersonal.

In this respect they provide the fifth, and final, major source of body intimacies. The five can be illustrated as follows. (1) When we are feeling nervous or depressed, a loved one may attempt to reassure us by giving us a comforting hug or a squeeze of the hand. (2) In the absence of a loved one, it may have to be one of the specialist touchers, such as a doctor, who pats our arm and tells us not to worry. (3) If our only company is our pet dog or cat, we may take it in our arms and press our cheek to its furry body to feel the comfort of its warm touch. (4) If we are completely alone and some sinister noise startles us in the night, we may hug the bed-clothes tightly around us to feel secure in their soft embrace. (5) If all else fails, we still have our own bodies, and we can hug, embrace, clasp and touch ourselves in a great variety of ways to help soothe away our fears.

If you spend some time as an observer, simply watching the way people behave, you will soon discover that acts of self-contact, or auto-contact, are extremely common, much more common than you might at first suppose. It would be wrong, however, to consider all these contacts as substitutes for inter-personal intimacies. Some of them have other functions. A man scratching an itch on his leg, for instance, is not doing it as a mime of someone else doing it to him. He is doing it as a simple act of self-cleaning, performed in its own right, with no hidden intimacy factor. It is important, therefore, not to over-state the case for self-intimacies. In order to put them into their true perspective, it is best to start out with a basic question, namely how and why do we touch our own bodies?

With this question in mind, I analysed several thousand examples of human actions involving self-contact. The first fact to emerge was that the head region was the most important area for *receiving* these contacts, and the hand the most important organ for *giving* them. Although the head is only a small part of the total surface area of the human body, it nevertheless received approximately half the total number of self-contacts.

Surveying these head contacts first, it was possible to identify 650 different types of action. This was done by recording which part of the hand was used, how it made the contact, and which part of the head was involved. It soon became clear that there were four major categories. (The first three, although interesting in their own right, do not directly concern us here and will only be mentioned briefly. Their inclusion is important, however, in order to make it clear that they must be kept separate and not confused with the true self-intimacies.) The four categories are as follows.

1. *Shielding actions.* The hand is brought up to the head to cut off or reduce input to the sense organs. The man who wants to hear less puts his hands over his ears. The man who wants to smell less holds his nose. If the light is too bright, he shields his eyes, and if he cannot bear the sight in front of him, he covers them completely. Similar actions are used to reduce output, as when a hand comes up to cover the mouth and thereby conceal a facial expression.

2. *Cleaning actions.* The hand is brought up to the head to perform a scratch, rub, pick, wipe, or some similar action. A variety of hair-tidying actions also come under this general heading. Some of these movements are genuine attempts to clean and tidy the head region, but in many instances they are 'nervous' actions, caused by emotional tensions, and are similar to the 'displacement activities' described by ethologists in other species.

3. *Specialized signals.* The hand is brought up to the head to perform a symbolic gesture of some kind. A man who says 'I am fed up to here' holds the back of his hand to the underside of his chin, indicating that he is so full of symbolic 'food' that he cannot take any more. A boy who 'thumbs his nose' presses

his thumb to his nose and spreads his fingers out in the shape of a vertical fan. This insult originates from the symbolic act of imitating the comb of a fighting cock, which is how it has become a threatening gesture. This is also the reason why it is sometimes called 'cocking a snook'. Another animal symbolism used as an insult in certain countries is making a pair of horns by holding the hands to the temples, with the forefingers raised and slightly curled. A common form of self-insult is aiming a forefinger at the temple and firing an imaginary gun.

4. *Self-intimacies*. The hand is brought up to the head to perform some action that copies or imitates an interpersonal intimacy. Surprisingly, no fewer than four-fifths of the different hand-to-head actions fall into this self-intimacy category. It seems as if the main reason we have for touching our heads is one of obtaining comfort from unconsciously mimed acts of *being touched by someone else*.

The most common form that this takes is resting part of the head on the hand, with the elbow of the arm in question in contact with a supporting surface, and the forearm acting as a prop to take the weight of the head. It could, of course, be argued that this simply indicates that the neck muscles are tired. A little close observation of these actions soon reveals, however, that physical exhaustion cannot account for the majority of cases.

In this action, the hand is being used as more than a hand. By providing it with support from the elbow, it has become something more solid, and seems instead to be acting as a substitute for the shoulder or chest of the imaginary 'embracing companion'. When, as a child or a lover, we are held in another's arms, we frequently rest the side of our face against their body and feel their soft warmth through the skin of our cheek. By resting the side of our face on our supported hand, we are able to re-create that feeling in their absence, and thereby give ourselves a welcome sensation of comfort and intimacy. Furthermore, since the origin of the act is suitably obscure, we can do this in public without any fear of being thought of as infantile. Sucking a thumb in imitation of childhood breast-feeding might do as well, but there the disguise would wear too thin, and so we tend to avoid it.

Clasping an unsupported hand to the head is also a common act, like the one in the example given of the woman on the railway platform. When this is done, the head cannot lean so heavily, and it appears as if this type of action is more related to the caressing or clasping of the face or hair that is often performed by the embracing companion as an embellishment of the general intimacy. Here, the hand is acting as a symbolic companion's hand, rather than as a symbolic chest or shoulder.

The mouth is a region that receives a great deal of attention, but here the most common action is to touch it in some way with the fingers or thumb, rather than with the whole hand. When making oral contact, the fingers or thumb are being used as substitutes for the mother's breast and nipple. Full thumb-sucking, as I have said, is rare; but modified, less obvious versions of it are common. The simplest modification, and one that is frequently seen, is the pressing of the tip of the thumb between the lips. It is not inserted into the mouth or sucked, but the comforting contact is there nevertheless. The tip, side or back of the forefinger is also used a great deal in this way, and it is often held in contact with the lips for a considerable period of time, while its worried owner gains reassurance from its presence, as dim, unconscious echoes from the infantile past make themselves felt in the brain.

As an elaboration of this form of mouth contact, the finger or thumb is sometimes gently and slowly rubbed across the surface of the lips, re-creating the movements of the baby's mouth on the mother's breast. At more intense moments of anxiety, knuckle-biting and nail-biting put in an appearance. When frustrated aggression is added to the act in this way, it can, in the case of nail-biting, become so persistent as to cause near-mutilation, with the nails bitten down to tiny stumps and the nearby skin chewed raw.

Of all the many different kinds of hand-to-head contact,

the most common, in order of frequency, are: (1) jaw rest, (2) chin rest, (3) hair clasp, (4) cheek rest, (5) mouth touch and (6) temple rest. All are performed by both adult males and females, but in two cases there is a strong sexual bias. Hair-clasping is three times as common in women as men, and temple-resting is twice as common in men as in women.

If we leave the head and move down the body, we soon find other forms of self-intimacy. We are all familiar with the tragic newsreel scenes of the aftermath of a disaster such as an earthquake or a mine collapse. A distraught woman in such a situation does not merely clasp one hand to her cheek. The act would be inadequate under the circumstances. Instead she goes much further, hugging her body with her arms and rocking herself pathetically from side to side, as she sits outside the ruins of her home or waits desperately at the pit-head. If she and another sufferer do not find comfort in a mutual embrace, she responds by embracing herself and by rocking herself gently back and forth as her mother once would have done when she was a frightened infant.

This is an extreme case, but we all use a similar device almost every day of our lives, when we fold our arms across our chest. Because the situation is less intense, so is the action, and the folding of arms on the chest is a much weaker form of self-embrace than the full self-hug of misery. It nevertheless provides a mildly comforting sensation of self-intimacy and is typically seen in moments when we are slightly on the defensive. If we are talking in a group of semi-strangers, for example, at a party or some other social gathering, and one of them is coming rather 'too close for comfort', we regain some of our lost comfort by bringing up our arms and folding them across our chest. Usually we are hardly aware that we have performed the act, or that it has any relation to the movements around us, but the fact that it operates in this way has led to its use as an unconscious social signal. For instance, a man who wishes to block a doorway against intruders may stand in front of it, fold his arms across his chest and say, 'No one is allowed inside.'

The act of arm-folding in this case, which comforts the man in question, begins to look positively threatening to those in front of him. It signals the fact that he is shutting them out of his embrace, and that he finds self-sufficient strength in his own private act of self-embrace.

Another act of intimacy we all indulge in daily is what can be described as 'holding hands with ourself'. One hand acts as our own, while the other, which clasps or grasps it, acts as the hand of an imaginary companion. We do this in several ways, some more intense than others. When, for example, we are in a particularly strong hand-holding mood with a real companion, we often interlock our fingers with theirs, making the interaction somehow more binding and complex. Similarly, in the absence of such a companion, we can re-create this sensation by interlocking the fingers of our left hand with those of our right. At moments of tension this is sometimes done with such force that the flesh shows white with the great pressure we are unconsciously exerting.

Similar pressures are exerted lower down on the body when we sit with one leg twined tightly around the other. Leg-crossing again seems to provide us with a remarkable degree of self-comfort, providing, as it does, the reassuring pressure of one part of the body against another, and reminding us perhaps of the comforting pressure we felt on our legs when, in a clinging embrace, we straddled the bodies of our parents.

In Victorian times, ladies were expressly forbidden—by the official rules of etiquette then applying—to cross their legs in public or social situations. Victorian males were less restricted in this way, but they were, nevertheless, requested not to hug their knees or feet when performing the act. Today there are no such restrictions, and a random count of a large number of leg-crossings revealed that 53 per cent were female and 47 per cent male, so that no sex difference has survived the passage of time from the last century into this. Two sex differences do exist, however, in the form which the act takes. If it is done by placing the ankle of one leg on the knee or thigh of the other, then it is nearly always a male performance, presumably because for the female this means an undue amount of crotch-exposure. It is intriguing that this applies even where women are wearing trousers, so that it would appear that a trousered woman is still mentally wearing her skirt. The second difference concerns the position of the feet of the crossed legs. If the foot of the 'upper' leg remains in contact with the surface of the 'lower' leg after the legs have been crossed, then the performance is almost always a female one. (The exception to this rule is the low-level ankle/ankle cross, where there are no sex differences, and where the feet are almost bound to be touching one another because of the nature of the act.)

A more intimate form of leg contact is leg-hugging. At its highest intensity this involves bringing the thighs up and the chest down until the two meet. The pressure is increased by embracing the knees or lower legs with the arms. As an addition, the head is lowered on to the knees and the chin or side of the face rested there. In such cases, the bent-up legs are being used as the substitute for the trunk of the imaginary companion, with the knees acting as the chest or shoulders. This is predominantly a female act—of a number of cases recorded at random, 95 per cent were female and only 5 per cent male.

Another typically female action is the clasping of the thigh with the hand, a survey of a large number of such contacts revealing that 91 per cent were female and only 9 per cent male. There appears to be an erotic element present here, the female hand acting as if it were a man's hand placed on her thigh in a sexual context, an act more typical of a courting male than a courting female.

In this survey of self-intimacies, it has nearly always been the hands and arms, and sometimes the legs, that have performed as the active organs, the ones making the contact, but there are a few exceptions to this rule. Sometimes, and again this is typically a female movement, the head is actively lowered on to one shoulder and pressed or rested there, the contact being made by the cheek, jaw or chin. Here it is the shoulder that is being used as the symbolic chest or shoulder of the imaginary companion. Another example concerns the tongue, which may be used to caress the lips, or some other part of the body, certain females even being capable of making contact with their own nipples in this way.

In addition to all these varied methods of making bodily contact with oneself, there is one important aspect of self-intimacy that remains to be discussed, and that is the auto-erotic stimulation usually referred to as masturbation. The word itself appears to be a corruption of *manu-stuprare*, 'to defile with the hand', and reflects the fact that the most common method of sexual self-stimulation involves a hand-genital contact. For males, this usually means grasping the penis with one hand and rhythmically raising and lowering the arm. The hand then takes on two simultaneous symbolic roles. Its movements up and down the penis mimic the male's own pelvic thrusts, whilst with its grip it acts as a pseudo-vagina. For females, the equivalent action is the stroking of the clitoris with the fingers. Here the fingers are acting as substitutes for the rhythmic pressure applied indirectly to the clitoris by the pelvic thrusting of the male during copulation. Alternative methods for the female are the stroking of the labia or the rhythmic insertion of the fingers into the vagina, with the fingers then acting as a substitute penis. Another technique is thigh-rubbing, in which the thighs are squeezed together, with an alternating tightening and relaxing of the inner muscles to produce a rhythmic pressure on the compressed genitals.

Surveys carried out in the middle of the present century revealed that masturbation is an extremely common form of self-intimacy and is indulged in by the vast majority of individuals at some time in their lives. Although it has always been little more than a harmless substitute for the inter-personal act of copulation, social attitudes towards it have varied considerably at different times. It appears to be widely practised amongst so-called 'primitive tribes', but is usually referred to as something of a joke, indicating that the masturbator is a failed copulator.

An entirely different and much less healthy view was prevalent in our own cultures in earlier centuries, when serious attempts were made to suppress the activity completely. In the eighteenth century, masturbation was denounced as 'the heinous sin of self-pollution'. In the nineteenth century, it became 'the horrid and exhausting vice of self-abuse', and young Victorian ladies were forbidden to wash their genitals in case the gentle friction of such an act, when regularly performed, 'might induce impure thoughts'. The wicked French bidet was not allowed to cross the English channel. In the early part of the twentieth century, masturbation declined in horror to the level of a 'nasty habit', but religious authorities were still seriously concerned that it might actually give some sensual reward to the masturbator. They did, however, allow that 'the effusion of semen would be legitimate for medical purposes if only it could be achieved without causing pleasure'. By the middle of the twentieth century, attitudes had undergone a dramatic change, and it was at last boldly announced that masturbation is 'a normal and healthy act for a person of any age'. In the past two decades this new approach has continued to gain ground to the point where, in 1971, a respectable women's magazine was able to publish the following words of advice, words which would have astonished a Victorian reader: 'Masturbation ... is wholesome, normal and sound ... you are training your body to become a superb instrument of love. Masturbate to your heart's content.'

Today's adolescent who, in the absence of copulatory opportunities, feels inclined to indulge in this form of sexual self-intimacy is lucky indeed. The adolescent of yesterday, far from being freely permitted to perform this activity, was often severely punished for doing so. During the past two centuries all kinds of harsh restraints have been applied, some of which we now find hard to believe. In some cases the young male offender was fitted with a silver ring that was slotted through holes pierced in his foreskin. Alternatively, he might have been equipped with a small penis-belt armed with spikes that automatically pricked the penis if it started to become erect. Blistering the penis with red mercury ointment was another 'remedy' that was sometimes recommended. Both sexes of maturing children were occasionally forced to sleep with their hands tied together or to the bed-posts, to prevent them from 'playing with themselves' at night, or were equipped with modern versions of chastity-belts. Young females might be forced to suffer the mutilation of having the clitoris cauterized or completely removed by surgery, and circumcision for males was advised by some medical authorities as an imagined aid to stamping out the 'evil act' of self-stimulation.

Happily, with the single exception of male circumcision, none of these painful hazards has survived to the present day as a common practice. Society's age-old urge to mutilate its growing juveniles seems, at long last, to be under control. Bearing this in mind, it is worth digressing for a moment to consider why the curious ritual of circumcision should have escaped this general change of attitude. Today the anti-masturbatory excuse is no longer given. Instead, the foreskin of the male infant is amputated for 'religious, medical or hygienic' reasons. The frequency of the operation varies from country to country; in Britain it is thought to be performed on fewer than half the male babies born, whereas in the United States a figure as high as 85 per cent has been quoted.

The medical reason given in favour of foreskin-removal is that it eliminates certain (extremely rare) disease dangers. These only occur, however, if the unmutilated adult male fails to keep his penis reasonably clean by the simple act of pulling back the foreskin and washing the tip of the organ. If this is done regularly, there is, according to medical authorities, no more of a health risk for an uncircumcised male than for a circumcised one. Since the vast majority of foreskin removals are not performed for religious reasons, and since the medical grounds are hardly worth considering, the true reason for the thousands of sexual mutilations carried out on male babies each year remains something of a mystery. Referred to recently by one doctor in America as 'the rape of the phallus', it appears to be a hang-over from our distant cultural past. It has, since early times, been a common practice in most African tribes and was adopted by the ancient Egyptians, whose priest-doctors made sure that no self-respecting male retained his foreskin. Because of the social stigma attached to an attached foreskin, the Jews borrowed the circumcision ritual from the Egyptians and made it even more obligatory for the male members of their religion. In becoming a social or religious 'law', the original significance of the operation had already been forgotten, and it is not easy today to trace it back to its source. Even amongst the African tribes where it is part of elaborate initiation ceremonies, it is usually merely referred to as being 'the custom', but a number of explanations have been forthcoming from modern investigators. One suggestion is that the male foreskin was considered to be a feminine attribute, presumably because it covered up the head of the male organ in the way that the female labia cover the female genital opening. By the same argument, the female's clitoris was considered to be a masculine organ, so that when boys and girls reached sexual maturity, they were both made more true to their sex by having the offending opposite-sex attributes removed. Another suggestion is that the shedding of the foreskin was a symbolic imitation of the shedding of a snake's skin, an action that was widely thought to endow that reptile with immortality, since it reappeared so shining and bright after each shedding. The symbolic equation was straightforward enough: snake = phallus, therefore snakeskin = foreskin.

These and many other ingenious explanations have been

put forward, but all seem to be inadequate when the phenomenon of sexual mutilation is viewed as a whole. It has occurred at some time or another in almost every corner of the globe, in literally hundreds of different cultures, and the precise form it has taken has varied considerably. It does not always involve simple foreskin or clitoris removal. In certain cases the parts removed are more extensive, or the mutilations are slits and cuts rather than amputations. In some tribes the female may be stripped of her labia as well as her clitoris, and in others the male may suffer the painful loss of the entire skin surface covering the lower belly, pelvis, scrotum and inner legs, or he may be subjected to the ordeal of having his penis split in two, down its whole length. The only overall common factor seems to be the act by human adults of perpetrating mechanical damage to the genitals of their juniors.

That this ancient form of adult aggression should have survived into present times in the form of male circumcision is something that might bear closer examination by the modern medical profession. Not since the anti-masturbatory assaults of the last century have young females been attacked in this way, presumably because, unlike the males, there was no hygienic justification left for the removal of any part of their genitals. It is fortunate that the situation was not reversed, for if the clitoris could have been proved to be unhygienic and a suitable medical excuse therefore found for its removal, the female would have suffered a considerable loss of sexual responsiveness. Recent careful tests have shown that the penis, by contrast, suffers little or no loss of sensitivity as a result of foreskin-removal, so that males who are mutilated in this way by the respectable modern equivalents of the ancient witch-doctors do not, at least, experience any reduction of sexual performance. These modern tests do, of course, make complete nonsense of the earlier, anti-masturbatory reason for surgically removing the foreskin. Mutilated or unmutilated, the adult male is still going to be able to obtain an unhindered sexual reward from his solitary indulgences in genital self-intimacy.

Summing up, then, it can be said that the reason why male circumcision has survived so widely, when virtually all other forms of archaic genital dismembering have been abandoned in 'civilized' communities, is that it is the only one which does not impair sexual activity and which, at the same time, has been able to acquire a respectable whitewash of medical rationalization.

Returning to masturbation itself, there only remains the question of whether, in the new-found self-stimulation freedom of the latter half of the twentieth century, there are any future hazards waiting in store for us. If we are all advised to 'masturbate to our heart's content' by popular magazine articles, has the pendulum of sexual opinion swung too far? Clearly the earlier rubbish about masturbation causing untold misery and sickness had to be thrown out with a vigorous propaganda campaign, and this has now successfully been done; but is there perhaps a danger that, in sweeping the ridiculous old ideas away, we may go too far in the opposite direction? Masturbation is, after all, a second-rate form of intimacy, like all the substitute social activities discussed in previous chapters. Anything done alone that is a mimic of something done with a companion must, of necessity, be inferior to the genuine act of body intimacy, and this rule must apply to masturbation as much as to any other form of self-intimacy. When there is nothing better available, then of course no justifiable argument can be brought against these substitute activities; but supposing something better is hoped for in the near future, is there not a danger of developing a fixation on the inferior substitute acts which later makes it more difficult to effect a transfer to the real thing?

Contemporary words of advice to a masturbating female stress that every woman should develop her own individual masturbation style, and that it is important to set aside several hours a week so that the new response pattern will become a stable one. She is informed that when she has educated her body in this way she will be able to guide the male, when making love, to positions that give her the maximum sensations. At least this approach is honest: the female works out and stabilizes her self-reward pattern and then it is up to the male partner to service her accordingly. This is recommended as a method of training the female body to become 'a superb instrument of love'. As a system for providing considerable sexual reward for a lonely or frustrated female it may be excellent, but as a system for enhancing love it perhaps leaves something to be desired. It overlooks completely the fact that human copulation is much more than an act of mutual sexual servicing. To approach a moment of intense, reciprocal body intimacy with a previously fixed pattern of reward-demand is to put the cart before the horse. It is no better than using the male's actions as substitutes for masturbation, rather than the other way around. Similarly, if a male has become too heavily fixated on a particular kind of manual masturbation, he may end up using the female vagina as a substitute for his hand, instead of the reverse. To approach copulation in this way is to reduce the partner to a small stimulation device, instead of a complete, intimate and loving person. Over-emphasis on the importance of advanced masturbatory techniques is therefore not perhaps as entirely innocent as the 'new liberalism' would have us believe.

This said, however, it cannot be stressed too strongly that such a warning must in no way be taken as an excuse for a return to the guilt-ridden restrictions of yesterday's forbidden self-intimacies. If the pendulum has perhaps swung a little too far, we are still in a much better position than our immediate ancestors, and we should be grateful for the sexual reformers of the twentieth century who have made this possible. In all probability the dangers of self-intimate fixations will not usually be too serious. If two people come to love one another sufficiently, the emotional intensity of their relationship stands a good chance of sweeping away the rigidity of their previous, solitary patterns of self-gratification, and allowing an increasingly free growth of the sexual interactions that occur between them. If their relationship is less intense and this does not happen, then they will at least be able to enjoy a mutual exchange of their stylized erotic stimulations, which is a good deal better than the Victorian situation, where the marriage partners felt themselves obliged to 'get the nasty business over' as quickly as possible before falling gratefully asleep.

9

RETURN TO INTIMACY

We are born into an intimate relationship of close bodily contact with our mothers. As we grow, we strike out into the world and explore, returning from time to time to the protection and security of the maternal embrace. At last we break free and stand alone in the adult world. Soon we start to seek a new bond and return again to a condition of intimacy with a lover who becomes a mate. Once again we have a secure base from which to continue our explorations.

If, at any stage in this sequence, we are poorly served by our intimate relationships, we find it hard to deal with the pressures of life. We solve the problem by searching for substitutes for intimacy. We indulge in social activities that conveniently provide us with the missing body contacts, or we use a pet animal as a stand-in for a human partner. Inanimate objects are enlisted to play the vacant role of the intimate companion, and we are even driven to the extreme of becoming intimate with our own bodies, caressing and hugging ourselves as if we were two people.

These alternatives to true intimacy may, of course, be used as pleasant additions to our tactile lives, but for many they become sadly necessary replacements. The solution seems obvious enough. If there is such a strong demand for intimate contact on the part of the typical human adult, then he must relax his guard and open himself more easily to the friendly approaches of others. He must ignore the rules that say,

'Keep yourself to yourself, keep your distance, don't touch, don't let go, and never show your feelings.' Unfortunately, there are several powerful factors working against this simple solution. Most important of these is the unnaturally enlarged and overcrowded society in which he lives. He is surrounded by strangers and semi-strangers whom he cannot trust, and there are so many of them that he cannot possibly establish emotional bonds with more than a minute fraction of them. With the rest, he must restrict his intimacies to a minimum. Since they are so close to him physically, as he moves about in his day-to-day affairs, this requires an unnatural degree of restraint. If he becomes good at it, he is likely to become increasingly inhibited in *all* his intimacies, even those with his loved ones.

In this body-remote, anti-intimate condition the modern urbanite is in danger of becoming a bad parent. If he applies his contact restraint to his offspring during the first years of their life, then he may cause irreversible damage to their ability to form strong bonds of attachment later on. If, in seeking justification for his inhibited parental behaviour, he (or she) can find some official blessing for such restraint, then it will, of course, help to ease the parental conscience. Unhappily, such blessings have occasionally been forthcoming and have contributed harmfully to the growth of personal relationships within the family.

One example of this type of advice is so extreme that it deserves special mention. The Watsonian method of child-rearing, named after its perpetrator, an eminent American psychologist, was widely followed earlier in this century. In order to get the full flavour of his advice to parents, it is worth quoting him at some length. Here are some of the things he said:

> Mothers just don't know, when they kiss their children and pick them up and rock them, caress them and jiggle them upon their knee, that they are slowly building up a

human being totally unable to cope with the world it must later live in ... There is a sensible way of treating children. Treat them as though they were young adults ... Never hug or kiss them, never let them sit on your lap. If you must, kiss them once on the forehead when they say goodnight ... Can't a mother train herself to substitute a kindly word, a smile, in all of her dealings with the child, for the kiss and the hug, the pickup and the coddling? ... If you haven't a nurse and cannot leave the child, put it out in the backyard a large part of the day. Build a fence around the yard so that you are sure no harm can come to it. Do this from the time it is born ... If your heart is too tender and you must watch the child, make yourself a peephole so that you can see it without being seen, or use a periscope ... Finally, learn not to talk in endearing and coddling terms.

Since this was described as treating a child like a young adult, the obvious implication is that the typical Watsonian adults never kiss or hug one another either, and spend their time viewing one another through metaphorical peepholes. This is, of course, precisely what we are all driven to do with the *strangers* who surround us in our daily lives, but to find such conduct seriously recommended as the correct procedure between parents and their babies is, to say the least, remarkable.

The Watsonian approach to child-rearing was based on the behaviourist view, to quote him again, that in man 'There are no instincts. We build in at an early age everything that is later to appear ... there is nothing from within to develop.' It therefore followed that to produce a well-disciplined adult it was necessary to start with a well-disciplined baby. If the process was delayed, then 'bad habits' might start to form which would be difficult to eradicate later.

This attitude, based on a totally false premise concerning the natural development of human behaviour in infancy and childhood, would merely be a grotesque historical curiosity were it not for the fact that it is still occasionally encountered at the present day. But because the doctrine lingers on, it requires closer examination. The main reason for its persistence is that it is, in a way, self-perpetuating. If a tiny baby is treated in this unnatural manner it becomes basically insecure. Its high demand for bodily intimacy is repeatedly frustrated and punished. Its crying goes unheeded. But it adapts, it learns—there is no choice. It becomes trained and it grows. The only snag is that it will find it hard ever to trust anyone again, in its entire life. Because its urge to love and be loved was blocked at such a primary stage, the mechanism of loving will be permanently damaged. Because its relationship with its parents was carried on like a business deal, all its later personal involvements will proceed along similar lines. It will not even enjoy the advantage of being able to behave like a cold automaton, because it will still feel the basic biological urge to love welling inside it, but will be unable to find a way of letting it out. Like a withered limb that could not be fully amputated, it will go on aching. If, for conventional reasons, such an individual then marries and produces offspring, the latter will stand a high chance of being treated in the same way, since true parental loving will now, in its turn, have become virtually impossible. This is borne out by experiments with monkeys. If an infant monkey is reared without loving intimacies with its mother, it later becomes a bad parent.

For many human parents the Watsonian regime appeared attractive, but far too extreme. They therefore employed a softened, modified version of it. They would be stern with their baby one moment, then give in the next. In some ways they applied rigid discipline, in others they coddled it. They left it to cry in its cot, but they gave it lots of expensive toys and cooed over it at other times. They forced it into early toilet training, but they kissed and cuddled it. The result, of course, was a totally confused baby which grew into what was called a 'spoilt child'. The fundamental error was then made of ascribing the 'spoiltness', not to the confusion, or to the early baby-stage disciplinary elements, but entirely to the moments of 'softness'. If only they had stuck to the rigid regime and not given in so often, the parents told themselves, then all would have been well. The growing child, now being awkward and demanding, was therefore told to 'behave itself', and discipline was strengthened. The result, at this stage and later, was tantrum and rebellion.

Such a child had seen what love was, in those early 'softer' moments, but, having been shown the entrance, had then had the gate repeatedly slammed in its face. It knew how to love, but it had not been loved enough, and in its later rebellions it repeatedly tested its parents, hoping to prove at last that they loved it no matter what it did – that they loved it for itself and not for its 'good behaviour'. All too often it got the wrong answer.

Even when it got the right answer, and the parents forgave its latest outrage, it still could not believe that all was well. The early imprints were too deeply engraved, the early, intermittent disciplines too unloving for a baby's mind. So it tested them again, going further and further in its desperate attempt to prove that, after all, they really did love it. Then the parents, faced with chaos, either finally applied strict discipline and confirmed the child's darkest fears, or they gave in over and over again, condoning increasingly anti-social acts out of a sense of dawning guilt – 'Where did we go wrong, how have we failed? We have given you everything.'

All this could have been avoided if only the baby had been treated as a baby in the first place, instead of a 'young adult'. During the first years of life, an infant requires total love, nothing less. It is not 'trying to get the better of you', but it does need the best of you. If the mother is unstressed, and has not herself been warped in infancy, she will have a natural urge to give her best, which is why, of course, the disciplinarian has to repeatedly warn mothers against giving in to those tender 'weaknesses' that 'tug at their heart-strings', to use a favourite Watsonian phrase. If the mother *is* under pressure, as a result of our modern way of life, it will not be so easy; but even so, without an artificially imposed regime, it is still not impossible to come close enough to the ideal to produce a happy and well-loved baby.

Far from growing into a 'spoilt child', such an infant will then be able to mature into an increasingly independent individual, remaining loving, but with no inhibitions about investigating the exciting world around it. The early months gave it the assurance that there is a truly safe and secure base from which to venture forth and explore. Again, experiments with monkeys bear this out. The infant of a loving monkey mother readily moves off to play and test the environment. The offspring of a non-loving mother is shy and nervous. This is the exact opposite of the Watsonian prediction, which expects that an 'excess' of early loving, in the intimate, bodily sense, will make for a soft, dependent creature in later years. The lie to this can even be seen by the time the human child has reached the third year of life. The infant that was lavished with love during its first two years already begins to show its paces, launching out into the world with great, if unsteady, vigour. If it falls flat on its face it is not more, but less, likely to cry. The infant that was less loved and more disciplined as a tiny baby is already less adventurous, less curious about what it sees, and less inclined to start making the first fumbling attempts at independent action.

In other words, once a totally loving relationship has been established in the first two years of life, the infant can readily move on to the next stage in its development. As it grows, however, its headlong rush to explore the world *will*, at this later phase, require some discipline from the parents. What was wrong at the baby stage now becomes right. The Watsonian distaste for the doting, over-protective parents of *older* children has some justification, but the irony is that where protection of this type occurs to excess, it is probably a reaction against the damage caused by earlier Watsonian baby-training. The child that was a fully loved baby is less likely to provoke such behaviour.

During later life the adult who, as a baby, formed a strong bond of attachment with its parents in the primary phase of total love, will also be better equipped to make a strong sexual bond of attachment as a young adult and, from this new 'safe base', to continue to explore and lead an active, outgoing, social life. It is true that, in the stage before an adult bond of attachment has formed, he or she will be much more sexually exploratory as well. All exploring will have been accentuated, and the sexual sphere will be no exception. But if the individual's early life has been allowed to pass naturally from stage to stage, then the sexual explorations will soon lead to pair-formation and the growth of a powerful emotional bond, with a full return to the extensive body intimacies typical of the loving baby phase.

Young adults who establish new family units and enjoy uninhibited intimacies within them will be in a much better position to face the harsh, impersonal world outside. Being in a 'bond-ful', rather than a bond-starved, condition, they will be able to approach each type of social encounter in its own terms and not make inappropriate, bond-hungry demands in situations which, inevitably, will so often require emotional restraint.

One aspect of family life that cannot be overlooked is the need for privacy. It is necessary to have private space in order to enjoy intimate contacts to the full. Severe overcrowding in the home makes it difficult to develop any kind of personal relationship except a violent one. Bumping into one another is not the same as performing a loving embrace. Forced intimacy becomes anti-intimate in the true sense, so that, paradoxically, we need more space to give body contact greater meaning. Tight architectual planning that ignores this fact creates unavoidable emotional tension. For personal body intimacy cannot be a permanent condition, like the persistent impersonal crowding of the urban world outside the home.

The human need for close bodily contact is spasmodic, intermittent, and only requires occasional expression. To cramp the home-space is to convert the loving touch into a suffocating body proximity. If this seems obvious enough, then it is hard to understand the lack of attention that has been given to private home-space by the planners of recent years.

In painting this picture of the 'intimate young adults', I may have given the impression that, if only they can acquire an adequate private home-space, have a loving infancy behind them, and have formed strong new bonds of attachment to one another, then all will be well. Sadly, this is not the case. The crowded modern world can still encroach on their relationship and inhibit their intimacies. There are two powerful social attitudes that may influence them. The first is the one that uses the word 'infantile' as an insult. Extensive body intimacies are criticized as regressive, soft or babyish. This is something that can easily deter a potentially loving young adult. The suggestion that to be too intimate constitutes a threat to his independent spirit, summed up in such sayings as 'the strongest man is the man who stands alone', begins to make an impact. Needless to say, there is no evidence that for an adult to indulge in body contacts typical of the infant stage of life necessarily means he will find his independence impaired at other times. If anything, the contrary is the case. The soothing and calming effects of gentle intimacies leave the individual freer and better equipped emotionally to deal with the more remote, impersonal moments of life. They do not soften him, as has so often been claimed; they strengthen him, as they do with the loved child who explores more readily.

The second social attitude that tends to inhibit intimacies is the one which says that bodily contact implies sexual interest. This error has been the cause of much of the intimacy restraint that has been needlessly applied in the past. There is nothing implicitly sexual about the intimacies between parent and child. Parental love and infantile love are not sexual love, nor need the love between two men, two women, or even between a particular man and a particular woman be sexual. Love is love—an emotional bond of attachment—and whether sexual feelings enter into it or not is a secondary matter. In recent times we have somehow come to overstress the sexual element in all such bonds. If a strong, primarily non-sexual bond exists, but with minor sexual feelings accompanying it, the latter are automatically seized upon and enlarged out of all proportion in our thinking. The result has been a massive inhibition of our non-sexual body intimacies, and this has applied to relationships with our parents and offspring (beware, Oedipus!), our siblings (beware, incest!), our close same-sex friends (beware, homosexuality!), our close opposite-sex friends (beware, adultery!), and our many casual friends (beware, promiscuity!). All of this is understandable, but totally unnecessary. What it indicates is that in our true sexual relationships we are, perhaps, not enjoying a sufficiently erotically exhausting degree of body intimacy. If our pair-bond sexual intimacies were intensive and extensive enough, then there should be none left over to invade the other types of bond relationships, and we could all relax and enjoy them more than we seem to dare to do at present. If we remain sexually inhibited or frustrated with our mates, then of course the situation is quite different.

The general restraint that is applied to non-sexual body contacts in modern life has led to some curious anomalies. For example, recent American studies have revealed that in certain instances women are driven to use random sex simply for the purpose of being held in someone's arms. When questioned closely, the women admitted that this was sometimes their sole purpose in offering themselves sexually to a man, there being no other way in which they could satisfy their craving for a close embrace. This illustrates with pathetic clarity the distinction between sexual and non-sexual intimacy. Here there is no question of body intimacy leading to sex, but of sex leading to body intimacy, and this complete reversal leaves no doubt about the separation between the two.

These, then, are some of the hazards facing the modern intimate adult. To complete this survey of intimate human behaviour, it remains to ask what signs of change there are in the attitudes of contemporary society.

At the infant level, thanks to much painstaking work by child psychologists, a greatly improved approach to the problems of child-rearing is being developed. A much better understanding now exists of the nature of parent/offspring attachments, and of the essential role that warm loving takes in the production of a healthy growing child. The rigid, ruthless disciplines of yesterday are on the wane. However, in our more overcrowded urban centres, the ugly phenomenon of the 'battered baby syndrome' remains with us to remind us that we still have a long way to go.

At the level of the older child, constant gradual reforms are taking place in educational methods, and a more sensitive appreciation is growing of the need for social as well as technical education. The demands for technological learning are, however, heavier than ever, and there is still a danger that the average schoolchild will be better trained to cope with facts than with people.

Amongst young adults, the problem of handling social encounters seems, happily, to be solving itself. It is doubtful whether there has ever before been a period of such openness and frankness in dealing with the intricacies of personal interaction. Much of the criticism of the conduct of young adults, on the part of the older generation, stems from a heavily disguised envy. It remains to be seen, however, how well the new-found freedom of expression, sexual honesty and dis-inhibited intimacies of present-day youth survive the passage of time and approaching parenthood. The increasingly impersonal stresses of later adult life may yet take their toll.

Amongst older adults there is clearly a growing concern about the survival of resolved personal life inside the ever-expanding urban communities. As public stress encroaches more and more on private living, a mounting alarm can be felt concerning the nature of the modern human condition. In personal relationships, the word 'alienation' is constantly heard, as the heavy suits of emotional armour, put on for social battle in the streets and offices, become increasingly difficult to remove at night.

In North America, the sounds of a new rebellion against this situation can now be heard. A new movement is afoot, and it provides an eloquent proof of the burning need that exists in our modern society for a revision of our ideas concerning body contact and intimacy. Known in general terms as 'Encounter Group Therapy', it has appeared only in the last decade, beginning largely in California and spreading rapidly to many centres in the United States and Canada. Referred to in American slang as 'Bod Biz' (for 'show business' read 'body business'), it goes under a number of official titles, such as 'Transpersonal Psychology', 'Multiple Psychotherapy' and 'Social Dynamics'.

The principal common factor is the bringing together of a group of adults for sessions lasting from roughly one day to one week, in which they indulge in a wide variety of personal and group interactions. Although some of these are largely verbal, many are non-verbal and concentrate instead on body contacts, ritual touchings, mutual massage, and games. The aim is to break down the façade of civilized adult conduct, and to remind people that they 'do not *have* bodies; they *are* bodies'.

The essential feature of these courses is that inhibited adults are encouraged to play like children again. The avant-garde scientific atmosphere licenses them to behave in an infantile manner without embarrassment or fear of ridicule. They rub, stroke and tap one another's bodies; they carry one another around in their arms and anoint one another with oil; they play child-like games and they expose themselves naked to one another, sometimes literally, but usually metaphorically.

This deliberate return to childhood is explicitly expressed in the following words, in connection with a four-day course entitled 'Become as You Were':

The adjusted American achieves a dubious state of 'maturity' by burying many child parts under layers of shame and ridicule. Relearning how to be a child may enrich the man's experience of being masculine and the woman's experience of being feminine. Re-experiencing being child with mother may shed light on one's approaches to loving, love-making and love-seeking. Paradoxically, making contact with childish helplessness releases surges of power and contacting childish tears opens the channels for expression and joy.

Other similar courses called 'Becoming More Alive through Play' and 'Sensory Reawakening: Rebirth' also emphasize the need to return to the intimacies of childhood. In some cases the process is taken even further with the use of 'womb-pools' kept at precisely uterine temperature.

The organizers of these courses refer to them as 'therapy for normal people'. The visitors are not patients; they are group members. They go there because they are urgently seeking some way of finding a return to intimacy. If it is sad to think that modern, civilized adults should need official sanction to touch one another's bodies, then it is at least reassuring that they are sufficiently aware that something has gone wrong to actively do something about it. Many of the people who have been through such sessions repeatedly return for more, since they find themselves loosening up emotionally and unwinding in the course of the ritual body contacts. They report a sense of release and a growing feeling of warmth in connection with their personal interactions at home.

Is this a valuable new social movement, a passing fad, or a dangerous, new, drugless addiction? With dozens of new centres opening up every month, expert opinions are varied. Some psychologists and psychiatrists vigorously support the encounter-group phenomenon, others do not. One argues that group members 'don't improve – they just get a maintenance dose of intimacy'. If this is true, then even so the courses may at least see certain individuals through a difficult phase in their social lives. This puts group attendance at the intimacy level of going dancing, or going to bed with a cold and being comforted there, but there is nothing wrong with that. It merely adds one more string to the bow of a person seeking a 'licensed to touch' context. Other criticisms, however, are more severe. 'The techniques that are supposed to foster real intimacy sometimes destroy it,' says one. A theologist, no doubt sensing a new form of serious competition, comments that all that people learn in encounter groups is 'new ways to be impersonal—a new bag of tricks, new ways to be hostile and yet appear friendly'.

It is certainly true that, listening to the leaders of the movement talking to the general public about their methods and their philosophy, there is sometimes an unmistakable air of smug condescension. They give the impression of having discovered the secret of the universe, which they are gracious enough to impart to other, lesser mortals. This point has been stressed as a serious criticism by some, but it is probably no more than a defence against anticipated ridicule. It is reminiscent of the tactics of the world of psycho-analysis in earlier days. Like encounter-group veterans, those who had been through analysis could not help smiling smugly down at those who had not. But analysis is past this stage now, and if encounter groups survive the novelty phase, the attitude will no doubt change, as the new cult matures to become an accepted pattern.

The more severe criticism that the group sessions actually do serious harm has yet to be proved. 'Instant intimacy', as it has been called, does, however, have its hazards for the returning devotee when he steps back, fully or partially 're-awakened', into his old environment. He has been changed, but his home companions have not, and there is a danger that he may make insufficient allowance for this difference. The problem is essentially one of competing relationships. If an individual visits an encounter group, has himself massaged and stroked by total strangers, plays intimate games with them, and indulges in a wide variety of body contacts, then he is doing more with them than he will have been doing with his true 'intimates' in his home setting. (If he is not, then he had no problem in the first place). If—as will inevitably happen—he later describes his experiences in glowing detail, he is automatically going to arouse feelings of jealousy. Why was he prepared to act like that at the encounter centre, when he was so remote and untouching at home? The answer, of course, was the official, scientific sanction for such acts in the special atmosphere of the centre, but that is no comfort to his 'real life' intimates. Where couples attend intimacy sessions together, the problem is greatly reduced, but the 'back home' situation still requires careful handling.

Some have argued that the most distasteful aspect of the encounter groups is the way in which they are converting something which should be an unconscious part of everyday life into a self-conscious, highly organized, professional pursuit, with the act of intimacy in danger of becoming an end in itself, rather than as one of the basic means by which we can intuitively help ourselves to face the outside world.

Despite all these understandable fears and criticisms, it would be wrong to scorn this intriguing new trend. Essentially, its leaders have seen an increasing and damaging shift towards impersonality in our personal relationships and have done their best to reverse this process. If, as so often happens, by the 'law of reciprocal errors', they are swinging the pendulum rather wildly in the opposite direction, then this is a minor fault. If the movement spreads and grows to a point where it becomes a matter of common knowledge, then, even for the non-enthusiasts, it will exist as a constant reminder that something is wrong with the way in which we are using—or, rather, not using—our bodies. If it does no more than make us aware of this, it will be serving its purpose. Again, the comparison with psycho-analysis is relevant. Only a small proportion of the general population have ever been directly involved in analysis, and yet the basic idea that our deepest, darkest thoughts are not shameful or abnormal, but are probably shared by most others, has permeated healthily throughout our culture. In part, it is responsible for the more honest and frank approach to mutual personal problems in young adults today. If the encounter-group movement can provide the same indirect release for our inhibited feelings concerning intimate bodily contact, then it will ultimately have proved to have made a valuable social contribution.

The human animal is a social species, capable of loving and greatly in need of being loved. A simple tribal hunter by evolution, he finds himself now in a bewilderingly inflated communal world. Hemmed in on all sides, he defensively turns in on himself. In his emotional retreat, he starts to shut off even those who are nearest and dearest to him, until he finds himself alone in a dense crowd. Unable to reach out for emotional support, he becomes tense and strained and possibly, in the end, violent. Lost for comfort, he turns to harmless substitutes for love that ask no questions. But loving is a two-way process, and in the end the substitutes are not enough. In this condition, if he does not find true intimacy—even if it is only with one single person—he will suffer. Driven to armour himself against attack and betrayal, he may have arrived at a state in which all contact seems repellent, where to touch or to be touched means to hurt or be hurt. This, in a sense, has become one of the greatest ailments of our time, a major social disease of modern society that we would do well to cure before it is too late. If the danger remains unheeded, then—like poisonous chemicals in our food—it may increase from generation to generation until the damage has gone beyond repair.

In a way, our ingenious adaptability can be our social undoing. We are capable of living and surviving in such appallingly unnatural conditions that, instead of calling a halt and returning to a saner system, we adjust and struggle on. In our crowded urban world, we have battled on in this way, further and further from a state of loving, personal intimacy, until the cracks have begun to show. Then, sucking our metaphorical thumbs and mouthing sophisticated philosophies to convince ourselves that all is well, we try to sit it out. We laugh at educated adults who pay large sums to go and play childish games of touch and hug in scientific institutes, and we fail to see the signs. How much easier it would all be if we could accept the fact that tender loving is not a weakly thing, only for infants and young lovers, if we could release our feelings, and indulge ourselves in an occasional, and magical, return to intimacy.

CHAPTER REFERENCES

It is impossible to list all the many works that have been of assistance in writing *Intimate Behaviour*. I have therefore included only those which either have been important in providing information on a specific point, or are of particular interest for further reading. They are arranged below on a chapter-by-chapter and topic-by-topic basis. From the names and the dates given, it is possible to trace the full references in the bibliography that follows. The bibliography also contains the titles of several broader works, not listed below against specific topics, which have proved of value in relation to the general subject.

Most of the statements concerning body contacts are, however, based on my own personal observations. Where specific statements are made, such as that a particular action is, say, three times as common in females as in males, they are based on a sample of 10,000 randomly selected units of behaviour collected during the past year. A detailed report on human contact actions, based on this study, is now being compiled.

CHAPTER ONE. THE ROOTS OF INTIMACY

Foetal behaviour: Munn, 1965; Tanner and Taylor, 1966.
Behaviour at birth: Prechtl, 1965; Smith, 1968.

Rocking: Ambrose, in Bowlby, 1969; Bowlby, 1969; Morris, 1967.
Heartbeat: Morris, 1967; Salk, 1966.
Swaddling: Smith, 1968; Spock, 1946.
Discipline: Watson, 1928.
Crying and smiling: Ambrose, 1960; Bowlby, 1969.
Transitional objects: Spock, 1963; Vosper, 1969.
Adolescence: Cohen, 1964; Freud, 1946.

CHAPTER TWO. INVITATIONS TO SEXUAL INTIMACY

Crotch: Morris, 1967.
Codpiece: Broby-Johansen, 1968; Fryer, 1963; Rabelais, 1653.
Human self-mimicry: Morris, 1967; Morris and Morris, 1966a; Wickler, 1967.
Prehistoric buttocks: Ucko, 1968.
Bustle: Broby-Johansen, 1968; Laver, 1963.
Breast variations: Ford and Beach, 1952; Levy, 1962.
Depilation: Gould and Pyle, 1896.
Chin: Hershkovitz, 1970.
Blush: Darwin, 1873.
Belladonna: Wedeck, 1962.
Pupil dilation: Coss, 1965; Hess, 1965.
Hair in Egypt: Murray, 1949.
Dancing: Bloch, 1958; Fryer, 1963; Licht, 1932.

CHAPTER THREE. SEXUAL INTIMACY

General: Kinsey *et al.,* 1948, 1953; Masters and Johnson, 1966; Morris, 1967, 1969.
Oral-genital contacts: Legman, 1969.
Sexual prudery: Fryer, 1963.
Primate copulation: Carpenter, 1934, 1942; Goodall, 1965; Hall and DeVore, 1965; Morris and Morris, 1966; Reynolds and Reynolds, 1965; Simonds, 1965; Southwick, Beg and Siddiqui, 1965; Yerkes, 1943.
Cross-cultural variations: Ford and Beach, 1952; Rachewiltz, 1964.

CHAPTER FOUR. SOCIAL INTIMACY

General: Morris, in preparation (see above).
Baby clapping: Ainsworth, 1964.

Hand-waving nationalities: Brun, 1969.
Men holding hands: Froissart, 1940.
Non-nutritional sucking: Bowlby, 1969; Wolff, 1969.
Bow and curtsy: Wildeblood and Brinson, 1965.
Religious kiss: Beadnell, 1942; Wildeblood and Brinson, 1965.
Handshake: Sorell, 1968; Wildeblood and Brinson, 1965.
Modern etiquette: Lyons, 1967; Page, 1961; Sara, 1963; Vanderbilt, 1952.

CHAPTER FIVE. SPECIALIZED INTIMACY

Microbes on man: Rosebury, 1969.
Physical illness: Morris, 1971 (in press).
Mental illness: Szasz, 1961.
Hairdressers: Williams, 1957.
Dancing: Bloch, 1958; Brend, 1936; Fryer, 1963; Lewinsohn, 1958; Licht, 1932.
Midwives: Forbes, 1966; Fryer, 1963.
Groupie girls: Fabian and Byrne, 1969.

CHAPTER SIX. SUBSTITUTES FOR INTIMACY

Man/animal relationships: Morris, 1967, 1969; Morris and Morris, 1965, 1966a, 1966b.
Petishism: Szasz, 1969.
Animal experiments: Heim, 1971; Matthews, 1964; Russell and Burch, 1959.

CHAPTER SEVEN. OBJECT INTIMACY

Dummies and pacifiers: Bowlby, 1969; Spock, 1946.
Hand sculpture: Miller, 1942.
Dildoes: Bauer, 1926; Dearborn, 1961; Henriques, 1963; Masters and Johnson, 1966.
Copulation machine: Lacey, 1967.

CHAPTER EIGHT. SELF-INTIMACY

General self-contacts: Morris, in preparation (see above).
Female leg-crossing: Birdwhistell, 1970.

Masturbation: Comfort, 1967; Dearborn, 1961; 'J', 1970; Kinsey et al., 1948, 1953; Lewinsohn, 1958; Malinowski, 1929; Masters and Johnson, 1966; Morris, 1969.

Circumcision: Comfort, 1967; Lewinsohn, 1958; Mollon, 1965; Morris and Morris, 1965; Rachewiltz, 1964; Smith, 1968; Spock, 1946; West, 1966.

CHAPTER NINE. RETURN TO INTIMACY

Child discipline: Watson, 1928.
Monkey rearing: Harlow, 1958.
Overcrowding: Morris, 1969; Russell and Russell, 1968.
Sex as comfort: Hollender et al., 1969; Hollender, 1970.
Encounter-group therapy: Gunther, 1969; Howard, 1970.

BIBLIOGRAPHY

AINSWORTH, M. D. 'Patterns of infantile attachment to the mother', *Merrill-Palmer Quart.* 10 (1964), pp. 51–8

AMBROSE, J. A. 'The smiling response in early human infancy' (Ph.D. thesis, London University, 1960)

ARGYLE, M. *Social Interaction* (Methuen, London, 1969)

BAUER, B. A. *Woman* (Cape, London, 1926)

BEADNELL, C. M. *The Origin of the Kiss* (Watts, London, 1942)

BIRDWHISTELL, R. L. *Kinesics and Context* (University of Pennsylvania Press, Philadelphia, 1970)

BLOCH, I. *Sexual Life in England Past and Present* (Arco, London, 1958)

BOWLBY, J. *Attachment and Loss* (Hogarth Press, London, 1969)

BREND, W. A. *Sacrifice to Attis* (Heinemann, London, 1936)

BROBY-JOHANSEN, R. *Body and Clothes* (Faber, London, 1968)

BRUN, T. *The International Dictionary of Sign Language* (Wolfe, London, 1969)

CARPENTER, C. R. 'A field study of the behavior and social relations of Howling Monkeys', *Comp. Psychol. Monogr.* 10 (1934), pp. 1–168

CARPENTER, C. R. 'Sexual behaviour of free ranging Rhesus Monkeys', *J. Comp. Psychol.* 33 (1942), pp. 113–62

COHEN, Y. A. *The Transition from Childhood to Adolescence* (Aldine, New York, 1964)

COMFORT, A. *The Anxiety Makers* (Nelson, London, 1967)

COSS, R. G. *Mood Provoking Visual Stimuli* (University of California, 1965)

CRAWLEY, E. *Dress, Drink and Drums* (Methuen, London, 1931)

DARWIN, C. *The Expression of the Emotions in Man and Animals* (Murray, London, 1873)

DEARBORN, L. W. 'Autoerotism', in *The Encyclopedia of Sexual Behavior* (Hawthorn, New York, 1961)

FABIAN, J., and J. BYRNE. *Groupie* (New English Library, London, 1969)

FAST, J. *Body Language* (Evans, New York, 1970)

FORBES, T. R. *The Midwife and the Witch* (Yale University Press, New Haven, 1966)

FORD, C. S., and F. A. BEACH. *Patterns of Sexual Behaviour* (Eyre & Spottiswoode, London, 1952)

FRANK, L. K. 'Tactile Communication', in Carpenter and McLuhan (eds), *Explorations in Communication* (Cape, London, 1970), pp. 4–11

FREUD, A. *The Ego and Mechanisms of Defense* (International Universities Press, New York, 1946)

FROISSART, J. *The Chronicles of England, France and Spain* (Everyman Library, London, 1940)

FRYER, P. *Mrs Grundy* (Dobson, London, 1963)

GOODALL, J. 'Chimpanzees of the Gombe Stream Reserve', in DeVore (ed.), *Primate Behavior* (Holt, Rinehart and Winston, New York, 1965)

GOULD, G. M., and W. L. PYLE. *Anomalies and Curiosities of Medicine* (Saunders, Philadelphia, 1896)

GUNTHER, B. *Sense Relaxation* (Macdonald, London, 1969)

HALL, K. R. L. 'Baboon social behaviour', in DeVore (ed.), *Primate Behavior* (Holt, Rinehart and Winston, New York, 1965), pp. 53–110

HASS, H. *The Human Animal* (Putnam, New York, 1970)

HARLOW, H. F. 'The nature of love', *Amer. Psychol.* 13 (1958), pp. 673–85

HEIM, A. *Intelligence and Personality* (Pelican, London, 1971)

HENRIQUES, F. *Prostitution in Europe and the New World* (MacGibbon & Kee, London, 1963)

HERSHKOVITZ, P. 'The decorative chin', *Bull. Field Mus. Nat. Hist.* 41 (1970), pp. 6–10

HESS, E. H. 'Attitude and pupil size', *Sci. Amer.* 212 (1965), pp. 46–54

HOLLENDER, M. H. 'The need or wish to be held', *Arch. Gen. Psychiat.* 22 (1970), pp. 445–53

HOLLENDER, M. H., L. LUBORSKY and T. J. SCARAMELLA. 'Body contact and sexual excitement', *Arch. Gen. Psychiat.* 20 (1969), pp. 188–91

HOWARD, J. *Please Touch* (McGraw-Hill, New York, 1970)

'J'. *The Sensuous Woman* (Lyle Stuart, New York, 1970)

JOURARD, S. M. 'An exploratory study of body accessibility', *Brit. J. soc. clin. Psychol.* 5 (1966), pp. 221–31

KINSEY, A. C., W. B. POMEROY and C. E. MARTIN. *Sexual Behavior in the Human Male* (Saunders, Philadelphia, 1948)

KINSEY, A. C., W. B. POMEROY, C. E. MARTIN and P. H. GEBHARD. *Sexual Behavior in the Human Female* (Saunders, Philadelphia, 1953)

LACEY, B. 'An evening with Bruce Lacey' (Lecture-demonstration at the Institute of Contemporary Arts, London, 1967)

LAVER, J. *Costume* (Cassell, London, 1963)

LAVER, J. *Modesty in Dress* (Heinemann, London, 1969)

LEGMAN, G. *Rationale of the Dirty Joke* (Cape, London, 1969)

LEVY, M. *The Moons of Paradise* (Barker, London, 1962)

LEWINSOHN, R. *A History of Sexual Customs* (Longmans, Green, London, 1958)

LICHT, H. *Sexual Life in Ancient Greece* (Routledge & Kegan Paul, London, 1932)

LOWEN, A. *Physical Dynamics of Character Structure* (Grune & Stratton, New York, 1958)

LYONS, P. *Today's Etiquette* (Bancroft, London, 1967)

MALINOWSKI, B. *The Sexual Life of Savages* (Routledge & Kegan Paul, London, 1929)

MASTERS, W. H., and V. E. JOHNSON. *Human Sexual Response* (Churchill, London, 1966)

MATTHEWS, L. H. 'Animal Relationships', *Med. Sci. and Law* (1964), pp. 4–14

MILLER, D. C. (ed.) *Americans 1942* (Museum of Modern Art, New York, 1942)

MOLLON, R. *The Nursery Book* (Pan, London, 1965)

MORRIS, D. *The Naked Ape* (Cape, London, 1967)

MORRIS, D. *The Human Zoo* (Cape, London, 1969)

MORRIS, D. 'The Biology of Illness' (1971, in press)

Morris, R., and D. Morris. *Men and Snakes* (Hutchinson, London, 1965)

Morris, R., and D. Morris. *Men and Apes* (Hutchinson, London, 1966a)

Morris, R., and D. Morris. *Men and Pandas* (Hutchinson, London, 1966b)

Munn, N. L. *The Evolution and Growth of Human Behavior* (Mifflin, Boston, 1965)

Murray, M. A. *The Splendour that was Egypt* (Sidgwick & Jackson, London, 1949)

Page, A. *Etiquette for Gentlemen* (Ward, Lock, London, 1961)

Prechtl, H. F. R. 'Problems of behavioral studies in the newborn infant', in Lehrman, Hinde and Shaw (eds), *Advances in the Study of Behavior* (Academic Press, New York, 1965)

Rabelais, F. *The Works of Mr Francis Rabelais* (Navarre Society, London, 1931)

Rachewiltz, B. de. *Black Eros* (Allen & Unwin, London, 1964)

Reynolds, V., and F. Reynolds. 'Chimpanzees of the Budongo Forest', in DeVore (ed.), *Primate Behavior* (Holt, Rinehart and Winston, New York, 1965)

Rosebury, T. *Life on Man* (Secker & Warburg, London, 1969)

Russell, C., and W. M. S. Russell. *Violence, Monkeys and Man* (Macmillan, London, 1968)

Russell, W. M. S., and R. L. Burch. *The Principles of Humane Experimental Technique* (Methuen, London, 1959)

Salk, L. 'Thoughts on the concept of imprinting and its place in early human development', *Canad. Psychiat. Assoc. Jour.* 11 (1966), pp. S296–S305

Sara, D. *Good Manners and Hospitality* (Collier, New York, 1963)

Simon, W., and J. H. Gagnon. 'Pornography — Raging menace or paper tiger?', in Gagnon and Simon (eds), *The Sexual Scene* (Aldine, New York, 1970)

Simonds, P. E. 'The bonnet macaque in South India', in DeVore (ed.), *Primate Behavior* (Holt, Rinehart and Winston, New York, 1965), pp. 175–96

Smith, A. *The Body* (Allen & Unwin, London, 1968)

Sorell, W. *The Story of the Human Hand* (Weidenfeld & Nicolson, London, 1968)

Southwick, C. H., M. A. Beg and M. R. Siddiqi. 'Rhesus

monkeys in North India', in DeVore (ed.), *Primate Behavior* (Holt, Rinehart and Winston, New York, 1965), pp. 111–74

SPOCK, B. *Baby and Child Care* (Giant Cardinal, New York, 1946)

SPOCK, B. 'The striving for autonomy and regressive object relationships', *Psychoan. Study Child* 18 (1963), pp. 361–4

SZASZ, K. *Petishism* (Holt, Rinehart and Winston, New York, 1969)

SZASZ, T. S. *The Myth of Mental Illness* (Hoeber-Harper, New York, 1961)

TANNER, J. M., and G. R. TAYLOR. *Growth* (Time-Life, New York, 1966)

TOMKINS, S. S. *Affect, Imagery, Consciousness* (Springer, New York, 1962–3)

UCKO, P. J. *Anthropomorphic Figurines* (Szmidla, London, 1968)

VANDERBILT, A. *Complete Book of Etiquette* (Doubleday, New York, 1952)

VOSPER, J. *Baby Book* (Ebury, London, 1969)

WATSON, J. B. *Psychological Care of Infant and Child* (Norton, New York, 1928)

WEDECK, H. E. *Dictionary of Aphrodisiacs* (Peter Owen, London, 1962)

WEST, J. *Parent's Baby Book* (Parrish, London, 1966)

WICKLER, W. 'Socio-sexual signals and their intra-specific imitation among primates', in Morris (ed.), *Primate Ethology* (Weidenfeld & Nicolson, London, 1967), pp. 68–147

WILDEBLOOD, J., and P. BRINSON. *The Polite World* (Oxford University Press, London, 1965)

WILLIAMS, N. *Powder and Paint* (Longmans, Green, London, 1957)

WOLFF, C. *A Psychology of Gesture* (Methuen, London, 1945)

WOLFF, P. H. 'The natural history of crying and other vocalizations in early infancy', in Foss (ed.), *Determinants of Infant Behaviour*, vol. 4 (Methuen, London, 1969)

YERKES, R. M. *Chimpanzees. A Laboratory Colony* (Yale University Press, New Haven, 1943)